THE **HIST** SOLUT

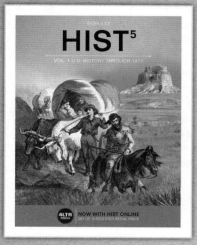

HIST⁵

VOL. 1: U.S. HISTORY THROUGH 1877

4LTR PRESS
NOW WITH HIST ONLINE
$65 US SUGGESTED RETAIL PRICE

Print
+
Online

MANAGE MY COURSE ⌄ | 👤 STUDENT

HIST5

CHAPTER
1

Three Societies on the Verge of Contact

CHAPTER
2

Contact and Settlement, 1492–1660

HIST⁵ delivers all the key terms and core concepts for the **U.S. History** course.

HIST Online provides the complete narrative from the printed text with additional interactive media and the unique functionality of **StudyBits**— all available on nearly any device!

What is a StudyBit™? Created through a deep investigation of students' challenges and workflows, the StudyBit™ functionality of **HIST Online** enables students of different generations and learning styles to study more effectively by allowing them to learn their way. Here's how they work:

COLLECT WHAT'S IMPORTANT Create StudyBits as you highlight text, images or take notes!

WEAK

FAIR

STRONG

UNASSIGNED

RATE AND ORGANIZE STUDYBITS Rate your understanding and use the color-coding to quickly organize your study time and personalize your flashcards and quizzes.

StudyBit™

TRACK/MONITOR PROGRESS Use Concept Tracker to decide how you'll spend study time and study YOUR way!

85%

PERSONALIZE QUIZZES Filter by your StudyBits to personalize quizzes or just take chapter quizzes off-the-shelf.

CORRECT

INCORRECT

INCORRECT

INCORRECT

HIST5, Volume 1
Kevin M. Schultz

Senior Vice President, Higher Ed Product,
   Content, and Market Development:
   Erin Joyner

Product Manager: Joseph D. Potvin

Content/Media Developer: Sarah Keeling

Product Assistant: Alexandra C. Shore

Marketing Manager: Christopher Walz

Sr. Content Project Manager: Colleen A. Farmer

Sr. Art Director: Bethany Bourgeois

Text Designer: Chris Miller, Cmiller Design

Cover Designer: Lisa Kuhn/Curio Press, LLC/Chris
   Miller, Cmiller Design

Cover Image: Robert Holmes/Alamy Stock Photo

Back Cover and Special Page Images:
   Computer and tablet illustration:
   © iStockphoto.com/furtaev; Smart Phone
   illustration: © iStockphoto.com/dashadima;
   Feedback image: © Rawpixel.com/
   Shutterstock.com

Intellectual Property Analyst: Alexandra Ricciardi

Intellectual Property Project Manager:
   Reba Frederics

Production Service: MPS Limited

For product information and technology assistance, contact us at
Cengage Customer & Sales Support, 1-800-354-9706

For permission to use material from this text or product,
submit all requests online at **www.cengage.com/permissions**
Further permissions questions can be emailed to
permissionrequest@cengage.com

Library of Congress Control Number: 2017949025

Student Edition ISBN: 978-1-337-29417-1

Student Edition with Online ISBN: 978-1-337-29416-4

Cengage
20 Channel Center Street
Boston, MA 02210
USA

Cengage is a leading provider of customized learning solutions with employees residing in nearly 40 different countries and sales in more than 125 countries around the world. Find your local representative at **www.cengage.com.**

Cengage products are represented in Canada by Nelson Education, Ltd.

To learn more about Cengage platforms and services, visit **www.cengage.com**

To register or access your online learning solution or purchase materials for your course, visit **www.cengagebrain.com**

Printed in the United States of America
Print Number: 01   Print Year: 2017

SCHULTZ
HIST⁵   BRIEF CONTENTS

CONTENTS

John Sfondilias/Fotolia

The Granger Collection, NYC

Eon Images

Picture History/Newscom

8 Securing the New Nation, 1789–1800   142

North Wind Picture Archives

Fotosearch/Getty Images

John Parrot/Stocktrek Images/Getty Images

About the Author

Kevin M. Schultz is an award-winning historian and bestselling author. He is currently a Professor of History at the University of Illinois at Chicago (UIC), where he has won several awards for his teaching and writing. He is the author of two other books: *Buckley and Mailer: The Difficult Friendship that Shaped the Sixties* (W.W. Norton & Co., 2015), which was an Amazon #1 New Release in American History; and *Tri-Faith America: How Postwar Catholics and Jews Helped America Realize Its Protestant Promise* (Oxford University Press, 2011), which is used in both graduate and undergraduate classes across the country. He has published widely for popular audiences, too, including having had a journal article appear immediately before one written by the Pope. He received his BA from Vanderbilt University and his PhD from UC Berkeley.

1 | Three Societies on the Verge of Contact

John Standidge / Fotolia

LEARNING OBJECTIVES

After reading this chapter, you should be able to do the following:

1-1 Explain current beliefs about how the first peoples settled in North America, and discuss the ways in which they became differentiated from one another over time.

1-2 Describe the African societies that existed at the time the first Africans were brought to the New World as slaves.

1-3 Describe Europe's experiences during the last centuries before Columbus made his first voyage to the New World in 1492.

AFTER FINISHING
THIS CHAPTER
GO TO **PAGE 20**
FOR STUDY TOOLS

People have been living on the landmass we now know as the United States for at least the past 12,000 years—long before civilizations emerged among the ancient Egyptians, the ancient Greeks, and the ancient Romans. It was even 10,000 years before the birth of Jesus Christ, whose estimated time of arrival, however incorrect, is the measure by which western European time came to be measured. As a political nation, however, the United States is less than 250 years old, encapsulating roughly just nine or ten generations. Although this book is mostly about that relatively recent political nation and the people who lived in it, this chapter examines the three groups of people—Indians, West Africans, and Europeans—who came together in North America more than five hundred years ago, setting in motion the process by which the United States would become an independent nation. This chapter begins in the Ice Age and ends as Christopher Columbus sets foot in North America in 1492, an arrival initiating the contact of cultures that would thereafter shape the development of the continent.

1-1 NATIVE AMERICA

Early human life in North America can be divided into three periods: (1) the Paleo-Indian, (2) the Archaic, and (3) the pre-Columbian.

1-1a The Paleo-Indian Era: The First Settlers (10,000–15,000 years ago)

The first settlers of the Americas appeared in what we call the Paleo-Indian era. Although we will probably never know when the first people set foot on what we now call the United States, it seems they may have come earlier than was thought not too long ago.

ARRIVAL

For a long time, archeologists believed that the first people came not for fame, fortune, or freedom (as subsequent

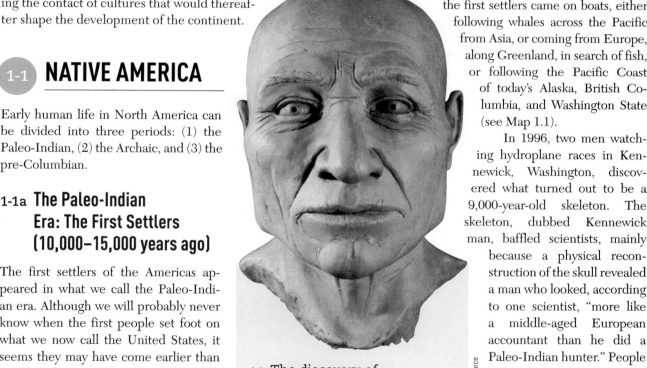

>> The discovery of "Kennewick man" in 1996 challenged scientists to rethink when people first came to North America.

Emmanuel Laurent/Science Source

immigrants would), but simply because they were hungry. According to this theory, about 12,000 years ago, thousands of young adults and their families left their homes in Asia and crossed a narrow passage of iced-over land called Beringia, southwest of today's Alaska. These people were supposedly following herds of woolly mammoths, intending to hunt the animals to feed and clothe their families. Many of these hunters followed herds south along the western coast of present-day Canada and ended up in what is now the United States. Many of their latter-day ancestors continued southward and, after many generations, made it all the way to the southernmost tip of South America, a place now called Tierra Del Fuego.

Recent evidence casts doubt on this theory. Carbon dating suggests that the first people on the continent were probably here much earlier than 12,000 years ago. This has prompted a reevaluation of the Beringia theory, with some scholars suggesting that the first settlers came on boats, either following whales across the Pacific from Asia, or coming from Europe, along Greenland, in search of fish, or following the Pacific Coast of today's Alaska, British Columbia, and Washington State (see Map 1.1).

In 1996, two men watching hydroplane races in Kennewick, Washington, discovered what turned out to be a 9,000-year-old skeleton. The skeleton, dubbed Kennewick man, baffled scientists, mainly because a physical reconstruction of the skull revealed a man who looked, according to one scientist, "more like a middle-aged European accountant than he did a Paleo-Indian hunter." People with European features were not thought to have been in North America for another 8,500 years, so Kennewick man presented the possibility that North American

◀◀◀ **As people moved their way south and inland into the interior of North America, they had to be creative in securing housing. Here, the "Cliff Palace" from the twelfth or thirteenth century is one of the best preserved dwellings of the Ancestral Pueblo peoples, located in Mesa Verde National Park, Colorado.**

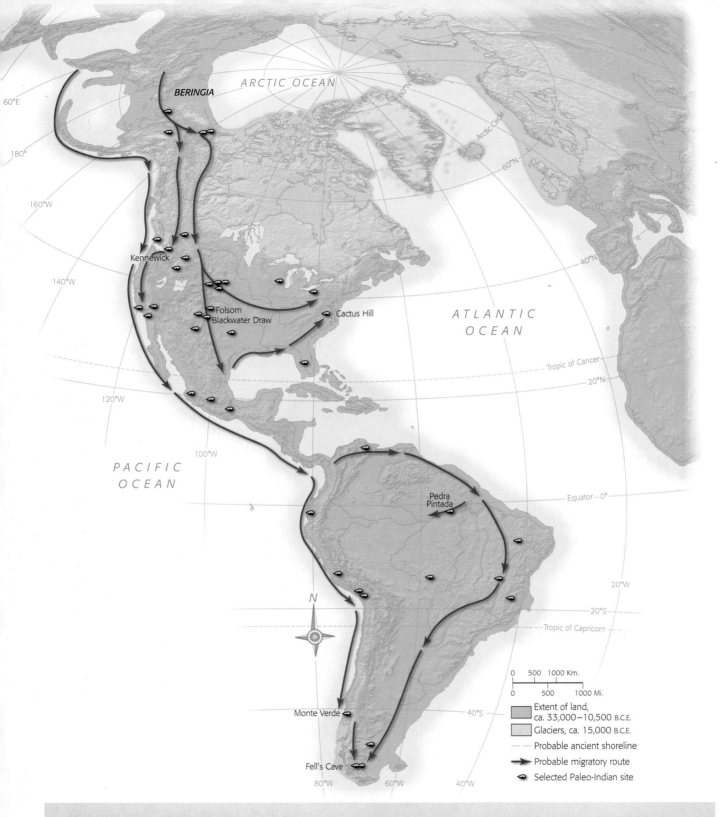

Map 1.1 Settlement of the Americas

>> This map details the imagined southward migration of the first peoples to inhabit the Americas and shows their journey from Beringia, through today's Canada and United States, ending all the way in the southern tip of South America.

settlement happened in different waves from a variety of locations, with older groups dying out and being replaced by yet newer immigrants. Another scientist then suggested that Kennewick man's features resembled those of people living in specific parts of Asia rather than Europe, further complicating our understanding of the origins of humankind in North America. Was he a man with European origins, an Asian man, or did he resemble one of America's indigenous Indians? As the battle raged on among scientists, white supremacists claimed Kennewick Man demonstrated that the first people in North America were "white" and thus served as the foundation for American civilization. Native American tribes, meanwhile, sued to have the man's remains returned to ancient burial grounds. Finally, in 2015, conclusive DNA evidence demonstrated the Kennewick Man was, in fact, of Native American origin, thus upholding the validity of the Beringia theory.

Regardless of the dispute, and regardless of when or from where Kennewick man came, his age suggests that calling North America the "New World" might be a mistake. England, for instance, was not inhabitable until 12,500 B.C.E., suggesting that the "New World" may actually have a much longer human history than what we now think of as the "Old World." Today we call these initial North American settlers the **Paleo-Indians**.

Although the initial origins and timing are in question, what is known for certain is that the greatest flow of people in this early period came between 20,000 and 10,000 B.C.E.; we also know that sometime between 9500 and 8000 B.C.E. the ocean level rose because of what we would today call global warming. With water covering the Bering Strait that connected Asia to North America, the first major wave of immigration came to an end. The path has remained submerged ever since.

EXPANSION AND DEVELOPMENT

As these migrants moved from region to region across North America, they adapted their lifestyle according to the climate and the land, as people do. The people of the **Paleo-Indian era** (10,000 to 15,000 years ago) thus lived a wide range of lifestyles, developing many languages

>> Stone tools for grinding maize. The complex genetic engineering of maize some 6,000 years ago was vital to the development of sedentary cultures.

Nancy Carter/North Wind Picture Archives

and belief systems along the way. Some of the most ancient peoples made spears by flaking stones and then chose "kill sites" where large herds traversed. Others hunted herds of animals across great distances. Still others slowly began to cultivate complex systems of sustainable agriculture that allowed them to remain in a single area for years. And still others depended on fishing and the riches of the seas to provide a stable life for their families. Over time, the population of Native North America grew.

1-1b The Archaic Era: Forging an Agricultural Society (2,500–10,000 years ago)

Between 5,000 and 8,000 years ago, a monumental transition occurred in how people lived. During the **Archaic era**, agriculture, not hunting, gradually became the primary source of sustenance for most of the people of Native North America. This trend was perhaps the most significant development in American prehistory, because settled agriculture permitted the establishment of a **sedentary existence**, without the need to pursue herd animals. Maize, a form of corn, was one key element of this existence. Maize is a highly nutritious cereal, containing more nutrients than wheat, rice, millet, and barley. Its development was a remarkable feat of genetic engineering. Some 6,000 years ago, Indians in today's southern Mexico cultivated the crop through the careful selection of desirable seeds, ultimately producing corn. It still stands as one of the most significant instances of crop cultivation in world history.

Paleo-Indians The first people to settle North America, roughly 10,000 to 15,000 years ago

Paleo-Indian era Era beginning about 15,000 years ago and ending about 10,000 years ago, characterized by initial North American settlement

Archaic era Era beginning about 10,000 years ago and lasting until about 2,500 years ago, characterized by increased agricultural development

sedentary existence Life in which settlers can remain in one place cultivating agriculture, instead of pursuing herd animals

Over time, populations grew larger, not only because food supplies increased, but also because group size was no longer limited by the arduous demands of hunting. Many tribes became semi-sedentary, settling in camps during the growing season and then breaking camp to follow the herds at other times of year. Others became increasingly centralized in their development, building permanent cities, some of monumental proportions.

The Archaic era was the formative period of the first settled tribes in North America—the immediate ancestors of many of the Indian nations with which we are most familiar today. The Mesoamerican civilization, founded and developed by the Olmec people, thrived in today's Mexico and served as a precursor to the many maize-based societies that developed throughout North America. Some 5,000 years ago, another successful ancient civilization—the people of Norte Chico in today's Peru—flourished by cultivating cotton, which they used to weave nets and catch the plentiful fish off the Pacific Coast; they then transported the fish to high-altitude cities in the Andes. Although nature has reclaimed much of what these early civilizations created, their developments and accomplishments are testaments to the capacity of humankind to create and develop monumental societies. One historian has argued that the only way to fully grasp the earth-changing significance of these early civilizations is to take a helicopter ride over undeveloped parts of Mexico and Central and South America, realizing that many of the hills and creeks below are actually the buried remains of temples and canals built by those early civilizations.

Paulo Afonso/Shutterstock.com

>> A gigantic, 20-ton Olmec head. Under the canopies of the rain forest, the mysterious Olmec developed the oldest of all Mesoamerican civilizations.

civilizations of the pre-Columbian world (the phrase means "before Columbus") usually based their economy on agriculture and for that reason were able to endure in a single location long enough to create complex, hierarchical societies and to develop long-standing trading networks.

The largest Indian civilization in this period was that of the Incas, who lived on the western coast of South America, from the equator to the southern tip of Chile. The Incas built large cities and fortresses on the steep slopes of the Andes Mountains (and were the beneficiaries of fish deliveries from the people of Norte Chico). Other impressive pre-Columbian societies include the Maya, who, with their step-tiered temples, dominated southern Guatemala and the Yucatan Peninsula (in present-day Mexico) from the fifth to the eighth centuries until an internal civil war weakened the civilization so much that it dissipated. The Teotihuacán society built a city (named Teotihuacán, about an hour's bus ride from Mexico City) that accommodated perhaps as many as 200,000 souls during the fifth century. The Mexica (later labeled "the Aztecs") developed a complex urban society that ruled central Mexico from the ninth to the fifteenth centuries. These were all large, complex societies that, in scientific knowledge, governing capacities, and artistic and architectural development, rivaled any in the world at the time of their particular dominance.

THE ANASAZI

In the present-day United States, two of the largest pre-Columbian cultures were the Anasazi and the Mississippians. In the American Southwest, the Anasazi founded a vast civilization by combining hunting and gathering with sedentary agriculture in order to sustain a large population in the arid desert of present-day New Mexico. As a testament to the grandness of their civilization, between 900 and 1150 c.e. the Anasazi built fourteen "great houses" in the Chaco Canyon, each one several stories tall and containing more than two hundred rooms. They were perhaps used as large apartment buildings, as the canyon served as the major trading post for turquoise and other material goods. Several of these great houses still stand near Albuquerque, New Mexico.

1-1c The Pre-Columbian Era: Developing Civilizations (500 B.C.E.–1492 C.E.)

Of all the people living in North America before contact with Europeans, we know the most about the people of the **pre-Columbian era** (500 B.C.E.–1492 C.E.). The great

pre-Columbian era North American era lasting from 500 B.C.E. to 1492 C.E., before Columbus landed

>> The Serpent Mound in Ohio, nearly a quarter of a mile long, is the largest and finest surviving serpentine earthwork, putting on dramatic display the pre-Colombian peoples' capacity to transform their world.

THE MISSISSIPPIANS

A second large, pre-Columbian culture to develop on the land now known as the United States was that of the Mississippians, whose many different tribal groups lived at about the same time as the Anasazi, from 700 to 1500 C.E., with their civilization reaching its peak at around 1100 C.E. The largest Mississippian city was called Cahokia, located eight miles east of present-day St. Louis. Inhabited by more than 20,000 people (comparable in size to London at that time), Cahokia served as the civilization's crossroads for trade and religion. Webs of roads surrounded the city, connecting rural villagers for hundreds of miles in all directions. The Mississippians developed an accurate calendar and built a pyramid that, at the time, was the third largest structure of any kind in the Western Hemisphere. The Mississippians also left many earthen mounds dotting the landscape.

> Scholars estimate that in 1491 North and South America had perhaps as many as 100 million inhabitants, making it more populous than Europe at the time.

Some of these early civilizations, like the Anasazi, declined about two hundred years before the first contact between Europeans and Africans. Others, such as the Aztecs and some of the Mississippians, were still thriving in 1492. Why did these powerful civilizations decline? There is no single answer to the question. Some scholars say that certain civilizations outgrew their capacity to produce food. Others say that battles with enemy tribes forced them to abandon the principal landmarks of their civilization. Still others cite major droughts.

And indeed, not all of these civilizations did decline by the time of first contact with Europeans. Scholars estimate that in 1491 North and South America had perhaps as many as 100 million inhabitants—making it more populous than Europe at the time. Although these numbers are greatly disputed, the idea that the Americas were barren "virgin" land before first contact with Europeans is clearly wrong.

In 1491, American Indians were thriving and transforming the land to suit their needs.

1-1d North America in 1491

By the late 1400s, then, North America was home to numerous civilizations and tribes, some of which were sizeable, dominating large swaths of land. More than two hundred languages were spoken among hundreds of tribes. It would be as if each of today's cities spoke its own language and had unique social rituals. Diversity abounded in this land. So did conflict.

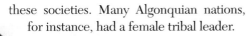

>> Aztec calendar.

iStock.com/SorenP

SOME SOCIAL SIMILARITIES OF NATIVE NORTH AMERICANS

Despite the wide variety of lifestyles developed by the pre-Columbian peoples, there were some broad general similarities among the tribes in North America during the late 1400s. Most of the tribes, for instance, were based on a **clan system**, in which a tribe was divided into a number of large family groups. They were also mostly **matrilineal**, meaning that children typically followed the clan of their mother and that a man, when married, moved into the clan of his wife. Matrilineal societies usually develop when agriculture is the primary food source for a society. In these societies women are in charge of farming (Europeans were universally surprised to see women working in the fields). Thus Indian women maintained the tribe's social institutions while men were hunting, fishing, or off to war. This system was by no means universal in Native North America, but it does signify a level of sexual equality absent from Europe at the time. Indeed, women were just as likely as men to wield political power in some of

these societies. Many Algonquian nations, for instance, had a female tribal leader.

Land was customarily held in common as well, although there are some instances in which individual rights are said to have existed and others where clan rights existed. Enslavement (usually of captured enemies) was relatively common, especially in the tribes of the American Southeast, but Indian enslavement varied in severity, and it is unlikely that enslavement was inherited, meaning that the children of slaves were usually not, by accident of birth, born as chattel.

Most Indian religions were **polytheistic** (believing in many deities) and **animistic** (believing that supernatural beings, or souls, inhabit all objects and govern their actions). Indian religions were usually closely related to the physical world, and local terrain was naturally imbued with spiritual meaning. Placing an emphasis on this world (and not on the next), typical ceremonies featured rain and fertility prayers. Many New England tribes, for example, believed in a ruling deity whom they called Manitou and looked to a dramatic local site (such as Mount Katahdin in Maine) as the source of divine power.

REGIONAL VARIATIONS

These broad similarities aside, the tribes of Native America were rich in regional variety (see Map 1.2). Most variations depended on how a tribe adapted to its surrounding terrain, and thus it is possible to make generalizations based on region.

The Northeast Several sizeable societies lived in the northeast corner of the United States, in the area now called New England. These nations included the Wampanoag, Narragansett, Massachusetts, Mohawk, Oneida, Erie, and Pequot. In general, these groups subsisted on hunting and agriculture, although most of their foodstuffs derived from agriculture. Those that lived along the coast relied on the riches of the ocean. Most of these nations lived in small villages that were closely surrounded by forests that protected them from attack—something that was always a possibility in the congested northeastern region. Indeed, fear of attack was part of the reason that several of these northeastern tribes came together to create the **Iroquois Confederacy**, a political

clan system Living arrangement in which a tribe was divided into a number of large family groups

matrilineal Family arrangement in which children typically follow the clan of their mother and married men move into the clan of their wives; most often seen in agricultural societies

polytheistic Belief system consisting of belief in many deities

animistic Belief system consisting of belief that supernatural beings, or souls, inhabit all objects and govern their actions

Iroquois Confederacy Group of northeastern tribes that joined to form a political and trading entity and later created an elaborate political system; also known as the Haudenosaunee Confederacy

Map 1.2 Native American Nations of North America

>> This map of North America details the numerous Indian nations that resided there, and the various forms of economic activity they engaged in, including agricultural, hunting and gathering, or fishing.

and trading entity that maintained relations between several tribes. (*Iroquois* is actually the European name for the Haudenosaunee Confederacy.) The local forests provided the raw materials for wooden houses crafted by the tribes of the Haudenosaunee, who called them "longhouses." Most of these tribes remained small, however, only occasionally trading with one another.

Other tribes developed cross-regional alliances. The tribes within the Haudenosaunee Confederacy developed an elaborate political system that incorporated villages into nations, then nations into a large confederation. The confederation's leaders were charged with keeping peace among the tribes under its auspices to ensure continuous trade and peaceful

relations. The proximity of one's tribal neighbors in the populous Northeast led many tribes to embrace the politics of the Haudenosaunee. Others, however, viewed the tribes of the Haudenosaunee as bitter enemies.

The Mid-Atlantic In the Mid-Atlantic region, where New York, New Jersey, Pennsylvania, Delaware, Maryland, and Virginia are today, lived the Lenni Lenape (Delaware), Susquehannock, and Nanticock, among others. The people in these tribes lived on a mixture of agriculture, shellfish, and game. They lived a semi-sedentary life, occasionally leaving their stable villages to follow herds of roaming animals. They, too, remained mostly local, aware of, but

>> In 1616, the French explorer Samuel de Champlain described an Iroquois longhouse (pictured here) as follows: "Their cabins are in the shape of tunnels [tonnelles] or arbors, and are covered with the bark of trees. They are from twenty-five to thirty fathoms long, more or less, and six wide, having a passage-way through the middle from ten to twelve feet wide, which extends from one end to the other. On the sides there is a kind of bench, four feet high, where they sleep in summer, in order to avoid the annoyance of the fleas, of which there are great numbers. In winter they sleep on the ground on mats near the fire, so as to be warmer than they would be on the platform."

rarely venturing into, the lands of another tribe. Disputes over boundaries routinely led to violence. The Indians who lived in the woodlands of the Northeast or Mid-Atlantic were collectively called "Woodlands Indians."

The Southeast The Southeast was perhaps the most heavily populated area of Native America at the time of first contact with the Europeans, a fact that would have profound consequences when the Europeans tried to settle there. In today's Florida, Georgia, North Carolina, South Carolina, Alabama, Mississippi, and Louisiana lived the Cherokee (actually named the Tsalagi), Creek, Choctaw, Biloxi, Chickasaw, and Natchez, among others. These tribes subsisted on agriculture, though those living in Florida and the Gulf Coast relied on fishing as well. They developed strong traditions in ceramics and basket weaving; they traded over long distances; and some, such as the Natchez, developed stable, hierarchical political organizations.

The Prairies The prairies, which stretch from today's

>> Totem pole from Stanley Park, Vancouver.

Dakotas south to Oklahoma, were the home of the bison and the tribes that subsisted on them, including the Omaha, Wichita, Kichai, and Sioux. These tribes usually lived on the edges of the plains, where they lived in semi-sedentary agricultural villages and held major hunting parties every year to hunt bison, the chief game animal of the Great Plains. They produced no pottery or basketry, or even much agriculture, as they depended almost entirely on the bison and the local rivers for their subsistence.

The High Plains The Indians of the High Plains, which extend from today's Montana all the way south to northwestern Texas, included the Blackfeet, Crow, Cheyenne, Arapaho, and Comanche. Like the Native Americans of the prairies, these tribes too depended on bison for a large part of their subsistence (especially after contact with European settlers drove them further west), and their only agricultural crop was usually tobacco (again, after contact), which they used for religious purposes and for pleasure.

The Southwest In the Southwest, in today's New Mexico and Arizona (and where the Anasazi had lived), lived the Apache and Navajo tribes, and a large conglomeration of tribes that included the Hopi, Taos, and Zuni, which made up what the Europeans called "the **Pueblo people**." These Indians subsisted almost entirely on agriculture, which is a testament to their ingenuity, considering the slight amount of rain that falls in this region. By about 1200 C.E., several of these tribes had developed villages made up of several multistory buildings built on strategically defensive sites in canyons and river valleys. By the time Columbus had reached the West Indies, some of the Pueblos had developed canals, dams, and hillside terracing to control and channel the limited amount of rainwater. Ceramic pots, which were elaborate and

> Women were just as likely as men to wield political power in some of these societies.

sophisticated during this precontact period, were used to transport water as well. According to one European observer in 1599, the Pueblo people "live very much the same as we do," although he may have said this simply because the Pueblos were one of the few Indian societies to have men, not women, practice agriculture.

The Northwest Thriving off the riches of the Pacific Ocean in the American Northwest, in today's Oregon and Washington, lived the Chinook, Tillamook, Yuki, and Squamish, to name just a few. These peoples ate fish and shellfish in addition to fruits, nuts, and berries. They made plank houses of cedar, which they sometimes surrounded with dramatic carved totem poles. Accomplished artists, they placed a priority on the arts of carving and painting and developed the elaborate ornamentation we commonly see on totem poles. Other prized creations were their artistically designed masks. Many of these tribes celebrated annual holidays, maintained social welfare programs, and adhered to a well-developed view of the cosmos.

INTERTRIBAL HARMONY AND HOSTILITY

Most tribal villages coexisted with their neighbors in a fairly stable balance between peace and warfare, at least until territorial disputes, competition for resources, or traditional rivalries set off battle, which happened often. Indians also went to war to bolster their numbers; male captives taken in war were usually integrated into the victorious tribe's village as slaves, while females and children were commonly integrated as full members.

Jejim/Shutterstock.com

>> Hogans, rounded earthen mounds in which lived many Indians from the American Southwest, were the traditional dwelling units for the Navajo people. They still dot parts of the American Southwest today. The doors typically faced east to welcome the rising sun.

Pueblo people Southwestern conglomeration of tribes including the Hopi, Taos, and Zuni, who lived in today's New Mexico and Arizona

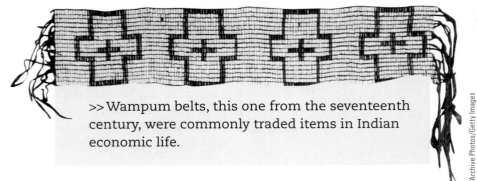

>> Wampum belts, this one from the seventeenth century, were commonly traded items in Indian economic life.

MPI/Archive Photos/Getty Images

Some societies, such as the Maya and Aztecs, developed an entire culture around warfare. The fact that some Indian groups forged defensive alliances, such as the Iroquois Confederacy, demonstrates that protective measures were necessary in a sometimes violent Native America.

But the Haudenosaunee (Iroquois) Confederacy demonstrates something else as well: the Indians' interest in and ability to promote peaceful and productive interactions. In many parts of the land, neighboring tribes traded fruitfully with each other. A network of dirt and stone roads traversed the continent, and towns became centers for trade and commerce. Although such trade was small in scale by European standards, the goods exchanged were vital to each village's way of life: arrowheads, furs, **wampum** (beads made of polished shell), **roanoke** (bracelet-like bands made of wampum), and food. Trade networks could extend over hundreds of miles. For instance, copper goods from the Southwest have been found at Eastern Woodlands sites, and how they got there, we presume, was via trade.

Despite their willingness to barter in portable goods, a sizeable majority of the people of Native America did not believe that property could be privately owned. Bequeathed to all, land could be used by any people so long as they cultivated it properly. In practice, however, tribal leaders granted specific parcels of land to a family for a season or two, and tribes frequently fought bloody battles for control of certain plots of land. When large numbers of Europeans arrived in the 1600s, the tribes of Native America would be forced to reconsider their conception of private property.

wampum Beads made of polished shell, used as currency in trading for goods

roanoke Bracelet-like bands made of wampum

Islam Modern religion that flourished throughout the world beginning in the fourteenth and fifteenth centuries; its adherents are called Muslims

Ghana West African kingdom that prospered from the eighth to the thirteenth centuries; famous for its gold deposits

1-2 AFRICA

Of all the immigrants who came to North America between the sixteenth and eighteenth centuries, roughly 250,000 of them came from Africa as slaves. This was not a huge percentage of all immigrants, but it was a significant one, dramatically influencing labor, social, and cultural relations in the New World. Understanding Africa's social customs is thus critical to understanding the development of the American nation. A large majority of the transplanted Africans were from West Africa (Map 1.3), and most of the West Africans were from a place called Lower Guinea, so our discussion will focus there.

1-2a Politics

Africa, the second largest continent on earth (after Asia), is as varied in climate and geography as North America. It follows, then, that there was great variety in the way Africans lived their lives. By the time of the first sustained contact with Europeans, in the 1400s and 1500s, some African societies had developed vast civilizations, as trade routes wound through the continent's various regions. Africans had also witnessed the spread of **Islam**, which, in the fourteenth and fifteenth centuries, was probably the most powerful and vibrant religion in the world, expanding rapidly throughout Africa, the Middle East, and Spain. One part of the continent transformed by the rise of Islam was West Africa.

GHANA

The kingdom of **Ghana** ruled West Africa from the eighth to the thirteenth centuries, beginning a tradition of expansive trade throughout western Africa using horses, camels, and advanced iron weapons to transport goods and ideas. A kingdom as rich in arts and commerce as any in Europe at the time, Ghana was made up of several large cities, where the people produced elaborate works of art and maintained a stable and complex political structure. Ghana was especially famous for its gold.

But the kingdom's extensive trade routes caused its eventual demise. In the twelfth century, it lost its trade monopoly, and gold was discovered elsewhere in West Africa. In addition, during the first half of the thirteenth century, North African Muslims used Ghanaian trade routes to invade the kingdom, and by 1235 C.E. they had conquered the ruling parties of Ghana.

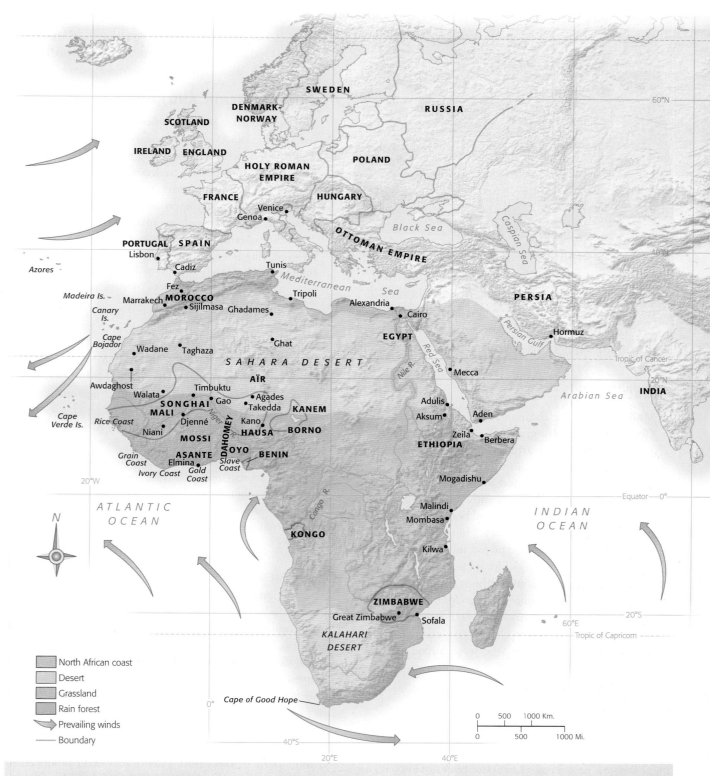

SWEDEN

DENMARK-
NORWAY

SCOTLAND

RUSSIA

IRELAND ENGLAND

POLAND

HOLY ROMAN
EMPIRE

FRANCE

HUNGARY

Venice

Genoa

OTTOMAN EMPIRE

Black Sea

Caspian Sea

PORTUGAL SPAIN

Lisbon

Azores

Cadiz

Tunis

Mediterranean   Sea

PERSIA

Fez

Madeira Is.

Marrakech MOROCCO

Tripoli

Alexandria

Canary
Is.

Sijilmasa Ghadames

Cairo

EGYPT

Hormuz

Cape
Bojador

Wadane   Taghaza

Ghat

SAHARA   DESERT

Nile R.

Mecca

Tropic of Cancer

AÏR

Adulis

Arabian Sea

INDIA

Awdaghost

Timbuktu

Agades

Walata

SONGHAI   Gao

Takedda

KANEM

Aksum

Aden

Cape
Verde Is.

MALI

Niger R.

Kano

BORNO

Zeila

Berbera

Rice Coast

Djenné

HAUSA

Niani

MOSSI

DAHOMEY

OYO

ETHIOPIA

Grain
Coast

ASANTE

BENIN

Mogadishu

Elmina

Ivory Coast

Gold
Coast

Slave
Coast

Equator

20°W

ATLANTIC
OCEAN

Congo R.

Malindi

INDIAN
OCEAN

N

Mombasa

KONGO

Kilwa

ZIMBABWE

20°S

Great Zimbabwe

Sofala

60°E

Tropic of Capricorn

KALAHARI
DESERT

	North African coast
	Desert
	Grassland
	Rain forest
→	Prevailing winds
----	Boundary

0°

Cape of Good Hope

0   500   1000 Km.

0   500   1000 Mi.

40°S

20°E

40°E

Map 1.3 **Africa in 1500**

>> This map of the African continent in the year 1500 shows the major geological features, including deserts, grasslands and rain forests, and the predominant cities of that time.

>> The recent finding of numerous medieval manuscripts in Mali, collectively called "the Timbuktu Manuscripts," promises to teach us more about thirteenth- and fourteenth-century West Africa, before contact with Europeans began in earnest.

MALI

Mali, a flourishing Islamic kingdom, rose in power as Ghana declined. Its principal city, **Timbuktu**, became Africa's cultural and artistic capital, drawing students from as far away as southern Europe. Timbuktu's cultural wealth was demonstrated in its rich artistic and economic resources, and the recently discovered Timbuktu Manuscripts reveal the depth and beauty of the Mali culture. By the thirteenth century, Mali had enveloped the Ghanaian kingdom and expanded mightily. However, Islam did not permeate all of Mali's territories. In contrast to what was happening in northern Africa, Islam spread slowly in the southernmost part of Mali. This southernmost part, called **Lower Guinea**, was the home of the majority of the Africans who came to America. This meant that many of the Africans who were forced to come to

Mali Flourishing Islamic kingdom; it enveloped the kingdom of Ghana by the thirteenth century

Timbuktu Principal city of the kingdom of Mali; cultural capital of Africa in the thirteenth century

Lower Guinea Southernmost part of Mali; home to the majority of the Africans who came to America

Songhay Empire Portion of Mali after that kingdom collapsed around 1500; this empire controlled Timbuktu

Benin African empire on the Malian coast

Kongo African empire on the Malian coast

North America via the slave trade maintained their local religions rather than Islam. Thus, Islam was hardly present in North America during the earliest years of contact.

SONGHAY, BENIN, AND KONGO

The kingdom of Mali collapsed around 1500—just as sustained contact with Europeans was beginning. Mali was divided, with the largest portion replaced by the **Songhay Empire**, which took control of Timbuktu. Farther along the Malian coast, the empires of **Benin** and **Kongo** were similarly approached by European traders in search of goods and, eventually, slaves. Indeed, by 1500, the ruler of the Kongo people converted to Catholicism, having been impressed by the Portuguese traders he had encountered.

1-2b Society

If political control over the region remained in flux in western Africa during the fifteenth and sixteenth centuries, social customs were slightly more stable. Most of the Africans in Lower Guinea lived in kinship groups and, through them, in villages, which were part of larger kingdoms and woven together by a web of roads. The Africans of Lower Guinea were mostly farmers, living in settled agricultural areas. The success of their agriculture allowed some to become artists, teachers, tradesmen, and storytellers—professions that earned their society's respect. Above this group of professionals were nobles and priests, who were mostly older men. Below them were farmers and slaves.

As with many North American tribes, family descent in Lower Guinea was typically matrilineal. Gender roles were generally complementary in Lower Guinea, as women frequently worked as local traders, participated in local politics, and played leading roles in the agricultural society. And, as with the agricultural societies of North America, the presence of stable agriculture meant the development of gendered roles. These cultural systems would all be challenged by sustained contact with Europeans and European-based societies.

The Africans of Lower Guinea also possessed slaves—usually captives from wars or debtors who had sold themselves into slavery to pay off their debt. As in most parts of the world, slavery had been practiced in Africa since prehistoric times. But unlike the type of slavery that developed in the New World, the African system of slavery did not enslave captives for life, nor did it necessarily deny them access to education. Significantly, the children of slaves were not routinely predestined to become slaves themselves; African slavery also was not based on a system of racial classification, as

Ariadne Van Zandbergen/Alamy Stock Photo

would develop in the United States. In fact, most slaves in Africa may have been women, who performed mostly field labor. Not all were laborers, though. Some slaves were servants, others soldiers, and some were artisans. Most slaves in Africa were treated like peasants or tenant farmers rather than human chattel.

1-2c Religion and Thought

Religiously, most of the Africans in Lower Guinea did not embrace Islam; they still believed in their traditional African religions. These religions were as varied as those of Native America, but generally they consisted of belief in a single supreme ruler and several lesser gods. Many of these lesser gods served in worldly capacities—to bring rain and to ensure good harvests, for example. Africans honored these gods elaborately, through their art and their celebrations. There was no single transcendent spirit (such as Christ) mediating between this world and the next, but deceased ancestors served as personal mediators between a person and the gods. This emphasis, in turn, nourished a strong tradition of family loyalty.

1-2d Africa on the Eve of Contact

On the eve of European contact, then, West Africa was, in general, an agricultural society divided into villages organized along matrilineal kinship lines. Some of its people were extremely skilled in the arts, and a class of intellectuals existed who were positioned in houses of learning and supported by kings. Politics advanced in large kingdoms that oversaw and protected their citizens and that allowed for expansive lines of trade. On the whole, West Africans participated in sophisticated societies that had highly developed skills for coping with the diverse geographical settings where they lived.

1-3 EUROPE

While Africans constituted one large block of immigrants between the sixteenth and eighteenth centuries, the vast majority of newcomers to North America came from Europe. These settlers came with a variety of goals and ambitions. Many, but not all, were disappointed in what they found.

1-3a Europe Up to 1492

Europeans were the initiators of the clash of cultures that would take place in the New World. But until the twelfth century, most of Europe was an economic and intellectual backwater in comparison to China, the countries of northern Africa, and parts of the Middle East. Intellectual and religious life thrived in Christian Byzantium (encompassing today's Turkey), and the burgeoning Islamic world was spreading episodically through the Middle East, North Africa, and Spain.

A significant factor in Europe's withdrawal from world affairs was feudal lords' domination of large plots of European land called **manors** (see Map 1.4). These men presided over a system of labor that came to be called **feudalism**, in which a lord granted control over a piece of land to an upper-class ally, or vassal. The vassal's grant included authority over all the land's inhabitants. The vassal treated these laborers as servants, guaranteeing them a level of protection in return for a portion of the fruits of their labor. In reality, these servants, called **serfs**, forfeited nearly all of their freedoms to the lord and vassal. With the exception of the Catholic Church, the nobleman was the sole authority on the land, serving as governor, judge, and war leader. The lords' overwhelming authority meant that serfs were not free and could not act autonomously. They could not change their profession or even move without approval from their lord.

Medieval Europe was therefore split into myriad feudal territories, which divided it linguistically and economically. For instance, England, Scotland, and Wales all had their own languages, fiefdoms, and cultures, and they all existed in just half the size of current New England. Europe also suffered from political instability due to Muslim expansion from the south and Viking raids from the north. Trade and learning virtually disappeared as a result of the battles among feudal lords and between feudal lords and various invaders. The Catholic Church was the sole overarching institution, and during parts of the medieval period, the Church was at its most powerful. As long as Europe was composed of hundreds of these feudal fiefdoms and under threat from raiders abroad, there were no entities that could operate like strong nations.

manor Agricultural estate operated by a lord and worked by peasants in exchange for protection and sustenance

feudalism System of labor in which a lord granted control over a piece of land, and authority over all the land's inhabitants, to an upper-class ally, or vassal

serf Laborer in the feudal system; protected and controlled by the vassal of the estate

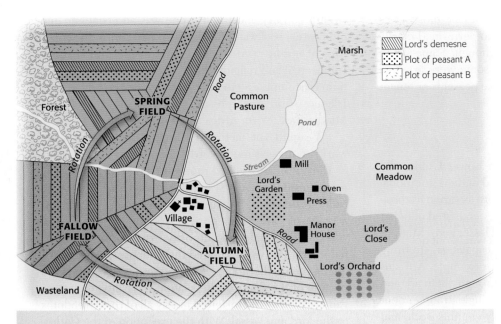

Map 1.4 A Typical European Manor

>> A drawing of a feudal manor, including the village, the shared fields, the common meadow, and the Lord's manor house. Before 1492, most Europeans lived on feudal manors, which were small fiefdoms ruled by lords or vassals and labored on by serfs. The preponderance of manors throughout Europe meant that, until the fifteenth century, Europe was politically unstable and economically divided.

1-3b The Decline of Feudalism

By the fifteenth century, the feudal system was rapidly declining in western Europe. In its stead, nations were becoming more powerful. The four causes for this transition were economic, religious, biological, and political

Renaissance Intellectual and artistic reconnection to the age of Greco-Roman antiquity, starting in the fourteenth century, that lionized the individual

mercantilism Theory that a nation or state's prosperity was determined by the total volume of its trade

Crusades Series of campaigns in which Europeans marched to the Middle East in an effort to seize the Holy Land of Jerusalem, which at the time was controlled by Muslims; battles lasted from 1096 to at least 1291

Black Death Bubonic plague, which started to spread in 1346 and eventually killed one-third of all Europeans

Hundred Years' War War waged between France and England in the fourteenth century over who controlled the French throne

(see "The Reasons Why..." box in this section). Together, these changes would lead to the rise of nations, and the competition among these nations would eventually prompt them to look outward and expand from Europe, sparking an Age of Discovery that would lead to sustained contact with the "New World."

SOCIETY

Socially, most Europeans in the fourteenth and fifteenth centuries still lived in an agrarian society on remnants of the feudal system, although towns and even some great cities had developed since the eleventh century. To ensure a regular food supply, all the members of European villages usually shared their year's crops. As with any society based on agriculture, there were gendered roles in European society. Unlike in some African and Indian cultures, women rarely participated in a town's political life or tilled the fields (but they did have lighter duties in the fields, as did children). Women's power was mostly limited to their influence on their husbands, children, and servants. In contrast, some women in religious orders (Catholic nuns) operated abbeys and wielded significant power in that realm.

Perhaps the greatest change during the thirteenth through fifteenth centuries was the expansion of European cities, where intellectual life prospered. Cities demanded surplus agriculture, which could be supplied only when rural farmers expanded their production to bring food to the market. This development further challenged feudal society because it gave serfs the ability to earn money at the market and thus purchase their freedom from the declining feudal lords.

THE RENAISSANCE

By the late fourteenth century, the forces of economic expansion and the development of urban life allowed for a high level of material well-being in the great European cities and the general decline of closed-off feudal living. It was this wealth and expansive mindset that engendered the **Renaissance**, an intellectual and

The Reasons Why...

There were four causes for the decline of feudalism:

Expanding trade. The first inklings of the transition away from feudalism can be seen around 1000 C.E., when Italian coastal traders began to exploit long-distance trade routes. The riches earned at these trading posts gave several city-states the wealth and power to free themselves from feudal lords. Similarly, merchants began to develop a theory of **mercantilism** (although it would not get that name until Adam Smith coined it in the late 1700s), which suggested that a nation or state's prosperity was determined by the total volume of its trade. Mercantilism was based on the idea that the amount of trade in the world was fixed at a certain level; those who traded favorably simply had a larger piece of the pie. This economic theory gained credence as nations increased in power throughout the sixteenth and seventeenth centuries and as European powers competed to develop colonial empires. It would propel these nations overseas and across continents in search of cheaper or more valuable raw materials.

The Crusades. The second reason for the decline of feudalism was religious. The search for riches fused with the power of the Catholic Church to prompt the **Crusades**, a series of campaigns in which Europeans marched to the Middle East to seize the Holy Land of Jerusalem, at that time controlled by Muslims. These bloody battles were intermittent, lasting from 1096 until at least 1291, and the Europeans never fully succeeded in their mission of permanently capturing the Holy Land. After their bloody excursions, though, crusaders brought back luxuries rarely available to medieval Europe, including spices, silks, and gems. Before long, Europeans deemed these goods invaluable (especially the spices). The Italian merchants who supplied these goods grew fabulously wealthy and began to yearn for greater autonomy and freedom from the feudal system.

The Black Death. The **Black Death**, or bubonic plague, which started to spread in 1346, also advanced the

>> The Black Death killed one-third of all Europeans.

Fine Art/Getty Images

decline of the feudal system. It did so in two principal ways. First, it caused the death of at least one-third of all Europeans, and it did not discriminate by class, meaning that feudal lords died at the same rate as did the poorer members of the continent. Because no one could stop this "Great Pestilence" (as it was called), Europe's leaders appeared weaker and more vulnerable than before. Second, the death of so many farmers meant that those who survived became more valuable; as a result, feudal lords were forced to grant them more allowances, including greater personal freedom, in order to maintain their loyalty. It would take 150 years for Europe's population to recover.

The Hundred Years' War. The fourth reason for the decline of feudalism was rooted in politics. The **Hundred Years' War**, waged between France and England in the fourteenth century, was, at its core, a battle over who controlled the French throne, but it is significant for two reasons.

First, it prodded Italian and Iberian merchants to find water routes that connected southern and northern Europe, as they could no longer safely travel by land through France. This situation spurred several technological advances that would make possible the exploration of North America.

Second, the war allowed the kings to further consolidate their power at the expense of the feudal lords, leading to the rise of several large kingdoms. By the fifteenth century, kings who had long been subjected to the whims of the feudal lords and who did not possess the financial or military power to become absolute rulers began to assert themselves and respond to the mercantilists' demands for organization and protection. The kings did this with considerable popular support; few feudal lords had endeared themselves to their subjects. By the end of the fifteenth century, three strong dynasties had emerged: the Tudors in England, the Valois in France, and the Hapsburgs in Spain. As the power of feudal landlords diminished and that of the kings increased, one idea gained currency: that a person could belong to or identify with a unified nation. This, in some ways, was when the idea of nationalism was born.

artistic reconnection to the age of Greco-Roman antiquity, when humankind was considered to be more cosmopolitan and not merely a source of labor for feudal fiefdoms. Central to Renaissance artists and thinkers was the idea of humanism, which lionized the individual and therefore directly challenged the declining feudal system.

1-3c The Decline of Catholic Europe

If the system of feudalism was declining in the fourteenth and fifteenth centuries, **Catholicism** was still the undisputed religious force in western Europe. Indeed, the artists of the Renaissance usually used Christian images to celebrate the new, more open atmosphere. The Church exerted its greatest power amid the divided feudal society as the sole institution with moral authority and even political power over all of Europe. The later medieval years witnessed Catholicism's greatest thinker, Thomas Aquinas (1225–1274), and its most powerful popes, Innocent III (pope from 1198 to 1216) and Boniface VIII (pope from 1294 to 1303). Catholicism covered Europe like a cloak, unifying many disparate feudal lands.

North Wind Picture Archives

>> Martin Luther took advantage of the invention of the printing press to advocate that scripture be read in local vernacular languages like German and English rather than Latin. Luther's ideas sparked the Protestant Reformation, which challenged the Catholic cloak over Europe, leading to numerous "Wars of Religion" and hastening the development of nationalism.

CHANGE

By the first quarter of the sixteenth century, two impulses collided to challenge the authority of the Catholic Church. The first was a new attitude toward humankind brought about by the slow urbanization of Europe, the consolidation of monarchical powers, and the rise of popular piety. Merchants did not like priests moralizing about their profits, and rulers did not like their authority challenged. In addition, the Church's total incapacity to confront and respond to the crises of the fourteenth century, which included famine, plague, and the Hundred Years' War, prompted several movements of popular piety. Together, these challenges led to the development of **Christian humanism**, defined as a renewed belief in the importance of the single individual as opposed to the institution of the Church. Optimism, curiosity, and emphasis on naturalism were components of the humanistic worldview. These factors led to renewed interest in the sciences, which began to challenge Christianity for worldly authority.

The second event concerned humans' relationship with God, and the Church itself helped invite this second challenge. Beginning during the Crusades of the eleventh century, the Church had grown increasingly secular in its discipline; it had even begun to sell its favors. For instance, some popes used their authority to limit the amount of time a person's soul spent in purgatory; the cost of this divine favor was usually cash. This practice, which grew throughout the thirteenth and fourteenth centuries, was called the **selling of indulgences**.

THE REFORMATION

These dual challenges—the rise of Christian humanism and corruption within the Catholic Church—sparked

Catholicism Central religious force in western Europe; sole institution with moral authority and political power over all of medieval Europe

Christian humanism Belief in the importance of the singular individual, as opposed to the institution of the Church; characterized by optimism, curiosity, and emphasis on naturalism

selling of indulgences Practice of popes using their authority to limit the time a person's soul spent in purgatory, in exchange for cash

the **Protestant Reformation**. At its core, the Reformation was a movement that challenged the Catholic Church to return to its unornamented origins. In addition to questioning the selling of indulgences, the leaders of the Reformation were critical of Church rituals, including the Mass, confession rites that reinforced the hierarchy by putting absolution at the discretion of a priest, and pilgrimages to holy sites. In short, the reformers felt it was faith in God that led to salvation, not the works one did to demonstrate that faith. As protesters (root of the word *Protestant*), the leaders of the Reformation sought a simpler church defined by an individual's relationship to God and the Christ. In Protestantism, the central authority was the Bible; in Catholicism, authority lay with the Bible and also with tradition as espoused by the hierarchy of the Church.

The leaders of the Reformation, most importantly Martin Luther (the moral conscience of the movement) and John Calvin (its great organizer), took advantage of the invention of the **printing press** (developed in the 1440s, although not used widely until the 1450s) to advocate that scripture be read in local vernacular languages like German and English rather than Latin.

The Reformation was important for at least two reasons. First, the Reformation hastened the development of nationalism by fragmenting the unity of Catholic authority over Europe. Freed from that yoke, European nations began to develop unique identities and consolidate wealth, which, in the creed of mercantilism, spurred aggressive attempts to expand in search of greater wealth. This would lead to the Age of Discovery and to sustained contact with both Africa and the New World. Second, the Protestant Reformation triggered several vicious and bloody battles over religion, many of which bled over into the New World and provoked people to leave Europe in search of greater religious freedoms. The Reformation meant that many countries would come to be defined by, and form alliances and enemies based on, the accepted faith of the rulers.

>> Martin Luther became the iconic symbol of the Protestant Reformation in 1517 when he posted his 95 Theses (or Protests) on the door of a Catholic Church in Germany.

Pictorial Press Ltd/Alamy Stock Photo

1-3d Europe in 1492

By 1492, Europe was a dramatically different continent from that of just a century earlier. Europeans had fundamentally altered their political, social, economic, and religious structures. Feudalism, headed by hundreds of feudal lords and vassals, had collapsed, and nations, headed by a handful of kings and queens, had become the most powerful political structures on the continent, covering vast territories and allowing for the easy movement of goods and peoples. Spain was the most powerful nation in Europe at the time, France was the largest, and Portugal had the advantage of superior nautical craftsmanship. Reformers, meanwhile, challenged the righteousness of Roman Catholicism, creating schisms and, eventually, new religious traditions. And in 1492, Spain took control of the city of Granada, ending the northward spread of Islam that had lasted at least five hundred years. Merchants had arisen as a powerful force across the continent too, paving the way for capitalism to flourish and for the market to penetrate more deeply into society than it ever had before. The printing press helped democratize knowledge, allowing scientists to share discoveries and news in many vernacular languages.

England was not as powerful as most of the rest of the countries at the time, mainly because it had been divided by internal religious wars for several decades, as Catholics and Protestants brutally vied for control of the country. It would become a powerful force only later, after Queen Elizabeth muted religious conflict, stabilized the economy, and prepared the country to challenge Spain as the most powerful nation in Europe. All that would take place after 1492.

Protestant Reformation Movement that challenged the Catholic Church to return to its unornamented origins; protesters criticized Church rituals, including the Mass, confession rites, and pilgrimages to holy sites

printing press Invention of the 1440s using metal letter faces to print words on paper, allowing for the quick, widespread dissemination of ideas, opinions, and scientific findings

At the end of the fifteenth century, three societies, long separated from one another and uniquely developed, stood on the verge of sustained contact. The location of this contact would be the "New World," which included North America, as well as Central and South America. Europeans would be the principal catalysts, as their world was in the middle of dramatic changes that led to outward expansion. But the peoples of West Africa and Native America would struggle to shape the outcome of sustained intercultural contact, too. The battle, both physical and ideological, would begin in earnest in 1492.

STUDY TOOLS 1

READY TO STUDY? IN THE BOOK, YOU CAN

❏ Rip out the Chapter Review Card, which includes key terms and chapter summaries.

ONLINE AT WWW.CENGAGEBRAIN.COM, YOU CAN:

❏ Prepare for tests with quizzes.

❏ Review the key terms with Flash Cards.

❏ Read more about the Paleo-Indians.

❏ Read about Kennewick Man

❏ Learn more about why Chaco Canyon declined.

❏ Learn more about feudalism.

❏ Learn about the fall of the Mali and Songhay kingdoms.

CH1 TIMELINE

		What Else Was Happening

8000–13,000 B.C.E. People of Paleo-Indian era develop different languages, economies, beliefs.

c. 200,000 B.C.E.: *The earliest humans appear in Africa.*
16,000 B.C.E.: *The last Ice Age reaches its coldest point; people in Asia, across Beringia, live in huts made from woolly mammoth bones.*

c. 7000 B.C.E. Kennewick man dies.

c. 500–8000 B.C.E. Agriculture and sedentary existence become dominant in Archaic era.

2500 B.C.E.: *Age of the Egyptian pyramids.*

500 B.C.E.–1492 C.E. Pre-Columbian societies develop trade, cities, social hierarchies, science.

1 C.E. Rise of the Roman Empire, birth of Jesus Christ.

900–1150 Anasazi build multistory "apartment houses" in Chaco Canyon.

1000 Italian long-distance trade begins, empowering rich mercantilist city-states.

1096–1291 European crusaders try to capture Jerusalem; return with spices and luxury goods.

1023: *Paper money is printed in China.*

1100 Mississippian city of Cahokia has 20,000 inhabitants—the size of London.

1225–1274 Life of Thomas Aquinas marks the height of Catholic power in Europe.

1235 North African Muslims conquer trade and gold empire of Ghana.

1300s–1600s Modern religion of Islam spreads rapidly through Africa, Middle East, Spain.
Urban wealth and expansion engender Renaissance of culture and humanism.

1300: *Timbuktu is Africa's cultural and artistic capital. Corsets for women are invented.*
1300s: *The Aztecs make "animal balloons" by creating inflated animals from the intestines of cats and present them to the gods as a sacrifice.*

1337–1453 French and English Hundred Years' War prompts new trade routes, larger kingdoms.

1346 Bubonic plague kills one in three Europeans and weakens feudal order.

1440s Invention of printing press.

1500 Empires of Benin and Kongo rise with Mali's demise; first Catholic conversions.

1489: *The symbols + (addition) and − (subtraction) come into general use.*

1517–1648 Christian humanism and secular church practices trigger Protestant Reformation.

2 | Contact and Settlement, 1492–1660

LEARNING OBJECTIVES

After reading this chapter, you should be able to do the following:

2-1 Explain the reasons Europeans explored lands outside Europe, and trace the routes they followed.

2-2 Describe the founding of Europe's first colonies in the New World.

2-3 Trace the expansion of England's holdings in the southern colonies.

2-4 Outline the reasons for and timing of England's founding of colonies in New England.

AFTER FINISHING
THIS CHAPTER
GO TO **PAGE 42**
FOR STUDY TOOLS

In the collision of cultures that took place in the New World, Europeans were the initiators. Their desire to find wealth and spread Christianity brought Indians, West Africans, and Europeans into sustained contact for the first time. At first, the results of contact were generally bad: the tale is mostly one of hunger, disease, and death. After this difficult start, however, the "New World" grew into an increasingly stable confluence of peoples struggling to make a life for themselves under dramatically new circumstances.

2-1 EXPLORATION AND DISCOVERY

Beginning in the fourteenth century, Europeans took advantage of the new technologies developed during the previous century, especially the nautical advances made during the Hundred Years' War, when large parts of central Europe became battlegrounds that required circumvention. They did so for at least two reasons: (1) to alleviate a trade deficit and (2) to spread Christianity (see "The Reasons Why . . ." box below).

2-1a The Eastern Route: The Portuguese

The search for riches and for lands not already in the hands of Christians drew European explorers to several locations around the globe, many of which they encountered quite accidentally. (Indeed, the Americas were perhaps the largest pieces of land ever discovered by mistake.) In 1298, the adventurer Marco Polo wrote that the Orient was the source of many desired goods and that there might be a western route there across the Atlantic Ocean. Others still believed in the existence of an eastern route, through Africa. Both beliefs propelled explorers into the unknown.

Portuguese leaders were among those who still believed that an eastern route could be found. Led by Prince Henry the Navigator (1394–1460), Portuguese sailors traveled down the western coast of Africa searching for the dramatic left turn that would lead them to India and the Middle East. After several failures, and after overcoming fears of mythic ocean monsters or possibly even the fabled edge of the world, in 1498 they finally succeeded. In that year, Vasco da Gama (1469–1524) reached India by rounding the Cape of Good Hope in southern Africa and then heading north to India. His success made Portugal a

The Reasons Why...

Europeans sought to explore lands outside Europe primarily for two reasons:

To alleviate a trade deficit. After the Crusades, many Europeans began to consider spices and other luxuries from the Middle East, India, and parts of Africa true necessities. To reach Europe, the goods had to be shipped from the Far East, through Middle Eastern and then Italian traders. This sequence of middlemen drove prices up, leading to a problem: because Europeans had few commodities to trade in return, they had to use gold to pay for the goods, and gold supplies quickly diminished. This trade deficit led to a depression throughout Europe, as a great deal of money was going out and very little was coming in. The depression sparked a scramble to find another way to obtain the desired goods, namely, a cheaper route to the Far East that would avoid Muslim and Italian middlemen.

To spread Christianity. The second factor in European expansion was the mission to spread Christianity, initially Catholicism, around the world. Like many other religions, Christianity has a missionary message within it, and many of the first explorers thought they could simultaneously search for riches and spread the gospel. Competition from the rapidly growing Islamic faith provided further motivation for spreading Christianity, as did the continuing battles between Catholics and Protestants that began during the Reformation. An important consequence of Christianity's messianic message was that Europeans sought not only trade relations with those whom they came into contact with, but also dominion over them.

◀◀◀ This engraving from 1590 depicts Christopher Columbus' first landing in North America, bringing Christianity (note the cross) and being greeted with gifts of jewels and gold as native people dance with joy in the background. First contact between Europeans and those already in North America was, of course, considerably more complicated.

> "Plenty of rubies, plenty of emeralds! You owe great thanks to God, for having brought you to a country holding such riches!"
>
> —VASCO DA GAMA

wealthy nation throughout the sixteenth and seventeenth centuries (see Map 2.1).

2-1b The Beginnings of European Slavery

Before da Gama's success, however, in the 1440s Portuguese sailors made a discovery that would be critical for the development of future relations between cultures. African kings wanted to trade with the Portuguese along the shore, and both sides benefited from the trade in goods. But in the process, the Portuguese also bartered for African slaves. They carried them back to Portugal as living novelties, thus introducing the system of African slavery to Europe during the fifteenth century.

Slavery had long been a prominent form of labor throughout the fifteenth century, though it was almost never based on one's race. By the 1490s however, the Portuguese had taken control of a previously uninhabited island off the west coast of Africa called São Tomé.

São Tomé had the perfect soil for growing sugar, a product much in demand in Europe. Sensing profits, in the 1500s the Portuguese began using African slaves to harvest sugar in São Tomé, and in the process established the first modern economy dependent primarily on race-based slave labor. While the preoccupation with race-based slavery would become paramount a few centuries later, it is vital to remember that the vast majority of people in the New World in the sixteenth and seventeenth centuries were unfree laborers, whether they were indentured servants, Native American prisoners of war held in captivity, or slaves held by opposing kingdoms. Slavery was simply the most extreme form of unfree labor at the time; only in the New World did it eventually become based almost entirely on one's race and passed down from generation to generation.

2-1c The Western Route: The Spanish

With Portugal's numerous successes along the African coast and into India, rival Spain acted like a jealous neighbor, and Spanish sailors began advocating the search for a western route to the Orient. After years of delay, the Spanish monarchy finally agreed to fund the costly venture. The first voyage that Spain reluctantly funded, in 1492, was that of Christopher Columbus (1451–1506), a Portuguese-trained Italian sailor. The Spanish monarchs, Ferdinand and Isabella, sent him westward with three small ships, the *Niña*, the *Pinta*, and the *Santa Maria*. On October 12, 1492, after ten long weeks at sea, Columbus and his crew sighted land in

>> This fifteenth-century exploring ship shows the angel of the Lord leading the ship forward with its full sails and bountiful surrounding fish. No matter where they went, European explorers often felt God was on their side.

© Eon Images

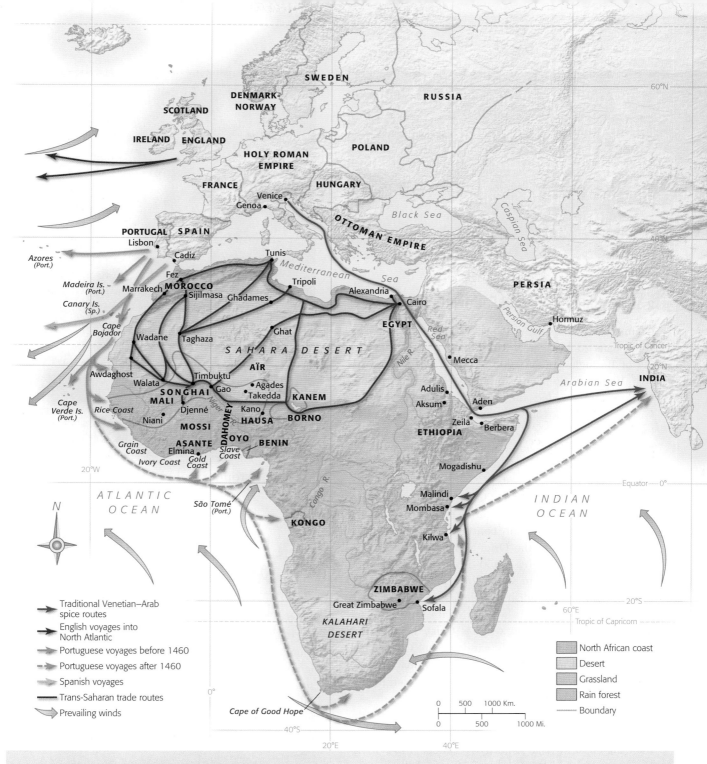

Map 2.1 **Routes of Early Exploration**

>> Starting in the fifteenth century, Europeans embarked on sea voyages that eventually circum-navigated the globe. This map shows several voyages from Europe to North America and Africa.

Map legend:

- Traditional Venetian–Arab spice routes
- English voyages into North Atlantic
- Portuguese voyages before 1460
- Portuguese voyages after 1460
- Spanish voyages
- Trans-Saharan trade routes
- Prevailing winds

- North African coast
- Desert
- Grassland
- Rain forest
- Boundary

the present-day Bahamas. Thinking this was an outlying portion of Asia and India, he called the local inhabitants "Indians." Columbus returned to Spain shortly thereafter, bringing some treasures and, more importantly, tales of the possible riches via the western route. In fact, of course, he had not found Asia or India at all; he was the first European in several centuries to set foot in North America.

> "They ought to be good servants. Our Lord pleasing, I will carry off six of them at my departure . . . in order that they may learn to speak."
>
> —CHRISTOPHER COLUMBUS, ON NATIVE NORTH AMERICANS

2-1d Predecessors and Followers

Columbus and his crew, however, were not the first Europeans to land in North America since the closing of Beringia some 10,000 years earlier. Around the year 1000 C.E., Leif Ericson and a cadre of Scandinavian explorers sailed their brightly colored ships to Greenland and possibly as far south as Cape Cod in today's Massachusetts. During the following decade or two, Scandinavians made several expeditions to North America, but they established neither lasting settlements nor substantive trading posts.

And so it was only after Columbus that a host of other explorers set out in search of treasures in the Middle and Far East. Many continued to search for the lucrative "passage to the Orient" by sailing west from Europe. John Cabot (ca. 1450–1499), like Columbus, was an Italian sailor in search of a patron. He found backing from the English merchants of Bristol, a city in southern England. He set sail in late May 1497 and landed a month later in what is today northeastern Canada. Riding the easterly winds home, Cabot landed in England just two weeks after he departed from Canada. His stories and his rapid return fueled further interest in exploration.

The Americas got their name from the first sailor to realize that he had reached a "new world" rather than the coast of Asia: Amerigo Vespucci (1454–1512). Vespucci explored the Caribbean Sea and the coast of South America from 1497 to 1502. Vasco de Balboa (ca. 1475–1519) was the first European to sail the Pacific (1513). Ferdinand Magellan's (1480–1521) crew completed the first circumnavigation of the world from 1519 to 1522 (although Philippine tribespeople killed Magellan shortly before the end of the journey). All these men, and others who explored North America, were prominent players in what historians have dubbed the "Age of Exploration."

iStock.com/Wynnter

>> Christopher Columbus.

2-2 EARLY SETTLEMENTS AND COLONIZATION

Most of these early voyages were intended simply to create trading networks. Few sought to create lasting settlements, and even fewer sought to colonize these exotic lands. However, each European power competitively sought the profits of sustained contact, and this competition for wealth drove them to create encampments that would enable them to defend their claims to those faraway natural resources.

2-2a Portuguese

After Columbus's voyage, Spain claimed possession of all of North America. Predictably, the Portuguese would have none of it. They protested Spain's claim. To prevent open conflict between the two Catholic nations, Pope Alexander VI intervened. In 1493, he drew a line on a map that extended from north to south, proclaiming that all land east of the line belonged to Portugal, all land west of it to Spain. The effect of this line, called

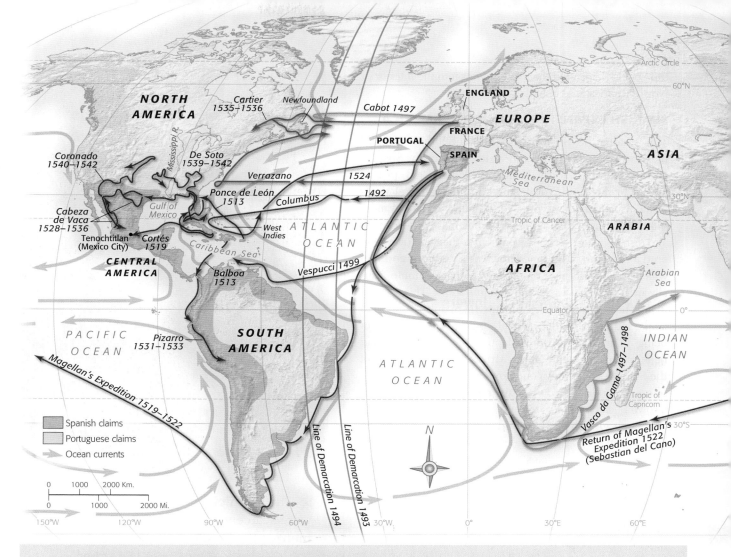

Map 2.2 Exploration in the New World, 1492–1542

>> This map details the expansive exploration of the fifteenth and sixteenth centuries.

the **Line of Demarcation**, was to grant all of Brazil to Portugal, while Spain had claim to Central and North America. In 1500, the Portuguese explorer Pedro Cabral accidentally landed in Brazil, beginning what would be Portugal's most profitable colonial venture. As perhaps the first act of modern European colonialism, the pope made his arbitration with no consideration of the peoples already inhabiting the land (see Map 2.2).

2-2b Spanish

Despite Portugal's early ambition, it was the Spanish that established the first colonies in North America. In the process, they began one of the bloodiest chapters in the history of the world, as disease and warfare nearly vanquished the native populations of the Caribbean, Mexico, and North and South America. The advent of disease was so bad that

the entire world's population dropped by perhaps as much as 20 percent in the fifteenth and sixteenth centuries. Furthermore, Spain, searching for gold and other sources of wealth, brutally abused the native populations, often enslaving them and forcing them to work in gold mines. Just two decades after Columbus first crossed the Atlantic, the Spanish had established permanent settlements in Hispaniola, Cuba, Puerto Rico, Jamaica, and Panama. By 1513, the enslaved natives of Hispaniola were producing $1 million worth of gold annually. It would be only a few years before

Line of Demarcation Line drawn by Pope Alexander VI through a map of the Western Hemisphere; granted the eastern half to Portugal and the western half to Spain, in what could be considered the first act of modern European colonialism

the Spanish expanded their settlements into the interior of North America in search of greater riches.

SPANISH EXPANSION INTO NORTH AMERICA

The system the Spanish used to develop their colonies was distinct. In the early sixteenth century, Spanish **conquistadors**, mostly minor noblemen, led private armies to the New World. These armies were relatively small, usually made up of fewer than one thousand men, but they devastated indigenous populations with weapons and disease wherever they went. Once they had overpowered a kingdom, it became known as an **encomienda**, in which Indian villages were obliged to pay a tribute, usually in gold or slaves, to the conquistadors. This system, in essence, enslaved the Indians in Spanish-controlled lands, although no one actually owned another human being. (The Spanish were adapting the system that had been enforced by the North African Muslims to control the Spanish when they conquered Spain.) As the number of encomiendas grew, **viceroys** reporting directly to the Crown began to govern them.

Their growth also inspired a stern opposition to the brutal manner in which the conquistadors exerted their control over the Indians. Of these critics, Bartolomé de las Casas, a Spanish priest, is the most famous. His book, *A Short Account of the Destruction of the Indies* (1552), serves as a key beginning point for humanitarian concerns about the potential for cruelty inspired by imperialism, although it must be quickly added that de las Casas proposed expanding the enslavement of Africans in order to reduce the perpetual mistreatment of Native Americans, hardly a humanitarian tradeoff.

Despite protests like that of de las Casas, Spanish imperialism continued. The most successful of the conquistadors were Hernán Cortés (1485–1547) and Francisco Pizarro (ca. 1475–1541), whose adventures sparked widespread interest in the New World.

Cortés and Mexico Between 1519 and 1521, Hernán Cortés led an expedition of six hundred men against the Triple Alliance (better, if incorrectly, known as the Aztecs) in Mexico and their ruler, Montezuma. Cortés was greatly aided by a slave given to him by the natives of Tabasco, a

conquistador One of the Spanish noblemen who sailed to the New World with small armies to vanquish kingdoms there

encomienda Tribute, usually payable in gold or slaves, that was demanded of conquered Indian villages by the conquistadors

viceroy Representative of the Spanish crown who governed conquered Indian villages

North Wind Picture Archives/Alamy Stock Photo

>> The sacrificial practices of the Aztecs were scarcely more brutal than their treatment at the hands of Cortés and his men.

woman who came to be known as La Malinche, who eventually served as his interpreter, guide, and lover. In addition to La Malinche, four weapons allowed Cortés and his men to overrun the huge civilization: (1) horses, which allowed mobility; (2) firearms, which terrorized their victims; (3) the support of other Indian tribes who had suffered under Aztec rule; and (4), by far the most important weapon, disease. Smallpox was first introduced to the New World by one of Cortés's men in 1519 and by 1520 had decimated the Aztecs. Under assault from these four weapons, the great Aztec civilization fell into Spanish hands within two years of Cortés's arrival, and, to Cortés's delight, so did the Aztecs' gold and silver. The Spanish built Mexico City on the ruins of the Aztec capital, Tenochtitlán. Hoping to find the same plunder that Cortés had found, Spanish colonists soon arrived in large numbers, and Mexico City became the largest "European" city in America.

Pizarro and Peru By the 1530s Francisco Pizarro, well aware of Cortés's triumph, explored the western coast of South America from a base he established in Panama. In 1532, he and his army of just 168 men (mostly untrained soldiers) encountered the tremendous Inca Empire of Peru. Initially, like the Aztecs, the Incas welcomed the army, but the relationship quickly soured. Many of the Inca soldiers were off at battle with another tribe caused in part because the ravages of smallpox had created political strife for the Incas. In the meantime, Pizarro kidnapped the Inca leader, amassed a huge fortune by ransoming his life, killed him anyway, and seized the Inca capital of Qosqo. With the Inca warriors away, Pizarro faced only mild resistance from what would have been formidable foes. When the Inca soldiers returned, Pizarro and his men were already entrenched in the empire. He founded the city of Lima as his capital in 1535 and ruled from there until his death in 1541. Internal battles within the Indian populations and especially smallpox had once again contributed to the decline of what had been a vibrant civilization.

The Caribbean In addition to Mexico and Peru, throughout the sixteenth and seventeenth centuries the Caribbean islands were some of the most prized New World possessions. From the time of Columbus, Europeans had attempted to subjugate the local Caribbean Indians to mine gold, search for food, and, in the case of the Spanish, serve as sexual companions. When sugar production began in earnest in the mid-1600s, Europeans devoted vast amounts of resources to grow the valuable cane. By the late 1600s, huge numbers of African slaves worked in the Caribbean. Without the presence of significant numbers of native inhabitants, the Spanish turned several sugar-producing Caribbean islands into some of the greatest generators of wealth in the world.

Florida Although of second-rate importance to the Spanish (because there was no gold), in today's United States the Spanish developed settlements in Florida and the Southwest. The Spanish initially had little interest in Florida, but when French adventurers began to use eastern Florida as a base from which to attack Spanish ships traveling to Mexico and Peru, Spain sent soldiers to drive out the French pirates. In 1565, in order to secure the region and protect their ships traveling to and from Mexico and the valuable Caribbean, the Spanish conquered the city of St. Augustine from the French. St. Augustine, now a part of Florida, is the oldest continually occupied European-established city in the continental United States. Under Spain's control, it was largely a town ruled by military leaders and Catholic clergymen, serving as an anchor for Spain's northernmost imperial designs.

The American Southwest The Spanish also explored the American Southwest, heading north from Mexico as far as present-day Colorado. As with St. Augustine in Florida, the Spanish occupied the town of Santa Fe to secure the region against intruders but had little other use for it. In 1598, Juan de Oñate, a Spanish conquistador, became the first European governor of a future American state—New Mexico. But again, other than a first line of defense and a missionary outpost, Spanish developments in today's United States were of secondary importance.

RESULTS OF SPANISH CONQUEST

By the middle of the 1500s, Spanish conquistadors controlled numerous areas surrounding the Gulf of Mexico. There were five principal results of this initial Spanish conquest: (1) biological, (2) financial, (3) racial, (4) religious, and (5) geopolitical.

Biological The most important result was the **Columbian Exchange**, in which agricultural products, domesticated animals, and microbial diseases crossed over from one civilization to the other, creating a vast "exchange" that would forever change the world, for good and for ill. As more Spanish came to the New World, they unknowingly carried with them microbes for several diseases to which Indians had not been exposed, smallpox being the most destructive. The direct result of the spreading of these microbes was the death of perhaps as much as 95 percent of the Indian population. The numbers tell the story. Historians estimate that more than 25 million people lived in central Mexico before Cortés arrived. Fifteen years after his arrival, more than 8 million had perished, almost one out of every three people. And within a few generations, diseases had eliminated two-thirds of the native population. And a century after first contact, the Indian population of central Mexico was around 700,000. It took less than one hundred years for this population to fall from more than 25 million to 700,000.

Diseases also spread far from the location of their initial inception, debatably stretching as far north as New England. This is perhaps one reason why English explorers found so few Indians when they first landed on the Atlantic Coast in the 1600s, although diseases affecting New England's tribes may also have come from contact

Columbian Exchange Biological crossover of agricultural products, domesticated animals, and microbial diseases from Europe to the New World and vice versa

>> This image titled "How Indians Treat Their Sick," from *Neue Welt und Americanische Historien* by Johann Ludwig Gottfried, demonstrates not only the prevalence of illness in Native America but also the high level of care and attention Indians gave to their sick, a counterpoint to the alternate image of them being generally inhuman.

chocolate, and potatoes, all of which had been first cultivated by Indians, came to Europe. The development of sugar plantations in the Caribbean Islands was also a product of the Columbian Exchange, although their dependence on slaves was a corrosive element of the exchange. The number of foods and animals that traversed the globe for the first time is truly astounding.

Financial Financially, the economic impact of the flow of silver from the mines of these lands was enormous. The influx of minerals made Spain one of the wealthiest nations in the world. Spain could now afford to defend a three-way trade between West Africa, the Americas, and Europe. But the sudden abundance of silver also meant that many people had access to money, causing prices to rise. The result was an inflationary **price revolution**, which badly hurt European laborers and landless agricultural workers, whose wages could not keep up with rising prices. Increased numbers of impoverished Europeans were driven to emigrate to the Americas in search of a new life.

Racial Another component of the Columbian Exchange concerns race, as Spanish exploration began the process of mixing various races of people. For one, the Spanish explorers procreated with Indian women. The child of Cortés and La Malinche, a boy named Martin, is considered one of the first Mestizos, or people of mixed European and indigenous American ancestry. For another, the depopulation of Native America by disease expedited the introduction of African slaves as a labor force in the New World. By 1600, the multiracial character of the New World was firmly established.

Religious A fourth result of the Spanish conquest concerns religion. In order to convert the Indians, the Spanish often destroyed Indian temples and replaced them with Catholic cathedrals. Catholic friars tried to use the religious symbols of the Indian religions to teach the lessons of Catholicism. But often the Indians transformed Catholic saints into spiritual likenesses of their preexisting gods and goddesses. The most famous example of this religious meshing was the Indian corn goddess and the Virgin Mary. Many Indians were able to accept the Catholic

with European fishermen off the coast of Canada. For their part, Indians may have introduced syphilis to Europeans, but even if syphilis did originate in the New World, it was hardly as deadly as smallpox or measles proved to be. Lest this part of the exchange be used to induce latter-day guilt in Europeans or European-Americans, most historians believe that, due to complex genetic dispositions within the Indian population, there would have been no way to prevent this microbial transmission. Furthermore, the recent work of Mexican epidemiologist Rodolfo Acuña suggests that many Indians in today's Mexico might have died from a disease called cocoliztli, which had nothing to do with smallpox and which was likely not imported from Europe.

If the exchange of microbes had horrifying ramifications, the mutual transfer of plants and animals led to a more positive biological exchange between the Americas and Europe. Contact allowed the cultures to expand the kinds of food they could grow and the animals they could domesticate. Horses and livestock were introduced to the Americas by the Europeans; maize, tobacco, tomatoes,

price revolution Inflationary event, such as the huge influx of silver to Spain in the mid-1500s, that causes the price of goods to surpass the wages paid to laborers and landless agricultural workers

faith on their own terms once it had been hybridized in this way. Still, this was typically not what the Europeans considered a pure understanding of the faith.

Geopolitical Meanwhile, Spanish successes meant that other European nations became hungry for conquest. Rivalries grew as nations sought resources they lacked at home. Of the five major results of the Spanish conquest, geopolitical concerns were the most significant in bringing the French and the English into New World exploration.

2-2c French

Like the Spanish and the Portuguese, French explorers, too, had been searching for the fabled route to the Orient. They focused on looking for the Northwest Passage that would lead them through today's Canada to the Pacific Ocean. The French never found this nonexistent route, but they did find valuable products, mainly furs, that they could return to France.

The result was the creation of several encampments in present-day Canada that served as French trading posts in the New World. The largest was Quebec, founded in 1608. At these encampments, the French traded for furs with the Indians and spread Catholicism. However, the French were beleaguered by disease, by warfare with the Iroquois (who resented the Frenchmen's successful trade with the Algonquians), and by the weather of the Northeast. Thus they remained a small but sturdy presence in North America, with holdings that extended great distances but vanished quickly after challenges from the more entrenched English throughout the 1700s. In the mid-1600s, there were only about four hundred French colonists in North America.

2-2d Dutch

The Dutch too quickly got into the game of North American colonization. By the late sixteenth century, they had concentrated their settlements in the Caribbean, trying to win a share of the wealth created in the sugar colonies. They colonized St. Croix, Tobago, Tortuga, and St. Maarten in the 1620s and 1630s. Also in the 1630s, the Dutch won a large chunk of northern Brazil from the Portuguese. They had also begun to explore further north, when a Dutch trading company hired the English sailor Henry Hudson to sail up

>> The Dutch were among the most adventurous travelers to the Americas. In 1615, the Dutch navigator Willem Cornelis Schouten, depicted here, became the first European to explore the southern tip of South America, giving it its name, Cape Horn.

what is now the Hudson River in New York. As an example of the bloody competition between the rivaling European powers, the Dutch were often knocked off their most valuable holdings by Spain and France.

The existence of all these forces—competing European powers criss-crossing the ocean, the peoples of the New World engaged in battles with Europeans and themselves, goods and people imported from Africa—has led scholars to see this area as a unique place, a place they have called the **Atlantic World**.

2-2e English: Planting Colonies, Not Marauding for Wealth

The English were slow to enter into New World exploration because the Tudor family was still consolidating their Crown in the early 1500s, when Portugal, Spain, and France were busy traveling abroad. Furthermore, the Tudors at this time were closely allied with Spain (both were still Catholic) and did not want to challenge Spain's dominance in the New World. Also, during the

Atlantic World The complex interactions among the peoples and empires bordering the Atlantic Ocean from about 1450 to the 1800s

early 1500s, the English textile industry was booming, so wealthy Englishmen chose to invest in textile businesses rather than in high-risk overseas ventures. Furthermore, young adventurous Englishmen could find opportunities for colonial exploration closer to home in Ireland.

By the middle of the 1500s, this English disinclination toward North American exploration began to change. There were at least four reasons for this: (1) religious; (2) economic; (3) social; and (4) geopolitical (see "The Reasons Why . . ." box).

Despite hopes to the contrary, England (and all other European nations other than Spain) did not find great wealth through quick plundering of existing civilizations in the Americas. England's wealth from the New World came instead through prolonged colonization, the development of substantial economies, and the exploitation of agricultural resources. As illustrated by Sir Walter Raleigh's explorations, it would take time and experience for the English to learn to focus on such endeavors. The desire for quick riches has persisted as a human flaw through the ages.

SIR WALTER RALEIGH AND ROANOKE

Sir Walter Raleigh was the first Englishman to found a New World colony. Raleigh received a royal patent to claim New World lands in the name of the queen, who was eager to check Spain's colonial expansion. In 1585, he established his first colony, using the Spanish conquistadors as his model. Like the Spanish adventurers

The Reasons Why...

There were four key reasons why the English became more interested in exploration in the mid-1500s:

Religious. After several contentious decades during which Catholics and Protestants fought bitterly over whose faith was the rightful inheritor of the Bible, Protestant Queen Elizabeth I came to the throne. Queen Elizabeth's support of the Reformation suddenly turned England into Europe's leading opponent of powerful Catholic Spain. Their rivalry increased after Spain supported two unsuccessful Roman Catholic plots to assassinate Elizabeth for her support of the Reformation (whether Pope Sixtus V was aware of these attempts remains an open question). Making matters worse, in 1588 Spain tried unsuccessfully to invade England. This intense rivalry meant that the English were unwilling to allow Catholic Spain to convert all the non-Christians of the New World without competition from the surging English Protestants.

Economic. The second motive for English expansion was that the textile markets of Antwerp, Belgium, failed in the late 1500s, a development that left English producers without this market for their cloth. As a result, many wealthy individuals stopped investing in textiles and looked for new opportunities, such as New World exploration. In addition, England had begun to import large quantities of raw materials, which created a dangerous trade imbalance. The New World had the potential to supply the English with raw materials at cheaper prices.

Social. Meanwhile, the enclosure of farms and the inflationary price revolution created a glut of impoverished Englishmen seeking to escape poverty by leaving England. But the poor were not the only English affected by limited economic possibilities. The English gentry was growing, and after the Church of England separated from the Catholic Church, traditional opportunities for the younger sons of nobles to serve in the Catholic Church were closed. With little unsettled land remaining in England, many members of the English upper class were willing to seek their fortune in the colonies.

Geopolitical. Fourth, Queen Elizabeth's durability as a monarch, reigning for over fifty years, stabilized the Tudor throne, meaning that England could now participate wholeheartedly in New World ventures. The bitter relations between Spain and England had erupted into war after Elizabeth knighted the English pirate Francis Drake for his raids on Spanish treasure ships from 1578 to 1580. The Anglo-Spanish war, most noted for the defeat of the Spanish Armada, led to an English victory. For our purposes, the Anglo-Spanish war is significant for two reasons. First, it established England as ruler of the sea, prompting it to begin exploring the New World, and second, it signaled the decline of Spain as a world power. Now other nations could more successfully capitalize on the promises of the New World.

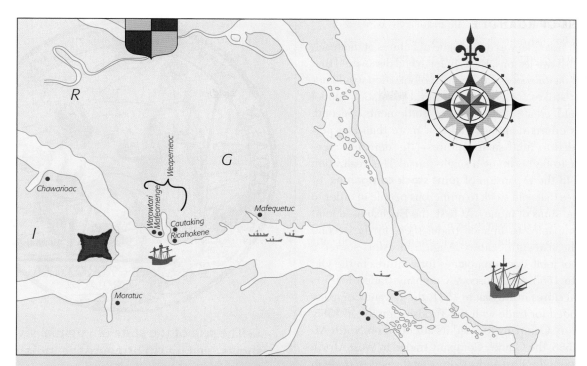

R

G

Chawarioac

I

Warowtari
Mateomenge

Weapemeoc

Cautaking
Ricahokene

Mafequetuc

Moratuc

>> In 2012, researchers looking at an old map of Roanoke discovered that someone had placed a piece of paper over a bright red mark, which might have been a place where members of the "lost colony" went to. Excavations are ongoing.

who had conquered the Aztecs and Incas, Raleigh and his men sought gold and silver, and he planned to exploit native labor to mine these treasures.

But there was a hitch in Raleigh's plan. Hoping to avoid conflict with the Spanish, Raleigh decided to focus his search to the north of Spain's territories in Mexico and South America. He and his men established their base at Roanoke, on the outer banks of modern-day North Carolina, a region lacking mineral wealth. Frustrated in their search for New World gold and silver, Raleigh's men abandoned the colony within a year and returned to England.

After the first Roanoke settlement failed, Raleigh decided to continue his efforts on a different basis. He returned to the same region because he still wanted to avoid the Spanish, but this time he declared that he would not seek easy treasure. Learning from his initial failure and drawing on the experience of English settlements in Ireland earlier in the century, Raleigh decided that his second colony would consist of **plantations**. Instead of sending conquerors, he sent whole families to the New World, hoping to recreate English society and its agricultural economy. Poor English farmers would perform the labor on the plantations, while transplanted gentry would perform their traditional functions of land ownership and governance.

But Raleigh's second Roanoke colony ultimately failed as well. Voyages to resupply the colonists were delayed by wars between England and Spain, and by the time a ship finally reached Roanoke in 1590, the outpost was deserted, perhaps after an attack by a local Indian tribe. The fate of the roughly one hundred settlers has never been conclusively determined, and the second Roanoke settlement came to be known as the **lost colony of Roanoke**. Evidence discovered in 2012 by using modern technology to examine old maps suggests that there may have been a fort built further inland from the original colony, a place to which the colonists might have decamped until supplies arrived. Mysteriously, someone had pasted a correction over the site of the fort on the map, shrouding it from historians for more than 400 years, shown in the redrawn image of the original map in this section. Excavations are currently ongoing at the new location, which presently sits amid a golf course and homes.

plantation Large farm staffed by an entire family in an agricultural economy

lost colony of Roanoke Second settlement by English colonists at Roanoke; deserted sometime before 1590

LESSONS OF ROANOKE

Although Roanoke was a catalogue of failures, it did teach the English two lessons. First, Raleigh had discovered that the formula for successful English colonization would not be quick strikes for gold but rather a plantation model that would create self-sustaining settlements. Second, Raleigh's efforts demonstrated that more than one person needed to fund such ventures—the demands were too great to be borne by a single purse. This realization resulted in the expansion of **joint stock companies**, or companies that sold stock to numerous people in order to raise large sums of money. At first, the English used joint stock companies to finance trade; then, in the second half of the sixteenth century, English investors started a number of joint stock companies for ventures in the Old World. In 1553, the Muscovy Company traded for furs and naval stores in Russia; in 1581, the Levant Company was founded for trade with the Turkish Empire; in 1585, the Barbary Company focused its attention on North Africa; in 1588, the Guinea Company traded in West Africa; and in 1600, the East India Company formed to trade in Asia. Many of these British companies were highly successful, and they encouraged many English investors to consider establishing colonies overseas by the early 1600s.

>> The seal of the state of Virginia, vividly shows the English bringing the Indians Christianity in return for the gift of New World tobacco.

Florida Center for Instructional Technology

 2-3 # ENGLAND FOUNDS THE SOUTHERN COLONIES, 1607–1660

After learning (if not always adhering to) these two lessons—using the plantation model rather than one of the conquistadors, and spreading the financial risk around by using joint stock companies— the English began to expand their holdings in the New World. Between 1600 and 1660, more than 150,000 English people left for the New World. Most went to the sugar islands of the West Indies, while perhaps slightly less than a third crossed the Atlantic to settle the eastern coast of North America.

> From 1607 to 1609, more than 900 settlers arrived in Jamestown. Only 60 survived the first few years.

2-3a Virginia: Jamestown

Despite 115 years of contact, the year 1607 is often regarded as the first year of American history. It was in that year that the English established their first lasting colony in the land that would become the United States: **Jamestown**, in present-day Virginia.

Begun by the Virginia Company of London (a joint stock company), Jamestown began with 104 colonists, some of whom favored the plantation model of settlement, others of whom favored the conquistador model. Failure bedeviled them, however, mainly because of a harsh drought and because this group of settlers included too many English gentlemen who had little desire either to work the soil or to build fortifications. Most notably, John Smith attempted to unite this first group of settlers, but his rise to power insulted many of the gentleman explorers, who had him shipped back to England. The first years for these settlers were difficult, as disease, lack of food, poor management, and hostile relations with Indian tribes took a toll. Historians now call the winter of 1609–1610 the

joint stock company Company that sold stock to numerous investors in order to raise large sums of money

Jamestown English settlement of 1607 in present-day Virginia

starving time, when food supplies were so scarce that at least one colonist resorted to cannibalism. Only the continued arrival of new colonists kept the settlement functioning. From 1607 to 1609, more than 900 settlers arrived in Jamestown. Only 60 survived the first few years.

JAMESTOWN FINALLY SUCCEEDS

Jamestown eventually succeeded, and its success depended on two things: Indian relations and tobacco.

The Powhatan Confederacy First, the English settlers, badly in need of food, relied on a group of six Algonquian villages known as the **Powhatan Confederacy** (named after its leader). Powhatan and his people saw the English settlers as allies who would accept food in return for knives and guns, which would help Powhatan secure his confederacy against other Indian nations. This was likely a difficult decision, because the Indians had little idea of what the colonists had in mind regarding the kind of life they wanted to develop in the New World. Other Indians deemed it less troublesome to simply attack and kill the newcomers. The relationship between Powhatan's people and the Virginians was sometimes violent, especially when crops were limited. But the Powhatan Confederacy did assist the English settlers throughout their struggling early years.

Tobacco Second, in the early 1610s, the English settlers hit a jackpot: they successfully cultivated tobacco. The Spanish had introduced the crop to Europe in the late 1500s after first encountering it in the Caribbean. Tobacco had been a tremendous success in the markets of Europe, making it, along with sugar, one of the most profitable **cash crops** of the New World. By 1612, the Virginia settler John Rolfe (best known for making peace with the local tribes by marrying Pocahontas, the daughter of a local chieftain) had successfully cultivated an imported strain of tobacco in Jamestown. The colonists shipped the first crop to England in 1617, and by 1620 they had delivered 40,000 pounds of the cured plant back to England. Within a few years, shipments had climbed to 1.5 million pounds. Virginia was about to boom.

JAMESTOWN GROWS

The success of tobacco made Jamestown a more appealing place to be. But cultivating tobacco requires labor. To meet this need, early tobacco growers attempted to follow the Spanish model and force Indians to work in their fields. Such efforts were hampered by several problems: Indians objected to the concept of growing surplus crops for cash; language barriers made it difficult for English

POCAHONTAS.

iStock.com/traveler1116

>> At the age of twenty-one, Pocahontas visited London, where she was presented to King James I and the court. In March 1617, she and her husband, John Rolfe, departed for home, but it soon became clear that Pocahontas would not survive the voyage. She died of pneumonia or tuberculosis and was taken ashore and buried far from her home.

planters to explain their demands; and, chiefly, the colonists lacked the military force required to enslave Indians. In 1619, Dutch traders imported a small number of Africans to Jamestown, who performed much of the back-breaking work of establishing a town. However, because it was so expensive to transport, then feed, house, and force African slaves to work for free, the institutionalized

starving time Winter of 1609–1610 in Jamestown, when food supplies were so scarce that at least one colonist resorted to cannibalism

Powhatan Confederacy Group of six Algonquian villages in present-day Virginia, named after its leader

cash crop Agricultural product grown primarily for sale. Examples include sugar and tobacco harvests

England Founds the Southern Colonies, 1607–1660   35

importation of Africans was slow to progress throughout the seventeen century.

The result was the expansion of a system of labor called **indentured servitude**, in which English and Irish poor sold their labor for four to seven years to a farmer who would fund their voyage across the Atlantic. To encourage their importation, the Virginia Company offered a **head right** of 50 acres to individuals who paid their own passage, which put more property in private hands. Throughout the 1600s, close to an amazing 80 percent of the immigrants to Virginia were indentured servants, most of whom were young lower-class males. These servants had to endure several years of "**seasoning**," a period of time during which they were exposed to the New World's microbes. Many did not survive.

CONSEQUENCES

Jamestown continued to grow in size and in population. This expansion had two major consequences: (1) increased hostility with Indians and (2) a change in leadership of the colony.

Increased Hostility with Indians Local Indian tribes were leery of the growth of Jamestown, which was rapidly encroaching on lands that previously had been open to them. After Powhatan died in 1618, his successor, Opechancanough, began planning an attack to expel the

>> Tobacco was a currency used to pay fines and taxes. For example, persons encouraging slave meetings were to be fined 1,000 pounds of tobacco; owners letting slaves keep horses were fined 500 pounds of tobacco; and if a person wanted to become married, he had to go to the rector of his parish and pay so many pounds of tobacco.

Willierossin/Shutterstock.com

colonists. A fierce assault in 1622 resulted in the death of 357 English colonists, or one-quarter of the Jamestown settlement. Angered, the settlers felt the attack gave them justification to destroy every Indian they encountered. Hostilities brewed. For the colonists, it seemed that at any moment the Native Americans could turn against them; for the Indians, a tireless cancer had seemed to settle on their shores, and it threatened the only way of life they had ever known.

Change to Royal Control A second result of Jamestown's growth was a change in who controlled the colony. Opechancanough's attack of 1622 wiped out vital infrastructure and subsequently bankrupted the Virginia Company of London, which had a grant for the land from the Crown. This, combined with internal conflicts within the company, led England's King James I to seize the colony and place it under royal control. Virginia thus became a **royal colony**, with a governor chosen by the king. But the colonists fought for their liberties and forced the governor to work with an assembly that would be chosen by the landholders (a more democratic method carried over from the Virginia Company). This assembly was called the **House of Burgesses**. Although the king maintained ultimate control, the colony enjoyed self-government and had its own political body within which it could air grievances. The struggle for political liberty in North America had begun.

2-3b Maryland: Founding and Politics

Following Virginia's success, based as it was almost entirely on the cultivation of tobacco, in 1632 the King of England granted the region that we now call Maryland to George Calvert, a lord whose aristocratic name was Lord Baltimore. Lord Baltimore created the first of the **proprietary colonies**, or colonies overseen by a proprietor who was

indentured servitude System of labor whereby farmers paid the Atlantic passage for English and Irish workers in exchange for four to seven years of their work on farms or plantations

head right A grant by the Virginia Company of 50 acres of land to any individual who paid his or her own passage across the Atlantic; put more property in private hands

"seasoning" Period of several years during which indentured servants were exposed to the New World's microbes; many did not survive

royal colony English settlement whose governor was chosen by the king

House of Burgesses Assembly of landholders chosen by other landholders, with which the royal governors were forced to work

proprietary colony Colony overseen by a proprietor who was allowed to control and distribute the land as he wished

allowed to control and distribute the land as he wished. The King granted Lord Baltimore the land in part to end a religious problem, because Lord Baltimore was a prominent English Catholic looking for a haven for members of his faith. Maryland was imagined to be that Catholic haven. The first settlers landed in Maryland in 1634, with large numbers of Catholics but a slightly larger number of Protestants. Learning from the mistakes of Roanoke and Jamestown, the colonists under Lord Baltimore developed an economy based on the plantation model, raising corn and livestock for food and tobacco for profit.

Although Lord Baltimore and his sons at first attempted autocratic rule over Maryland, they quickly opted to create a legislature in the model of the House of Burgesses, which allowed the colonists a good amount of self-rule. Self-rule had its problems, though: as more Protestants came over from England and openly rebelled against being ruled by Catholics, Lord Baltimore realized that he must protect his fellow Catholics. The result was one of the major landmarks in the history of liberty: the **Toleration Act of 1649**, which granted freedom of worship to anyone who accepted the divinity of Jesus Christ. The act did not end religious disputes between the colonists, as Protestants continued to battle Catholic rule in the colony. And it did not protect non-Christians at all. But it did prevent legal action from being taken on account of one's Christian faith. In Maryland, Christians, whether Catholic or Protestant, could not be imprisoned for their faith.

2-3c Life on the Chesapeake

Although Maryland and Virginia prospered, mainly due to tobacco, life on the Chesapeake was generally miserable. Virginia and Maryland remained a collection of tiny villages made up of numerous small farms worked by indentured servants (Map 2.3). Three-quarters of those who came over were young males, and most died during their seasoning period. Families were unstable: marriages were fragile, childbirth risky, and growing up with both parents a rarity. In this atmosphere, the population was slow to establish churches and schools. Most homes were crudely built, with few partitions, and the quality of life could be described as bleak.

 2-4 # FOUNDING THE NEW ENGLAND COLONIES, 1620–1660

Despite the harshness of life in the colonies, the promise of wealth and freedom fueled England's desire for more colonies, for two main reasons.

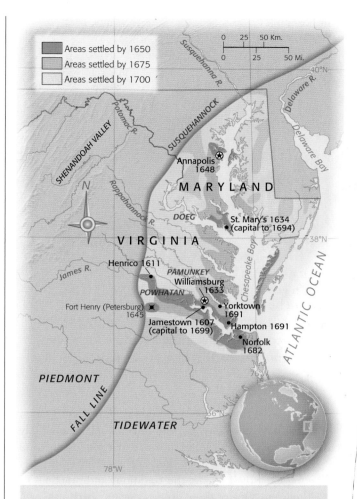

Map 2.3 **Settlement of the Chesapeake**

>> This map shows the expansion of English settlement in the Chesapeake.

The first was financial. Having seen the wealth that successful cultivation of a cash crop like tobacco could generate, English investors became more interested in colonial development. When money arose to fund exploration and colonization, explorers and laborers willingly took on the new adventure.

Toleration Act of 1649 Act granting freedom of worship to anyone who accepted the divinity of Jesus Christ; meant that neither Catholics nor Protestants could be imprisoned for their faith

Puritans Protestants who wished to reform or purify the Church of England by removing its hierarchy, its emphasis on work as payment to God, its allowance of prayers for communal salvation, and its promotion of missions

>> The Puritans embarked for North America with hopes they could purify their church and be a shining example for others around the world. Their hopes faded quickly.

There were religious reasons as well. In 1559, Queen Elizabeth reestablished the Church of England as a body distinct from the Catholic Church. Nevertheless, several groups in England felt she had not gone far enough in freeing Christianity from the traditions and practices of Catholicism. One of these groups was the **Puritans**, who wished to reform, or purify, the Church of England by removing its hierarchy, its emphasis on work as payment to God, its allowance of prayers for communal salvation, and its promotion of missions. Another dissenting group was the **Separatists**, who wished to separate completely from the Church of England because they believed it was irrevocably corrupted. Both these groups were buttressed by England's social problems, which created a large number of poor people who feared the power of an overarching institution such as the Church of England.

Separatists Group of believers who wished to separate completely from the Church of England because they believed it was irrevocably corrupted

Mayflower Ship containing Separatists who sailed from Holland and landed in Plymouth, in present-day Massachusetts, in 1620

Mayflower Compact An agreement that bound each member of the Separatist group in Plymouth to obey majority rule and to promise to defend one another from potential eviction; set a precedent for democratic rule in Massachusetts

2-4a Massachusetts

In order to escape the Church of England and worship according to their understanding of the Christian faith, a group of Separatists departed from England. First, they went to Holland; then, after receiving a land grant from the Virginia Company of London, they sailed on the ship *Mayflower* in 1620, destined for Virginia. The winter winds caught them, and they were blown off course, landing in present-day Massachusetts on a site they called Plymouth. Weakened by the crossing and fearful of storms, they decided to establish their pure Christian community there. The Plymouth colony was born.

These Separatists had no title to land this far north, however, and they knew this would be a problem if other settlers arrived with a proper patent. To remedy this problem and to establish ground rules for governing once they landed, they signed an agreement that bound each member to obey majority rule and to promise to defend one another from potential eviction. This was the **Mayflower Compact**, an agreement that set a precedent, in rhetoric if not always in reality, for democratic rule in Massachusetts. It was also grounded in the notion of Christian unity, lending a messianic fervor to the mission: in their minds, they were there because God wanted them to be there. One year later, in 1621, they secured from the Crown a patent to the land.

SETTLEMENT

After a difficult first winter in 1620, during which half of them died or returned to England, the Separatists established farms and developed a fur trade farther north. The local Wampanoag Indians viewed their presence—and the presence of all Europeans—as an opportunity to enjoy trading for a short time, after which they would expel the intruders. By 1621, however, the Wampanoag had been ravaged by disease and needed help fending off their rivals from further west. Their leader thus made a deal: they would allow the European visitors to stay if the English settlers would agree to ally with the Wampanoag. Once the agreement was settled, a harvest festival enjoyed by the two peoples in 1621 became the symbol for the event we today know as Thanksgiving.

In 1623, the settlers divided their land among the people, rewarding those who were willing to work hard. The ingenuity and drive of these early settlers, in addition to some help from London benefactors, helped them pay off their debts to the Virginia Company by 1627, a remarkably quick repayment that encouraged others to migrate to Massachusetts. They also had stable governmental self-rule, especially after one of the new settlers,

William Bradford, ruled with a strong, level hand and consulted numerous colonists before making decisions.

EXPANSION

Encouraged by the developments at Plymouth, English Puritans (not Separatists) sought to formalize Massachusetts as a royal colony and colonize it themselves. This was done in 1629 under the name of the Massachusetts Bay Company. Its charter was special, however, in that it did not stipulate that decisions about the colony had to be made in England, thus implying that those who lived under the charter would enjoy self-rule. The charter encouraged a larger group of Puritans, who were under increasing assault in England for their religious beliefs, to migrate.

Led by John Winthrop, 1,000 Puritans set out for their religious haven of Massachusetts; between 1630 and 1640, 25,000 more followed, melding with the Separatists who were already there. Their combined successes, supported by the cultivation of cereals and livestock, made the Puritans believe that "God hath sifted a nation"—that God had wished the Puritans to settle the Americas as the world's Promised Land. As John Winthrop told them before they arrived, "We shall be as a city upon a hill [and] the eyes of all people are upon us." Their so-called "errand into the wilderness," as it was described in a 1670 sermon, was an attempt to form an exemplary religious community, one that would inspire reform in Old England.

POLITICS

Politically, the Puritans were not democrats, believing instead in a state that forced all of its inhabitants to hold a specific religious orthodoxy within an established church. This unity of belief, combined with the fact that most of the immigrants came as families, allowed the development of tightly knit communities based on a less rigid hierarchy of labor exploitation than that found in the Chesapeake.

By 1634, the people of Massachusetts began to reject the absolutism of Puritan control (it had not lasted long), although the colonists did not reject the religious nature of the colony. They also demanded a legislature, which had been approved in the royal charter. The legislature was composed of two separate houses:

>> Replica of the *Mayflower*, the ship that transported the Separatists to Massachusetts in 1620.

Mary Evans Picture Library/Alamy Stock Photo

one an elite board of directors, the other a larger house made up of popularly elected deputies. This was a less-than-representative form of representative government, though: only selected church members were allowed to vote for the deputies who represented them.

SOCIETY

Massachusetts slowly began to prosper through the cultivation of grains and cereals, and shortly thereafter small towns began to appear throughout present-day Massachusetts, Maine, New Hampshire, Connecticut, and Rhode Island (see Map 2.4). Small villages composed of several families were the central institutions of Massachusetts, dotting the New England coast and the central New England rivers. Large farmlands surrounded the villages, and the villagers would trudge each morning from their homes to work the outlying lands, then return to the central village at nightfall. These settlement patterns were directly related to both the primary religious mission of the original colonies and also to the New England environment, where cold winters necessitated easy transportation and proximity to town centers. This pattern clearly contrasted with life on the Chesapeake, where the warmer climate allowed larger, more distant plantations to arise.

In Massachusetts, the town's land was often parceled out to families depending on each family's size and needs. Successful families were expected to give back to their community by helping out the poor or the unlucky. Importantly, disease was much less of a problem than in the Virginia and Maryland colonies. Indeed, infant mortality in Massachusetts eventually fell below that of Europe, resulting in a remarkable population boom during which the population doubled every twenty-seven years.

During the early years, biblical orthodoxy was demanded of all settlers, and even the most successful colonists often remained less powerful than the town's minister. Single men and women were required to live with a family so as not to appear promiscuous. In response to a need for religious education, the Puritans founded Harvard College in 1636. New England also was fertile ground for famous writers and poets during this period.

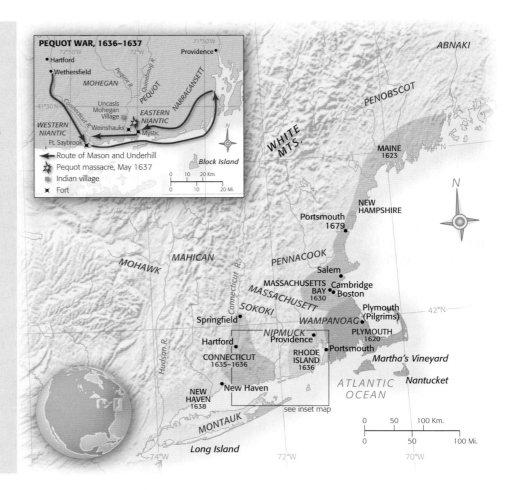

Map 2.4
Seventeenth-Century New England

>> This map shows how New England in the seventeenth century consisted largely of coast-hugging colonies surrounded by a variety of often hostile Native Americans. The threat of further English encroachment led to several vicious battles, including, most brutally, the Pequot War of 1636-37 (inset).

2-4b Rhode Island

In Massachusetts, the persistent demands of religious orthodoxy rankled some settlers, and one of the biggest troublemakers was Roger Williams, the minister of Salem, Massachusetts, who hoped for a "purer" form of religion than even the Puritan founders had institutionalized. Most importantly, he suggested that there should be a clear division between the practice of religion and the politics of state. He believed that politics necessarily impeded the soul's progress toward perfection. Williams's teachings obviously contradicted the Puritan notion of a common-wealth based on devotion to God, and Williams was eventually expelled from Massachusetts. He left Massachusetts

Antinomianism Theological philosophy stressing that only God, not ministers, determined who merited grace and that humankind's relationship with God was a continual process of divine revelation and not dependent on a single orthodox scripture; Anne Hutchinson led a group of Antinomian dissenters and was banished from Massachusetts for these beliefs

with a small band of followers, walking to what is today Rhode Island and founding the town of Providence.

A second group of dissenters was also destined for Rhode Island. The leader of this second group was a charismatic woman named Anne Hutchinson. Hutchinson, a married woman who worked as a midwife, defied the orthodoxy of Massachusetts by stressing that only God determined who merited grace, not ministers or powerful men. More importantly, she disputed the notion of a single orthodox scripture, suggesting instead that humankind's relationship with God was a continual process of divine revelation, rather than based solely on a fixed scripture from thousands of years ago. This theological turn came to be called **Antinomianism**. Hutchinson was an able leader and a persuasive preacher who won over many followers, and Boston's clergy saw her and her Antinomianism as a threat to their community and their leadership. To silence her, they put her on trial, found her guilty of sedition and contempt, and banished her. She and her followers left Massachusetts and founded Portsmouth, Rhode Island, just southeast of Providence.

North Wind Picture Archives/Alamy Stock Photo

>> Anne Hutchinson's trial, where she was found guilty of sedition and contempt and banished from Massachusetts.

NEW ENGLAND IN THE 1660s

In Providence, Roger Williams promised religious and civil freedom to all settlers. Hutchinson's town of Portsmouth was less tolerant, although it continued to attract those unwilling to follow Massachusetts's orthodoxy. This situation encouraged other religious "heretics" to found towns in Rhode Island, such as Newport and Warwick. A preliminary charter founding Rhode Island as a colony independent of Massachusetts was granted in 1644. It was followed by another in 1663 that granted political and religious freedoms to the settlers; this charter attracted a wide range of dissenters from other colonies and Europe.

2-4c Continued Expansion and Indian Confrontation

Puritan dissenters continued to expand outward from Massachusetts, and by the 1630s they had founded towns in what are now Connecticut, Maine, and New Hampshire. The combination of these dissenters and the remarkable growth of New England meant that the ideal of puritanically pious communities was untenable. What grew instead

Stock Montage/Getty Images

>> New Englanders effectively exterminated the Pequot tribe in the bloodbaths of the 1630s.

was a dynamic agricultural society fueled by a seemingly insatiable land hunger. Almost as soon as Puritans had started to proliferate, their hope of a "pure" society began to fade.

As had happened in Virginia, New England's growth led to confrontation with the land's previous inhabitants, the tribes of Indians. Although the Puritans had several Indian allies, John Winthrop had prepared New Englanders quite early for the possibility of conflict, agreeing to train all male colonists to use firearms, forbidding Indians from entering Puritan towns, and forbidding Puritans' from selling firearms to Indians.

During the first years of settlement, conflict was sporadic and light, no doubt in part because European diseases had killed off as much as three-quarters of the Indian population before the colonists arrived at Plymouth. In fact, the Puritans viewed this dying as the work of God, who, they felt, divinely wished to transform New England's wilderness into a shining work of the Lord. One tribe remained strong, however, and by the 1630s conflict between the New Englanders and the Pequot became inevitable. The result was a series of bloody battles collectively called the **Pequot War**, in which the supposedly pious New Englanders effectively exterminated the tribe, gruesomely killing men, women, children, and the elderly. With the Pequot Indians now removed from power, the colonists were assured control over all the southern tribes of New England. The blood shed during the Pequot War foreshadowed the dark nature of Indian–colonist relations that was just over the horizon.

Pequot War Bloody battles of the 1630s between New England colonists and the Pequot tribe of Indians

Historians still debate the legacy that modern America inherited from this initial phase of colonial development, but some parallels are clearly visible. For instance, the freedom to worship as one pleased had its origins in both Maryland and Rhode Island during a time when that level of religious tolerance was little known elsewhere in the world. Politically, there was a considerable amount of self-rule, which one would have never encountered in England. And economically, it was much easier in the colonies to increase one's wealth and escape the class into which one was born. This sense of economic mobility also transcended any similar experience one might encounter in Europe.

On the other hand, each of these democratic impulses had considerable limitations. By 1660, every colony besides Rhode Island had restrictions on what faith one could hold; the exception existed because minority sects had founded it in order to find freedom from harshly restrictive colonial magistrates. In politics, the right to participate in political life was limited to landholding farmers or orthodox religious adherents (depending on whether one lived in the South or the North). Economically, although there was some mobility, one had to endure tremendous hardships to realize it. Most who came seeking great wealth were promptly disappointed. Nevertheless, with the Chesapeake in the South and New England in the North, these were America's colonial beginnings. They were part of a much larger web of New World exploration, and just a tiny part of the interactions of the bustling Atlantic World. But England's North American colonies would grow from these origins, as we will see in the next chapter.

STUDY TOOLS 2

READY TO STUDY? IN THE BOOK, YOU CAN

❑ Rip out the Chapter Review Card, which includes key terms and chapter summaries.

ONLINE AT WWW.CENGAGEBRAIN.COM, YOU CAN:

❑ Collect StudyBits while you read and study the chapter.
❑ Quiz yourself on key concepts.
❑ Find videos for further exploration.
❑ Prepare for tests with HIST5 Flash Cards as well as those you create.
❑ Read Columbus's 1493 letter about his findings.
❑ Read a firsthand account of Vasco da Gama's travels.
❑ Read firsthand descriptions of Cortés's first contact with the Aztecs.
❑ Read more about the founding of Santa Fe.
❑ Read an account of the capture of St. Augustine.
❑ Read John Smith's Generall Historie of Virginia.
❑ Read Rolfe's firsthand account of conditions in Jamestown at the end of its first decade.
❑ Take a tour of Jamestown.
❑ Learn more about what life was like in 1628 New England.

What Else Was Happening

▶ **c. 1000** Scandinavian expeditions to North America.

1405–1433: *Chinese explorer Zheng He goes on seven expeditions to Arabia, East Africa, India, and Indonesia.*

▶ **1440s** Portuguese begin trade with Africa.

1492: *First Spanish voyage of discovery: Christopher Columbus.*

▶ **1493** Pope Alexander VI draws Line of Demarcation.

▶ **1497** Englishman John Cabot lands in Canada.

1498: *Vasco da Gama reaches India via Cape of Good Hope.*

▶ **1512** First permanent Spanish settlements in New World.

▶ **1519–1522** Cortés conquers Mexico. Magellan completes first circumnavigation of the world.

▶ **1532** Pizarro overthrows Incas in Peru.

1540: *The first horses arrive in North America, when Spanish explorer Francisco Vasquez de Coronado, traveling through Kansas, lets about 260 of them escape.*

1551: *What is now the National Autonomous University of Mexico is founded.*

▶ **1565** Spanish seize St. Augustine from French.

1585: *First Roanoke settlement.*

Sir John Harrington invents the first flushing toilet and puts one inside the palace of Queen Elizabeth, who deems it too loud.

▶ **1607** Jamestown founded by Virginia Company of London.

▶ **1608** Quebec founded as French trading post.

▶ **1620** Settlement of Plymouth.

▶ **1629** Massachusetts becomes a royal colony.

▶ **1630s** Pequot War in New England.

▶ **1632** Founding of Maryland.

▶ **1644** Rhode Island receives preliminary charter as independent colony.

3 | Expansion and Its Costs, 1660–1700

LEARNING OBJECTIVES

After reading this chapter, you should be able to do the following:

3-1 Describe the development of the North American colonies from 1660–1700, and analyze the four distinct areas that began to emerge in British North America.

3-2 Describe and analyze the British colonists' interactions up to 1700 with Native American peoples.

3-3 Understand the British colonists' interactions up to 1700 with African slaves.

3-4 Describe and analyze the European wars that had an impact on North America.

AFTER FINISHING
THIS CHAPTER
GO TO **PAGE 60**
FOR STUDY TOOLS

During the hundred-plus years between 1660 and 1763, the English colonies in North America not only scratched out a living in a harsh environment, but also grew and expanded into a sizeable power central to the British Empire. In 1660, Britain had just a few colonies in the land that would become the United States. They were merely a tiny part of Europe's New World holdings, vastly overshadowed by colonial possessions in the Caribbean and South America. They were largely concentrated in just two regions: in New England, with its numerous small towns, and in the Chesapeake, in its large tobacco-producing farms that sprawled along the region's riverbanks. In total, there were about 70,000 people of non-Indian origin living in these regions. There was not much commerce between the two settlements, and no matter where one lived, daily life in the early colonies was grueling.

One hundred years later, the landscape had changed considerably. By 1763, there were thirteen English colonies in four distinct regions: New England, the Middle Colonies, the Chesapeake, and the Southern Colonies. Each of these regions enjoyed a vibrant economy based on commerce, agriculture, and industry. Intellectually and culturally, the English colonies on American soil had begun to develop a style all their own, too. The colonial non-native population reached 1 million by 1750, with colonists pushing toward lands in the west that would accommodate their growing numbers.

This chapter explores this development from 1660 to 1700, paying particular attention to the expansion of British America, the decline of the Indian populations along the Atlantic Coast, and the subtle transition from indentured servitude to race-based slavery. It also examines how the growing North American colonies became crucial players in the "Wars for Empire" between the European powers. Chapter 4 will focus on the solidification of the four distinct colonial regions, the development of the American slavery system, and the attempts by the British crown to reassert control over colonial America, efforts that would ultimately trigger the Revolutionary War.

3-1 EXPANSION OF ENGLISH HOLDINGS IN NORTH AMERICA, 1660–1700

3-1a English Motives for Further Expansion

There were several reasons for Britain's colonial expansion in North America. Some related to the English civil war, others to the issue of royal control, and still others to financial concerns.

THE ENGLISH CIVIL WAR

The initial impetus for the expansion of England's colonial holdings came from the homeland. In 1642, revolutionaries led by Oliver Cromwell began a series of revolts that led, in 1649, to the execution of the English king Charles I which ignited a decade of conflict and upheaval in England. The revolutionaries intended to create a kingless republican government called a **commonwealth**, founded on concepts like taxation only with representation, limited government, and antimonarchical beliefs—all of which would become central ideas of the American Revolution more than a century later. Because English Puritans formed the backbone of the revolutionary forces, the civil war greatly slowed Puritan migration to Massachusetts. They were more interested in fighting battles at home.

When Cromwell died in 1658, the commonwealth he founded dissolved into chaos, leaving the revolution without a leader. Conservative military men took control of the country, and, in 1660, a group of generals invited Charles II to fill his late father's position as king of England. After twelve years of civil war, the Stuarts (the family that had controlled the throne since 1603) regained power. The period of British history that followed is called the **Restoration** (1660–1685), and it was significant for colonial North America because King Charles II used the colonies: (1) to tighten control of his initially unstable leadership and (2) to pay off debts incurred during his fight to recover the throne.

TIGHTENING ROYAL CONTROL

To reinforce control over the colonies (which, in general, had been sympathetic to Cromwell and which had engaged in more trade with the Dutch because of the decline in British trading), Charles II first enacted strict trade regulations. Passed by Parliament in 1651, the first version of these regulations, known collectively as the **Navigation Acts**, dictated where colonial

commonwealth A kingless republican government

Restoration Period of English history when the Stuarts were restored to the throne (1660–1685)

Navigation Acts Regulations that dictated where colonial producers could ship their goods, stipulated that colonists must transport their goods in British ships, and listed a group of products that colonists were permitted to sell only to Britain

◄◄◄ **This engraved English tobacco label displays a colonial Virginia planter at ease while his slaves labor in the tobacco fields.**

>> Tobacco ships in the James River, Virginia Colony, 1600s.

North Wind Picture Archives

had a guaranteed buyer in Britain. Proprietors could become extremely wealthy while the king could be assured of having supporters whose wealth depended on preserving his favor.

3-1b The Creation of Colonies During and After the Restoration

Proprietary colonies were the chief means of colonial expansion between 1660 and 1700, and it was through them that the large gap of land between Massachusetts and Virginia, as well as the lands between Virginia and Florida, were colonized (Map 3.1). During the Restoration, friends of Charles II created five proprietary colonies: (1) Carolina (present-day North and South Carolina); (2) New York; (3) Pennsylvania; (4) East Jersey; and (5) West Jersey (later joined to become New Jersey). The proprietary colony of Georgia was founded after the Restoration. The proprietors of these colonies were free to establish any sort of government they wished, so long as their laws did not contradict those of Britain. Given this freedom, each of the proprietary colonies developed quite differently. The expansion of colonial America had begun.

CAROLINA

Three years after returning to his father's throne, Charles II granted the vast territory of Carolina to a group of eight noblemen who had supported him during the revolution. According to the grant, the Carolinas extended from Virginia south to the northern tip of today's Florida and west all the way to the Pacific Ocean. The eight proprietors set up elaborate rules (in a constitution drafted by the philosopher John Locke) and encouraged the establishment of large plantations. Two-fifths of each county was to be set aside for the proprietors, thus ensuring the continued wealth of the founders.

The Failure of Proprietorship Things did not turn out as Carolina's proprietors had hoped. Basically, they did not understand that the American context of abundant land would not accommodate the hierarchical society of England, with its noble titles and haughty proprietors. Many of the earliest

producers could ship their goods and stipulated that colonists must transport their goods in British ships. In 1660, Parliament passed a second version that listed a group of **enumerated articles** (tobacco, sugar, cotton, indigo) that colonists were permitted to sell only to Britain. The goal of these measures was to prevent the transfer of resources from Britain to its rivals, France and the Dutch Republic. They were also intended to curb the industrial growth of colonial North America, which the Crown saw as a potential competitor to British producers.

PAYING OFF DEBTS

Because the Navigation Acts ensured an British monopoly on the first sale of all colonial goods, anyone who controlled a colony could grow quite wealthy. To pay off his debts, Charles II offered his supporters land in the New World so that they could establish **proprietary colonies**—colonies owned and ruled by an individual or a private corporation rather than by the Crown. If the proprietors ruled them successfully, they

enumerated articles Goods (tobacco, sugar, cotton, indigo) listed in the Navigation Acts that colonists were permitted to sell only to Britain

proprietary colonies Colonies owned and ruled by an individual or a private corporation, rather than by the Crown

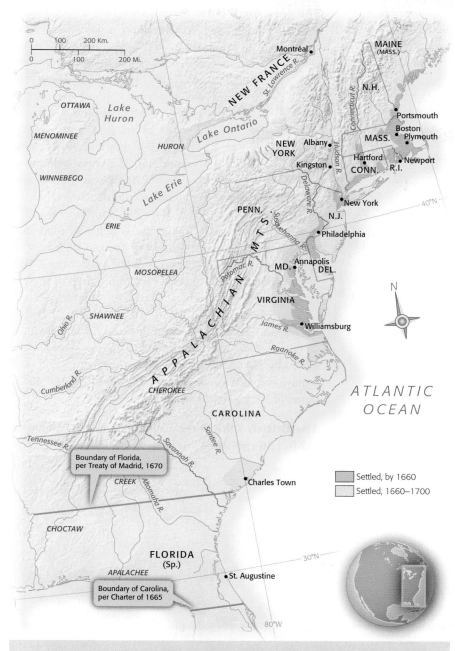

hierarchical society the proprietors intended to emulate. The settlers from the Caribbean also brought slaves with them, meaning that, from its earliest history, Carolina was powered by small-scale entrepreneurs and slave laborers. It later had the ignominious distinction of being America's first colony dependent on slave labor. Charles Town (later Charleston) was founded in 1670 after the decimation of Indian nations in the area, but Carolina was considered highly undesirable; its weather was hot and humid, and tobacco did not thrive in the colony's soil. Everything was going badly.

Rice The colony's fortunes reversed in 1693, when Carolinians discovered from their African slaves that rice could be grown easily in the fertile soil. The cultivation of rice spread rapidly and farms popped up quickly, making Carolina lucrative and suddenly creating an urgent need for more labor. This labor crunch meant that by 1720 the southern part of the colony, where the soil was most fertile, was populated by twice as many slaves as European freemen or indentured servants. Most of these slaves had been brought from Barbados, in the West Indies, which had become a key marketplace for the worldwide slave trade. The large number of slaves in Carolina made Charles Town the center of North America's early slave trade, which would begin to prosper in the 1680s and 1690s.

Map 3.1 European Settlements and Indian Nations in Eastern North America

>> This map of the east coast settlement in British America shows areas of conflict between the British and the various Indian nations.

settlers of Carolina came from the Caribbean rather than Britain because a temporary dip in sugar prices made the Caribbean islands less appealing. These settlers were accustomed to self-rule, not the

Life in Carolina Few Europeans lived in the southern part of Carolina because life there was so miserable. Diseases spread rapidly, and population growth remained low. Despite the proprietors' hopes for a harmonious existence with the Indians, before rice made Carolina lucrative, its principal export was captured Indian slaves who were sold in New England and the West Indies. This meant continued warfare with Indian nations—yet another reason to avoid the southern part of Carolina. Yet for the Englishmen the battles were successful: within the first three decades of the colony's founding, the two largest Indian nations on the Carolina coast were largely extinct.

> Carolina had the ignominious distinction of being America's first colony dependent on slave labor.

In the northern part of the colony, where there were fewer diseases and lower humidity, a different kind of society developed. Tobacco farmers from Virginia developed small farms and advocated self-rule there. Although slavery existed, it never became the main labor supply. By 1698, the differences between the south and the north had become so marked that the proprietors chose to divide the colonies in two; in 1712, they became South Carolina and North Carolina.

NEW YORK

New York was also a proprietary colony, but from the beginning it was polyglot and diverse and developed very differently to Carolina.

The New York Dutch New York began as a Dutch colony founded in 1624, when the Dutch claimed New Jersey and New York. The Dutch based their claims on the voyage of Henry Hudson in 1609 and Peter Minuit's purchase of the island of Manhattan for a small amount of trinkets and jewelry. They called their territory New Netherland. This was a bold move because Britain was developing colonies south of New York in Virginia and north of it in New England.

During the early 1600s, the Dutch had moderate success trading furs with the Iroquois. But their biggest success lay in the port town of New Amsterdam (later New York City). There, a multicultural group of traders gathered to trade and barter near the Atlantic. No one was better at it than Adriaen van der Donck, a Dutch lawyer who became an eager advocate for and political leader of New Amsterdam and the New World more generally. He created maps, wrote travelogues, and paid to have colonists come to Manhattan. By 1660, the population of New Amsterdam reached 10,000.

The British Take Over Competition over commerce led to bitter relations between the English and Dutch,

A Carolina Rice-field.

>> This engraving shows a Carolina rice field. African slaves taught Carolinians that rice could be grown there easily.

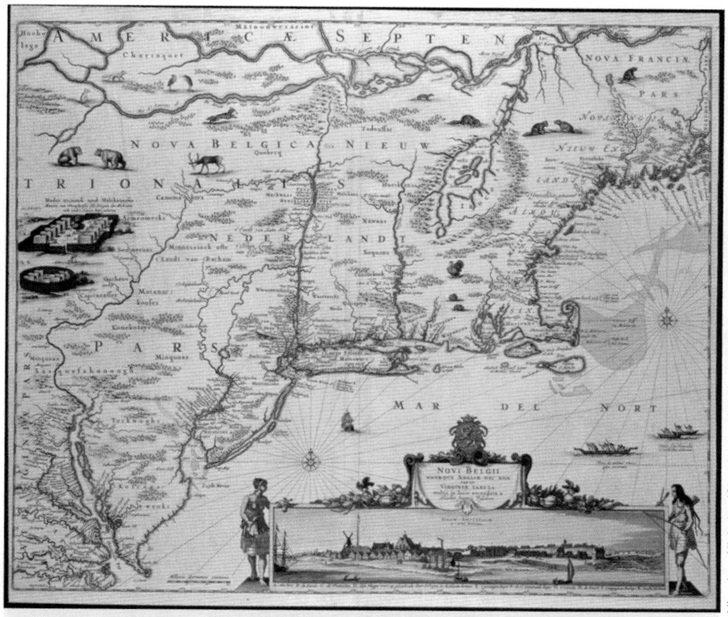

Visscher, Nicholas (Claes) Jansz (1586–1652)/The Art Gallery Collection/Alamy Stock Photo

>> This map of New Netherland, by N. J. Visscher, 1650–1651, was based on a map compiled by Adriaen van der Donck in 1648. van der Donck's map inspired continued growth to what would become New York.

and three small "Anglo-Dutch" wars broke out between the two nations, fought mostly in the English Channel between 1652 and 1675. In 1664, Britain's Charles II wrested New Amsterdam from the Dutch and granted it to his brother, the Duke of York. Renaming the colony New York, the duke ruled it severely and autocratically for two decades. But his attempts to restrict the rights of New Yorkers were resisted by the diverse mix of settlers and traders, who, by 1700, included not only British and the Dutch, but also Swedes, French, and Germans, as well as local native populations and African slaves. Together, the merchants fought to keep New York free for commerce and expression. New York did, however, allow slavery. By 1703, 42 percent of New York's households had slaves, the second highest percentage of any North American city at the time, bested only by Charles Town (today's Charleston).

PENNSYLVANIA

Outdoing even New York's polyglot character, Pennsylvania, founded by William Penn, became the most diverse of the proprietary colonies. Penn was named after his father, a royal courtier to whom the king had become indebted because of gambling losses. When the elder Penn died, the younger William Penn inherited claim to the debt. And when Charles II began imprisoning religious minorities in the 1670s, Penn, a newly converted Quaker, traded the debt for a North American colony, where he could safely take his co-religionists.

Quakers The **Quakers** are Protestants who believed that God's will was directly transmitted to people through "the inner light" of divine knowledge that a person possesses within his or her being. This belief was in opposition to the Protestant mainstream, which made the Bible the center of religious experience. The Quakers also rejected the concepts of Original Sin and predestination, further alienating them from the Protestant core.

In the 1600s, there were also social differences between Quakers and Protestants. Quaker meetings employed no professional ministers (whom they derisively called "hireling ministers"), relying instead on laypeople (nonordained faith-community members). Quakers, sometimes called the Society of Friends, rejected class distinctions as well, which prevented them from deferring to social superiors. Furthermore, the Quakers argued that any believer was as capable as any other of transmitting the truth about God's will, including women, a policy that threatened traditional Christian distinctions between the sexes. In an era of religious intolerance and political instability, the egalitarianism of the Quakers was distrusted and even outlawed.

Fleeing Britain In 1674, Penn, along with ten other Quakers, purchased the proprietary rights to West Jersey. Penn drafted a constitution for the colony that protected the right of trial by jury, prohibited capital punishment, allowed almost all free males the right to vote, and sought to ensure good relations with the Indians. His constitution required settlers to purchase any land taken from Indian inhabitants and extended the right of trial by jury to Indians (with the stipulation that juries in the trial of an Indian would be half Indian, half English).

Although many considered such policies radical, Penn enjoyed good relations with both Charles II

Quakers Protestants who believed that God's will was directly transmitted to people through "the inner light" of divine knowledge that a person possesses within his or her being; this belief was in direct opposition to the Bible-centered Protestant mainstream

and the Duke of York. In 1681, Charles granted him Pennsylvania (which means "Penn's wood")—which he named after Penn's father. The sale of "Penn's wood" relieved the king of two things: his gambling debt to Penn's father and the Quakers. In 1682, the Duke of York sold Penn three additional counties from his own vast New World landholdings. In time, these counties would become Delaware.

Creating Pennsylvania Recruiting settlers was the key to fulfilling Penn's idyllic vision. Penn's promotion of the colony rested on two factors: religious freedom and a liberal land policy that allowed easy access to land. Penn dispatched agents throughout Europe to advertise the colony, and the response was overwhelming. In 1682, the population was about 1,000; two years later, it had grown to 4,000; by the end of the 1680s it had risen to 12,000. Although not yet as large as the Massachusetts Bay colony, Pennsylvania's population was increasing rapidly. Penn was also successful in promoting peaceful relations with the Indians; in fact, Indian refugees migrated to Pennsylvania from other lands where they had faced violence from colonists.

Penn did permit slavery. He owned slaves personally and allowed other colonists to do the same. Like most northern slaves, slaves in Pennsylvania were Africans used primarily as domestic workers. Although some Quakers spoke out publicly against slavery as early as 1688, slavery lasted in Pennsylvania until the 1780s.

NEW JERSEY

In 1673, the Duke of York granted the southern portion of his colony to two friends, one of whom sold his portion to a group of Quakers. This led to the creation of East Jersey, which bordered New York, and West Jersey, which bordered Pennsylvania. Although they

>> William Penn had more generous feelings toward Native Americans than most of the other European colonists. This image commemorates a 1680s treaty between Penn and the Lenni-Lenapi Indians.

North Wind Picture Archives/Alamy Stock Photo

retained certain differences, by 1702 both areas had grown substantially, earning a single royal charter. To attract settlers, the proprietors of New Jersey promised both generous land grants and a limited freedom of religion. For these reasons, Puritan New Englanders and Dutch New Yorkers migrated there, prompting significant growth by 1726. The two colonies were united and renamed New Jersey.

GEORGIA

Georgia was founded after the Restoration as a proprietary colony. The chief motives for its settlement were to create a buffer between Spanish Florida and the Carolinas and, perhaps more interestingly, to create a haven for British debtors and persecuted British Protestants. James Oglethorpe, the utopian lead proprietor, led the first settlers to Savannah in 1733. Oglethorpe opposed Britain's policy of imprisoning those who could not pay their debts, and his vision fashioned Georgia as a colony where the "worthy poor" could start anew.

The colony grew slowly because the charter stipulated that no one could own enough land to develop a large-scale plantation. Furthermore, slavery was initially prohibited because of Oglethorpe's vision for the colony and because the Spanish in Florida had promised freedom to any slave who would serve in their military, which would have meant a collection of slaves eager to desert Georgia for Florida. It was only in the 1750s that the Crown, to whom the proprietors had returned the charter, succumbed to local demands of English planters and allowed slavery.

3-1c Where Were the Spanish?

As the British planted deeper roots in colonial North America, even tossing the Dutch from New York, the Spanish were pulling their roots out. The main reason was an unwillingness to develop colonial settlements, preferring instead to bring home quick profits after a brief period of having conquered and controlled resource-rich lands. They established some settlements, like those founded by Catholic friars eager to convert Indians, but these permanent settlements frequently conflicted with local Indian nations and persuaded Spain that permanent settlement was not worth the investment. Their colonial conflicts thus tended to be about labor relations and faith, rather than a struggle for land, which was paramount to the British.

NEW MEXICO

In New Mexico, for example, the Pueblo people rejected the forced piety of the Spanish Catholic friars, and in a dramatic 1680 rebellion, a shaman named Popé led the **Pueblo Revolt**—an uprising of several villages spanning several hundred miles across the New Mexican landscape. The villagers burned Spanish farms, destroyed churches, and killed half the friars. Reeling from the revolt, the Spanish left the Southwest for more than a decade. They returned in the 1690s with a more tolerant outlook, and the Pueblo people welcomed them only because they felt they needed European weaponry to fight their enemies.

FLORIDA

The Spanish faced similar resentments in Florida. But here the resentments were compounded by the proximity of colonial competitors, the British and the French.

> "I received information that a plot for a general uprising of the Christian Indians was being formed and was spreading rapidly. This was wholly contrary to the existing peace and tranquillity in this miserable kingdom, not only among the Spaniards and natives, but even on the part of the heathen enemy."
>
> —Don Antonio de Otermin, governor of New Mexico during the Pueblo Revolt

When Britain and France went to war in the War of Spanish Succession in 1701, British Carolinians attacked Spanish Florida (the British feared that Spain and France were becoming too closely allied). The result was the devastation of all Spanish strongholds in Florida except St. Augustine. And, because British colonists outnumbered Spanish settlers, the Spanish were slow to resettle Florida. By 1700, the Spanish presence in the future United States was limited to a few Catholic missions and a few increasingly smaller settlements.

3-1d By 1700

Between 1660 and 1700, Britain had crafted the beginnings of a large colonial empire in North America. It had seeded permanent colonies and established itself as the European nation claiming the biggest stake to the land, ahead of the Dutch, French, and Spanish, whose primary colonial interests lay elsewhere. These British colonies were not yet wholly stable, nor were they unified. Furthermore, each colony comprised a mix of people, including Europeans from different countries, Indians from many nations, and, increasingly, slaves.

Pueblo Revolt An uprising of several villages spanning several hundred miles across the New Mexican landscape in 1680, led by the shaman Popé

3-2 INDIANS

As Britain's colonial holdings expanded into the American interior, they encroached on lands that were already inhabited. The initial encounters between Europeans and the peoples of Native America had mixed outcomes. In their search for gold and other riches in the 1500s, the Spanish annihilated many Indian nations with violence and disease. The French, without a large settled presence in the New World, had mostly positive trade arrangements with the Indians near Quebec. The British had at first cautiously engaged the Indian peoples for trade and protection, but as their settlements expanded, suspicion and enmity between the two groups increased. In Jamestown, for instance, relations between the Powhatan Confederacy and the first settlers were generally nonviolent until the expansion of Jamestown provoked Powhatan's successor, Opechancanough, to attack. In New England, the Pequot War symbolized the violent direction relations were taking.

These first encounters had elements of both trust and suspicion, but the situation worsened over time. By the beginning of the 1700s, it was clear that the two peoples would not share the New World. Most British colonists believed that any Indian who stood in their path to settlement could rightfully be exterminated. Indians responded in kind. Competition for land was the key motive. Violence, disease, and the market economy were the principal means of effecting change.

3-2a What Went Wrong?

There were four general reasons why the situation deteriorated so drastically after 1660 (see "The Reasons Why . . ." box).

3-2b The Middle Ground

Although the decimation of Native America is by far the most significant story of Euro-Indian relations, positive interactions occurred during the colonial era as well, usually over trade. In this "middle ground," as historians have called it, the two groups operated as equals. Indians and Europeans shared rituals, such as tea and rum drinking, gift giving, and pipe smoking. This middle ground was noticeable whenever colonists encountered large groups of Indians, meaning that the groups were close to equal in number, and it allowed contact that benefited both Indians and colonists. Although these middle grounds were prominent places for trading, they were also spaces for cultural interaction and sharing. These spaces existed most prominently around the Great Lakes and the upper Mississippi River basin.

3-2c Colonial Land Lust, Colonial Democracy

But the central story of Indian relations with European colonists is one of violence. In the first half of the 1600s, most outbreaks of violence between

The Reasons Why...

There were four general reasons why relations between British colonists and the various Indians they came into contact with dissolved into violence:

Land lust. Land lust of the British colonists grew as the initial colonies succeeded, prompting perpetual incursions on lands occupied by Indians.

Religion. Religious differences between the two groups prevented each group from having a common understanding of the other and led to each one seeing demons and devils in the other.

Culture. Cultural differences about land use, gender roles, and language created further misunderstandings and resentments.

European alignments. Perhaps most important, the European powers were viciously protective of their lucrative New World holdings. Throughout the 1700s Europeans fought several wars to defend them, and the battleground of this "great war for empire" (as historians have called these wars) was often the New World, forcing colonists and Indians to take sides. In the short term, Indians could profit by selling their support to one European power or the other. But as Britain won increased dominion, the nations of Native America could no longer play one side against the other, and Britain (and eventually the United States) could subject the Indians to their will, at times violently.

>> In an area historians have called the "middle ground," Indians and Europeans shared rituals, such as tea and rum drinking, pipe smoking, and gift-giving, as shown in this painting of a gift exchange.

British colonists and Indians were short-lived. The deadlier conflicts occurred between various Indian nations seeking to win European trade. The bloodiest of these intertribal battles were the **Beaver Wars** (1640–1680s), in which the Iroquois, seeking beaver pelts to trade with the French, forced the Huron and their supporters out of the Northeast altogether, leaving the Iroquois Confederacy as the single most significant collection of Indians between northern Canada, southern Virginia, and the Mississippi River. They decimated their competition and forced the survivors to flee across the Mississippi River.

By the 1670s, enough British settlers had moved to the colonies that colonists and Indians could engage in prolonged wars. These wars established a pattern of violence that would last for the duration of contact between the two groups. Although highlighted by several large-scale battles, conflict between Indians and North American colonists was continual, making every outing a potentially perilous adventure. Two events of the 1670s, however, greatly influenced colonist–Indian relations: Metacom's War and Bacon's Rebellion.

METACOM'S WAR (KING PHILIP'S WAR), 1675–1676

The first large-scale conflict was **Metacom's War** (sometimes called "**King Philip's War**"), which broke out in Plymouth, Massachusetts, in 1675. "King Philip" was the name the British gave to Metacom, the son of the Wampanoag chief, Massasoit. Massasoit had befriended the Plymouth settlers in the 1620s (his generosity thus giving Americans the model for today's Thanksgiving), but by the 1670s the British settlement in Massachusetts had grown to 50,000. The New Englanders had expanded onto Indian territories and forced the Wampanoag and other Indians to obey English law. The settlers' cattle trampled native cornfields, demonstrating the differences in concepts of land use between the two peoples and the arrogance of some New Englanders, who felt God had granted them the land to cultivate. The younger generation of Indians had had enough.

The result was a vicious war. Many Indian nations joined Metacom in battling the settlers, although several Indians that had converted to Christianity sided with the British. Over a period of fourteen months in 1675 and 1676, Metacom and his followers attacked fifty-two of the ninety Puritan towns, destroying thirteen of them completely. They attacked towns in four colonies: Plymouth, Massachusetts Bay, Rhode Island, and Connecticut (see Map 3.2). Before the tide of battle had turned, Metacom's forces had pushed the area of British colonization in New England almost back to the coast. The story of Mary Rowlandson, a young New England settler, dates from King Philip's War. Metacom's forces kidnapped her and held her hostage for three months before ransoming her back to her family; she wrote a wildly popular account of her tribulations, giving many colonists a firsthand look at Indian life.

The tide of war turned against the Indians in 1676. The British retaliated against them for Metacom's assaults, and the colonists' most significant victory came after a New England boy escaped captivity, returned home, and then led the colonists to the exact location of the Indians. The fighting ended in 1676 when Metacom fell in battle at the hands of an Indian acting as a scout for the colonists.

Beaver Wars Intertribal battles in the 1600s in which the Iroquois forced the Huron out of the Northeast

Metacom's War First large-scale conflict between colonists and Native Americans, waged in Plymouth, Massachusetts Bay, Rhode Island, and Connecticut (1675–1676)

King Philip's War British colonists' name for Metacom's War, because they referred to the Wampanoag leader Metacom as King Philip

Map 3.2 New England During Metacom's War, 1675–1676

>> This map of the Massachusetts Bay Colony and Connecticut shows the numerous battles of Metacom's War.

Legend:
- Indian village
- Town destroyed
- Town damaged
- Other town
- Major battle

The colonists placed Metacom's head on a stake and let it stand in Plymouth town square for twenty-five years.

New England's Indians paid a heavy price for their resistance. Algonquian communities were decimated from Narragansett Bay to the Connecticut River Valley. Many died from disease and starvation, in addition to the thousands who were killed in battle. Both sides suffered: Metacom's War killed one in ten of New England's colonists. It also led to a further decline of Puritan leadership, as many colonists viewed the war as a sign of God's displeasure. More obviously, the war exposed a ferocious undercurrent of racism among the British colonists, many of whom were eager to attack and kill any Indian they encountered. Metacom's War also showed

an early, if uneven, willingness of Indian nations to unite to fight colonists.

BACON'S REBELLION, 1676–1677

The impact of Metacom's War was felt beyond New England. Metacom's message of pan-Indian resistance to British settlement spread (aided by the fact that all Indians faced the same frustrations as Metacom). By 1676, the warriors from the Potomack and Susquehannock nations of the Chesapeake began to raid English outposts in Virginia. The British governor of the colony, Sir William Berkeley, showed a reluctance to retaliate, favoring instead a policy of keeping a strict boundary between Indian and colonial land (and of keeping his bountiful trade

>> In perhaps the most dramatic moment of Bacon's Rebellion, in 1676 Nathaniel Bacon's supporters attacked and burned Jamestown itself, forcing Governor William Berkeley to flee. Bacon's Rebellion would help lead to the decline of indentured servitude and the rise of racialized slavery.

relations with several Indian nations going). His disinclination to fight, and his unwillingness to compromise with (or even listen to) the demands of the laboring people, or "middling sorts," who aspired to own land, sparked a revolt among the colonists, called **Bacon's Rebellion**.

Nathaniel Bacon was a young, well-educated, and charismatic member of the Virginia colony council. He was also related to Berkeley through marriage. In opposition to Berkeley, Bacon advocated immediate retaliation against the Potomack and Susquehannock. But Berkeley denied Bacon's bid for a commission to attack the Indians, recognizing that arming hundreds of young colonial men—mostly former indentured servants—would pose a threat to the colonial leadership. Bacon ignored Berkeley's command and raised his own militia to fight the Native Americans.

Bacon's Laws Bacon's militia quickly vanquished the Indians in the area. Fearful of where Bacon might go next, Governor Berkeley dispatched three hundred militiamen to stop him. Bacon himself was captured and released, and then continued to seek a commission to attack the Indians again. Berkeley resisted. A series of standoffs ensued, with Bacon variously being imprisoned or on the run. In the process, Berkeley became acutely aware of Bacon's popularity among the settlers and, to quell the potential uprising, passed a series of laws that democratized the politics of Virginia. Commonly called **Bacon's Laws**, the new rules granted the franchise to all freemen (not just landowners), inaugurated elections of the members of the legislature (rather than offering legislators lifetime appointments), and granted greater representation in taxation. In sum, Bacon's Laws reduced the influence of the ruling elite in Virginia, setting a precedent for free white man's democracy. This was a

Bacon's Rebellion Revolt among colonists, led by Nathaniel Bacon, that was triggered by Virginia governor Sir William Berkeley's unwillingness to listen to the demands of the laboring people who wanted to attack several nearby Indians (1676–1677)

Bacon's Laws Series of laws that democratized the politics of Virginia, granted the franchise to all freemen, inaugurated elections of the members of the legislature, and granted greater representation in taxation

meaningful step in the expansion of colonial liberty, although it was of course brought about by the desired subjugation of Indians.

Berkeley's new laws were also an attempt to win back some of the popularity Bacon had attracted. After the passage of Bacon's Laws, Berkeley persisted in his attempts to quell any rebellion, but it seemed that would be impossible to do without granting the militia a commission to kill local Indians and cultivate their lands—something he would not allow.

Eventually, and despite the passage of Bacon's Laws, the continued standoff prompted Bacon and his army to attack Jamestown itself in the summer of 1676, forcing Berkeley to flee. Bacon invited his troops to plunder the plantations around Jamestown, especially those of Berkeley's supporters, and throughout the summer, Bacon's ragtag army fought with Indians and British alike.

During the late summer of 1676, Berkeley organized a counterattack against Bacon's anti-Indian, anti-upper-class forces. Berkeley's men, with superior arms, chased Bacon around eastern Virginia, capturing several of his supporters but not the rebel himself. When 1,100 English troops arrived to help Berkeley, Bacon went on the run, contracted an infectious fever, and died. Other rebels tried to maintain control of the colony, but Bacon's death brought the rebellion to a rapid close. Berkeley remained in power and later tried to repeal several of Bacon's Laws, but these efforts were overruled by more moderate members of the Burgesses, who were afraid of what might happen should they try to restrict the rights of the common people.

Results Bacon's Rebellion succeeded in pushing the Potomack and Susquehannock Indians farther west, opening up more land for Euro-American settlement. But Bacon's Rebellion is significant to American history for other reasons as well (see "The Reasons Why . . ." box).

3-3 THE EXPANSION OF AMERICAN SLAVERY

Europe's slave trade with Africa began in the 1400s and increased in the 1500s and 1600s as a means of relieving a labor shortage in the areas surrounding the Mediterranean. Labor needs arose in the New World during the late 1500s and 1600s after Europeans realized that sugar could be grown easily in the West Indies and South America. (Europeans had discovered sugar in their travels during the Crusades, and it became so popular and expensive in Europe that it was among the first items Columbus transported from the New World, in his second voyage of 1493.) Cultivating sugar is incredibly labor intensive though, and once Europeans had exhausted and exterminated native populations in the West Indies and South America, their search for labor led them to African slaves. This was made easier by the fact that the established trade routes between Europe and Africa had made Africans eager for European goods, especially guns. Thus, in a mutually beneficial trade

The Reasons Why...

Bacon's Rebellion is significant to American history for at least three reasons:

Land lust. Bacon's Rebellion reflected the land lust of the growing colonial population.

Demonstrable violence. It demonstrated that the settlers were willing to use violent means to gain that land, usually against Indians, but sometimes against the English gentry.

Rise of slavery. It made wealthy colonists less willing to import indentured servants, who, as the

rebellion proved, would do nearly anything to get land once they were freed from their condition of servitude. This was one factor that led to a rise in the importation of African slaves beginning in the 1680s. It also initiated an upper-class proclamation of the similarity of all men perceived to be white, no matter their wealth or class; by importing more slaves and creating a racially divided population, the upper classes of Virginia sought to limit class conflict between white people. This was a turning point in the history of North American race relations that led to the expansion of the American slave system and the decline of indentured servitude. But, of course, this decline in awareness of hierarchical class distinctions was solidified by the darkening of the lines between races.

system, beginning in the early 1600s West African kingdoms competed with one another to supply slaves to Europeans in return for European goods.

But what began so easily was not so easily stopped. As the Atlantic slave trade grew, West African kingdoms grew leery of supplying Europeans with more slaves because they were fearful of the overwhelming demand. Some Europeans resorted to kidnapping slaves from West African villages. The horrifying results of the modern racialized slave system were becoming increasingly apparent.

3-3a Why the Transition from Indentured Servitude to Slavery?

In the early 1600s, the North American colonies relied mainly on European (and some African) indentured servants for labor. At least 70 percent of those in the Chesapeake came as indentured servants from Britain. By the 1680s, however, African slaves had begun to replace indentured servants as the colonists' preferred labor source, and by the early 1700s, there were few indentured servants in the colonial labor pool.

Despite the variety of benefits of indentured servitude (the ability of landowner and laborer to communicate easily, similarities in culture and religion between the two), it posed several problems in North America. First, many servants simply ran away once they landed in the New World, and, as Europeans, once they escaped, they blended in easily. Second, most of those who did remain confronted the wet climate of the Chesapeake, which was so unhealthy that many servants died shortly after arriving in America. Those who survived were habitually sick and unable to work. And third, indentured servants also earned their freedom once their term of indenture (usually seven years) expired. At that point, some of them acquired land and began competing with their former masters, a situation that most masters did not welcome, as proved by Bacon's Rebellion. Finally, as Britain's economy improved, fewer people signed up to become indentured servants in the first place.

By the 1680s, the practice of indentured servitude diminished rapidly. In need of labor, North American colonists tapped into the slave trade system that had developed during the 1600s.

3-3b Africans' Transition from Servants to Slaves

In 1619, when the first Africans arrived in Virginia, they were treated like indentured servants, which meant not generously, but not inhumanely either. They lived alongside European colonists in their landowner's house, and some earned their freedom after their term of service. But as the number of Africans in the Chesapeake increased during the 1680s, European and Euro-American colonists began to craft a slave-based society, developing laws that would make slavery an enduring, race-dependent institution.

By the late 1630s, colonists had already begun to differentiate between indentured servants and slaves, but the first major law specifically regarding slavery emerged in Virginia in 1662. It stipulated that the condition of the mother determined the condition of the child; if a mother was a slave from Africa—or had African heritage—her child was to be a slave as well. This allowed male slaveholders to exploit African American females and, at the same time, produce new slaves.

In 1664, Maryland enacted an "anti-amalgamation" law, which outlawed interracial sex and marriage, rendering any relationship between a male colonist and a female slave illegal, and any relationship between an African American male slave and a European female colonist intolerable. Virginia followed suit, declaring in 1691 that any colonist who married a "Negro, mulatto, or Indian" would be banished from the colony. In 1682, Virginia passed a law that used specific racial differences to differentiate between servants and slaves, thus ensuring that African Americans and Euro-Americans were treated differently by the law. Thus, even before the rapid expansion of slavery in the 1680s and 1690s, colonial laws differentiated people by strict racial classifications. These differences grew markedly after slaves were brought to the American colonies in greater numbers throughout the 1700s.

3-3c Slave Codes

Slowly race became the central factor determining who was perceived as a freeman worthy of "natural rights" and who was not. In 1705, Virginia codified the racial orientation of the new system of labor with a series of **slave codes**. These codes meant that, in most areas, especially in the Southern Colonies and the Chesapeake, it became impossible for an African American to live as a free person. The codes declared

slave codes Laws meant to govern the slave system of labor; these laws made it impossible for an African American to live as a free person

Some Slave Codes...

Virginia, 1639

Act X. All persons except Negroes are to be provided with arms and ammunitions or be fined at the pleasure of the governor and council.

Maryland, 1664

That whatsoever free-born [English] woman shall intermarry with any slave . . . shall serve the master of such slave during the life of her husband; and that all the issue of such free-born women, so married shall be slaves as their fathers were.

Virginia, 1667

Act III. Whereas some doubts have arisen whether children that are slaves by birth . . . should by virtue of their baptism be made free, it is enacted that baptism does not alter the condition to the person as to his bondage or freedom; masters freed from this doubt may more carefully propagate Christianity by permitting slaves to be admitted to that sacrament.

Virginia, 1682

Act I. It is enacted that all servants . . . which [sic] shall be imported into this country either by sea or by land, whether Negroes, Moors [Muslim North Africans], mulattoes, or Indians who and whose parentage and native countries are not Christian at the time of their first purchase by some Christian . . . and all Indians, which shall be sold by our neighboring Indians, or any other trafficing with us for slaves, are hereby adjudged, deemed, and taken to be slaves to all intents and purposes any law, usage, or custom to the contrary notwithstanding.

INTRODUCTION OF SLAVERY.

North Wind Picture Archives/Alamy Stock Photo

>> **Buyers inspecting the product.**

---

that all "Negro, mulatto, and Indian" servants brought into the region were slaves, or "real estate." This guaranteed slaveholders *permanent* ownership of the black bondspeople they purchased. It also allowed masters to punish their property, and, because no one would deliberately destroy his own property, Virginia lawmakers said there was no need to enact laws prohibiting slaveholders from killing their slaves. The codes stated that slaves needed written permission to leave their plantation, would receive severe physical punishments for any wrongdoing, and no longer had any legal standing. Virginia's slave codes served as a model that other states emulated. British colonists were constructing a legalistic slave society based entirely on perceived racial distinctions.

 ## 3-4 WARS FOR EMPIRE

Propelled by the desires of landless young men and attracted by the potential profits of a slave-based economy, British colonists continued their seemingly perpetual march westward into North America. There, they ran into an obstacle other than Indians: the French. Beginning in the late 1600s, the French recognized the rich potential of North America and fortified their posts from the Great Lakes to New Orleans, traveling down the Mississippi River and usually developing friendly relations with Indians along the way, especially the Algonquians. Their only significant settlements, however, were at Quebec and New Orleans. Nevertheless, the increased French presence brought them into conflict with the British. When France and Britain had disputes in Europe, their battles had New World ramifications. Beginning in the late 1600s, European wars had North American fronts as well as European ones.

3-4a King William's War and Queen Anne's War, 1689–1713

The first of these carryover battles lasted from 1689 to 1697, and its most significant theaters were in Europe and the Caribbean. But it also reached the North American mainland, where it was called **King William's War**. King William's War began when New York's governor, Thomas Dongan, goaded the Iroquois into attacking Indian nations that were friendly with France. The French fought back by attacking the Iroquois and, eventually, British colonists in northern New England and New York. Britain in turn attacked various French outposts, with minimal success. The New World front had stalemated without significant gains for either side.

Nevertheless, King William's War was influential for three reasons. First, it prompted the French to fortify their New World position, creating a stronghold of settlers for the first time. Second, it demonstrated the ways Europeans manipulated Indians (and vice versa) in efforts to conquer the land. And third, in its wake, the Iroquois established better relations with the French and agreed to remain neutral in future conflicts.

The second British–French war started shortly thereafter, in 1702, when the French king angled to put his grandson on the newly vacant Spanish throne. The other European powers rejected this power play and attacked France. This was the War of the Spanish Succession, called **Queen Anne's War** in the New World (1702–1713). Twelve years of battle between the Spanish in Florida, the French in the North American interior, the British along the coast, and the various Indians friendly to one group or another finally ended with a British victory.

Queen Anne's War was significant for two reasons. First, success gave the British a base on the Hudson Bay, further promoting their expansion westward, into the interior of America. Second, it ushered in a period of relative peace in Europe, which allowed France and Britain to fortify their positions in the New World, so that when later Atlantic World battles came, both sides were better entrenched. Over time, the increasing economic and social strength of British colonies threatened the

THE WITCH No2

The Granger Collection

>> The Salem Witch Craft Trials contained both fear and frivolity. In this later drawing, convicted "witches" are carried to their punishment, which included time in the stockades and, for some, death.

French, who feared that the alliances they had built with the Indians would falter.

3-4b Salem Witchcraft Trials

It should also be noted that historians have recently attributed the Salem witch trials to fears triggered by the Indian wars. Because these witch trials were prosecuted in 1692–93, during King William's War, they suggest how the European Wars for Empire were felt in even the smallest of New World hamlets.

Trouble began in 1692 when two girls were playing with an older female slave who taught the girls African voodoo tales. The girls later became seized with fits, and soon other girls in Salem were behaving strangely as well. Searching for an explanation, the town's leaders accused the female slave and two other women of practicing witchcraft. Soon, the village elders accused several others of being witches, too. Once started, accusations flew wildly.

King William's War Battles between the Iroquois, French, and English colonists (1689–1697)

Queen Anne's War The New World name for the War of the Spanish Succession; twelve years of battle between the Spanish in Florida, the French in the North American interior, the English along the coast, and various Indian nations (1702–1713)

Before long it became apparent that divisions relating to social class, gender, commercial profession, and religiosity determined who was accused and who was not, as the poor were accused more readily than the wealthy, as were those who had fallen away from the church. Recent research demonstrates that unmarried women of property were prominent targets as well. Before the accusations slowed, twenty people had been executed. The strangeness of the Salem witchcraft episode reveals the anxiety of the time, sparked at least in part by wars with Indians. It also reflects the widespread willingness to believe in witches, spirits, and ghosts, a prominent feature of what one historian has called the colonial "worlds of wonder."

>LOOKING AHEAD...

By 1700, then, the North American colonies had developed into established, but not yet prospering, outliers in Britain's colonial web. They were securely situated along the Atlantic seaboard, and it seemed inevitable they would continue to settle farther into the interior of the continent. It was also clear that Europeans (and especially the British) would not blend into the lands of Native America or mix with its inhabitants, but would seek dominion over the areas they controlled. Also by 1700, the colonists had established slavery as the primary system of labor in the New World. From these roots, a system of racialized slavery would expand on American soil.

These trends would only continue from 1700 to 1763 as the colonies developed economically and socially. The four distinct regions became stronger and more established, so that when later "Wars for Empire" broke out, the North American colonists could ponder independence. But in 1700 those thoughts were still years away.

CH3 TIMELINE

What Else Was Happening

▶ **1640–1680s** In Beaver Wars over French fur trade, Iroquois Confederacy defeats Huron.

▶ **1649** Oliver Cromwell's execution of King Charles I prompts English civil war.

1651 Parliament passes first of colonial trade regulations known as Navigation Acts.

1655 *The Dutch of New Amsterdam use lotteries to raise money for the poor.*

1660–1685 Charles II's return to his father's throne signals a new era of royal Restoration.

1662–1690s Colonial assemblies make slavery matrilineal, prohibit miscegenation, separate slaves from servants by race.

1664 Charles II invades Dutch colony New Amsterdam, grants it to brother, Duke of York.

1666 *The Great Fire destroys three-fourths of London, killing only sixteen and helping halt the spread of the bubonic plague.*
1670 *Paris café starts serving ice cream.*

1674 Penn and Quakers purchase West Jersey.

1675–1676 Wampanoags lead pan-Indian fight against Puritan encroachment in Metacom's War.

1676–1677 British freemen fight colonial nobility over Indian and land policies in Bacon's Rebellion.

1680 Pueblo Revolt expels and kills Spanish Catholic friars.

1681 William Penn exchanges father's royal debt claim for colony that offers religious freedom.

1686 *Christian Gabriel Fahrenheit invents the thermometer.*
1688 *The start of the Japanese Edo Renaissance, a cultural flowering that saw the development of Kabuki theater.*

1689–1697 French–English rivalries reach colonies and Indian allies in King William's War.

1693 Rice cultivation expands rapidly in the Carolinas.

1698 Rapid growth of southern slave plantations prompts Carolina's split.

1701–1713 Europeans fight over French claim to Spanish succession, leaving English victorious in Queen Anne's War.

1705 Virginia slave code ties slavery to African origin.

1720 African slaves make up two-thirds of South Carolina's population.

1726 East and West Jersey unite as New Jersey.

1733 James Oglethorpe leads settlers to Georgia to create haven for "worthy poor."

1750 Non-native population in colonial America reaches 1 million.

4 | Expansion and Control, 1700–1763

LEARNING OBJECTIVES

After reading this chapter, you should be able to do the following:

4-1 Describe the development of the British colonies during the 1700s, including a discussion of each of the four distinct groups of colonies: New England, the Middle Colonies, the Chesapeake, and the Southern Colonies.

4-2 Discuss the impact of the Enlightenment and the Great Awakening on colonial America.

4-3 Chronicle the development of slavery in the American colonies, and analyze the reasons for changes in attitudes and in the legal system that helped the distinctively American slave system flourish.

4-4 By 1763, American colonists had become used to making their own decisions and taking care of their own needs. Describe the events in Britain that contributed to this situation, and explain their effects on the colonists.

AFTER FINISHING THIS CHAPTER GO TO **PAGE 84** **FOR STUDY TOOLS**

As discussed in the last chapter, from 1660 to 1700, British colonial America gradually evolved into four unique regions. This chapter explores the development of these regions from 1700 to 1763 as well as the expansion of an intellectual and cultural life distinct from that of Britain, and the ways in which African slavery became ingrained in the life of colonial North America. It concludes with Britain's attempts to regain control of its increasingly feisty and independent-minded colony, an effort that would eventually foster a revolution.

4-1 EXPANSION OF COLONIAL ECONOMY AND SOCIETY, 1700–1763

By 1700, four distinct regions had developed in colonial North America: (1) New England (Massachusetts, Rhode Island, New Hampshire, Connecticut), (2) the Middle Colonies (New York, New Jersey, Pennsylvania, Delaware), (3) the Chesapeake (Virginia and Maryland), and (4) the Southern Colonies (North Carolina, South Carolina, Georgia) (see Map 4.1). Each region had a unique economy based on its geographical location and its founding ideology, and each region's society developed in response to those two factors. The idea that all colonists possessed "natural rights" as Englishmen was perhaps the only unifying feature among the colonists, as they tried from afar to demonstrate their "Englishness" and unify the diverse population under the banner of Britain. Otherwise, they lived incredibly distinct lives, based largely on the region in which they resided. These regional distinctions would remain significant, and would perhaps even lead to the American Civil War nearly a century later.

4-1a New England

New England's terrain, climate, and founding ideology encouraged the development of certain types of agriculture, business, trade, and society.

ECONOMY

Like most other colonists, most New Englanders were farmers. New England's hilly land and short growing season encouraged **diversified farming**, a system in which a single home could farm many different crops that would sustain the household throughout the year. Farmers lived in towns and walked each day to their fields to tend their crops. Livestock was allowed to graze on community-owned land, such as the town common.

New Englanders, however, were consistently alert to new economic opportunities. They grew surplus agricultural goods to trade for tools and other finished goods such as furniture. At first their surplus was limited to grains and cereals, but by the early 1700s New Englanders were trading meat, dairy, and orchard products as well. In the mid-1600s and throughout the early 1700s, New Englanders also maintained an active trade in furs, fish, and timber.

New Englanders also often produced their own furniture and agricultural implements, and they spun their family's flax and wool to make clothing. Over time, some small industries developed around New England's two principal products: fish and lumber. New Englanders used local timber to establish a shipbuilding industry, and by the mid-1700s, one-third of all ships used by Britain were built in New England, a truly remarkable statistic.

Developing industries require money, salesmen, and trade routes, too, and the merchants who met these needs became prominent players in the development of New England from 1700 to 1763, as some of the first in a developing commercial class. They brought in capital and managerial expertise, and when land opened up to the west, the commercial leaders of New England were some of the first speculators, originating the practice of western land speculation around 1670.

These commercial adventurers also participated in a pattern of trade that has come to be called the **Triangular Trade**, although it was much more complicated than a simple triangle. The New England colonies traded fish and grains to Britain and to southern Europe in return for wine, spices, and gold. They also sold their goods to the West Indies in return for sugar and molasses. The New Englanders then distilled the molasses to make rum and traded it, along with other manufactured goods,

diversified farming   System in which a single home could farm various crops to sustain the household throughout the year

Triangular Trade   Pattern of trade in which fish, grains, spices, sugar, ships, slaves, and gold were traded between the New England colonies, England, southern Europe, the West Indies, and Africa

◄◄◄ **During the first half of the eighteenth century, Britain's colonies in North America grew socially, economically, and culturally—so much so, in fact, that they began to appear increasingly distinct from their mother country.**

>> By the mid-1700s, one-third of all ships used by Britain were built in New England. This fact alone signified that the North American colonies were no longer simply providing raw materials for Europe, but were developing large, complex industries on their own. This image shows the development of the shipping industry in colonial New England.

North Wind Picture Archives

to Africa in return for slaves and gold. The gold from this trade allowed New Englanders to purchase manufactured goods, tools, and linens from Britain, which in turn bought New England's manufactured ships. The Atlantic World was a dynamic and boisterous place throughout the eighteenth century.

By 1763, New England was a thriving arena of commerce that gave the colonies a good deal of economic independence, which later supported their insistent demands for increased political independence. New Englanders had also established a diversified economy that possessed but was not dependent upon slave labor.

SOCIETY

In 1660, New England had a population of more than 30,000 people of European descent. These people lived a mostly provincial life in small, family-centered towns. By 1700, the population had tripled to 90,000, and by 1760 it had reached 450,000.

Still, most of these people lived in small towns. Nevertheless, the dramatic increase in population reflected the stability and importance of families and an environment hospitable to life and commerce. Some immigrants came, and slaves were forced to come, but most of the growth was due to a high birthrate. This burgeoning population was the impetus for rapid westward expansion. A family with six sons could not divide its land six ways and bequeath a plot of land large enough for each son to ensure his prosperity or success. Some of the children had to strike out on their own.

One British import that crossed the Atlantic successfully was a social system demarcated by class, which was defined not only by the amount of wealth a person had but also by their mannerisms, their ancestry, and their power. Theoretically at the top of the system was a small group of aristocrats—governors, judges, and wealthy businessmen, often with distinguished British backgrounds—who endeavored to live a properly refined life above the rest of the population. The wealthiest attempted to recreate the privileged life of urban Britain, building large homes and filling them with British furnishings. To flaunt their wealth, some possessed slaves.

A slightly larger group consisted of what the colonists called the "natural aristocracy"—merchants and wealthy landholders who made their fortunes in the New World and usually did not possess noble titles. These men dominated economic affairs and owned an increasing percentage of the area's wealth.

A group of commercial middlemen, farmers, and artisans constituted the class in the middle and made up the majority of the population. They may have owned their own farms or small businesses producing handmade goods.

Beneath them was a laboring class that consisted mostly of young men waiting to inherit land from their fathers or preparing to enter a craft. In time, most of this laboring class would own property and enjoy some level of wealth. Slaves, employed by the wealthiest members of the natural aristocracy, dwelled at the bottom of the social structure.

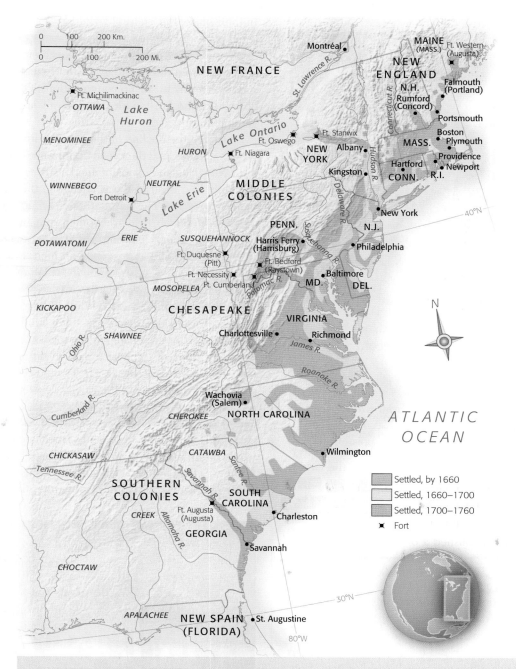

Map 4.1 British Settlement by 1760

>> This map details the progressive settlement of areas along the Atlantic coast, showing the dramatic growth between 1660 and 1760 in British North America.

Legend:
- Settled, by 1660
- Settled, 1660–1700
- Settled, 1700–1760
- ✳ Fort

LIFE IN NEW ENGLAND

With the growth that occurred between 1660 and 1763, the now-idealized image of an agricultural and religiously orthodox New England receded into the past. In its place emerged an increasingly commercialized society characterized by economic mobility and social differentiation. Although New England remained overwhelmingly agricultural, the small towns became increasingly connected to one another.

>> Life in colonial New England, as merchants discuss the most recent business developments.

This was a significant transition from a century earlier. In the 1660s, colonial New England was a provincial land freckled with unconnected towns. There were few roads in the 1660s, and they connected only the largest towns. By the 1700s, that had begun to change. Commerce had grown exponentially, and colonists tracked the markets in Britain and knew which ships were carrying which goods. One historian has called this developing society "an empire of goods" because of the large number of goods criss-crossing the Atlantic Ocean in order to become available for purchase.

As the population multiplied, colonists pushed westward and developed one town after another, creating a large half-circle of small towns around any large Atlantic port city. These hinterland towns lay on the margins of the bustling economic and social world of New England's cities.

Such robust growth meant that the religious and social orthodoxy enforced by the Puritans could not last. Prosperity weakened the younger generations' commitment to the strict religious practices of their forefathers. Ministers slowly lost stature, no longer defining New England life as they had when the Puritans first arrived.

jeremiad A long speech or literary work emphasizing society's fall from purity and grace to its current, depraved state

In their place, the "natural aristocracy" assumed a privileged place. By 1700, many Puritan ministers had begun to rely on the jeremiad—a long speech emphasizing society's fall from purity and grace to its current depraved state—as a way to stir up congregations. Often they had little luck. The Puritan ideal had hardly lasted beyond a generation or two.

Despite the decline of the church's importance, the growth of cities, and the rise in importance of commerce, most New Englanders maintained a strong commitment to family life. If all else was changing, these values remained constant. The sexual division of labor continued (as imported from Britain): women remained in charge of "indoor affairs" (raising children, preparing food, cleaning house, doing laundry) and men took charge of "outdoor affairs" (cultivating fields, chopping wood, and conducting the daily business transactions, such as buying horses and selling crops). While most of their waking hours consisted of working on their family farm, New Englanders often recreated in the town's common, what we might think of today as a park in the middle of the town that was shared by all. They would read books and gather information from the slowly developing newspaper industry. Courtship was always done carefully, and could only proceed with the approval of the woman's parents. If the parents approved of the match, the couple would often "bundle" together for one night, or sleepover at the woman's house, staying up as late as possible and never removing one's clothes (sometimes the couple was

>> By 1760 New England no longer looked like the Puritan ideal. Instead it looked a lot like Britain, with mansions such as Vassall House, pictured here, in Cambridge, Massachusetts, though with greater economic and social mobility and a higher rate of literacy.

separated by a piece of wood called a "bundling board" to ensure nothing overly intimate could happen). If the couple remained enamored with one another after their night together, they would then proceed to get married.

In sum, New England consisted mostly of stable, agriculturally based families, an expanding economy that led to the growth of some cities, and a rapid westward migration to accommodate the growth of the population. And, of course, there continued to be the presence of Indians, who, although being pushed west, still occupied significant terrain in all the colonies.

4-1b The Middle Colonies

The warmer climate and distinct foundings of the Middle Colonies created some important differences from New England.

ECONOMY

In the Middle Colonies, farms were larger than in New England, and farmers lived on their farms rather than in the village. Many of the Middle Colonies' farms achieved relative self-sustenance, and some were so bountiful they exported goods. Fruit, livestock, and wheat were the principal exported crops of the region, wheat being the biggest export. Indeed, by the early 1700s, New York and Pennsylvania were sometimes known to British traders as the "bread colonies." Agricultural production grew 2 to 3 percent every year from 1700 to 1770, and the best farmers in the Middle Colonies could afford to bring nearly 40 percent of their produce to market, meaning that this area quickly grew wealthier than New England as money from Britain poured in.

As in New England, families in the Middle Colonies produced their own furniture and agricultural implements and spun their family's flax and wool to make clothing. Clay from the riverbeds allowed them to build houses of brick, usually two stories high. Unlike the many small towns of New England, commerce focused on the two urban hubs of the Middle Colonies: New York and Philadelphia. The chief industries developed around corn and wheat, and mills built alongside rivers ground these grains into flour. Nearly all of these goods passed through New York or Philadelphia to

>> Wheat.

iStock.com/Tjanze

>> Slave auctions like the one drawn here on the New York waterfront in the late 1600s, almost always drew quite a crowd. Throughout the 1700s, American slavery grew tremendously, and by 1750 New York City had become a major hub of the worldwide slave trade.

North Wind Picture Archives/Alamy Stock Photo

be traded overseas. If you lived in the Middle Colonies during these years, it is likely you would have either lived on a wheat farm or in the commercial cities of New York or Philadelphia.

The success of the mills allowed the Middle Colonies to participate in the Triangular Trade by supplying wheat, grain, and excess fish to Britain and southern Europe, where they were traded for wine and gold. They traded other surplus items, such as meat and horses, to the West Indies in return for sugar and molasses. As in New England, they turned the molasses into rum, which they shipped with other goods to Africa in return for slaves and gold. Some families were slaveholders, and by the 1760s slavery was generally well established in the Middle Colonies, although most families owned only small numbers of slaves.

SOCIETY

In 1660, just 5,000 non-Indian people lived in the Middle Colonies. In 1710, that number had grown to 70,000, and by 1760 it was 425,000. This growth was fueled by a high birthrate and also (unlike New England) continued immigration from Scotland, Ireland, Germany, and Britain.

>> In most areas, the division of labor by gender continued, with women controlling indoor activities, such as cooking as shown here, and men controlling outdoor activities.

In the Middle Colonies, several members of the natural aristocracy owned enormous tracts of land. These people grew wealthier and wealthier throughout the 1700s as they sold some of their extensive lands. Below them socially were urban merchants and small family farmers, who comprised the majority of the population. Below these groups were tenant farmers who rented the farms they worked. And in the cities there was a growing number of poor. There were also around 35,000 slaves in the Middle Colonies in 1770, most of whom worked in the agricultural areas of New York, usually cultivating wheat. Slavery was also visible in the cities, usually because the wealthiest colonists liked to have a servant in tow to show off their wealth. By 1750, New York City was a major hub of the American slave trade.

LIFE IN THE MIDDLE COLONIES

Life in the Middle Colonies can be differentiated by looking at the big cities (Philadelphia and New York) on the one hand, and everywhere else on the other. Family farms owned and worked by one family produced huge amounts of grain. In New York, however, large landowners owned baronial estates and had tenants work their lands. As in New England, the population boom propelled youngsters off family plots and farther west. Some tried to purchase farms, and some were reduced to tenant farming. In most areas, the sexual division of labor continued, with women controlling indoor activities and men controlling outdoor activities. Families remained generally stable, and, in the absence

of large villages, the number of people living on a farm grew. Courtship typically occurred between neighboring farm families, and games and recreation were often rural and included hunting, fishing, and other outdoor games.

The cities were booming as well. In 1765, almost one out of every five Pennsylvanians lived in a sizeable town. A professional class of lawyers, craftsmen, and millers emerged. The populace founded urban institutions such as centers of public education, newspapers, theaters, fire departments, and libraries. More so than the other colonies, the Middle Colonies' thriving population was diverse. In New York City and Philadelphia, many languages were spoken, and people often grouped together by language. There was also a growing diversity of religious groups in the Middle Colonies, including Presbyterians, Lutherans, Anglicans, Congregationalists, Baptists, Roman Catholics, and Jews. In general, the laboring people of the Middle Colonies exerted an impressive amount of control over civic life, as a ruling elite was slow to emerge. This civic input combined with devotion to family and individual happiness to form the cornerstone of society.

4-1c The Chesapeake

Further south, the Chesapeake, with more fertile soil than either New England or the Middle Colonies, had fewer towns and more land devoted to a single crop: tobacco. Life there largely centered around the cultivation of that single crop.

ECONOMY

Tobacco was the chief product of the Chesapeake area, and, rather than developing a diversified economy, farmers in the Chesapeake remained tied to this single lucrative crop. For instance, in the late 1600s, tobacco generated 90 percent of the enormous wealth in Virginia and Maryland. Flour and grains came in a distant second as exports, growing in importance only in the mid-1700s. From 1660 to 1763, tobacco was king of the Chesapeake, its production influencing everything else in the colony.

Because people lived on huge stretches of land that grew tobacco, there were few towns and hardly any developed industries in the Chesapeake. Virginia did mine some iron ore, and after 1730, when grain became profitable, mills sprang up along the rivers. Indeed, just before the American Revolution, the Chesapeake's mills had developed into one of the strongest sectors of the economy. But this was a late development.

> Tobacco was king of the Chesapeake.

The Chesapeake relied on its staple crop for its wealth, and the growth of other industries would suffer because of it.

Cities, too, failed to develop. By the middle 1700s, the Chesapeake had only one sizeable city in Baltimore, which was developed as a port town for the area's grain. Other than that, most of the Chesapeake's cities (such as Norfolk) were little more than small towns.

Instead of living in cities or towns, the people of the Chesapeake settled on farms. Key to a farm's success was access to a riverbank where product could be transported to market. Thus, a developmental map of the Chesapeake would show a number of large farms moving farther and farther up the major rivers. In 1660, there were around 35,000 non-Indians living in the Chesapeake. By 1760 that number had reached 500,000. Just below two-fifths of this total (about 190,000) were slaves, most of whom worked on tobacco plantations that lined the major waterways.

SOCIETY

In this economically minded society, social relations were based on knowing one's place in the social hierarchy and deferring to one's superiors. At the top of the structure were the few families with access to land who profited from selling tobacco and grain. They increased their wealth throughout the 1700s, constructing a visible structure of leadership and power and modeling their lives after those of the landed British gentry, not wealthy Londoners. By setting themselves up as an elite class with social responsibilities, they gained total control over political and religious institutions. By the mid-1700s, commentators were noting the extravagance and indulgences of this elite. They sat high above the less affluent free colonists, who were usually small landholders and who were, in turn, socially above the increasingly large number of slaves.

LIFE IN THE CHESAPEAKE

The majority of the people in the Chesapeake lived on widely scattered farms and plantations. Because settlements were scattered, individual households grew larger and larger in size, and it was common to live with one's siblings for most of one's life. Throughout the 1700s, kinship networks among neighbors prospered.

As roads slowly developed, settlements began to spring up farther from the rivers. Horses provided the main mode of transportation. By the 1750s, the Chesapeake supported a rural commercial network along these roads, where merchants, innkeepers, and traders could hawk their wares. Life was slowly moving away from being entirely agricultural, although in contrast to New England and the Middle Colonies, urban life in the Chesapeake was nonexistent.

Until 1700, there were also many more men than women in the Chesapeake. This meant that many people married late and that women possessed ample power. The region suffered from high death rates, economic inequality among free people, and weak social institutions, such as churches (where a sense of community could develop).

This began to change around 1700. A temporary lull in tobacco prices slowed the rush of new arrivals, allowing Chesapeake society to settle down as its sex ratio evened out. In addition, after 1675 slavery replaced indentured servitude as the preferred type of labor. By 1720, slaves made up 25 percent of the population, a percentage that stabilized at about 40 percent by 1760, when almost 50 percent of white families owned slaves, usually in small numbers. The declining number of indentured servants meant the eventual decline of a class of free white laborers, who would have constituted the region's middle rung of society. Because of the growth of

>> The governor's palace at Williamsburg, Virginia, the seat of royal power in the colony, exemplified the standard to which wealthy Virginia families aspired.

slavery, this middle rung remained narrow in the Chesapeake; there was little middle class to speak of.

For women, this meant a changed domestic life, and a less influential one. Following the model of the landed British gentry, Chesapeake society viewed men as benign patriarchs presiding over their flock of dependents. The result was that women's public roles in the region declined in importance from 1660 to 1760.

As opposed to the variety of religions in the Middle Colonies and, increasingly, New England, throughout the 1700s the Anglican Church became entrenched in the life of the Chesapeake. Unlike Puritans, Anglicans did not demand strict adherence, and the Chesapeake institutions remained generally secular. This situation was aided by the fact that there were few ministers in the growing region, and the gentry did not care to pay for more to come.

Throughout the 1700s, then, the Chesapeake developed a strongly aristocratic social structure and a largely rural, British model of living. This pattern stood in contrast to New England, which featured small towns and social mobility. It also stood in contrast to the Middle Colonies, which relied on New York and Philadelphia as central urban hubs to support the many middle-rung farmers. Life in the Chesapeake was more deferential regarding status, more rural, and, at the top, more luxurious and comfortable.

4-1d The Southern Colonies

Impressive as the wealth of the Chesapeake was, it could not compete with that of the Southern Colonies. Like the Chesapeake, the Southern Colonies relied overwhelmingly on a few staple crops, but life was generally so miserable that few colonists resided there permanently. Only two towns of any size were established, and no social models of leadership developed. The wealthy landowners enjoyed the profits emerging from the rich soil, but they typically chose to live elsewhere.

ECONOMY

The staple crops of the Southern Colonies were tobacco, rice, and indigo, and they dominated the region's economic life. Cotton would become significant only after 1793, when Eli Whitney invented the cotton gin, which allowed the cultivation of the crop on lower-quality land,

> By the mid-1700s, commentators were noting the extravagance and indulgences of the Chesapeake elite. They sat high above the less affluent free colonists.

thus expanding the amount of cotton that could be grown. By the early 1700s, however, large plantations started springing up to grow those staple crops. Slave labor was the key to their development, allowing a few successful farmers to develop large plantations of more than a thousand acres.

There was little industrial development in the Southern Colonies. Local artisans and their apprentices developed small establishments for manufacturing guns and other ironware. For the most part, however, the people of the Southern Colonies relied on trade with Britain for their industrial goods. Indeed, the Southern Colonies were key players in the Triangular Trade, shipping their tobacco, rice, and indigo to Britain in return for manufactured goods and slaves.

SOCIETY

Because of the miserable living conditions, including heat, humidity, and insects, the population of the Southern Colonies was slow to grow. In 1660, there were very few non-Indian settlers. In 1710, there were 26,000, and in 1760 there were just 215,000, about 95,000 of whom were slaves. The social structure reflected this differentiation. Plantation bosses were heads of large fiefdoms. Under them was a tiny middle class of lawyers, merchants, and skilled workers who usually lived in the region's few small towns or worked in the lumber mills of North Carolina. The bulk of the working class was made up of slaves imported from Africa.

LIFE IN THE SOUTHERN COLONIES

There was a difference in lifestyle between the upper and lower Southern Colonies. In the lower colonies (today's South Carolina and Georgia), life expectancy continued to be perilously short. Few people lived to be sixty, and many died before they were twenty. This meant that, for the most part, those who could live elsewhere did.

Nevertheless, the lucky and the entrepreneurial amassed great wealth in the Southern Colonies. The commercial gentry who enjoyed this wealth lived a stylish life, usually in the manner of the British elite, enjoying West Indian accent pieces for their home's furnishings. They customarily owned two homes: one on their plantation (where they spent little time), and one in either Charleston or Savannah. To make use of the gentry's wealth and leisure time, these two cities developed such

>> Town homes in Charleston, South Carolina.

institutions as libraries, theaters, social clubs, and concert houses.

Throughout the Southern Colonies, communities were not always based around families, mostly because there was no certainty that parents would survive long. Law enforcement was slack, depth of religious commitment was shallow, and interest in public education was limited. The wealthy frequently sent their children to Britain to be educated.

In dramatic contrast to the pleasant life they were leading, elite white Southerners developed draconian slave codes to govern the lives of their slaves. Punishment for slave insurrections was severe, travel for slaves was limited, and accumulation of wealth denied. Yet, there were few slave revolts, probably because most slaves did not yet work in gangs. The single major uprising, the Stono Rebellion of 1739 in South Carolina, was put down brutally and spurred the reinforcement of strict slave codes (see Section 4-3c). However, because of the high rates of white absenteeism from plantations, there was little owner oversight, meaning that slaves actually led a slightly freer life than the laws dictated.

4-2 EXPANSION OF COLONIAL INTELLECTUAL AND CULTURAL LIFE

The expanding economic and social life of the 1700s gave some people the time and inclination to engage in intellectual and cultural pursuits. It also allowed Americans to participate in a monumental transition affecting much of the Western world, a movement away from medieval thought toward that of what has come to be called the Enlightenment. This was important for the history of the United States because Enlightenment ideals played a substantial role in the American Revolution and in the development of the American political system that was to come.

4-2a The American Enlightenment

The American **Enlightenment** stemmed from the European Enlightenment, which was a movement to prioritize human capacity for reason as the highest form of human attainment. In the early 1600s, most people of the Western world believed: (1) in the unquestioned primacy of rulers (spiritual and secular); (2) in humans' incapacity for social change; and (3) that our time here on earth is a temporary interlude on our journey toward either eternal salvation or damnation. But as early as the 1500s, European scientists, most notably Copernicus who argued that the earth revolved around the sun, not the other way around, began to question some of these foundational beliefs. By the 1600s educated people were postulating whether natural laws (not divine ones) governed society and the universe, and whether these natural laws were accessible to humans through the use of reason.

The most prominent of the Enlightenment thinkers were, perhaps, John Locke and Jean-Jacques Rousseau. Locke argued that one's environment was more significant than divine decree in the development of one's character, and that individuals had "natural rights" to life, liberty, and property, which even a king or a pope

Enlightenment A movement to prioritize the human capacity for reason as the highest form of human attainment

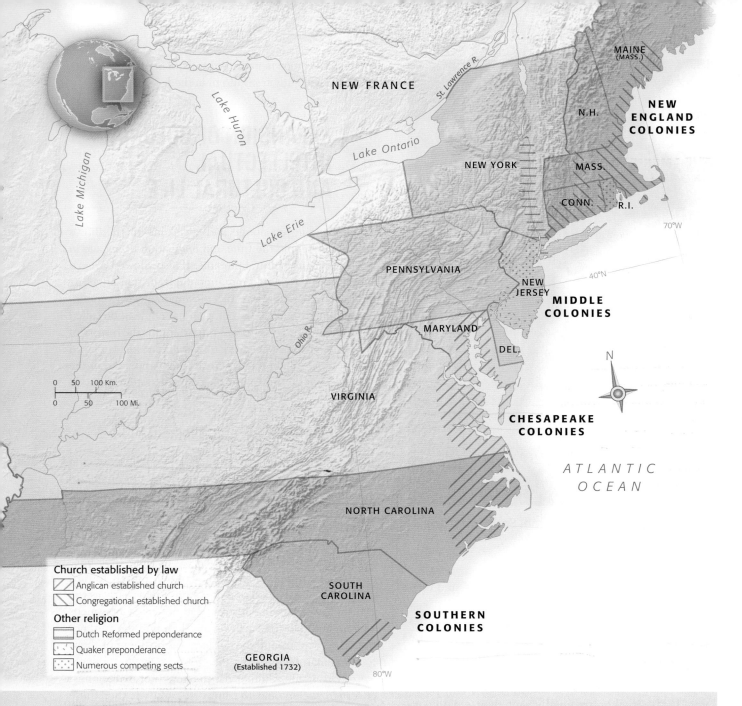

Map 4.2 **Religion in the Colonies, 1720**

>> From the very beginning, there were competing religious sects in the British colonies, although Anglicanism was generally predominant in the Chesapeake and the South, while Congregationalism prevailed in New England. This map shows the various places where faiths were either dominant or established by law.

could not deny. For his part, Rousseau famously argued that humans were born virtuous and therefore had a responsibility to use their virtue to check the growth of social institutions that would inevitably become premised on inequality and favoritism. The key Enlightenment economist was Adam Smith, who, among other things, postulated a natural balance in the economy determined by laws of supply and demand. Each of the central ideas implied that progress was possible as people achieved more and more of their natural rights and that people had a stake in their own life and were entitled to reject authority if certain rights were denied. The Enlightenment was a fundamental transformation in the way people in the Western world thought about themselves and the societies in which they lived.

THE AMERICAN ENLIGHTENMENT AND RELIGION

These ideas inspired both harmony and conflict with religious leaders, and many of the most consequential American intellectual outpourings from the colonial period are either rejections of or support for the Enlightenment. Cotton Mather, for instance, produced important sermons as he refined a Puritan theology that articulated the centrality of God to an individual's well-being. William Bradford, John Winthrop, and Edward Johnson wrote histories of New England, giving special testament to the sacrifices made to religion by the colonial founders, and also hedging a bit toward the Enlightenment by praising the individual fortitude of those founders. They seemed to be trying to balance the imperatives of reason with those of revelation. Religion, meanwhile, animated the poems of Anne Bradstreet, Edward Taylor, and Michael Wigglesworth. The American Enlightenment did not produce many atheists or agnostics, but it did begin a process whereby religious thinkers tried to find a balance between science and religion.

It also produced several generations of thinkers who, despite being across the Atlantic Ocean from most of the progenitors of these ideas, engaged with them thoughtfully. Colonists debated how the Enlightenment idea of "natural rights" might influence their actions as colonists under the rule of the British crown. They discussed how far an individual's reason could push them away from established faiths, as they rejected authoritarianism, irrationality, and obscurantism. Some became deists, a faith holding that God had merely set up this world and then allowed humans to develop it as their reason allowed. Famous American Enlightenment thinkers include Benjamin Franklin, Thomas Jefferson, and Thomas Paine.

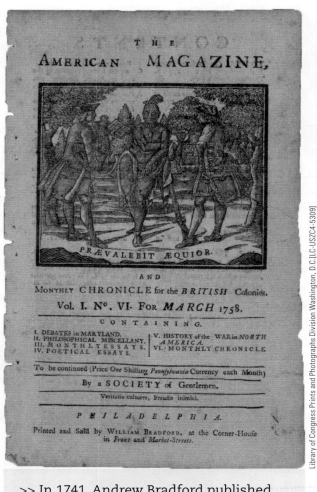

>> In 1741, Andrew Bradford published the colonies' first magazine. Its title, The American Magazine, reflects the sense of distinctiveness felt by the colonists.

EDUCATION

The necessity of training ministers, especially in New England, had led to the creation of an educational system, and the Enlightenment ideals of individual progress via human reason prodded the slow democratization of the system over the course of the seventeenth and eighteenth centuries. Reflecting this balance between religious and secular ideals, America's first college, Harvard, was founded in 1636, not as an official church school, but under the prevailing Puritan philosophy and with a mission to create a literate ministry. In 1642, Massachusetts passed a law requiring parents to teach all children to read. In 1647, it passed a law requiring towns to maintain a primary school. Although they did so more slowly than New England, the Middle Colonies also launched endeavors in public education.

Over time, the presence of schools grew, especially in New England. Secondary schools opened there in the 1700s. They would not be established southward in significant numbers until after the American Revolution. Nine colleges were founded during the colonial period, four of them in New England. All, like Harvard, were in some way church schools.

>> John Peter Zenger's trial.

THE SECULAR PRESS

Enlightenment ideals also took hold with many laypeople, as did the secular practices of politics and commerce. This trend was reflected in the expansion of nonreligious newspapers throughout the 1700s, especially in New England. In Boston, Benjamin Harris published the first North American newspaper in 1690, and the first regularly published paper was the *Boston News-Letter*, begun in 1704. By the middle of the 1700s, every major town had its own newspaper (although they published more about events in Europe than about those in the colonies). In 1741, Andrew Bradford published the first magazine, the *American Magazine*. The title alone reflects the unity that the colonists were beginning to feel.

The freedom encouraged by Enlightenment ideals also led to expansion of individual liberties, as in the case of John Peter Zenger, a New York newspaperman who was arrested after publishing an attack on the governor. Zenger was acquitted of the crime (because his attack was factually correct), setting a crucial precedent for freedom of the press. Truth

became a legitimate defense against a charge of libel, no matter how elevated in rank the alleged libel victim was. Illustrating the deep anti-authoritarianism that ran through the case (and the Enlightenment in general) the jury, in coming to its decision, defied the wishes of the judge. Enlightenment ideals about the value of the individual regardless of his or her station in life had won out.

4-2b The Great Awakening

During this expansion of Enlightenment ideals, American churches perhaps surprisingly experienced something of a revival. A combination of the threat of Enlightenment ideals and a general unhappiness with social and economic developments bred dissatisfaction with the direction American life was taking. Many colonists felt that the established religions had overly accommodated the rise of rational thought, allowing rationalization too much free rein in the spiritual world. Many colonists had also begun to feel alienated from the mainstream establishment and the traditions that ensconced them in power; the social hierarchies they had perhaps hoped to leave behind had made their way to the colonies.

In response, ministers and laypeople alike fomented a Protestant revival that emphasized the notion that individuals could find heaven if they worked hard enough (not just if they were predestined to go to heaven) and that allowed—even invited—emotional expressions of religion. Ignoring tradition, this new group of preachers

>> In this painting, George Whitefield preaches with both hands raised to a motley crew of listeners. Historians estimate that roughly 80 percent of all American colonists heard him preach at least once, leading him to often be called "America's first celebrity."

stressed that all were equal in Christ. The result was the growth and development of several new Protestant denominations that invariably emphasized the laity's role in matters both spiritual and temporal, as well as a more emotional type of religion. Called the **Great Awakening**, it was America's first large-scale religious revival.

Jonathan Edwards was the intellectual leader of the Great Awakening, although itinerant evangelical preachers such as George Whitefield played a considerable role in spreading the revival. These itinerants advocated an emotional style of religion and sometimes attacked local ministers. And by the time it had run its course (by about 1745), the Great Awakening had opened a tremendous rift among Protestants. On one side were the **Old Lights**, who condemned emotionalism and advocated a more rationalistic theology favored by elements of the Enlightenment; on the other side were the **New Lights**, who supported evangelism, the new methods of prayer, and equality before Christ. The revival slowed during the 1750s, but it is significant for at least five reasons (see "The Reasons Why . . ." box).

 ## 4-3 AFRICAN SLAVERY

Perhaps ironically, perhaps not, alongside the American Enlightenment and the Great Awakening, an intricate and harsh slave system grew and developed during

> "The congregation was extraordinarily melted by every sermon; almost the whole assembly being in tears for a great part of sermon time."
>
> —JONATHAN EDWARDS ON GREAT AWAKENING PREACHER GEORGE WHITEFIELD'S SERMONS

the first half of the eighteenth century. Although slavery existed everywhere in colonial North America, it was especially brutal in the Southern Colonies. Numerically speaking, the colonies that would become the United States were a tiny part of a much larger

Great Awakening America's first large-scale religious revival, originated by preachers who stressed that all were equal in Christ

Old Lights Protestant leaders who condemned emotionalism and advocated a more rationalistic theology favored by elements of the Enlightenment

New Lights Protestant leaders who supported evangelism, the new methods of prayer, and equality before Christ

The Reasons Why...

The Great Awakening provoked changes in colonial life for at least five reasons:

Growth of churches. As ministers formed new sects to meet the demands of the population, they greatly increased the number of churches in colonial America.

Rise of new churches. Many of these new churches emerged from evangelical sects, such as the Baptists, who became prominent in the Chesapeake and sought to overturn the aristocratic social structure, setting the stage for a battle with the established Anglican Church of England.

Development of colleges. Seeking to train all these new ministers, many religious orders established several colleges, many of which still exist today (such as Princeton, Brown, Rutgers, and Dartmouth).

Religion and science. Unlike in Europe, in the North American colonies, the Great Awakening made accommodations with the Enlightenment, allowing the persistence of religion in conjunction with Enlightenment ideals. This compromise was vital because, although contrarian faiths like deism did arise, there was never any widespread atheism or agnosticism.

Decline of authority. The Great Awakening also severed colonial ties to established structures of authority (religious authority, in this case), serving in some ways as a precursor to revolution, although such conclusions must be made with caution.

>> To meet the labor demands of the New World, European merchants developed the Atlantic slave trade, which would eventually force as many as 12 million Africans to cross the Atlantic to work as human property. Of this huge number, roughly 5 percent came to land that would eventually become the United States.

Atlantic slave trade, a huge system of trade and migration that brought millions of slaves to the New World and Europe and that served as a pillar in the world economy. Europeans and colonials forced perhaps as many as 12 million Africans to cross the Atlantic (many died during the arduous passage, masking the true number of forced migrants). A vast majority of the Africans went to colonies controlled by Spain or Portugal: about 2 million to Brazil and 3 million to the West Indies, usually to work on sugar plantations. Of these many millions, just 350,000 Africans, less than 5 percent of the total, came to the future United States. Of this 350,000, Europeans forced 10,000 Africans to come during the 1600s and the remainder during the 1700s. Although some would become free after earning enough money to

purchase their freedom, more than 95 percent of colonial Africans remained slaves for life.

4-3a Enslavement

Enslavement was a brutal process in all three of its stages: (1) initial capture in Africa; (2) the middle passage across the ocean; and (3) the period of adjustment to the New World.

CAPTURE

The process by which captured slaves came to North, South, and Central America was rationalized by the profits to be made. Acquired either through barter between a European slave trader and an African kingdom or through kidnapping, the enslaved Africans were often bound at the neck in a leather brace. The slave trader connected a gang of slaves together by chains attached to the neck braces. Then the chained gang was marched to the coast, a journey sometimes as long as 550 miles, which could take up to two months. Once on the African coast, the traders

---

Atlantic slave trade Huge system of trade and migration that brought millions of slaves to the New World and Europe in the 1600s and 1700s

herded their captives into stucco pens to be inspected and sorted by desirability. Some traders branded the slaves with hot irons to mark them as their property. Then the slaves waited in captivity for cargo ships to arrive.

THE MIDDLE PASSAGE

When the ships arrived, slave traders forced the slaves from their pens onto canoes and then paddled them out to the larger ships. At this point, some slaves jumped overboard, keeping themselves under water long enough to drown.

Once aboard the transport ship, slaves faced the "**middle passage**," their horrible journey across the Atlantic. Traders packed the ships until they were over-filled. They cuffed the slaves and kept them below decks, away from fresh air. The captives were denied access to latrines, and the stench in the holds typically became unbearable. Many captives vomited in response, making the stench even worse. The Europeans also fed the slaves paltry food and threw sick slaves overboard to try to prevent the spread of diseases. They force-fed with a mouth wrench those who sought to starve themselves. Because the slaves came from varied tribes, it was likely they did not speak one another's language, cutting them off completely from the life they once knew. The middle passage took between four and eight weeks, and more than one in four captives died along the way. In the seventeenth and eighteenth centuries, any trans-Atlantic journey was perilous and potentially fatal, but especially so for the captured Africans.

TO A NEW LIFE

Once in the New World, slave traders auctioned off their cargo in public squares, chiefly in New York and Charleston, but in several other cities as well. Potential buyers inspected the captured men and women's teeth, underarms, and genitals. Strong young men were the most valuable, but women of childbearing age were also prized because they could have children who, by law in the 1700s, were also the slaveholder's property. Then the buyer transported the slaves to what lay ahead: a life of ceaseless labor. In total, the journey from African village to New World plantation routinely took as long as six months.

This process began in the 1600s and continued into the 1800s, although the 1780s were the years of the Atlantic slave trade's peak. Before the American Revolution, there were only a few scattered movements to protest the slave trade and the practice of slavery (primarily by the Quakers, the Mennonites, and a few other religious groups). Much of European society simply accepted the horrors of slavery as a necessary cost of colonial expansion.

North Wind Picture Archives

>> Slave traders packed their ships tightly to maximize profits.

4-3b The Spread of Slavery

Tobacco, rice, and indigo—the three staple crops of the Southern and Chesapeake colonies—all demanded significant labor, and by the late 1600s, the favored form of labor in the American colonies was rapidly becoming African slaves. Between 1680 and 1700, the average number of slaves transported on British ships rose from 5,000 slaves a year to more than 20,000.

Although slavery was most common in the Southern Colonies and the Chesapeake, it was legal in *all* British colonies in North America. In the North, slaves worked as field hands on farms and as domestic servants, dockworkers, and craftspeople in cities. But because of their labor-intensive cash crops, the market for slaves was much more lucrative in the South and the Chesapeake. Nevertheless, many northerners were involved in the trade. Northern traders, especially from Massachusetts, New York, and Rhode Island, engaged in and profited from the slave trade before the United States outlawed the importation of slaves in 1808.

middle passage The perilous journey across the Atlantic endured by captives from Africa

TO BE SOLD on board the Ship *Bance-Island*, on tuesday the 6th of *May* next, at *Ashley-Ferry*; a choice cargo of about 250 fine healthy NEGROES, just arrived from the Windward & Rice Coast. —The utmost care has already been taken, and shall be continued, to keep them free from the least danger of being infected with the SMALL-POX, no boat having been on board, and all other communication with people from *Charles-Town* prevented.
Austin, Laurens, & Appleby.

N. B. Full one Half of the above Negroes have had the SMALL-POX in their own Country.

>> A 1780s newspaper ad for a slave auction held near Charleston, South Carolina.

4-3c Life Under Slavery

The daily life of a slave in colonial America depended on where he or she lived. In New England, where only about 3 percent of the population was African during the colonial era, slaves worked as field hands on small farms, as house servants for wealthy colonists, or as skilled artisans. Slaves could be isolated from one another (and most were), or they could live in a port town like Newport, Rhode Island, where slaves made up 18 percent of the population. In the Middle Colonies, some slaves worked as field hands on small farms, while smaller numbers worked in cities in nearly every labor-intensive occupation. Neither of these regions relied on gang labor.

In the Southern Colonies and the Chesapeake, on the other hand, most slaves were field hands who grew sugar cane, rice, tobacco, or cotton. Some were house servants who cooked, cleaned, and helped care for children. A very few were skilled artisans. As arduous as the southern labor system was, however, plantation life allowed for development of a slave culture. This was possible because of the large number of slaves who could gather together after working hours.

Stono Rebellion Slave rebellion in South Carolina in 1739, the largest slave uprising of the century

PLANTATION LIFE

The plantations where slave life developed most fully were entirely in the South, especially in the lower South, where slaves outnumbered other colonists. Many slaves here spoke Gullah, a hybrid language of several African tongues. They preserved several African religious traditions, such as a couple's jumping over a broomstick to seal a marriage. Over time, these traditions merged with Christianity in the same way that Catholic images merged with the traditional beliefs of Native America.

For slaves, family life was unpredictable, fragile, and subject to the arbitrary whims of their owners. Children typically stayed with their family until they were eight, at which time they were sometimes sold. Masters occasionally raped or coerced female slaves into sexual relations, further demonstrating their limitless power over their property. Nevertheless, families did struggle through, and wherever possible, strong family structures emerged. The hazards and difficulties inherent in the process of sustaining a family life under these conditions led slave men and women to take on roles different from those of their masters. Slave women, for instance, worked both in the field and in the home. Slave men, meanwhile, took on occasional domestic duties.

REBELLION AND RESISTANCE

Despite the horrific nature of slave life, slave rebellions were infrequent, principally because slave owners had taken such drastic measures to maintain control over their slaves. The few slave rebellions that did arise met with violent resistance and led to even tighter controls. One planned insurrection in New York City in 1740 ended with the burning of thirteen slaves and the hanging of eighteen others (along with four white allies).

The most notable slave revolt of the 1700s—the **Stono Rebellion**—occurred in Stono, South Carolina, in 1739, when, on a quiet Sunday morning, a group of mostly newly arrived slaves marched into a firearms shop, killed the colonists manning the shop, stole several firearms, and marched south, probably in an effort to get to Florida, where the Spanish government promised Britain slaves freedom. After traveling only a few miles, the number of slaves had grown to more than one hundred. They marched from house to house, murdering slave owners and their families as they went. After 10 miles, the band was eventually met by an armed white militia, which killed at least thirty of the rebelling slaves and captured almost all of the rest. Nearly all who were captured were killed.

The response came quickly. Shortly after the rebellion, South Carolina passed the **Negro Act**, which consolidated all of the separate slave codes into one code that forbade slaves from growing their own food, assembling in groups, or learning to read. This sharp response to the Stono Rebellion continued a pattern of harsh legal retributions for slave insurrections.

4-3d Slavery and Racism

In the end, slavery promoted the rise of extreme, sustained racism against African Americans in North America. Since their arrival in the Chesapeake in 1619, dark-skinned people had been considered of lower status by Europeans. But because until the 1680s there were so few African slaves in the American colonies, they were generally not treated especially harshly. During this early period, a few slaves broke the bonds of enslavement and became landowners and politically active freedmen. Yet as the cost of indentured servants went up and that of slaves went down (for the reasons why this happened, see Chapter 3), slaves were employed as the central labor force of the South and the Chesapeake.

> Religious writers, philosophers, scientists, and lay writers (among them, Thomas Jefferson) concocted theories about the "inferior" nature of African Americans.

As the number of slaves rose, so did restrictions on Africans and African Americans. Rabid manifestations of racism emerged out of owners' growing fears. The result was the creation of a caste-like system of segregation in which African Americans were considered inherently inferior to Europeans and Euro-Americans, and sometimes less than human. At the same time, religious writers, philosophers, scientists, and lay writers (among them, Thomas Jefferson) concocted theories about the "inferior" nature of African Americans, thus creating an intellectual framework to support the economic reality. Slavery lasted until the American Civil War of the 1860s, and elements of this racial caste system have persisted to the present day.

4-4 ATTEMPTED EXPANSION OF BRITISH CONTROL

Slavery was, of course, a huge part of the North American economic expansion of the early 1700s—an expansion that led to increased interest in the colonies by the British crown. Most importantly, the exceptional production of raw materials had propelled the colonies into a second stage of economic development, whereby manufacturing and industry began to prosper (and not just the cultivation of raw materials). This development stimulated economic competition between the North American colonies and Britain, something the Crown could not tolerate.

4-4a Salutary Neglect

But any attempt by the Crown to reassert control of the colonies was bound to aggravate the colonists, though, because they had become accustomed to a hands-off style of relations between the Crown and the colonies, a relationship that came to be labeled **salutary neglect**. The principle developed in the late 1680s, when, upon King Charles II's death in 1685, his brother, James II, became king and promptly attempted to make England a Catholic country once again. This change created such a severe rift within England that it almost fell into civil war. Unlike the Cromwellian revolution of the 1650s, however, this second revolution was bloodless, and in the so-called **Glorious Revolution of 1688**, Protestant factions forced James II to flee England. His exit left the Crown to his Protestant daughter and son-in-law, William of Orange and Mary II, more commonly referred to as William and Mary.

For the colonists, the result of the Glorious Revolution was looser governance by the Crown and the removal of many of the proprietors who had founded the colonies. William and Mary continued to have a definite economic interest in the colonies, establishing a Board of Trade to oversee affairs and collect data. They also established a privy council to administer colonial laws. But, in general, royal administration over the colonies grew much looser with the decline of the proprietors. The relationship of salutary neglect had begun.

Negro Act South Carolina state law that consolidated all the separate slave codes into a single code that forbade slaves from growing their own food, assembling in groups, or learning to read

salutary neglect Hands-off style of relations between the Crown and the colonies; a loose system of oversight whereby the Crown ignored governance of its colonies and enforcement of its trade laws so long as the colonies provided England with cash and crops

Glorious Revolution of 1688 Overthrow of King James II by Protestant factions; his exit left the crown to William and Mary

The colonists loved, advocated, and fought for this loose system of oversight. The concept was simple: the Crown would essentially ignore governance of its colonies and enforcement of its trade laws so long as the colonies continued to provide Britain with sufficient cash and produce. Politically, this system gave colonial assemblies a high level of legitimacy, which was accomplished at the expense of the royal governors. Of course, the risk of salutary neglect was that, if Britain ever decided to enforce the laws on its books, a serious conflict was inevitable. And this is exactly what would happen during the French and Indian War, which was yet another of the "Wars for Empire" that occurred in the Atlantic World from 1754 to 1763.

4-4b The French and Indian War, 1754–1763

The truce from Queen Anne's War lasted nearly thirty years, but the battles between the European powers were hardly over. In **King George's War** (1744–1748),

King George's War Continued New World battles between Britain and France (1744–1748)

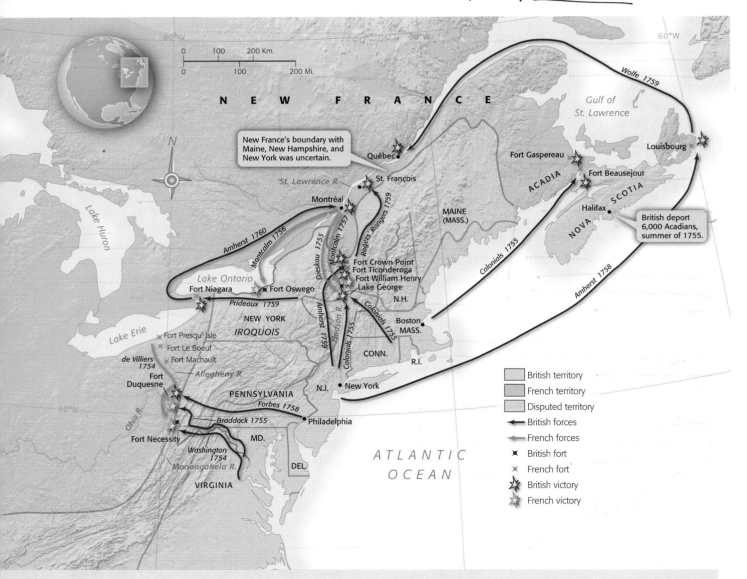

Map 4.3 French and Indian War

>> This map shows the various battles of the French and Indian War, which was the North American component of a larger war between France and Britain called the Seven Years War.

Britain and France continued their New World spat, but the war ended with resolutions concerning only Europe; in the New World, the ramifications remained unclear.

Meanwhile, British colonists continually pushed deeper into the Ohio Valley, further infuriating the French, who were already established traders there. Eventually the French attempted to build a series of military strongholds that would intimidate the BRITISH, the largest of which was Fort Duquesne in today's southwest Pennsylvania. They wanted to keep the British out. Virginia colonists who were speculating on lands to the west retaliated against the French forts by building Fort Necessity nearby. When the Virginians sent an inexperienced young militia colonel named George Washington to deter the French from building more forts, a skirmish between the French and the British ignited yet another war, with greater consequences than before.

George Washington was swiftly forced to surrender, and it seemed the French were going to control trade relations in the American interior for the foreseeable future. But British merchants in London lobbied to use this backwoods dispute over fort-building to forge a war to eject the French from North America once and for all. Without the French, London merchants would have a monopoly on much of the North American trade, which promised to be incredibly lucrative. They succeeded in their lobbying, and a hesitant Crown used this minor provocation to start a major war. It was in this contrived way that a skirmish on the Pennsylvania frontier exploded into a world war that eventually involved France, Britain, Austria, Russia, Prussia, Spain, and numerous Indian nations. In Europe, the war was called the **Seven Years' War**; in North America, it was the **French and Indian War**.

4-4c The Albany Congress

The coming war put the British colonists on high alert. To discuss the matter, seven of the colonies sent representatives to Albany, New York, in the summer of 1754. The meeting, called the **Albany Congress**, represented the first time the mainland English colonies met for a unified purpose.

THE ALBANY PLAN

Part of their purpose was to convince the Iroquois to join with Britain in the battle, but the Iroquois chose to remain neutral in order to preserve their trade routes. Another part of the colonists' strategy was to develop what would have been the first-ever colonial union under the **Albany Plan**, drafted by the printer, scientist, and, later, politician Benjamin Franklin. The Albany Plan would have placed all of Britain's colonies in America under a single president-general, appointed by the Crown, whose responsibility would be to manage all activity on the frontier and handle negotiations with Indians. It also would have created a single legislature, made up of representatives from each of the colonies, whose number would depend on how much in taxes each colony paid.

The union failed to materialize, however, mainly because the colonists felt allegiance only to their particular colony and (to a lesser extent) to the Crown. They did not yet fully identify with their fellow colonists. Despite the failure of the proposal, it put Britain on high alert. It was fearful of the prospect of colonial unity. But slowly the colonists were beginning to perceive the need for it. The French and Indian War did much to solidify the feeling that the British colonies along the Atlantic Coast would share one fate and should, perhaps, unite.

RESULTS

As the colonists had foreseen, the French and Indian War came, and under the leadership of General Edward Braddock, the British fared badly. Braddock's attempts to raise money from the colonists to help supply his troops provoked colonial ire, and his patronizing attempts to work with Indian tribes also failed. Worse, he bumbled his way from one military defeat to another. Within three years, two-thirds of his troops were dead, including Braddock himself (Map 4.3).

In 1758, the British began to take the conflict more seriously and sent a large army under the leadership of Jeffrey Amherst. What followed was warfare marked by extreme brutality on all sides. After a year, the British began to shift the tide of war, and a year later, in 1760, hostilities largely ended. In 1763 the three warring nations (Spain, Britain, and France) signed the **Treaty of Paris (1763)** (Map 4.4), which

Seven Years' War European label for the world war (1754–1763) between France, Britain, Austria, Russia, Prussia, Spain, and numerous Indian tribes

French and Indian War Colonial label for the Seven Years' War

Albany Congress Meeting of representatives from seven colonies in Albany, New York, in 1754, the first time the mainland British colonies met for a unified purpose

Albany Plan Concept for the first-ever colonial union, drafted by Benjamin Franklin

Treaty of Paris 1763 Agreement between Spain, Britain, and France that made the Mississippi River the boundary between Britain's holdings and Spain's, and evicted France from North America

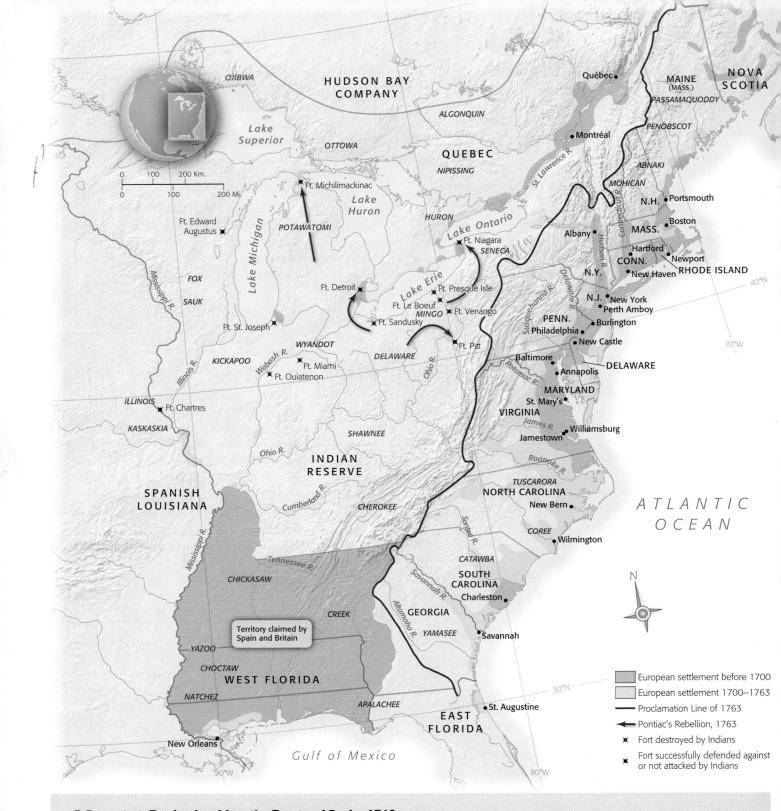

Map 4.4 Territories After the Treaty of Paris, 1763

>> This map shows the various territory claims settled in the Treaty of Paris (1763). It also highlights the land occupied by the various Indian nations, and the major battles in the various wars in the west of the middle 1700s.

Map labels

HUDSON BAY COMPANY

OJIBWA

Lake Superior

OTTOWA

ALGONQUIN

QUEBEC

NIPISSING

Québec

MAINE (MASS.)

NOVA SCOTIA

PASSAMAQUODDY

PENOBSCOT

Montréal

ABNAKI

MOHICAN

Ft. Michilimackinac

Lake Huron

HURON

St. Lawrence R.

N.H. • Portsmouth

Ft. Edward Augustus

POTAWATOMI

Lake Michigan

Lake Ontario

Ft. Niagara

SENECA

Albany

MASS. • Boston

Hartford

CONN. • Newport

New Haven • RHODE ISLAND

FOX

SAUK

Ft. Detroit

Lake Erie

Ft. Presque Isle

Ft. Le Boeuf

MINGO • Ft. Venango

Ft. Sandusky

Ft. Pitt

N.Y.

N.J. • New York

Perth Amboy

PENN.

Philadelphia • Burlington

New Castle

Ft. St. Joseph

WYANDOT

Wabash R.

Ft. Miami

Ft. Ouiatenon

KICKAPOO

DELAWARE

Ohio R.

Baltimore

Annapolis • DELAWARE

Susquehanna R.

Delaware R.

Potomac R.

Mississippi R.

Illinois R.

ILLINOIS • Ft. Chartres

KASKASKIA

SHAWNEE

INDIAN RESERVE

MARYLAND

St. Mary's

VIRGINIA

James R.

Williamsburg

Jamestown

SPANISH LOUISIANA

Ohio R.

Cumberland R.

CHEROKEE

Roanoke R.

TUSCARORA

NORTH CAROLINA

New Bern

ATLANTIC OCEAN

Tennessee R.

CHICKASAW

CATAWBA

COREE

Wilmington

CREEK

Territory claimed by Spain and Britain

Savannah R.

Altamaha R.

SOUTH CAROLINA

Charleston

GEORGIA

YAMASEE

Savannah

YAZOO

CHOCTAW

WEST FLORIDA

NATCHEZ

APALACHEE

EAST FLORIDA

St. Augustine

New Orleans

Gulf of Mexico

90°W   80°W   30°N   70°W   40°N

Legend

- European settlement before 1700
- European settlement 1700–1763
- Proclamation Line of 1763
- Pontiac's Rebellion, 1763
- Fort destroyed by Indians
- Fort successfully defended against or not attacked by Indians

Scale: 0 100 200 Km. / 0 100 200 Mi.

N

The Reasons Why...

The French and Indian War provoked a stronger colonial response compared to any other New World conflict for several reasons:

Colonial ire toward Britain. During the war, the colonists gained experience dealing with the British army. They disliked its hierarchical style, especially after having experienced extensive self-rule in the colonies. For their part, the British saw the colonists as ragtag and undisciplined, and contempt between the two peoples increased, even though they were both subject under the British crown.

Colonial unity. The French and Indian War allowed the British colonies to see themselves as a united body distinct from Britain. The Albany Congress proved to be the first demonstration of an increasingly unified colonial identity. It would take time, but that sense of unity would grow.

The British financial burden. Meanwhile, the war was costly for Britain, and its attempts to recoup its losses through taxes on the colonies led directly to the Revolution.

French anger. Fourth, the French wanted revenge against the British for this battle, a chance they would get by helping the Americans during the American Revolution.

Pan-Indianism. And fifth, with the French removed, the British could dictate the terms of trade and land possession in much of North America. This did not bode well for the future of the northeastern Indians. Looking for a response, many Indians participated in pan-Indian resistance movements. In a similar way in which the French and Indian War had brought the British colonists together, it also began the process of bringing together various enemy tribes.

laid out the so-called Proclamation Line giving Britain the western interior of North America, Canada, and Florida. Spain had already received Louisiana from France, and the Mississippi River became the boundary between Britain's holdings and Spain's. France had been evicted from North America.

The French and Indian War was widely significant for at least five important reasons (see "The Reasons Why . . ." box).

4-4d Pan-Indianism

The outcome of the French and Indian War would prove to be a disaster for the Indians of North America. With all the lands east of the Mississippi River now belonging to Britain, Indian tribes lost the ability to negotiate with one group of colonists and play the European nations off one another in order to win concessions. Now Indian–colonial relations were centralized in London. Many Indian leaders recognized this transition and began to realize the importance of an increased unity between the various Indian nations in opposition to the British. Simply put, in the aftermath of the French and Indian War, many of the Native American nations shifted from

favoring a tribal identity to assuming a racial one, something called **pan-Indianism**. This was especially true in the Northwest, between the Great Lakes and the Appalachian Mountains, where contact with the colonists was most sustained.

NEOLIN

In the late 1750s and 1760s, **Neolin**, a Delaware prophet, took up the call of pan-Indianism and began preaching a return to old Indian ways, as things were before Europeans had come to America. Central to this revitalization movement was the notion of purging all European habits, including reliance on material goods, use of alcohol, and belief in Christianity. Neolin traveled to several

pan-Indianism Movement in which many of the tribes of Native America shifted from favoring a tribal identity to assuming a racial one; a way in which the various Indian nations of North America came together to oppose the British

Neolin Prophet from the Delaware tribe who began preaching a return to old Indian ways

North Wind/North Wind Picture Archives

>> Chief Pontiac, leader of the Ottawa nation, led a pan-Indian revolt against the continued encroachment of the British. Here, he addressed a group of Native Americans.

Indian nations preaching his message of pan-Indianism and anti-Europeanism.

PONTIAC'S REBELLION

By 1763, several Indians had followed Neolin's advice and come together to present a unified front against the colonists. Under the leadership of Pontiac, chief of the Ottowa, they were ready to protest British intrusion into their lands and attempt to drive the colonists back across the Appalachians. The resulting battles in **Pontiac's Rebellion** were brutal, with the British attempting to introduce smallpox into Indian communities (through infected blankets) and Indians deliberately poisoning British troops' drinking water (by putting rotten meat in springs upriver from British camps). The British troops were better equipped for warfare, however, and the Indian nations of Native America, without the French available to help, could not withstand the British armies. They were beaten back and pushed farther west, in yet another battle of what one historian has called "the long war for the West."

Pontiac's Rebellion Brutal battles between Ottowa Indians and British troops in 1763

Little did Britain suspect that, although it had won the Wars for Empire throughout North America, it had done so at great cost: it had sparked the process of colonial unification. The fight for political freedom was about to begin. During the years between 1700 and 1763, the North American colonies had developed into a stable, manufacturing economy that could potentially rival many European nations. It had large numbers of free white farmers and slave laborers performing much of the backbreaking labor. It also had a growing class of merchants and wealthy landowners who provided leadership and governance.

As the French and Indian War was fought on American soil, many colonists began to feel themselves a people apart from their mother country. Many colonists could not, or would not, fathom the idea of independence—they had too much to lose. But many outspoken colonists felt that if Britain persisted in proclaiming the end of salutary neglect and intended to intrude upon colonial affairs more pointedly, there would be trouble.

STUDY TOOLS 4

READY TO STUDY? IN THE BOOK, YOU CAN:

❑ Rip out the Chapter Review Card, which includes key terms and chapter summaries.

LOCATED AT WWW.CENGAGE.COM/LOGIN

❑ Collect StudyBits while you read and study the chapter.

❑ Quiz yourself on key concepts.

❑ Find videos for further exploration.

❑ Prepare for tests with HIST5 Flash Cards as well as those you create.

❑ Read Jonathan Edwards on the Great Awakening.

❑ Learn more about the Stono Rebellion.

❑ Read Cotton Mather on the need for education.

❑ Read a doctor's account of the middle passage.

▶ **1688** Protestants replace James II with William and Mary in Glorious Revolution.

▶ **1696** The Salem witchcraft trials signal demise of Puritans' religious utopia.

1709: *Bartolomeo Cristofori invents the piano.*

1712: *The last execution of an accused witch takes place in Britain.*

▶ **1720** Slaves make up 20 percent of Chesapeake population.

▶ **1734** New York Weekly Journal editor J. Peter Zenger is punished for government criticism.

▶ **1738–1745** In Great Awakening, itinerant preachers such as George Whitefield promote emotional Protestantism.

▶ **1739** South Carolina whites quell slaves' Stono Rebellion and in turn pass Negro Act.

▶ **1740** Fearful of slave insurrection, New York City convicts, burns, and hangs 35 suspects.

▶ **1744–1748** France and Britain continue imperial rivalries in King George's War.

1751: *Benjamin Franklin sends up a kite during a thunderstorm and discovers that lightning is a form of electricity.*

1752: *The first eraser is put on the end of a pencil.*

▶ **1754–1763** French and Indian war over trade in the North American interior escalates into a worldwide battle.

▶ **1754** At Albany Congress colonists for the first time discuss common concerns with war.

▶ **1760** Slaves make up 40 percent of Chesapeake population.

▶ **1773** Treaty of Paris evicts France from America, draws Proclamation Line, sets borders with Spanish Empire.

Brutal pan-Indian Pontiac Rebellion against growing British colonial empire fails.

5 | Toward Revolution, 1763–1775

LEARNING OBJECTIVES

After reading this chapter, you should be able to do the following:

5-1 Explain Britain's main reasons for attempting to overturn salutary neglect.

5-2 Explain the colonists' responses to the new acts, and trace the evolutionary process that brought the colonies closer to rebellion.

5-3 Trace the path to revolution from the Townshend Acts of 1767 to the meeting of the First Continental Congress in 1774.

5-4 Explain how the American Revolution finally began, and describe the first battles of the conflict.

AFTER FINISHING THIS CHAPTER GO TO **PAGE 102** **FOR STUDY TOOLS**

Getting the colonies organized for the French and Indian War exposed a number of problems for Britain, the most serious of which was the lax enforcement of royal policies in the colonies, the principle labeled "salutary neglect." The tradition of salutary neglect meant that the colonies were slower to mobilize when the British demanded adherence to their dictates. It also meant the colonists paid few taxes. After the expensive French and Indian War, the British came to see the colonists not only as resistant to the demands of their mother country, but also as getting free armed protection by the world's most powerful army. The British, meanwhile, were being taxed pretty stiffly, in part to help secure American economic development. Moreover, the British Army had removed the colonists' most powerful competition (the French) from the land. Shouldn't the colonists pay for these benefits?

As the French and Indian War came to a close in 1763, Britain decided to remedy these problems through a series of reforms that tightened control over the colonies and limited the areas where colonists could settle. The colonists resisted these encroachments because they had become accustomed to the self-rule implied in salutary neglect. In addition, since the Enlightenment, Englishmen had sought to protect their "natural rights" from encroachment by their rulers. It did not matter if the ruler was a king or a parliament: if either institution violated one's rights to life, liberty, and property, all Englishmen felt they could reasonably rebel. The colonists hoped Britain's King George would protect them from what they saw as the enmity of a jealous Parliament. The British, on the other hand, saw the colonists as a bunch of headstrong upstarts, demanding rights without assuming the responsibilities inherent to them. As this rhetoric escalated, conflict escalated as well.

5-1 BRITISH ATTEMPTS TO REIN IN THE COLONIES

The British plan to reform colonial relations had three main goals: (1) to tighten control by eliminating absenteeism and corruption of royal officials in the colonies and by limiting smuggling, which colonists were using to avoid taxes, tariffs, and regulations; (2) to limit the areas where colonists could settle; and (3) to raise greater revenue.

5-1a Tightening Control

Britain began its attempts to rein in the colonies in 1760, shortly before the end of the war with France. In that year, the **Privy Council**, which advised the Crown on various matters, issued the "Orders in Council," which required absentee officials to occupy their posts instead of collecting a salary and then paying a substitute to occupy the post. The Privy Council also rewarded officers and crews of naval vessels for seizing smuggling ships. British officials were going to be more present in the colonies.

5-1b Limiting Settlement

The next major reform was the Proclamation of 1763, which did three things: (1) it placed a moratorium on government sale of western lands; (2) it put trade with Indians under royal control; and (3) it forbade settlement west of the Proclamation Line, which followed the crest of the Appalachians (refer back to Map 4.4 in Chapter 4). The purpose of the law was to control British settlement into the western interior and push the colonists into the newly acquired colonies of Canada and Florida. Royal officials also believed that the policy would protect British manufacturing, because if colonists moved too far from the Atlantic Coast, they would be forced to develop their own manufacturing industries rather than import British goods.

Many colonists were merely frustrated by the Orders in Council but they were infuriated by the Proclamation. In their minds, the French and Indian War had been fought to *allow* the colonists to move farther west. And many colonists believed that the removal of the French from the region would make westward colonial expansion a possibility. King George's Proclamation of 1763 directly contradicted this belief. Ultimately, the law was impossible to enforce. Settlers moved across the line anyway, and the royal government lacked the resources to stop them. But colonial ire was piqued.

Privy Council A group of close advisors to the Crown that offered suggestions on how the Crown should best exercise its executive authority

◄◄◄ Compared to the more organized and unified British "Red Coats," the colonists were a rag tag bunch of fighters. But unlike the British, the colonists came to think that they were fighting for their freedom.

>> British soldiers were harassed by colonial boys.

5-1c **Raising Revenue**

The final piece of reform was George Grenville's plan for paying off Britain's debt. The British had tried to prevent the colonists' evasion of royal taxes earlier in the 1700s, most notably with the 1751 Writs of Assistance, which gave British officials the right to inspect not only places of work, but also private homes. The colonists fought this infringement on their liberties, although they did not persuade the Crown to reverse the decision. George Grenville, who became Britain's

prime minister in 1763, contributed to these woes. He convinced Parliament to pass several specific acts in the 1760s that significantly increased the Crown's interference in the economy of its colonies. It was these revenue acts as much as anything else that signaled the end of salutary neglect.

The first of these acts was the **Sugar Act of 1764**, which was technically a cut in taxes on molasses and sugar brought into the colonies from non-British colonies in the West Indies. But it was troublesome to the colonists because, even though it reduced the assessment on sugar, it increased enforcement of tax collection. Furthermore, the act taxed items besides sugar, including indigo, pimento (allspice), some wines, and coffee. Britain was now evidently looking to the colonies as a source of direct revenue.

The next intrusive act, the **Quartering Act of 1765**, required the colonies to feed and house British troops stationed in their territory. Colonists bristled at the idea of British soldiers living in their houses, and the colonial assemblies often refused to provide the money required to feed and house these soldiers.

Most disruptive of all, however, was the **Stamp Act**. Passed by Parliament in 1765, the Stamp Act mandated the use of stamped paper for all official papers, including diplomas, marriage licenses, wills, newspapers, and playing cards. The stamp, embedded in the paper (not a topical stamp), indicated that a tax had been paid on the document. Grenville insisted

Sugar Act of 1764 Act that reduced taxes on molasses and sugar, laid taxes on indigo, pimento (allspice), some wines, and coffee, and increased enforcement of tax collection; signaled the end of the era of salutary neglect

Quartering Act of 1765 This act required the colonies to feed and house British troops stationed in their territory

Stamp Act of 1765 This act mandated the use of stamped (embedded) paper for all official papers, including diplomas, marriage licenses, wills, newspapers, and playing cards

>> This 1872 engraving depicts the rioting provoked by the Stamp Act. The Act seemed to undermine colonial self-rule, and many colonists took to the streets in protest.

that revenues from the tax go directly to soldiers protecting the North American colonies. He also mandated that those who avoided using taxed paper would be tried in a Crown-operated vice admiralty court, rather than by a trial of one's peers. Not only had the Crown declared its intention to raise revenues from the colonists, but it also indicated it was ready to enforce its actions—in courts of its own control.

5-2 BEGINNINGS OF AMERICAN RESISTANCE

The Sugar Act was widely unpopular. New Englanders in particular saw that the new regulations threatened their profitable (though now illegal) rum trade. And the Quartering Act seemed wildly intrusive. But the Stamp Act provoked a much stronger backlash than the Sugar Act had, for at least three reasons (see "The Reasons Why . . ." box).

In general, there were a wide variety of reasons why colonists began to resist the end of Britain's salutary neglect. Affluent southern tobacco planters, for example, were deeply in debt to British banks by the 1760s, and they saw the crown's attempts to regulate the colonial economy as threatening to their ability to pay off their debts. In Boston, on the other hand, many colonists hated the fact that British military men, who were paid poorly by the crown, took on extra jobs that were normally done by the colonists. Regardless of motivation, though, the end of salutary neglect signaled the beginning of colonial revolt.

5-2a The Stamp Act Congress

To try to force Parliament to repeal the Stamp Act, opponents in Massachusetts initiated a **circular letter** inviting all the colonies to send representatives to a congress to discuss resistance to the Stamp Act. This was a radical move. Convening an intercolonial congress without British authorization was an illegal act. Nevertheless, the **Stamp Act Congress** convened in New York City in October 1765, with representatives from nine colonies in attendance.

Although it began as an act of defiance, the Stamp Act Congress was largely conciliatory to the Crown. It acknowledged that the colonies were "subordinate" to Parliament in matters of administration, but it maintained that the colonists' rights as British men were infringed upon when Parliament levied taxes without providing the colonists with representation in Parliament. Resolutely noninflammatory, the Stamp Act Congress avoided words like *slavery* and *tyranny*, which were common in editorials of the day. Nevertheless, it did declare that taxes had never been imposed on the colonists by anyone other than colonial legislatures. It also differentiated between the Crown, to which the colonists pledged allegiance,

> **circular letter** Communication among a number of interested parties that was sent from colony to colony to keep the disparate colonies together, or united; a primary form of communication for the colonies during the revolutionary period
>
> **Stamp Act Congress** Gathering of colonial leaders from nine states in New York City in October 1765 to discuss resistance to the Stamp Act; one of the early instances of collaboration between colonies and of identifying Parliament as the opposition rather than the king

The Reasons Why...

The Stamp Act provoked a stronger colonial response than the Sugar or Quartering Acts for three principal reasons:

An educated resistance. The Stamp Act applied to the kinds of goods used by merchants and lawyers, which stirred up an educated and powerful opposition.

Time to organize. Although Parliament passed the Stamp Act in March, the act did not go into effect until November 1, 1765. This gave colonists time to organize a resistance, which they did.

Undermining colonial self-rule. The Stamp Act was also a direct tax on the colonists (instead of a regulation of trade), and the proceeds were meant to pay the salaries of colonial officials, something the colonists themselves had done in the past. Taxing the colonies so that the Crown could pay these salaries undermined colonial control over royal officials and seemed to indicate that Parliament was limiting colonists' liberties, becoming a key marker that the time of salutary neglect by the crown was coming to an end.

and Parliament, to which they acknowledged a grudging "subordination." In the end, the Stamp Act Congress showed the colonists' increasing tendency to collaborate as a single unit; it also began a pattern of finding fault with Parliament rather than with the king.

5-2b Boycotts

In addition to these legalistic declarations, there were other, more potent forms of protest. In Boston, New York, Philadelphia, Charleston, and smaller ports, merchants signed agreements not to import British goods until the Stamp Act was repealed. In New England, women's groups called **Daughters of Liberty** organized local boycotts against cloth and tea imported from Britain. These women also held "spinning bees" that encouraged American women to show loyalty to the resistance by producing homespun cloth. Locally produced clothing was a sign that one was a "patriot," and colonial women like Abigail Adams and Sarah Franklin "Sally" Bache were the key to making it happen.

The boycott proved effective, especially in New York, where boycotters shut down the port. British exports to the colonies declined, and the opposition party in Parliament began to advocate repealing the Stamp Act. The boycotts were also meaningful because simple participation in a colonywide boycott radicalized the population, forcing people to choose sides.

>> Tax stamp.

North Wind Picture Archives/Alamy Stock Photo

The very clothes people wore became a form of protest.

This was becoming larger than a protest of elite lawyers. The very clothes people wore became a form of protest.

5-2c Rioting

Although the Stamp Act Congress and boycotts proved fruitful, rioting proved to be the most effective means of protest. To coordinate the riots, several colonists formed groups called the **Sons of Liberty**. Typically led by men of wealth and high social standing, the Sons of Liberty served as leaders in organizing protests and intimidating stamp officials. Mobs in Massachusetts, New York, Rhode Island, and South Carolina burned the homes of stamp officials and hanged effigies of tax collectors. Occasionally, they even tarred and feathered them, a brutal form of humiliation in which a mob gathered its victim, poured tar on him or her (usually pine tar) and then rolled them in feathers before parading them around town. As a result of these various forms of intimidation, all known stamp officials resigned before the Stamp Act went into effect on November 1, 1765. When the Crown offered the positions to others, many simply refused the job. Furthermore, when the stamps and stamped paper arrived in America, colonists sent them back to Britain, destroyed them, or locked them away.

5-2d Ideological Opposition

In addition to these physical forms of protest, several colonial assemblies sent Parliament written protests, called "resolves." The wording of the resolves was usually influenced by British political pamphlets that circulated at the time. Both the pamphlets and the resolves are significant because they became some of the most important articulations of the ideas of liberty that positioned the colonists against Britain all the way to the Revolution.

The central drafters of the pamphlets called themselves **Radical Whigs** (which referred to the opposition

Daughters of Liberty Group of colonial American women who organized boycotts of tea and other imported British goods and who produced homespun clothes as a protest of British imported clothing

Sons of Liberty Groups of colonial leaders who organized protests and intimidated stamp officials; their actions caused the resignation of all known stamp officials

Radical Whigs Political activists and pamphleteers who vigorously defended the rights and liberties of Englishmen and who coined the phrase "no taxation without representation"

party in Britain, the Whigs). Radical Whigs in Britain cast a suspicious eye on any infringement of personal liberties, and Radical Whigs in colonial America, such as James Otis of Massachusetts, argued that, because the colonists were not represented in Parliament, Parliament had no authority to tax them. These were the men who coined the phrase "no taxation without representation." The Radical Whigs claimed that the principle that taxation required representation had precedent in British law (in the Magna Carta) and was one of the basic British liberties.

In Virginia, Patrick Henry followed this line of reasoning. He argued that the Stamp Act was unconstitutional because only the Virginia legislature had the authority to tax Virginians. He introduced a series of *Resolutions Against the Stamp Act* to the Virginia legislature and asserted that anyone who supported the Stamp Act was an enemy to Virginia. Several of his *Resolutions* were passed by the Burgesses and forwarded to Parliament, indicating the high level of radicalization provoked by the Stamp Act.

John Adams of Massachusetts framed another argument against Parliament's right to tax the colonists. In his *Instructions of the Town of Braintree to Their Representative*, Adams argued that allowing Parliament to tax the colonists without their consent threatened the sanctity of private property and personal liberty. If Parliament could seize colonists' property, Adams argued, then colonists were dependents of Parliament and not free men. Furthermore, Adams railed against Parliament for creating the specific courts (called vice admiralty courts) that denied the colonists the right to a trial by a jury of one's peers. More than anything else, Adams argued, the colonists wanted the liberties promised through Enlightenment thought; they did not want to become slaves to the whim of a Parliament over which they had no control.

Benjamin Franklin and Daniel Dulany (a celebrated Maryland attorney) promoted another argument against the Stamp Act. They insisted that colonists accept Parliament's right to regulate trade through the use of duties—a form of taxation they called **external taxes**. What the colonists objected to, according to these writers, was the Stamp Act's imposition of an **internal tax** that directly affected the internal affairs of the colonies. Dulany and Franklin feared that internal legislation threatened private property. Both the Crown and many colonists questioned the validity of this distinction between the two forms of taxation. Although this was a milder argument than that of Adams, who

>> This depiction of a stamp collector being tarred and feathered was a brutal occurrence, especially with the threatening noose hanging from the "liberty tree" in the background.

Fotosearch/Getty Images

rejected all taxes, it also demonstrated strong opposition to the Stamp Act.

5-2e Opposition to the Opposition

Not all colonists agreed with these dissenters. In fact, a large portion of colonists did not care one way or another about the Stamp Act. Meanwhile, some, such as James Otis, opposed the Stamp Act *and* resistance to it, favoring instead to advocate for a parliamentary repeal. Still others, such as Lieutenant-Governor

external taxes Duties designed to protect the British Empire; part of Parliament's right to regulate trade, as argued by Benjamin Franklin and Daniel Dulany

internal taxes Duties that directly affected the internal affairs of the colonies; according to Benjamin Franklin and Daniel Dulany, this internal legislation threatened private property

>> Many colonists rioted in protest of the Stamp Act. No one paid more dearly than Thomas Hutchinson, shown in this engraving fleeing his burning house.

Thomas Hutchinson of Massachusetts, defended the Stamp Act. Hutchinson personally disliked the Stamp Act but believed that, because Parliament was the supreme legislative body in the empire, everything it did was constitutional. Hutchinson said that no matter how inconvenient the Stamp Act was, duty and law required obedience. Hutchinson became a focal point of the rioters, who viewed him as a stooge of the Crown. They sent Hutchinson fleeing, and a mob eventually pulled the roof off his house and trashed all his possessions. In 1765, resentments were heating up.

In Britain, few people accepted any of the colonists' arguments. Because they shouldered a heavy tax burden already, most of them felt the colonists were asking for a better deal than that received by those living in the mother country. The British regarded the colonists' arguments as mere rationalizations to avoid paying taxes.

Members of Parliament also rejected the opposition to the Stamp Act. They argued the dubious point that the House of Commons represented the interests of all the king's subjects, wherever they might reside. This theory of **virtual representation**, they said, was vital to parliamentary legitimacy because many regions within Britain itself were not directly represented in Parliament. In addition, in some areas that *were* represented in the House of Commons, the people had no say in who represented them. Instead, the local nobility or the king selected their representative. King George himself owned the right to appoint more than fifty members to the House of Commons—more than 10 percent of the entire body. Under this theory, Parliament rejected the colonists' demand for actual or **deputy representation**.

virtual representation Theory endorsed by Parliament that said the House of Commons represented the interests of all the king's subjects, wherever they might reside; this was the pretext for rejecting the colonists' demand for actual representation

deputy representation The practice of the people's interests being advocated by a deputy; also known as actual representation

5-2f Repeal of the Stamp Act

A trade recession in late 1765 ended the bitter dispute. With a downturn in the economy, the king withdrew his tacit support of the Stamp Act for fear that opposition to it would damage revenues too much, sending the British economy into a steeper decline. His withdrawal of support doomed the Stamp Act, and Parliament eventually repealed it. In repealing the act, however, Parliament stated it was yielding not to the colonists' demands, but to the king's. To make this clear, on the same day it repealed the Stamp Act, Parliament passed the **Declaratory Act**, which affirmed its authority to legislate for the colonies "in all cases whatsoever." Although it was largely symbolic, the Declaratory Act became one of the nonnegotiable claims Parliament was unwilling to relinquish throughout the struggle. Parliament's leaders would rather go to war than be stripped of its authority over the colonies.

News of the Declaratory Act perplexed American leaders, leaving them to wonder whether Parliament had accepted the distinction between internal and external taxation. If the distinction was not accepted, the Declaratory Act asserted Parliament's raw power over the colonies because it gave no concessions on the issue of representation. Most colonists, however, overlooked such abstruse concerns and simply celebrated the Stamp Act's repeal. When Parliament passed few new taxes in 1766, many colonists believed that the crisis was over. They were wrong.

>> John Adams.

iStock.com/Wynnter

5-3 TAXATION WITHOUT REPRESENTATION, 1767–1773

In 1766, Charles Townshend, a British politician who believed it was fair for Britain to tax the colonies "to provide their own safety and preservation," was installed as Britain's Chancellor of the Exchequer. The first act he sponsored did not impose a new tax on the colonies, but it did alert colonists that their struggle with Parliament was not over. In the **Restraining Act**, Townshend suspended the New York Assembly for failing to comply with the Quartering Act. This move bred suspicions that Townshend would deal

"No freeman should be subject to any tax to which he has not given his own consent"

—JOHN ADAMS, 1765

harshly with the colonies. It also pushed the debate beyond mere revenue issues, such as taxation without representation. Now Parliament was infringing on the colonists' self-government and self-rule. Townshend had upped the ante. But it was only the beginning.

5-3a The Townshend Acts of 1767

Townshend confirmed colonists' worst fears in the summer of 1767, when he steered new taxes through Parliament. Although he considered the colonists' distinction between internal and external taxes invalid, he saw how he could use it to his advantage. He intended to raise revenue with new, *external* duties on the goods that the colonists imported from Britain. The resulting **Townshend Acts** laid duties on glass, lead for paint, tea, paper, and a handful of other items. The Townshend Acts also demanded the collection of duties and bolstered the importance of colonial governors friendly to the Crown. Once again, the acts threatened the previous status quo of salutary neglect and signified that Britain would continue its attempt to increase its powers over the North American colonies.

Declaratory Act Passed by Parliament in 1766, this act affirmed its authority to legislate for the colonies "in all cases whatsoever"; largely symbolic, it became one of the nonnegotiable claims that Parliament was unwilling to relinquish throughout the struggle

Restraining Act In this act, Chancellor of the Exchequer Charles Townshend suspended the New York Assembly for failing to comply with the Quartering Act

Townshend Acts These acts of 1767 instituted duties on glass, lead for paint, tea, paper, and a handful of other items

OPPOSITION

Opposition to the Townshend Acts followed the pattern of the Stamp Act opposition—although more slowly, largely because of internal splits among merchants. But many colonists eventually began to boycott British goods again. Women stopped wearing silks and satins or serving tea and wine, making fashionable what they saw as a modest, patriotic life. By 1769 the boycotts were effective in every colony, having been spread by colonial newspapers, which shared information and important essays.

One essay, published simultaneously in seven separate colonial newspapers, offered a distinctive ideological protest to the Townshend Acts. Posing as a simple country gentleman resisting a corrupt government, the prominent lawyer John Dickinson wrote a series of essays called *Letters from a Farmer in Pennsylvania*—published in both Britain and America. Dickinson explained that the colonies had tolerated earlier duties because they accepted the idea that Parliament should regulate trade. The purpose of the Townshend duties, however, was not regulation, but revenue. Dickinson considered this unconstitutional. His letters were yet another argument against Britain's attempts to overturn salutary neglect.

> The British regarded the colonists' arguments as mere rationalizations to avoid paying taxes.

THE BOSTON MASSACRE

Opposition to the Townshend Acts triggered rioting as well. Radicals in the Massachusetts legislature drafted a circular letter rejecting the Townshend Acts that was sent to all the colonies. Written primarily by Samuel Adams, the letter urged all merchants to enforce the boycott. In one case, colonist John Hancock's sloop *Liberty* arrived in port in Boston with a cargo of wine. Colonists held the customs official hostage as the wine was unloaded without payment of the required duties. Similar protests followed in other towns.

In response, the British sent troops to restore order, and by 1770 British troops were quartered in New York, Boston, and other major towns. The conflict was growing increasingly tense. Now there was a seemingly permanent British military presence in the colonies.

On March 5, 1770, a crowd of Boston rebels began throwing snowballs, oyster shells, and other debris at a British sentry in front of the Customs House, prompting the British captain to order more guards outside. When a stick hit one of the soldiers, he fell, and someone shouted, "Fire!" prompting a British guard to shoot into the crowd. Hearing the report, other soldiers shot into the crowd, and in the end, five colonists lay dead and six were wounded. The colonists called this the **Boston Massacre**. Nine British soldiers were tried for the act, and two were convicted of manslaughter (they were all defended by future president John Adams). The "Massacre" served as important propaganda for the colonial agitators, despite the fact the British had followed the rule of law and that most of the soldiers were found innocent in a colonial court of law. Furthermore, responses to the "Boston Massacre" sparked a vigorous debate within the colonies about how far rebellion should go. Many colonists remained on the side of the soldiers. They were, after all, still subjects of the British crown.

REPEAL

The same day as the Boston Massacre, Parliament repealed most provisions of the Townshend Acts. But,

>> A color print of the Boston Massacre by Paul Revere, showing British soldiers firing on a crowd of colonists, used as propaganda to spur on the cause of colonial rebellion.

Boston Massacre Incendiary riot on March 5, 1770, when British soldiers fired into a crowd and killed five people

as a symbol of its continued control, Parliament left the tax on tea in place; the colonists accepted the tea tax and dropped their boycott, claiming victory in the conflict.

But this sort of compromise meant Parliament and the rebelling colonists had not reached a clear agreement, leaving the situation ripe for future conflicts. For the next several years, no major issue emerged to galvanize colonial opposition, lulling many in Britain and in the colonies to believe the crisis was over. This was a relief to the Crown, as well as to the many colonists who were content with the colonies' relationship to the royal government. Furthermore, royal officials in America did their best to foster this pacified view, asserting that subordination of the colonies had finally been achieved. This, however, was merely the surface view.

5-3b Local Conflicts, 1770–1773

If unified colonial opposition declined between 1770 and 1773, local conflicts continued, demonstrating that colonists remained assertive and that royal control was tenuous.

THE *GASPÉE* INCIDENT

The most noteworthy local conflict was the **Gaspée incident**. In Rhode Island, colonists from Providence boarded and burned an British naval vessel, the *Gaspée*, that had run aground while in pursuit of a colonial ship accused of smuggling. Charring a British naval ship was quite a radical move. Britain assembled a royal commission of British officials in America to identify the perpetrators and remand them to Britain for trial. The local commission, however, shortly became the target of colonial protest. **Committees of correspondence**, or organized groups of letter writers, coordinated opposition to the extradition of the suspects, and, as a result, the perpetrators of the *Gaspée* incident were never identified or tried.

COMMITTEES OF CORRESPONDENCE

Massachusetts colonists also continued their resistance to royal policies. In 1772, several Bostonians set up a committee of correspondence to inform other Massachusetts towns and other colonies of their grievances, "as Men, as Christians, and as Subjects." These protestors aimed to stir up dissent and unite the colonists in their opposition. Several other colonists from towns outside of Boston joined these committees, creating a method for the relatively quick transmission of information between the colonies. As letters circulated from one committee to the next, they passed along information, helping unify colonial opposition to the Crown.

Although local opposition to Crown policies was significant between 1770 and 1773, it was not as widespread as the protests that emerged in response to the Stamp Act or the Townshend Acts. And, although some colonial leaders tried to transform local concerns into colonywide grievances, most issues never achieved more than local prominence, mainly because most colonists were reluctant to engage in a full-on confrontation with the Crown.

Within cities like Boston, New York, and Philadelphia, wealthy people remained mostly supportive of the Crown, while artisans and merchants, who had been financially stung by several economic acts passed by the Crown, were the most avid patriots. Many people did not favor conflict and could not imagine rebellion. New England's slaves, meanwhile, attempted to use the language of political freedom to their benefit, and in 1773 and 1774 they petitioned the Massachusetts government for their freedom. When the legislature passed a bill on their behalf, the royal governor Thomas Hutchinson vetoed it. Regardless, the slaves made it clear that whoever promised to free them would earn their support.

In the Southern Colonies and the Chesapeake, many of the most powerful families remained supportive of the Crown, whose policies had enriched them in the first place. Meanwhile, those living in rural areas were more supportive of the rebels, mainly because they felt slighted by the meager amount of self-rule the colonial elite granted them. These internal cleavages would persist through the Revolutionary War, although between 1770 and 1773, they were less visible because no single issue stoked the fires of dissent. In 1773, however, an issue emerged that would prod more and more colonists toward open opposition to royal control.

5-3c The Tea Act, 1773

In 1773, Parliament passed the **Tea Act**. The act was designed not to anger the colonists, but to give the East India Company a monopoly on the sale of tea to North

> **Gaspée incident** Conflict that occurred when colonists from Providence boarded and burned the British naval vessel *Gaspée*
>
> **committees of correspondence** Organized groups of letter writers who would provide quick and reliable information throughout the colonies
>
> **Tea Act** Passed in 1773, this act was designed to give the East India Company a monopoly on the sale of tea to North America

America (the company was badly in debt and had influence in Parliament).

The Tea Act had three provisions: (1) it lowered colonists' duty on tea; (2) it granted the East India Company the monopoly; and (3) it appointed royal agents who were to pay a duty on tea based on profits made in the colonies. This last provision meant that colonial merchants could no longer sell tea. Prior to the Tea Act, most colonists had bought smuggled Dutch tea because it was cheaper than the British variety. The Tea Act was designed to bring British tea to the colonies at a lower price, thus undercutting the illegal Dutch trade. Because tea was the most common beverage consumed by colonists, Parliament and the East India Company hoped the colonies would be pleased with the measure and buy more tea.

COLONIAL RESPONSE

This did not turn out to be the case, for two reasons. Naturally, powerful colonial tea merchants were upset at losing the business. Whether or not the tea they were selling was smuggled or legal, tea merchants were upset the Tea Act replaced them with royal agents; in short, they had lost their livelihood. But in addition, the timing of the act meant that many colonists interpreted it as yet another move to establish Parliament's authority. Radical Whigs pointed out that until 1773 the duty on tea had been paid in Britain. But now, under the Tea Act, the duty would be collected from British agents who had collected the revenue from North American colonists. Instead of a tax laid in Britain and collected in Britain, it was a tax laid in Britain and collected in North America.

The colonists responded as they had before, only more violently. They published protests and pressured anyone concerned with enforcement of

> Women were the key players in reducing tea consumption, while men were the staunchest advocates of using violent means.

the law to send tea back to Britain. More violently, they forged a campaign of intimidation by threatening anyone who tried to enforce the act. In short, the colonists planned to nullify the Tea Act by refusing to comply. Women were the key players in reducing tea consumption, while men were the staunchest advocates of using violent means.

THE BOSTON TEA PARTY

Most of the tea-bearing ships that encountered resistance when they tried to dock or unload simply returned to Britain. But in Boston, the tea issue was especially sensitive because Governor Thomas Hutchinson's son was one of the major consignees, and Hutchinson was determined to support his son's enterprise. In addition, Hutchinson viewed the Tea Act as a chance to demonstrate his fidelity to the Crown in the face of the most rebellious colony in North America. Thus, when Bostonians pressed to have the imported tea returned to Britain, Hutchinson said that was fine, so long as the colonists paid the tax on the tea first.

The rebelling colonists refused, and in this impasse, the ship simply sat in Boston Harbor. The deadlock could not last: by law, the tax had to be paid within twenty days, which, in this case, meant December 17, 1773. Governor Hutchinson vowed to have the tea unloaded and the tax paid on the day of the deadline. To prevent this, on the night of December 16, an organized squad of roughly sixty colonists dressed as Mohawk Indians boarded the ship and dumped the entire cargo—342 chests of tea—into Boston Harbor. Historians are unsure why the rebels chose that particular disguise to commit their act of protest. Perhaps it was to distinguish themselves from others? Perhaps costumes promoted unity? Perhaps Native Americans symbolized both savagery and radical democracy, freed from the constraints of British "civilization"?

For Boston radicals like the Sons of Liberty, the **Boston Tea Party** was momentous. Bostonians were proud they had made a powerful strike against the Crown, and they noted that discipline among their ranks had been maintained throughout. Beyond the tea, the

Boston Tea Party Protest staged December 16, 1773, when an organized squad of roughly sixty colonists dressed as Mohawk Indians boarded Hutchinson's ship and dumped 342 chests of tea into Boston Harbor

>> It wasn't the tax on tea that caused the colonists problems, but the enforcement.

iStock.com/Jaume Ribera

North Wind Pictures Archives

>> This nineteenth-century image of the 1773 Boston Tea Party highlights the Indian costumes worn by the radical protestors.

squad did not commit vandalism or destroy any other property.

But the rebels also recognized they had pushed the conflict to a new level. After the destruction of British property, colonists could only speculate how the British government would react. Refraining from buying tea was essentially a passive protest; destroying an entire ship's worth of cargo was something altogether different.

5-3d The Coercive and Quebec Acts, 1774

Parliament's response came quickly. A few members of Parliament argued that the Tea Party's ringleaders should be arrested. The majority disagreed, recalling the failure of the government to bring to trial the perpetrators of the *Gaspée* incident. To avoid the difficulties of prosecuting the individual Bostonians, Parliament opted to pass punitive legislation against the entire colony of Massachusetts—the so-called Coercive Acts—in 1774.

"I immediately dressed myself in the costume of an Indian, equipped with a small hatchet . . . and a club, after having painted my face and hands with coal dust in the shop of a blacksmith, I repaired to Griffin's wharf, where the ships lay that contained the tea."

— EYEWITNESS TO THE BOSTON TEA PARTY

THE COERCIVE ACTS

The laws that came to be called the **Coercive Acts** actually comprised four separate acts, most of which simply attempted to punish Massachusetts for the Tea Party. Parliament thought it could attack Massachusetts and thus divide the colonists in order to reconquer them. The four acts were (1) the Boston Port Act, which closed Boston's harbor until the town paid for the destroyed tea; (2) the Massachusetts Government Act, which terminated most self-government in the colony; (3) the Administration of Justice Act, which dictated that any British official charged with a capital offense in the colonies could be tried in Great Britain (this issue had arisen after the trials that resulted from the Boston Massacre); and (4) the Quartering Act, which applied to all the colonies and allowed the British Army to house troops wherever necessary, including private buildings.

THE QUEBEC ACT

A fifth act followed the same year. The Quebec Act not only straightened out several legal issues in Canada but also did two other things: (1) it guaranteed French Canadians the right to practice Roman Catholicism, which appalled the colonists in the future United States, especially in New England, where almost everyone was a Protestant unaccustomed to accommodating other

Coercive Acts Four separate acts, passed in 1774, that were meant to punish Massachusetts for the Tea Party: the Boston Port Act, the Massachusetts Government Act, the Administration of Justice Act, and the Quartering Act

religions; and (2) it declared that much of Britain's holdings across the Proclamation Line of 1763 (everything west of the Appalachian Mountains) would be governed from Quebec. The colonists were infuriated that the Crown had decided to govern this land from the north rather than the east. After all, many colonists felt they had fought for the right to occupy this land during the French and Indian War. The colonists' widespread anti-Catholicism and their land lust led them to link the Quebec Act and the Coercive Acts, referring to them together as **Intolerable Acts**.

COLONIAL RESPONSE

The various acts of 1774 were intended to break the colonists' spirit, to dissolve colonial unity, and isolate Massachusetts. The actual results were quite different. At the most basic level, Bostonians refused to pay the penalties required by the Port Act. A small number of pro-British merchants offered to pay the fines on the city's behalf, but a group of rebellious colonists threatened them, too. The rejection of the offer was a strong measure of the colonists' convictions because the closure of the port of Boston inflicted considerable suffering on the people who depended on trade to maintain their economic well-being.

Through committees of correspondence, colonists everywhere heard of Massachusetts's plight. Virginia, South Carolina, and Connecticut even sent food. Thus, rather than isolating Massachusetts and splitting colonial resistance, the acts unified the colonies.

THE FIRST CONTINENTAL CONGRESS

This colonial unity is best seen in the meeting of the First Continental Congress. In May 1774, Rhode Island, Pennsylvania, New York, and Virginia called for an intercolony congress to address the growing crisis (doing so without consent from the Crown was still illegal). In September, delegates from twelve colonies met in the **First Continental Congress** at Philadelphia to consider the American response to the Coercive Acts. Only Georgia was absent, principally because Creek Indians were

actively fighting Georgians over western expansion, and the colonists in Georgia felt they needed British support to keep the Creeks at bay.

The delegates considered several plans of action. Ultimately, the Congress created the **Continental Association**, which supervised a boycott of British trade. The Association was prefaced with a "Declaration of Rights" that asserted the natural-rights foundation of the colonists' resistance, affirming the trio of natural rights put forward by John Locke—"life, liberty, and property." This was not yet independence, though. The delegates at the First Continental Congress tried to maintain a balance between supporting colonists' rights and affirming the authority of the Crown. In 1774 they were pursuing autonomy, not independence. They agreed to meet again the next year.

5-4 THE SHOT HEARD 'ROUND THE WORLD

Meanwhile, throughout Massachusetts, local militias were preparing for battle. Parliament, these men felt, had pushed far enough; they would no longer tolerate more infringements on their liberties. Furthermore, who knew what the Crown would do next to plague their economic existence? Indeed, by mid-1774 colonists in western Massachusetts had essentially taken over the towns and evicted British officials. Like many colonists, they really did believe the British were coming to take away their freedoms, and they had acted in firm accordance with this belief. Indeed, so radical were these actions that one historian has called this the Revolution of 1774.

5-4a Militia Preparations

To ready themselves for battle, Massachusetts colonists stockpiled guns in several locations outside Boston and militia groups drilled defiantly in town squares. They developed a "Provincial Congress" that assumed the role of a colonial government outside the Crown. Other Massachusetts counties organized conventions to unify the resistance. In some areas, colonists opposed the Administration of Justice Act by closing courts rather than permitting the governor's appointed judges to sit.

Other colonies followed Massachusetts's lead, organizing their own provincial congresses, committees, and conventions. Patriots near urban centers formed committees of correspondence to circulate news, information, and instructions throughout the colonies. Although not all colonists were enthusiastic for war, especially outside the cities

Intolerable Acts Colonists' collective label for the Quebec Act and the Coercive Acts

First Continental Congress Meeting of twelve colonies at Philadelphia in May 1774 to consider the American response to the Coercive Acts

Continental Association Group that supervised a boycott of British trade; the association was prefaced with a "Declaration of Rights" that affirmed the natural rights of "life, liberty, and property"

that were affected the most by Britain's policies, there was a growing sense that the conflict between Britain and its North American colonies might result in a full-scale rebellion.

5-4b Britain's Response to the Preparations

The colonists' military preparedness became evident to the British in September 1774, when Massachusetts patriots responded to false rumors that the royal governor had ordered the British Army to seize colonial gunpowder and that British troops had fired on the people of Boston. In this "Powder Alarm," rumors also circulated that six colonists had been killed in skirmishes, and that Boston was ablaze. None of this was true, but still, more than 20,000 armed colonists left their homes for Boston to fight. News eventually came that the rumors were unfounded. Even still, 3,000 colonists continued to march to Cambridge, Massachusetts, just outside Boston, forcing two Crown-appointed council members and the lieutenant governor of Massachusetts to resign.

The royal governor, Thomas Gage, realized his army was outnumbered in Massachusetts and that the colonists were prepared to actually fight. In response, he ordered the construction of fortifications across the small strip of land that connected Boston to the mainland (see Map 5.1) and asked Parliament for 20,000 more British troops.

5-4c Lexington and Concord

By the spring of 1775, tensions were at a fever pitch. Feeling threatened, the British secretary of state pressured Gage to curb the colonists' military planning, and so, in April 1775, Gage sent troops to the town of Concord, about 20 miles northwest of Boston, to capture the colonial military supplies hidden there and to arrest patriot leaders John Hancock and Samuel Adams.

The British soldiers were armed and resolute when they left Boston on April 18, 1775. Despite British efforts to move quietly, Boston patriots detected the troop movement and sent Paul Revere, William Dawes, and Samuel Prescott on horseback to alert colonists in the countryside between Boston and Concord (only Prescott made it all the way to Concord; Revere was captured on the way while Dawes was chased off the route). On the morning

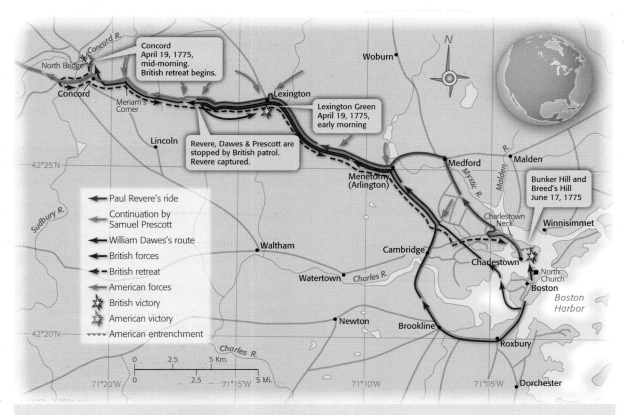

Map 5.1 Lexington, Concord, and Boston, 1775

>> This map of eastern Massachusetts shows the major events of the battles of Lexington and Concord.

of April 19, a militia assembled in Lexington in order to stop the British before they reached Concord. The British, still the most powerful army in the world at the time, did not back down. The American militia captain ordered his men (called "**Minutemen**" because they supposedly were ready on a minute's notice) to retreat after the much stronger British forces ordered them to disperse. As some of the rebelling colonists began to fall back, someone fired a shot (both sides later claimed the other side had fired first). Regardless of who fired first, British soldiers opened fire on the militia. The colonists suffered eighteen casualties (eight killed and ten wounded), while the British suffered only one, after this, the supposed "shot heard 'round the world."

After this initial rout of the Minutemen, the British continued their march to Concord, but by the time they arrived, Hancock and Adams had fled, and it is uncertain whether the cautious British would have exacerbated the already explosive situation by carrying out the capture of these two prominent colonists anyway. Instead, when they took their position at one end of the North Bridge in Concord, they were met by another armed militia that positioned itself at the opposite end of the bridge. The colonial militia fired on the British troops and forced them to alter their route back to Boston. This was the first time Americans had fired against the British Army (colloquially referred to as the Redcoats because of the color of their uniforms) in a formal confrontation. It was also the first time the Redcoats had been forced to retreat in the face of an American enemy.

The Minutemen made the Redcoats' return to Boston a nightmare. Militiamen gathered from surrounding towns to pursue the British the entire way, firing from behind stone walls and trees. The British suffered heavy casualties and, once in Boston, found themselves besieged by thousands more militiamen. Over the course of the day, the Americans suffered 95 casualties, while the British suffered 273, including 73 dead. This was a marked escalation of the conflict; for the first time, Americans had killed British soldiers in battle and indeed, arguably even won a major skirmish.

Minutemen Nickname for American militia soldiers because of their reputation for being ready on a minute's notice

Second Continental Congress Gathering of colonial leaders in May 1775 to determine the colonies' response to the battles of Lexington and Concord; they passed resolutions supporting war that included a sharp rejection of all authority under the king in America

Olive Branch Petition A 1775 declaration to King George III that the colonists were still loyal to him and imploring the king to seek a peaceful resolution to the conflict

5-4d Colonial Response to Lexington and Concord

Following the battles of Lexington and Concord, colonists had to decide what their best response might be. Had an all-out war begun? What about the many colonists who did not support the rebellion?

On May 10, 1775, the **Second Continental Congress** gathered in Philadelphia to answer this question. The Congress enacted several policies, including acknowledging the militia companies surrounding Boston as the core of a new "Continental Army" and appointing as its general a Virginian, George Washington. (The selection of a Virginian was meant to balance the predominance of Massachusetts militiamen in the army, thus showing colonial unity.) The Second Continental Congress also passed resolutions supporting war, which included a sharp rejection of all authority under the king in America. And it adopted the "Declaration of the Causes and Necessity of Taking Up Arms." These were bold, brave actions, although no one was sure whether this was a battle over grievances against Parliament or one with a goal of complete independence.

Regardless, without formally declaring independence, the Continental Congress was beginning to behave more like the government of an independent nation than that of a territory within an empire. The Congress remained cautious about the word *independence*, though, and in July 1775 it approved the "**Olive Branch Petition**," written by John Dickinson, which declared that the colonists were still

Table 5.1 Pre-Revolution Chronology	
1763	French and Indian War ends
1764	Sugar Act
1765	Quartering Act
March 22, 1765	Stamp Act passed
Summer/Fall 1765	Colonial protests and riots
August 1765	Sons of Liberty
October 1765	Stamp Act Congress meets
March 1766	Stamp Act repealed
1767	Townshend Acts
1770	Boston "massacre"
May 10, 1773	Tea Act passed
December 16, 1773	Boston Tea Party
Spring 1774	Coercive, or Intolerable, Acts
May 1774	First Continental Congress
April 19, 1775	Lexington and Concord
May 10, 1775	Second Continental Congress
June 17, 1775	Battle of Bunker Hill

THE RETREAT FROM CONCORD.

North Wind Picture Archives/Alamy Stock Photo

>> The Minutemen made the Redcoats' return to Boston a nightmare. If the Massachusetts' revolutionaries couldn't best the British army in formal battle, it would use guerrilla warfare to fight for what they believed, as shown in this image.

loyal to King George III and implored the king to seek a peaceful resolution to the conflict. The king ignored the petition, viewing the colonists as insubordinate subjects of the Crown.

5-4e The Battle of Bunker Hill

Within weeks, the hesitancy toward independence shown at the Second Continental Congress vanished. Local battles inspired this change. Throughout May of 1775, thousands of men from throughout the colonies joined the Minutemen around Boston to besiege the British military, peppering British ships with cannon fire. On June 17, 1775, the British Army sent troops across the Charles River to capture the colonists' cannons located on Breed's Hill, which overlooked Boston and was connected to nearby Bunker Hill by a saddle of land. The colonists had fortified Breed's Hill because they could fire their cannons at British ships in Boston Harbor from there. The ensuing battle was fought primarily on Breed's Hill but came to be known as the **Battle of Bunker Hill**. It was the first all-out battle of

the Revolutionary War. Although British troops forced the colonial rebels to abandon their hilltop position, the colonists inflicted heavy casualties on the British. In one particularly brutal episode, the British lost 1,000 men in an hour. The British killed around 400 Minutemen.

>LOOKING AHEAD...

When news of the Battle of Bunker Hill spread through the colonies and reached Britain, it had two key effects. First, it prompted thousands of additional colonists to join the opposition to Britain, and small conflicts spread across the land. Second, it convinced Britain that many colonists, not just a handful of troublemakers, were part of the rebellion. Because of this realization, Parliament issued the

Battle of Bunker Hill Outbreak of fighting on June 17, 1775, near Boston Harbor; the first all-out battle of the Revolutionary War

American Prohibitory Act, which declared the colonies to be "in open rebellion," forbade commerce with the colonies by blockading their ports, and made colonial ships and their cargo subject to seizure as if they were the property "of open enemies." Now that Parliament had declared the colonies to be in rebellion, any leaders who were caught could be tried for treason and executed. This development raised the stakes dramatically. A rebellion was turning into a revolution. What had begun in the early 1760s as the Crown's attempt to tighten control over its North American colonies had led those colonies to unite in order to claim their independence. The result would be the American Revolutionary War.

> **American Prohibitory Act** This act declared the colonies to be "in open rebellion," forbade commerce with the colonies by blockading their ports, and made colonial ships and their cargo subject to seizure as if they were the property "of open enemies"

STUDY TOOLS 5

READY TO STUDY? IN THE BOOK, YOU CAN:

❑ Rip out the Chapter Review Card, which includes key terms and chapter summaries.

ONLINE AT WWW.CENGAGEBRAIN.COM, YOU CAN:

❑ Collect StudyBits while you read and study the chapter.

❑ Quiz yourself on key concepts.

❑ Find videos for further exploration.

❑ Prepare for tests with HIST5 Flash Cards as well as those you create.

❑ Learn more about (and read) the Resolutions of the Stamp Act Congress.

❑ Read some of Patrick Henry's Resolutions Against the Stamp Act.

❑ View a short film about Benjamin Franklin's life.

❑ Read Adams's Instructions of the Town of Braintree to Their Representative.

❑ Read an eyewitness account of the Boston Massacre.

❑ Read a participant's eyewitness account of the Tea Party.

❑ Watch a film about Lexington, Concord, and the "shot heard 'round the world."

CH5 TIMELINE

▶ 1751	Writs of Assistance allow British search and seizure in private homes.	
▶ 1760	Privy Council issues "Orders of Council" to rein in smugglers and absentee officials.	

What Else Was Happening

1700s: *American innkeepers think nothing of requesting that a guest share his bed with a stranger when accommodations become scarce.*

1760s: *Because the British Macaroni Club's members are known for having affected manners and long, curled hair, "macaroni" becomes a slang term for "dandy." The song "Yankee Doodle" is invented by the British to insult American colonists. The section where Doodle puts a feather in his cap and calls it macaroni is a slap at the ragged bands of American troops.*

1763   Proclamation Line tries to stop western land sales and settlement, makes Indians royal subjects.

1764   Sugar Act cuts taxes and increases enforcements.

1765   Quartering Act requires colonists to house and feed British troops.

Stamp Act stirs powerful opposition against direct taxation of official paper.

1766   Declaratory Act asserts Parliament's right to legislate colonies.

Restraining Act suspends New York Assembly for violating Quartering Act.

1767   New external duties in Townshend Act stir boycotts, revolutionary ideology.

1769: *Shoelaces are invented in Britain.*

1770   In Boston Massacre, British soldiers shoot into rowdy crowd, killing five.

1772: *Joseph Priestley invents soda water.*

1773   Tea Act cuts duties but establishes monopoly for East India Company.

Colonists in Indian disguise board ship to destroy tea cargo in Boston Tea Party.

1774: *Coercive Acts close Boston harbor and Massachusetts government, tightening Quartering Acts to protect British officials from colonial courts.*

Parliament grants Quebec jurisdiction over land west of Proclamation Line.

First Continental Congress signals colonial unified resistance, not submission.

Empress Catherine II's Russian troops defeat Turkey, adding the Southern Ukraine, the Northern Caucasus, and Crimea to the Russian Empire.

1775   In Concord and Lexington, Minutemen engage Redcoats in guerrilla tactics.

Second Continental Congress creates Continental Army under Washington.

Battle of Bunker Hill triggers colonists' solidarity and British resolve.

6 | The Revolution

LEARNING OBJECTIVES

After reading this chapter, you should be able to do the following:

6-1 Describe the long-term causes and more immediate events that led the colonists into a true war for independence against Britain.

6-2 Enumerate the various phases of the American Revolution, and analyze the circumstances that eventually helped the colonists win a conflict that Britain, by rights, should never have lost.

6-3 Assess the significance of the American Revolution to the following groups: colonists, slaves, Native Americans, and women.

AFTER FINISHING
THIS CHAPTER
GO TO **PAGE 122**
FOR STUDY TOOLS

After the "long train of abuses" that led to the Declaration of Independence, from 1776 to 1783 American patriots fought a long and difficult war with Britain. Ostensibly, the battle was between freedom and tyranny (if you were a patriot), or about the responsibilities of being British (if you were a Loyalist). In reality, choosing sides was much more personal, depending, for instance, on whether your landlord was a Loyalist or a patriot, whether you thought political freedom would improve your economic situation, or whether you felt the earnings you made from a slave-based economy were threatened. All colonists were forced to choose sides, although many remained ambivalent. Loyalists were scorned, but revolutionaries would be punished brutally if their side lost. Choosing sides was no small matter, and the consequences could be deadly.

But the war and the political independence that followed made up only one of several transitions that took place during these years. The Revolutionary War brought with it fundamental questions about freedom and liberty, and about what kind of society Americans wanted. How far would the American Revolution go in promoting equality? Would economic and educational differences be eradicated by a leveling state? Would slavery be abolished? How different would the new society look compared to the old? How revolutionary would the American Revolution be?

6-1 FROM REBELLION TO REVOLUTION

As in most revolutions, the American Revolution had long-term, underlying causes that finally came to a head because of short-term, precipitating events.

6-1a Underlying Causes

In the 103 years between 1660 and 1763, the colonies had formed a unique society distinct from that of Britain. Perhaps most important, they had developed a dynamic economy in manufacturing and processing goods, as well as supplying raw materials to trading partners in both the Old and New Worlds. In other words, the colonies were not just a primary economic supplier (supplying raw materials to a mother country), but a well-rounded economic system unto themselves. Of course, many wealthy southerners owed their fortunes to slave-based cash crops that were then traded with Britain, so these colonists shied away from confrontation with the Crown. Nevertheless, large sectors of the North American economy were becoming increasingly independent of Britain.

Along similar lines, property ownership was more common in the colonies than in Britain. This meant that, with the notable exception of slaves, the people working the land owned it, which gave them something to fight for should their position be threatened. The colonies also had developed without the titled aristocracy or widespread poverty found in Britain, two further factors that made them an entity unique from Britain. And, in fact, each colony had developed a self-elected government, something it was not willing to give up easily.

6-1b Precipitating Events

But these long-term causes could not have detonated into a war without several immediate sparks. Three were vital: (1) increased local conflicts; (2) the uncompromising attitude of Britain; and (3) a shift in opinion among the colonists—toward revolution.

THE WIDENING WAR

At the local level, the war's scope was widening even before any official declaration of war. In 1775, for instance, Ethan Allen and his "Green Mountain Boys" attacked and captured Britain's Fort Ticonderoga and Crown Point in backwoods New York. At about the same time, the patriots' Continental Army invaded Canada and captured Montreal but failed to capture Quebec. In Charleston, meanwhile, patriots beat back an attack by a British fleet. In Boston, patriots surrounded and laid "siege" on the city after the British had taken control in the aftermath of the Battle of Bunker Hill. Perhaps most dramatically, Virginians forced the royal governor, Lord Dunmore, to retreat from the mainland to a British warship in the harbor at Norfolk. These local conflicts, organized without the assistance of any unified colonial body, indicated a widening war between Britain and the colonies, and signaled the transformation of grassroots opinion toward war.

Lord Dunmore's story is significant, however, for another reason. After retreating to an offshore ship as he awaited British military support, Dunmore issued a

◄◄◄ **The first shots of the American Revolution were fired in Lexington, Massachusetts on April 19, 1775, pictured here. Little did anyone know then that this initial skirmish would lead the colonies to declare their independence and strike out on their own. Even less known was what kind of nation would form in wake of a historic revolution.**

proclamation offering freedom to any slave who agreed to fight for the British. His program, "Liberty to Slaves," angered the colonists, who would later cite Dunmore's actions in the Declaration of Independence. To many colonists, liberty was meant only for Europeans and Euro-Americans, and it stung that the governor was offering it to slaves. Within weeks of Dunmore's call, between five hundred and six hundred slaves responded, and before the Revolutionary War was over, several thousand more fought for Britain and for their freedom. In contrast, George Washington refused to use black soldiers during the first years of the war. Indeed, only during the final months of the war were colonists forced to press slaves into service, delaying the action because they feared arming them.

UNCOMPROMISING BRITAIN

As the war widened, King George III grew increasingly angry at the colonies for their continued insubordination. He rejected the "Olive Branch Petition" of the Second Continental Congress and in August 1775 denounced the colonists as rebels. He also hired mercenaries from Germany, called "**Hessians**," to fight the colonists. And in December 1775 he closed all American ports.

This last action was particularly significant because it made independence absolutely necessary to open trade with other countries. The king's uncompromising attitude presented the colonists with few options other than revolution. Each step amplified the conflict.

THE SHIFT IN AMERICAN OPINION

Finally, popular opinion in the colonies had gradually shifted toward independence. The decline of salutary neglect and the spread of local violence led many colonists to side with the revolutionaries. These economic and social events pushed the war of ideas about freedom

>> The king's uncompromising attitude presented the colonists with few options other than revolution. Here the king is dressed in his royal best.

The National Trust Photolibrary/Alamy Stock Photo

and sovereignty into the lives of everyday Americans, and the more the Crown proved uncompromising, the more American opinion shifted toward revolution.

6-1c Choosing Sides

There was, however, never unanimity, and thus, in addition to this being a revolutionary war, it was also very much a civil war.

THE LOYALISTS

Why remain loyal? In the end, somewhere between one-fifth and one-third of the colonists remained loyal to Britain throughout the war (see "The Reasons Why . . ." box). Most prominent in this group were wealthy landholders and slave owners, who had the most to lose in a revolution. Furthermore, a large percentage of colonists remained indifferent to both the British and the revolutionaries.

Although all the colonies had some pro-Crown families, geographically most Loyalists lived in the southern colonies and New York.

THE REVOLUTIONARIES

Why revolt? Each rebelling colonist had a different motive for supporting a break with Britain, and these reasons were just as complicated as those for remaining loyal.

iStock.com/raclro

>> Fort Ticonderoga stamp, celebrating a local conflict of 1775.

Hessians German soldiers hired by Britain to fight against the rebelling American colonies

The Reasons Why...

Colonists were reluctant to withdraw from the British Empire for at least six reasons:

Personal connections in Britain. Many still felt a strong attachment to Britain and the king, and many still had family and friends in Britain.

Economic ties. Many also had strong commercial ties with Britain (the slave-based economy of the southern colonies was particularly dependent on such trade). To rebel was to risk their present and future wealth.

Geopolitical concerns. Some feared that France or Spain might take over if Britain were driven out of the colonies, and they preferred British rule to that of some other European nation.

Fears of what American independence might mean. Some of the smaller religious groups felt that Britain had protected them from more powerful denominations that could potentially flourish if the new American state adopted a national religion.

Personal motives. Economically, it was often a matter of settling small scores. If, for instance, your landlord was a revolutionary, you were likely to be a Loyalist; if your landlord was a Loyalist, you were likely to be a patriot.

Uncertainty about American success. Some colonists doubted the colonies' ability to throw off British rule. After all, Britain was the most powerful nation in the world, with the mightiest army.

Personal and commercial considerations were vitally important. But perhaps most influential was the ideology of **republicanism**, the idea that government should be based on the consent of the governed and that the people had a duty to ensure that their government did not infringe on individual rights. The American Revolution was the first serious modern attempt to craft a government based on these principles.

Republicanism set down deep roots in Britain before it flowered on American soil. The British Radical Whigs of the 1600s, for example, harked back to the classical Roman ideal of a "republican society," in which governmental power was curtailed by the actions of the people, who were presumed to be virtuous and willing to sacrifice for the public good. Drawing on these Roman ideals, the Radical Whigs outlined a theory according to which a government was legitimate only when it was based on an agreement between the members of a society and government. In this formulation, members of society would agree to sacrifice a degree of liberty in exchange for the government maintaining security and order, but otherwise avoid infringing on a person's life, liberty, or property. Any ruler who transgressed natural laws was considered a tyrant, and under tyranny the rebellion of a people was justifiable. (Republicanism was different from liberalism, which viewed any government as an unwanted infringement on individual liberty.)

Republican ideas spread throughout the colonies in the 1700s, mainly by the work of two British authors—John Trenchard and Thomas Gordon—who wrote a short book called **Cato's Letters**. In America, *Cato's Letters* and other Radical Whig writings were quoted every time Britain attempted to raise taxes after the French and Indian War.

But the best-known expression of republican ideas in revolutionary America was corset maker Thomas Paine's political pamphlet **Common Sense**, published in January 1776. Its simple wording of republican ideals nudged the colonists further toward independence. Paine asserted that the king never had the welfare of his subjects in mind and that he was entirely concerned with his own exercise of power. Paine also argued that independence was the only answer to this problem, using language so powerful that it made any other course of action seem absurd. He set forth a vision of America as a dynamic, independent nation, growing in population and prosperity, with a kindly government doing a substantial amount of economic and political leveling to ensure equality. Pointing

republicanism The theory that government should be based on the consent of the governed and that the governed had a duty to ensure that their government did not infringe on individual rights

Cato's Letters Book that spread republican ideas throughout the colonies; written by British authors John Trenchard and Thomas Gordon

Common Sense Influential political pamphlet written by Thomas Paine, published in January 1776, containing a simple wording of republican ideals

to the tremendous growth of the American colonies in the eighteenth century, Paine argued that America was more than just capable of maintaining independence from Britain; America was so strong, he claimed, that independence was inevitable. "Until an independence is declared," Paine wrote, "the continent will feel itself like a man who continues putting off some unpleasant business from day to day, yet knows it must be done, hates to set about it, wishes it over, and is continually haunted with the thoughts of its necessity."

>> Loyalist Flag.

Powered by Light/Alan Spencer/Alamy Stock Photo

Paine's pamphlet was enormously influential in changing the minds of those who had opposed independence, especially in extending republican ideals to colonists beyond the educated elite. Emerging just as local conflicts spread throughout the colonies, *Common Sense* was reprinted several times; in total, Paine estimated that 150,000 copies were distributed throughout the colonies—a number that would be equivalent to 15 million copies being distributed in the United States today. Historians have recently downgraded Paine's estimates by half if not more, with its influence most widely felt in the north. Still, all of them credit *Common Sense* with providing layman's terms for the case of independence.

6-1d The Declaration of Independence

The increase in local conflicts, Britain's inflexibility, and the spreading of republican ideals made a break with Britain seem practically inevitable by 1776. But independence was expedited further by events on the ground. In March 1776, the Continental Army forced the British to evacuate Boston, ending the eleven-month siege of the city that had begun after Lexington and Concord and the Battle of Bunker Hill. Rather than sail for home, however, the British Army headed to New York, where more Loyalists resided than in any other colony. Choosing not to establish their base where colonists were united in opposition (Boston), the British hoped to divide the colonies by setting their base of operations in an area less committed to independence (New York).

THE DRAFTING

With this crisis at hand, Richard Henry Lee, a Virginia delegate to the Continental Congress, proposed, on June 7, 1776, that the colonies officially declare their independence. With regional balance in mind, the Congress created a committee of five to draft a declaration. The committee consisted of John Adams of Massachusetts, Roger Sherman of Connecticut, Robert R. Livingston of New York, Benjamin Franklin of Pennsylvania, and Thomas Jefferson of Virginia, who was selected as the principal draftsman. After the committee made minor revisions to Jefferson's first draft, it presented the **Declaration of Independence** to the Congress on June 28, 1776.

North Wind Picture Archives

>> This woodcut image from 1776 shows patriots tearing down a statue of King George III, symbolically declaring their independence.

Declaration of Independence Statement adopted by the Second Continental Congress declaring that the thirteen American colonies, then at battle with Britain, constituted a free and independent state; drafted primarily by Thomas Jefferson and adopted in 1776

>> As commemorated on today's two-dollar bill, John Trumbull's 1819 painting shows the five-man drafting committee presenting the Declaration of Independence to the Continental Congress.

THE DECLARATION

The document consisted of two parts: (1) a preamble justifying the revolution on the basis of natural rights, as espoused in the language of republicanism; and (2) a list of grievances accusing George III of tyranny and therefore justifying revolt. Heretofore, the colonists' complaints had all been directed toward Parliament. By accusing the king of tyranny, the Declaration signified a tremendous, even treasonable, break.

THE SIGNING

Once the Congress had read the Declaration, they debated it and made several major changes (the most important was deleting Jefferson's tortured assertions that Britain had been responsible for implanting the institution of slavery in the New World and then, through Lord Dunmore, provoking slave rebellions). On July 2, the Continental Congress voted to dissolve ties with Britain, essentially declaring independence, which is why John Adams later wrote that July 2 could be called the birthday of the United States. But on July 4, Congress chose to adopt the document we now call the Declaration of Independence. On that date, two people signed it: John Hancock as president of the Congress, and Charles Thomson, the Congressional secretary. On August 2, approximately 50 others signed a clean copy of the Declaration, with six more adding their names later. With the July 2 declaration, the Revolution had a goal—political independence

> The main way they raised money was simply to print it and hope people would accept the bills.

from Britain. With the July 4 Declaration of Independence, however, American colonists had declared their intention not just to seek nationhood, but to do so in the belief that all men were created equal and that all people possessed certain rights that nobody could deny.

6-2 THE WAR FOR INDEPENDENCE

6-2a The Opposing Sides

The colonists had declared their independence, but now they would have to fight for it. But how could they? They had long been protected by the British, and, other than a few small colonial militias, they had no standing army.

THE CONTINENTAL ARMY

Efforts to build a bona fide army began even before the Declaration of Independence. It was an uphill battle from the start. Throughout the war, the army of the patriots, called the Continental Army, was often ill equipped, undermanned, and hungry. Recruitment was always a problem. Many colonists wanted freedom, but few wanted to give their lives for it. The Continental Congress had to offer large bounties of land to induce men to enlist, and eventually it reduced the term of service to just three months. Although the Congress set enlistment quotas for all the new states, the states rarely met them. At any given time, there were usually 10,000 poorly trained troops in the Continental Army. They were often hungry and unpaid, but the Continental Congress could not help because it did not have much money itself. As fighting progressed, the army had to live off the kindness of surrounding farmers (hoping they were patriots and not Loyalists).

The Continental Army acted under the orders of George Washington, a patrician Virginia tobacco farmer whose wealth came from his wife's family. He believed in the republican ideology to the very marrow of his bones. He also had a brilliant grasp of the war's military strategy. He recognized that, because of the ideological nature of

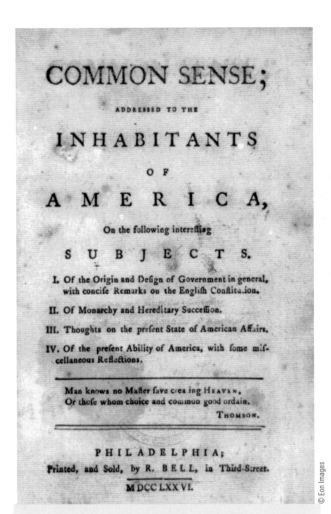

COMMON SENSE;

ADDRESSED TO THE

INHABITANTS

OF

AMERICA,

On the following interesting

SUBJECTS.

I. Of the Origin and Design of Government in general,
with concise Remarks on the English Constitution.

II. Of Monarchy and Hereditary Succession.

III. Thoughts on the present State of American Affairs.

IV. Of the present Ability of America, with some miscellaneous Reflections.

Man knows no Master save creating HEAVEN,
Or those whom choice and common good ordain.

THOMSON.

PHILADELPHIA;

Printed, and Sold, by R. BELL, in Third-Street.

MDCCLXXVI.

© Eon Images

>> Shown here is the original cover of the pamphlet, *Common Sense*. The pamplet was reprinted several times; in total, Paine estimated that 150,000 copies were distributed throughout the colonies, although historians have cut that number in half. Nevertheless, it put the conflict in layman's terms, helping increase support for declaring independence.

the Revolution and the condition of his ragtag army, his chances would be better if he did not try to win every battle. Indeed, if he refused to engage the British at all and made them wear themselves out pursuing him, he could win simply by surviving. This strategy, of course, depended

bills of credit Currency printed by the Continental Congress during the Revolutionary War; printing these bills in huge numbers and without any backing led to high inflation

on nonmilitary colonists continuing to resist and harass the British governors and troops. Without grassroots support in colonial cities and towns, the British might have starved the colonists into submission. But Washington knew, or at least hoped, that he could find support from a large number of colonists. He also knew that to not lose was his best chance to win.

THE REVOLUTIONARY GOVERNMENT AND FINANCES

Despite his tactical savvy, Washington received his orders from the Continental Congress, the only centralized authority in the colonies, although it had no legal standing or charter document. The Continental Congress could only request assistance from the various states, which had no obligation to grant those requests. Although the revolutionaries planned a national government in 1777, its founding charter (the Articles of Confederation) was not completed until 1781. Throughout the Revolutionary War, then, the revolutionaries had no official central authority.

This hindered them organizationally, and worse, it meant that the revolutionaries could not easily raise money. They had neither the power to levy taxes nor the infrastructure of a treasury. The main way they raised money was simply to print it and hope people would accept the bills. The Continental Congress issued these **bills of credit** throughout the war. The states issued their own money as well, almost all of which was generally more stable than the Continental dollars. Toward the end of the war, the phrase "not worth a Continental" became common, suggesting the centralized currency's lack of buying power and the widespread lack of faith in it. Only after 1781, when Robert Morris became superintendent of finance for the fledgling nation, did monetary conditions improve, mainly because he could borrow from friendly European nations. But throughout the war, the United States endured the highest inflation in its history. This took a tremendous toll on consumers, which is to say, all colonists.

THE BRITISH ARMY

The British, on the other hand, had the most powerful army in the world, supremacy of the seas, and an organized hierarchy of authority that extended all the way to the king. But they also had the more difficult military task of trying to destroy Washington's army, which was adept at running up hills and into forests to avoid being captured. The Crown sent seasoned British troops who were well armed and accustomed to large battles on vast battlefields. It also hired German mercenaries, the Hessians, to fight the revolutionaries. Many times, the British outnumbered the revolutionaries and were better trained and better armed, but they nonetheless confronted three insurmountable problems: (1) Britain could never supply its troops adequately, especially as Washington prolonged the war by constantly retreating inland, away from places where British ships could easily resupply British troops; (2) Washington avoided directly engaging the British troops, so the regimented British Army was subjected to unaccustomed guerrilla warfare as it chased him around the countryside; and (3) other European nations (notably France) eventually supported the revolutionaries. These other nations were only too glad to see mighty Britain humbled by upstart New World backwoodsmen.

>> George Washington.

6-2b The Second Phase of the War, 1776–1779

Historians have identified three phases of the war. The first took place mostly in New England from 1774 to 1777 and was viewed by Britain mostly as a police action. The pursuits in Lexington and

>> Continental Congress bills of credit were unpredictable and sometimes worthless. Pictured here are several varieties of the bills of credit.

Concord, as well as the Battle of Bunker Hill, represented Britain's attempts to bring their colonial upstart back into line. The second phase, which began in 1776, was generally fought in the Middle Colonies and was a more traditional battle, with the British trying to fight large military battles and take what was then the capital city, Philadelphia (see Map 6.1). The third and final phase was fought in the South and led to widespread guerrilla warfare. Generally speaking, the Americans' strategy was to run and survive. They attacked only when they were convinced of victory.

EARLY BRITISH SUCCESSES

After evacuating Massachusetts in March 1776, the British Army repositioned on Long Island and pressed to drive patriot forces from New York City, thus initiating the second phase of the war. Their goal was to isolate New England (which it saw as the center of resistance) by taking control of New York City and the Great Lakes, then subduing the South, leaving Massachusetts stranded in its revolutionary fervor.

In July 1776, 34,000 British troops delivered a crushing defeat to the patriots on Long Island and forced the revolutionary army of 18,000 to give up New York City. The patriots withdrew all the way to New Jersey, then to Pennsylvania. Fleeing was militarily embarrassing and bad for morale, but it was tactically sound: so long as the Continental Army remained intact, the colonies were still fighting for independence.

CROSSING THE DELAWARE

As recruitment suffered because of the demoralizing loss at New York, Washington realized he needed a victory. Furthermore, most of his soldiers were enlisted only through the end of 1776, and he feared that without a victory before the end of the year, the majority of his soldiers would not reenlist. Washington decided on a bold, brilliant action. On Christmas night 1776, the army crossed the ice-filled Delaware River and captured Trenton, New Jersey, which at the time was held by 1,500 Hessian mercenaries working for the British Army. The American victory at Trenton had little strategic significance, but it boosted morale and energized the Revolution.

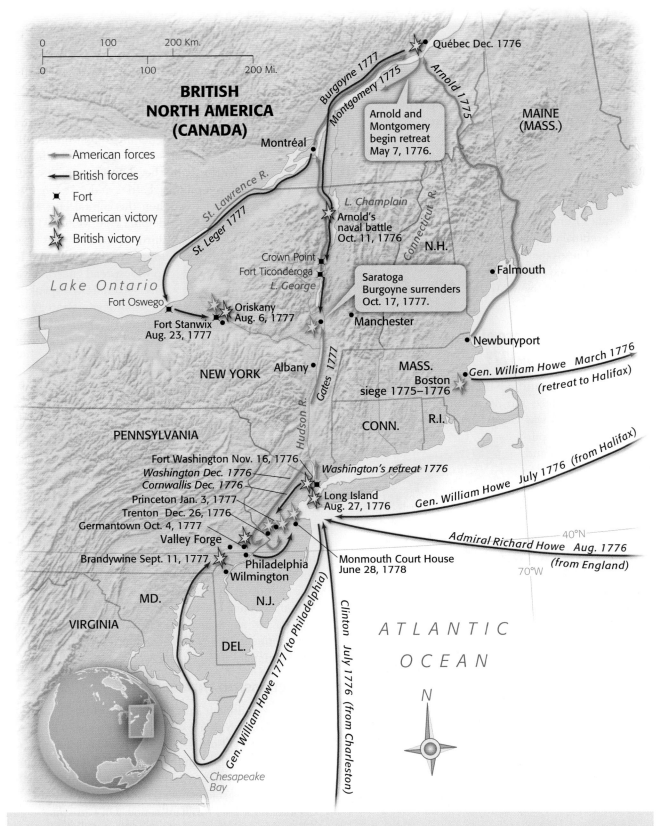

BRITISH NORTH AMERICA (CANADA)

Legend:
- American forces
- British forces
- ■ Fort
- ✦ American victory
- ✦ British victory

0   100   200 Km.
0   100   200 Mi.

Burgoyne 1777
Montgomery 1775
Arnold 1775
Québec Dec. 1776
MAINE (MASS.)

Montréal

Arnold and Montgomery begin retreat May 7, 1776.

St. Lawrence R.

L. Champlain

Connecticut R.

Arnold's naval battle Oct. 11, 1776

St. Leger 1777

Crown Point
Fort Ticonderoga
L. George

N.H.

Saratoga Burgoyne surrenders Oct. 17, 1777.

Lake Ontario

Fort Oswego

Oriskany Aug. 6, 1777

Fort Stanwix Aug. 23, 1777

Manchester

Falmouth

Newburyport

NEW YORK

Albany

Gates 1777

MASS.
Boston siege 1775–1776

Gen. William Howe   March 1776
(retreat to Halifax)

PENNSYLVANIA

Hudson R.

CONN.

R.I.

Fort Washington Nov. 16, 1776
Washington Dec. 1776
Cornwallis Dec. 1776
Princeton Jan. 3, 1777
Trenton Dec. 26, 1776
Germantown Oct. 4, 1777
Valley Forge
Brandywine Sept. 11, 1777

Washington's retreat 1776

Long Island Aug. 27, 1776

Gen. William Howe   July 1776 (from Halifax)

Admiral Richard Howe   Aug. 1776
(from England)

40°N

70°W

Philadelphia
Wilmington

Monmouth Court House June 28, 1778

Gen. William Howe 1777 (to Philadelphia)

Clinton July 1776 (from Charleston)

MD.

N.J.

VIRGINIA

DEL.

ATLANTIC OCEAN

N

Chesapeake Bay

Map 6.1 Revolutionary War in the North

>> This map details the major battles of the Revolutionary War in the northern colonies and shows both land and water battles stretching from New Jersey to New York, and demonstrates the revolutionaries' attempts to win the war by fleeing inland to prevent being captured.

>> The American victory at Trenton, after Washington's crossing the Delaware, depicted in the Currier and Ives lithograph, had little strategic significance, but it boosted morale and energized the Revolution.

THE BATTLE OF SARATOGA

Because the loss at Trenton was of minor strategic importance, the British let it go, and, in 1777, British leaders planned a two-pronged invasion that they hoped would finish off the war. British general John Burgoyne was to lead his army south from Canada. At the same time, General William Howe was to capture Philadelphia, the seat of the colonial government, and then sail up the Hudson River to join Burgoyne, completely isolating New England and testing the revolutionaries' unity.

At first, the plan was successful. Burgoyne's army captured outposts in upstate New York (Fort Ticonderoga) and began moving south. Meanwhile, Howe drove the patriots from Philadelphia on September 26, 1777 (forcing the Continental Congress to flee the capital), and headed north.

But then the British faced obstacles. General Burgoyne's troops were slowed by assorted Loyalists seeking protection from the revolutionary fervor of the northern states, and the delay in managing supporters fleeing from the retribution of patriots allowed guerrilla fighters and an organized camp of the Continental Army to catch up and harass the British troops. By the time Burgoyne neared the Hudson River, the Americans had forced him to halt, and, while he waited for reinforcements, he found himself surrounded by 6,000 Continental soldiers and up to 11,000 militiamen who left their homes in order to join the battle. Recognizing their advantage, the Americans attacked.

At the end of the fighting, Burgoyne surrendered all 5,700 men remaining in his army. This was the **Battle of Saratoga**. The American victory there proved two things: (1) that the patriots could in fact defeat sizeable regiments of the larger British Army and (2) that, if the British were to win this war, it was going to be a long, expensive affair.

THE FRENCH ALLIANCE

The Battle of Saratoga was also significant in that it convinced several European powers, including Spain and the Dutch, to fight against the British. Obtaining the support of France, however, was key. The French allied themselves with the Americans for two reasons: (1) they wanted to help weaken the British Empire, and (2) they wanted access to New World trading posts, which they had lost in the French and Indian War. Up until this point, the French had been reluctant to support what had looked like a losing cause. The victory at Saratoga helped alleviate these concerns.

In addition to France's backing, the Americans also received aid from an influential Frenchman. The Marquis de Lafayette, a nineteen-year-old nobleman committed to the republican cause in France, volunteered for the American fight. Lafayette became an instrumental leader in the American Army and played a key role in several pivotal American victories. The youngest of all the generals in the war, he successfully lobbied the French to more fully support the patriots' cause.

In the end, French support was vital. The French naval fleet battled Britain's mighty navy in both the eastern (European) and western (American) Atlantic. The French also fought naval battles in the West Indies, the Mediterranean, and India, further diverting British efforts from the American Revolution. With the French involved, the British now had to defend their entire empire, not just their North American colonies. By 1780, French armies were actively fighting alongside Washington's army, giving a considerable boost to the revolutionaries.

Battle of Saratoga Battle in New York State in 1777 between the Continental Army and General Burgoyne's British Army troops; Burgoyne surrendered, giving hope to the revolutionary effort

>> Victory at the Battle of Saratoga was so significant that Congress commissioned this 1821 painting, showing Burgoyne's surrender, to display in the rotunda of the U.S. Capitol, where it hangs today.

United States Architect of the Capitol

THE WAR IN THE WEST

In the American West—west of the Appalachian Mountains, south of the Great Lakes, and east of the Mississippi River—the Revolutionary War was a brutal and violent "Indian War," where the British and the revolutionaries vied for Indian allies and control of the various forts European settlers had built since first contact. Like the colonists, many Indians were greatly divided as to which side to support, and the stakes for them were incredibly high, considering their already plummeting fortunes in North America. If they picked the wrong side, they could easily be destroyed. Several major Indian nations, including the Iroquois, Cherokee, and Shawnee, divided into factions over which side to support.

The British, in general, had more success finding allies and establishing forts near the Great Lakes, and they often used those forts as staging grounds for raids into western New York and Pennsylvania. As always during the war, as they advanced, they encountered a variety of Indians and settlers, and they never could be quite sure whose side these people were on. This uncertainty made the war in the West a violent and unstable concoction.

In western New York, for instance, where there were numerous Iroquois sympathetic to the British, Congress in 1779 authorized the use of 4,500 soldiers to fight under the command of General John Sullivan to eradicate all Indian villages. The troops succeeded. Not only did they destroy up to forty villages, but they also chopped down every fruit tree and confiscated every

domesticated plant they could find. In the midst of battle, Sullivan's officers offered a toast: "Civilization or death to all American Savages."

In Ohio country, the Virginian George Rogers Clark sought to end British control in Detroit and in other vital throughways to the West. In 1779, Clark captured some key British and Indian troops and controlled parts of Ohio territory. Despite this advantage, a decisive victory proved ephemeral, and uncertainty reigned.

In perhaps the most horrific example of the brutality of the war in the West, on one occasion in 1782, more than 150 Pennsylvania militiamen were on the hunt for enemy warriors. Instead, they came across nearly 100 Delaware Indians who had converted to Christianity and were noncombatants in the war. The Indians were starving and were in an unexpected location searching for food. Uncertain of the veracity of the Delaware Indians' story, the militiamen held a council and voted to massacre the whole lot, leading to the execution (they were scalped) of 28 men, 29 women, and 39 children. Two boys escaped the vicious execution, telling the story of what has come to be called the Gnadenhutten Massacre, named after the Pennsylvania town in which it occurred. Several militiamen refused to participate in the slaughter, but the violence and the uncertainty that surrounded it suggest the frightful nature of the war in the West.

THE WINTER OF 1777–1778

Aside from the victory at Saratoga and the French commitment to enter the conflict, the Americans were slowly losing the war. General Howe's forces were continually besting George Washington's troops, enabling the British to capture Philadelphia and other locations. And Washington, keeping with his chief tactic, kept on running. As a result, while Howe's army wintered in the comforts of Philadelphia, Washington and his army stayed 20 miles away in the wilderness of Valley Forge, Pennsylvania. It was a harsh winter, too, and Washington's men were close to starvation. They were poorly equipped, and, although the country had enjoyed one of its best harvests ever, the Congress had allowed the military supply system to deteriorate to the point of almost non-existence. The men's clothes were threadbare and the troops were losing heart. From the perspective of the winter at Valley Forge, the Revolutionary War would not last long. The British would win easily and quickly.

And Valley Forge wasn't alone. Later in the war, in 1779, the army encamped at Morristown, New Jersey, nearly disbanded so that soldiers could search for food and clothes during a particularly harsh spell of winter. For most soldiers who experienced it, Morristown was truly the low point of the war.

6-2c The Third Phase of the War, 1778–1781

But the victory at Saratoga had still another surprising effect, one that would change the shape of the war. When the snow finally melted, colonists realized the British had changed tactics once again, this time in response to Saratoga. The patriots' victory there made it apparent that Britain would have to commit more troops in order to win, and to do this it needed to raise money, most plausibly by raising taxes in Britain. This was wildly unpopular in Britain, and the people's resistance to increased taxes forced Parliament to make a peace offering to the revolutionaries. Parliament's peace offering would have maintained the colonial status of America but abandoned British attempts to tax the colonists—returning things to the way they had been in 1763. In some ways, it was an offer to return to the days of salutary neglect. But to the patriots, this offer was unacceptable; they now wanted freedom.

GIVING UP ON NEW ENGLAND

Instead of attempting the costly venture of replacing Burgoyne's troops in an effort to capture New England, the British planned to contain New England by holding New York while harassing the coastline and the South (see Map 6.2). They also aimed to demoralize the patriots and break the will of the fighters. For example, the British recognized that the American treasury had little to offer its generals, so they tried to "buy" major American leaders, hoping the defection of prominent patriots would spread disaffection. The purchase of General Benedict Arnold in 1779 (for £20,000) was their chief victory on this front. Arnold had been a revolutionary hero, serving in many of the war's major battles, including Ticonderoga and Saratoga, where he had been badly injured. After having invested his personal fortune in

> "I saw several of the men roast their old shoes and eat them, and I was afterwards informed by one of the officers' waiters, that some of the officers killed and ate a favorite little dog that belonged to one of them."
>
> —Joseph Plumb Martin, Continental soldier, on northern campaigns of the winter of 1780

the war effort, he was somewhat suddenly charged with corruption by political adversaries and was investigated by the Congress. He thus was a ready, bitter target for bribing. But aside from Arnold, Britain's bribery policy proved largely unsuccessful.

BRITAIN'S SOUTHERN PLAN

Meanwhile, the British prepared to invade the southern colonies. Understanding that the South possessed more natural resources than the North, they sought to preserve their claim to at least that region. They also believed that Loyalists were abundant in the South, so they hoped to exacerbate divisions along Loyalist–patriot lines. They had several reasons to believe this, the main one being that, in the South, the Revolutionary War really was a civil war between frontiersmen, who generally favored independence, and landholders, who usually sided with the British in order to protect their assets.

The British miscalculated the amount of Loyalist support in the South, however. For one thing, Loyalists lacked the fervor and militancy of the patriots. For another, Loyalists were not as prevalent as British leaders had hoped. The British plan was therefore doomed from the beginning.

Indeed, throughout the colonies, north and south, it had become a dangerous thing to admit sympathy to the British this late in the war. As the British moved through the area hoping to unearth Loyalist support, the region broke into what has to be called civil war, as old grudges and family squabbles led to widespread violence. Patriots often subjected Loyalists to public humiliation, as they looted their land and ransacked their homes.

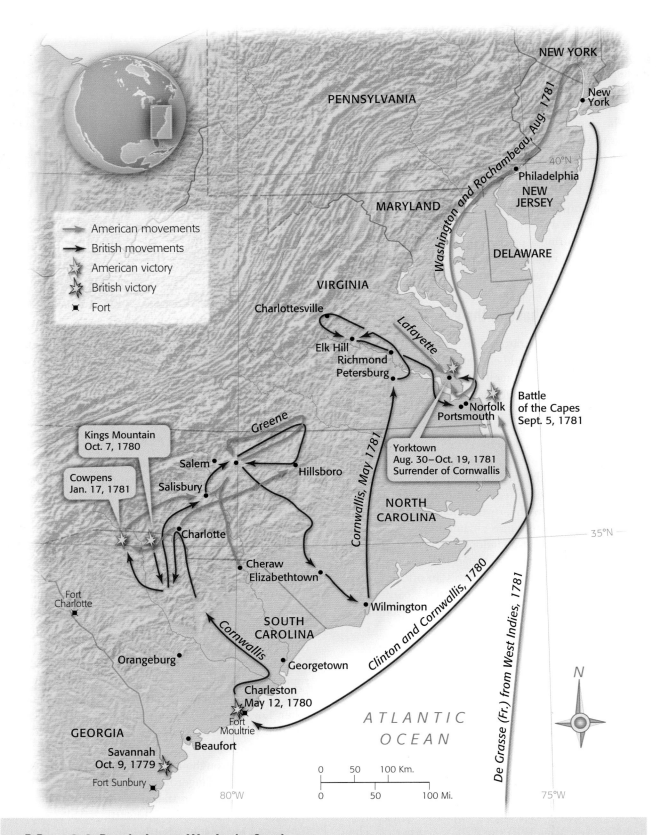

Map 6.2 **Revolutionary War in the South**

>> This map details the American Revolutionary War in the southern colonies, stretching from New York to Georgia, and shows how far inland many of the battles extended.

In 1779, the British landed a large army at Charleston. Commanded by General Sir Charles Cornwallis, the army speedily captured Savannah, Georgia, and Charleston, South Carolina. Through 1780, Cornwallis continued to capture southern towns, and he planned to march north to subdue the rest of the colonies, particularly Virginia, which he viewed as crucial to holding the South.

WASHINGTON AND GREENE'S STRATEGY FOR VICTORY

In 1780, the Continental Army in the South, now led by Nathanael Greene, attempted to counter Cornwallis's successes by fleeing inland and thus sucking the British Army farther into the continent, away from the coast. This approach served two purposes: (1) it stretched British supply lines, and (2) it countered British attempts to rally Loyalist opposition. By drawing the British away from their supplies, Greene hoped to force them to "live off the land," a military euphemism for stealing food from the people. Greene and Washington expected that any support for the British would evaporate as hungry British soldiers began to raid farms.

Their plan succeeded. For several months, Cornwallis pursued the Continental Army across the Carolinas (note Cornwallis's movements in Map 6.2). British supplies gradually ran low and, just as Washington and Greene had predicted, the troops began stealing from once-sympathetic farmers. On top of this, when the two armies actually fought, the Continental soldiers inflicted major casualties on the British. Although the British won most of the engagements, meaning they took control of the territory being fought over, the Continental strategies made British victories costly.

In early 1781, Cornwallis was forced to cease his pursuit and take his army north, into Virginia, to await reinforcements. Faced with mounting casualties, he planned to reunite with his naval fleet at Chesapeake Bay.

YORKTOWN AND VICTORY

The problem with Cornwallis's plan was positioning: while Cornwallis waited for the British fleet (which the French had forced to retreat to New York), his army was stranded at the tip of the Yorktown peninsula in Virginia. Seizing the opportunity to attack, Washington moved a combined force of American and French troops across the lower peninsula; the American victory was complete when the French naval fleet arrived just before the British fleet could rescue Cornwallis's 27,000-man army. The British found themselves trapped on the peninsula.

After a night of bombardment, on October 19, 1781, Cornwallis turned his sword over to Washington. More accurately, an emissary for Cornwallis handed it to American general Benjamin Lincoln, whom Washington appointed to accept the surrender when he learned that the British commander had refused to offer his sword personally. When news of Cornwallis's surrender reached Britain, King George III refused to accept defeat, leading to a tremendous rift between the king and a growing minority in Parliament who saw the efforts to keep the rebelling colonies as a poor investment. Despite the surrender, then, smaller battles continued for more than a year.

NEWBURGH CONSPIRACY

Nonetheless, after Yorktown, peace negotiations began, and yet because of the king's refusal to admit defeat, discussions went nowhere for more than a year. The armies remained mobilized, pitched for battle, sometimes even engaged in skirmishes. And as always, American troops continued to be underpaid and under-supplied. In this atmosphere, several American military leaders proposed a coup, seeking to take control from the relatively impotent Continental Congress in order to implement a tax to pay for unpaid expenses, including their own salaries. The Continental Army was at the time positioned in Newburgh, New York, about 60 miles north of New York City, which was still occupied by the British, and thus their plan became called the Newburgh Conspiracy.

With the British in close striking range, any hint of turmoil within the Continental Army might have provoked Britain to resume hostilities. But Washington rapidly quashed the whispered conspiracy, principally by demonstrating the costs of the war on him personally. The generals were not the only ones who had suffered during the war, he said, reminding them that independence was more consequential than worldly gain. Washington's words derailed the revolt, but the unrest demonstrated the significance of the peace treaty that was to come.

6-2d Peace Negotiations, 1782–1783

With battle mostly over, the American team of negotiators—Benjamin Franklin, John Jay, and John Adams—found themselves in a difficult situation. They traveled to Paris for the talks in 1782, with instructions to consult with the French. However, the Americans knew that both France and its ally, Spain, had territorial goals of their own in the New World, goals that the Americans did not want to encourage. As a result, Franklin, Jay, and Adams determined that it was in their best interest to negotiate with the British separately and deal with the French later.

THE TREATY OF PARIS (1783)

The treaty that Franklin, Jay, and Adams fashioned in 1782 included so many provisions favorable to the Americans that it has frequently been called the greatest triumph in the history of American diplomacy. Britain had its own interests at heart, too, of course: To guarantee that France did not have the best trading rights to the New World, Britain willingly offered generous terms to the Americans in terms of land and trading rights. America and Britain signed a treaty in November 1782. In doing so, Franklin, Adams, and Jay violated one of the provisions of the Franco-American Alliance of 1778: namely, that neither France nor America would negotiate a separate peace with the British. Nevertheless, the French were eager to end the war, and on January 2, 1783, preliminary treaties were signed between Britain and France and Britain and Spain, and on February 4 hostilities formally ceased. All parties signed the Treaty of Paris (1783) in September 1783.

There were five major parts to the Treaty of Paris of 1783: (1) American independence; (2) American expansion west to the Mississippi River and north to the Great Lakes (a much greater area than Americans had thus far settled); (3) freedom of all parties to travel the Mississippi River; (4) Spanish control of Florida; and (5) "no lawful impediment" placed on British merchants seeking to recoup debts from America. The war was finally over.

6-3 SIGNIFICANCE OF THE WAR

The six long years of the Revolutionary War were filled with suffering. A doctor in the Continental Army suggested that American losses totaled 70,000, but the number of war-related deaths was more likely 25,000, with perhaps another 25,000 injured. Disease and infection killed off many more. Indeed, the war took place in the midst of a widespread smallpox epidemic, which may have killed as many as 130,000 colonists. (Washington wisely had his troops inoculated, perhaps his smartest move in the entire campaign.) But it was nevertheless a long war, longer than the Civil War, World War I, or World War II.

Furthermore, the war had divided the colonists between Loyalists, rebels, and those indifferent to either side. It had also greatly disrupted daily life, as soldiers were recruited to join the army and leave their families for extended periods of time, women were asked to shoulder a heavier burden in their household and in civic life, and slaves ontemplated their future in a new American republic, one that showed little sign of granting them freedom. Beyond these tremendous disruptions in daily life, the American war for independence had six major results.

6-3a The Impact on Politics

Politically, the American Revolution was the first world conflict whose winners embraced the promise of the Enlightenment. In promising the "natural rights" of life, liberty, and property, the American Revolution served as an ideological model for later revolutions in France and in Central and South America, among others.

But the Revolution was a bellwether of not only liberty but also republican democracy. The American revolutionaries hoped their struggles would curb the system of Old World aristocracy. They no longer wanted to be ruled by a few powerful people with long-entrenched methods of perpetuating their wealth and status. Many rebels also did not want an established church that denied freedom of belief. No one was sure what would arise in the place of Old World aristocracy, but they knew that, after the Revolution, the old system was dead.

>> The experience of fighting for their political independence was the impetus for the mounting tide of patriotism and patriotic imagery that followed the Revolutionary War. As shown here, the bald eagle became a stalwart symbol of American strength.

American School/The Bridgeman Art Library

Eventually, this awareness would lead to the formal separation of church and state and limited (but growing) access to the ballot. During the revolutionary era, access to the ballot was still dependent on owning property, which usually excluded women and African Americans, but the Revolutionary War geared up the machinery for a more expansive democracy in the future.

6-3b The Impact on American Nationalism

Before the American Revolution, the colonists living in what became the United States did not think of themselves as having a national culture fundamentally unique from Britain's. In terms of nationality, most colonists considered themselves as their great-grandfathers were, British. But the French and Indian War and the American Revolution unified the colonists under a new, ideological definition of what it meant to be an American.

A nation is composed of people who recognize that they share certain qualities that set them apart from other nations, whether those qualities are ideological, political, linguistic, religious, cultural, racial, or historical. For Americans, in the revolutionary era and after, a strong belief in democracy and the experience of fighting for their political independence were the impetus for the mounting tide of patriotism that followed the Revolutionary War. The question of what it meant to be an American was now defined largely by a commitment to republican ideals and a desire to fight for them. It would, however, take time for that ideological meaning to take hold. Most Americans still emphasized local, state, and regional identities over that of their nation. But the seeds of a national identity premised on the belief in a set of ideas were planted during the Revolutionary War.

6-3c The Impact on Slavery

By illustrating the contradiction between slavery and freedom, the Revolutionary War triggered the abolition of slavery in the North. During the war, slaves participated in the fight on both sides, although the British welcomed them more willingly than the revolutionaries. Cornwallis himself enlisted 5,000 slaves, promising to free them after the war. At the same time, many slaves simply fled their masters during the confusion of battle. In all, there were about 50,000 fewer slaves after the war than before it. Some former slaves went to New England, some went to Canada, and many stayed in the South to live freely.

The progress of formal abolition after the war was slow and gradual, but it was progress nonetheless. Most of the changes were in the North, where slavery was slowly, state by state, abolished. But some advances were even made in the South, where the vast majority of slaves lived

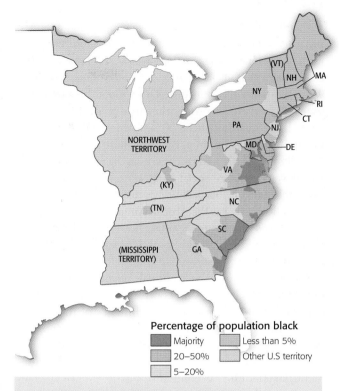

Percentage of population black

- Majority
- 20–50%
- 5–20%
- Less than 5%
- Other U.S territory

Map 6.3 Distribution of African American Population, 1790

>> This map shows the percentage of population in the states that was black, demonstrating that most of the northern states had fewer than five percent of their population as black, and increases as the further south you look.

(see Map 6.3). Virginia and Maryland made it easier for owners to **manumit** (or willingly free) their slaves, and some if not many revolutionaries chose to do so. By 1800, one in ten African Americans in the Chesapeake region was free. This meant there were large communities where escaped slaves could hide in the growing cities of the Chesapeake. Nevertheless, slavery had not been abolished in the South, and leaders like Thomas Jefferson, who were well aware of the contradiction between the practice of slavery and the rhetoric of independence, never freed more than a tiny number of their slaves.

The most dramatic changes occurred in the North when abolition was set in motion legally. Vermont outlawed slavery in its first constitution in 1777. In Massachusetts and

manumit To willingly free one's slaves

New Hampshire, slaves sued for their freedom—and won. In the Middle States, where the slave population was larger, progress was slower, but both Pennsylvania and New York favored gradual emancipation, which, in Pennsylvania's case, meant that all slaves born in 1780 or later were free when they turned twenty-one. Throughout the North, five states allowed African Americans to vote, and in total, by 1810, three-quarters of the 30,000 African Americans living in the North were free. By 1840, there were only 1,000 slaves in the North, and the freed slaves and their children had developed large social institutions, including various sects of historically black churches and numerous fraternal organizations, such as the African American Masons.

Perhaps most importantly, however, by 1790, all states except Georgia and South Carolina had outlawed the importation of slaves from abroad. As Americans began to consider the political meanings of liberty and freedom, they were confronted by the obvious contradiction of having freed themselves of the Crown while others in their midst lived in slavery. After the Revolution, only compromise would keep the issue of slavery at bay, as the North and South took different tactics in handling the contentious issue.

6-3d The Impact on Native America

The war also greatly affected the fate of Native Americans, who were generally worse off after the war than before it. By the time of the Revolution, there were few Indian nations still living on the Atlantic Coast, as disease and violence had decimated the Indians of that region. The most powerful Indian nations in contact with the colonists lived between the Appalachian Mountains and the Mississippi River, where the Iroquois dominated in the North and the Choctaw, Seminole, Creek, and Cherokee dominated in the South. The battles throughout Native America were unspeakably harsh on them, though, as the war often served as a pretext to remove Indian nations and empty Indian land for land-hungry colonists. Anyone could become a casualty on the frontier. By the end of the war, nearly one-third of the Iroquois nation was dead. Their supremacy in the land between the Appalachians and the Great Lakes did not survive long after the war.

In addition to these violent encounters, with the war over, the nations of Native America had to contend with an expanding nation of settlers who respected no practical western boundary and answered to no governmental authority preventing them from moving farther west. This situation portended a grim outlook for American Indians. Where once they could play the varying European nations off one another to their advantage, now they had to contend with a single expansive nation that had shown them little respect in the past.

6-3e The Impact on Women

Women played key roles during the Revolution. They enforced boycotts, sewed clothing made of nonimported fibers, raised impressive funds for the Continental Army, and sometimes even engaged in battle. This was a significant shift from the colonial era, when women only rarely protested their total exclusion from politics. New Jersey's constitution of 1776 opened the franchise to "all free inhabitants" who were worth at least fifty pounds, thus allowing many New Jersey women to vote for the first time.

But immediately after the war, women generally lost out politically as the new nation decided how far it would extend the rewards of citizenship. In many states,

North Wind Picture Archives

>> Sybil Ludington, shown here, was just 16 years old when she traveled 40 miles from her home, watching out for British soldiers and loyalists, in order to warn the revolutionary militia that British soldiers were burning the town of Concord in 1777.

women were not eligible to own property. And, in every other state besides New Jersey, there is no evidence that women were ever offered the vote. In 1807, even New Jersey rescinded its offer of the franchise.

Similarly, men often confined women's role to that of "republican motherhood," which historians now describe as a double-edged identity—one that put women in charge of raising young male republicans through a demanding path of education, religious adherence, and political engagement but that also confined women's role to familial relations outside the realm of direct intervention in the public sphere.

6-3f The Impact on Religious Minorities

Many historians have pointed to the Great Awakening of the 1730s and 1740s as laying part of the foundation for the revolutionary events of the 1760s and 1770s. With its emphasis on personal religious experience rather than the authority of the ministers, and as one of the first events to create a shared experience for people from New England to the southern colonies, some have viewed the Great Awakening as an early form of revolutionary activity. Colonists were also afraid that, around 1763, Parliament was planning to establish a bishop of the Anglican Church for America. They feared that any such appointment would extend Britain's official church to the colonies.

Two American actions after the war reflected their concerns about an established church: (1) Most of the new state constitutions included some guarantee of religious toleration, although a few states that already had an official tax-supported church (like Massachusetts) moved more slowly toward disestablishment and many allowed tolerance for Christians only; and (2) the democratic ideals of the Revolution called into question public financial support of churches that were not attended by everyone.

The best-known representation of these ideas came in 1786, when the Virginia legislature passed a Thomas Jefferson-drafted bill that called for the disestablishment of the Episcopal Church. Jefferson's **Virginia Statute on Religious Freedom** was one of the accomplishments that Jefferson himself was most proud of. The statute said that no Virginians would be "compelled" to go to any church or form of religious worship against their will and that all Virginians were free to profess their own opinion "in matters of religion." It immediately influenced several state constitutions, and several states made their ratification of the United States Constitution in 1787 contingent upon an amendment promising the federal government would

Table 6.1 Revolutionary War Chronology	
1763	End of salutary neglect
1775	Local conflicts escalate
January 1776	Tom Paine's *Common Sense*
July 1776	Declaration of Independence
December 25, 1776	Crossing the Delaware
September–October 1777	Battle of Saratoga
1778	France enters war on the side of the United States
1779	Britain invades the South
1780	Inland battles force British away from supply lines
October 1781	Yorktown and American victory

not infringe on religious liberties (in what turned out to be the First Amendment).

At the same time, the Revolution led to the creation of several divisions of American churches, such as the Methodist Episcopal Church of America and the Presbyterian Church of the United States. Two "freedom churches" also opened, both of which stressed the brotherhood of man and the freedom of conscience: the Universalist Church (1779) and the Unitarian Church (1785). Thus, not only did the Revolution inspire laws mandating the separation of church and state, but it also encouraged the creation of two major antidogmatic sects.

>LOOKING AHEAD...

Historians have long weighed the question of how revolutionary the Revolutionary War really was. At a basic level, the war set the patriots free from British political control, but it did not necessarily overturn economic or gendered structures that had been in place long before the war. For the most part, a working man was still a working man, a woman's role was largely confined to the domestic sphere, and the racial hierarchy that was in place since Bacon's Rebellion (if not long before) still stood. But the

Virginia Statute on Religious Freedom Bill passed in 1786 that was originally drafted by Thomas Jefferson, articulating distrust of an established state church and the value of religious liberty

war provoked the question of how far republicandemocracy would extend. Many revolutionary leaders feared that too much freedom might lead to chaos: if everyone were free, who would ensure order? On the other hand, too little freedom might trigger a second revolution.

With the war over, the leaders of the new nation confronted yet another daunting task: forming a new government that embodied the revolutionary spirit without letting that spirit extend to anarchy. It would be no easy task.

STUDY TOOLS 6

READY TO STUDY? IN THE BOOK, YOU CAN

❏ Rip out the Chapter Review Card, which includes key terms and chapter summaries.

ONLINE AT WWW.CENGAGEBRAIN.COM, YOU CAN:

❏ Collect StudyBits while you read and study the chapter.

❏ Quiz yourself on key concepts.

❏ Find videos for further exploration.

❏ Prepare for tests with HIST5 Flash Cards as well as those you create.

❏ Learn more about Lord Dunmore and read his proclamation.

❏ Read Common Sense.

❏ View a film about the drafting of the Declaration of Independence.

❏ Read the Declaration of Independence.

❏ View a film about the life of George Washington.

❏ Read one Quaker's attempt to point out inconsistencies between American freedom and slavery.

CH6 TIMELINE

What Else Was Happening

▶ **1775**

August: King George III denounces colonists as rebels.

November: Dunmore promises slaves freedom for fighting alongside British.

▶ **1776**

January: Thomas Paine's pamphlet *Common Sense* calls for independence.

March: Continental Army forces British to evacuate Boston, ending eleven-month siege.

June 7: Committee for Declaration of Independence forms, with Jefferson as draftsman.

June 28: Continental Congress debates and edits Declaration of Independence.

1776

July 2: Continental Congress unanimously approves Declaration of Independence.

August–December: Continental Army escapes British in New York.

December 26: General Washington defeats British with surprise move in Trenton, New Jersey.

1777 September 19: *Patriot victory at Battle of Saratoga leads to Franco-American Alliance.*

September 26: *Under General Howe, British take the new capital of Philadelphia.*

July 4: *The United States celebrates its first birthday. Ships lined up on the Delaware River discharge thirteen cannon shots in honor of the thirteen states.*

Franco-American Alliance against British expands the war to the Atlantic.

New Orleans businessman Oliver Pollock creates the $ symbol.

1779

Under Cornwallis, British land in South Carolina and advance quickly.

1780

To weaken British, patriots draw fighting deeper into South Carolina.

1781

Cornwallis gives up South Carolina and awaits reinforcements in Virginia.

October 19: American and French forces trap Cornwallis army on Yorktown peninsula.

1782

John Jay, Benjamin Franklin, John Adams travel to Paris for peace talks.

1783

September: Treaty of Paris grants American independence and rights to the West.

1784: *A new trade route opens for Americans when the* Empress of China *sails from New Jersey around Cape Horn in South America to China.*

1785

Revolution inspires formation of freedom churches such as the Unitarians.

1787: *The first U.S. penny, designed by Benjamin Franklin, is minted.*

1789: *The French Revolution begins, initiating a long battle in France over "liberty, equality, and fraternity."*

1790: *All states but South Carolina and Georgia outlaw slave import from abroad.*

The cornerstone of the mansion known as the White House is laid.

7 | Confederation and Constitution, 1783–1789

Picture History/Newscom

LEARNING OBJECTIVES

After reading this chapter, you should be able to do the following:

7-1 Describe the first state constitutions written and adopted after the United States declared its independence.

7-2 Analyze the federal government as it existed under the Articles of Confederation.

7-3 Enumerate the most significant issues the United States confronted under the Articles of Confederation, and explain how the Articles failed to live up to the needs of the new country.

7-4 Explain the need for the Constitutional Convention that met in Philadelphia in 1787, and describe the process of writing the Constitution.

7-5 Describe and explain the major provisions of the Constitution, especially concerning the separation of powers and the rights given to individual states.

7-6 Explain the procedure established for ratification of the Constitution, describe the actions of its supporters and its opponents, and explain how and when ratification was achieved.

AFTER FINISHING THIS CHAPTER GO TO **PAGE 140** **FOR STUDY TOOLS**

By 1783, the nation was officially independent, but it had three immediate problems: (1) it had amassed a huge debt from fighting for independence; (2) it suddenly had vast lands to control in the West; and (3) it had to recreate a system of trade after Britain's protections had been withdrawn. These problems were intensified because the ideology that had propelled the revolution—republicanism—strenuously warned against a strong central authority. Most Americans wanted their day-to-day freedoms. They wanted the liberties promised in the Declaration of Independence. Which begs the obvious question: What were those freedoms, and, just as important, what price were people willing to pay for them? Could Americans design a government able to provide liberty, but strong enough to protect that liberty?

Their first attempt to find an appropriate balance, through a government established under the Articles of Confederation, proved unsuccessful. The Articles made the federal government too weak to address the nation's pressing needs. By 1787, Americans had scrapped the Articles and designed an entirely new structure of government. This new government, as defined in the United States Constitution, placed more power in a central authority than most Americans had anticipated or wanted. But a Bill of Rights protected the liberties Americans sought to preserve. Although not perfect, what they created in the Constitution has served the nation for more than two hundred years.

This chapter explores the development of the American government between 1783 and 1789. It begins by examining the state constitutions that served as testing grounds for the federal constitution; then it examines the strengths and weaknesses of the Articles of Confederation before addressing the current U.S. Constitution and its Bill of Rights.

7-1 STATE CONSTITUTIONS, 1776–1780

Between 1776 and 1780, while the fighting still raged, all of the thirteen new states except Connecticut and Rhode Island drafted their own constitution. Most changed their constitution several times, meaning

that there was a good deal of experimentation going on. The ideas laid out by John Locke, Jean-Jacques Rousseau, John Trenchard, Thomas Gordon, the British Parliament, and the colonial legislatures were put to the test at the state level during these years. These state constitutions worked out ideas that would later influence the federal system.

7-1a Content

While experimentation was the word of the day, most state constitutions had several common elements. For instance, all were attempts to fashion a government that offered some form of representation to the people. Gone were the days of non-elected leaders. Almost all of the state constitutions also shared three other things: (1) bills of rights; (2) limits on participation; and (3) separation of powers.

BILLS OF RIGHTS

Seven of the eleven new state constitutions had a **bill of rights** that protected the "natural rights" that many Americans felt were threatened by Britain's prerevolutionary laws. The other four had these rights scattered within them, but no separate list. Most of the bills of rights guaranteed the freedom of the press, the right of popular consent before being taxed, and protections against general search warrants. Most states guaranteed the freedom of religion, although many limited political participation to Christians only.

LIMITS ON PARTICIPATION

Almost universally, the state constitutions also broadened the base of people who could participate in government by relaxing property-holding qualifications. Pennsylvania, for instance, gave the vote to anyone who paid taxes. And New Jersey opened the vote to "all free inhabitants" worth at least fifty pounds. Nevertheless,

> **bill of rights** In the American context, a list of "natural rights" that many Americans felt were threatened by Britain's prerevolutionary laws; most of the bills of rights included in early state constitutions guaranteed the freedom of the press, the right of popular consent before being taxed, and protections against general search warrants

◄◄◄ **The US Constitution, signed and drafted in 1787, has ever since been a contested hallmark in American history, with people constantly debating the original intent of the signers—or even whether their original intent should still matter. This early twentieth-century painting shows reverence for George Washington, Benjamin Franklin, and several other signers of the US Constitution.**

>> New Jersey's constitution of 1776 opened the franchise to "all free inhabitants" who were worth at least fifty pounds, thus allowing many New Jersey women and African Americans to vote for the first time. This drawing shows women and African Americans exhibiting their right to vote.

The Art Gallery Collection/Alamy Stock Photo

each state maintained limits on who could vote and who could hold public office. These limits usually concerned owning property or adhering to a particular religion. Women and teenagers were almost universally excluded from voting, except, sometimes, when they owned property.

SEPARATION OF POWERS

As they tinkered with various forms of government, each state recognized that creating several different branches of government and giving each different responsibilities prevented one person or one body from becoming overly tyrannical or exerting an excess of authority. This was called the **separation of powers**. In the 1780s, John Adams of Massachusetts developed the theory behind separation of powers, one he called "mixed government." Most of the states operated according to separation of powers, in that they had a weak elected governor, a powerful legislature that changed membership frequently, and courts whose judges were named for life to ensure they were beholden to no one. Despite the ideal of separation of powers, the legislative branches were almost always more powerful than the executive and judicial branches.

separation of powers The concept of creating several different branches of government and giving each of them different responsibilities so as to prevent any one body from exerting an excess of authority

7-1b Results

The various state constitutions were valuable forums for working out different types of government. Many worked well for their citizens. The constitutions drafted earlier in the process tended to be more radical and democratic (like Pennsylvania's 1776 constitution), while the constitutions adopted later (like Massachusetts' 1780 constitution, or even Pennsylvania's revised constitution of 1790) increased limits on political participation. Still, none addressed the issue of how the states would participate in a national body. The states were keen to keep their powers. And most Americans were leery of a large national government, uncertain it could prevent itself from becoming tyrannically powerful.

7-2 THE ARTICLES OF CONFEDERATION, 1777–1787

Americans managed to fight more than half the Revolutionary War without any legitimate federal government. That was unsustainable, and the problem was rectified in 1777 with the Articles of Confederation.

7-2a Origins

In the absence of a federal government, the Continental Congress had assumed a number of rights and responsibilities, such as creating the Continental Army, printing

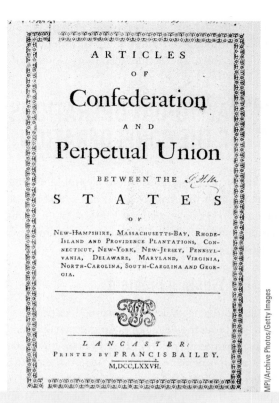

>> The Articles of Confederation and Perpetual Union, pictured here, was the nation's first attempt to establish a centralized government. Its weaknesses, including granting too much power to the individual states, led to calls for its revision and, eventually, its replacement.

money, managing trade, and dealing with debt. But it had done these things without having been granted authority by the people or some other sovereign power. Feeling the need to legitimate their actions and define the colonies' collective sovereignty, the revolutionaries realized they had to form a governing body. So between 1776 and 1777 the Continental Congress drafted the **Articles of Confederation**. The following year, it presented the document to the states for ratification, and, by July 1778 eight states had ratified the document. But full unanimity of the thirteen states, which was required before it could go into effect, would not be reached until 1781.

The experimentation that had taken place in the states did not really affect the Articles of Confederation, which were drafted too early to be substantially influenced by the state constitutions. Thus the Articles did not innovate; they basically codified the way things were in the late 1770s. John Dickinson, the prominent lawyer who had drafted the ideological tract *Letters from a Farmer in Pennsylvania*,

was the principal author of the Articles. Although he refused to sign the Declaration of Independence (he felt the colonies were ill prepared), the Continental Congress invited him to draft the new system of government.

7-2b Division of Powers

Leery of a strong federal power, the Articles provided for each state's independence, and granted very little power to the overarching federal government. The central government was simply supposed to be an administrative agency that provided a meeting place for debate and enacted some very minimal, hard-to-enforce rules.

POWERS RESERVED FOR THE FEDERAL GOVERNMENT

Dickinson's Articles placed all governing power in a single legislature, which was the system followed under the Continental Congress. This meant there was no separation of powers, because there was no president, monarch, or prime minister to serve as the executive power. Instead, there was a "Committee of the States," in which one representative from each state was seated. This was the most centralized authority, and its powers were minimal. The Continental Congress, on the other hand, had five powers under the Articles: (1) to declare war and make peace; (2) to make international treaties; (3) to control Indian affairs in the West; (4) to establish a currency; and (5) to create and maintain a postal service.

POWERS RESERVED FOR THE STATES

The states, meanwhile, maintained the all-important rights to: (1) levy taxes and (2) regulate commerce. Unfortunately, these were perhaps the two most pressing needs of a nation conducting a war, precisely because they are the actions that keep the money rolling in. If the states would not provide enough funds to fight a war, what could the federal government do? Under the Articles of Confederation, it could do nothing.

7-2c Achievements of the Articles

We can already begin to guess at the flaws and limits of the Articles, but they also represented significant achievements. From a philosophical perspective, two stand out: (1) the Articles established the United States as a government of laws that placed limits on the government's

Articles of Confederation Document that defined the colonies' collective sovereignty; drafted by the Continental Congress between 1776 and 1777, then ratified by the thirteen states by 1781

authority, and (2) the Articles created a national citizenship, which gave equal rights to qualifying members (although deciding who was and was not a citizen was still determined by each state). There would be no titles or codification of classes in America. These were major accomplishments well within the ideals of republicanism. A third accomplishment of the Articles, the greatest in its day-to-day operations, was its utility in organizing the newly acquired western lands.

7-2d Weaknesses of the Articles

But the weaknesses of the Articles outweighed its achievements. Three stand out: (1) the inability to raise funds; (2) the need for complete unanimity to make changes; and (3) the lack of authority over internal trade.

INABILITY TO RAISE FUNDS

The war had sunk the new nation badly in to debt, and the Articles declared that Congress could not levy taxes. Furthermore, with a massive debt, it was hard to find creditors. This combination spelled immediate trouble for the new nation. For instance, how could it afford to pay an army? Who would regulate currency? Under the Articles, the nation could not manage its fiscal affairs.

THE NEED FOR UNANIMITY TO MAKE CHANGES

To help remedy this problem, in 1781, nationalists in Congress chartered a national bank to help consolidate the national debt and facilitate credit. In order for the bank to operate, however, Congress needed money to create a system of reserves. To get that capital, Congress passed a bill that put a 5 percent tax on all imported goods. However, the Articles of Confederation required that all bills receive unanimous approval before becoming law. Tiny Rhode Island, reliant on foreign trade for its economy, would not assent to the tax. Without Rhode Island, the bill died, as did these early plans for a national bank. In matters legislative, the need for unanimity was a clear problem.

LACK OF AUTHORITY OVER INTERNAL TRADE

Finally, commerce between the states suffered because there was no central authority to manage it. Because each state had its own currency, its own levels of inflation, and its own taxes, it was difficult to transport goods across state lines or engineer large programs that would encompass an entire region. The Articles provided no national policy on commerce, and throughout the first half of the decade, delegates from southern states resisted efforts to devise one. They feared that such a policy would allow northern merchants to monopolize the trade of southern

agricultural products, bypassing southern merchants and traders. Without an overarching government to oversee commerce, the entire nation's economy would suffer.

7-3 DAY-TO-DAY OPERATIONS OF THE CONFEDERATION

In addition to these constitutional problems, the government under the Articles faced three other significant challenges: (1) managing western expansion, (2) foreign relations, and (3) debt. These further underscored the Articles' strengths and weaknesses.

7-3a The Western Problem

The most pressing challenge concerned land in the West. During and after the Revolution, Americans continued their seemingly perpetual push westward, and in the 1780s large numbers of Americans moved to western Pennsylvania, Kentucky, and the Nashville region. They were slowly populating the area between the Appalachian Mountains and the Mississippi River, further dispossessing the Indians who lived there already. As these pioneers moved west, they began to enrich the states that had charters in the West (since many of the original colonial charters specified northern and southern boundaries but usually made the western boundary the Pacific Ocean). These stipulations bred jealousy among states that had no claims on western land. Maryland, in fact, refused to ratify the Articles of Confederation until the largest western landholder, Virginia, ceded its western holdings to the federal government (Map 7.1).

LAND CESSIONS

In 1784, Congress finally persuaded Virginia to cede much of its land to the federal government. But Virginia and other large landholders did so only on the condition that they be allowed to keep small "reserves" of land for later use, a condition the Continental Congress had to grant. By 1802, eighteen years later, all states had ceded their western lands to the federal government. The inability of the federal government under the Articles to make this happen sooner showed it could not bully the states into doing what it needed, even if what it wanted was best for the young nation.

ORGANIZING TERRITORIES

With continued westward migration and calls for the federal government to oversee that expansion, Congress devised several plans to organize the western

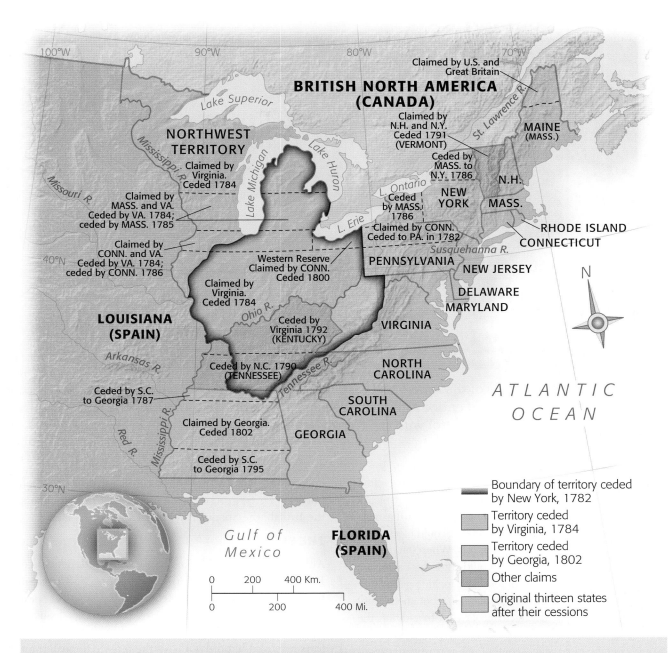

Map 7.1 Western Land Claims After the Revolution

>> A map of the new United States of America, highlighting the large western lands claimed by Virginia, Georgia, and other states, land they would eventually cede to the federal government.

territories. The Land Ordinance of 1785, which surveyed the immense western territory, divided it into townships 6 miles square and set prices for its sale to individuals. This plan favored wealthy speculators because small farmers could not afford an entire "township," thus requiring speculators to act as intermediaries, which drove prices up. These speculators, not small farmers, were the real beneficiaries of this system.

Furthermore, two years later Congress passed the **Northwest Ordinance of 1787**, which established territorial governments in the Great Lakes region and set a pattern

Northwest Ordinance of 1787 Legislation that established territorial governments in the Great Lakes region and set a pattern for future western development

>> Like other images of the American West, this "Plan of an American New Cleared Farm" from 1793 helped entice Americans to move further west, something the federal government sought to control with the Northwest Ordinance of 1787.

for future western development. The Ordinance crafted boundaries for territories and developed laws by which a territory could be included in the nation. When the male population of a territory reached 5,000, it could elect a legislature and send a delegate to Congress. When the population reached 60,000, the territory could enter the Union as a state, on equal status with all other states, including the original thirteen. The Northwest Ordinance also contained something absent from the Articles: a bill of rights. In addition, the Ordinance prohibited slavery in the territories, a point that would become increasingly contentious as westward expansion continued throughout the first half of the 1800s. It did, however, act with blatant disregard for the native inhabitants of the land, creating a system for white expansion that would be defended by the federal government.

But, of course, because the federal government could not fund a standing army, it had little capacity to protect those settlers who moved there. War with Indians would continue to rage for the next century.

7-3b The Problem of Foreign Relations

The second important issue confronted by the government under the Articles of Confederation had to do with foreign relations. Most significantly, with a weak federal government, Americans found it difficult to secure their borders. Three groups took advantage of this weakness: the British, the Spanish, and pirates.

THE BRITISH

Although the United States had won its independence, Britain retained a few forts along the U.S.–Canadian border. They did this to protect their lucrative fur trade and to ensure the United States paid off its loans to British creditors. The United States badly wanted these forts removed but did not have the muscle to push them out. Again, the United States had no standing army and could not afford to maintain one.

THE SPANISH

The second grating interloper was Spain, and, from a foreign relations perspective, there were three problems with Spain: (1) the Treaty of Paris was unclear about who controlled a piece of land called the Yazoo Strip, which was the boundary between Spanish Florida and American Georgia; (2) the Spanish controlled the mouth of the Mississippi River and were able to close off this central access point to the American interior, should they ever wish to; and (3) the Americans wanted access to Spanish traders in the West Indies, but Spain was reluctant to allow this because it did not want the United States to become dominant in the Western Hemisphere.

In 1784, Spain made a proposition to the United States: Spain would grant Americans access to the Spanish West Indies (which would benefit American traders), but it would cut off access to the Mississippi River (so Spain could limit the amount of goods coming down the Mississippi into the open market). Needing nine votes in Congress to approve the measure, the treaty floundered, winning only seven. It was revealing that all seven votes came from northern states, infuriating southerners and westerners, both of whom would be hurt economically if the Mississippi River were closed off to American traders. The Spanish eventually reopened the Mississippi but charged high duties to American merchants.

PIRATES

In the 1780s, American forces were also impotent in the face of Mediterranean pirates, who preyed on American trade ships in the Atlantic and the Caribbean. Without the capital to maintain a strong navy, the government under the Articles could do little to stop the marauding of American ships.

7-3c The Debt

Despite these two serious issues (the West and foreign relations), the most immediate problem facing the new nation was debt. This had three visible political ramifications: (1) those who held the debt wanted to be repaid; (2) the rank-and-file of the army grew angry when the government could not pay all the backpay it owed the soldiers; and (3) farmers grew angry because inflation had priced them out of the life to which they were accustomed.

PROMISSORY NOTES AND BONDS

To finance the Revolutionary War, the American government had sold bonds, which had to be repaid, plus interest, at a certain time in the future. Furthermore, the government had issued several promissory notes, mostly to farmers whose land was used during the war, and usually after the army had seized farmers' property in order to wage battle. Both types of debt-holders wanted to be paid back to prevent them from defaulting on their own loans.

AN ANGRY ARMY

The problem escalated when, shortly after the war, it became evident that the government could not pay its soldiers they pay it owed them. Officers petitioned on behalf of soldiers' grievances, sometimes threatening violence if the payments were not made. In one standoff,

troops protested in front of Philadelphia's Independence Hall, forcing the Continental Congress to abandon Philadelphia (it moved to Princeton, New Jersey, until the threat quieted down). Only George Washington's words could soothe the troops. But this signaled troubles to come; after all, the Continental Congress was still unable to raise revenue, and soldiers were angry.

ANGRY FARMERS

Meanwhile, the economy remained incredibly turbulent, and farmers were hit hardest. They had enjoyed rising prices for their goods during the war and had increased their spending, sometimes to the point of indebtedness. After the war, with no army to feed, markets suddenly shrank. At the same time, Britain prohibited American ships from trading in the West Indies, further limiting the size of the market.

As a result, American agricultural goods flooded American markets, lowering prices and dropping farm wages by as much as 20 percent. When creditors demanded payment from the farmers in gold or silver (a form of payment called **specie**), most farmers were unable to pay their debts. Although most of the farmers' debts were small, foreclosure threatened many. Some were about to lose their farms or were imprisoned after being convicted in debtors' court.

SHAYS' REBELLION

The financial burden seemed unbearable to those who had just fought for independence. In Massachusetts, a tax increase compounded these problems. In 1786, rural towns in Massachusetts petitioned its state assembly for a moratorium on taxes and on lawsuits against debtors. In doing so, they relied on the republican revolutionary language that had fueled the revolution in 1776. When the assembly rejected their petitions, angry crowds gathered at several county courthouses to stop the courts by force. Daniel Shays, a former Continental Army officer, emerged as one of the leaders of the rebellion, and was later vilified as a crazy anarchist by the press, which named the rebellion after him.

Fed up with the Massachusetts government's failure to address the problem of inflation and with its apparent favoritism toward coastal merchants who did not require the large and costly infrastructure that farmers did, on January 26, 1787, Shays and several others led 1,200 men

specie Gold or silver, which has intrinsic value, used as payment instead of paper money, which has extrinsic value

>> Shays' Rebellion, depicted here showing federal troops firing on the rural rebels, leading six men to die, demonstrated not only the dire problem of the federal debt, but also the dangers of true democracy.

to seize control of the federal arsenal in Springfield, Massachusetts. This potential coup was formally called **Shays' Rebellion**.

The Massachusetts government, however, had prepared for such a move (after protesters had stormed the debtors' courts), and a force of 4,400 soldiers from New England was ready to defend the arsenal. Tellingly, these troops were funded and led into battle by East Coast merchants, not country farmers. The troops opened fire on Shays' army. Six died. This seemed to be the beginning of a civil war between the commercial class and the farming class, the wealthy and the poor. But, unprepared for formal combat, the rebels quickly abandoned their siege, and during the next few weeks Shays' Rebellion waned.

Despite the rebellion's quick but violent dissolution, unrest continued to haunt leaders in Massachusetts and other states. Shays' Rebellion was a warning that the federal government would have to address the problem of debt in order to prevent a lower-class uprising. Under the Articles it was impossible to do so. Shays' Rebellion was also a warning about the dangers of true democracy, dangers that

Shays' Rebellion Potential coup of January 26, 1787, when Daniel Shays led 1,200 men to seize control of the federal arsenal in Springfield, Massachusetts, to protest the state legislature's inability to address the debt problems of small farmers

made many leading intellectuals incredibly nervous. How could order be preserved in a country that lionized liberty?

7-3d The Failure of the Articles of Confederation

Despite these underlying problems with the Articles of Confederation, a financial collapse was the last straw. In 1783, Britain banned all American ships from the West Indies and put limitations on specific competitive items coming into Britain. Few other countries granted protective treaties with the United States, knowing that America was too weak to honor them. The United States, therefore, had few places to export its goods. Meanwhile, the individual American states began to levy their own tariffs to raise money. The result was that the states with the lowest tariffs received the most trade, which led to hostile competition between the various states within the Union. The federal government's attempt to pay off its debt by simply asking the states for help was not working and was in fact promoting further discord by leading them to compete with each other. With a single veto, both New York and Rhode Island rejected proposed revenue-raising tariffs. Change had to come.

At the urging of Virginia and Maryland, in 1786 (months before Shays' Rebellion), congressional representatives made plans to meet in Annapolis, Maryland, to discuss the problem of commerce. Only five states sent delegates, but several prominent figures were there, including James Madison, Alexander Hamilton, and George Washington. The convention's main success was in reaching a consensus to call a general meeting of delegates for the purpose of amending the Articles of Confederation. They agreed to meet again in May 1787, in Philadelphia.

 ### 7-4 THE CONSTITUTIONAL CONVENTION

Although it started as an effort to amend the Articles of Confederation, the meeting in Philadelphia rapidly became a Constitutional Convention, aimed at creating an entirely new government. There were substantial differences of opinion, however, and the Constitutional Convention debated these issues throughout the summer of 1787. The goings-on were kept secret, thus allowing each member to speak his mind without fear of political retribution. Only through participants' notes, most notably James Madison's, do we know what happened at the Convention.

>> Most delegates were young (average age: forty-two), wealthy, and wanted to strengthen the national government to protect trade and promote economic and social stability. Here is a latter-day reproduction of their deliberations.

THE VIRGINIA (LARGE STATES) PLAN

James Madison of Virginia was one of the most vocal at the Convention and, because it is from his notes that we know much of what we know about the Convention, he is also often deemed to be its star. A thirty-six-year-old Princeton graduate, Madison was well read in political science. He came to the Convention with an agenda, summarized as the Virginia Plan. The **Virginia Plan** sought to: (1) scrap the Articles of Confederation; (2) create a Congress with two houses, known as a bicameral legislature; (3) establish a federal judiciary; (4) establish a president who was elected by Congress; and (5) in general create a centralized system of government in which Congress had veto power over the actions of the states. Membership in Congress would be determined by population, which would clearly favor the large states.

THE NEW JERSEY (SMALL STATES) PLAN

For obvious reasons, smaller states objected to the Virginia Plan. Under the Articles of Confederation, all states had received an equal voice in Congress, regardless of size, and states could veto the actions of the federal government. To counter the Virginia Plan, New Jersey delegate William Paterson proposed an alternative—the **New Jersey Plan**—that called for revising the Articles of Confederation rather than replacing them altogether. Paterson's plan strengthened the federal government in many ways, but it proposed giving each state equal representation in a single, or unicameral, legislature, and ensured the federal government couldn't veto the actions of the state.

7-4c Drafting the Constitution

The Convention was deadlocked over apportionment of representatives until Roger Sherman of Connecticut came up with a compromise.

Virginia Plan This proposal, known as the large states plan because it favored those states, sought to scrap the Articles of Confederation and create a Congress with two houses, with representation in Congress being determined by population

New Jersey Plan This proposal suggested revising the Articles of Confederation rather than replacing them altogether

7-4a Membership

One matter on which there was complete agreement was that George Washington should be the president of the Convention. Washington's reputation and integrity protected the Convention from accusations it had usurped the authority of the Congress.

Along with Washington, fifty-four other delegates attended. Members had been elected by their state, and they were, for the most part, members of the social and educational elite. Most were young (average age: forty-two), wealthy, and wanted to strengthen the national government to protect trade and promote economic and social stability. They were leery of democracy, because, as Shays' Rebellion had just demonstrated, democracy could be messy. Most of the delegates were also lawyers (more than half were college graduates), which meant they would respect and honor the rule of law.

7-4b Preliminary Plans

There were several key divisions at the Convention (northern states versus southern, merchants versus farmers), but none was as important as that between the large states and the small ones. Two plans, prepared before the Convention even began, highlighted the differences between the two.

THE GREAT COMPROMISE

Sherman suggested granting each state equal representation in the upper house (to be called the Senate) and representation that was proportional to population (1 representative for every 30,000 people) in the lower house (the House of Representatives). This plan was ultimately approved (after Benjamin Franklin reproposed it and conceded to the larger states the power to have all funding bills originate in the lower house). Sherman's plan is called the **Great Compromise** because it broke a stalemate that could have been fatal to the development of a new federal constitution.

SLAVE STATE VERSUS FREE STATE

The large states versus small states debate was only one of the many divisions that bedeviled the Convention, and indeed, the Great Compromise had raised another problem. How do you count the population of each state? Should only voters count? Only taxpayers? Should women count? Although the conventioneers had ready answers for many of these questions, the issue became volatile when it touched on slavery.

In the early 1780s the Atlantic slave trade was at its height. But the spread of antislavery sentiment in the North seemed to threaten their labor supply. In addition, southerners feared that freed slaves would seek vengeance against their former masters. And so southern delegates wanted a constitutional guarantee that slavery would be legal in the new nation, and they needed political power to ensure that

> George Mason, a Virginia slaveholder himself, predicted that slavery would cause "the judgment of heaven" to fall upon the nation.

slavery would continue. Thus, in a stroke of historical irony, this demand meant that southerners wanted slaves to be included in the counting of their population, which would grant the South more representatives in the House. Northerners objected, arguing that, because slaves would not have an active political voice, their numbers should not be included.

Yet another compromise emerged, allowing southerners to include three-fifths of their slave population for both representation and the apportionment of federal taxes. This "**three-fifths clause**" demonstrated that, despite the new nation's stated commitment to freedom and equality, white Americans still treated African Americans as far less than equal—and that this perceived inequality would be enshrined in the American Constitution.

Delegates also had to forge a compromise regarding the slave trade. Some southerners threatened to secede if the slave trade was abolished, but many delegates (both northern and southern) considered the trade inhumane. George Mason, a Virginia slaveholder himself, even predicted that slavery would cause "the judgment of heaven" to fall upon the nation. But the majority of delegates felt the survival of the nation was at stake and agreed to yet another compromise. Ultimately, antislavery delegates agreed to permit the slave trade for twenty more years, until 1808. In exchange, proslavery delegates granted Congress the authority to regulate commerce with a simple majority (rather than the two-thirds vote desired by most southerners).

EAST VERSUS WEST

The final compromise of the Convention was made between eastern and western states. Easterners were afraid that western expansion would allow the government to be controlled by agricultural interests rather than commercial ones. To compromise, the Convention granted Congress (and not the president) the power to admit new states to the nation, which meant that the eastern states that were already a part

Great Compromise Plan to grant each state equal representation in the upper house (to be called the Senate) and representation that was proportional to population (1 representative for every 30,000 people) in the lower house (the House of Representatives)

three-fifths clause Section of the Constitution that allowed southerners to include three-fifths of their slave population for both representation and the apportionment of federal taxes

>> James Madison of Virginia.

iStock.com/Wynnter

of the nation would have the power to regulate the number of new (western) states that could enter.

 ## THE CONSTITUTION

Once these compromises were agreed upon (after the Convention had gone on for four hot summer months), the Convention established the structure of the new government in a constitution. The U.S. Constitution developed mostly out of the Virginia Plan, although considerable concessions were made to small states, southern states, and eastern states. Indeed, James Madison was furious the federal government wasn't as strong as he'd hoped. In the end, the Convention created a government of three branches—executive, legislative, and judicial—granting unique powers to each branch.

7-5a The Powers Given to Congress

The Convention allocated several specific powers to Congress. The Convention's intention was to make Congress the most powerful branch, allowing it to do five vital things: (1) collect taxes and raise revenue; (2) regulate commerce, both foreign and domestic (except on the issue of slavery, where compromise meant that it could not touch the issue until 1808); (3) declare war; (4) maintain an army; and (5) make any changes "necessary and proper" to pursue these powers, and, it added, "all other Powers vested by this Constitution in the Government of the United States." By controlling the government's purse strings and by demanding that all laws originate in Congress, the Constitutional Convention wanted to ensure no single authority would possess too much power. This was a testament to the republican ideology of the war, although somewhat tempered by the compromises made at the Convention.

7-5b The Executive Branch

The Convention also created an executive branch, consisting of a president and his cabinet.

HOW ELECTED

Because of their experience with King George III, most Americans initially favored keeping power in the hands of elected legislators. Yet, after the failure of the Articles of Confederation, those at the Constitutional Convention realized that this system did not work. As an alternative, the Virginia Plan proposed having Congress elect the president. Another plan would have the president serve a life term. A third plan would have three presidents serving simultaneously. Finally, Gouverneur Morris, an influential delegate from Pennsylvania, insisted that the executive should not depend on Congress for his office. Instead, Morris proposed having him elected directly by the people to two terms of substantial length.

Although this plan had its merits, the framers of the Constitution remained fearful of true democracy. They remembered Shays' Rebellion. So in the Constitution they created an **Electoral College** that was composed of delegates from each state equal in number to its total apportionment in Congress (number of senators plus number of representatives). The college was designed to ensure that only qualified candidates, not populist hooligans, got elected. Originally, each delegate in the Electoral College was to vote for two people. The person who received the most votes would be president; the one with the second most votes would be vice president. Anticipating that several people would run for president (and not anticipating the two-party system), the House of Representatives would decide the president if no one received a majority of the votes.

POWERS

The Constitution also gave the president the power to do five important things (although perhaps not as important as the powers granted to the legislature): (1) make treaties, but only if two-thirds of the Senate approved them; (2) oversee the army and navy as commander-in-chief; (3) name diplomats with the consent of the Senate; and, most important, (4) execute the laws passed in Congress and (5) veto acts of Congress that he did not feel were constitutional (or, as it was understood after Andrew Jackson, in the country's best interests). The president was to be powerful, and also somewhat deferential to Congress.

7-5c The Judicial Branch

The Constitution also provided for a federal system of courts, headed by a Supreme Court and several regional courts. The president was to name the judges to the courts to serve lifetime appointments. The judges had jurisdiction over constitutional questions, cases in which the United States itself was a party, and

Electoral College Group composed of delegates from each state equal in number to its total apportionment in Congress (number of senators plus number of representatives); these delegates cast votes for president

cases between two or more states or between the citizens of two or more states. The framers also included a "supreme law of the land clause" (or Supremacy Clause), which made the Constitution supreme over state laws in all legal matters.

7-5d Federal and State Powers

Conscious of the necessary balance between state and federal powers, the framers of the Constitution forbade states from making their own money, levying customs, or infringing on the obligation of contracts (all things that the states had done during the era of the Articles of Confederation). Other than that, states maintained significant power. By design, if a power was not specifically given to the federal government, the states controlled it.

7-5e Relationship of the Government and the Governed

There were other transitions as well. Under the Articles, the central government was not permitted to reach the individual—that was the sovereign right of the states. But under the new Constitution, the federal government could rule individuals directly. Perhaps the most significant change in this regard was granting the federal government the power of taxation. The revolutionary commitment to representation was not abandoned, however, as the legislative branch of government, which represented the people most directly, held the exclusive right to tax.

7-6 THE RATIFICATION DEBATE

In September 1787, the framers of the Constitution presented their work to the states for ratification. The Constitution needed the states' approval to become the law of the land. Otherwise, the Articles of Confederation would still rule. The conventioneers urged each state to hold a special convention to discuss ratifying the new document, and they voted that approval by nine states was enough for the Constitution to take effect—deliberately avoiding the need for unanimity.

7-6a A Slow Start

A few states ratified the Constitution almost immediately: smaller states, such as Delaware, Connecticut, and New Jersey, supported the Constitution because it promised to strengthen their position in conflicts with their larger, more populous neighbors. The Great Compromise had secured their votes. Georgia ratified quickly as well because it felt threatened by Indian conflicts and the Spanish presence in Florida. The people of Georgia needed protection. But the only large state to ratify the Constitution before the end of winter 1788 was Pennsylvania. In the other states with a large population—particularly New York, Massachusetts, and Virginia—concerns about the loss of sovereignty generated opposition. Citizens in those states wanted to ensure they kept the rights they felt they had won during the Revolution.

Library of Congress Prints and Photographs Division

>> This cartoon from the 1787 ratification debate shows Connecticut as the wagon, buried under debt and sinking into the mud of the hapless Articles of Confederation. The Federalists are pulling the wagon into sunshine (it is a Federalist cartoon). Connecticut became the fifth state to approve the U.S. Constitution.

7-6b The Federalists

Factions speedily formed. It was never a foregone conclusion that the Constitution would be passed, especially after reflecting that the Revolution had been fought to get rid of an overarching government. In an effort to undercut opposition, supporters of the Constitution took the name **Federalists** and began openly campaigning for the Constitution's ratification. The Federalists, mostly composed of young men whose careers had been made by the Revolution and who generally favored a larger commercial platform, emphasized that the new government would not end state autonomy. They also contemplated a bill of rights that would prevent the new centralized government from infringing on what were considered natural rights.

To influence the debate in the key state of New York, in 1787 the Federalists John Jay and Alexander Hamilton wrote a series of essays that came to be called the **Federalist Papers**. The essays appeared in pamphlets and were condensed in newspapers. Soon James Madison of Virginia added his own essays to the series. The Federalist Papers were to become a tool in the ratification debate, as well as America's most significant contribution to political theory. They defended the Constitution article by article, demonstrated to Americans how the Constitution would work, and addressed many of the complaints of opponents, such as the concerns about the size of the new nation. The papers were a tool of ideological warfare in the name of the new Constitution. And the Federalist Papers weren't alone. Indeed, they are simply the most famous (and perhaps not even the most influential at the time) in a river of polemical literature arguing about ratification.

The Federalists' choice of a name was meaningful too. Supporters of the Constitution emphasized that the new government was designed around the principle of **federalism**, which is the philosophy of government in which states and nation share the responsibility of government, with no one group or agency possessing sufficient power to dominate the other. This was an attempt to assuage notions that the new government would slide into tyranny.

7-6c The Anti-Federalists

The name *Federalists* impelled opponents to take the name *Anti-Federalists*. The **Anti-Federalists**, who came from a variety of factions and included many prominent patriots, including Patrick Henry, John Hancock, and Samuel Adams, preferred a weaker confederation of states and a more direct democracy. They sought to protect the "spirit of '76," the language they used to make sure democracy was preserved despite the obvious need to govern. In fact, Anti-Federalists did not really oppose federalism, but they did object to the concentration of power in a centralized government regardless of how it divided power. They believed that centralized governments threatened the sovereignty of the states and the liberties of individuals. At the very least, the Anti-Federalists wanted an explicit bill of rights to safeguard those liberties. Because of their steadfast defense of individual rights, historians often view the Anti-Federalists as idealistic patriots concerned about how much liberty they would have to sacrifice in order to earn federal security. The Federalists, on the other hand, are seen as those more comfortable with a stronger national government, with more to gain by having a stronger, overarching government and more to lose by the occasional violent flourishings of true democracy.

7-6d The Debate

The Federalists attempted to address the concerns of their opponents by arguing that the rights of the states and of individuals were adequately protected by state bills of rights. However, the Anti-Federalists maintained that, if the Constitution were the supreme law of the land, its provisions would have preeminence over any state legislation. Thus, Anti-Federalists—especially those from the powerful states of New York and Virginia—insisted on the addition of a federal Bill of Rights before they would consent to ratification. The Federalists, on the other hand, resisted any amendments because they knew the addition of new sections to the Constitution meant the entire process of ratification would have to start over.

Compromise ultimately broke the deadlock. In Massachusetts, the Anti-Federalist leader, John Hancock, changed his position after Federalists promised him that

Federalists Framers of the Constitution who emphasized that the new government would not end state autonomy; they also contemplated a Bill of Rights that would prevent the new centralized government from infringing on what were thought of as natural rights

Federalist Papers Essays written by John Jay, Alexander Hamilton, and James Madison in 1787, meant to influence the Constitution ratification debate in New York State; the essays defended the Constitution article by article and addressed many of the complaints of opponents, such as the concerns about the size of the new nation

federalism Philosophy of government in which states and the nation share the responsibility of government, with no one group or agency possessing sufficient power to dominate the other

Anti-Federalists A group of American patriots who preferred a weaker confederation of states and a more direct democracy; they objected to the concentration of power in a centralized government regardless of how it divided power

Table 7.1 Ratification of the Constitution

Date	State	Votes Yes	Votes No
December 7, 1787	Delaware	30	0
December 12, 1787	Pennsylvania	46	23
December 18, 1787	New Jersey	38	0
January 2, 1788	Georgia	26	0
January 9, 1788	Connecticut	128	40
February 6, 1788	Massachusetts	187	168
April 28, 1788	Maryland	63	11
May 23, 1788	South Carolina	149	73
June 21, 1788	New Hampshire	57	47
June 25, 1788	Virginia	89	79
July 26, 1788	New York	30	27
November 21, 1789	North Carolina	194	77
May 29, 1790	Rhode Island	34	32

the insertion of a Bill of Rights in the Constitution would be the first order of business for the new government. Such conditional ratification provided New York and Virginia with an acceptable formula for their own voting; they shortly consented to the new Constitution, although the voting remained incredibly close. Virginia passed the Constitution by a vote of 89 to 79. New York's vote in favor was 30 to 27 (see Table 7.1).

The compromise came just in time. In June 1788, New Hampshire voted to ratify the Constitution, becoming the critical ninth state and putting the Constitution into functional operation. But it was crucial for the new government to have the support of the larger states of Massachusetts, New York, and Virginia if it was going to succeed. With these larger states now supporting the document, by the end of 1788, twelve states had accepted the Constitution (Rhode Island finally ratified the Constitution in 1790). The new United States government was launched (see "The Reasons Why..." box).

7-6e The Bill of Rights

Massachusetts, Virginia, and New York had all agreed to ratify the Constitution only if Congress hastened to the task of drafting a Bill of Rights that would protect individual freedoms from the threat of a potentially tyrannous federal government. It began the task of crafting these rights even before the Constitution was fully ratified. Congress pondered a dizzying number of protections, many of which were borrowed from the various state constitutions. In the end, twelve were proposed, and ten passed.

The first two amendments, which specified the number of constituents of each representative and compensation for congressmen, respectively, did not pass. The remaining ten became the Bill of Rights.

We can see in each amendment a specific grievance that emerged during the "long train of abuses" that led to the Revolution, including the fear of an established church, abridgements to free speech and peaceful gatherings, attempts to disarm the people, the quartering of soldiers in private homes, the forcible removal of private property, unreasonable searches by the federal government,

>> Each of the initial ten amendments addressed specific grievances the colonists had with the British. Courts have constantly adapted their meanings over the course of the life of the nation.

MPI/Archive Photos/Getty Images

·The Reasons Why...

There were at least four reasons why the states ratified the Constitution:

Small states got apportionment. Several small states, such as Delaware, Connecticut, and New Jersey, supported the new Constitution immediately, mainly because the Constitution strengthened their position relative to the larger, more populous states. The Great Compromise had secured their votes.

Georgia needed protection. Georgia supported the Constitution quickly too, mainly because it needed protection from the Spanish in Florida and the Indians to its south and west.

Rivers of polemical literature like the Federalist Papers. The Federalist Papers, drafted by John Jay, Alexander Hamilton, and James Madison during the ratification debate in New York, argued that the new Constitution would not abridge the "natural rights" that were fought for and thought to be secured by the American Revolution. More than just a series of polemical pamphlets, the Federalist Papers addressed many of the most important questions in political theory at the time, including how much liberty should be sacrificed for the protection of a governing state, how the rights of minority groups could be protected in a democracy, how the Constitution could prevent one of the three governing powers from growing too strong, and how a nation could expand its borders without sacrificing the liberty of those already members. The Federalist Papers are perhaps the most important contributions in political theory ever to emerge from the United States. But the Federalist Papers were hardly alone, and were in fact just one small part of a flowing polemical literature at the time.

The promise of a Bill of Rights. And fourth, impelled by the writers who came to be known as the "Anti-Federalists," who were afraid the Constitution would make the national government too strong, the framers agreed to attach a Bill of Rights to the Constitution, which ensured that some of the liberties deemed sacred would be protected in the Constitution. By agreeing that the new government's first order of business would be to draft a Bill of Rights, the framers of the Constitution won the support of the three most important states at the time: Massachusetts, New York, and Virginia. The state legislatures in each of these three states, however, still endured incredibly close votes.

iStockphoto.com/Bonniej

>> The Constitution.

the denial of a trial by one's peers, and the suspension of protections under the law. The First Amendment's prohibition against establishing a national religion was especially important because of the sectarian battles happening between the various Protestant denominations. The Congregationalists in New England were afraid the Anglicans in the South might win federal power, while the Anglicans were equally afraid of the Congregationalists. The Baptists, meanwhile, were bitter that some states maintained control over certifying who could become a minister, making them fearful that one day they might be barred from practicing their faith. The First Amendment ended many of these debates and assuaged most of these fears, at least at the federal level.

The Bill of Rights was to defend against the kind of tyranny that the revolutionaries had encountered in the run-up to the Revolutionary War. Indeed, the final amendment making up the Bill of Rights pronounced that any power not delegated to the federal government by the Constitution was reserved for the states, thus ensuring a balance of power between the new government and the state governments.

>LOOKING AHEAD...

The Constitution has survived, relatively unchanged, as the basis of the United States's republican government for more than two hundred years. The first ten amendments—the Bill of Rights promised by the Federalists—were added in 1791. Since then, only seventeen more amendments have become law. Some of the fundamental debates, including the question of the balance of power between the states and the federal government, continue today. Interpretations of the framers' intentions have changed over time, but the American frame of government created in 1787 has demonstrated impressive flexibility and longevity.

More than just a political document, the Constitution also sparked essential debates that would continue to preoccupy the American nation. What would be the role of African Americans? Was America a nation only for white people? And what about women as citizens? Was there any justification for

their exclusion from voting? And what would be the nature of the relationship between the Americans and the Indians, both of whom had good reasons to think of the land as theirs? Who would decide? The Constitution took a stand on many of these issues, coming out in ways that make it look anything but democratic. Slaves were to be counted as merely three-fifths of a person (and only so that their owners could possess more power in Congress), women were not explicitly granted the right to vote, and Indians were not made citizens.

Through amendment and custom, though, the American nation would slowly achieve greater democracy. The initial steps were taken in the first years of the new nation, a period that historians today call the Federalist era.

STUDY TOOLS 7

READY TO STUDY? IN THE BOOK, YOU CAN:

❑ Rip out the Chapter Review Card, which includes key terms and chapter summaries.

ONLINE AT WWW.CENGAGEBRAIN.COM, YOU CAN:

❑ Collect StudyBits while you read and study the chapter.

❑ Quiz yourself on key concepts.

❑ Find videos for further exploration.

❑ Prepare for tests with HIST5 Flash Cards as well as those you create.

❑ Read the Articles of Confederation.

❑ Read the Northwest Ordinance.

❑ Learn more about the Constitutional Convention and read Madison's original notes.

❑ Read the U.S. Constitution.

❑ Read the Federalist Papers.

❑ Read the Bill of Rights.

▶ **1777–1781** States ratify Articles of Confederation.

▶ **1783** Continental Congress demobilizes Continental Army.

▶ **1784** Virginia cedes western land claims to federal government.

1785: *Frenchman J. P. Blanchard is said to be the first to actually use a parachute by dropping a dog in a basket, to which the parachute was attached, from a hot-air balloon. The dog survived, but fourteen years later, Blanchard suffered a heart attack, fell from one of his own balloons, and died of his injuries.*

▶ **1786** In vain, Massachusetts farmers petition for debt relief.

1787: *Northwest Ordinance creates territorial governments, orders western development.*

January 26: *In Shays' Rebellion, Massachusetts farmers try to seize federal armory.*

May: *State delegate meeting in Philadelphia turns into Constitutional Convention.*

September: *Delegates present new Constitution to states for ratification.*

December: *Delaware, Pennsylvania, New Jersey ratify Constitution.*

Mozart composes his opera Don Giovanni.

1788 June: *New Hampshire becomes ninth state to ratify Constitution.*

Australia is first settled by Europeans as a penal colony.

1789 September: *Congress sends Bill of Rights to states for ratification.*

Mutiny takes place on H.M.S. Bounty.

▶ **1790** **May:** Rhode Island is last state to ratify Constitution.

▶ **1791** **December:** Bill of Rights goes into effect.

1793: *Reign of Terror begins in France, as rival revolutionary factions battle over the proper ways in which "liberty, equality, and fraternity" can be implemented in a modern nation-state. Between 15,000 and 40,000 French lose their lives during the fourteen-month Terror, many by the blade of the guillotine, which earns the nickname "National Razor."*

8 | Securing the New Nation, 1789–1800

LEARNING OBJECTIVES

After reading this chapter, you should be able to do the following:

8-1 Describe the creation of the federal government under the new Constitution.

8-2 Show how disagreements over how the United States should be governed led to political divisions, and discuss some of the individuals who took strong stands on each side.

8-3 Outline the country's development of a two-party political system.

8-4 Discuss the issues of John Adams's presidency, and explain how he and the country dealt with them.

8-5 Explain the convoluted political process that made Thomas Jefferson president in 1800.

AFTER FINISHING
THIS CHAPTER
GO TO **PAGE 158**
FOR STUDY TOOLS

Although the war had been won and the Constitution ratified, the debate about the size, shape, and duties of the federal government continued. A blueprint, after all, is not a building. Some, like New York's Alexander Hamilton, were worried that common people could not handle democracy and would be confused by the challenges of running a nation. Others, like Thomas Jefferson, were concerned that a powerful centralized federal government would take away coveted liberties and the sovereignty of the states.

The stakes were high, as the unformed nation struggled to establish itself on the periphery of the European economic system. Daily life went on, of course: people went to school, got married, had families, bought slaves, moved west, and built new homes. But they did so during a time of heightened worries about the political stability of their new nation. Was American independence going to be temporary? Could the country's leaders pull the nation together? Politics of the 1790s was fraught with questions, anxiety, and passion. It led to disagreements, and even duels.

In the end, the political center held, but not in a way that anyone had predicted. Nearly all the founders disliked political partisanship, yet they helped usher in the two-party system that we know today. They also preached the virtues of liberty and equality but went to great extremes to safeguard both the practice of slavery and the continued seizure of Native American lands. Thomas Jefferson advocated a rural, agrarian republic, yet the stability enjoyed and the land acquired during his presidency helped foster an economic revolution. But, first, to the decade following the ratification of the Constitution, when the central role of the federal government was to secure the new nation. This chapter examines the development of the new government, the rise of the two-party political system, and the first peaceful turnover of power in the "bloodless revolution" of 1800.

> From 1789 to 1800 the federal government was remarkably small.

8-1 CREATING A NEW GOVERNMENT

From 1789 to 1800 the federal government was remarkably small. In 1800, the Department of State had only three employees, plus representatives in London, Paris, Madrid, Lisbon, and The Hague. The entire Treasury had a total of about seventy-five employees. The War Department consisted of the secretary of war, two clerks, and a messenger. The Post Office numbered seventy-five offices. The legislative branch had only twenty-six senators and sixty-four representatives. For a nation suspicious of centralized power, a small federal government was appropriate.

As the new government began operations in 1789, it became clear that, although the Constitution outlined a framework of government, the exact roles of its three branches were not clearly defined. Establishing precedents would be the mission of the first group of federal politicians.

8-1a The First Citizens

According to Article 4, Section 2 of the Constitution, the states dictated who was and was not a citizen. More or less, they all confined citizenship to white, property-holding males, although there were a few exceptions to this generalization. Immigrants could become citizens as well, and in the **Naturalization Act of 1790**, Congress declared that, among immigrants, only "free white persons" could become citizens of the United States. This obviously limited black people, Native Americans, and Asians. (These restrictions continued

> **Naturalization Act of 1790** Legislation which declared that, among immigrants to the United States, only "free white persons" could become citizens

◄◄◄ **The view from the U.S. Capitol down Pennsylvania Avenue in 1800. Reflecting the fear of having too strong of a federal government, Washington, D.C. remained a small town for much of the first half of the nineteenth century.**

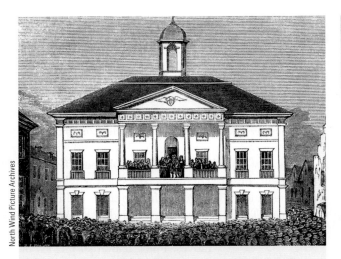

>> Federal Hall in New York City, the first capitol building of the United States, on the day of George Washington's inauguration as first president.

for almost a century, until 1870, when African Americans were allowed to become citizens.) White women also had few property rights, and, once she was married, anything a woman owned became the property of her husband. It was not until 1920 that women were granted the federal right to vote.

8-1b The First Congress

The first federal election under the new Constitution was held late in 1788. Most of the men elected were sympathetic to the arguments laid out in the Federalist Papers. At its first meeting in the capital city of New York, the first Congress had four major tasks: (1) setting up a system of federal courts; (2) securing the Bill of Rights that had been promised during the ratification period; (3) establishing the executive department; and (4) raising revenue. By addressing these pressing issues in a relatively tidy manner, the first Congress demonstrated its strength compared to the Continental Congress under the Articles of Confederation. The new government seemed to be working.

patronage System of granting rewards for assisting with political victories

Hamilton Tariff of 1789 Act that imposed a 5 to 10 percent tariff on certain imports to fund the new government

COURTS

The Judiciary Act of 1789 created three circuit courts and thirteen district courts to accompany the Supreme Court established by the Constitution.

THE BILL OF RIGHTS

James Madison proposed to Congress seventeen amendments to the Constitution, twelve of which Congress approved and ten of which the states later ratified. These ten amendments are known as the Bill of Rights.

EXECUTIVE DEPARTMENT

Congress created five executive posts: (1) the secretary of state, (2) the secretary of war, (3) the secretary of the Treasury, (4) the attorney general, and (5) the postmaster general. These positions were to be filled by the president, meaning the president would control **patronage**, defined as the granting of rewards for assisting with political victories (although, in these early years, these jobs were not viewed as lucrative because the federal government was so small). Under President George Washington, these positions (except that of postmaster general) would serve as his cabinet of advisors.

REVENUES

James Madison, who had played an important role at the Constitutional Convention, was elected to the House of Representatives from Virginia. In 1789, he persuaded Congress to pass the **Hamilton Tariff of 1789**, which imposed a 5 to 10 percent tariff on certain imports. By coming up with a safe, nationwide way to generate revenue, the act's success freed the federal government from constant worry about economic shortfalls.

8-1c The First President

The least surprising outcome of the nation's first election was the installation of George Washington as president. His stature as an honest war leader made him the obvious choice to lead the new government. He never ran for the office, and indeed, had retired from public life altogether before he was elected. Washington had to be talked into coming back to serve his country once again.

As he formulated his approach to the office, Washington was aware that he had no contemporary role models; the American republic was truly an experiment. "I walk on untrodden ground," he said. "There is scarcely any part of my conduct which may not hereafter

>> Washington in retirement at Mount Vernon after the war. He would have to be persuaded to reenter public life and become the new nation's first president.

be drawn in precedent." He was right. Washington established several important precedents while in office. Three of the most significant concerned the presidential manner, the cabinet, and relations with Congress.

THE PRESIDENTIAL MANNER

Washington displayed a dignified and formal manner as president, but it certainly wasn't royal. In the debate about how people should address him, Washington remained quiet. Federalists proposed calling him "His Excellency" or "His Highness," but Anti-Federalists rebuffed the proposal, favoring a less lofty title. Without any insistence from Washington himself, he came to be called simply "Mr. President." This endowed him with importance, but not regal entitlement. Washington also dressed formally (never in military attire, always in American-made suits), conducted affairs in a formal manner, and decided not to use his veto power unless he deemed a law unconstitutional. He wanted people to take the office of president seriously, but without encouraging the office to usurp the will of the people as expressed by Congress.

It was not until 1920 that women were granted the federal right to vote.

THE CABINET

Washington's second important precedent concerned his cabinet. Congress voted to create several departments within the executive branch, but the Constitution did not explicitly outline the responsibilities of these departments (which were collectively known as the president's "**cabinet**"). With the cabinet's role open to interpretation, Washington assembled this group with an eye toward gathering differing viewpoints. He hoped that including a range of opinions within the government would keep leaders working together in the nation's interests rather than fighting among themselves for power.

Washington appointed Thomas Jefferson the first secretary of state. In addition to heading American diplomatic relations, Jefferson's office was in charge of the census, patents and copyrights, public lands, and the mint. Washington's Treasury secretary was Alexander Hamilton, a close friend who had served as his aide-de-camp during the Revolution. Henry Knox was secretary of war, as he had been under the Continental Congress during the 1780s. Knox commanded an army of 5,000 men, most of whom were deployed for defense against Native Americans in the western territories. Samuel Osgood was the postmaster general, in charge of mail delivery. Edmund Randolph was the attorney general, who met with the cabinet as Washington's personal advisor.

Reflecting the balance of perspectives that Washington sought, Hamilton and Knox favored a strong centralized government, whereas Jefferson and Randolph favored greater power at the state level. Jefferson and Randolph were from Virginia, Hamilton from New York, Knox and Osgood from New England. When Washington began consulting them on official matters (or, more commonly, asking Randolph to solicit their opinions), the cabinet system was born.

cabinet Group of the heads of departments within the executive branch; one of George Washington's innovations as president

>> General George Washington, lionized war hero and president.

RELATIONS WITH CONGRESS

The Constitution required that the executive branch draft treaties with the "advice and consent" of the Senate, but the first time Washington endeavored to make a treaty, the resulting bickering with Congress led to an inconclusive treaty. From then on, Washington decided to negotiate treaties first and then submit them to Congress for approval. This established a precedent. Washington also took seriously his role of informing Congress of the state of the union once a year, thus demonstrating his attentiveness to the will of the people.

8-2 POLITICAL DIVISIONS

During its first decade, this small government had serious problems to confront, and the confrontations sparked factionalism. Whose side you chose in the debate depended on your vision for the nation. Some, like Washington, Hamilton, and Adams (who, as a political group, would come to be called the Federalists), wanted a strong federal government that would assist merchants and industry in order to create a buoyant, market-based nation. Alexander Hamilton was the true visionary of the bunch. Born out of wedlock on a Caribbean island, the ambitious Hamilton was determined to utilize what he saw as the bustling spirit of Americans in order to create a first-class capitalist nation that was important to the world's economy. He wanted an assertive government that encouraged economic investment and entrepreneurship. He wanted all the states to buy into this vision, and he proposed a series of creative and far-sighted economic measures that would transform the United States from an economic outpost to a true international powerhouse. Many of his proposals appeared in his famous "Report on Manufactures," a plan that would eventually become government policy.

Others, like Jefferson and Madison (who would come to be called the Democratic-Republicans), preferred a weaker federal government that would allow the preservation of "natural rights" and of slavery. Often, but not always, the Democratic-Republicans were Anti-Federalists in the debate about the Constitution. The most brilliant of this lot was Thomas Jefferson, the author of the Declaration of Independence. Jefferson came from Virginia and was an agrarian aristocrat. He sought a decentralized government made up of small farmers. He feared that the expansion of commerce and industry via Hamilton's plan would create a class of wage workers who were dependent on others for their income and thus unable to participate in democratic political processes.

Although no party set out to create calcified political divisions, that would be the end result. Two issues illustrated these competing visions of the nation: (1) problems over government finance and (2) foreign policy. Together, they would help form the nation's first two-party system.

8-2a The Problem of Finance

During the Revolutionary War, the Continental Congress had taken out loans to fund the war. Foreign investors held $12 million worth of notes; domestic bondholders were owed $48 million. To establish good credit and to maintain authority over the states, the federal government had to pay off the loans.

HAMILTON'S FINANCIAL PLAN

Hamilton, in an effort to promote economic policies aligned with his vision for a strong, centralized government, proposed an economic plan to remedy the problem, one that quite naturally favored the interests of the commercial and mercantile elite. His plan had four key components: (1) consolidating the loans that Congress

The Reasons Why...

The Democratic-Republicans had three problems with Hamilton's plan:

Speculators would benefit. The Democratic-Republicans thought that honoring all debts was unfair because many of the Americans who had purchased bonds to fund the Revolutionary War—often widows and soldiers—had been forced to sell their bonds for less than their face value during the hard economic times of the 1780s. Commercial speculators bought the bonds from them at low prices, and Hamilton's plan would reward these speculators unfairly.

Some had already paid off their debts. They also believed that nationalizing state debts was unfair because some states (especially southern states like Jefferson's Virginia) had already made headway in paying off their debts by selling western lands. If the debts of all states were pooled together, the residents of the states that had already reduced their debts would have to pay a disproportionate share of the national debt.

A fear that financiers were given preferential treatment. Creating a bank was contentious because many Americans—particularly southerners—argued that the creation of a national bank would serve the interests of only financiers and merchants. They believed it would offer little aid to farmers and plantation owners. The Democratic-Republicans considered these groups the most virtuous citizens of an agrarian republic. Arguing that the creation of a bank was not within the purview of the federal government, the opponents of Hamilton's plan favored a more literal interpretation of the Constitution—a position called **strict constructionism.**

---

took out during the Revolutionary War into one national debt, which would importantly commit the wealthy people who were owed money to the success of the federal government; (2) consolidating the individual states' loans into the national debt; (3) raising revenue through the sale of bonds, the sale of public lands, the establishment of tariffs, and the imposition of an excise tax on whiskey; and (4) creating the First Bank of the United States, which would hold the government's revenue and issue bank notes (paper money) that would be legal tender throughout the country.

The bank was the linchpin of the plan. It would benefit the business classes, who could capitalize on the stability provided by a bank. It would organize the loans and the debt as well. But it would also expand the power of Congress and, therefore, of the federal government. A national bank was not mentioned in the Constitution, but the Constitution did grant Congress the power to do anything "necessary and proper" to carry out its delegated powers. If Congress could successfully charter a bank (which it did in 1791), it would assume a vast amount of **implied powers** through a loose interpretation of the words in the Constitution—a position called **loose constructionism.** This would in turn make the federal government much more powerful. Some of the founders had envisioned this all along, while others had not, thus making the "original intent" of the founders difficult if not impossible to decipher.

OPPOSITION TO HAMILTON'S PLAN

Thomas Jefferson and James Madison led the faction that immediately opposed Hamilton's policies. Because Jefferson was a towering figure in the new government, this faction came to be called the Jeffersonians, although they preferred to be called the **Democratic-Republicans**. The Democratic-Republicans had three problems with Hamilton's plan (see "The Reasons Why . . ." box).

implied powers Congress's power to do anything "necessary and proper" to carry out its delegated powers, even if those actions are not explicitly named in the Constitution

loose constructionism Interpretation of the Constitution suggesting that the Constitution should be flexible to accommodate new demands

Democratic-Republicans Faction that coalesced in opposition to Alexander Hamilton's economic policies and Jay's Treaty; led by Virginians like Thomas Jefferson and James Madison; also known as the Jeffersonians

strict constructionism Literal interpretation of the Constitution, arguing that the original meaning of those at the Constitutional Convention should not be adapted to fit more recent times

>> This fresco, appearing in the US Capitol Building in Washington, D.C., shows Alexander Hamilton and Thomas Jefferson vying for President George Washington's attention.

Jefferson, Madison, and their supporters envisioned an agrarian nation made up of independent farmers, not laborers and industrialists dependent on others. Their plan for an agrarian nation, of course, also allowed for, indeed depended on, the perpetuation of slavery. (Hamilton, meanwhile, ardently opposed slavery, believing that it denied individual liberty and favored the established aristocracy of the South over the merchants of the North.)

CONGRESSIONAL IMPASSE AND WASHINGTON, D.C.

The deadlock over Hamilton's plan was ultimately broken by a compromise on an entirely separate issue: the location of the national government. Between 1789 and 1793, the federal government of the United States was in New York City. In 1793, the government moved south to Philadelphia, but southern leaders wanted the government to be located even farther south, in Virginia. They also wanted it to be located *outside* a big city, because many of Jefferson's supporters considered big cities sinkholes of corruption.

Over dinner and wine one night, Jefferson and Hamilton struck a deal: Hamilton would instruct supporters of his economic plan to favor relocating the seat of government along the Potomac River, and Jefferson would allow Hamilton's plan to pass through Congress. With this compromise, Hamilton's economic legislation passed, the First Bank of the United States was created (it lasted until 1811), and the stage was set for the national government to move to Washington, D.C. It was a true victory for Hamilton, as his economic plan would transform the nation and little would come from the fact that the capital city was located further south.

THE WHISKEY REBELLION

Opposition to Hamilton's economic policies was not limited to Democratic-Republicans in the government. In western Pennsylvania, Hamilton's decision to tax whiskey

>> George Washington sent a newly organized army of almost 13,000 to quell the Whiskey Rebellion. Here, a man is tarred-and-feathered for his attempts to collect the Whiskey tax before Washington's troops restored order.

proved divisive. Before railroads or canals were built, western farmers depended on slow, halting, horse-based transport and had difficulty transporting their crops without spoilage. They found it easier to distill their grain to whiskey and ship it in that form. A tax on whiskey was thus a serious threat to their livelihood. To make matters worse, Hamilton's plan taxed small producers of whiskey more than it did large producers, in part because the tax was an effort to demonstrate to small farmers and westerners the government's authority to tax them. This gave rise to accusations of East Coast elitism.

In 1794, many westerners attacked the tax men who tried to collect the whiskey tax. When Washington and Hamilton attempted to bring some of the rebels to justice, they chose whiskey producers in western Pennsylvania as their test case. The rural Pennsylvanians fought back, eventually rioting and overrunning the city of Pittsburgh, where they were to be tried for tax evasion. This was the **Whiskey Rebellion**. Alarmed by the direct refusal to adhere to the dictates of the federal government, George Washington issued a proclamation declaring the farmers in rebellion and sent a newly organized army of nearly 13,000 to quell the revolt. Washington himself at times led the troops. But by the time the army reached western Pennsylvania, the rebels had gone home. Washington ultimately pardoned the two men who were captured in the dispute.

There were two main results of the Whiskey Rebellion. First, from this time forward, the western provinces were firmly Anti-Federalist, favoring the small-government approach of the Democratic-Republicans. Hamilton's economic plans had indeed exacerbated sectional differences between those who most obviously benefited from them (East Coast elites, bankers, and educated businessmen) and those who did not (southern and western farmers). But second, Washington's message was clear: the national government would not allow extralegal protests to effect change. In a nation of laws, change would come only through peaceful means.

8-2b The Problem of Foreign Policy

Through the 1790s, there were still no formal political parties, but clear divisions were apparent. Both politicians and everyday Americans had to determine what kind of nation they wanted. In the Whiskey Rebellion, the Pennsylvania farmers sought to defend their idea that the federal government should not reach too deeply into the pockets of everyday Americans. They lost that particular battle, but the sympathy they aroused from the future Democratic-Republicans showed their complaints did not go unheard.

As a new nation, the United States also had to travel the often-treacherous terrain of foreign policy. And here too, almost every decision made by the federal government was liable to be framed in divisive language. Would the nation support other Enlightenment-based revolutions, like the one taking place in France? Would it challenge Britain when it infringed on American liberties in the seas? Plus, there were still divisions in the West, with the Spanish still in control of the Mississippi River and Florida, the British still possessing forts in the western hinterlands and Canada, and Indians still living on and claiming lands throughout the vast terrain. The answers to these questions only increased political divisions.

THE FRENCH REVOLUTION AND THE CITIZEN GENÊT AFFAIR

One of the first flash points occurred in France. In 1789, growing discontent with the French king spurred the

Whiskey Rebellion Conflict in which Pennsylvania farmers fought a tax on whiskey, eventually rioting and overrunning the city of Pittsburgh in 1794, where they were to be tried for tax evasion

>> The bank was the linchpin of Hamilton's plan to strengthen the federal government. Pictured here is the U.S. Treasury building.

iStock.com/RobertDodge

Table 8.1 The Differences Between Jefferson and Hamilton

	Jefferson	Hamilton
Party	Democratic-Republican	Federalist
National vision	An agrarian republic of independent farmers	A capitalist, industrial power
Federal government	Small, subservient to states	Strong and centralized
Labor	Free and enslaved	Free
National bank	Against	For
Constitution	Strict interpretation	Loose interpretation

French people to overthrow their monarchy, inciting the French Revolution. Most Americans were initially pleased with the news, thinking they themselves had been on the front line of an inevitable transition toward republican governments around the world. But by the early 1790s, the news from France grew worse: the country had erupted into violence, and one leader after another had been deposed, creating chaos and a reign of terror. The French could not agree on what liberty was, who was deserving of it, or how the nation could be governed fairly.

Public opinion in America was divided over the French Revolution. The disorder in France alarmed many Federalists, and criticism increased when in 1793 the French revolutionaries executed their former king, Louis XVI, and his wife, Marie Antoinette. At the same time, many Federalists (especially in New England) viewed Britain as the United States's natural trading partner. When Britain and France declared war on one another in 1793 (other European nations saw France's chaos as an opportunity to make territorial gains, prompting Europe-wide battles), many New Englanders were concerned that too much support for France's revolution would sour trade relations with Britain. On the one hand, the Democratic-Republicans continued to sympathize with the revolution, supporting its attempt to create a republican government. On the other hand, Federalists in New England supported Britain.

In the United States, the conflict came to a head when an ambassador from the revolutionary French Republic, Edmond Genêt, arrived in the United States on April 8, 1793. Genêt's mission was to raise support for the new French government, particularly because the revolution had brought France into conflict with

impressment Practice of capturing and forcing sailors from other nations into naval service

Britain and Spain, key trading partners of the United States. Genêt received a mixed reception. Many Americans remembered the French contribution to the American Revolution and welcomed him. Others pointed out that America's alliance had actually been with the now-deposed French king, not the new French Republic. To avoid entanglement, Washington issued a neutrality proclamation two weeks after Genêt's arrival, on April 22, 1793.

But Genêt ignored the proclamation and very publicly tried to recruit American soldiers and advocate American attacks on British ships. Since this was a direct challenge to Washington's stance on neutrality, the president issued a proclamation in August 1793 that France recall Genêt. (Genêt was allowed to stay in America, however, after a new French government demanded his arrest and Washington became aware that Genêt would likely be executed if he returned to France. Washington opposed Genêt's methods, not Genêt himself.)

Besides creating a diplomatic nuisance, what came to be called "the Genêt affair" was significant because it delineated further distinctions between Washington's Federalists and Jefferson's Democratic-Republicans. Jefferson, who had long supported the French Revolution, opposed President Washington's neutrality and realized that Washington had started looking more to Hamilton for advice on foreign affairs than to him. Recognizing his loss of influence, Jefferson resigned as secretary of state in July 1793, a sign of growing divisions within American political leadership.

U.S. NEUTRALITY AND JAY'S TREATY

The rebuke of Genêt did not end Washington's problems maintaining neutrality. Indeed, neither France nor Britain respected American neutrality, with the British sometimes performing the terrible act of **impressing** (capturing and forcing into service) American sailors into its navy. Other British policies, unrelated to the war with France, also aggravated Americans. For example, the treaty that ended the American Revolution decreed that the British evacuate their forts on the American frontier, but a decade after the agreement was reached, Britain still occupied the forts. In addition, Britain closed its ports in the West Indies to American ships.

To address these issues, in 1794, Washington sent New York's John Jay to Britain. Jay had served as the first chief justice of the Supreme Court and helped negotiate the treaty that ended the American Revolution.

In 1795, Jay returned with **Jay's Treaty**. In it the British agreed to evacuate military posts along the frontier in the Northwest Territory and make reparations for the cargo seized in 1793 and 1794. But Jay made several concessions; for instance, the United States lifted duties on British imports for ten years. Furthermore, the treaty avoided addressing other important issues, such as the impressing of American sailors.

Jay's Treaty brought the conflict over foreign relations (whether to support France or Britain) to a boiling point. Jefferson's partisans were brutal in their attacks on the Federalists, claiming that Jay's Treaty was a betrayal of the 1778 alliance with France and a humiliating capitulation to the British. At public rallies, protesters even burned Jay in effigy. The vehemence of the opposition caused Washington to hesitate in signing the treaty, although he did sign it eventually. Nevertheless, Jay's Treaty indicated growing divisions within American politics, passionate divisions over the direction of the nation that would contribute to the rise of a two-party political system.

THE PINCKNEY TREATY

In one rare instance, the **Pinckney Treaty of 1796** (also called the Treaty of San Lorenzo) was an accomplishment everyone could celebrate. The tax on whiskey remained after the Whiskey Rebellion, but opposition to the policy cooled when this treaty with Spain gave Pennsylvania farmers an easier way to get their crops to market. The Pinckney Treaty opened the Mississippi River to American shipping and allowed Americans the "right of deposit" at New Orleans, which meant that American merchants could warehouse goods in the city. The Pinckney Treaty was popular, a notable foreign policy achievement in a decade of political controversy.

8-2c Indian Relations

If problems of finance and foreign policy were crafting two political factions, both parties could at least agree on the policies toward Indians. Once again, it was the Americans' westward expansion that provoked conflict.

INDIAN RESISTANCE IN THE NORTHWEST

In 1790, a huge coalition of Indian nations (including the Chippewa, Ottawa, Shawnee, Delaware, Pottawatomi, and others) attacked American settlers north of the Ohio

>> Washington, D.C., in 1800 was not a large city at all.

River, in what is today Ohio. Buttressed by British promises of support, the Native Americans were successful in defeating several American battalions until 1794, when the American Army finally secured a victory in the Battle of Fallen Timbers. President Washington intended to clear the Ohio River Valley of Indians for American settlement and had finally done so at that battle. The resulting **Treaty of Greenville** (1795) forced the Indian nations of the old Northwest westward across the Mississippi River (Map 8.1). This development signaled peace in the Ohio River Valley and white settlement there for two decades.

THE SOUTH

At about the same time, the Creeks near Georgia were battling to prevent further American encroachment on their lands, in the so-called Creek War. The Spanish were the real beneficiaries of the Creek war, because the Creeks served as a buffer between Spain's Florida territory and American settlers in Georgia.

Jay's Treaty Treaty in which the British agreed to evacuate military posts along the frontier in the Northwest Territory and make reparations for the cargo seized in 1793 and 1794 while the United States lifted duties on British imports for ten years

Pinckney Treaty of 1796 Agreement with Spain that opened the Mississippi River to American shipping and allowed Americans the "right of deposit" at New Orleans, which meant that American merchants could warehouse goods in the city

Treaty of Greenville Agreement that forced the Indians of the Old Northwest westward across the Mississippi River in 1795

Map 8.1 The West, 1783–1800

>> This map shows the seemingly perpetual westward expansion of territory by American citizens, who, from 1783–1800 settled all the way to the Mississippi River.

Anxious to avoid continued attacks by the Creeks, George Washington called the Creek leader, Alexander McGillivray, to New York to pursue a treaty. The parties agreed to terms that legitimated the Creek presence and ended hostilities until 1792, when McGillivray accepted better terms from the Spanish. Small wars continued in the South and Southwest until 1794, at which time Tennesseans, hoping to establish Tennessee as a state, successfully pushed the Creeks farther west and south.

A NEW POLICY

The seemingly endless violence led the United States to revise its Indian policy. In 1790, Congress passed the first of the **Indian Trade and Intercourse Acts**, which made it illegal for Americans to trade with Native American nations without formal consent from the federal government. The acts also made it illegal to sell land to or buy land from Native Americans without similar federal

Indian Trade and Intercourse Acts Laws that made it illegal for Americans to trade with Native Americans without formal consent from the federal government and also made it illegal to sell land to or buy land from Native Americans without similar federal consent

consent. This last part began the process of defining "Indian territory," the lands where Indians could live and work. The acts once again made it clear that the United States had no intention of integrating Indians into their new nation.

8-3 THE RISE OF TWO-PARTY POLITICS

Despite Americans' willingness to come together to fight Indians, by 1795, after the uproars caused by the Citizen Genêt affair and Jay's Treaty, two major divisions of opinion had crystallized into political parties: the Democratic-Republicans and the Federalists. Each party considered itself the inheritor of America's revolutionary ideology and viewed its opposition as bastardization of the cause.

8-3a The Democratic-Republicans

The Democratic-Republican Party (often called the Republican Party or the Jeffersonian-Republicans) coalesced in opposition to Hamilton's economic policies and Jay's Treaty. James Madison and a few other Virginians were the architects of the new organization. They transformed a loose collection of "Democratic-Republican societies" into a disciplined party whose members voted with consistency. In 1792, Thomas Jefferson assumed the party's leadership.

In general, the Democratic-Republicans favored limited government. They opposed the national bank and other measures that enhanced the power of the federal government, and they sided with France over Great Britain because of the feeling of shared republican brotherhood with France. It should be noted, however, that their sense of self-rule also included the right to own slaves if one so desired. Jefferson found supporters among southern landholders and among free workers and laborers everywhere.

8-3b The Federalists

The **Federalist Party**, meanwhile, grew out of the faction of American leaders that endorsed Hamilton's economic policies and Jay's Treaty. They supported Washington's presidency and helped John Adams succeed him in 1796. In general, the Federalists supported the stability provided by a centralized government and were suspicious of the whims of the populace. The Federalists supported a strong governmental role in economic affairs and the stability of trade with Britain. They were mostly wealthy merchants, large property owners, or conservative farmers. New England and the Middle Colonies were Federalist strongholds.

8-3c Slavery

Aside from finance and federalism, another issue caused a rift between the two parties: slavery. To be sure, most Federalists were not abolitionists, but many of them were less committed to the continuation of slavery than the Democratic-Republicans. This division was illuminated in each party's reaction to the Haitian Revolution.

THE HAITIAN REVOLUTION

In 1791, slaves in Santo Domingo, a Caribbean island nation just south of Florida, revolted, killing planters and burning sugar plantations. Led by Toussaint L'Ouverture, the slaves eventually declared independence from their French overlords and created the nation Haiti. In the United States, the Federalists supported the revolution (in this instance, *they* were the ones mindful of their own republican roots). George Washington kept up trade relations with Haiti and sought to recognize the independent nation made up mostly of former slaves.

Democratic-Republicans were aghast at Washington's actions. The Haitian Revolution had forced a flood of white landholders to decamp to America's southern states, who told of the violence and warned against the potential creation of a black republic near the coast of America. When Thomas Jefferson became president in 1800, he reversed the nation's position on the Haitian Revolution and supported French attempts to crush the slave rebellion. (The French lost this effort in 1803, and Haiti became the first black republic and Latin America's first independent state.)

There were three results of the Haitian Revolution in the South. First, lawmakers in southern states tightened black codes, citing fear of slave insurrections in America. Second, the revolution hardened planters' conviction that the South was meant to maintain slavery. This reliance on slavery had deepened after the invention of the cotton gin in 1793, which made labor-intensive cotton profitable in much of the South. Finally, the revolution underscored France's increased reluctance to maintain its possessions in the New World, a sentiment that led to the Louisiana Purchase of 1803 (see Chapter 9).

Federalist Party Faction of American leaders that endorsed Hamilton's economic policies and Jay's Treaty

>> In 1791, slaves in French-controlled Haiti declared their independence from France. Led by Toussaint L'Ouverture, pictured here on a 1989 banknote from Haiti, the bloody revolution led France to pull up its roots in the New World, ultimately leading to the Louisiana Purchase in 1803.

Georgios Kollidas/Shutterstock.com

GABRIEL'S CONSPIRACY

Yet another result of the Haitian Revolution was the spread of revolutionary fervor among American slaves, which sparked **Gabriel's Conspiracy** in 1800. After the American Revolution, New York and Philadelphia became havens for free black people, and nearly all of the northern states developed plans to free their slaves. The opposite was happening in the South, where slavery was becoming more and more entrenched.

In 1800, several churchgoing African Americans learned of the events in Haiti and planned a similar attack on Richmond, Virginia. They intended to burn the town and capture the governor, James Monroe. After heavy rain postponed the attack, several conspirators leaked the plan. State leaders hanged twenty-six rebels, including the leader, a slave named Gabriel. A second attack in 1802 (led by a slave named Sancho) was also preemptively stopped.

These two attempts to overthrow the slave system resulted in the further tightening of the laws governing slaves. Most significantly, all talk of emancipation in the South (though admittedly limited) ended due to white fears of black insurrection. The increasingly harsh measures were meant to stifle slaves' hopes of escaping the system, and the measures worked.

> Adams's opponent, Thomas Jefferson, became his vice president. From 1797 to 1800, there would be no harmony in the federal government.

Gabriel's Conspiracy Slave rebellion in 1800 in Richmond, Virginia; twenty-six rebels were hanged

8-4 ADAMS'S PRESIDENCY AND DEALING WITH DISSENT

George Washington easily won reelection as president in 1792, but as the election of 1796 approached, Washington decided not to run for a third term. Exhausted by his years as president and by the continual attacks of the Democratic-Republican press, Washington encouraged Americans to come together under a nonpartisan system. In his Farewell Address, Washington called the emerging political parties "a frightful despotism" that would lead to series of abuses and counter-abuses, all to the detriment of the nation.

His hopes for non-partisanship were quickly dashed. The Democratic-Republicans and the Federalists both began organizing local meetings of supporters, and both parties were sufficiently well organized to field candidates in the election of 1796. The two-party political system we have known ever since was born.

8-4a Adams's Election

When Washington's vice president, Federalist John Adams, announced his candidacy for president, the Democratic-Republicans nominated Thomas Jefferson to oppose him. After a particularly partisan campaign, rife with intense bickering, Adams received 71 electoral votes and became president. According to the Constitution, the candidate with the second highest number of electoral votes was to be vice president, and, by previous arrangement among Federalist electoral voters, Adams's running mate, Thomas Pinckney of South Carolina, was meant to receive the same number of votes as Adams less one, with one supporter withholding his vote. This would have given Pinckney 70 votes and the vice presidency. Confusion and trickery muddled the plan, though, and communications were slow. No one was sure who was supposed to hold back his vote for Pinckney, and so several did. The result was that, instead of Pinckney, it was Jefferson who took second place, with 68 electoral votes. Thus, Adams's opponent, Thomas Jefferson, became his vice president. From 1797 to 1800, there would be no harmony in the federal government.

>> John Adams.

iStock.com/Wynnter

8-4b The XYZ Affair

Upon entering office in 1797, Adams immediately faced a foreign policy crisis called the **XYZ Affair**, which further divided the two parties. Upon reviewing Jay's Treaty, the French interpreted it to mean that the United States was siding with Great Britain in the trade wars. They retaliated by raiding American merchant ships. France was angry at what it saw as a rebuke to the clan of republican brotherhood. To defuse the situation, Adams sent three envoys to France, and the French foreign minister sent three agents to meet them (designated X, Y, and Z in official French documents). It quickly became evident, however, that X, Y, and Z's real purpose was to extort money from the Americans as a prerequisite for negotiations. When news of "the XYZ Affair" reached the United States, Americans were outraged at France's galling lack of respect.

> Lyon retaliated by spitting in Griswold's face, and the two men began wrestling on the floor of the House of Representatives.

RESULT—THE QUASI-WAR

Meanwhile, the French continued to raid American ships. The Adams administration responded to these raids by repudiating America's 1778 alliance with France, and a "quasi-war" erupted between the two nations. From 1798 to 1800, the naval fleets of both countries openly plundered each other's ships. As Franco-American relations deteriorated, Adams feared the outbreak of a full-scale war between the two nations. This was significant because it put Adams on the defensive regarding dissent within the American government. In his mind, America was on the verge of an international war, and the Democratic-Republicans, who were already sympathetic to the French cause, would not stop badgering him about it.

8-4c The Alien and Sedition Acts

Adams's concerns about dissent became problematic because partisanship had escalated significantly during his term. For example, in 1798, a fight broke out on the floor of the House of Representatives when Matthew Lyon, a pugnacious Democratic-Republican congressman from Vermont, declared that aristocratic Federalist representatives were perpetually duping the people. Roger Griswold, a Federalist representative from Connecticut, asked Lyon if he meant to defend the people with a wooden sword. (Griswold was referring to the fact that, during the American Revolution, Lyon had been court-martialed for cowardice and forced to wear a wooden sword as punishment.) Lyon spat in Griswold's face, and the two men began wrestling on the floor of the House of Representatives.

Attempting to bring such bitter conflicts under control, Adams pushed a series of measures through Congress known collectively as the **Alien and Sedition Acts**. They turned out to be his undoing.

The Alien and Sedition Acts consisted of three separate acts, the third of which would have the

XYZ Affair Foreign policy crisis with France over the trade wars; three agents designated X, Y, and Z attempted to extort money from American envoys as a prerequisite for negotiations

Alien and Sedition Acts Legislation signed by President John Adams; included the Alien Enemies Act, the Alien Friends Act, and the Sedition Act; opponents called them a violation of the First Amendment's guarantees

Library of Congress Prints and Photographs Division Washington, D.C. LC-DIG-ppmsca-19356

>> In 1798, dissent between the two political parties became so heated that there were fisticuffs on the floor of Congress. This political cartoon details the most famous, between Matthew Lyon, a Democratic-Republican, and Roger Griswold, a Federalist, who were fighting over which party was most deliberately trying to dupe the American people. However, John Adams' attempts to quell the dissent with the Alien and Sedition Acts would only fan the flames more.

biggest impact on Adams's future. (1) The Alien Enemies Act authorized the deportation of the citizens of enemy nations. (2) The Alien Friends Act allowed the government to detain and deport noncitizens for almost any cause; because many of the most active Democratic-Republicans were recent British immigrants, this was regarded as a deliberate assault on the party. Finally, (3) the Sedition Act set fines and prison sentences for anyone found guilty of writing, speaking, or publishing "false, scandalous and malicious" statements against the government.

Virginia and Kentucky Resolutions Declarations written by Thomas Jefferson and James Madison and adopted by the legislatures of Virginia and Kentucky, proclaiming that the Sedition Act was an infringement on rights protected by their state constitutions and that states had the right to nullify federal laws within their borders

doctrine of nullification The theory that each state had the right to nullify federal laws within its borders

The two Alien Acts had little impact, but the Sedition Act was explosive. Several Democratic-Republican newspaper editors were jailed for violating the new law. Federalists even used the law to jail Matthew Lyon, the Democratic-Republican representative who had wrestled on the House floor. Not only did the act make political martyrs out of the jailed Republican-Democrats, but it also provoked their party colleagues to fight back.

Calling the Alien and Sedition Acts a violation of the First Amendment's guarantee of free speech, Thomas Jefferson and James Madison collaborated anonymously to pen a set of resolutions denouncing the acts. In 1798, the legislatures of Virginia and Kentucky adopted resolutions—called the **Virginia and Kentucky Resolutions**—proclaiming the Sedition Act an infringement on rights protected by their state constitutions. Even more powerfully, the resolutions declared that each state had the right to nullify federal laws within its borders.

This bold challenge to federal authority was called the **doctrine of nullification**. No other state endorsed the resolutions, and several openly rebuked them, but they provided the intellectual framework for sectional divisions that were to come. They also set the stage for the bitter election of 1800.

8-5 THE "BLOODLESS REVOLUTION" OF 1800

The candidates in the election of 1800 were the same as those in 1796, Jefferson and Adams. Four years of controversy, however, had intensified the rivalry between the two. Citing the Alien and Sedition Acts, Democratic-Republicans accused Adams of harboring monarchical ambitions and called him a slave to British interests. Federalists castigated Thomas Jefferson as an atheist (he had in fact composed his own personal copy of the Bible by cutting out everything but the words spoken by Christ, but he was not an atheist) who would follow the lead of the French revolutionaries and instigate a reign of terror in the United States. The campaigning was vitriolic, to say the least.

8-5a The French Again

John Adams gave his opposition unexpected help by reopening negotiations with France. In terms of international relations, the negotiations were a success; they resulted in a peace treaty that brought the quasi-war to an end. But in terms of his candidacy, because most of his fellow Federalists were pro-British, his efforts to smooth things over with France divided his own party. The Federalist Party had already suffered in the controversy over the Alien and Sedition Acts. Now they were divided over whether the United States should negotiate with France. In putting the priorities of the nation over the interests of his party, Adams won a victory for statesmanship but created a political problem he could not overcome.

8-5b The Election

As the election of 1800 approached, the Federalists were too divided to give Jefferson any real competition. Hamilton, in fact, jockeyed to get the Federalists to dump Adams as their candidate. In contrast, the Democratic-Republican Party was well organized, and the final tally in the Electoral College gave Jefferson and his running mate, Aaron Burr of New York, a clear margin of victory.

8-5c Results

The assumption of power by the Democratic-Republicans did not go off without a hitch, however. Ironically, the Democratic-Republicans were, in a way, *too* organized. Jefferson and Burr received 73 votes apiece in Electoral College voting. This was a problem because the Constitution did not provide for a two-person ticket (with one designated as president and the other as vice president). Rather, it stated that the candidate with the most electoral votes became president and the candidate with the second most votes assumed the vice presidency. In the event of a tie, the decision was placed in the hands of the House of Representatives.

In the election of 1800 (Map 8.2), Democratic-Republican candidates had also won control of both

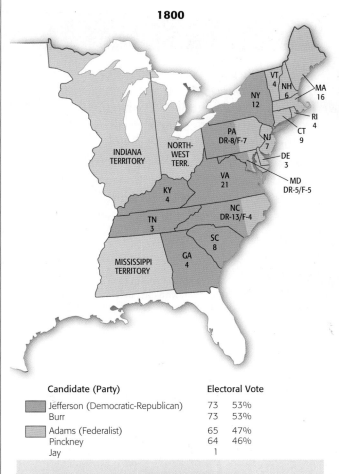

1800

Candidate (Party)	Electoral Vote	
Jefferson (Democratic-Republican)	73	53%
Burr	73	53%
Adams (Federalist)	65	47%
Pinckney	64	46%
Jay	1	

Map 8.2 The Election of 1800

>> The electoral map of 1800, showing that most of Adams support came from New England.

houses of Congress, but the new Congress did not sit until after the presidential election was settled. Therefore, it was the **lame-duck** (or, soon-to-be-out-of-office) Federalist Congress that would make the decision. Some Federalists decided to support Burr and deny Jefferson presidency, and, although Burr did not openly support this movement, he also did not denounce it. Hamilton, however, distrusted Burr more than he disliked Jefferson. Using his influence among the Federalists, Hamilton helped his old rival Thomas Jefferson to victory on the thirty-sixth ballot. To ensure that the shenanigans of the 1800 election would never be repeated, in 1804 the United States adopted the Twelfth Amendment to the Constitution, allowing electors to vote for president and vice president separately.

>LOOKING AHEAD...

Although party politics had increased tremendously between 1796 and 1800, the election of 1800 was valuable in demonstrating that an opposition party could defeat the party in power without causing a total breakdown of government or a civil war. This was a tremendous accomplishment. When Adams and the Federalists handed over the reins of power peacefully, optimism ran high that the nation had passed a critical test. Jefferson himself declared in his Inaugural Address, "We are all Republicans. We are all Federalists," thus suggesting that the survival of the nation should trump political differences. After 1800, opposition became a cornerstone of the American system of government, as did the two-party system. The so-called bloodless revolution of 1800 paved the way for active, peaceful political dissent in American life.

lame-duck Politician who is not returning to office and is serving out the rest of his or her term with little influence; a soon-to-be-out-of-office politician or Congress

STUDY TOOLS 8

READY TO STUDY? IN THE BOOK, YOU CAN:

❏ Rip out the Chapter Review Card, which includes key terms and chapter summaries.

ONLINE AT WWW.CENGAGEBRAIN.COM, YOU CAN:

❏ Collect StudyBits while you read and study the chapter.

❏ Quiz yourself on key concepts.

❏ Find videos for further exploration.

❏ Prepare for tests with HIST5 Flash Cards as well as those you create.

❏ Read Washington's First Inaugural Address.

❏ Read the Naturalization Act of 1790.

❏ Take a virtual tour of the activities of the First Federal Congress.

❏ Read Washington's Farewell Address of 1796.

❏ See documents related to Gabriel's Conspiracy.

1788 First federal election.

Judiciary Act creates three circuit and thirteen district courts.

1790 Naturalization Act limits citizenship for immigrants to free white persons.

Indian coalition attacks American settlers north of Ohio River.

Indian Trade and Intercourse Act puts trade with natives under federal control.

1792 Jefferson becomes leader of Democratic-Republican Party.

1793 Genêt affair further splits Democrat-Republicans and Federalists.

1794 Western settlers resist federal authority in the Whiskey Rebellion.

1796 Pinckney Treaty with Spain opens Mississippi River to American trade.

Federalist John Adams becomes second president of the United States.

1797 XYZ Affair prompts quasi-war with revolutionary France.

What Else Was Happening

1791: *Congress charters First Bank of the United States.*

Haitian Revolution becomes only successful slave rebellion in hemisphere.

Early bicycles are made in Scotland.

France begins using the metric system.

1795: *Conciliatory Jay Treaty with Britain angers Democratic-Republicans.*

Treaty of Greenville forces Indians west out of Ohio Valley.

Tula Slave Rebellion in the Dutch Caribbean colony of Curacao lasts a month before finally being suppressed. August 17 is still celebrated in Curacao as a day of freedom.

1798: *Adams tries to control political conflict with Alien and Sedition Acts.*

In response, Virginia and Kentucky formulate doctrine of nullification.

The first soft drink is invented.

1800: *Virginians crush Gabriel's slave conspiracy and tighten slave laws.*

Jefferson's election demonstrates peaceful political change in republic.

9 | Jeffersonian Democracy, 1800–1814

Wai Chan Chan/EyeEm/Getty Images

LEARNING OBJECTIVES

After reading this chapter, you should be able to do the following:

9-1 Define Jeffersonian Democracy, and explain how Jefferson's presidency both defined and contradicted that political philosophy.

9-2 Discuss the reasons for and results of the War of 1812.

AFTER FINISHING
THIS CHAPTER
GO TO **PAGE 172**
FOR STUDY TOOLS

of federal laws, a right called the **doctrine of judicial review**. Based on that ingenious decision, the Supreme Court refused to engage in the partisan bickering of the time, while at the same time carving out its position as the ultimate interpreter of constitutional questions. Since *Marbury*, the Court has struck down more than one thousand acts of Congress or state legislatures, declaring them unconstitutional.

The Legality of Partisanship The second important judicial precedent was established when Jefferson sought to impeach the most politically biased Federalist judges. To Jefferson's chagrin, in 1805, the Senate refused to convict Federalist judge Samuel Chase on purely political grounds. This set the precedent that partisanship was not a crime and that, once appointed, judges could be as partisan as they wished in their decisions without facing rebuke or retribution.

EXPANDING THE AGRARIAN REPUBLIC

Given the republican belief that farming provided the moral basis for good citizenship, Jefferson felt it essential that the United States continue to open new territory to settlement. Without access to new land, Jefferson reasoned, crowding would pressure people into working for others as urban wage laborers. In contrast, territorial expansion would allow every American the chance to be a self-sufficient farmer. Jefferson believed the new nation should dislodge Spanish claims to territory in Florida and northern Mexico, and French claims in the Mississippi.

The Louisiana Purchase The first step Jefferson took to realize this vision was to purchase the city of New Orleans from France. New Orleans was a vital port city at the mouth of the Mississippi River, and the Mississippi was the country's main north–south inland waterway, providing a means of transportation from the Gulf of Mexico to present-day St. Paul, Minnesota. The United States could never guarantee control of the Mississippi unless it controlled New Orleans as well.

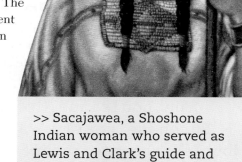

>> Sacajawea, a Shoshone Indian woman who served as Lewis and Clark's guide and translator, as depicted in a nineteenth-century painting.

In 1803, Jefferson sent emissaries to France to negotiate the purchase. Much to Jefferson's surprise, the French emperor, Napoleon Bonaparte, wanted to sell not only New Orleans, but also the rights to all of Louisiana, which was at the time a huge tract of land stretching from the Mississippi River to the Rocky Mountains, land that was of course occupied and claimed by a variety of Native American nations but that was nevertheless laid claim to by the French. The French treasury was nearly empty, and another war loomed between France and Britain. In addition, after the Haitian Revolution (see Chapter 8), France had learned how costly it was to maintain colonial possessions. Napoleon asked only $15 million for the claim to 828,000 square miles of Louisiana.

The Constitution did not give the president power to buy new territory, but Jefferson nonetheless pushed ahead with the **Louisiana Purchase**. Although he claimed to believe that federal power was dangerous and that the Constitution had to be followed strictly, Jefferson was willing to bend his own rules in order to expand America's western boundary (see Map 9.1). The purchase nearly doubled the geographic size of the nation.

> The Lewis and Clark expedition inspired generations of Americans to move westward.

Lewis and Clark Jefferson took responsibility not only for acquiring new territory, but also for exploring it. In 1803, before the Louisiana Purchase was completed, Jefferson sent his private secretary Meriwether Lewis with William Clark as

doctrine of judicial review Right of the courts to judge the constitutionality of federal laws; established the Supreme Court as the ultimate interpreter of constitutional questions

Louisiana Purchase Tract of 828,000 square miles that stretched from the Mississippi River to the Rocky Mountains; Jefferson bought the rights to it from Napoleon for $15 million in 1803

>> William Clark's diary of the Lewis and Clark expedition.

co-commander on an exploratory mission to the Pacific. In 1804, Lewis and Clark, along with forty-eight other men, left St. Louis and journeyed northwest toward the Rockies. With the help of Sacajawea, a Shoshone Indian woman who served as their guide, Lewis and Clark traveled to the Pacific. Their journey lasted two-and-a-half years. They encountered Indians friendly and fierce, unknown wildlife, and brutal weather, both hot and cold. In 1806, three years later, the expedition returned to St. Louis with an immense amount of information about the American West, including a valuable map. Their journey and the stories from it inspired generations of Americans to move west and lay claim to the nation's interior.

Land Policies Jefferson also made access to western lands easier through a revised land policy. The Land Act of 1800, signed by President Adams, had set up land-selling offices in the West, made the parcels smaller (and more affordable), and allowed for payment over time

> The Louisiana Purchase nearly doubled the geographic size of the nation.

(rather than in a single large lump sum). In 1804, the Democratic-Republicans again reduced the minimum amount that could be purchased, making western land even more affordable. In a sense, the federal government had become the real estate agent for the nation's interior. And, as always, increased westward expansion meant increased contact, and battles, with Native Americans.

TECUMSEH AND THE PROPHET

In the early 1800s, two Shawnee brothers, Tecumseh and the Prophet, proposed to unite all the Native American nations from the Old Northwest (in Ohio and Michigan) and the South (Georgia) to resist the seemingly perpetual encroachment of American settlers. The brothers toured across the land preaching a revival of old ways in a **revitalization movement** reminiscent of Neolin's (Chapter 4). The brothers opposed the acceptance of European and American habits, including whiskey and guns. They set up pan-Indian towns across Indiana, the most famous of which was called "Prophetstown" by the surrounding American settlers and was situated alongside the Tippecanoe River. As white Americans moved further west, they would eventually run into an increasingly united force of Indians.

REELECTION

Taking advantage of the new culture of politics, the expansion of the nation, and the good economic times of the early 1800s, Jefferson coasted to an easy reelection in 1804. The Federalists had once again been beaten badly, and some Federalists were so dismayed at their reversal of fortune they persuaded Aaron Burr to run for governor of New York

revitalization movement
Revival of old ways of tribal life and pan-Indianism preached by Tecumseh and the Prophet

>> Tecumseh and the Prophet (shown here), Shawnee Indian brothers who led a revitalization movement among Indians of the Old Northwest, saw their movement decimated after the Battle of Tippecanoe.

and then, if victorious, to separate New York and New England from the rest of the nation. This, in 1804, was the country's first serious plot of secession. Alexander Hamilton—ever the nationalist—learned of the plot and politicked against Burr in New York, leading to Burr's defeat.

The discord between the two men grew worse and worse, and, in a rage of fury, Burr challenged Hamilton to a duel. The two had a long-standing feud, and this would be its final episode. In the duel, on a desolate hill in New Jersey (they had deliberately left New York, where dueling was illegal), Burr shot and killed Hamilton, who had fired first but missed, perhaps as a form of protesting duels, deliberately firing into the air. Burr, hearing a shot whiz by his head and crash into the trees behind him, fired a fatal bullet into Hamilton's gut. Burr, the sitting vice president, subsequently lost all political respectability because most Americans believed politics was meant to occupy the realm of discussion and law, not violence and vigilantism. Deemed a relic of an older age and cast out from distinguished political society, Burr moved west, perhaps plotting further secession attempts, until he was tried for treason in the nation's first "Trial of the Century." He was found not guilty by Chief Justice John Marshall, but his widespread unpopularity prompted him to decamp to Europe.

Although Burr is an extreme case, his actions illustrate the bitter divisions between the Federalists and the Democratic-Republicans. His very extremity and singularity, however, also demonstrate that, despite partisanship, the new nation was a nation of laws.

9-1c Jefferson's Foreign Affairs

While the new nation was weathering the few internal storms that arose (and enjoying good economic times), international events seized attention during Jefferson's two terms.

JEFFERSON'S PROBLEMATIC DIPLOMACY

Shortly after the Louisiana Purchase, the long-expected war between France and Great Britain erupted. At first, the United States benefited. With Britain and France fighting each other, America (as a neutral power) took control of the shipping trade between the Americas and Europe. Many American traders grew wealthy. Soon, however, the United States found itself caught in the middle.

In the battle, Britain controlled the seas, and France controlled the continent of Europe. With no land to fight on, each nation attempted to starve the other into submission. They restricted other nations from trading with their enemy, raided ships, and prevented them from entering European ports. In 1806, France passed the Berlin Decree, which forbade trade with Britain by neutral parties, at the risk of French attack. In return, in 1807, Britain passed the Orders in Council, which required all ships coming to northern Europe to stop in British ports first, or risk being seized by Britain. American shipping was particularly punished. By 1807, about eight hundred American ships had been raided by French and British fleets. Meanwhile, the British began impressing American sailors into the Royal Navy, much as they had in the early 1790s. Estimates of the number of Americans eventually impressed range from 4,000 to 10,000. After one highly publicized attack on the U.S.S. *Chesapeake*, Americans were so angered that some called for war, but it was not to be, for the simple reason that Jefferson had dismantled the U.S. military and was sure to lose any such battle.

The Right of Neutrality Eager to save face, Jefferson reiterated the rights of a neutral party and initiated a program of "peaceable coercion," which he hoped would get both Britain and France to stop tormenting America's shipping industry. His plan turned out to be his administration's biggest mistake. The plan centered on the **Embargo Act of 1807**, which stopped American exports from going to Europe and prohibited American ships

>> This illustration depicts Burr assassinating Hamilton, who, disapproving of duels, had perhaps fired his gun into the air.

Embargo Act of 1807 Legislation that stopped American exports from going to Europe and prohibited American ships from trading in foreign ports from trading in foreign ports. Jefferson reasoned that depriving France and Britain of American commerce would force them to recognize America's neutral rights. In essence, he was saying that, if Britain and France would not respect American rights, Jefferson would punish them by denying them American trade. It would turn out, however, that Jefferson underestimated the impact his Embargo Act would have on American traders.

Results The Embargo Act was a disaster. Europe was not deprived of very much, and British ships took over the Atlantic sea trade. The act imperiled the American economy, though, especially in the Federalist stronghold of New England, where shipping was a major part of the local economy. Angered by the embargo, American traders began smuggling goods out of the country, an act Democratic-Republicans denounced.

The Embargo Act was a disaster. Europe was not deprived of very much, and British ships took over the Atlantic sea trade.

Despite the policy's shortcomings, Jefferson refused to admit his mistake. He reasoned that foreign trade necessarily led to foreign entanglements, and his vision of a yeoman farmer's republic was supposed to shun such engagements. All of these frustrations bubbled into the presidential election of 1808.

9-2 JAMES MADISON AND THE WAR OF 1812

The Federalists hoped to capitalize on the unpopularity of the Embargo Act to reclaim the presidency in 1808, but, despite solid support in New England, they did not have the national strength to defeat the Democratic-Republicans.

9-2a The Election of 1808 and Declaration of War

Like Washington, Jefferson chose not to run for a third term. Instead, he ensured the nomination would go to his friend and fellow Virginian, James Madison. Madison handily defeated the Federalist candidate, Charles Pinckney, but Pinckney did better than projected, worrying Democratic-Republicans, who became aware of the widespread anger stirred up by Jefferson's Embargo Act.

THE REPEAL OF THE EMBARGO ACT

To prevent the Federalists from gaining ground on the issue of the Embargo Act, Congress repealed it in 1809, shortly before Madison became president. In its place, Congress passed the **Non-Intercourse Act**, which allowed American ships to trade with all nations except Britain and France, and authorized the president to resume trade with those countries once they began respecting America's neutral trading rights.

FRANCE MAKES AMENDS

In a brilliant tactical move, France's emperor, Napoleon, announced that he would respect America's neutrality rights, whereupon Madison resumed trade with France and vehemently prohibited trade with Britain. With British trade banned from both continental Europe and the United States, the British economy suffered a depression. On June 16, 1812, the British vowed to respect American neutrality. But it proved to be too little, too late.

IN THE WEST

But it was events in the West that would turn what was a simmering frustratation between the United States and England into a full-scale war. The revitalization movement spurred by Tecumseh and the Prophet had grown popular with young Indians, and the few British who remained in the American West encouraged its growth, hoping it would prove too formidable for the American frontiersmen and curb further expansion. But American settlers had likewise developed a strong presence in Indiana. In 1811, Indiana governor William Henry Harrison attacked Prophetstown, setting the town ablaze.

DECLARATION OF WAR

Madison had been incensed by Britain's refusal to recognize American neutrality. Moreover, he had been influenced by westerners who wanted war with Britain

Non-Intercourse Act Legislation passed in 1809 that allowed American ships to trade with all nations except Britain and France and authorized the president to resume trade with those countries once they began respecting America's neutral trading rights

The happy Effects of that Grand System of shutting Ports against the English !!

>> Jefferson's Embargo Act closed ports across the east coast of the United States, provoking anger and resent that Jefferson had not foreseen.

because they felt the British were to blame for increased Indian violence in the Midwest. These westerners, led in Congress by Kentuckian Henry Clay, were called "war hawks." They wanted the British evicted from the West, and they hoped to annex Canada as well. Their influence meant that war, if it came, would be fought against both the British in the Atlantic and hostile Indians to the west.

Under these pressures, James Madison went to Congress on June 1, 1812 (two weeks before Britain pledged to honor America's neutrality), to ask for a declaration of war. Congress split over the question along party lines, with Democratic-Republicans favoring war and Federalists condemning it. Federalists were convinced that war would only hurt American trade further. They believed an expansionist war would not address the problem of impressments or the violation of neutrality rights. In contrast, Democratic-Republicans were convinced that a "second war for American independence" was necessary before Britain would finally recognize America's rights as a neutral nation. Despite Federalist opposition, the Democratic-Republicans carried the vote, and the United States declared war against Britain on June 14, 1812. (For more, see "The Reasons Why . . ." box.)

Support for the war not only appeared along partisan lines, but regional ones as well, a fact that emerged a few months later, in the presidential election of 1812. Madison and the Federalist candidate DeWitt Clinton split the votes of all the eastern states, while the five western states voted solidly for Madison, catapulting him to a second term.

9-2b The War of 1812

With Britain still embroiled in conflict with France, many Americans expected to win the War of 1812 handily. In reality, winning the war proved more difficult.

EARLY DEFEATS

Jefferson's reduction of the American military had left the United States poorly prepared. American troops numbered only 12,000 men, and they quickly tried to recruit 35,000 more, although pay was poor and many soldiers refused to fight beyond the boundaries of their own state. Nevertheless, American forces initiated an assault on British-controlled Canada in 1812, hoping to conquer it quickly and make it one of the United States (Map 9.2).

Despite the fact that the British military was occupied with France and instructed to only fight defensive battles against the Americans, the invasion of British Canada was a complete fiasco. Instead of striking directly at the St. Lawrence River—the lifeline that linked Canada's principal cities to the Atlantic Ocean—the Americans split into three forces, each too small to crush a small but trained opposition. They were further handicapped by Britain's willingness to sign treaties with Native Americans if they would fight against the Americans. When the United States was forced to surrender the village of Detroit, the British forced them to surrender not only to a British Major General but also the Shawnee leader Tecumseh.

·The Reasons Why...

There were four reasons why the War of 1812 began:

A violation of neutrality rights. In 1803, Britain and France began fighting what came to be called the Napoleonic Wars. At first the United States benefited from a battle between two of its primary economic competitors, and it remained officially neutral in the war. These benefits dissipated, though, once both sides began restricting American ships from trading with their enemy. The British raided and attacked American ships bound for France, and France did the same to ships bound for Britain. The United States was an unwilling participant. Its rights as a neutral power were being violated.

Impressment. Furthermore, in need of soldiers, the British began forcing Americans into British naval service, an act called impressment. Americans were obviously angered by the practice. The British impressed between 4,000 and 10,000 Americans in the buildup to the War of 1812.

Napoleon's smarts. In a brilliant tactical move, the French emperor Napoleon Bonaparte saw the increasing American resentment against the British and recognized that France would benefit if Britain were distracted by a war with the United States, so he announced that he would respect America's neutrality rights, leaving Britain as the lone violator of American neutrality rights.

Battles for the West. In the West, meanwhile, the British offered encouragement to a pan-Indian revitalization movement led by Tecumseh and the Prophet in the Indiana territory. Expansive-minded Americans were unimpressed, and western congressmen such as Henry Clay from Kentucky became known as "war hawks" because they saw a potential war against Britain as a way to remove the British from the American West and from Canada too.

SURPRISING VICTORIES AND INDIAN DECIMATION

The following year, the picture brightened for the United States. After replacing the Secretary of War, and focusing on the development of warships that could travel the Great Lakes, American forces finally won a crucial naval battle at Put-in-Bay on Lake Erie. American naval control of the waters in the region made defense of the area north of Lake Erie impossible for the British. The British defeat also spelled disaster for a group of Indian nations that had united with the British to fight for tribal rights, as the victorious Americans now felt entitled to plunder their villages. For his part, Tecumseh was killed a few months later, in the Battle of the Thames.

In the South in 1813, a frontier army under Andrew Jackson defeated the Creek Indians (who viewed the War of 1812 as an opportunity to take advantage of a distracted American army and finally secure its land in Georgia). In March 1814, at the Battle of Horseshoe Bend in today's Alabama, Jackson's troops forced the Creeks to accept a treaty ceding their best lands to the Americans. The Creeks had divided over the issue of whom to support in the war, leading to a civil war between the Upper Creeks and the Lower Creeks. This division did not matter much to Jackson, who, upon winning, took the land of all the Creeks, including those who had helped him at Horseshoe Bend.

CULMINATION

Just as the Americans had seemed to turn the tide of battle, their position teetered when the British forced the abdication of France's Napoleon, briefly ending European hostilities and freeing the British to focus on their war with the United States. British leaders planned a three-pronged strategy to win the War of 1812: attacking Lake Champlain, Washington, D.C., and New Orleans.

At Lake Champlain, in September 1814, the British ground force of 15,000 men faced stiffer-than-expected resistance from American advance units, while U.S. naval forces under Captain Thomas Macdonough defied all expectations and destroyed the British fleet as it waited for ground support. The British assault on Washington, D.C., was more successful. The U.S. militia was overwhelmed and essentially vanished during the fight, leaving only a small force of American soldiers and sailors to serve as the region's defense. President Madison and his wife Dolley were among those compelled to flee the city. The British burned the White House, the Capitol, and other government buildings, but the ultimate objective of the invasion—to capture the port city of Baltimore—eluded them. During the failed invasion of Baltimore, Francis Scott Key wrote the poem "The Star-Spangled Banner." Later set to the tune of an English drinking song, it became the national anthem.

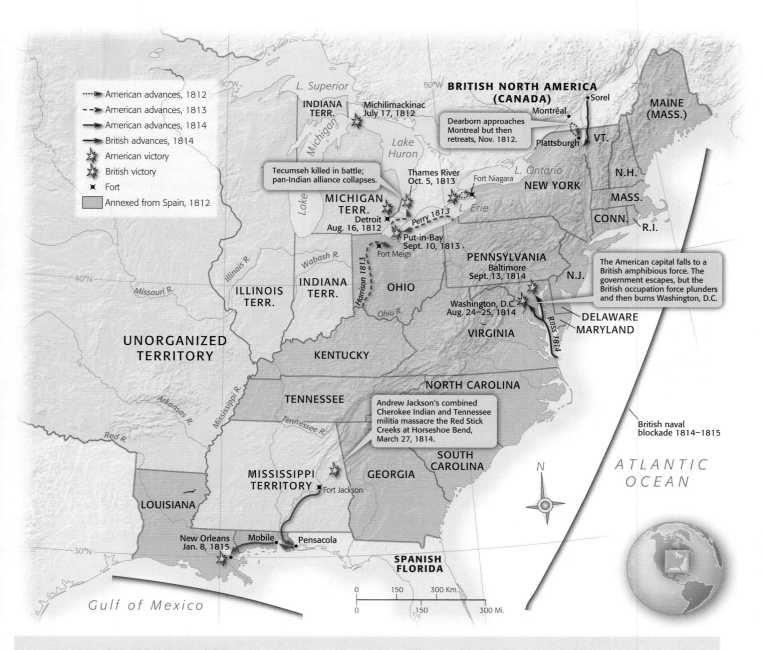

Map 9.2 The War of 1812

>> A map of the eastern half of the United States, showing the major battles of the War of 1812, including battles at Dearborn and Washington, D.C., and Andrew Jackson's famous victory at New Orleans.

ANDREW JACKSON AND THE BATTLE OF NEW ORLEANS

The most startling upset took place in January 1815 at New Orleans, where the British bungled their invasion plans and were mowed down by American troops serving under Andrew Jackson. Because of previous skirmishes, Jackson knew the British were coming and ordered a fortified line of soldiers and artillery batteries to confront the invading army. On the day of the largest attack, January 8, 1815, the British hoped to use a thick fog to disguise their onslaught, but as they advanced, the fog lifted. The Americans suffered only 21 casualties in the Battle of New Orleans, but the British incurred more than 2,000. Jackson became an instant national hero and

>> In January 1815, General Andrew Jackson knew the British were coming, so he ordered a fortified line of soldiers supported by heavy artillery. His tremendous victory made Jackson an instant national hero, one that would elevate him to the presidency and continue through the years (as in this 1890 painting), despite the several controversial things he did as president.

a symbol of America's determination to be permanently independent of Great Britain. The irony was that the Battle of New Orleans took place several weeks after a peace treaty had been negotiated, thus accomplishing little other than establishing Jackson's national reputation and ruining Federalist efforts to label the war a failure.

THE HARTFORD CONVENTION

The timing was vital too, because, as Jackson and his men defended New Orleans, Federalists in New England held a meeting at Hartford, Connecticut, to discuss their problems with the war and with the Democratic-Republicans, who had by then been in power for 15 years. At the meeting, called the **Hartford Convention**, Federalist leaders expressed their frustrations with the War of 1812, which they had protested from its inception. They were

Hartford Convention Meeting of New England Federalists in 1814 in which they proposed constitutional amendments limiting the government's ability to restrict American commerce and repealing the three-fifths clause to limit the power of the South in Congress

"Era of Good Feelings" Period of nonpartisan politics following the implosion of the Federalist Party, roughly 1815–1824

fed up with the government's economic policies, which had hurt the mercantile interests of New England. They had also witnessed their increasing alienation from southerners and westerners. To remedy this problem, some Federalists proposed a series of constitutional amendments that would have limited the government's ability to restrict American commerce and repealing the three-fifths clause in order to reduce the power of the South in Congress. Some representatives even broached the idea of seceding if these measures failed.

Jackson's victory, followed by the announcement that the United States and Britain had negotiated terms for peace, made a mockery of the Hartford Convention. The Federalist Party was immediately tainted with treason, and nearly all support for the party vanished across the country. The nation's first two-party system was over, as only the Democratic-Republicans remained viable. The period of nonpartisan politics that followed became known as the **"Era of Good Feelings."** This only lasted a few years, and, although the seeds of factionalism would blossom again in 1819 and 1820, historians generally consider the Era of Good Feelings to have lasted until the presidential election of 1824.

THE TREATY OF GHENT

It was the Treaty of Ghent of 1814 that formally ended the War of 1812, but it did not settle any of the significant issues, principally naval impressments and America's right to neutrality. Almost all land taken was returned, and all ships and soldiers imprisoned were sent home. "It was as if no war has been fought" wrote a historian. "For nothing has changed." The treaty did, however, end hostilities, which was a relief to both sides. With the war over, the United States was able to turn its attention away from Europe and back to affairs at home.

9-2c The Significance of the War of 1812

The War of 1812 was however significant for at least four reasons: (1) in politics, it affirmed the importance of a strong national government; (2) it vacated the British from the West; (3) it shaped America's role in world affairs; and (4) it unified the nation and boosted American patriotism.

Political Changes Politically, the War of 1812 demonstrated the weakness of the Democratic-Republicans' insistence on a small federal government. It prompted four immediate changes from James Madison: (1) he recognized that having a stronger standing army and navy would have served the country better than the scanty forces that had eked out a victory against Great Britain; (2) he recognized the need for a new national bank to centralize banking, which he chartered as the Second United States Bank in 1816; (3) he agreed to new protective tariffs designed to support the growth of American industries; and (4) he realized the need for a system of national improvements, such as roads and canals to facilitate transportation between the newly settled West and the East Coast. Each of these lessons (some of them very Hamiltonian) would play an integral role in the future development of the United States. The Democratic-Republicans had learned the importance of having at least a modest-sized federal government.

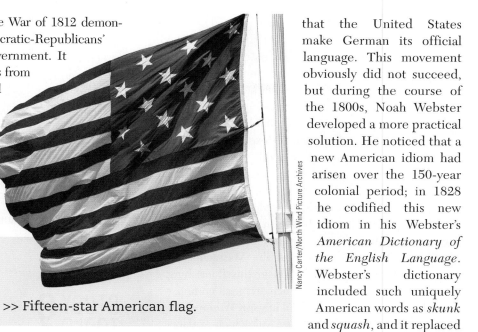

>> Fifteen-star American flag.

Nancy Carter/North Wind Picture Archives

Vacating the West In the West, the War of 1812 produced decisive defeats against the most powerful Native American nations in the Southwest (in today's Tennessee and Alabama) and the Northwest (in the Ohio River Valley). The conclusion of the war also meant Britain would no longer impede settlement in the American interior, leaving the United States free to expand in the West—at the continued cost of Native Americans, who were running out of room after being forced to perpetually move west.

America's Role in the World The War of 1812 also showed the European powers that the United States was a relatively strong, modern nation. Twice in three decades the United States had defeated Britain. The United States earned greater respect and entered a prolonged period of relative isolation, safe from invasions and incursions from abroad.

American Patriotism and American Culture And fourth, pride in their victory in the War of 1812 generated a strong urge to define the United States as finally and fundamentally different from Britain. Hatred of the British prompted some to propose that the United States make German its official language. This movement obviously did not succeed, but during the course of the 1800s, Noah Webster developed a more practical solution. He noticed that a new American idiom had arisen over the 150-year colonial period; in 1828 he codified this new idiom in his Webster's *American Dictionary of the English Language*. Webster's dictionary included such uniquely American words as *skunk* and *squash*, and it replaced British spellings, such as *colour*, with American versions, such as *color*.

At the same time, a group of poets called the "Hartford Wits" became the first well-known creative authors on American soil. The most prominent of the Hartford Wits was Francis Scott Key. Other "Wits" composed such enduring songs as "Hail Columbia." At the same time, the first American magazine of note—the *North American Review*—began publication in 1815. The very title of the magazine denoted Americans' attempt to separate culturally from Europe.

In the graphic arts, talented painters in early America crafted pictures with patriotic themes, expressing their gratitude for liberty. The best remembered are portraits

iStock.com/Cheng Chang

>> Thomas Jefferson's home, Monticello, is a prime example of the neo-classical style that flourished after the War of 1812.

of the founding fathers, many of them painted by Gilbert Stuart (1755–1828) and John Trumbull (1756–1843). Trumbull was also known for his patriotic images, the most popular of which is *Declaration of Independence* (1819), a depiction of a fictional gathering of founding fathers (no such meeting ever took place) that today appears on the back of the two-dollar bill.

The most notable artistic expression of early American nationalism developed in architecture, though, as American architects, identifying with the ancient republican Romans, revived classical architecture styles and motifs, a style known as neo-classicism. Both Thomas Jefferson, who designed the University of Virginia and his home, Monticello, and Charles Bulfinch, who designed the Massachusetts State House in Boston, excelled in this flourishing realm. Pierre l'Enfant, the French architect commissioned to design the capitol buildings in Washington, D.C., also participated in this revival, which explains the plethora of classical architecture found today in Washington, D.C.

>LOOKING AHEAD...

With the rise of the Democratic-Republicans in the early 1800s, the American nation had survived its first significant transfer of power. The Democratic-Republicans had also introduced a new, livelier style of politics into the political culture, one that prioritized the advocacy of a yeoman farmer's republic and the assertion of a specific kind of patriotism.

But Jefferson's attempts to create an idealized agrarian republic proved highly problematic. By curbing the size of the military and limiting federal income to only tariffs, Jefferson exposed the nation to a variety of geopolitical upheavals taking place in Europe. Only heroic fighting and some good luck during the War of 1812 kept the young nation politically solvent.

Shortly thereafter, the nation would turn another corner and embark on a period of economic growth that ran counter to the image idealized by Jefferson. In place of an agrarian republic, the nation would soon develop into an international trading center, bustling with markets and commerce. America was still largely a nation of farmers, but these farmers became more intent on bringing their product to market than on merely remaining self-sufficient. Although the Democratic-Republicans had established much of the political and diplomatic security for the new nation, their vision would not carry the day. It is to the Market Revolution and its manifestations that we now turn.

STUDY TOOLS 9

READY TO STUDY? IN THE BOOK, YOU CAN:

❏ Rip out the Chapter Review Card, which includes key terms and chapter summaries.

ONLINE AT WWW.CENGAGEBRAIN.COM, YOU CAN:

❏ Collect StudyBits while you read and study the chapter.

❏ Quiz yourself on key concepts.

❏ Find videos for further exploration.

❏ Prepare for tests with HIST5 Flash Cards as well as those you create.

❏ Read Lewis and Clark's journal.

❏ Read the lyrics to "The Star-Spangled Banner."

❏ View a satirical cartoon poking fun at the Hartford Convention.

❏ View more pictures of the classical revival in America.

CH9 TIMELINE

1800 Land Act creates federal offices for sale of western land to settlers.

1801–1835 Chief Justice John Marshall builds Supreme Court's constitutional authority.

1803 John Marshall introduces judicial review in *Marbury v. Madison*; Napoleon Bonaparte sells Louisiana territory.

1804 Aaron Burr kills Alexander Hamilton; his supposedly secessionist plans lead to trial for treason.

1804–1806 Lewis and Clark expedition sparks Americans' fascination with the West.

1807 Embargo Act stops American exports and foreign trade, and imperils economy.

1808: *End of legal slave importation in the United States.*

1810: *Peter Durand invents the tin can.*

Father Miguel Hidalgo begins the movement for Mexican independence.

1811: *William H. Harrison attacks Tecumseh's tribal alliance at Tippecanoe.*

Steamboat service begins on the Mississippi River.

1812 War with Britain over American neutrality, alleged collusion with Indians.

Invasion of British Canada a fiasco.

1813 Andrew Jackson defeats Creek Indians in battle over land in Georgia.

1814 Treaty of Ghent ends hostilities without resolving causes of war.

1815: *Battle of Waterloo ends the Napoleonic Wars and the reign of Napoleon.*

March: Creeks lose their land to United States after Battle of Horseshoe Bend.

August: British burn White House in assault on Washington, D.C.

October: Defense of New Orleans against British forces makes Jackson national hero.

December: New England Federalists invoke states' rights at Hartford Convention.

1815–1824 Decline of Federalist Party ushers in nonpartisan "Era of Good Feelings."

10 | The Market Revolution

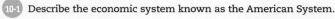

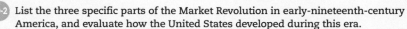

PROCESSION OF VICTUALLERS

OF PHILADELPHIA, ON THE 15.TH OF MARCH 1821. CONDUCTED UNDER THE DIRECTION OF M.R WILLIAM WHITE.

LEARNING OBJECTIVES

After reading this chapter, you should be able to do the following:

10-1 Describe the economic system known as the American System.

10-2 List the three specific parts of the Market Revolution in early-nineteenth-century America, and evaluate how the United States developed during this era.

10-3 Describe the growth of America's middle class during the first half of the 1800s, and discuss some of the stronger movements toward reform during the era.

AFTER FINISHING
THIS CHAPTER
GO TO **PAGE 193**
FOR STUDY TOOLS

In the years following the War of 1812, the United States became relatively isolated from Europe. It focused inward. There was a strong feeling that the country needed to strengthen its economy in order to protect itself against further incursion from outside powers. This view took tangible form as politicians and citizens designed what they called an "American System" of economics that focused on keeping American goods within the United States.

The American System of economics was a fantastic success, and it facilitated so many economic and social changes between 1812 and the 1860s that historians see this period as the social and economic equivalent of the political revolution of the 1770s. Indeed, they describe all these transitions under the term **Market Revolution**. Aided by numerous transportation, communication, and technological innovations, the Market Revolution refers to the time when an increasing number of farmers willingly turned away from the ideal of being self-sufficient in order to focus on a single crop that could be sold at market. This change encouraged specialization and the growth of a dynamic string of market hubs within the United States. The United States had always been a part of the colonial world market, and between 1810 and 1860 the markets simply moved closer to home. Instead of American commerce focusing on transactions between the Atlantic seaboard and Europe, it shifted, focusing now on transactions between the East Coast and the lands extending to and beyond the Mississippi River.

The rise of commercial agriculture changed the way Americans lived their lives. It moved them closer to the world of the marketplace and allowed many to leave the world of agriculture altogether. At the dawn of the 1800s, more than 80 percent of the American labor force worked in agriculture. By 1850, that figure had declined to 55 percent. By the 1880s, less than half of America's workforce was engaged in farming. Local markets needed local salesmen, lawyers, factories, marketers, economists, and bookkeepers. The expansion of the American marketplace was also profoundly reliant on slave labor, as large commercial enterprises required significant amounts of labor. Thus the expansion of American capitalism not only aided in the growth of a new middle class, but it also deepened the country's reliance on slavery. The changes associated with this transition affected nearly every American, and America in 1860 looked dramatically different than it did in 1810.

This chapter examines the Market Revolution, its causes and effects, and the variety of responses to it.

10-1 ECONOMIC NATIONALISM

The second generation of American politicians (James Monroe was the last American revolutionary to be president, serving from 1817 to 1825) did not have the distrust of centralized authority that characterized the revolutionary era. Several men of this younger generation developed a nationalist program for economic growth similar to the one proposed by Alexander Hamilton during the Federalist era. Updated to fit the demands of the 1810s and 1820s, they called this economic plan the **American System**.

10-1a The American System

The American System came from a surprising source: young Democratic-Republican politicians from the West, the South, and the Middle Atlantic states who had superficially embraced Jefferson's vision of a small federal government but in fact eagerly sought the patronage that a large federal government could dole out. Henry Clay from Kentucky and John C. Calhoun from South Carolina led this group. Together, they advanced a vision that the federal government should encourage economic enterprise in three ways: (1) by creating roads and canals, collectively called **internal improvements**; (2) by developing secure economic institutions, such as banks; and (3) by providing for the security of America's economic interests through high tariffs. After seeing the weaknesses of Jefferson's vision of a disparate collection of states, the leaders of the American System wanted to strengthen the nation and secure the advancement of the West through the creation of tremendous public

Market Revolution A series of innovations that led to the creation of an integrated national marketplace; it included the long-distance coordination of the production, distribution, and consumption of goods

American System Economic plan based on the idea that the federal government should encourage economic enterprise

internal improvements Building of roads and canals by the federal and state governments

◀◀◀ **Between 1810 and 1860 the United States underwent an economic transformation, a transition from being largely a producer of raw materials and goods for overseas buyers to being a self-sustaining, vibrant location of economic growth. Here, the expansive marketplace in Philadelphia reviews a procession of cattle coming to be sold at local markets.**

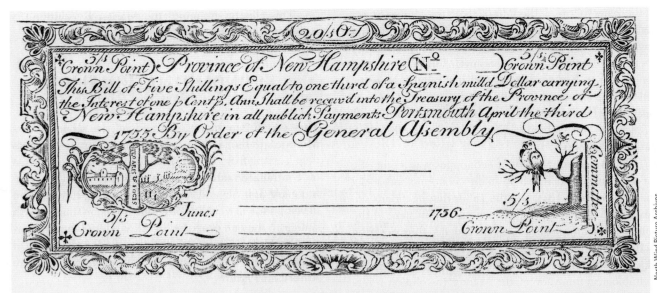

>> The states chartered their own banks, offering a bewildering variety of currencies and credit, such as this banknote from New Hampshire. It was, to say the least, unstable.

works projects. Despite the Democratic-Republican's Jeffersonian origins, their plan was very much in the Hamiltonian mold.

10-1b A New National Bank

One of the key components of the American System was the creation of a national bank. When Congress, before the War of 1812, refused to recharter the First National Bank in 1811, the states chartered their own banks, offering a bewildering variety of credit and currencies. More than four hundred banks were operating in 1818, each offering its own form of currency and credit. Speculation ran rampant, as investors attempted to pick which currency would appreciate the quickest. Fortunes were won and lost very quickly, and investors had little idea which currencies would be the most durable.

To end the mayhem and strengthen the national government, proponents of the American System designed the **Second Bank of the United States**. In a bill drafted by Calhoun, the Second National Bank was established with support from western and southern congressmen. New Englanders, who had adequate and secure banks in the North, opposed the creation of the bank. With Democratic-Republicans

Second Bank of the United States National bank established in 1816 to curb rampant currency speculation

mostly supporting a national bank and former New England Federalists opposing it, times had changed since the Federalist era; now each party was advocating what it had opposed just two decades prior. The new bank was chartered in 1816.

10-1c A Protective Tariff

Calhoun and Clay also supervised the passage of the Tariff of 1816, which taxed all incoming goods at the stiff rate of 25 percent. They designed the tariff to limit consumption of foreign goods in the United States and to encourage the development of American commerce and industries. This meant that the goods in the American System were to be American.

10-1d Court Cases

During these years, the Supreme Court issued a number of decisions that advocated economic growth at the expense of the states or of previous contracts. One of the most consequential cases was *Dartmouth College v. Woodward* (1819), which forbade state legislatures from altering college charters in order to gain control over them, because a corporation (the university) had drafted the charter. This decision prioritized the rights of a corporation over those of the state, thus clearing the path for increased economic development. In *Gibbons v. Ogden* (1824), a steamboat operator named Aaron Ogden argued that his business license from the state of New York entitled him to a monopoly on transporting commerce along the New York coastline. The U.S. Supreme Court disagreed, however, arguing that Thomas Gibbons, whose steamboat company had been chartered by the U.S. Congress, could navigate there as well, suggesting that the federal government's power to regulate commerce overruled that granted by states.

10-1e A Protected Hemisphere

The War of 1812 and the resulting economic nationalism made the United States a stronger force, allowing it to assert greater dominance throughout the Western Hemisphere. To solidify and expand its border, in 1819 the United States negotiated a treaty with Spain, which wanted to cut some of its colonial possessions in order to

>> James Monroe. Although the Monroe Doctrine was little noted at the time, it later became a foundation for American foreign policy.

Library of Congress Prints and Photographs Division [LC-USZC4-12215]

strengthen its control over modern-day Mexico. The resulting Adam-Onis Treaty granted the United States possession of Florida and a large swath of land extending from today's Oklahoma all the way to Oregon, all in exchange for parts of Texas. Now the United States extended from the southern tip of Florida to the current-day northern boundary with Canada, and from the Atlantic almost to the Pacific (although it still did not claim today's American Southwest).

The new dominance was expressed most clearly in the **Monroe Doctrine** of 1823. This doctrine, which emerged as many Latin American countries were clamoring for independence from their European colonizers, declared that any European nation attempting to re-colonize Latin America would be treated as a party hostile to the United States. President James Monroe announced that the Western Hemisphere was the domain of the United States and was to remain separate from the affairs of Europe. At the same time, Monroe agreed to refrain from any interference with

existing European colonies or with the internal affairs or wars of the European powers. Although the Monroe Doctrine was little noted at the time, it later became a foundation for American foreign policy, used to justify American expansion into and involvement with the countries of Latin America.

10-1f Opponents of the American System

Not everyone favored the American System. Some southerners saw it as merely an attempt to wrangle taxes from wealthy cotton planters and give the money to northern and western business interests. Others liked the American System well enough when the money was spent in their home state but opposed it when resources were spent elsewhere. War-hero-turned-politician Andrew Jackson at first enjoyed the fruits of the plan but eventually came to see it as a vehicle for corruption. Despite these mounting complaints, which would increase throughout the first half of the 1800s, the American System was the prevailing economic plan for the nation until the 1830s and 1840s.

 ## THE MARKET REVOLUTION

Combining tariffs, internal improvements, and a national bank, the American System of economics facilitated the Market Revolution. Farmers, more than ever before, could focus on producing what they produced best, bring their goods to local American markets, and purchase the items they could not grow or make themselves. The result was that people's notions about their role in the economy changed. Leaving behind the idea that they had to be self-sustaining farmers, they instead began to think of themselves as participants in the national and international marketplace.

Monroe Doctrine Declaration of 1823 proclaiming that any European nation attempting to colonize Latin America would be treated as a party hostile to the United States; President James Monroe announced that the Western Hemisphere was the domain of the United States and was to remain separate from the affairs of Europe

This made them more accepting of commercial and capitalist goals, for they were becoming not only producers, but also *consumers*. For the most part, the Market Revolution had to do with commercialized agriculture and not with industrialization (although the beginnings of the Industrial Revolution can be identified in this period).

The Market Revolution was made up of three parts, in roughly this order: (1) a transportation and communications revolution, (2) a transition to commercialized farming, and (3) industrialization. Each transition provoked significant social changes.

10-2a The Transportation and Communications Revolution

Along with friendly government policies, the Market Revolution could not have happened without a revolution in the way people and goods moved around and the way people communicated with one another. Since the start of European settlement in North America, long-distance travel had meant using rivers or the sea. Water offered the quickest and most reliable means of moving goods from their place of origin to a market where they could be sold. However, America's rivers run primarily from north to south, making travel from east to west difficult. For instance, there was not a single navigable river connecting the northeastern cities of New York, Philadelphia, or Boston to the farmlands of the Ohio River Valley.

Recognizing the importance of speedy transportation, in the years after 1800 some states began internal improvements. They financed, for the most part through tax dollars, the construction of toll roads, canals, and other modes of transportation. This funding sparked four eras of transportation innovation: (1) the turnpike era, (2) the canal era, (3) the steamboat era, and (4) the railroad era (Map 10.1).

THE TURNPIKE ERA

The first improvements were roads and turnpikes (private roads with tolls), and the 1810s were the turnpike era. Between 1800 and 1825, hundreds of miles of toll roads crisscrossed the nation. The Cumberland Road was the best known, extending from Maryland to West Virginia. But these early roads were mostly unpaved, and huge ruts and tree stumps made them dangerous and slow going. The roads were too unpredictable for Americans to use reliably to transport large amounts of commercial goods.

Erie Canal Artificial river connecting the New York State cities of Buffalo and Albany; provided a continuous water route from the shores of the Atlantic to the Great Lakes; measured 364 miles long and 40 feet wide

THE CANAL ERA

To solve this problem, human ingenuity provided the country with something nature had not—a series of east-to-west canals—and the 1820s were the canal era. New York led the way in 1817. New York governor DeWitt Clinton helped nurture a partnership between the state government and private entrepreneurs in order to undertake the monumental task of constructing the **Erie Canal**, an artificial river connecting Buffalo—on the shore of Lake Erie—to Albany. Because Albany was linked to New York City by the Hudson River, the Erie Canal provided a continuous water route from the shores of the Atlantic to the Great Lakes. This was an immensely complex project. At the time, the longest canal in the world was 28 miles long. The Erie was 364 miles long and 40 feet wide. New Yorkers completed construction in eight years. When it was done, mules on paths along the shore could tow with a rope a barge filled with more than a ton of goods. The barge moved as fast as the mules. The Erie Canal opening was a landmark development for four reasons (see "The Reasons Why . . ." box).

THE STEAMBOAT ERA

Despite the general reluctance of the South to invest in transportation improvements, there were innovations in the South and the West as well. There, steamboats,

>> Early roads like the one pictured here were mostly unpaved, and huge ruts and tree stumps made them dangerous and slow going.

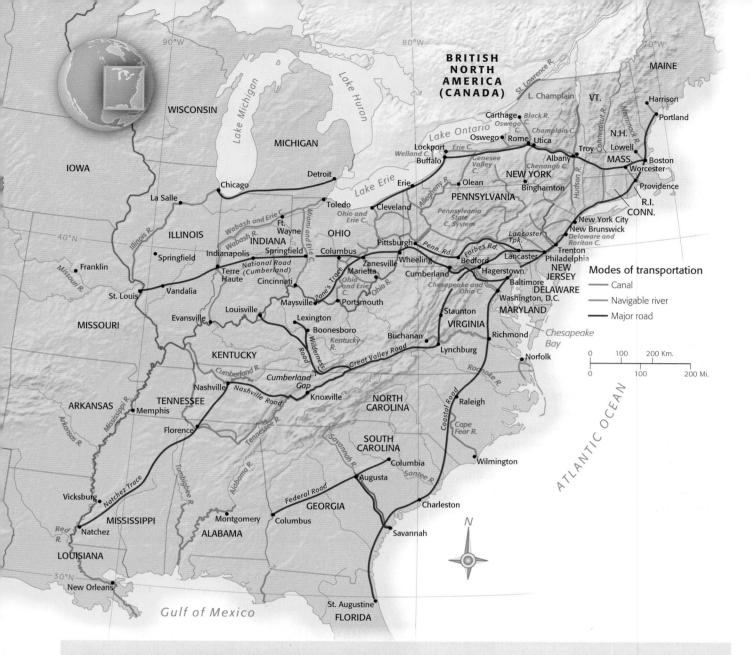

Map 10.1 Rivers, Roads, and Canals, 1825–1860

>> The first fifty years of the nineteenth century witnessed four separate revolutions in transportation: the turnpike era, the canal era, the steamboat era, and the railroad era. All but the steamboat era were concentrated in the North and the West. This map shows each of those four developments.

developed in the early 1800s, proved to be effective transport on the regions' broad rivers. By the 1830s, they carried much of the commerce in those regions and succeeded in reducing cargo rates across the country. Their fabulous success made many southerners consider the funding of other internal improvements unnecessary.

THE RAILROAD ERA

The most transformative new form of transportation was the railroad, which became the cornerstone of the American transportation revolution of the 1840s and 1850s. The development of railroads further extended the transportation improvements begun during the canal

The Reasons Why...

There were four reasons why the Erie Canal was a landmark development:

Financial. First, the project was a tremendous economic success. The cost of moving one ton of goods from Buffalo to New York City dropped from nineteen cents per mile to a little more than one cent. The canal cut the time it took to move goods between Buffalo and New York City from twenty days to six. The state of New York charged tolls on the canal, which yielded a huge profit.

Copycats. Second, these profits pushed other states to invest in transportation. Many states chartered private corporations to build those internal improvements, which greatly politicized the role of corporations in American life. This process became political because it was profitable to run a canal, so winning a charter to build one was comparable to winning the lottery. Significantly, all but three of the largest canals were built in the North, signifying a northern commitment to the Market Revolution. Southern leaders, who were usually wealthy landowners, remained content to rely on the rivers that transported cotton and other staple crops.

Creating a major metropolis. Third, it spurred the growth of New York City. As the major trading link between the interior of the United States and the Atlantic Ocean, New York City became the nation's major economic center.

A change in farming. Fourth, the creation of a cheap way to move goods to market made it more enticing to farmers in the interior to produce only the few items that would be the most profitable.

>> The Erie Canal, shown here, provided a continuous water route from the shores of the Atlantic to the Great Lakes.

North Wind Picture Archives

and steamboat eras, but railroads had three crucial advantages over water travel: (1) unlike canals, rail lines did not depend on natural waterways as their end points; (2) railroads did not freeze; and (3) trains traveled significantly faster than mules.

For these reasons, railroads helped complete the full transition to a market-based economy. In the 1830s, American builders laid more than 3,000 miles of track. By the 1860s, more than 30,000 miles of track ran through the country. As with canals, most of the nation's railroads were concentrated in the North, laid by merchants and state governments eager to develop a diversified economy. The South, meanwhile, maintained its plantation-based culture and its dependence on natural waterways to move its key staple crops.

From 1810 to 1850, the speed with which goods and people could be moved across vast stretches of land increased considerably. In the 1810s, a journey via horseback from the Atlantic Coast to the Great Lakes would have taken several weeks. In the 1850s, one could take either the Erie Canal or a railroad and be there in a matter of days, if not hours.

THE COMMUNICATIONS REVOLUTION

At the same time, in the early 1830s Americans were inventing and incorporating new methods of communication. The key development was Samuel F. B. Morse's successful transmission via the first telegraph, which used electric wires to send a message nearly instantaneously from one place to another. Now news about politics, the price of goods, and arrival of new products could be known throughout the nation in a matter of seconds. The telegraph facilitated nationwide commerce and lowered the cost of communication. It also symbolized the energy of the era, when, for the first time in human history, communication was set free from the realm of physical transit. Americans at the time were unaware of the kinds of communications that would emerge in future years, but they were aware that they were living at a transformative time in human history. Morse emphasized this notion

>> This image of Louisville, Kentucky, circa 1850, with the numerous steamboats dotting the shore of the Ohio River, shows how prevalent steamboats were in the era, especially in the South, and how numerous factories and warehouses oriented themselves to transporting their goods via the area's rivers.

The Filson Historical Society, Louisville, KY

when, in 1844, he chose the first words to be transmitted via his brand new code: "What Hath God Wrought?"

10-2b Commercialized Farming

The transportation and communications revolutions caused a transition in how farmers (that is, most Americans) farmed their land. No longer did each family have to produce almost everything it consumed. This transition was not entirely new to farmers in the South and in areas of the Middle Colonies, where colonial-era farmers had already oriented their production around staple crops. But the rest of the nation had concentrated on self-sufficiency and diversified farming, and this market transition led to dramatic changes in the South, the West, and New England.

CHANGES IN THE SOUTH

Before 1793, southern agriculture consisted of the staple crops of tobacco

>> "What Hath God Wrought?"—Samuel F. B. Morse. Morse's first transmission via the telegraph spoke to the transformative nature of instant communications.

villorejo/Shutterstock.com

and rice, but farmers had added a few more varieties of crops during the 1700s. After 1793, when Eli Whitney promoted a new invention called the cotton gin, everything changed. The cotton gin allowed for the profitable cultivation of cotton even in land with poor soil by allowing the harvesting of "short staple" (or hard-to-clean) cotton. Thus cotton became easy and profitable to produce throughout the South (not just in areas rich in nutrients), and cotton production rapidly took over southern agriculture and the southern economy. By 1825, the American South was the world's largest producer of the fiber. Between 1816 and 1840 southern cotton constituted more than half the value of all American exports.

This development created obvious opportunities for white southerners. If you could get a little land and a few slaves, you could earn huge profits. The ease with which wealth could be generated spurred a large westward migration throughout the South, as small farmers searched for land to grow cotton. The development of the cotton gin also reinforced the farmers' dependence on slaves because it made their labor even more valuable (slaves could be used profitably on even poor land). At the same time, slavery moved west with the cotton farmers, making the slave trade profitable even after the importation of slaves from Africa had stopped in 1808, per the agreement reached in the U.S. Constitution. These farmers revived the domestic slave trade. Any ideas that emancipation might be plausible in the South during these years vanished after the introduction of the cotton gin.

This cotton boom had two other key outcomes. First, cotton impeded any significant internal improvements in the South because wealthy southerners considered waterways sufficient to transport cotton. This hurt small farmers, who could not afford land along waterways, and it stalled the development of any major railroad lines in the southern states. Second, the roaring success of cotton, in combination with the Market Revolution elsewhere in the nation, hindered southerners from developing a diversified economy. They could rely on other parts of the nation for the goods they needed. This meant that if the South's cotton production was ever threatened, the southern economy would be in trouble.

CHANGES IN THE WEST

The Market Revolution also meant that farmers in the Midwest (Ohio, Indiana, and Illinois) could take maximum advantage of the land's rich soil and plentiful rain. Reflecting the Market Revolution's transition to commercialized agriculture, a wheat belt stretched from western New York to Wisconsin, a corn belt reached from Ohio to Illinois, a tobacco belt extended from Kentucky to Missouri, and a cotton belt spread from Georgia to Mississippi. Each area continued to grow a diverse range of crops, but each increasingly specialized in what it grew best.

The commercial development of these regions prompted a huge shift of the American population (Map 10.2). With the **Land Act of 1820**, the federal government helped promote settlement of land west of the Appalachians

Land Act of 1820 Legislation that promoted settlement west of the Appalachians by setting affordable prices for manageable plots of land

by setting affordable prices for manageable plots of land. This prompted one of the largest internal migrations in American history. In 1789, two-thirds of all Americans (about 3 million people) lived within 50 miles of the Atlantic Ocean, while only 5 percent lived west of the Appalachians. By 1840, one-third of the population (more than 5 million people) lived in new states west of the Appalachians. Several new areas applied for statehood, almost all of them as a result of westward migration: Indiana (1816), Mississippi (1817), Illinois (1818), Alabama (1819), Maine (1820), Missouri (1821), Arkansas (1836), Michigan (1837), Florida (1845), Texas (1845), Iowa (1846), and Wisconsin (1848). During these years, between 5 and 10 percent of all Americans moved each year.

THE WEST AND SLAVERY

Westward migration provoked a significant question: What to do about slavery? In 1819, Missouri sought entry into the union as a slave state. Its request provoked a debate in Congress that Congress wished desperately to avoid. Even the aging Thomas Jefferson wrote that the issue of slavery frightened him like a "fire bell in the night."

The issue of whether slavery would be allowed in Missouri was pivotal for two reasons: (1) Missouri lay along the same latitude as several free states, and its entry into the Union as a slave state would move slavery

>> By allowing the cultivation of cotton in less-than-ideal soil, the cotton gin, pictured here in action, revived the internal slave trade in the United States, while also curtailing the development of a diversified economy in the South.

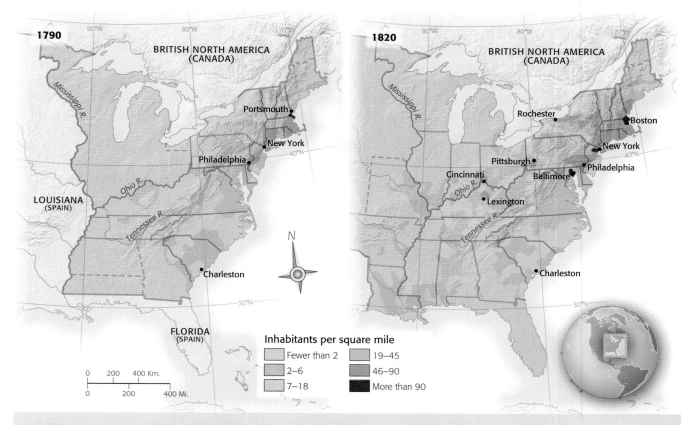

Map 10.2 Population Density, 1790–1820

>> Two maps, side-by-side, showing the dramatic increase in population density of the American Northeast from 1790 to 1820.

Inhabitants per square mile
- Fewer than 2
- 2–6
- 7–18
- 19–45
- 46–90
- More than 90

northward; and (2) the admission of Missouri as a slave state would upset the congressional balance of eleven slave states and eleven free states. Northerners, mindful of the ideals of the Revolution and intent on avoiding a large black population in the North, sought to keep slavery in the South. Southerners sought to expand the development of cotton, which, they felt, required the labor of slaves.

When Representative James Tallmadge, Jr., proposed the **Tallmadge Amendment**, which would have enforced gradual emancipation in Missouri, a vicious debate broke out on the floor of Congress. Henry Clay brokered a compromise: Missouri could enter as a slave state if Maine could enter as a free state. In addition, Clay drew a line at the latitude of 36°30′. Territories

The aging Thomas Jefferson wrote that the issue of slavery frightened him like a "fire bell in the night."

THE NEW ENGLAND TRANSITION

Since colonial times, New England farmers had developed diversified farms that could fulfill many of their families' needs,

north of the line would remain free, while territories south of it could maintain slavery. This was the **Missouri Compromise**, passed in 1820, which would dictate the spread of slavery in the West for the next thirty years.

Tallmadge Amendment
Proposal that would have enforced gradual emancipation in Missouri

Missouri Compromise
Arrangement brokered by Henry Clay that set 36°30′ as the divider between free and slave territories and that allowed Missouri to enter the nation as a slave state if Maine were allowed to enter as free

while local markets provided items that could not be grown or manufactured easily. The Market Revolution (combined with soil exhaustion) slowly eroded this lifestyle. Rocky, cold New England had never been a great place to farm, and access to cheap western agriculture furthered the decline in farming during the 1820s.

Without a central profitable crop to turn to, New Englanders reorganized their economy. Giving up on corn and wheat, they began to grow garden vegetables, fruit, dairy products, meat, eggs, and other perishable goods that could be sold in the growing urban markets. They also took advantage of the new methods of transportation to get their goods to market. In 1820, about one-third of all New England produce was sent to market. By 1850, that proportion had jumped to about one-half.

The result was dazzling success—for those who owned land. Those who did not own land confronted rising land prices. Many headed west, where land was cheaper. Others worked as wage laborers on farms, hoping one day to earn enough money to buy land of their own.

Women's output was similarly affected. Many women stopped weaving clothes, because store-bought cloth was cheaper. Many churned butter and made cheese instead, participating in the new market economy by selling dairy products at market.

10-2c Industrialization

The first two facets of the Market Revolution (the transportation revolution and the conversion to commercial agriculture) required a third: machines. Railroads needed machinery to fabricate engines, cars, and tracks; cotton crops required factories to turn the raw product into cloth; and specialized farming in the West demanded large reapers and tough plows. Thus, the third aspect of the Market Revolution was the rise of industrialization and the creation of factories. It is

>> Cotton.
iStock.com/Craftvision

important to remember that this was not yet the full-scale industrialization associated with today's large factories. But it was the beginning of that process.

THE MECHANIZATION OF AGRICULTURE

Cyrus McCormick's development of the reaper in 1831 was the most significant industrial development in agriculture. A twenty-five-year-old Virginia farmer, McCormick developed a machine that harvested grain much faster than manual labor could. This was a boon for the western states because they had miles of flat farmland that was perfect for the reaper. In 1837, McCormick moved his factory from Virginia to Chicago, the principal city of the booming Midwest, and sold his reapers to farmers there. In the same way, John Deere's steel plow (1837) made it easier to plow tough fields, and of course the cotton gin (1793) sped up the process of separating short-staple cottonseed from its fiber.

THE MECHANIZATION OF MACHINE TOOLS

McCormick and Whitney noted the precise specifications of the many moving parts that made up their machines. They then reproduced those parts in large quantities, thus introducing the system of interchangeable parts. Eli Whitney was chiefly credited for this development (more than he deserved) and won government contracts to develop muskets that used interchangeable parts. With interchangeable parts, producers could make products more quickly and cheaply instead of handcrafting each item one by one. Watches, clocks, and locks—all luxury items in 1800—became inexpensive household goods by 1840 because of the use of interchangeable parts.

FACTORIES

Factories were the most efficient way to produce the large quantities of goods needed to accommodate the Market Revolution, but they did not prosper as quickly as one might imagine. Before 1800, most production was done in a decentralized system of family- or artisan-based manufacturing. Large manufacturers would pay one family to perform one task and then pass the item on to the next family or artisan to perform the next task. This was called the **"putting out" system**.

"putting out" system Division of labor in which large manufacturers would pay one family to perform one task, then pass the item on to the next family or artisan to perform the next task

>> The cotton gin easily separated cotton fibers from the seed, a mechanizing process that led to the dramatic expansion of the cotton industry.

The rise of the factory in the 1820s altered this system by bringing nearly all aspects of production under one roof. Samuel Slater was the first to develop the workings of a factory on American soil, designing in 1789 a factory that spun cotton into thread. Within its first ten years of operation, Slater's textile mill hired more than one hundred people, mostly women and young children. The amount of thread produced by Slater's mill prompted a rise in the volume of thread-based goods (mainly clothes, and also towels and curtains) and a drop in their price.

Entrepreneurs opened other factories, and these new factories continued to improve production. Slater could not weave thread into cloth at his mill, for example (he still had to "put out" his thread to home workers for this task). In 1813, Boston merchants developed a power loom to weave cloth. Headed by Francis Lowell, the new factory brought all the processes of clothmaking under one roof, thereby quickening the pace of work and cheapening the price of production. Between 1820 and 1860 textile mills sprouted up all over the northern and Middle Atlantic states, harnessing the power of swift-moving rivers. Americans began purchasing their clothing rather than making it, a change that boosted the rise of retail clothing stores. Other manufacturing industries, such as shoemaking and clockmaking, followed.

10-2d Social Changes Associated with the Market Revolution

The Market Revolution had many social ramifications. The six most significant were (1) the growth of cities; (2) the impact on the environment; (3) the changing face of the labor force; (4) an increase in religious divisions; (5) the beginnings of a working class and a middle class; and (6) increased protest movements.

THE GROWTH OF CITIES

The expansion of markets and the growth of factories led to a slow process of urbanization. In 1830, only 5 percent of Americans lived in towns of 8,000 people or more. By 1850, that number had more than tripled, to 16 percent. With the development of the Erie Canal, New York City solidified its position as the largest city in the nation, with a population in 1840 of more than 300,000. Philadelphia, Boston, and Baltimore experienced robust growth as well. Of the ten largest cities in 1860, only one, New Orleans, was in the South.

ENVIRONMENTAL COSTS OF THE MARKET REVOLUTION

There were significant environmental costs of the Market Revolution as well. Steamboats and early railroads burned wood as a source of power, which caused rapid deforestation in the Northeast. Similarly, as the transportation revolution enabled more people to move west, new settlers cleared land and chopped wood, destroying animal habitats and western landscapes. Sawmills and textile mills, relying on waterways for their power, interrupted the paths of spawning fish. And in the South, enslaved workers cleared land to make way for cotton fields, thus forever dispossessing Native Americans from those lands. These costs would only increase as industrialization expanded through the rest of the century.

WOMEN AND IMMIGRANTS IN THE LABOR FORCE

There was also a dramatic change in the composition of the labor force. Setting a pattern followed by other factory owners, Francis Lowell hired single women from New England farms to work in his clothmaking factory. He needed cheap labor, and young women would work for lower wages than men. To present a wholesome image to the farm families who might send their daughters to work there, Lowell built boarding houses for his "mill girls," where they were taught Christian ethics and monitored by chaperones. This was called the

Lowell System. Factory life was harsh for these workers, however, and most sought to return home to start families after a short tenure in a Lowell mill. Most stayed just five years. They worked without insurance, wage guarantees, or legal protections of any kind, and when times were hard, these factory workers were the first to suffer.

For the most part, working in a factory was arduous, and wages were low. People often worked fifteen-hour days, six days a week, and usually an entire family had to work in order to get by. Men, women, and young children spent long hours in the hot, noisy factories.

But mill owners were not obligated to listen to complaints; they could always find eager replacements. After 1840, the number of immigrants arriving in the United States suddenly soared, causing the nation's population to increase a whopping 36 percent in the 1840s. Roughly two-thirds of these new arrivals were Irish, fleeing years of miserable poverty and hunger that peaked during the **Great Irish Famine** of 1845–1851. The majority of Irish immigrants settled in northeastern cities and worked at industrial jobs, replacing New England women and children. By the 1860s, half of the employees in most American factories were immigrants, most of them Irish. The Irish became a distinct underclass in the nineteenth-century United States.

Anonymous/The Art Gallery Collection/Alamy Stock Photo

>> "The early millgirls were of different ages," "said Harriet Hanson Robinson, a mill worker in Lowell, Massachusetts for fourteen years, starting at age ten." "Some were not over ten years old; a few were in middle life, but the majority were between the ages of sixteen and twenty-five." This image depicts workers very much like Robinson.

CHALLENGES TO THE PROTESTANT CONSENSUS

Along with a willingness to work for cheap wages, the Irish immigrants brought Roman Catholicism. Catholicism had been present in the United States since the first European settlements, but Catholics had always been a small minority compared to the Protestant majority (roughly 1 percent at the time of the Revolution). With the wave of Irish immigrants, Catholics formed the first sizeable religious minority in American history. Many Protestant Americans feared this development, believing that rising levels of Catholic immigration threatened the character of America, which they considered a "Protestant nation." Catholics, most nineteenth-century Americans believed, were too bound to the teachings of the pope to behave like free and independent republicans. They were also prone to the excesses of drinking and licentiousness, or so claimed Protestant nativists.

To counteract the growing Catholic presence, some Protestants began seeking an official proclamation of Protestantism as the official religion of the nation. Such efforts never succeeded, but they did stir controversy. For instance, the efforts of Protestant educators to introduce Protestant religious study into the curriculum of the nation's public schools prompted the development of the first Catholic parochial schools.

A NEW WORKING CLASS

In their new jobs, Irish workers earned little pay. Indeed, what made Irish laborers so attractive to factory owners was their willingness to work for low wages. Moreover, the

Lowell System A labor and production model for manufacturing textiles that, for the first time, brought all stages of textile production under one roof, with employees living near the factory in employee housing, away from their families; featured mostly female employees, young women seeking to earn wages before getting married

Great Irish Famine Years of miserable poverty and hunger in Ireland that peaked during 1845–1851 and led millions of Irish to the United States

Irish were forced to accept the worst housing available. Irish families crowded together in basement apartments or in attics, and Irish slums became hotbeds for diseases like cholera and tuberculosis. To the eyes of native-born Americans, these conditions served as unhappy notice that the squalor of Britain's industrial towns had been transplanted to America. In fact, the Irish slums were simply a part of the new working class that worked in the factories, earned day wages, and were increasingly removed from the fruits of their labor. Over the course of the 1800s, these laborers would begin to feel aligned with one another, creating a sense of belonging to a particular class.

PROTEST MOVEMENTS

Several movements arose to protest the living and working conditions experienced by the working class. Protest movements of the early nineteenth century were usually one of two kinds: (1) an organization of middle-class reformers seeking to safeguard the morality of workers or (2) laborers fighting for economic and work-related protections, such as a shorter workday. The two movements often opposed each other, usually because the middle-class reformers were anti-immigrant, while the labor movement was made up of Irish and non-Irish immigrants. Furthermore, the federal and state governments firmly supported economic development, so ceding to the demands of laborers did not seem to offer immediate gains for the economy.

Despite these hurdles, the laborers enjoyed some successes. Neighborhood groups began to meet up in citywide trade assemblies that delved into politics and rallied to elect politicians sympathetic to their cause. They then attempted to unify the citywide assemblies into nationwide unions. One such union, the **Workingmen's Party**, was formed in 1828 and spread through fifteen states. It was surpassed in 1834 by the **National Trades' Union**, which is usually regarded as the nation's first large-scale union. And, although the power of the trade unions varied depending on the economy, in 1840, President Martin Van Buren instituted the ten-hour day for federal employees, yielding to one of the long-standing demands of the laboring classes.

 ## REFORMERS

But the most influential reform movement of the early nineteenth century emerged from the middle class. Spurred by a religious revival known as the Second Great Awakening, a large group of middle-class social reformers attempted to control the changes brought about by the Market Revolution. The men and especially the women who led the reform movement promoted a vision

>> A woman's first priority was making the family home a sanctuary for her laboring husband, a "haven in a heartless world." This image, a wood cutting, shows a mother teaching her daughters how to do domestic chores.

of a more caring nation, one more considerate of human life. In doing so, these reformers broached some of the most consequential issues the nation would face during the next two hundred years, including racism, the rights of workers, and the rights of women.

10-3a The Creation of the Middle Class

Where did these reformers come from? As more and more unskilled laborers transitioned to factory work, a need arose for paper-pushing bureaucrats who could manage others, balance the books, and sell goods. This

Workingmen's Party Union of laborers, made up from citywide assemblies, that formed in 1828; eventually spread through fifteen states

National Trades' Union First large-scale labor union in the United States; formed in 1834

was new. In 1800, a shoemaker would have made shoes himself, selling them at his own shop. By 1860, however, many "shoemakers" did not actually make shoes at all. Rather, they supervised a group of semiskilled or unskilled laborers, each of whom completed a part of the shoemaking process. Similarly, large factories needed bookkeepers, accountants, salesmen, and clerks.

This management class formed the backbone of an emerging middle class. Before 1800, Americans had hardly ever used the term *middle class*. By 1850, the term was part of the popular vocabulary. The middle class began to develop a culture distinct from that of the elite property owners or that of the workers.

In the middle class of the mid-1800s, men were presumed to be the sole income earners, usually working outside the home. Their wives, meanwhile, transitioned from income providers to guardians of the home and family, a concept that came to be called the "cult of female domesticity." Middle-class women developed their own social and cultural outlets. Manufacturers were quick to recognize this trend, providing products exclusively geared to women, in a feminization of consumerism. Publishers introduced a "ladies" literature, a feminization of culture. But a woman's first priority was making the family home a sanctuary for her laboring husband, a "haven in a heartless world."

10-3b The Second Great Awakening

For most people, and especially for women, new evangelical churches lay at the center of middle-class culture. More than any other group in American society, the middle class—the shopkeepers, clerks, and managers—was most active in the evangelical sects that developed in the 1830s and formed the center of what historians call the Second Great Awakening. The Second Great Awakening was a Protestant religious revival that began in the West but shortly moved to the Northeast and the South. It lasted from the 1790s to the 1840s and reached its high point between the 1820s and 1840s.

THE THEOLOGY

The central theological idea behind the Second Great Awakening was that an individual's soul could be saved through human agency (meaning hard work) and his or her acceptance of responsibility for a sinful nature. This meant that divine revelation was not the only path to salvation. This stood in contrast to Jonathan Edwards's and George Whitefield's theology of relying on divine benevolence for salvation, which was paramount during the First Great Awakening. The ideas behind the Second Great Awakening were that humans could achieve a level of perfectibility—both individual and social—by doing good works and by promoting what they understood to be God's intent. Action was the key. Humans had the power to choose good or evil, and, by choosing good, they could eventually alleviate sin or, put another way, become perfect. The name for the idea that humans can accept or reject divine grace is Arminianism.

HOW IT SPREAD

The Second Great Awakening spread through a series of three- or four-day revivals orchestrated by itinerant preachers. The most prominent was Charles G. Finney, a New York lawyer who gave up the law in 1821 to convert souls. Finney was a spellbinding orator whose sermons were particularly effective in the towns that had experienced the most changes during the Market Revolution. One area in upstate New York had so many converts

>> The beauty and seclusion of Walden Pond helped lead writer Henry David Thoreau to consider the costs of the Market Revolution. This replica of his cabin is far sturdier than the original.

it was called the **burned-over district**, having been penetrated by fiery orators speaking the Word of God. Many people genuinely believed God had touched them, and the habits they developed because of their faith—thrift, sobriety, obedience—led them to succeed in the new market-based economy. In the South, women and African Americans were particularly moved by the Christian message of salvation and hope. American Catholics and Jews responded to the newfound fervor as well, usually by upgrading the importance of the sermon in their worship ceremonies, although Catholics and Jews were still not widely accepted by the mainstream. The Methodists and the Baptists, both reform-minded low-church traditions, capitalized on the religious fervor to the greatest extent. By the 1820s, both denominations had surpassed all others to become the two largest churches in America. Meanwhile, the Second Great Awakening led to a "Christianization" of African Americans, both free and enslaved, during this era.

Oneida Community Mansion House

>> Among the "perfectionist" communities that popped up in the 1840s, none was more famous than that in Oneida, New York, where men and women experimented with non-traditional living arrangements in search of a perfect community. Here, a group of men and women work collectively for the good of the community.

WHY A REVIVAL?

Some historians have argued that middle-class interest in religion stemmed from a desire for economic security. As the American economy became more competitive, those who aspired to succeed embraced religion for a sense of hope and confidence in the future. In addition, evangelical religion promoted the values—frugality, sobriety, diligence, and zeal—that Americans needed to achieve their economic goals. More prosaically, church membership also bestowed social respectability, and those who joined were more likely to impress their superiors at work, which might lead to promotions. Both religion and the cult of female domesticity were central aspects of the emerging American middle class.

THE TRANSCENDENTALISTS

The theology of perfectibility appeared in secular form in writings by the **Transcendentalists**, a group of thinkers and writers in the Northeast who believed that ultimate truths were beyond human grasp—that they "transcended" our capacity for understanding. This being so, they turned inward—to themselves and to their society—asking what could be done to improve the human condition. The best-known Transcendentalists were Ralph Waldo Emerson and Henry David Thoreau, two genuine celebrities of the time. Seeking to live by Transcendentalist ideals, Thoreau attempted to return to nature and narrated his experiences in his book *Walden*. Telling the tale of his two-year journey living in the wilderness, the book demonstrated Thoreau's desire for self-sufficiency and for the conservation of nature. He also protested slavery and war, and he advocated civil disobedience, starting a tradition that would influence later reformers like Martin Luther King, Jr. His friend Emerson, meanwhile, critiqued economic competition and social conformity. Their critiques of a market-based society, with the manufacturing of desire and economic disparity, still resonate with many Americans.

burned-over district Area in upstate New York that had many converts who had been inspired by the fiery orators speaking the Word of God during the Second Great Awakening

Transcendentalists Group of thinkers and writers in the Northeast who believed that ultimate truths were beyond human grasp

The purity of Thoreau's and Emerson's ideals struck a chord with their generation and with the generation that followed, whose luminaries included Nathaniel Hawthorne and Herman Melville. These writers debated in their fiction the perfectibility of humankind. Perhaps ironically, all of these thinkers were speakers on the **lyceum circuit**, a touring lecture circuit that was made possible only by the transportation breakthroughs of the Market Revolution.

UTOPIANISM

Utopianism provided another response to the quest for perfectibility. After their inception in Europe, several "perfectionist" communities popped up in the 1840s and 1850s, mostly in the Northeast and also in the Midwest. One was in Oneida, New York, where John Humphrey Noyes led a group of fifty-one followers to develop what he viewed as a perfect community. The Oneida community had open sexual mores, communal child rearing, a unique division of labor, and a therapeutic milieu where people freely offered constructive criticism of one another under the watchful eye of Noyes.

The Shakers, who developed from a group of Quakers, also believed in perfectionism and communal property. Their communities developed a tradition of rejecting commercial endeavors, one result being their creation of beautiful handcrafted furniture, which continues to be sold today. There were many more of these groups. More than one hundred utopian communities were established between the 1820s and the 1850s.

THE LATTER-DAY SAINTS

Creating a utopia was not for everyone. Some preferred to anticipate the Second Coming of Christ, when perfection would reign for the chosen. The most significant group was the Mormons, founded by Joseph Smith, a Protestant convert who witnessed one of Charles Finney's revivals. After his conversion in the burned-over district, Smith claimed to have been visited by the angel Moroni, who showed him several golden tablets that revealed the foundations for a new religion based on the lost tribe of Israel. According to Smith, these

lyceum circuit Schedule of lectures in which clergymen, reformers, Transcendentalists, socialists, feminists, and other speakers would speak to large crowds in small towns

The Granger Collection Ltd.

>> The revivals of the Second Great Awakening proved fertile ground for new religions, the largest of which is Mormonism, which began when Joseph Smith claimed to be visited by the angel Moroni, as depicted here, who led Smith to golden tablets upon which were written the Book of Mormon.

tablets contained *The Book of Mormon*. (After showing a handful of friends and family, Smith said he returned the tablets to the angel, so they are no longer of this world. The witnesses' testimonies appear in the beginning of *The Book of Mormon*.) Smith asserted that the tablets possessed an ancient revelation of God that predicted the "end-times," making the Mormons "saints" called out by God to usher in the new millennium; this is why Mormons called themselves the Latter-Day Saints.

Smith's vision appealed to a growing number of people who were either convinced by Smith's vision or dissatisfied with the new social order unfolding during the Market Revolution. Chastised as a heretic, Joseph Smith led his congregation to Ohio, then Missouri, then Illinois. By 1844, Smith was tried for treason and assassinated, and facing persecution once again, the Mormons, under

>> Persecuted almost everywhere they went, the Mormons eventually set out west, finally finding a home in the territory of Utah. Here, a group of Mormon pioneers take a rest on their trek west en route to Utah.

the leadership of Brigham Young, headed west in 1846, ultimately settling in the territory of Utah. (For more on the Mormons, see Chapter 13.)

10-3c The Reform Impulse

While movements striving for perfectibility continued to blossom throughout the first half of the 1800s, most Americans preferred more subtle attempts at reform.

THE BENEVOLENT EMPIRE

Instead of drastically altering the entire society, most Americans sought to change one element at a time, leading to a series of single-issue reforms. Many of the reformers felt that, all together, their various efforts would create a "Benevolent Empire" on American soil. Led by individuals like Arthur and Lewis Tappan, evangelical brothers who advocated numerous reforms, the reformers of the 1820s, 1830s, and 1840s sought social change with a messianic fervor. In their advocacy, they sometimes patronizingly questioned the morality of impoverished immigrants and non-Protestants, but they claimed to do so only in an effort to improve American society.

FEMALE REFORM SOCIETIES

The reforming impulse was particularly meaningful for nineteenth-century women. Politics were thought of as men's arena, but social reform was considered within women's sphere, and thus activist women played a large role in the movement for social reform. This role was most dramatically illustrated by the **American Female Moral Reform Society**, which by 1840 had more than five hundred local chapters throughout the country and had successfully lobbied for legislation governing prostitution.

TEMPERANCE

By far the largest reforming effort went into moderating the consumption of alcohol in America. In 1800, Americans per capita drank five gallons of alcohol every year (today we drink about two gallons per capita). Booze was especially integral to the new culture of politics, but it permeated the rest of American culture as well. At the same time, the Irish immigrants who streamed into the country in the 1840s brought with them a tradition of alcohol consumption and of gathering in saloons.

Female reformers attacked the habit, claiming that men who drank often beat their wives and children. They maintained that drinking also affected their work habits, sometimes forcing families into financial hardship. In 1826, temperance workers founded the **American Temperance Society**, and by the middle of the 1830s, 5,000 local and state temperance organizations had appeared. In 1851, Maine prohibited the sale of alcohol. By 1855, temperance and prohibition laws spread throughout New England and the Midwest. The temperance movement also played a prominent role in the presidential elections of the 1840s and 1850s, as temperance workers vigorously promoted candidates who shared their ideals.

American Female Moral Reform Society Women's activist group that had more than five hundred local chapters throughout the country by 1840 and had successfully lobbied for legislation governing prostitution

American Temperance Society Group founded by temperance workers in 1826; they promoted laws prohibiting the sale of alcohol

EDUCATION

Between 1800 and 1860, free public education expanded across parts of the United States. Overcoming the mainstream perception that free schools were only for poor people, reformers such as Horace Mann and Henry Barnard fought to establish the public elementary school as a fixture in antebellum America. By the 1820s, public secondary schools had increased in number, although they were generally reserved for those interested in a profession. Schools expanded in every region, with the South being the slowest to adopt the institution. A few state-supported colleges also opened in these years. Women gained access to public education as well, highlighted by the founding of a series of coeducational colleges. Most schools took for granted America's Protestant majority and subsequently instituted courses in Protestant moral theology and Bible readings from the King James, or Protestant, Bible.

PRISON REFORM

Prisons also attracted significant attention from middle-class reformers. Before 1800, punishment was usually doled out financially (in fines) or physically (in lashes). But during these reform years, reformers, including large numbers of female reformers and Quakers, designed a criminal justice system whereby criminals were incarcerated for a fixed period of time. Solitary confinement—another old-time punishment—was limited to extreme cases. Inmates were allowed (mostly forced) to work together in the daytime, a practice thought to bring about personal reform. The reformer Dorothea Dix was crucial in focusing public interest on the criminal justice system and in removing large numbers of the mentally ill from prisons.

ABOLITION

Of deeper importance was the small but growing movement for abolition. The moral perfectibility preached during the Second Great Awakening openly exposed the greatest sin of the nation: slavery. And, as the cotton gin enabled cotton production to expand westward, slavery became firmly established in the expanding South during the first quarter of the 1800s. Opposition to slavery in the form of a full-fledged abolitionist movement would develop in the North especially during the 1830s (for more on the abolitionist movement, see Chapter 12). But by far the largest antislavery movement in the first decades of the nineteenth century was the **American Colonization Society**, a group founded in 1816 to advocate for the complete removal of America's black population, repatriating them to Africa. The establishment of the nation of Liberia in 1847 was the result of the ACS's efforts, although the organization failed to thrive because of divisions between good-hearted antislavery advocates, who felt African-Americans would succeed better in Africa than America, and slaveowners, who sought to rid America of its free black population.

10-3d The Women's Movement

Women, both black and white, were some of the most ardent abolitionists. The sisters Angelina and Sarah Grimké, Lydia Maria Child, Maria Chapman, and Lucretia Mott were all active in the crusade. For many of these women, advocating the rights of African Americans highlighted the absence of basic civil rights for women. In one notable instance, the Grimké sisters were criticized for their abolitionist activism by Congregationalist ministers who circulated a letter outlining the "proper" duties of women in the church. This criticism quite pointedly turned the Grimkés' attention to the condition of women. In response, in 1838, Sarah Grimké published *Letters on the Equality of the Sexes and the Condition of Men* and Angelina Grimké published her *Letters to Catherine E. Beecher*, both landmark tracts in the struggle for women's equality.

In 1848, several women, including the leading abolitionists mentioned previously and Elizabeth Cady Stanton, organized the Women's Rights Convention at Seneca Falls, New York, normally called the **Seneca Falls Convention**. The convention adopted a Declaration of Sentiments, which was modeled after the Declaration of Independence and articulated the injustices that women faced in American society. As a political tactic, the women's movement put securing the vote for women atop their list of demands. But they faced two challenges: (1) from men reluctant to admit women into the raucous world of nineteenth-century politics, and (2) by the rising

American Colonization Society Organization founded in 1816 to advocate removing America's black population and repatriating them to Africa; the Society established the colony of Liberia on the West African coast for this purpose in the 1820s

Seneca Falls Convention Gathering of women activists in Seneca Falls, New York, in 1848; their goal was securing the vote for women

Elizabeth Cady Stanton and Women's Rights

>> Elizabeth Cady Stanton, an abolitionist and women's rights advocate, organized the Seneca Falls Convention of 1848.

issue of racial equality, which would culminate in the Civil War and make all other attempts at social reform seem less pressing. The movements for justice by African Americans and women have always been linked (for example, Frederick Douglass spoke at the 1848 Seneca Falls Convention), but the thorny issue of whether to concentrate on establishing African American rights or women's rights perpetually divided the various women's movements, at least until the latter half of the twentieth century.

>LOOKING AHEAD...

Between 1812 and the 1860s, the nation's social and economic life changed dramatically. With the American system of economics as a model, the United States became increasingly market oriented. Production was implemented on a larger scale and became more and more mechanized. The transportation and communications revolutions altered the way people thought of the vast expanse that was their nation. And urbanization, the creation of a working class, and the expansion of slavery served as reminders that certain advances come with costs.

The significant changes associated with the Market Revolution provoked various reactions, from the perfection seekers of the Second Great Awakening to calls for social reform from the working class, American Catholics, African Americans, and women. A new form of politics also arose during these years, moving away from the politics associated with "Jeffersonian Democracy" and toward that prominently associated with one dynamic character. It is to Andrew Jackson and the politics of the Market Revolution that we now turn.

STUDY TOOLS 10

READY TO STUDY? IN THE BOOK, YOU CAN:

❑ Rip out the Chapter Review Card, which includes key terms and chapter summaries.

ONLINE AT WWW.CENGAGEBRAIN.COM, YOU CAN:

❑ Collect StudyBits while you read and study the chapter.

❑ Quiz yourself on key concepts.

❑ Find videos for further exploration.

❑ Prepare for tests with HIST5 Flash Cards as well as those you create.

❑ Read a firsthand description of the Lowell mills from one young female worker.

❑ Read more about roads, canals, steamboats, and railroads.

❑ View an online exhibition of the American Temperance Society.

❑ Read more about Horace Mann and his address to the Massachusetts Board of Education.

❑ Read more about Mormonism.

❑ Read more about Seneca Falls.

❑ Read portions of Thoreau's *Walden*.

Bettmann/Getty Images

CH10 TIMELINE

		What Else Was Happening

1789 Samuel Slater builds first American spinning factory.

1793 Cotton gin makes fiber a profitable cash crop and revives plantation slavery.

1800 Land Act creates federal offices for sale of western land to settlers.

1807 First steamboats introduced to American rivers.

1811 Congress fails to recharter First Bank of the United States.

1813 Lowell system combines all processes in textile production in one factory.

1815: John Roulstone writes the first three verses of "Mary Had a Little Lamb" after his classmate Mary Sawyer comes to school followed by her pet lamb.

1816 Democratic-Republicans push for Second Bank of the United States.

Congress discourages foreign imports with high tariff.

1817 State of New York begins construction of canal from Albany to Buffalo.

1819 Supreme Court protects contract clause in *Dartmouth College v. Woodward*.

Spain yields Florida and claims to Pacific Northwest in Adams-Onís Treaty.

1820 Federal Land Act promotes western migration and farm settlements.

Compromise admits Missouri as slave, Maine as free, states; sets slavery's northern boundary at 36° 30'.

1820s–1840s Second Great Awakening promises salvation through good works.

1823: Monroe Doctrine claims Western Hemisphere as American domain.
The game of rugby is invented.

1825 364-mile-long Erie Canal connects eastern seaboard with Great Lakes.

1826 American Temperance Society becomes century's largest reform movement.

1828 Workingmen's Party formed; eventually spreads to fifteen states.

1831 Cyrus McCormick's mechanical reaper transforms commercial agriculture.

1833: *Britain outlaws slavery in response to the continued efforts of evangelical Christians and the politician William Wilberforce.*

1834 National Trades' Union formed.

1837 Horace Mann becomes secretary of the Massachusetts Board of Eduation, eventually developing the foundations for American public schools.

1838: *Grimké sisters publish landmark tract in struggle for women's equality.*

Massachusetts prohibits the sale of liquor. One man gets around the law by painting stripes on a pig and advertising that, for 6 cents, a person could see the pig and get a free glass of whiskey.

1844 Samuel P. Morse "wires" first message "What Hath God Wrought?"

1845 Irish potato famine further pushes European immigration to United States.

1846 Mormons migrate west to escape persecution.

1847: *Hanson Gregory, a New England mariner, invents the donut.*

1848 Women's Rights Convention at Seneca Falls adopts Declaration of Sentiments.

1854 Thoreau's *Walden* typifies Transcendentalist response to Market Revolution.

11 | Politics of the Market Revolution

Library of Congress Print and Photographs Division [LC-USZC4-9701]

LEARNING OBJECTIVES

After reading this chapter, you should be able to do the following:

11-1 Describe the changes that took place in American politics during the first decades of the 1800s, and explain the reasons for these changes.

11-2 Explain how Jackson's approach to the "spoils system," the nullification crisis, the National Bank, Indian removal, and the Panic of 1837 reflected his vision of federal power.

11-3 Explain the development of America's second two-party political system between the Democrats and the Whigs.

AFTER FINISHING THIS CHAPTER GO TO **PAGE 210** **FOR STUDY TOOLS**

The first half of the 1800s saw political developments almost as momentous as the social and economic changes brought on by the Market Revolution. While the American economy was booming and busting and booming again between 1814 and 1850, American politics were becoming more and more democratic. The politics of deference—in which people were expected to defer to the wisdom of the educated elite—was dying out. Historians have called it "the era of the common man," in which politics expanded beyond its elite origins and the vote was extended to more and more of the population.

To be sure, the America of the early 1800s considered the "common man" to be white and, quite literally, a man. However, while racial minorities and women were still excluded from the franchise, many states ceased requiring property ownership as mandatory for full citizenship. This meant that a much higher percentage of Americans could vote in 1840 than in 1790. Large political parties arose to woo the new voters. The result was a vibrant, sometimes raucous political life for men that featured the rise of two new parties to replace the Federalists and the Democratic-Republicans from the founding era. These new parties—the Democrats and the Whigs—mostly argued about the best way to manage the economy during the Market Revolution. Because Andrew Jackson symbolized this new style of politics, the period is often called the Age of Jackson.

11-1 POLITICS IN THE AGE OF JACKSON

11-1a A New Kind of Politics

Four factors contributed to the rise of this new kind of politics in the 1820s and 1830s: (1) economic booms and busts caused Americans to feel that the government should be more responsive to their needs; (2) the expansion of the franchise, or vote, allowed greater numbers of men to participate in politics; and (3) a contentious presidential election of 1824 led the entire nation to become increasingly political, which (4) led to the rise of mass parties and the second two-party system.

THE PANIC OF 1819

As we saw in the last chapter, during the first half of the nineteenth century, the United States became a more market-driven society, with increasingly rapid communications and transportation. At the same time, Americans were on the move, settling western lands and building railroads to connect the new settlements with eastern cities. The South was booming as well, becoming Europe's principal supplier of cotton. With these developments, many Americans felt they were destined to reap continued economic success.

Such optimism did not last. In 1819, global demand for American agricultural production (particularly cotton) plummeted, in part because of Europe's recovery after the end of the Napoleonic Wars in 1815. At the same time, the Second Bank of the United States tightened credit due to fears about overinvestment in factories and land. With fewer people buying American goods and credit tightened, the United States entered its first major economic depression. Land values tumbled across the nation, and the demand for goods and foodstuffs slackened. Every bank south and west of Pennsylvania failed except two. Thousands of people declared bankruptcy or were sentenced to debtors' prison.

The Panic of 1819 deeply affected the average American. Farmers in the West were particularly hard pressed. Having bought their farms on credit, many could not make their payments, and banks foreclosed the loans. In desperation, people turned to their state governments, demanding financial assistance during these tough times. In Kentucky and other states, voters agitated in vain for the government to declare a moratorium on the collection of debts. In general, Americans began to feel that the government should protect its constituents from economic disaster and, more importantly, from the topsy-turvy nature of a market-based economy.

EXPANSION OF THE FRANCHISE

This push to make government more responsive to the common people coincided with the opening up of the political process. In the first years after the Revolution, most states limited the vote to white men who owned a certain amount of property. Such requirements were designed to place political power in the hands of men who were considered to have a "real stake" in society.

These limits did not last long. During the first part of the 1800s, almost every state removed property restrictions on citizenship. By 1824, most states had liberalized their laws so that every free white man was allowed to vote; only Rhode Island, Virginia, North Carolina, and Louisiana still maintained property restrictions.

◄◄◄ **Andrew Jackson's inauguration was a famously raucous affair, reflecting the new politics of the common man.**

As states expanded the franchise to all white men, legislators of the early 1800s simultaneously developed restrictions that prevented African Americans from voting. If slavery had slowly departed from the North following the American Revolution, racism had not. For example, the New York Constitution of 1777 did not mention race at all, but in 1821, the revised New York Constitution restricted the vote to all white men and to wealthy African Americans. Women and poor black men were specifically excluded. The world of politics was becoming more democratic, and more people were allowed to participate, but it still maintained significant barriers to participation.

THE ELECTION OF 1824

Nowhere was this new politics better reflected than in the election of 1824 (see Map 11.1). Since the Federalist Party fell apart in the late 1810s (after contemplating secession at the Hartford Convention), all national politicians of the 1820s considered themselves Democratic-Republicans. Five Democratic-Republicans were nominated to the presidency in 1824, for example, and each had strong regional support. Yet no single candidate was able to muster a majority.

Per the Constitution, the election was handed over to the House of Representatives, which was, by law, instructed to consider only the top three candidates. They were Andrew Jackson, John Quincy Adams, and William H. Crawford. The candidate who had come in fourth place (and was thus no longer on the ballot) was Henry Clay. Clay instructed his backers to support Adams—an action that infuriated Jackson, who had won the most popular and electoral votes. With Clay's support, then, John Quincy Adams, the son of former president John Adams, leapfrogged Jackson in the election and was elected president of the United States on the next vote of the House.

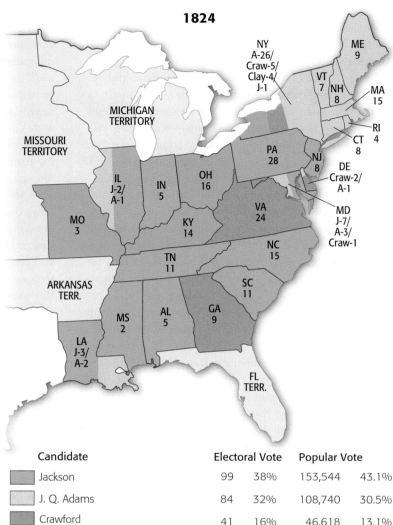

1824

Candidate	Electoral Vote		Popular Vote	
Jackson	99	38%	153,544	43.1%
J. Q. Adams	84	32%	108,740	30.5%
Crawford	41	16%	46,618	13.1%
Clay	37	14%	47,136	13.2%
Territories, unsettled, etc.				

Map 11.1 The Election of 1824

>> An electoral map from the election of 1824 showing that, despite winning the most votes, Andrew Jackson had not earned a majority, thus allowing the election to be decided by the House of Representatives, a majority of whom favored John Quincy Adams.

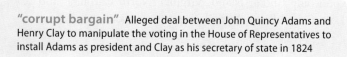

"corrupt bargain" Alleged deal between John Quincy Adams and Henry Clay to manipulate the voting in the House of Representatives to install Adams as president and Clay as his secretary of state in 1824

When Adams shortly thereafter appointed Clay secretary of state (a frequent stepping-stone to the presidency), Andrew Jackson and his followers protested that there had been a **"corrupt bargain"** between the two men. Jackson and his supporters vowed revenge, and revenge they would get, but it would have to wait until 1828.

The split between Clay and Adams on the one hand and Jackson on the other was a key step in the development of the **second two-party system**. By 1824, the followers of Jackson called themselves Jacksonians, and they advocated a strong executive branch, perpetual westward expansion, and an aggressive democratization of the political process, especially opening the franchise to all white men. A few years later, the followers of Clay and Adams chose to be called the National Republicans. They later changed their name to the Whigs, in honor of Britain's Whigs, who had protested the authoritarian actions of the king of Britain (thus insinuating that Jackson yearned to be a dictatorial king). They advocated a strong legislature, government-funded internal improvements, economic protectionism, and the American System of economics.

But the more immediate effect of the "corrupt bargain" was to stimulate partisanship and get more people interested in politics. In the election of 1824, national voter turnout was just 24 percent of eligible voters. By 1840, turnout was nearly 80 percent. National parties had developed in the intervening years to capitalize on and profit from the newfound interest in politics.

A NEW CULTURE OF POLITICS

These national parties fed a new culture of politics in the 1820s and 1830s. Between the increased number of eligible voters and the expansion of political parties, popular interest in politics soared. Because most "common men" now had the right to vote, political candidates had no choice but to mingle with the masses and earn their respect and attention. As a result, politics for the first time became mass entertainment. Partisan newspapers flourished. Campaigns were conducted to appeal to popular tastes. They featured public rallies, picnics, and elaborate parades with marching bands. Alcohol flowed freely at these events. What better way for a candidate to prove he was a man of the people than to raise a glass of whiskey to their health? In this jovial atmosphere, no one charmed the people better than Andrew Jackson.

11-1b Andrew Jackson and the Politics of the "Common Man"

Resentful of the "corrupt bargain," in 1828 Jackson and his newly emerging Democratic Party set out to mobilize voters and achieve the presidential victory he felt he deserved.

THE ELECTION OF 1828

Jackson had a busy four years between 1824 and 1828, barnstorming all twenty-two states. Jackson's opponent

>> A depiction of Andrew Jackson on the campaign trail. Note his roughly worn attire and his engaged, aggressive stance.

in 1828 was the incumbent president, John Quincy Adams, an old-style, patrician politician in the mold of his father. He made no effort to reach out to the people, relying instead on his record as president, which mostly included a successful series of internal improvements in the West. In his platform, he proposed even more internal improvements, funding explorations of the western interior, and leveraging American manufacturing, but he made his case to the electorate mostly from the White House, not the campaign trail.

Jackson took a different route. Instead of focusing on specific issues, he used a campaign strategy all too familiar to American voters today: mudslinging. While Jackson defamed the personal character of his political adversaries, his fellow Democratic leaders organized rallies and barbecues to attract and mobilize voters. The Democrats amplified Jackson's biography as a hero of the War of 1812, and his biography changed slightly depending on where he campaigned. He was most successful with three groups: (1) southerners, who appreciated the fact that some of the Indians he had killed were Florida's Seminoles, who were hated by southerners because the Indian nation had invited slaves to escape to freedom on Seminole lands; (2) westerners, who viewed him as a hearty frontiersman (his supporters avoided revealing the fact that his frontier lifestyle depended largely on the hundred slaves he owned); and (3) the working classes of the North, who had come to resent what they called the "elitism" of the Federalists

second two-party system Evolution of political organizations in 1824 into the Jacksonians and the Whigs

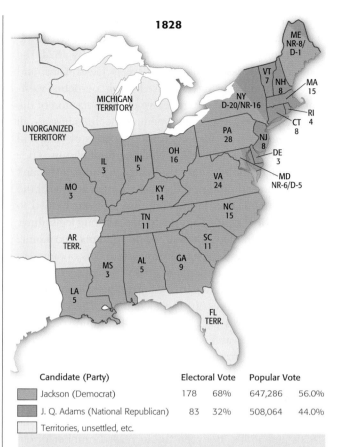

Mary Evans Picture Library/Alamy Stock Photo

>> John Quincy Adams, pictured here, made no effort to reach out to the people, relying instead on his record as president. It didn't work out so well for his re-election in 1828.

1828

Candidate (Party)	Electoral Vote		Popular Vote	
Jackson (Democrat)	178	68%	647,286	56.0%
J. Q. Adams (National Republican)	83	32%	508,064	44.0%
Territories, unsettled, etc.				

Map 11.2 The Election of 1828

>> An electoral map from the election of 1828 showing Andrew Jackson handily defeating the incumbent, John Quincy Adams.

and their political offspring. Jackson won the election of 1828 (Map 11.2) by a wide margin—all the more impressive because the total number of voters had tripled in just four years. He did not make the customary visit to President John Quincy Adams before taking office, and, to return the snub, Adams refused to attend Jackson's inauguration, a rollicking affair that was open to the public (for the first time) and that led to significant damages to the White House. Indeed, the inauguration has come to symbolize how politics had shifted to embrace the "common man."

WHITE MALE DEMOCRACY

Jackson's ascendance to the presidency is often described as the dawning of the age of the common man, or the revolt of westerners and southerners against a northeastern elite. Both interpretations are somewhat misleading. Jackson was a successful lawyer

and a wealthy slaveholder and, in political acumen at least, he was far from common. And, in the 1828 triumph, he won sections of large northern states such as New York.

Nevertheless, it was Jackson's appeal to the American masses that got him elected in 1828. More than anyone else, Jackson symbolized the power of the people in the new political system. He was the first president from the West (Tennessee) rather than from the aristocracy of New England or Virginia. He was supported by a coalition of western frontiersmen, southern planters, and the northern working class who supported manhood suffrage (extending the vote to all white men regardless of property ownership) and opposed anyone they considered an aristocrat, even if those aristocrats were interested in extending rights to other, less privileged minorities.

RACISM IN THE NORTH

One group that did not support Jackson, largely because they did not have the legal right to do so and also because of the racism of Jackson's supporters, was African Americans. Slavery remained legal in the South, and although Jackson did not design any policies specifically against free blacks, the Democrats were hostile to any suggestion of improving the condition of free blacks living in the North. These northern free blacks were usually denied basic civil rights. Only in Massachusetts, for example, could a black person sit on a jury. Worse still, Ohio, Indiana, and Illinois passed laws that prohibited free blacks from settling within their borders. By custom, segregation was the rule in the North. Black people had to sit in separate sections on railroads, steamboats, and stagecoaches. They were barred from entering many hotels and restaurants. Thus, although the North had abolished slavery during the first quarter of the 1800s, societywide racism made the black population an underclass, separate from the "common men" Jackson represented.

11-2 JACKSON AS PRESIDENT

He may have symbolized the "common man," but Andrew Jackson's presidency was anything but common. Four issues dominated his presidency: (1) patronage, (2) the nullification crisis, (3) the Bank War, and (4) Indian removal. The way he handled each of them had long-lasting ramifications, some of which live with us today.

11-2a Patronage

When Jackson and his followers came to power, they sought to exact revenge on Adams, Clay, and their supporters. Following the advice of the masterful New York politician Martin Van Buren, Jackson took control of the federal government through a system of political **patronage**. Patronage is defined as the direct exchange of a government job in return for political campaign work. This means that, rather than seek out the best-qualified person for a job, a politician simply awards the job based on the campaign support one has provided. This system was routinely called the "spoils system," as in "to the victor go the spoils." Upon his victory in 1828, Jackson fired many federal workers and replaced them with committed Jacksonians, surrounding himself with like-minded men. Among other things, the open use

> "On your undivided support of your government depends the decision of the great question it involves, whether your sacred Union will be preserved, and the blessing it secures to us as one people shall be perpetuated."
>
> —ANDREW JACKSON, PROCLAMATION ON NULLIFICATION, DECEMBER 10, 1832

of patronage shifted the focal point of national politics squarely on the White House.

The one non-Jacksonian who could not be fired was Vice President John C. Calhoun, a former senator from South Carolina and a strong advocate of states' rights. The battles between Jackson and Calhoun were legendary, especially during what came to be known as the nullification crisis.

11-2b The Nullification Crisis

By far, the most serious crisis Jackson confronted—in fact, the most serious crisis in the nation between the Revolution and the Civil War—developed around the concept of states' rights and whether or not a state could "nullify" a federal law. Nullification emerged as a major issue during Jackson's first term.

THE CONTEXT OF NULLIFICATION

By the time Jackson was elected president in 1828, the Panic of 1819 was just an ugly memory, but Americans were still anxious about economic matters. The economy was changing so rapidly during the Market Revolution that many Americans felt they could hardly keep up. This was especially true in South Carolina, where the cotton market had been hit hard by the depression and by soil depletion. South Carolinians focused the blame for their economic problems on the high tariff placed on their goods.

patronage Exchange of a government job in return for political campaign work

TARIFFS

They were not entirely wrong. Congress had begun increasing America's tariffs in 1816 to protect American industries, especially the newly mechanized textile industry taking root in New England, which used southern cotton as its raw material. This was a key component of the American System. The western states also benefited from the tax on imported goods because taxes on European wheat, hemp, and other agricultural products made them more expensive; with the tariff, Americans would buy American goods.

The South, however, felt left out. American tariffs did not affect southern staple crops because Europeans did not grow competing crops. As southerners saw it, they were forced to pay higher prices for goods to subsidize the economic development of the North and West.

When Congress raised these tariffs in 1824, South Carolina and other southern states vigorously objected. Despite these complaints, Congress narrowly approved the tariff. Then in 1828, in a stunning move that backfired, Jackson, running for president against Adams, advocated a ridiculously high tariff, assuming it would not pass. Jackson's promotion of the tariff would have gained him the support of the West and the North (which might otherwise have supported Adams), while the South would be content that no tariff had been passed. Jackson's support was intended to be a political ploy.

To Jackson's shock, the Tariff of 1828, which came to be known as the "Tariff of Abominations," passed. Adams, the outgoing president, did not veto the measure, leaving Jackson with a tariff that made many of his own supporters unhappy. The South was furious and, in response, the South Carolina legislature issued a document called the *South Carolina Exposition*. The anonymous author of this document was John C. Calhoun, Jackson's incoming vice president.

WHAT WAS NULLIFICATION?

The *South Carolina Exposition* gave voice to a new political idea: **nullification**. Calhoun's concept of nullification was designed to answer a serious problem of political theory: how to protect the rights of a minority in a government based on the rule of the majority.

nullification Assertion that the United States was made up of independent and sovereign states; states did not agree to give up their autonomy; and every state reserved the right to reject any federal law it deemed unconstitutional

(This is something we have seen before, in Jefferson's Virginia and Kentucky Resolutions of 1798.) Calhoun's theory of nullification asserted that the United States was made up of independent and sovereign states. In joining the Union, Calhoun argued, states did not agree to give up their autonomy. Therefore, every state reserved the right to reject any federal law it deemed unconstitutional.

In 1828, South Carolina did nothing more than articulate the idea of nullification, but in 1832, after Congress failed to revise the Tariff of Abominations, South Carolina actually put nullification into practice. The state legislature authorized the election of delegates to a popular convention, and, in November 1832, that convention passed an ordinance declaring the tariffs of 1828 and 1832 null and void in South Carolina, effective February 1, 1833.

JACKSON'S RESPONSE

As an ardent nationalist, President Jackson was not about to let South Carolina challenge the authority of the federal government. In his Proclamation on Nullification, delivered in December 1832, Jackson emphasized that the states of the Union were not independent and that, therefore, no state had the right to reject a federal law; only the Supreme Court had the authority to do that. Moreover, Jackson declared that the Union was perpetual. By this logic, Calhoun's assertion that a state could withdraw from the Union was treason.

To demonstrate how seriously they took the threat, Jacksonians in Congress passed the Force Bill in March 1833, which confirmed the president's authority to use the army and navy to put down insurrection. But Jackson was wise enough to use the carrot as well as the stick. While threatening South Carolina with the possibility of force, Jackson also urged Congress to lower the tariff. By doing so, Jackson isolated South Carolina. No other state would defend South Carolina when the federal government was trying to be accommodating. As a result, Calhoun himself backed away from nullification and supported a compromise tariff bill. It went into effect on the same day as the Force Bill, March 1, 1833. South Carolina promptly repealed its nullification of the tariff, but, in a final display of spiteful defiance, it nullified the Force Bill. Jackson sagely ignored this and allowed the nullification crisis to die out. For the moment, Jackson's brand of nationalism had triumphed over the forces of nullification and secession.

11-2c The Bank War

As strong as Jackson's sense of nationalism was, it did not prevent him from attacking and eventually destroying one major national institution: the Second Bank of

SET TO BETWEEN OLD HICKORY AND BULLY NICK.

>> Political cartoons were ubiquitous in the early 19th century, including this one, which shows Andrew Jackson boxing Nicholas Biddle, the head of the Bank of the United States. In this sympathetic telling, Jackson fights for the common man while Biddle defends the fat and the wealthy.

the United States. The crisis surrounding the charter of the Second Bank of the United States was the third issue that polarized the politics of the 1830s (along with patronage and nullification).

THE BANK

The Second Bank of the United States, located in Philadelphia, had been created by Congress in 1816 and been granted a twenty-year charter. During its first years, the Bank extended credit easily, helping the economy to grow in the aftermath of the War of 1812. Americans were on the move, buying and cultivating new lands in the West, and credit from the Bank underwrote much of this economic activity. In 1819, however, the Bank reversed course and began calling in its loans, contributing to the Panic of 1819. People late on their payments now had to pay up. Many Americans went to debtors' prisons; others suffered bankruptcy. Although the Bank was not the sole cause of the panic, many citizens considered the Bank a dangerous institution.

In 1823, Nicholas Biddle, a Philadelphia businessman, assumed leadership of the Bank. Biddle believed that the Bank could serve as a stabilizing influence over the American economy by preventing the national credit supply from expanding too far or contracting too quickly. It is important to remember that America's monetary system in the nineteenth century was dramatically different from today's. Until 1863, there was no standardized national currency. Several forms of money existed, and payments were made in (1) specie (gold or silver); (2) barter (goods exchanged for other goods without the use of money); and (3) state bank notes (paper money issued by state-chartered banks). The problem with the paper money was that its value fluctuated depending on the status and solvency of the bank. When too many notes were in circulation, their value declined. Biddle promised to use the Bank to control fluctuations in the value of paper money by limiting the amount in circulation.

JACKSON'S OPPOSITION

Jackson personally distrusted the Bank. After losing his money in a bank in the 1790s, he viewed paper money as dangerous. In his eyes, only specie provided stability. Outright conflict between Jackson and Biddle erupted in 1832, when Biddle applied for a renewal of the Bank's charter four years before the charter was set to expire. Jackson presumed that Biddle was trying to make the Bank an issue in the presidential election of 1832. Already reeling from the nullification crisis, Jackson had no patience for Biddle's request and vowed to destroy the Bank altogether. Despite Jackson's objections, Congress renewed the Bank's charter in the summer of 1832. Undeterred, Jackson vetoed the charter. He justified his veto with a powerful message, arguing that the Bank was a nest of special privileges for the wealthy who were out to hurt America's humble poor. He also argued that the Constitution did not allow for the creation of a national bank or for the use of paper money. His veto was popular with the working classes, westerners, and southerners.

CRUSHING THE BANK

Once Jackson was reelected at the end of 1832, the Bank still had four years of its charter left. Jackson brashly resolved to crush the Bank before its charter expired. He ordered that all $10 million of federal deposits be withdrawn and redeposited in state banks. The Senate censured Jackson for defying its wishes, but

>> A drawing of the Second Bank of the United States in Philadelphia.

Jackson ruined the national currency, which did not revive again until the Civil War.

11-2d Westward Expansion and Indian Removal

While all this was happening, Americans continued their perpetual move west. Soil exhaustion in the Southeast, a shortage of land in New England, and the alluring expanses of the Midwest drew Americans to the Great Plains. Southerners usually moved west to find land where they could grow cotton. Cotton growers moved through Alabama, Mississippi, and Arkansas, eventually populating Texas (with free blacks and slaves) in the 1840s. Similarly, northerners moved in order to cultivate the fields of the Midwest, pushing as far as Iowa by the 1840s.

All this growth boosted the development of several cities that served as trading and transportation hubs for the growing West. Louisville, Cincinnati, Detroit, Chicago, and St. Louis grew into the largest cities in the region. Connected to the East Coast by a chain of steamboats, canals, or trains, these cities boomed as centers of America's westward expansion. Rapidly they, too, became industrial centers, with mills and factories lining their riverways.

INDIAN RESISTANCE

And, as before, the Native Americans were the chief obstacles to westward migration and settlement. Although the U.S. government pursued numerous treaties with the various Indian nations during the first part of the 1800s, such agreements proved untenable because the federal government would not keep its word. In addition, westward pioneers did not heed the restrictions placed on them; they often strayed into Indian territory. In some instances, Indians were invited to trade with the Americans at specified trading posts, but the result often plunged the Indians into debt, forcing them to sell their lands to find economic relief. The Choctaw, Creek, and Chickasaw nations all succumbed in this way. And, as Americans moved west, they introduced disease. Smallpox wiped out the Pawnee, Omaha, Otoe, Missouri, and Kansas nations in the Midwest during the 1830s and 1840s. And where debt and disease did not crush Indian resistance, war did. For example, the small Indian nations in the Midwest were decimated in the Blackhawk War of 1832, after which any significant Indian presence in today's Midwest disappeared.

it could not prevent the Bank from going under. When the Bank's charter expired in 1836, the weakened institution closed its doors for good.

WILDCAT BANKING

The result was not what Jackson had anticipated. Jackson deposited all of the government's money in several state banks, many of which were owned by his friends. (This was another example of Jackson's controversial use of political patronage.) The absence of a central bank allowed for the rise of many state and local banks that had less than adequate credit and little government regulation.

As a result, hundreds of paper currencies appeared, many of which were valueless. Counterfeiting was popular. Ironically, the only people who were knowledgeable about currencies were the commercial elite, reinforcing the notion that paper money only helped the wealthy. Jackson fulfilled his own prophecy—when he took away the regulations, his rhetoric about the insecurity of paper money made sense, and some states, such as California in 1849, outlawed paper money entirely. Quite predictably, the financial instability handicapped economic growth. Despite what his appearance on today's $20 bill might suggest, Andrew

>> The Trail of Tears, when, in 1838, the United States forced the Cherokee Nation from its home in Georgia to Oklahoma, even after the Cherokee had won a Supreme Court case affirming Cherokee sovereignty. It has since been remembered (as in this 20th century painting) as one of the most atrocious acts committed by the U.S. government.

Superstock/Glow Images

INDIAN REMOVAL ACT OF 1830

In the South, the Indian nations were larger and better organized. Constant battles raged, and complete Indian removal became established U.S. policy. After some harsh political debate, Congress passed the **Indian Removal Act of 1830**, which allowed the federal government to trade land west of the Mississippi River for land east of the river. Citing the act, Jackson forced several Indian nations, including the Creek and the Lower Creek, to move west throughout the 1830s. The remainder of the Indian nations, however, would not move so easily, most especially the Cherokee.

THE CHEROKEE NATION VERSUS GEORGIA

The Cherokee had accommodated to the American way of life more than any other Indian nation. They had adopted an American-style bicameral government, translated a Christian Bible into the Cherokee language, and adopted American rules regarding property and slaveholding. By 1833, the Cherokee owned 1,500 black slaves.

But when gold was discovered in western Georgia, white Georgians wanted the Cherokee removed so they could mine the gold. They therefore attempted to dissolve the Cherokee constitution and take away their property rights. To resist, the Cherokee took advantage of a primary American institution: they sued the Georgians in federal court. And they won. In *Worcester* v. *Georgia* (1832), which followed a similar case from the year before, *Cherokee* v. *Georgia*, the

Supreme Court ruled that the Cherokee nation was a sovereign nation and that the state of Georgia could not enter it without Cherokee permission. According to the Court, if the U.S. government wanted to move the Cherokee, it would have to do so in a treaty, not through the Removal Act.

Amazingly, Jackson simply ignored the decision. One newspaper reported the president as saying, "[Chief Justice] John Marshall has made his decision: now let him enforce it." With the prospect of violence looming and the federal government not willing to stand by a decision from its highest court, a tiny faction of Cherokee (500 out of 17,000) attempted to end hostilities by signing a treaty with Jackson. The treaty traded Cherokee land in Georgia for land west of the Mississippi, and when Congress ratified the treaty (by a single vote, over the strenuous objections of Henry Clay and Daniel Webster, who knew it to be illegitimate), the Cherokee lost title to their land. (The nation later murdered the Cherokee treaty makers, who were viewed by the majority as traitors.) After one American general resigned in protest, in 1838 General Winfield Scott invaded the Cherokee nation and forced the Cherokee to travel a thousand miles, from Georgia to Oklahoma, enduring hardship and death on what was

> **Indian Removal Act of 1830** Legislation that allowed the federal government to trade land west of the Mississippi River for land east of the river, allowing the federal government to move Indians further west

> "I have recommended them to quit their possessions on this side of the Mississippi, and go to a country in the west where there is every probability that they will always be free from the mercenary influence of White men, and undisturbed by the local authority of the states: Under such circumstances the General Government can exercise a parental control over their interests and possibly perpetuate their race."
>
> —ANDREW JACKSON, IN A LETTER TO CAPTAIN JAMES GADSDEN, 1829

called the **Trail of Tears**. About 4,000 Cherokee died along the way, and, when they arrived in Oklahoma, they faced conflict with the Indians already there. For more on why the Cherokee were pushed off their lands in Georgia, see "The Reasons Why . . ." box.

WAS JACKSON ANTI-INDIAN?

Jackson had a complicated relationship with Native Americans. His Indian Removal Bill of 1830 forced all Native Americans to move west of the Mississippi, clearing their lands for white settlement. But he defended these actions under the guise of paternalism—the idea that Jackson was moving Indians for their own good, saving them from the ravages and greed of the white man. He put this idea into practice when he adopted

Trail of Tears Forced removal of the Cherokee nation from Georgia to Oklahoma in 1838; the Cherokee were forced to travel more than a thousand miles

Specie Circular Executive order of 1836 requiring that the government cease accepting paper money as credible currency, accepting only gold or silver (specie) for all items, including public land

a Creek Indian as a son after the Creek War. On the whole, however, the evidence stacks up against Jackson. He ultimately believed any Indian presence east of the Mississippi River was illegitimate, and, in fact, he believed the Indian people as a whole were destined for extinction anyway. His policies nearly made him correct.

THE SEMINOLE REVOLT

Jackson's paternalism had limited appeal for those who were being patronized, though, and Jackson's Indian removal plan and his attitude toward African Americans combined to provoke what may have been the largest slave revolt in American history. Seminole Indians in northern Florida had long provided a refuge for escaped slaves. Beginning in 1835, Seminoles had been fighting a perpetual war with American settlers over land in Florida. In 1836, the Seminoles and their free black population (called Black Seminoles) attacked at least twelve white-owned sugar plantations. Enslaved plantation workers joined the fray, striking back at their slave masters.

In the mayhem that followed, many slaves freed themselves and burned all the sugar plantations in the region. The residents of St. Augustine watched the smoke drift from the south as the plantations burned to the ground. Sugar was never again a viable product in northern Florida. The war between the Seminoles and the settlers lasted until 1842 without a clear victor.

11-2e The Panic of 1837

The westward push, the Indian policy, and Jackson's bank policy all combined to create an economic panic in the mid-nineteenth century, one so deep it has been surpassed in severity only by the Panic of 1893, the Great Depression of the 1930s, and the Great Recession of 2008.

THE SPECIE CIRCULAR

As with the Panic of 1819, currencies were the provocation. Once Indian removal became official policy of the federal government in 1830, speculators began purchasing land in the West, knowing white Americans would quickly move there. To do so, many used paper money from the wildcat banks that had emerged in the aftermath of Jackson's Bank War. This proved a toxic combination because the cash was not stable, and it often lost much of its value. In an attempt to protect the settlers and to affirm his distrust of paper money, Jackson, in 1836, passed the **Specie Circular**, an

The Reasons Why...

There were four reasons why the Cherokee were pushed off their lands in Georgia:

White land lust. First, soil exhaustion in the Southeast sent farmers further west in search of land where they could grow staple crops such as cotton, which had been made considerably easier to do after the invention of the cotton gin in 1793.

Racism. Second, since the early colonial days, European colonists in North America (and later, white Americans) had rarely treated Indians with any decency, largely thinking of them as un-Christian, uncivilized dark-skinned heathens. By the 1820s and 1830s, many Americans, such as Andrew Jackson, simply felt the Indians were dying out, which would,

of course, open land in the West for settlement by white Americans.

Federal policy. In light of these two long-standing propositions, the Indian Removal Act of 1830 made it established U.S. policy to move Indians west of the Mississippi River, pushing them further away from the settled parts of the United States.

Andrew Jackson's ire. In 1832, the Cherokee nation sued the state of Georgia for allowing white Georgians onto their land while searching for gold, with the Cherokee claiming they were a sovereign nation beyond the bounds of the Indian Removal Act of 1830. The U.S. Supreme Court upheld the Cherokee claims, but, citing a controversial treaty with a tiny faction of Cherokee, Andrew Jackson ordered the U.S. military to march the Cherokee from Georgia to Oklahoma, on what has come to be called the "Trail of Tears." One general resigned in protest of Jackson's order.

---

executive order requiring that the government cease accepting paper money as credible currency, accepting instead only gold or silver (specie) for all items, including public land. The result of the federal government's saying it did not trust the value of paper money was of course to devalue paper money even further, abandoning settlers to worse economic trouble and sending much of America's specie west.

THE PANIC OF 1837

The Specie Circular could not have happened at a worse time. The rollicking economy of the Market Revolution experienced a boom in the early 1830s, mostly due to rampant speculation in the West along new transportation routes. The Specie Circular caused an immediate drop in demand for western lands and drained most of the specie from New York banks.

>> In 1837, the United States plummeted into an economic depression that was the worst the nation would endure for the first half of the nation's existence. Here, a cartoon drawing of a bunch of paupers, beggars, and drunkards reflects the hard times many Americans endured during the Panic of 1837.

>> Andrew Jackson's use of patronage jobs to ensure loyalty was not always loved. Here, a cartoon drawing shows a triumphant Jackson aloft a fat pig trampling over the bones of those he defeated. The base of the statue reads: "To the victors belong the spoils."

Library of Congress Prints and Photographs Division[LC-USZ62–100254]

Unable to match its paper money with specie reserves, several hundred banks in New York City closed their doors in April. In May 1837, every bank in New York refused to accept paper money for specie. Paper money lost nearly all of its value, and nearly a quarter of all banks in the United States closed. After the Bank War, there was no central bank to control the economic contraction, and the United States plummeted into an economic depression that would last nearly a decade.

 11-3
THE DEVELOPMENT OF THE SECOND TWO-PARTY SYSTEM

Jackson's contentious presidency and the rollicking economy stirred up a vibrant, flourishing political opposition, and during the 1830s the second two-party system in American history took hold, pitting Jackson's Democrats against Adams's and Clay's Whigs.

11-3a Jackson's Democrats

For their part, Jackson's Democrats were extremely nationalistic who nonetheless believed it was best to keep the federal government small. They fashioned themselves as the heirs of Jefferson, who considered government as nothing more than a necessary evil. To Jackson's Democrats, the government was not supposed to control the way people conducted themselves privately. This made them less aggressive in pushing America's economic development, viewing American society as being divided between two hostile camps: "the people" (farmers, planters, workers), who worked hard to make an honest living, and "the aristocracy" (merchants, bankers, financial agents), who manipulated markets for their own private enrichment. This, of course, did not preclude Jackson's Democrats from supporting America's westward expansion. Jackson's Indian Removal Bill secured much new territory for white settlement, and subsequent Democratic presidents would eventually push the boundaries of the United States all the way to the Pacific. Prominent Jacksonians included Martin Van Buren and James K. Polk.

11-3b The Whigs

The Whigs, on the other hand, favored a more active federal government. They supported using federal funds to finance internal improvements like turnpikes and railroads. They also believed that government power could be used to promote the moral health of the nation through temperance laws or antislavery legislation. And the Whigs were more comfortable with market capitalism. As they saw it, economic development made people richer, increased popular demand for foodstuffs and other agricultural products, and created jobs. The Whigs denied there was any conflict between the common people and big business. According to their view, banks were not evil; they were essential in controlling the flow of money. Many Whigs also opposed the expansion of slavery into new territory, but they did form alliances with southern states' rights groups. Prominent Whigs included Henry Clay, Daniel Webster, and William Henry Harrison.

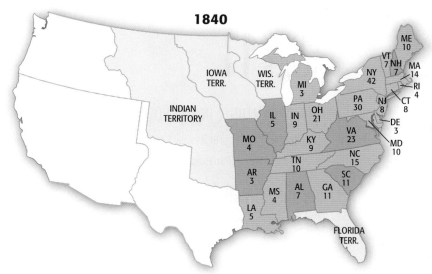

1840

State	Electoral Votes
ME	10
VT	7
NH	7
MA	14
NY	42
RI	4
CT	8
PA	30
NJ	8
DE	3
MD	10
VA	23
OH	21
IN	9
IL	5
MI	3
MO	4
KY	9
NC	15
TN	10
AR	3
SC	11
MS	4
AL	7
GA	11
LA	5

Candidate (Party)	Electoral Vote		Popular Vote	
Harrison (Whig)	234	80%	1,274,624	53.1%
Van Buren (Democrat)	60	20%	1,127,781	46.9%
Territories				

Map 11.3 The Election of 1840

>> An electoral map showing the electoral votes from the election of 1840, showing Harrison handily beating Martin Van Buren.

11-3c Constituencies

Although it is tempting to categorize the Democrats as the party of the poor and the Whigs as the party of the rich, this was not the case. Most Americans were farmers of the "middling sort" who were neither miserably impoverished nor impressively wealthy. It was true that most businessmen joined the Whig Party, but the Whigs had several other key constituencies: (1) farmers who wanted better methods to transport their produce to market; (2) workers who believed they would benefit from economic growth; and (3) planters who wanted the United States to have a stable bank system that would float loans. The Whigs also appealed to people concerned about the increasing numbers of Irish Catholics entering the country. In short, the Whigs did well in cities and rural areas that embraced market competition. Appealing to these various constituencies, and playing the new politics developed by the Jacksonians, the Whigs developed a solid party by the late 1830s, symbolized by William Henry Harrison's presidential victory over Martin Van Buren in 1840 (Map 11.3).

The Democrats, in contrast, attracted farmers and workers who felt alienated by America's increasingly commercialized economy, as well as small businessmen who hoped the Democratic Party would stand watch against monopolies and give "little guys" a chance to succeed. They also found a ready constituency in the Irish immigrants who immigrated in large numbers during the 1840s.

11-3d Political Stability

By the election of 1840, Americans had succeeded in building its second stable two-party system. Although the Jacksonians were always numerically superior to the Whigs, each party held together a coalition of northerners and southerners, and the party system helped relieve sectional tensions over slavery. (Basically, neither party wanted to talk about slavery and its westward expansion for fear of dividing their party.) As long as the second two-party system existed, hostilities between the North and South faded into the background. Such tensions never disappeared entirely, however, and territorial expansion in the 1840s set in motion a breakdown of America's second two-party system, leading to renewed sectional conflict and, ultimately, civil war.

Table 11.1 The Differences Between Jacksonians and Whigs

	Jacksonians	Whigs
Strength in government	Presidency	Legislature
Economics	Local growth	Nationalists
National Bank	Against	For
Internal improvements	Against	For
Constituents	Southerners, westerners, and the working class	Social conservatives, native born

As the Market Revolution stirred up numerous social and economic changes, politicians sought to manage the rapidly transforming republic. They expanded patronage and developed a new political culture that was expansive to greater numbers of Americans but which was also limited by race and gender. In one respect, the politicians were struggling to keep an increasingly disparate nation together through a series of political endeavors. At the same time, however, reformers were provoking questions that only increased sectional divisions, the most prominent of which was slavery.

In the end, the economic tugs of the Market Revolution would be too strong to preserve this unity. And, between the 1830s and the 1850s, America to a large degree fractured into a regionalized nation. This is the subject of the next chapter.

STUDY TOOLS 11

READY TO STUDY? IN THE BOOK, YOU CAN:

❏ Rip out the Chapter Review Card, which includes key terms and chapter summaries.

ONLINE AT WWW.CENGAGEBRAIN.COM, YOU CAN:

❏ Collect StudyBits while you read and study the chapter.

❏ Quiz yourself on key concepts.

❏ Find videos for further exploration.

❏ Prepare for tests with HIST5 Flash Cards as well as those you create.

❏ Read Andrew Jackson's First Annual Message, and see what might have appealed to the "common man."

❏ Hear music for an Andrew Jackson campaign song, and be sure to read the lyrics!

❏ Read President Jackson's report on Indian Removal.

❏ Read South Carolina's Ordinance of Nullification.

❏ Learn more about the Seminole Revolt.

1819 Europe's postwar recovery hits U.S. agriculture, leading to financial panic.

1821 *Mexicans finally win an eleven-year war for their independence from Spain.*

1822–1834 *British mathematician Charles Babbage proposes constructing machines to perform mathematical calculations: the Difference and Analytical Engines, forerunners of the modern computer. He runs out of money before completing either.*

1824 Most states have expanded franchise to all free white men.

Jackson's complaint of Adams's "corrupt bargain" starts second party system.

Michael Faraday invents the first toy balloon.

1826 July 4: *Both John Adams and Thomas Jefferson—longtime friends, rivals, and, in the end, correspondents—die, on the fiftieth anniversary of the Declaration of Independence.*

1828 Jacksonian Democrats win presidency with mass appeal.

1830 Jackson's Indian Removal Act forces Indians to move west of Mississippi.

Simón Bolívar dies of tuberculosis in Colombia, after contributing to the independence of much of Latin America, including Venezuela, Colombia, Ecuador, Peru, and Bolivia.

1832 Supreme Court confirms Cherokee sovereignty in *Worcester* v. *Georgia*.

Tariffs cause nullification crisis between South Carolina and Washington.

1836 Jackson refuses to renew charter of Second National Bank.

Jackson's Specie Circular forbids government from accepting paper currency.

1838 4,000 Cherokees die on the Trail of Tears from Georgia to Oklahoma.

1837 *Severe bank panic spreads from New York across the country.*

The first kindergarten, called "small child occupation institute," opens in Germany.

1842 Seminole Indians rebel against sugar planters in Florida.

12 | A Regionalized America, 1830–1860

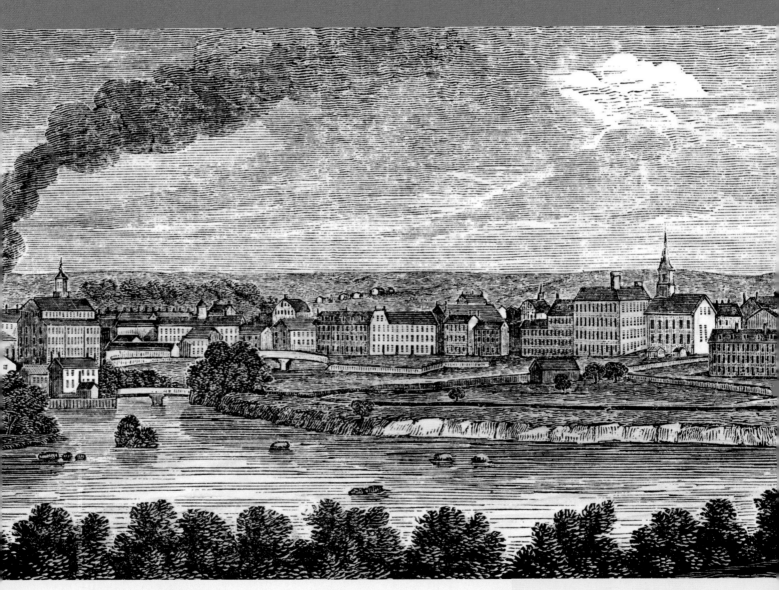

LEARNING OBJECTIVES

After reading this chapter, you should be able to do the following:

 Describe social life in the commercial North as it developed between 1830 and 1860.

 Describe social life as it developed in the South between 1830 and 1860 as a result of dependence on cotton.

AFTER FINISHING THIS CHAPTER GO TO **PAGE 230** **FOR STUDY TOOLS**

Between 1830 and 1860, American life became increasingly regionalized. As we have seen in previous chapters, this had always been the case. But with the arrival of the various transportation and communication revolutions of the early nineteenth century's Market Revolution, the North, South, and West drifted farther and farther apart, not only politically but also socially and economically. Different ways of living emerged in the three regions. Work relations were different, communities developed in different ways, and people often thought of themselves in regional terms. "I'm a northerner," they might say, "and I don't work for slave wages." Another might say, "In the West, we operate by a different law."

Slavery, western expansion, and commercial development were the vital issues that perpetuated regionalized identities, although the transportation revolution bound the West with either the North or the South. These regionalized identities persisted despite the best efforts of politicians to bridge sectional gaps (see Map 12.1).

This chapter describes social life in the North and the South as it developed during the Market Revolution. The next chapter describes life in the West, which had an identity all of its own.

12-1 SOCIAL LIFE IN THE COMMERCIAL NORTH

Three forces dramatically altered life in the northern United States between 1830 and 1860: (1) the Market Revolution, (2) immigration, and (3) urbanization.

12-1a The Market Revolution

First, although some protested the Market Revolution (recall Thoreau and others from Chapter 10), most northerners accommodated and even promoted the transitions associated with it. The beginnings of an industrial urban sector, the opening of the farmlands of the West, and the interconnectedness of the different groups living in the North affected the social life of every northerner. For the most part, northerners acclimated themselves to these changes. Railroads crisscrossed the North. Commerce blossomed. The Market Revolution ignited the processes that made the North look like what we think of today as a modern society.

12-1b Immigration

The second dramatic change was a wave of immigrants that came to the United States between 1830 and 1860. By 1860, about 20 percent of the total population of the North was foreign-born. Most of the immigrants came from Europe, and nearly two-thirds came from just two countries: Ireland and Germany. These immigrants settled largely but not entirely in the North, creating distinct immigrant neighborhoods in nearly every Northern city. As these immigrant groups became established and stable, they prompted new definitions of what it meant to be an American. They were of course not descendants of the American Revolution and thus had a different vision of what America meant.

12-1c Urbanization

The third dramatic change in the north was urbanization. In 1860, cities still housed a minority of the American population (most Americans were farmers), but within their borders the dramatic interplay of America's social divisions played out. Differences between black and white, rich and poor, and native-born and foreign-born all became flashpoints in early-nineteenth-century northern urban life. Each of these developments contributed to a unique and tumultuous social life in the antebellum North. And the cities would only continue to grow.

12-1d Life in the Northern Countryside

These three events had widespread ramifications for all groups, but life in the North varied depending on whether one lived in the cities or in the countryside.

COMMUNAL VALUES

For the most part, communal values still prevailed in the northern countryside. Farm families gathered regularly to raise barns, participate in politics, and attend church, an especially popular activity in the wake of the Second Great Awakening. Social networks were strong. Sewing bees and apple bees brought communities together. Most farming families in the "Old Northwest" of Illinois, western Pennsylvania, and Indiana (areas west of the Appalachians but east of the Mississippi River) found a balance between their roles as consumers and

◄◄◄ **The Erie Canal, at 363 miles long, cut transportation costs between the Eastern coast and the Great Lakes by ninety-five percent, lowered food costs in Eastern cities, and made shipment of manufactured goods to the Midwest much easier. The transportation revolutions of the early 19th century helped create the Market Revolution.**

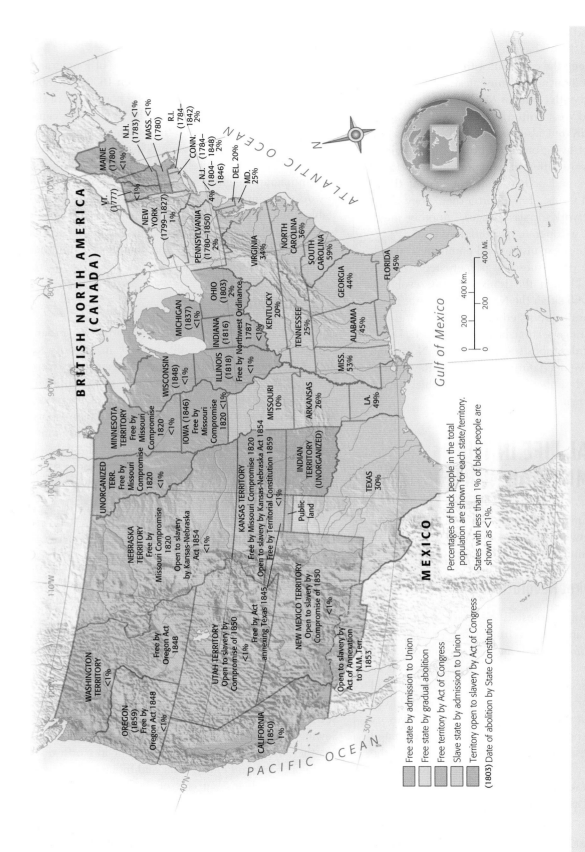

Map 12.1 Region and Race in Antebellum America, 1830–1860

>> This map, showing the land that would become the United States, displays not only the percentage of each state's or territories population that is African American, but also when and how it came into the union, and what its legal provisions were regarding slavery.

BRITISH NORTH AMERICA (CANADA)

MAINE (1780) <1%

N.H. (1783) <1%

VT. (1777) <1%

MASS. <1% (1780)

R.I. (1784–1842) 2%

CONN. (1784–1848) 1%

NEW YORK (1799–1827) 1%

N.J. (1804–1846) 4%

PENNSYLVANIA (1780–1850) 2%

DEL. 20%

MD. 25%

VIRGINIA 34%

NORTH CAROLINA 36%

SOUTH CAROLINA 59%

GEORGIA 44%

FLORIDA 45%

OHIO (1803) Free by Northwest Ordinance 1787 2%

MICHIGAN (1837) <1%

INDIANA (1816) <1%

KENTUCKY 20%

ILLINOIS (1818) Free by Missouri Compromise 1820 <1%

WISCONSIN (1848) <1%

TENNESSEE 25%

ALABAMA 45%

MISS. 53%

IOWA (1846) Free by Missouri Compromise 1820 <1%

MISSOURI 10%

ARKANSAS 26%

LA. 49%

MINNESOTA TERRITORY Free by Missouri Compromise 1820 <1%

UNORGANIZED TERR. Free by Missouri Compromise 1820 <1%

KANSAS TERRITORY Free by Missouri Compromise 1820 Open to slavery by Kansas-Nebraska Act 1854 Free by Territorial Constitution 1859 <1%

INDIAN TERRITORY (UNORGANIZED)

Public land

NEBRASKA TERRITORY Free by Missouri Compromise 1820 Open to slavery by Kansas-Nebraska Act 1854 <1%

TEXAS 30%

WASHINGTON TERRITORY <1%

OREGON (1859) Free by Oregon Act 1848 <1%

UTAH TERRITORY Open to slavery by Compromise of 1850 <1%

Free by Oregon Act 1848

NEW MEXICO TERRITORY Open to slavery by Compromise of 1850 <1%

Free by Act annexing Texas 1845 <1%

CALIFORNIA (1850) 1%

Open to slavery by Act of Annexation to N.M. Terr. 1853

MEXICO

Gulf of Mexico

PACIFIC OCEAN

ATLANTIC OCEAN

N

Percentages of black people in the total population are shown for each state/territory. States with less than 1% of black people are shown as <1%.

0   200   400 Mi.
0   200   400 Km.

- Free state by admission to Union
- Free state by gradual abolition
- Free territory by Act of Congress
- Slave state by admission to Union
- Territory open to slavery by Act of Congress
- (1803) Date of abolition by State Constitution

>> This picture shows a stone house typical of those built by the early German and Swiss immigrants in what is today called Pennsylvania Dutch country.

iStock.com/Dennis Guyitt

as producers. Some, like the utopians, rejected these impulses, but most northerners adapted to them.

DECREASED ISOLATION

Nevertheless, change did come to the northern countryside. For one thing, the countryside was less isolated than it had been. Markets sprang up at railroad depots, and mail and news traveled rapidly from one part of the country to the next.

Meanwhile, the transportation revolution communicated new ideas to once-isolated areas. The itinerant ministers of the Second Great Awakening, for example, moved across the country on canals and, later, railroads. The countryside also enjoyed an active lyceum circuit, where clergymen, reformers, Transcendentalists, socialists, feminists, and other provocative orators would speak. The North opened some public schools and enjoyed a burgeoning newspaper industry as well. The press, though, was heavily partisan, because it was usually financed by political parties. This meant that in almost every town there were at least two papers: one Democrat, one Whig. Meanwhile, the entire North, including in the countryside, achieved almost universal literacy in those years, a truly remarkable feat. And at the same time, immigrants from Germany and Scandinavia moved into the Old Northwest to continue the farming life they had left behind in Europe. These newcomers slightly altered midwestern accents, politics, and social life, while upholding steadfast rural ideals. Descendants of these immigrant groups still have a significant presence in these areas today. In sum, the communications and transportation revolutions that were associated with the Market Revolution had sewn together

> Immigrants from Germany and Scandinavia moved into the Old Northwest to continue the farming life they had left behind in Europe.

the vast stretch of lands in the northern United States, from Maine to the Mississippi, north of Tennessee.

12-1e City Life

Despite this increased connectedness, city life in the North was changing much more rapidly than life in the country. The cities were growing at a tremendous rate. Between 1830 and 1860, the number of towns with 10,000 or more people quintupled, totaling ninety-three in 1860. There were seven towns in the North with more than 100,000 people. In 1830, there had been just one city that large, New York City, which had just over 200,000 inhabitants. By 1860, more than 814,000 people lived in New York, making it by far the nation's largest city. The Market Revolution had increased the importance of commercial hubs, making cities singularly important and vibrant. Nevertheless, they were still dependent on and connected to the products being grown and produced in the northern countryside.

IMMIGRANTS

Immigrants contributed to much of the urban growth. In all, more than 5 million immigrants came to America between 1830 and 1860. The peak period of immigration came in the late 1840s and 1850s, when nearly 1 million Irish came to the United States to escape the potato famine. Many Germans came at this time too, especially in 1848, after a failed revolution in Germany forced

>> The difficult life endured by Irish immigrants, including challenges forced upon them by those who opposed their arrival, has been a constant feature in American culture, including in the 2002 film, "Gangs of New York," a scene from which is pictured here.

Miramax/courtesy Everett Collection

many political dissidents to flee. Unlike the Irish, these German immigrants, called **the 48ers**, were educated and often financially well off.

The immigrants arrived in such numbers that they changed the nature of the cities. For example, more than half of all the inhabitants of New York City were foreign-born in 1855. More than a third of Bostonians were. Within the cities, immigrants usually created enclaves of ethnic neighborhoods, starting their own churches, leisure societies, sporting clubs, and charitable organizations.

While most of these new immigrants stayed in the Northeast, some moved to the Midwest. In 1855, for example, more than 60 percent of St. Louis was foreign-born. And many of the 48ers moved to the rural western provinces, where they could farm and where they could vote after just one or two years of residency. These new immigrants largely avoided the South because of its dependence on slave labor, which limited access to jobs.

RACIAL AND ETHNIC IDENTITIES

With the arrival of these millions of immigrants, many Americans began to consider what it was that made

someone an American. One response was to define an American as someone with a British background who was born in the United States. The most ardent supporters of these views formulated a racial and ethnic identity that differentiated the various immigrant groups and proclaimed the superiority of their own group, usually labeled "native Americans." They chastised the Irish, equating them with black slaves in the South. And they were offended by the German tradition of gathering at beer gardens on Sundays, which these "native Americans," who were overwhelmingly Protestant, considered a day of worship. The "native American movement," sometimes called **nativism**, seeped into politics and the social and economic life of the nation as well. Nativists placed restrictions on what fields of business new immigrants could enter, where they could live, and where they could work. The influential temperance movement also contained within it a large amount of anti-Irish and anti-German nativism. This was the era when the term *yankee* came to have meaningful social significance, differentiating between those whose family lineage predated the Revolution and those who arrived later.

Related to this racial and ethnic stereotyping was a brutal form of anti-Catholicism. The Irish were usually willing to work for lower wages than anyone else, which provoked anti-Irish sentiment from workers who felt threatened by this cheap labor force. Because the Irish were identifiable by their Catholicism, mobs, angry at how the nation was changing, sometimes attacked Catholic churches, convents, and priests. In Boston, where large numbers of Irish had settled, anti-Catholic riots broke out regularly. Public education became more visibly imbued with Protestantism in the 1840s and 1850s, prompting many Catholics to establish a web of parochial schools.

the 48ers Germans who came to the United States in 1848, after a failed revolution in Germany forced many political dissidents to flee

nativism Political identity that defined an American as someone with a British background who was born in the United States; supporters formulated a racial and ethnic identity that proclaimed the superiority of their group, usually labeled "native Americans"

But identity formation went both ways. Upon their initial arrival, Irish and German immigrants routinely referred to themselves by the town or county from which they came. But after just a short time in America these immigrants began to consciously think of themselves as "Irish" or "German" or "Swedish." A common language was one feature that bound certain groups together. Religion also helped newcomers feel part of a cohesive group, especially for the Irish. Restricted to certain neighborhoods, immigrant groups developed communities that embraced cultural forms harking back to the homeland. For instance, Milwaukee and St. Louis maintain extensive brewing industries today, a legacy of the German immigrants who settled in these cities during the middle of the nineteenth century. Several of these communities also still have *Turnvereine*, or turnvereins, gymnasiums founded in the spirit of the German liberation movement that erupted in 1848.

CLASS CONSCIOUSNESS

In addition to the formation of racial and ethnic identities, the combination of ethnic enclaves, middle-class professions, and the incredible wealth earned by canal builders and others led to highly visible social divisions. While most of the working class lived in small apartments, wealthy Americans were constructing large mansions. By the 1850s, affluent neighborhoods had access to indoor plumbing and gas lighting. The wealthy moved through the cities via horse-drawn carriages and built neighborhoods away from industrial hubs. And the rich were getting richer, too: in 1845, almost 80 percent of New York City's individual wealth was owned by just 4 percent of the population. Poorer people had none of these luxuries and were often forced to live in the least desirable neighborhoods, near stockyards or slaughterhouses.

One result of these increasing economic distinctions was the creation of identities associated with being a member of a specific class. Although never totally distinct from ethnic, racial, and religious divisions, distinctions began to grow in how poor people talked, voted, and fought. Much of the lower-class consciousness developed not in the workplace but in places of leisure, where workers felt most free. It was in these locations that organizers had success developing the political parties of the working class.

WOMEN AND THE MIDDLE CLASS

Along with a slowly forming working-class consciousness, northern cities also became crucibles of the middle class, made up mostly of managers, desk workers, and educators. This group of educated middlemen and their families cultivated a middle-class identity between wealth and poverty. Their children slept one to a bed, they owned several pieces of large furniture, and their sons often went to college. Women were central to the formation of the middle class, and indeed, one hallmark of a middle-class family (in contrast to working-class families) was that its women rarely worked outside the home. As work moved out of the home and into factories and commercial centers, the

North Wind Picture Archives

>> For middle-class women in the 19th century like the one shown here surrounded by her charges, teaching was among the primary occupations open to them.

>> Milwaukee, Cincinnati, and St. Louis still maintain extensive brewing industries, a legacy of German immigrants. Here, this woodcutting depicts a brewer combining ingredients to make beer.

home became idealized as a haven in a heartless world, and middle-class women were expected to cultivate and maintain this idealized perception. In serving as the moral centerpieces of middle-class society, women became the backbone of reform efforts designed to improve the moral character of the nation. Consequently, teaching became the main profession open to middle-class women. Catharine and Mary Beecher headed up efforts to ensure that middle-class women were prepared to teach middle-class children the proper disciplines, and they were only two of the most famous female reformers of the era.

LEISURE

Also during this period, several forms of leisure

> Throughout the 1800s, audience participation was expected at plays, and the interaction between performer and audience made plays a democratic form of entertainment rather than a polished form reserved for the educated elite.

became commodities to be purchased rather than merely games to play. Although urban Americans still gathered at taverns and competed in physical contests, enterprising merchants developed networks of theaters and professional sports. Boxing, horse racing, track and field, and, in the 1850s, baseball all evolved into professional sports during this era, attracting large crowds and meriting their own pages in the newspapers. In contrast to male-dominated professional sports, theaters provided social spaces for both men and women. Towns routinely constructed theaters early in their development, featuring plays by Shakespeare and other luminaries. Perhaps the

>> This 1835 watercolor depicts the American minstrel tradition, a tradition that often featured white men in blackface poking fun at the South's backwardness and at African American people in general.

most popular form of entertainment was the minstrel show, featuring white men smeared with burnt cork (to make them look black) who lampooned slave life in the South. The joke was intended to be twofold, making fun of the South for its backward ways and also ridiculing African Americans for being, in the actors' minds, doltish and childlike. The most famous minstrel show featured an actor portraying a slave doing a silly dance and singing a song about "jumping Jim Crow." Despite the slow elimination of slavery in the North after the Revolution, northern racism held firm. The minstrel shows ran concurrently with Shakespeare's plays and other forms of what might today be thought of as high culture. However, throughout the 1800s, audience participation was expected at plays, and the interaction between performer and audience made

plays a democratic form of entertainment rather than a polished form reserved for the educated elite.

In the private spaces of their homes (and with increased access to indoor gas lighting), Americans also began to read more. The number of newspapers skyrocketed during these years (funded mostly by political parties), and American novelists flourished. Herman Melville, Nathaniel Hawthorne, and Fanny Fern were some of the most popular authors. The best-selling book of the period was Harriet Beecher Stowe's antislavery novel, **Uncle Tom's Cabin**; or, Life Among the Lowly (1852). Stowe and Fanny Fern were part of the growth of a "ladies' literature" in which middle-class women used their leisure time to cultivate what historians have since called a "sentimental culture." Despite the dismissive title, Stowe's Uncle Tom's Cabin emerged from the sentimental culture but had far-reaching political ramifications, enlightening people across the country to the conditions of southern slavery. Many of the other works of ladies' literature were less politically engaged, more often propagating middle-class morality.

FREE PEOPLE OF COLOR

The cities of the North were also home to free people of color, albeit in small numbers. In all, there were about 500,000 free people of color in the United States in 1860, about half of whom lived in northern cities. The remainder lived in border states, especially in and around Baltimore, Maryland. These enclaves were important not so much for provoking nativist opposition (as the Irish did), but because they created lasting institutions that perpetually supported movements for freedom. One institution was the organization of African American freemasons named after its founder, Prince Hall.

The most influential institution for free people of color, though, was the black church. During the Second Great Awakening, for the first time a majority of African Americans became Christians. Barred from worshiping in several houses of the Christian religion, black Americans founded the **African Methodist Episcopal (AME) Church** in the 1790s. By 1816, there were enough

Uncle Tom's Cabin Antislavery novel published by Harriet Beecher Stowe in 1852; best-selling book of that period

African Methodist Episcopal (AME) Church National African American Methodist religious denomination founded by Richard Allen and Absalom Jones in the 1790s; doctrinally Methodist, it was the first major religious denomination in the Western world to originate for sociological, not theological, reasons

branches to merit a national organization, and by 1824 the AME Church had several thousand congregants. More than just places of worship, the churches functioned as schools and community centers. Because white people were unwilling to block church development for fear they would be accused of preventing Christian worship, the churches developed a separate sphere of freedom for black Americans.

In the wake of the development of the black church, several African American voluntary groups appeared, promoting abolition, temperance, and other reform causes. Black social fraternities prospered as well. If free blacks could not successfully conquer white racism, they could create institutions that developed a class of black leaders and an ideology of independence. Leaders such as James Forten and Reverend Henry Highland Garnet became political advocates for the abolition of slavery during these years. And the educated members of this society began referring to themselves as "Colored Americans" rather than "Africans" in order to assert their membership in the American nation. Throughout the 1840s and 1850s, these black Americans swayed between optimism and pessimism about the place of black people in America, debating whether or not it would ever feel truly like home.

ABOLITIONISM

Free African Americans had long advocated the abolition of slavery, and in the 1820s they accelerated their efforts.

Richard Allen, head of the African Methodist Episcopal Church, and David Walker, a vocal pamphleteer, advocated immediate emancipation. Walker's essay *Appeal to the Coloured Citizens of the World* (1829) serves as the strongest statement from an African American during the era; its fiery rhetoric about the evils of slavery helped provoke many small slave riots across the South.

While African Americans advocated immediate emancipation, most white Americans favored gradual emancipation, or gradualism. In the North, slavery had been phased out after the Revolution, and the problem seemed less pressing to northern white reformers. Some white Americans participated in the American Colonization Society (as discussed in Chapter 10), although its motives were hardly clear even to those active in the organization.

GARRISON AND *THE LIBERATOR*

Public opinion in the North began to shift in 1831, when William Lloyd Garrison, a white journalist advocating immediate emancipation, began publishing the antislavery newspaper *The Liberator*. *The Liberator* served for thirty years as the central voice of the abolition movement. It drew together a group of antislavery advocates, many of whom were evangelical preachers affiliated with the Lane Theological Seminary in Cincinnati (men like Lyman Beecher and Theodore Weld). The ideas of the Second Great Awakening prodded these leaders to advocate immediate emancipation, although many other northern white

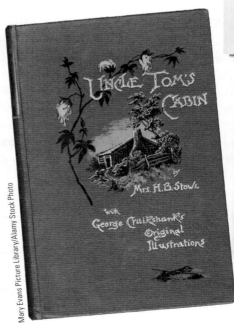

Mary Evans Picture Library/Alamy Stock Photo

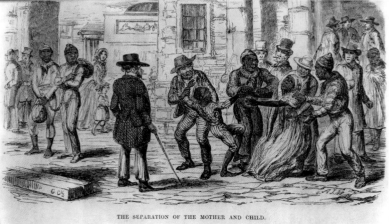

>> Pictured here is the caption of *Uncle Tom's Cabin*, with one of George Cruikshank's original illustrations from the book, which helped stir reactions to the book's antislavery message.

THE SEPARATION OF THE MOTHER AND CHILD.

" The old men of the company, partly by persuasion and partly by force, loosed the poor creature's last despairing hold, and, as they led her off to her new master's waggon, strove to comfort her."—Page 103.

Cruikshank, George (1792–1878) (after)/The Art Gallery Collection/ Alamy Stock Photo

churches were slower to adopt the cause of emancipation, prompting Garrison to attack them for their complicity. Garrison was clearly the most steadfast in his pursuit of abolition: at one point, he publicly burned a copy of the U.S. Constitution, suggesting that it too was complicit in allowing slavery (which, of course, it was). This action, and others like it, alienated Garrison from many white abolitionists who favored gradualism. In 1833, Garrison founded the **American Anti-Slavery Society**, an organization that served as a point of contact for escaped slaves like Frederick Douglass and Harriet Tubman. His secretary, the dynamic Maria Weston Chapman, edited *The Liberator* when Garrison was off doing other work.

> The wealthy got wealthier, and the middle class created a unique and comfortable life for itself.

RESISTANCE TO ABOLITION

Abolitionists faced fierce, stubborn resistance in both the South and the North. In northern states like New York and Illinois, merchants and laborers challenged abolitionists mainly because they were afraid that poor black people would be willing to work for low wages, thus depressing the economy. In 1837, vigilantes in Illinois even murdered the minister and journalist Elijah Lovejoy for perpetually publishing abolitionist tracts. In the South, southerners also sometimes violently prevented abolitionists from distributing antislavery tracts. Georgia offered a $5,000 reward to anyone who delivered Garrison to state authorities.

CONGRESSIONAL "GAG RULE"

Northern abolitionists continued to fight, though, sending thousands of petitions to Congress and fomenting a serious political movement. In an effort to prevent Congress from discussing slavery (and therefore threatening the free state/slave state balance established by the Compromise of 1820), the House of Representatives adopted, in 1836, what opponents called the "**gag rule.**" This was a legal provision that automatically tabled any discussion of abolition. Under this law, slavery was not open for discussion in Congress. Former president John Quincy Adams, now a member of the House of Representatives representing his home state of Massachusetts, repeatedly protested the rule, but persistent opposition frustrated his efforts for eight years, when Congress finally rescinded the rule.

By the 1850s, the northern movement for abolition was growing, and so was its opposition. As the debate became increasingly polarized, more and more people had to weigh the costs associated with slavery.

12-1f "Free Labor"

In general, most Americans in the North accommodated the Market Revolution. The wealthy got wealthier, and the middle class created a unique and comfortable life for itself. Immigrants poured in, and, although the working class faced brutal working hours, painstaking labor, and few benefits beyond a paycheck, all they had to do was look south to see that they were much better off than the laborers there, a great majority of whom were enslaved and had no hope of freedom. Indeed, it was around the idea of "**free labor**" that many northerners, diverse as they were, united. In the nineteenth-century North, "free labor" meant the ability to work without a master, to be free to leave one's employer if one wished, and to be able to move upward if one was successful. Ultimately, it promised to allow the laborer to gain enough capital so that one did not have to work for someone else, but could work on one's own "account." Impoverished as many were, these "free laborers" saw themselves as uniquely distinct from the slave society of the South, where most of the workers were distinctly unfree.

 # 12-2 SOCIAL LIFE IN THE COTTON SOUTH

Between 1830 and 1860, southerners experienced dramatically different developments than northerners. In every way, cotton became king. It constituted nearly half of the exports of the entire nation, and southerners knew they could get rich if they could succeed as cotton farmers. But growing cotton required slaves

American Anti-Slavery Society Organization founded by journalist William Lloyd Garrison in 1833 that served as a point of contact for escaped slaves like Frederick Douglass and Harriet Tubman

gag rule Legal provision of 1836 that automatically tabled any discussion of abolition in Congress; under this law, slavery was not open for discussion

free labor The concept that most unified the diverse collection of people in the northern states, centered on a society filled with those who worked without a master and possessed the freedom to leave a job if and when they wished

The Reasons Why...

There are three main reasons why popular images of the antebellum South as portrayed in venues like *Gone with the Wind* are misleading:

Most white Southerners did not own slaves. First, of the 8 million southern white people, only a quarter owned slaves, meaning that a large majority of southern white people were not slaveowners. Most were isolated yeoman farmers seeking self-sufficiency.

Most slave owners had only a few slaves. Second, of that quarter of the white population that owned slaves, most owned very few slaves. More than 60 percent of slave owners owned five or fewer slaves, and only 3 percent owned twenty or more slaves.

But most slaves lived on plantations. Finally, while a vast majority of southern white people had no connection to a plantation, the majority of slaves did. Indeed, the few massive plantations housed as many as half of all the slaves in the region. As such, plantations were vital in the development of a unique slave culture. On the other hand, the wealthy plantation life of *Gone with the Wind* was lived by only a very small minority of white southerners.

and land, so southerners brought slaves and slavery with them into the southwestern territories of the United States. This ended any potential talk of gradual emancipation during this period. Furthermore, southerners had little need for big cities, and, without jobs to offer, they did not attract immigrants in the same numbers as the North. This was the period when southerners solidified their plantation economy and developed a vehement defense of it—one based on the superiority of the white race.

When we think of the antebellum South, we are prone to think of images culled from the novel and film *Gone with the Wind*, which portrayed the leisurely lifestyle of a landed and cultured white elite being served by willing and subservient black slaves. But three facts are vital in understanding how the actual prewar South contrasted with this image (see "The Reasons Why . . ." box).

12-2a Southern White Society

While the North was notable for distinctions between the countryside and the city, there were no similar complexities in southern society, because there were so few cities. Instead, white southern society was stratified between yeoman farmers and wealthy planters. A group of landless white people consisting of perhaps 25 to 40 percent of the population ranked below the yeoman farmers (but above slaves), mostly working as laborers on farms or as frontiersmen settling the Southwest. But most white southerners were either wealthy planters or yeoman farmers.

>> Wealthy southern planters imagined themselves as the region's aristocracy, and built homes like this Greek revival style antebellum mansion, dramatically displaying their wealth and status in Southern society.

In new screen splendor...
The most magnificent picture ever!

DAVID O. SELZNICK'S PRODUCTION OF MARGARET MITCHELL'S
"GONE WITH THE WIND"

STARRING
CLARK GABLE
VIVIEN LEIGH
LESLIE HOWARD OLIVIA de HAVILLAND

A SELZNICK INTERNATIONAL PICTURE · DIRECTED BY VICTOR FLEMING · SCREEN PLAY BY SIDNEY HOWARD · METRO-GOLDWYN-MAYER INC. · Music by MAX STEINER

1939

Courtesy of The Advertising Archives

>> The vision of the antebellum South presented in Gone with the Wind (1936) correctly identifies only a tiny percentage of southerners living during the era. This movie poster from the 1939 film shows a romanticized version of the antebellum South in an effort to promote the movie. It worked. The film was the highest-grossing film ever at that point in time.

THE PLANTERS

The planters viewed themselves as paternalistic aristocrats managing preindustrial fiefdoms. They were deeply involved in national and international markets (for instance, the development of the telegraph in 1845 allowed them to monitor cotton prices in Britain). But they usually preferred to keep the marketplace at a distance. They spent their summers abroad and sent their children to schools in Europe and at the Ivy League colleges in the North. The planters also often entered politics, considering themselves the natural leaders of society. Financially and politically powerful, they fought all attempts to make their society more democratic. They resisted funding public education through taxation and defeated similar attempts to create internal improvements that would have invited more commerce and industry to the South. Content with the society they had created, southern planters resisted change unless it could earn them greater profits.

YEOMAN FARMERS

Only a tiny minority of white southerners were planters; the majority were yeoman farmers. Yeoman farmers were largely self-sufficient, living with their families on remote farms or in small towns, and missing out on much of the Market Revolution. They were usually forced onto less desirable plots of land, and, most of the time, these farmers used most of their land to plant cotton and the rest to grow crops needed by the household. They used the money earned from cotton to purchase items that could not be grown in southern soil, such as coffee.

Most yeoman farmers remained largely isolated from markets. A few acquired large plots, bought slaves, and became wealthy, but this was rare. Social mobility was limited in the antebellum South, and when it did occur, it mostly pushed people downward. At some point during their lives, nearly one-quarter of white southerners were landless and thus forced to search for work on someone else's farm or push west in search of work. With few public schools, most yeoman farmers were also uneducated. (At least 20 percent of white adult southerners could not read.) Consumed by the work of their farms, they remained isolated in their culture, which was centered on family, church, and region.

12-2b The Defense of Slavery

No matter what their station in society, nearly all white southerners were advocates of slavery. For the planters, this was an easy decision: slavery, while expensive to maintain, was profitable, and profits and social norms overcame any moral difficulties. For yeoman farmers and landless white people, the existence of slavery ensured that there was always a class of people below them socially, that there was always one rung farther down the ladder. The presence of slaves kept alive their hopes that maybe one day they too might own slaves and become wealthy. Thus, no matter their station in life, the vast majority of white Southerners took for granted the existence of black slavery and the superiority of what they understood to be the white race.

NAT TURNER

Of course, the vast majority of African Americans did not support the institution. Most violently, in 1831, Nat Turner, a Christian preacher, led a group of slaves through the Virginia countryside, murdering sixty white people of both sexes and all ages during a two-day stretch. Turner's plan was to raise an army of freed slaves and lead an insurrection against the southern white planters, hoping to end slavery once and for all.

The white response to Nat Turner's rebellion was overwhelming and brutal. White militiamen viciously

"And about this time I had a vision—and I saw white spirits and black spirits engaged in battle, and the sun was darkened—the thunder rolled in the Heavens, and blood flowed in streams—and I heard a voice saying, "Such is your luck, such you are called to see, and let it come rough or smooth, you must surely bear it."

—THOMAS R. GRAY, THE CONFESSIONS OF NAT TURNER

attacked the group associated with Turner, but they also indiscriminately killed slaves not involved in the insurrection at all. Perhaps more than two hundred slaves were killed in retaliation. Turner was eventually captured and hanged, but not before being interviewed by southern physician Thomas R. Gray, who published the interview as *The Confessions of Nat Turner*. The book sold well from its first publication, and it remains one of the most haunting tales of American slavery.

>> In 1831, Nat Turner led a slave revolt through the Virginia countryside, killing sixty white people with hopes of starting a massive slave revolt. It didn't work out as Turner had planned. Here, Turner and his accomplices plot.

Ullstein Bild/The Image Works

LEGAL RESTRICTIONS

Besides the violent damage done to black bodies, Nat Turner's insurrection also caused white southerners to pass further laws restricting black freedoms. Many states prohibited slave literacy. Others required all slave meetings to be supervised by whites. Slave behavior was monitored. In 1832, the Virginia legislature debated a plan that would simultaneously emancipate its slaves gradually and then deport them all to Africa. The plan did not pass, and no other open discussion of emancipation ever occurred in the South until the Civil War.

PROSLAVERY IDEOLOGY

Beyond punitive and legal ramifications, the reaction to Nat Turner and the growth of abolitionist sentiment in the North stimulated a change in the way slavery was understood in the South. In this period, southern writers developed a defense of slavery that suggested that slavery was good for both races, because black people were not equipped to take care of themselves and needed white, paternalistic masters to protect them. White slaveholders began to cite biblical references to slavery, suggesting that the institution was somehow sanctioned by God. Thomas R. Dew, George Fitzhugh, and J. D. B. DeBow all advocated the benefits of slavery in widely read publications. Through them, the South's understanding of slavery transitioned from being a "necessary evil" (as it was conceived during the revolutionary period) to being a "positive good." Paralleling the "free labor" ideology of the North, the development of a proslavery ideology in the South grounded many southerners' sense of who they were as a people and how they differed from those living just north of them.

>> This cartoon image, showing a white family standing in front of several peaceful and happy-looking slaves, reveals the idealized view of slavery that developed in the 1830s and 1840s. The caption reads:

Slaves: God bless you massa! you feed and clothe us. When we are sick you nurse us, and when too old to work, you provide for us!

Master: These poor creatures are a sacred legacy from my ancestors and while a dollar is left me, nothing shall be spared to increase their comfort and happiness.

12-2c Slave Society

Certainly no slave would agree with the notion that slavery was a positive good. Life for slaves was arduous, a relentless grind of forced labor in uncertain social conditions, shadowed by the constant threat of abuse. Most slaves were field hands growing sugar, rice, tobacco, and especially cotton. Some were house servants who cooked and cleaned for their masters and helped take care of their children. Some were skilled artisans, such as blacksmiths, carpenters, or ironworkers. A few worked as longshoremen or ship-builders in port cities such as New Orleans, Louisiana, and Charleston, South Carolina. Yet all were regarded as property, to be bought, sold, or bartered at the whim of their owner, a torturous form of uncertainty and inhumanity.

The law did not protect slave families either. Husbands and wives, as well as parents and children, could be separated from each other permanently, without notice. Although there were official limits on the treatment of slaves (the murder or unjustifiable mutilation of slaves was illegal in most states, and state laws set minimum standards for the amount of food, clothing, and shelter that must be provided for slaves), such laws were unenforceable because slaves were prohibited from taking their masters to court.

Despite severely restricting the rights of slaves, many slave masters believed it was in their best interest to treat slaves decently—as long as the slaves remained obedient. Masters were generally profit-minded men who understood that healthy laborers were more productive than those who were sick or abused.

Owners also recognized that healthy slaves were more likely to produce healthy offspring. Slave reproduction mattered to plantation owners because the United States had outlawed participation in the international slave trade in 1808. While Caribbean slaveholders frequently worked slaves to death only to replace them with new imports from Africa, this was impossible in the United States. This meant there was a greater interest and insistence on breeding. Nevertheless, the fact that slaveholders had an interest in keeping their slaves alive did not mean that slaves were treated humanely in the antebellum South.

During the major seasons of cotton cultivation, slaves labored in the fields for up to sixteen hours a day.

gang system Work arrangement under which slaves were organized into groups of twenty to twenty-five workers, supervised by an overseer

slavedriver Supervisor or overseer of slave labor, usually employed on a cotton plantation

task system Work arrangement under which slaves were assigned a specific set of tasks to accomplish each day; often employed on rice plantations and in domestic service situations

"I heard them [slaves] get up with a powerful force of spirit, clapping they hands and walking around the place. They'd shout, 'I got the glory. I got the old time religion in my heart.'"

—MOSE HURSEY, FORMER SLAVE FROM RED RIVER COUNTY, TEXAS

WORK

The work conditions endured by slaves were as varied as the tasks they performed, but plantation labor was usually organized in one of two ways. The first was the **gang system**. Under this system, masters organized slaves into groups of twenty to twenty-five workers, supervised by a white overseer or a black **slavedriver**. This method of organizing labor was most commonly used on cotton plantations. During the major seasons of cotton cultivation, slaves labored in the fields for up to sixteen hours a day. Although most masters, in keeping with their Christian beliefs, gave their slaves Sundays off and required only a half-day of work on Saturday, working under the gang system was backbreaking.

The second major labor system was the **task system**. As the name suggests, this system assigned each slave a specific set of tasks to accomplish each day. Once slaves had accomplished these tasks, their time was largely their own. The task system was common on rice plantations, because rice did not require the constant care and toil that cotton did. Slaves working as domestic servants also commonly labored under the task system. Although the task system typically gave slaves more freedom, slaveholders frequently set unrealistic expectations for slaves and then punished them for failing to finish their work.

Some slaves did not work in either of these two systems. Instead, they had special arrangements that allowed them an unusual amount of freedom. This

>> Pictured here is an unusual sight—five generations of a slave family, together, on Smith's Plantation, Beaufort, South Carolina, 1862.

QUARTERS

Despite the wide variety of possible slaving conditions, most slaves were owned by planters who lived on large plantations. In these conditions, most slaves lived in slave quarters, defined as a group of cabins set away from the master's home. The cabins were usually organized around families, who tended personal gardens and raised their own animals. On the largest plantations, slave quarters were significant communities with ample freedom away from the watchful eye of the master.

COMMUNITY

In slave quarters, slaves created a culture far removed from that dictated by white southerners. From the beginning, Africans came to America with their own cultures, and the experience of slavery did not completely obliterate those cultures. The influence of African cultures was especially strong in the music, dancing, and verbal expressions that slaves used in their everyday lives and religious ceremonies.

Family lay at the center of slave culture. Although masters retained the right to separate spouses, siblings, parents, and children from each other, most slaves remained determined to preserve a sense of family. Slave marriages were not legally recognized, but slaves entered marital unions with great joy and celebration. Some marriages were made by obtaining the master's verbal consent.

was especially common among slaves living in cities. Although urbanization did not occur as quickly as it had in the North, the South did possess a small number of cities, including Baltimore, Richmond, Charleston, Mobile, and New Orleans. Each city housed a large slave population, and, even though urban slaves remained the property of their masters, owners could not exercise complete authority over their slaves in the city. For instance, a skilled slave carpenter needed the freedom to move about the city to reach job sites. Craftsmen, such as blacksmiths or jewelers, often worked independently, sharing a portion of their earnings with their master. As these slaves' experiences attest, slavery was an adaptable economic institution, working in a variety of agrarian and urban settings. It wasn't simply a pre-capitalist ancient relic, but an institution capable of adapting to modern capitalism.

When possible, slaves maintained traditional nuclear families with a father, a mother, and children living together. Within this family unit, men and women followed traditional gender roles, although they worked side-by-side, doing the same work in the fields. At home, women usually did the indoor work, such as cooking, cleaning, sewing, and raising children, while men did chores outside the home, like hauling water and gathering wood. Although premarital sex was common in slave quarters, at some point every slave was expected to choose a mate and settle down. Maintaining a two-parent family was not within their control, however. Whenever it was convenient or profitable, many masters sold off married slaves, leaving mates behind. One estimate suggests that, in the four decades preceding the Civil War, around 600,000 slave husbands and wives were separated from each other in this way.

>> The Underground Railroad was composed of a chain of houses or other safe-houses where runaway slaves could hide as they escaped to freedom. Both white and black abolitionists aided the runaway slaves, as shown in this commemorative painting from 1893.

Religion served as another pillar of slave culture. Most slaves arrived in America holding some form of West African religious belief. They usually believed in a Supreme God or Creator, as well as in the existence of a number of lesser gods. During the colonial period most slaves continued to practice their native religions, and slave owners did little to introduce their slaves to Christianity, fearing that if slaves became Christians they would have to be freed.

During the Second Great Awakening, however, most slaves became Christians. And despite the controlling efforts of the masters, slaves formed their own ideas about Christianity, melding their native practices with Christian beliefs. Many slaves also maintained belief in benevolent spirits and in the practice of conjuring or foreseeing the future. Theirs was a jubilant faith, promising deliverance. Religious

services in slave quarters included dancing, singing, and clapping. Spirituals were the most significant form of African American music developed during this period. For obvious reasons, the biblical lessons slaves emphasized were not those that commanded obedience and docility, but those that inspired hope for the future. The God they worshiped was one who would redeem the downtrodden and lift them up to heaven on Judgment Day. The master might be rich and powerful in this life, but many slaves took solace in the conviction that they would attain glory in the next one.

RESISTANCE AND REVOLT

Although several slave revolts are well remembered today, it is worth asking why there were not more of them. Partly the answer has to do with the harsh

> Intelligent slaves often faked confusion to avoid being assigned certain tasks or to explain why work was not completed. They were resisting their condition in a subtle manner.

reaction southern whites had after slave revolts. Still, the low number of slave revolts in American history should not be interpreted as a lack of resistance on the part of American slaves. Most slaves who wanted to buck the system simply found less overt ways of insulting or irritating their masters, especially considering that punishments for revolt were so severe. Slaves broke tools and machinery in order to slow production. Some feigned illness and injury to avoid work. Still others stole goods from their master to sell or trade for other goods. Even in their everyday demeanor, slaves occasionally outsmarted their owners. They could pretend to be ignorant and happy, as whites believed them to be, and use white stereotypes of them as a way to escape work. For example, intelligent slaves often faked confusion to avoid being assigned certain tasks or to explain why work was not completed. They were resisting their condition in a subtle manner.

Those who wanted to resist white authority in more dramatic fashion, but did not want to take the chance of organizing widespread revolts, had another option. They could run away. However, few slaves found permanent freedom in this way, especially if they were trying to flee from states in the Deep South, defined as Alabama, Georgia, Louisiana, Mississippi, and South Carolina. White Southerners organized slave patrols to watch for runaways and used hunting dogs to track escaped slaves. Slave owners also used newspapers to alert white people across the South to be on the lookout for certain runaways. Because so few southern black people were free (only about 8 percent), slaves on the run were easily sighted.

Despite the odds, many slaves did flee, and a few, perhaps a couple hundred every year, found permanent freedom. Some runaways found help from the **Underground Railroad**, defined as a network of men and women (white and black) who opposed slavery, sheltered runaway slaves, and expedited their journey to freedom. One slave who successfully escaped bondage and settled in the North was Frederick Douglass. After his escape, Douglass became one of the foremost figures in the abolition movement. He wrote about his experiences in his autobiography, *Narrative of the Life of Frederick Douglass* (1845), which traces his personal journey from slavery to freedom.

>LOOKING AHEAD...

By the 1830s, the North and the South had begun to develop divergent societies. The Market Revolution and slavery served as obvious battle lines. And indeed, the two societies were growing increasingly at odds with one another, both politically and culturally. For instance, although most northerners did not favor abolition, they generally agreed that slavery contradicted the way of life that the Market Revolution was bringing about, one that underscored the presence and importance of labor that was free to choose its manner and place of employment. The North was also becoming increasingly urbanized and industrialized, with a large population of landless (often immigrant) workers. And it was sewn together by its general embrace of the communication and transportation revolutions of the previous decades.

Southerners, meanwhile, had begun to articulate the concept that slavery was not shameful, but essential to the protection and improvement of the black race. The region remained a predominantly agrarian society that depended on slave labor for the cultivation of its most profitable crop, cotton. Many in the South viewed the growth of cities and commerce in the North as a move away from the values on which the country had been founded and toward materialism and greed. Northerners, in turn, tended to view the South as a region stuck in

Underground Railroad Network of men and women, both white and black, who were opposed to slavery, sheltered runaway slaves, and expedited their journey to freedom

the past, venerating the kind of class system and aristocracy against which the revolutionary patriots had rebelled decades earlier.

In addition, the two regions had widely differing attitudes toward the role of the federal government. The North depended on the high tariffs of the American System to protect its growing manufacturing concerns, and the government used the income from the tariffs to finance the roads, canals, and other internal improvements that northerners needed to bring goods to market. Southerners opposed high tariffs. They did not need tariffs to protect their cotton production, so tariffs accomplished nothing for southerners beyond raising the cost of the imported goods they wanted to purchase. This distinction about the role the federal government should play would shape opinions for a long time to come.

Until the 1830s, most northerners had been content to tolerate slavery outside their own state borders, but, as the nation expanded geographically, Americans were repeatedly forced to confront the issue. Should slavery be allowed to move west? Over the next few decades, the question of whether or not slavery would be allowed into new western territories reappeared continually, and conflict over this question would lead to sectional tensions, political conflicts, and eventually, a civil war. What made the issue so pervasive was the continued move to the West, which had a culture and society all its own. This continued move westward is the subject of the next chapter.

STUDY TOOLS 12

READY TO STUDY? IN THE BOOK, YOU CAN:

❏ Rip out the Chapter Review Card, which includes key terms and chapter summaries.

ONLINE AT WWW.CENGAGEBRAIN.COM, YOU CAN:

❏ Collect StudyBits while you read and study the chapter.

❏ Quiz yourself on key concepts.

❏ Find videos for further exploration.

❏ Prepare for tests with HIST5 Flash Cards as well as those you create.

❏ Learn more about slave religion.

❏ Learn more about David Walker and his *Appeal*.

❏ View a Library of Congress exhibit about the American Colonization Society.

❏ Read more about *The Confessions of Nat Turner*.

❏ Read Harriet Ann Jacobs's account of life in the South after Nat Turner's rebellion.

❏ Read narratives from former slaves.

❏ Read a song written by a recent Irish immigrant about his struggle to find a job.

❏ Read a newspaper account of an anti-Catholic riot in Philadelphia.

❏ Learn more about *Uncle Tom's Cabin*.

❏ Read Chapter 1 of *Uncle Tom's Cabin*.

What Else Was Happening

▶ **1816** African Methodist Episcopal Church becomes national organization.

▶ **1821** American Colonization Society promotes slaves' return to Africa and founds Liberia.

▶ **1831** Nat Turner's deadly revolt breeds repression and new defense of slavery.

Lloyd Garrison becomes leading voice of abolitionists.

▶ **1838** Frederick Douglass escapes slavery with help of the Underground Railroad.

▶ **1840s–1850s** A peak period of immigration to America, with nearly 1 million Irish escaping the potato famine.

Catholic parochial schools are established, with public schools becoming more visibly influenced by Protestantism.

1848 *Revolutions occur throughout Europe protesting industrial disorder and aristocratic rule. Most fail.*

Karl Marx and Friedrich Engels publish The Communist Manifesto.

1849 *The first safety pin is patented.*

1850 *Beer is first sold in glass bottles. Before that, patrons had their beer poured into a bucket or cup that they brought with them.*

▶ **1852** Harriet Beecher Stowe's *Uncle Tom's Cabin* popularizes abolitionism.

1857 *Elisha Graves Otis demonstrates his passenger safety elevator at the Crystal Palace Exposition in New York by cutting the elevator's cables as it ascends a 300-foot tower.*

The words and music to "Jingle Bells" are registered, under the title "One Horse Open Sleigh"—which didn't stick.

13 | The Continued Move West

Fotosearch/Getty Images

LEARNING OBJECTIVES

After reading this chapter, you should be able to do the following:

13-1 Describe the conquest and development of the West between 1820 and 1850 by white Americans.

13-2 Explain how the expansionist spirit in the West led to political conflict.

AFTER FINISHING THIS CHAPTER GO TO **PAGE 246** **FOR STUDY TOOLS**

Beginning in the 1820s, white Americans began settling west of the Mississippi River for the first time. They did so for a variety of reasons, the three foremost being: (1) to flee religious persecution, (2) to pursue greater social freedom, and most often (3) to seek riches.

Between the 1820s and 1860, Americans' westward migration across the Mississippi occurred in two general phases. The first which lasted from the 1820s to 1844, saw Americans move west without their government's consent or decree; they moved mostly for personal reasons. The second phase of westward migration began in 1844, after the election of President James K. Polk, an active evangelist for American expansion. On his watch, the American nation doubled in size. This second, deeply nationalistic phase was promoted under the banner of "**manifest destiny**," the idea that America was destined by God to conquer North America and spread American civilization far and wide. In 1872, the artist John Gast captured the image perfectly (see the chapter opening image), showing an angel of the Lord carrying a school book (representing education and civilization) and telegraph wires (representing the Market Revolution) as she guides white Americans west, while Indians back away, cowering under the power of God's divine plan. The reality of America's westward expansion was of course much more complicated, but the idea of "manifest destiny" was a powerful propellant pushing white Americans west.

The continued westward movement of Americans had at least four significant consequences: (1) the further decimation of Native America; (2) the continued expansion of the Market Revolution; (3) the "opening" of the frontier, which kept alive the democratic promise that poor but free men could make it on their own instead of subjugating themselves to capitalist chieftains; and (4) perhaps most important, the explosion of the slavery issue onto the American political stage. After decades of cobbled-together political compromises, the question of whether slavery would be allowed in the new territories of the West helped lead to a political breakdown that ignited the Civil War. Thus, while nearly all Americans supported westward expansion under the banner of manifest destiny, they differed considerably in how they hoped the new land would be developed. Whose image of the United States would triumph, the North's or the South's? But, first, to the great westward expansion between the 1820s and 1860.

13-1 WESTERN CONQUEST AND DEVELOPMENT, 1820–1844

Americans developed four unique territories in the West between 1820 and 1844: Texas, Oregon, Utah, and California. Each territory was developed for a different reason, and each bore the imprint of its initial conquest long after the territory was settled.

13-1a Mountain Men

Before the development of these territories, however, the American presence west of the Mississippi River was marked mostly by a rugged group of explorers, the so-called mountain men. These mountain men roamed the Rocky Mountains and the various trails carved out by Indians through the years. They were frequently employed as trappers, working for one of the fur companies that bought and sold beaver pelts. But their main occupation was exploration. Men like Jim Bridger, James Beckwourth, and Christopher "Kit" Carson are some of the best-known mountain men. Their names are largely remembered in either the names of mountain passes and Rocky Mountain locales or in the folklore of the West that blossomed during these years, coloring the image of the West as a dangerous and exciting place. All of these mountain men married Native American women, and all at one point or another worked as scouts for the U.S. Army, which over time participated in the ongoing encroachment of Indian lands. And Beckwourth is today celebrated as one of the key African American mountain men of the Old West.

13-1b Texas

With the mountain men paving the way and spurring American imaginations about the promise of the West, before the late 1840s, the most popular destination of westward migrants was Texas. It was a Spanish colony until 1821, when it became part of the newly independent nation of Mexico. Americans seeking land for growing cotton had been hesitant to settle in Texas while it was a Spanish colony. But the new nation of Mexico seemed much less powerful than

manifest destiny Likely coined by journalist John L. Sullivan in 1845, refers to the idea that the United States was destined by God to expand from the Atlantic Ocean to the Pacific

◄◄◄ **Artist John Gast captured the idea of manifest destiny perfectly in this image, showing an angel of the Lord bringing education and commerce west for the benefit of white settlers, while Native Americans fearfully back away.**

Smithsonian Institution Archives

>> James Beckwourth, pictured here. One of the famous "mountain men" who dotted the Old West in the early nineteenth century.

Spain, and Americans in the 1820s seized their chance to settle in Texas, bringing with them their cotton gins and their slaves. During that decade, about 20,000 Americans streamed into the province, rapidly outnumbering the 5,000 Mexicans who were living there. A small handful of Anglo-Americans assimilated to Mexican culture, but most chose not to. Instead, they continued to speak English, creating separate schools and conducting most of their trade with the United States. When in 1829 Mexico abolished slavery, American cotton planters simply ignored it.

By 1830, the Mexican government became worried that it was losing control of Texas. Objecting to the continued and illegal persistence of slavery there, Mexico sought to curtail U.S. immigration to the region. It raised taxes there, built new military posts, and prohibited further American settlement. But it was too late. The floodgates had opened, and Americans, both free and enslaved, continued to pour into the province hoping to cultivate cotton. Predictably, they hated the new regulations and eventually demanded autonomy from Mexican rule. Mexico of course refused, setting the stage for bitter conflict.

MEXICAN-AMERICAN HOSTILITIES

Mexico had other problems, though. Between 1829 and 1834, Mexico suffered a series of internal political coups, leading up to General Antonio López de Santa Anna's seizing power in Mexico City. He abolished the Mexican constitution and declared himself absolute dictator. He also intended to rein in Texas's autonomy. Texans rebelled. Led by Stephen F. Austin and William B. Travis, and with Sam Houston as commander-in-chief of the new Texas army, Texans declared their independence from Mexico and created an interim government. Santa Anna refused to tolerate this insurrection, and in 1836 led 1,600 troops to San Antonio, attacking the American rebels at an abandoned mission called the Alamo. Some 187 Texans, including western pioneer legends David Crockett and James Bowie, were killed during the battle. But before they lost the Alamo, the Texans had killed between 400 and 600 Mexican troops. Their stand became a source of inspiration for the Texas military, which continued to "remember the Alamo" during later battles.

>> The famous Alamo Church (central right) still stands and is today the iconic "Alamo." When the Alamo was at its largest, however, it had been transformed from an abandoned mission to an armed compound held by the newly formed Texas Republic.

A VICTORY FOR TEXAS . . . AND FOR SLAVERY

Two months later, Texans scored the decisive victory over Santa Anna when Sam Houston surprised the Mexican forces at San Jacinto, near today's city of Houston. Santa Anna himself was captured (while dressed in the garb of a common soldier, and only identified as Santa Anna when other captured soldiers bowed to him), and the Texans forced him to sign treaties guaranteeing Texan independence. Soon after this victory, Texas drew up a new constitution that guaranteed its white citizens the right to own slaves and prohibited free black people from immigrating to the new nation of Texas. Texans formally petitioned the United States for immediate annexation. They thought of themselves as Americans and wanted Texas to be part of the United States. Plus, they needed protection.

Many northern members of Congress feared that admitting Texas as a slave state would disrupt the Missouri Compromise of 1820, which had crafted a delicate balance between slave and free states. Furthermore, many assumed that if they annexed Texas, Mexico would declare war, something most Americans did not want. American leaders therefore rebuffed the appeals for annexation and left the new Texas Republic to make its own way as an independent nation.

13-1c Oregon and the Oregon Trail

The next region colonized by American settlers was Oregon. The U.S. government had asserted its sovereignty over Oregon ever since maritime merchant Robert Gray's expedition to the region in 1792, which helped inspire Jefferson to send Lewis and Clark on their trip of exploration. But there were also prior British, Spanish, and Russian claims on the territory. In the early 1800s, as the Oregon fur trade competition increased, American diplomats took steps to ensure that their merchants would not

>> Almost all settlers who moved to Oregon were stunned by the region's natural beauty, but predictably, tensions between white settlers and those who already lived there led to violence. This painting shows the stunning beauty of the Oregon Trail, as American settlers moved west through the terrain.

be excluded from trading in the region. Before 1830, only a few American citizens (usually Protestant missionaries) ventured into distant Oregon, because most of it was controlled by Native Americans and British fur-trading companies. As the area's beaver population dwindled, the British slowly withdrew. Their departure left the territory open to settlement, and in the 1830s and 1840s American settlers began to move into Oregon's Willamette River valley. Between 1842 and 1845, the number of Americans in Oregon increased tenfold, from about 500 to about 5,000.

NEW SETTLEMENTS AND INDIAN VIOLENCE

Predictably, as the new settlements spread throughout the valley, tensions between Indians and settlers increased. Indians felt crowded out, and many were dying from diseases imported by American settlers. In 1847, discontent erupted into violence when a group of Cayuse Indians killed fourteen settlers, including a white doctor who had been treating infectious diseases in white people but refused to treat Indians. The violent attack prompted outrage in Washington, D.C., and provoked Congress to establish more direct control over Oregon by organizing it as a formal American territory.

OREGON FEVER

Although violence persisted between Indians and American settlers, increased government control prompted a surge of new arrivals. After the opening in the early 1840s of a new route through the Rockies, called the Oregon Trail, more and more Americans moved to the territory. They farmed in the bountiful valley, and by 1850 there were 12,000 American inhabitants (see Map 13.1).

13-1d Utah and the Mormons

Most American settlers in Texas and Oregon moved for economic reasons, taking advantage of the transformations of the Market Revolution, but another group—the Mormons—went west seeking a haven from religious persecution. The Mormons found refuge in the area around the Great Salt Lake, in what would become the state of Utah.

JOSEPH SMITH AND THE ORIGINS OF MORMONISM

As we saw in Chapter 10, in 1830 Joseph Smith organized a new religion called the Church of Jesus Christ of Latter-Day Saints, known colloquially as the Mormons.

polygamy   The practice of having more than one spouse

Like other new religious communities founded during the Second Great Awakening, Mormonism emphasized a direct and ecstatic connection with God. It attracted people who both believed in Joseph Smith's divine visions and who wanted to renounce the sinfulness and social disorder they saw all around them. Mormonism gained converts by the thousands. But many other Christians viewed Mormons with suspicion because of their community's isolated ways and curious practices, particularly **polygamy**, or the practice of having more than one spouse. Joseph Smith, for instance, was reputed to have had thirty-four wives between the ages of fourteen and sixty. Each time tension grew with neighboring "gentiles," the Mormons moved their headquarters, first from New York to Ohio, then to several locations in Missouri. In 1838, they settled in Commerce, Illinois, which they renamed "Nauvoo" (as it is known today).

Anti-Mormon poster advertising a book critical of 'Polygamy or, The Mysteries of Mormonism' (litho), American School, (19th century)/Private Collection/Peter Newark American Pictures/Bridgeman Art Library

>> Joseph Smith was reputed to have had thirty-four wives between the ages of fourteen and sixty, prompting responses such as this anti-Mormon poster advertising the book *Polygamy or, the Mysteries of Mormonism.*

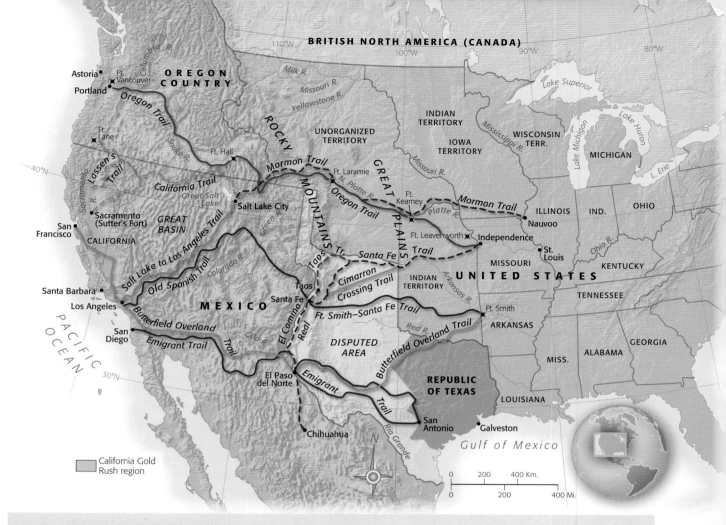

Map 13.1 Overland Trails

>> This map, focusing on the western half of the United States, shows the numerous overland trails that took settlers from the existing states of the union to the territories further west.

For five years, the Mormon community grew and prospered in Nauvoo. But in 1844 trouble erupted after a local newspaper, fearful of Smith's growing power, published an exposé of the polygamy practiced by Smith and other Mormon men. As the mayor of Nauvoo and the head of its court and its militia, Smith demanded that the newspaper be suppressed. His followers subsequently destroyed its press and other facilities. During the controversy, non-Mormons grew increasingly hostile and appealed to state authorities to help drive the Mormons out. Soon after, Joseph Smith and his brother Hyrum were arrested for treason, and on June 27, 1844, a lynch mob entered the jail where the men were being held and shot them both dead. In 1845, in what was referred to as "the Mormon War in Illinois," Mormon opponents torched more than two hundred Mormon-owned buildings in Nauvoo. Rumors surfaced that the federal government was planning a raid, and the Nauvoo city charter was revoked. The Mormons, now led by Smith's successor Brigham Young, negotiated a truce so they could leave Illinois peacefully.

BRIGHAM YOUNG

From published journals celebrating the western frontier, Young learned of an inland sea—the Great Salt Lake—that lay north of New Mexico. Although surrounded by inhospitable deserts and mountains, the land immediately next to the lake seemed ideal for settlement. To Young, the area also appeared sufficiently remote to guarantee that the Mormons would not encounter persecution. In addition, Utah was still under Mexican control and therefore outside U.S. jurisdiction. This meant that the Mormons could function relatively independently, following their own laws and customs. They set out to find their promised land on what came to be known as the Mormon Trek (see Map 13.1).

TO UTAH

A dynamic leader, Young had little difficulty persuading most of his followers that the Great Salt Lake area would be their home. In 1847 and 1848, thousands of Mormons settled in the Salt Lake basin. There they developed an irrigation system, which expanded their acreage of arable land, and laid the foundation for today's Salt Lake City.

But the Mormon dream of settling beyond the reach of the U.S. government did not last long. The United States won control of Utah in February 1848 as part of the settlement of the Mexican–American War, thus continuing the contentious relationship between Mormons and the federal government for the next fifty years. From 1856 to 1858, relations soured over the issue of who controlled the Utah territory, leading to a brief "Utah War." One notable episode of this conflict was the Mountain Meadows massacre of 1857. In the massacre, more than one hundred California-bound migrants from Arkansas were slaughtered by a collection of Mormon militiamen and Paiute Indians, both of whom feared the continued presence of American settlers in their territory.

North Wind Picture Archives/Alamy Stock Photo

>> In 1849, shortly after gold was found in California, approximately 80,000 fortune hunters descended onto the state, half Americans from the east, the other half from dozens of places around the globe. Here, Gold Rush prospectors wash sediment from a stream to find gold nuggets in California.

13-1e California: Ranches and Gold

Still farther west, American citizens were beginning to settle the Mexican state of Alta California. In the early 1840s, new Republican leaders awarded huge land grants in California to a handful of its American citizens and retired Mexican soldiers. Word of California's bountiful, fertile lands spread quickly. With the opening of the Oregon Trail and its offshoot, the California Trail (Map 13.1), more and more Americans made their way to the distant Mexican state. By early 1846, about 800 Americans and about 8,000 to 12,000 *californios* lived there.

This all changed in January 1848, when gold was discovered along California's American River. Emigration to California suddenly exploded. In 1849, an estimated 80,000 fortune hunters reached California, half of them Americans, the rest immigrants from around the globe. Gold, for instance, was the key attraction for numerous Chinese immigrants, beginning a long-standing Chinese presence in the West. Regardless of country of origin, though, most miners were young, unmarried men who had no intention of settling in California; they wanted to get rich and go home. But whether or not mines "proved out" and produced the riches expected of them, many of these "forty-niners" ended up staying in California. They set up temporary businesses, such as saloons, stores, and brothels, which soon surrounded the hastily erected shacks of mining camps. They also treated with scorn the surrounding Indians, viewing them as obstacles to their riches. Once miners had exhausted the gold supply, they abandoned the area, looking for the next profitable mine. Most of the booming settlements of the gold-rush days later decayed into ghost towns.

13-1f Tribal Conflicts

No matter where Americans went, they moved onto lands claimed by other parties, and sometimes by multiple other parties. While Mexicans in Texas and British settlers in Oregon suffered from American expansion, no group was more dislocated than Native Americans. Most dramatically, the nations of the Western Plains—the Arapahoe, Blackfoot, Cheyenne, Kiowa, and Sioux Indians—depended on the migratory hunting of buffalo for food. White settlers moving through buffalo ranges disrupted the natural hunting process, threatening these Indians' livelihood. The interference eventually prompted the Plains Indians (as these nations are collectively called) to attack white pioneers on the emigrant trails, sparking many bloody battles throughout the

The Reasons Why...

There were four reasons why the United States' official interest in westward expansion surged in the 1840s:

Route to China? The Market Revolution created a desire to have access to the Pacific Ocean and thus to the fabled Chinese and other Asian markets. (Americans were already establishing connections in Hawaii.) The West Coast was needed to serve as a staging ground.

Politically popular. Political leaders also discovered that proposals to annex new lands were popular with American voters, despite the festering question of whether to allow slavery there. Politicians, constantly seeking reelection, took note.

A new beginning. The financial Panic of 1837 led many Americans west in order to start their lives over.

National ambition. Finally, the U.S. government sought a rapid expansion of its power, which meant owning as much land as foreign powers, if not more. It used the notion of "manifest destiny" to spend its resources aiding those who sought to move west.

West. Indeed, throughout the 1830s and 1840s, nearly every pioneer would confront the powerful Comanche Empire. It dominated the American Southwest with weaponry and horses, and served as one of the key provocations for Mexico first allowing Americans to settle there (to help buffer Comanche raids). The Comanche Empire was by far the most powerful force confronting American westward migration. As for white settlers during the colonial era in New England and Virginia, conflict with the nations of Native America was part of daily life for the westward bound.

The U.S. government's response to this increased Indian conflict was typical: as the number of white settlers increased, the U.S. government continued to cajole or force Native Americans into giving up their land. In the 1851 **Fort Laramie Treaty** with the Plains Indians, the U.S. government agreed to make cash restitution for disruptions to the buffalo grounds, while tribal leaders in turn agreed not to attack the large number of settlers moving through the area. But in 1854 yet another transportation corridor for white pioneers was carved out of land that was once set aside as Indian territory. Following the development of this new route, the Plains Indians were relocated once again. As they were being shuffled from one area to another, the creation of a defined system of reservations for Native Americans was not far off.

13-1g Conclusion

Western settlement complicated matters reaching far beyond the lives of the settlers themselves. The haphazard manner in which the West was conquered forced politicians in the East to bring some form of governing order to the West. The independent-minded settlers, accustomed to managing their own affairs, did not always welcome the imposition of Eastern ideals. Friction was inevitable. Moreover, by taking responsibility for the actions of white settlers—particularly the rebels in Texas and the pioneers traversing Native American territories—government officials committed themselves to defending, and defining the course of, westward expansion. This led to westward expansion's second phase, a much more controlled and government-sanctioned project.

 ## 13-2 THE EXPANSIONIST SPIRIT REBOUNDS

During the 1840s, the United States' official interest in acquiring western territory surged for four principal reasons (see "The Reasons Why . . ." box). These arguments motivated the American government to aggressively resume territorial expansion. Journalists and others who favored national expansion embraced an ideology justifying the sometimes brutal methods used to expand American civilization: manifest destiny.

Fort Laramie Treaty Agreement of 1851 between Plains Indian nations and the U.S. government; the government agreed to make cash restitution for disruptions to the buffalo grounds, while tribal leaders agreed not to attack the large number of settlers moving through the area

13-2a Texas and the Rise of James K. Polk

The first significant debate concerned Texas. The Texas Republic, upon winning its independence from Mexico in 1836, had already applied to become a U.S. state. But the Texas constitution guaranteed the perpetuation of slavery, so if Texas entered the Union, it would disturb the balance between free and slave states established by the Missouri Compromise of 1820. Moreover, U.S. annexation of Texas would surely start a war with Mexico. Thus, by the late 1830s, Texans suspended all efforts to gain admittance to the Union and focused on developing their own political and economic institutions.

Foreign policy issues in the 1840s forced the issue of Texas annexation back into the limelight. Britain considered establishing relations with the independent Texas in order to gain a stronger foothold in North America. This prospect alarmed many Americans, and, fearful of increased British presence in North America, in 1843 Secretary of State John C. Calhoun signed a treaty with Texas that promised eventual admission to the Union. President John Tyler (who became president in April 1841) then sent the treaty to the Senate for ratification. Would Texas finally become a state? Northerners in Congress reasoned that the excuse of foreign diplomacy was just a thinly veiled power play by southern slave owners to tip the balance of power toward the slave states. The Senate thus defeated the proposed treaty. Texas would have to wait a little longer.

THE ELECTION OF 1844

The issue persisted and became a key division in the presidential election of 1844. The Whigs were divided, with many of them opposed to the introduction of a new

>> James K. Polk, during whose presidency the landmass of the United States increased by a third.

Eon Images

slave state while others more fully embraced the idea of manifest destiny. With the Whigs divided, the Democrats simply stole the issue and made overall territorial acquisition a key part of their strategy to spread American civilization far and wide. They blustered on and on about how America's territorial growth would make it a first-class nation. Their platform called for the "re-annexation" of Texas and the "re-occupation" of Oregon up to a northern boundary of 54°40′, an outrageous land grab that included nearly all of today's British Columbia, extending to the southern border of today's Alaska.

The Democrats' plan, though greedy, was perceptive. By offering to acquire both Texas and Oregon, they intended to give something to the North and to the South, thus unifying the nation and securing a Democratic victory. The party's presidential nominee was James K. Polk, a former Tennessee governor and congressman (whose nickname was "Young Hickory," aligning him with Andrew Jackson, who was called "Old Hickory"), and he became the loudest spokesperson for the benefits to be gained from American expansion.

TEXAS AND THE LIBERTY PARTY

Henry Clay was the Whig candidate. Like many Whigs, Clay initially opposed annexing Texas. But midway through the campaign, he decided the issue was too popular to resist, and he needed the votes. He changed his platform. Outraged at his reversal—and his political gaffe of not offering to acquire Oregon as well—a group of northern antislavery activists left the Whig Party and created the **Liberty Party**, which opposed admitting any new slave territory to the United States. The Liberty Party nominated James G. Birney, who attracted voters who would otherwise have supported Clay. This division strengthened the Democratic Party and allowed Polk to win the election fairly easily. But the introduction of the Liberty Party revealed hairline fractures in the second two-party system—fractures that would steadily grow into an outright break. And the issue that provoked all the dissent was whether or not to allow slavery to expand into the West.

Liberty Party Political party created by northern antislavery activists who left the Whig Party because they were outraged at Henry Clay's reversing his position against annexation of Texas; their departure revealed cracks in the second two-party system

TYLER AND TEXAS

President John Tyler, who had a few months left in his term before being succeeded by Polk, interpreted Polk's victory as a sign that the public did indeed support efforts to admit Texas. Thus, during his last months in office, in an effort to ensure himself a positive legacy, Tyler again pushed Congress to annex Texas through a congressional resolution. (A resolution is similar to a treaty but requires only a simple majority to pass instead of the two-thirds majority needed for a treaty.) This time, the Senate, swayed by the public enthusiasm it had witnessed during the election of 1844, narrowly passed the resolution. On March 1, 1845, the United States formally offered Texas statehood, which Texas accepted in December.

In response to admission of Texas as an American state, Mexico broke off diplomatic relations with the United States, setting the stage for conflict between the two nations.

13-2b Oregon and American Dominance in the West

POLK AS PRESIDENT

Despite Tyler's role in granting Texas statehood, it was Polk who would become the nation's staunchest supporter of acquiring new territory. Polk was an avid believer that Americans were destined to control the West, and he had the personality, vigor, and power to be a strong cheerleader. However, when it came to the West, Polk was less concerned about slavery and more concerned about a potential surge of British influence in North America. Thus his first action as president was to snuff out any plans Britain had for reentering North America, not only in Texas but also in Oregon and California. Polk also had to live up to his campaign promise of bringing a northern state into the Union in order to balance the recent addition of Texas.

54°40'

During Polk's presidential campaign, he pledged to fight for exclusive title to the Oregon Territory and to settle for nothing less than the entirety of American claims, which extended all the way up to a northern line of 548409—close to what is now the southernmost point of Alaska's border with British Columbia (see Map 13.2). Britain, however, would certainly not concede that

>> The California gold rush led thousands of fortune-seekers from around the world to California, most of them men, most of them eager to make a buck. As one gold miner put it, "There is a good deal of sin & wickedness going on here, Stealing, lying, Swearing, Drinking, Gambling & murdering. . . . Almost every public House is a place for Gambling. . . . Men make & lose thousands in a night, & frequently small boys will go up & bet $5 or 10—& if they lose all, go the next day & dig more. We are trying to get laws here to regulate things but it will be very difficult to get them executed." —S. Shufelt, gold miner

the United States owned a territory that Britain had long explored and claimed. After his inauguration in early 1845, Polk softened his position and returned to the demand made by every president since James Monroe: the United States would be willing to settle for a border along the 49th parallel—Washington state's northern border today. Britain rejected the offer; it wanted to control the Columbia River, 200 miles south of the 49th parallel. Angered at Britain's refusal and inspired by the partisan cry of **"Fifty-four Forty or Fight!"** Polk returned to his more aggressive position. In early December 1845, he asked Congress to extend U.S. military protection to the Oregon Trail. He hoped that feigning military intervention would persuade the British to concede the vast Oregon territory.

"Fifty-four Forty or Fight!" Rallying cry referring to the Americans' intended latitude for the contested border between the United States and Canada; Britain was willing to settle for the 49th parallel

49TH PARALLEL

Polk's tenacious talk was merely a bluff: he believed that the land north of the 49th parallel, where few American settlers had reached, was not that important. What he really wanted was Puget Sound and access to the ports of California for trading. Britain's government, meanwhile, decided that its interest in the region, originally based on the once-robust fur trade, which was now rapidly declining, was not worth a war. In late December 1845, the two parties reopened negotiations over the issue, intending to prevent what would have been the third war in seventy-five years between the two nations. The British proposed a treaty accepting the 49th parallel as a border, although it sought to retain the right to navigate the Columbia River. The Senate approved the resulting **Buchanan-Pakenham Treaty** in July 1846, and America now had uncontested access to the Pacific.

13-2c Manifest Destiny

Amid the frenzy stirred by the Oregon and Texas statehood issues, a new expression of the spirit of an American

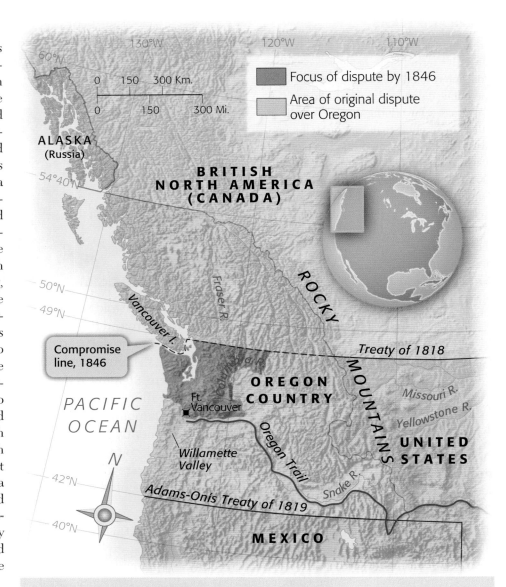

Map 13.2 The Oregon Boundary Dispute

>> A map of the Pacific Northwest showing the various demands and compromises made between the United States and Britain over what would become the boundary between Canada and the United States.

empire was born. The term manifest destiny—was coined by New York journalist John O'Sullivan. In July 1845, O'Sullivan wrote an editorial in his *United States Magazine and Democratic Review* urging Whigs and Democrats to join together in support of "the right of our manifest destiny to overspread and to possess the whole of the continent, which Providence has given us." Manifest destiny was popularized in political debates over Oregon, where it was used as an argument for why Britain should not block U.S. expansion. Soon the rhetoric made its way into American popular culture.

Though the term *manifest destiny* was newly coined, it reflected the much older American belief that divine

Buchanan-Pakenham Treaty Agreement of 1846 between the United States and Britain, agreeing on the 49th parallel as the border between the United States and Canada; the treaty gave the United States uncontested access to the Pacific

providence was directing the nation. Many Americans felt that their country—by virtue of its strong Christian faith, its commitment to "civilization" and democracy, and the supposed "emptiness" of the West—would dominate North America as a great Empire for Liberty, thriving under God's benevolent guiding hand. The phrase was explicitly chauvinistic, implying the need to "subdue" and "fertilize" the "virgin land" of the West. It was also explicitly racist, referring to the God-given rights of the white man to conquer the "red man's lands." Manifest destiny interpreted the conquest of the West as a story of triumph in the cause of freedom rather than a saga of conflict, death, and destruction. The concept grew in popularity throughout the 1840s, justifying westward expansion.

13-2d The Mexican–American War

With Oregon secure and the ideology of manifest destiny swirling throughout the American presses, Polk turned his attention once again to Mexico. When Texas won its independence from Mexico in 1836, the Mexican dictator General Antonio López de Santa Anna vowed that any move by the United States to annex Texas would be met with military force. When Texas did become the twenty-eighth state, in 1845, President Polk privately relished Mexico's threat. He hoped that by provoking Mexico to make good on its promise of war, the United States could crush the Mexicans and gain control of even more Mexican territory, particularly the far western prizes of California and New Mexico.

> If American lives were endangered, the president reasoned, it would be easy to declare war on Mexico.

POLK SEEKS A FIGHT

Mexican officials, though they would not accept the annexation of Texas as legal, did not want to wage war over the matter. Instead, they chose to haggle over the precise boundary of Texas's southern border. Texas state officials insisted that the proper boundary between Texas and Mexico was the Rio Grande. The Mexicans, however, considered the Nueces River (130 miles north of the Rio Grande) to be the border. Polk decided that the United States had a responsibility to defend Texas's land claims, and he stationed U.S. warships off the coast of Texas. In October 1845, Polk dispatched nearly 4,000 U.S. troops to the northern side of the Nueces River. By demonstrating American strength, he hoped to bully the Mexican government into ceding the disputed lands.

Despite these intimidation efforts, Mexico refused to respond militarily. So, in November 1845, Polk took another approach, attempting to pressure Mexico into selling not only Texas but also New Mexico and California to the United States. Polk's tactics failed once again. Mexico refused. Frustrated, Polk decided to make another show of force. In January 1846, he ordered General Zachary Taylor, head of the U.S. Army encamped along the Nueces, to move into the disputed region between the Nueces and the Rio Grande. Polk hoped to provoke the Mexican army into firing on the Americans. If American lives were endangered, the president reasoned, it would be easy to declare war on Mexico.

He finally got his fight. On April 25, 1846, Mexican forces crossed the Rio Grande and attacked Taylor's men, killing eleven soldiers. Polk immediately declared that Mexico had "shed American blood upon the American soil," even though the land was clearly disputed terrain between the two rivers. According to the president, Americans now had no choice but to avenge the lives of their slain countrymen.

PATRIOTIC FERVOR

On May 13, 1846, as patriotic fervor swept the country, Congress passed a declaration of war by an overwhelming majority, thus formally beginning the Mexican–American War. Volunteers responded en masse to fill the ranks of the army. The war was not universally popular, especially among northerners who considered the war a strategy to expand slavery into new western territories like New Mexico and California. Leading figures, such as Henry David Thoreau, Frederick Douglass, and William Lloyd Garrison, opposed the war, viewing it as an unjust aggression against Mexico and an opportunity for slave owners to annex new land for their plantations. In 1847, a young congressman from Illinois named Abraham Lincoln offered a resolution to Congress (which did pass) demanding to be shown the exact spot upon which American blood was spilled on American soil. Lincoln rightly thought the first shots had been fired on disputed territory, not American land, and the proposal came to be called Lincoln's "Spot Resolutions." Nevertheless, these countervailing views were overpowered by the louder voices advocating America's "manifest destiny."

CALIFORNIA AND NEW MEXICO

Now that the battle with Mexico had begun, Polk also planned to seize Mexico's other northern states,

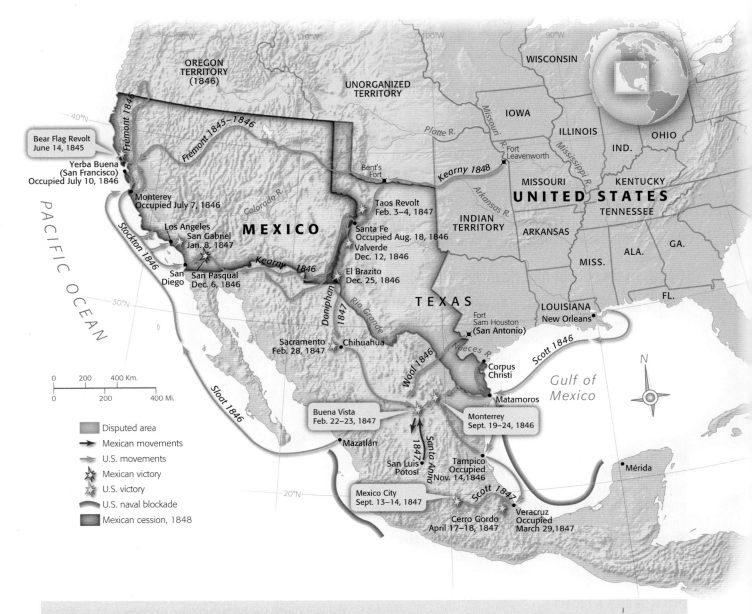

Map 13.3 War with Mexico, 1846-1848

>> A map of the United States and Mexico, showing the major battles of the Mexican–American War and the various territories eventually won by the United States, including what are today Texas, New Mexico, Arizona, and California.

California and New Mexico, some of his primary targets all along (see Map 13.3). In June 1846, a small group of American rebels, flying a flag decorated with a bear and a red star, seized the California town of Sonoma (north of San Francisco) and declared the state an independent republic. John C. Frémont led an armed expeditionary group in what came to be called the "Bear Flag Revolt." The California Republic was, however, short-lived. By the end of July 1846, Frémont's men were inducted into the U.S. Army as the "California Battalion." By August, the United States had taken control of California's key ports, and Frémont became a national hero. Polk's land grab proceeded apace.

Further south, a group of American troops marched through what is today New Mexico. In August, this force seized Santa Fé, the capital of the Mexican region, without

The San Jacinto Museum of History, Houston

El Fandango.

>> Inspired by patriotic fervor, seventeen-year-old Bostonian Sam Chamberlain joined the 1st Regiment of Dragoons and saw service in northern Mexico under the command of General Zachary Taylor. His illustrated account of the Mexican War, entitled "Recollections of a Rogue," has all the color of a young American's first experiences in a foreign conflict—not all of them military, as this watercolor of a Mexican dance hall demonstrates.

firing a shot. By January 1847, the troops had finished their mission and had moved to the southern California coast. They arrived just in time to put down a Mexican revolt against American rule that had been raging in Los Angeles since the previous September. Relatively easily, and within about six months, Americans had taken control of the large territories of California and New Mexico. Now all that was left was formalizing the land grab.

INVADING MEXICO

After the United States seized both territories, Polk was prepared to offer Santa Anna a deal. Overthrown in an 1844 coup, Santa Anna was now living in Cuba, plotting his return to Mexico. Polk offered him the chance to do so in exchange for a promise to end the war and to cede California, New Mexico, and Texas to the United States. Santa Anna agreed. Once he arrived in Mexico, however, he reneged on this promise and rallied Mexican forces against the Americans.

To counter this revolt, Polk ordered General Winfield Scott to invade Mexico from the sea, especially targeting the capital, Mexico City. With this daring move, he hoped to defeat the main forces of the Mexican Army and sap Mexican resolve to fight. He would also undercut Santa Anna and his men, who had moved north to attack Americans along the border. In March 1847, after capturing the Mexican port of Veracruz, 14,000 American troops marched inland toward Mexico City, and, after numerous battles and several bouts with yellow fever, on September 13 the American troops entered the Mexican capital. Within three days, Santa Anna, his army defeated and capital taken, surrendered to the American forces.

TREATY OF GUADALUPE HIDALGO

In February 1848, an American envoy named Nicholas Trist negotiated the **Treaty of Guadalupe Hidalgo**, which officially ended the Mexican–American War. The treaty gave the United States control of Utah, Nevada, California, western Colorado, and parts of Arizona and New Mexico, and it set the Mexican–American border at the Rio Grande. This was everything the U.S. government wanted, all in exchange for $15 million. It also safely ignored several arguments that the United States should swallow the entire nation of Mexico.

>LOOKING AHEAD...

The Mexican cession, comprising nearly 500,000 square miles of territory, turned the rhetoric of manifest destiny into reality. With Texas's annexation and the acquisition of Oregon, New Mexico, and California, the United States had become an empire spanning the width of the continent—all within four short years.

But the struggle involved in taking all this land provoked the issue that no American politician wanted to engage: slavery. The issue of whether or not slavery should exist in the western territories would lead to the political crisis of the 1850s, which would ultimately bring about the American Civil War. It is to this impending crisis that we now turn.

Treaty of Guadalupe Hidalgo Agreement ending the Mexican War in 1848, which gave the United States control of Utah, Nevada, California, western Colorado, and parts of Arizona and New Mexico and established the Rio Grande as the border, in exchange for $15 million

STUDY TOOLS 13

READY TO STUDY? IN THE BOOK, YOU CAN:

❏ Rip out the Chapter Review Card, which includes key terms and chapter summaries.

ONLINE AT WWW.CENGAGEBRAIN.COM, YOU CAN:

❏ Collect StudyBits while you read and study the chapter.

❏ Quiz yourself on key concepts.

❏ Find videos for further exploration.

❏ Prepare for tests with HIST5 Flash Cards as well as those you create.

❏ Read about some of the most famous mountain men.

❏ Read a dramatic antislavery letter by a member of the new Liberty Party.

❏ Read President Polk's "Message on War with Mexico."

❏ Read Whig senator Thomas Corwin's speech opposing the Mexican War.

❏ Read Democratic senator Donald S. Dickinson's speech justifying the U.S. acquisition of territory.

❏ Read John O'Sullivan's "Annexation" essay.

❏ View a map of California Gold Country.

❏ Read a letter from a gold miner in Placerville, California.

❏ Learn more about the Mexican War.

❏ Read the Fort Laramie Treaty.

CH13 TIMELINE

What Else Was Happening

1821 Mexico's independence draws American settlers to northern province of Texas.

1822: A yellow fever epidemic leaves New York City with 16,000 corpses and no readily available space to bury them.

1829: Mexico abolishes slavery.

1830 Joseph Smith forms Church of Jesus Christ of Latter-Day Saints.

1834 Texas settlers rebel against Mexican ruler Santa Anna.

1835: The Liberty Bell becomes cracked.

1836 187 Texan rebels perish in Alamo after killing over 1,200 Mexican troops.

1840: The saxophone is invented.

1842: The Treaty of Nanjing ends the First Opium War between Great Britain and China, which began when China protested the importation of opium by British merchants. The treaty mandates that China open trade relations with Great Britain, including the continued trafficking of opium, and it makes Hong Kong a British colony, which it remains until 1997.

1844 James K. Polk wins presidency with promise of annexing Oregon and Texas.

1845 Admission of Texas sets stage for war with Mexico.

July: *John O'Sullivan coins term* manifest destiny.

"Mormon Wars" follow 1844 murder of Joseph Smith in Nauvoo, Illinois.

The New York Baseball Club plays the Knickerbockers in the first recorded baseball game, at Elysian Fields in Hoboken, New Jersey.

1846 **April:** Polk provokes war with Mexico and seizes northern provinces.

June: Rebels under John C. Frémont declare California independent republic.

June: Buchanan-Pakenham Treaty establishes Canadian–U.S. border in Northwest.

1847 Clashes between Oregonians and Indians show need for territorial government.

September: U.S. forces march into Mexico City; Santa Anna surrenders.

1848 **January:** Gold discovery in California triggers global gold rush.

January: Gold discovery in California triggers global gold rush.

America gains control of the Utah Territory one year after Mormons settle there.

1851 Fort Laramie Treaty with Plains Indians secures settler migration westward.

14 | The Impending Crisis

Francis G. Mayer/Getty Images

LEARNING OBJECTIVES

After reading this chapter, you should be able to do the following:

14-1 Describe the arguments that took place over whether slavery should be allowed to expand into the new territories, and explain how the Compromise of 1850 was supposed to settle the issue.

14-2 Explain how the Kansas-Nebraska Act affected the territories of Kansas and Nebraska, and describe the events that made "Bleeding Kansas" an accurate description of the region.

14-3 Discuss the events that propelled the United States into civil war in 1861.

14-4 Explain why and how the southern states seceded from the Union, discuss President Lincoln's reaction, and describe the earliest physical conflict between the two sides.

AFTER FINISHING THIS CHAPTER GO TO **PAGE 266** **FOR STUDY TOOLS**

During the 1850s, the controversy over the spread of slavery to the West froze America's territorial expansion. The gains of the 1840s had been impressive: the United States had acquired California, Texas, Oregon, Washington, New Mexico, and more. But in the 1850s, except for a small stretch of land on the southern edge of today's Arizona (the Gadsden Purchase), the United States made no further territorial gains.

Nevertheless, the territorial expansion of the previous fifty years (and especially the previous ten) had made it nearly impossible for the two political parties to retain support from all the nation's various regions. In general, although northerners were not often hardcore abolitionists, they protested the spread of slavery in the West, favoring the expansion of free labor, in which men could choose the kind of labor they would perform. Most southern whites, meanwhile, fiercely supported the institution of slavery, seeing it as integral to the American economy and the cotton culture they had developed since the invention of the cotton gin in 1793. Indeed, for many southerners slavery had gone from being a "necessarily evil," as those of the founding era conceived of it, to being a "positive good." As for the political parties, neither Democrats nor Whigs could afford to alienate the South by appearing overtly against slavery or the North by seeming too supportive of the institution. The risk was that each party would become strictly regional or that it would implode while trying to find a balance.

This political conundrum provoked the development of splinter parties, and without the hedging and compromising of the two mainstream parties, the center of American politics could not hold. In the end, the election to the presidency of an antislavery northerner provoked many southerners to withdraw from the Union altogether. Considering that people in democratic societies ideally settle their differences without killing one another, how had things gone so wrong?

14-1 ARGUMENTS OVER SLAVERY IN THE NEW TERRITORIES

The Mexican-American War had, from 1846 to 1848, temporarily united the North and the South in a common enthusiasm for military conquest. But tensions between the two regions always lay just beneath the surface. During and after the war, American politicians became consumed with the issue of whether extensive territories won from Mexico should or should not permit slavery.

14-1a The Democrats on Slavery in the West

Andrew Jackson's Democratic Party had always claimed to defend the rights of the "common man." Yet southern Democrats, by demanding that new territories allow slavery, hardly seemed to be advocating policies that helped every common man, white or black. Northerners argued that if slavery were allowed in Texas and other parts of the West, wealthy plantation owners would buy up all the new land, leaving little left for less affluent farmers. How democratic was that? Southern Democrats were unable to substantively counter this argument.

RACIST, BUT ANTISLAVERY, NORTHERN DEMOCRATS

More importantly, new plantations in places like Texas and Kansas and Missouri meant that the western territories would be populated with black people. Despite the fact that many northern Democrats were opposed to slavery, they were quite openly racist and had no desire to live amid a large African American population.

The widespread belief in white supremacy led northern and southern Democrats to radically different conclusions. Many northern Democrats turned against slavery in order to avoid living and competing with black people in the western territories, whereas southern Democrats retained their proslavery stance in order to defend the plantation economy, which theoretically promised even the common man great wealth. This disagreement splintered the Democratic Party into southern and northern branches.

14-1b The Wilmot Proviso and the "Free Soil" Movement

The splintering intensified in 1846 when one of the alienated northern Democrats, Pennsylvania congressman David Wilmot, proposed that slavery be prohibited from any new territories that the United States might acquire from Mexico. Wilmot was no abolitionist. He wanted slavery kept out of the West so the land would be available to average white farmers (who could not afford slaves) rather than to wealthy slave owners who would establish massive

◄◄◄ **As the storm of civil war approached, perhaps and seemingly inevitably, many Americans felt conflicted and uncertain. Was war between the states inevitable?**

plantations. The **Wilmot Proviso** passed in the House of Representatives several times but was repeatedly rejected by the Senate, where southerners had the edge because of the support of several "**doughface**" senators, defined as senators from the North who supported southern slavery.

Meanwhile, each round of voting on the Wilmot Proviso exacerbated regional tensions. Many northern Whigs, such as Abraham Lincoln, joined northern Democrats in voting for the measure. At the same time, southern Democrats, such as John Calhoun (now a senator from South Carolina), argued that the Constitution guaranteed the option of slavery in federal territories. Thus he joined southern Whigs in voting against it. Now the Whigs were beginning to divide along regional lines, too. Southerners from both parties advocated introducing slavery in the new territories, while northerners from both parties opposed such an effort.

THE PRESIDENTIAL ELECTION OF 1848

The presidential election of 1848 deepened these tensions. At first, the campaigners tried to ignore slavery altogether. When this proved impossible, Democratic nominee Lewis Cass hoped to sidestep the issue by proposing the idea of **popular sovereignty**, which meant letting settlers in the territories decide whether or not they wanted slavery. The Whigs, meanwhile, who had nominated Mexican-American War hero and slave owner Zachary Taylor (who had never voted before, much less held political office), made no mention of slavery in their platform.

THE FREE SOIL PARTY

Neither of these positions satisfied all Democrats or all Whigs, and disaffected Democrats launched a political movement under the banner of the **Free Soil Party**. The new party was headed by former Democratic president Martin Van Buren and advanced a platform centered on the Wilmot Proviso. The party was antisouthern but not staunchly abolitionist. It argued that southern slave

---

Wilmot Proviso Legislation proposed in 1846 to prohibit slavery from any new territories that the United States might acquire from Mexico

doughface Derisive name for a northerner who openly supported the South

popular sovereignty Proposal for letting the settlers in the territories decide whether or not they wanted slavery

Free Soil Party Political movement started by disaffected anti-South Democrats and headed by former Democratic president Martin Van Buren; they wanted new lands to be made available to small, ambitious white farmers

---

owners were blocking the development of northern progress. Southern congressmen, said the Free Soilers, refused to advance national programs for internal improvements, which would facilitate access to the West and extend the progress made by the Market Revolution. Free Soilers wanted western lands to be available to ambitious white farmers, and they wanted to save the land for white people.

In its platform, the party called for "free soil, free speech, free labor, and free men," focusing not on abolishing slavery where it already existed but on keeping slave-based plantations from spreading into the West. Significantly, the Free Soil movement brought together all those who opposed slavery in the West. But of course these groups opposed the expansion of slavery for different reasons. Abolitionists sympathized with the slaves, while racists did not want to compete with African Americans economically in the new territories. The Free Soil Party also brought together northern Democrats, such as Wilmot, with northern Whigs, who were unhappy about their party's nomination of slave owner Zachary Taylor.

Taylor and the Whigs cobbled together enough votes to win the election of 1848, but they failed to win a congressional majority, and in the long run, they were greatly weakened by the rise of the Free Soil Party.

14-1c The Compromise of 1850

California provoked the next round of battles in Congress.

CALIFORNIA AS THE PROBLEM

When Zachary Taylor took office in 1849, California, brimming with new settlers driven by the gold rush, applied for statehood. But would it enter as a free or slave state? Either way, its statehood was destined to upset the balance between free and slave states that had held since the Missouri Compromise of 1820.

Taylor tried to address the crisis as soon as he took office. He hoped to simply bypass the slavery issue by granting immediate statehood to California and New Mexico without specifying whether they were free or slave states.

Southern politicians attacked Taylor's plan. They worried that once California was admitted, its citizens would vote to be a free state (again, not because they were overwhelmingly abolitionists, but because they wanted to keep black people and wealthy plantation owners from competing with them economically), thus setting a precedent for prohibiting slavery from all western territories. They also feared that someday slave states would be greatly outnumbered by free ones in

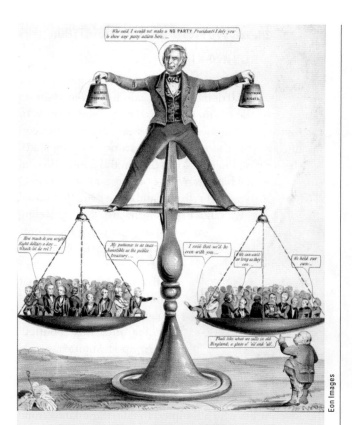

>> Political cartoonists recognized the balancing act performed throughout the 1850s by American politicians. Here, Zachary Taylor is depicted balancing the "Wilmot Proviso" with "Southern Rights" as everyone seemingly waits for the scales to tip.

Congress—an event that could lead to the permanent decline of southern interests and the permanent abolition of slavery.

THE COMPROMISE

To allay these fears, Henry Clay, author of the Missouri Compromise of 1820 and now a powerful senator, stepped forward with yet another compromise. In January 1850, Clay proposed a five-part bill, which came to be called the **Compromise of 1850**.

The Compromise of 1850 included five key components:

1. California would be admitted to the Union as a free state.

2. The remaining land won during the Mexican-American War would be divided into two new territories, New Mexico and Utah, and would remain open to slavery until they became states, at which time the state legislatures could vote on the issue.

3. To mollify antislavery northerners, the slave trade (but not slavery itself) would be banned in the nation's capital, Washington, D.C.

4. Texas would relinquish its claim to land that extended all the way to Santa Fe, which would become part of New Mexico (these parts of New Mexico would be called "little Texas"), and in return receive $10 million in compensation.

5. For southerners, the federal government would create and enforce a new and tougher **Fugitive Slave Law**. By punishing white northerners who helped slaves escape from the South, the measure sought to ensure that the North and the South would cooperate in protecting the slave system.

THE CONTROVERSY

The compromise contained elements to appeal to both sides, but it also set off a storm of political controversy. Opposed by hardliners on both sides of the slave-state issue, the compromise gave rise to the first focused talk of secession in the South. This alarmed President Taylor so much that he decided to oppose the compromise altogether. Months of impassioned arguments for and against the compromise went on in Congress. The debates marked the last time that the great triumvirate of powerful senators, Clay, Calhoun, and Daniel Webster, would discuss the nation's fate with their formidable oratorical skills. Clay and Webster allied in favor of the compromise, and Webster's "Seventh of March" speech rallied northern opinion for the compromise. On the opposite side, Calhoun, dying of tuberculosis, watched his friend James Mason deliver Calhoun's last speech in the Senate against the proposed compromise. But the compromise remained in limbo.

BECOMING LAW

When, in 1850, Zachary Taylor died of gastroenteritis and was replaced by Millard Fillmore, the compromise's

Compromise of 1850 Five-part bill proposed by Henry Clay, which outlined specific arrangements that accommodated both antislavery northerners and slave-owning southerners

Fugitive Slave Law Law passed as part of the Compromise of 1850 requiring that all runaway slaves be returned to their masters; those who willfully ignored the law were to be punished

>> "As much indisposed as I have been, Mr. President and Senators, I have felt it to be my duty to express to you my sentiments upon the great question which has agitated the country and occupied your attentions."—John C. Calhoun, debating the compromise in the Senate as read by his friend James Mason. Pictured here is a portrait of Calhoun, circa 1850.

Library of Congress Prints and Photographs Division[LC-USZ62-76296]

chances of passing improved. Fillmore favored the plan. With Fillmore's support, Clay's political lieutenant in the Senate, Stephen A. Douglas of Illinois, set to work dividing the bill in five parts and finding majorities for each of its separate proposals. By September 1850, the compromise had become law.

The peace that ensued would prove unstable, however, as many northerners resented the tough Fugitive Slave Law. In fact, during the next decade many northern states passed **Personal Liberty Laws**, which were designed to protect escaped slaves—for instance, by prohibiting the use of a state's jail to restrain runaway slaves. Vermont, Rhode Island, and Connecticut passed Personal Liberty Laws in 1854. Maine, Massachusetts, and Michigan did so in 1855, followed by Kansas and Wisconsin in 1858, Ohio in 1859, and Pennsylvania in 1860. Reaction to the Fugitive Slave Laws also created the sympathy that propelled the success of Harriet Beecher Stowe's *Uncle Tom's Cabin*.

The debates of 1849 and 1850 only worsened the mutual distrust between North and South. But the Compromise of 1850 bought some time before the ultimate dissolution of the nation's political order.

Personal Liberty Laws A variety of laws designed to protect escaped slaves, such as by prohibiting the use of a state's jail for runaway slaves; these laws passed in many northern states in the 1850s

filibusters Adventurers who attempted to invade the island of Cuba to bring it into the Union as a slave state

14-1d Western Destiny Deferred

BUYING CUBA?

As the debates over the Compromise of 1850 demonstrated, admitting new states to the Union was bound to be contentious. In addition, southerners immediately noticed that there was more territory open for statehood in the North than in the South. Fearful of what this might portend, southern leaders sought to expand America's territorial holdings southward, by expanding into Latin America. Presidents Polk and Pierce, in fact, had both tried to buy the island of Cuba from Spain, thinking it could, perhaps, one day become a slave state. When Polk's offer was rebuffed, a group of Americans tried to invade the island in order to bring it into the Union. They failed, but the adventurers who attempted to take these lands came to be called **filibusters**, after the Spanish *filibustero*, for "pirate" or "freebooter." The term was subsequently adopted to describe attempts to extend debate over a legislative proposal in order to hijack or delay its passage.

THE SLAVE CONSPIRACY

These reckless attempts to create more southern states heightened northerners' suspicions that the Democratic Party was plotting with slave owners. Abolitionists and Free Soilers viewed the Cuban plan as an indication that the South, rapidly being outpaced in population growth by the North, was desperate to acquire new slave states to maintain parity in the Senate. Sensing a conspiracy, northerners fought hard to prevent further accessions to slaveholders' power. Both sides were intensifying their opposition to the other.

14-2 THE KANSAS-NEBRASKA ACT AND NEW POLITICAL PARTIES

These sentiments erupted in the 1854 debate over the Kansas-Nebraska Act. And, again, it was expansion in the West that brought the issue of slavery to a head within the nation's corridors of power.

14-2a Slavery in Kansas and Nebraska?

By the early 1850s, plans were under way to build the nation's first transcontinental railroad, and Senator Douglas of Illinois wanted Chicago to serve as the new railway's major hub. But Chicago could not serve as the hub if the unorganized northern portion of the Louisiana Purchase remained unorganized and unpopulated; it wouldn't make any sense to put a railroad where there were no people and where the United States had little political presence.

Library of Congress Prints and Photographs Division[LC-DIG-cwpbh-00881]

>> "Senator Douglas was very small, not over four and a half feet height, and there was a noticeable disproportion between the long trunk of his body and his short legs. His chest was broad and indicated great strength of lungs. It took but a glance at his face and head to convince one that they belonged to no ordinary man. No beard hid any part of his remarkable, swarthy features. His mouth, nose, and chin were all large and clearly expressive of much boldness and power of will."—Journalist Henry Villard, 1858 describing Douglas, who is pictured here.

To eliminate this problem, Douglas began to push for the creation of several new territories in that northern region, where today sit Kansas and Nebraska.

The problem with Douglas's plan was that, according to the Missouri Compromise of 1820, slavery was prohibited in the northern part of the Louisiana Purchase. Southerners therefore resisted Douglas's efforts, fearing that when those territories eventually became states, they would become free states, once again tipping the balance of power in the Senate against the South.

THE KANSAS-NEBRASKA ACT

Douglas, a shrewd statesman, devised a compromise to ensure that southerners would support the development of the new territories. Douglas created two territories, Kansas and Nebraska (Map 14.1), and left the status of slavery in each territory open, to be decided by those who settled there. In the end, this meant that the Missouri Compromise of 1820 did not apply because slavery might have been allowed above 36°30', had the residents of Kansas or Nebraska so chosen. Many northerners were outraged at the prospect, but a coalition of northern Democrats (who wanted the transcontinental railroad) and southerners (who wanted a maintenance of slavery) passed the **Kansas-Nebraska Act** by a narrow margin.

14-2b The Death of the Second Two-Party System

The passage of the Kansas-Nebraska Act had two direct results: (1) it contributed to the demise of the Whig Party, and (2) it sparked a race to populate Kansas, because the fate of slavery in Kansas would be decided by voters there. The race would lead to tension, then conflict, and, ultimately, violence.

But the first result to become visible was the fatal weakening of America's second two-party system, splitting both parties along regional lines. Northern Whigs found themselves at odds with southern members of the party who opposed the Kansas-Nebraska Act; southern Whigs abandoned the party altogether to join the Democrats, which was more clearly supportive of slavery. Many northern Democrats, meanwhile, were increasingly sympathetic to parties like the Free Soilers. At the same time, several

Kansas-Nebraska Act The 1854 act that created two territories, Kansas and Nebraska, and left the status of slavery in each territory open, to be decided by the popular sovereignty of those who settled there

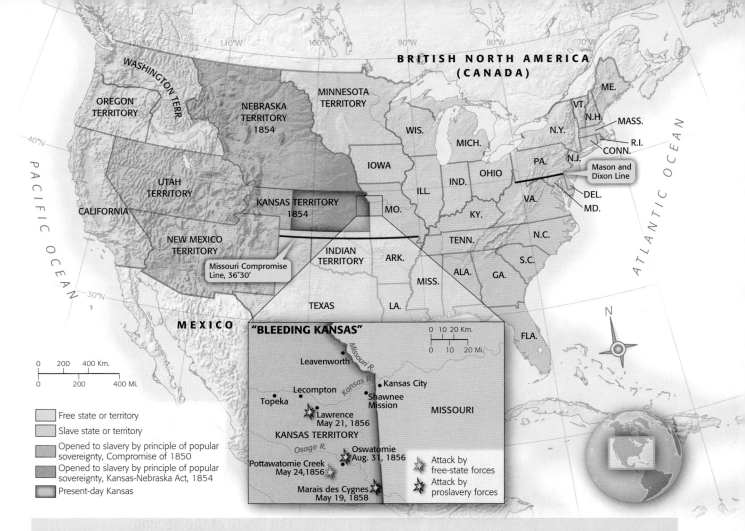

Map 14.1 Kansas-Nebraska and the Slavery Issue

>> This map of the US shows slave states and free states, and how the question of expanding slavery in the west broke down the nation's various efforts at compromise, including the violence provoked by the Kansas-Nebraska Act of 1854.

new political parties emerged, all of which spoke mostly for regional issues. By 1856, there were no longer any national political parties. The political system had crumbled over the issues of slavery and westward expansion.

THE KNOW-NOTHING PARTY

One of the new parties to arise in the 1850s was the American Party, which built its base of support on anti-immigrant and anti-Catholic sentiment. The American Party was an outgrowth of a secret society called the

Order of the Star-Spangled Banner. As a secret society, its members vowed to answer all inquiries about the Order with the response "I know nothing." Consequently, the American Party came to be known as the **Know-Nothing Party**.

Believing that "Americans should rule America," the Know-Nothings wanted to prevent new immigrants from gaining political rights. They advocated changing naturalization laws so that immigrants would be required to wait twenty-one years (as opposed to just five) before they could apply for citizenship, and they particularly targeted Irish Catholics. As they saw it, Catholics took their instructions from the pope and did not exercise the independence of mind necessary to function as democratic citizens. The Know-Nothings prided themselves on disdaining the very things the Irish stereotypically

Know-Nothing Party The American Party, a new political party of the 1850s that built its base of support on anti-immigrant and anti-Catholic sentiment

embraced: alcoholism, urban disorder, and poverty. The party appealed to middle-class and working men who saw immigrants as their main competition for jobs.

Very quickly, the Know-Nothings won several elections, suggesting the appeal of nativist ideas in mid-nineteenth-century America and the faltering status of the two-party system. In 1853, just a year after they formally established their party, the Know-Nothings won important electoral victories in New York, Pennsylvania, Massachusetts, and Ohio, the states that had experienced the most dramatic influx of immigrants. By 1855, the Know-Nothings had more than 1 million voters enrolled in their various lodges. Although they were never a commanding national party, the rise of the Know-Nothings is significant not only as a testament to the appeal of anti-Catholic nativism in the 1850s, but also because its rise killed off the Whig Party. Southern Whigs had deserted the party to join the Democrats, and many northern Whigs flocked to more locally oriented parties like the Know-Nothings.

After its meteoric rise, the popularity of the Know-Nothings plummeted just as rapidly. When the Know-Nothings failed to achieve their goals of changing naturalization laws and restricting political rights of immigrants, many members became disillusioned. And by that time there were also other parties to join.

THE REPUBLICAN PARTY

Most of the disaffected Know-Nothings joined another political party that was forming at the time, the **Republican Party**. Unlike any other party except the Free Soilers, the Republican Party was explicitly antislavery; its main goal was to prevent any further expansion of slavery in the West. Its platform included support for homesteading rights, a protective tariff, and internal improvements—most of the components of the American System. The Republicans succeeded in unifying numerous antislavery groups, including the Free Soilers. They also drew support from northern Whigs and Democrats who were infuriated by the Kansas-Nebraska Act and the idea of popular sovereignty wherein voters from each of those territories would get to decide if they were to become slave states or free states.

TWO PARTIES FROM TWO REGIONS

The Republicans were a purely sectional party, drawing almost all of their strength from antislavery sentiment in the North. Because the North had a significantly larger population than the South, the Republicans expected that they could eventually win the presidency without courting southern voters. Therefore, by the late 1850s, after the downfall of the Know-Nothings, a new, completely sectional

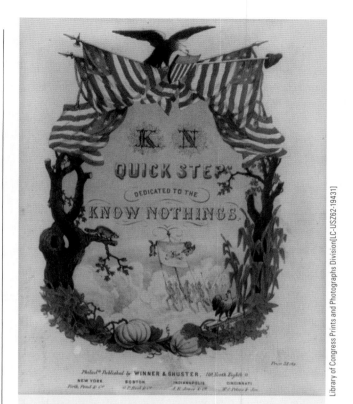

>> Popular music was on the rise during the 1850s, so it was inevitable that someone would compose a song for the new political party. Its sheet music cover, pictured here, is loaded with symbols of Americanism, from the eagle and flags to native pumpkins and corn.

party system was established, pitting antislavery northern Republicans against proslavery southern Democrats. This decline of national parties and the rise of sectional ones would accelerate the political crisis of the 1850s.

14-2c "Bleeding Kansas"

So what would become of Kansas? Would it enter the Union as a slave state or a free one? Under the doctrine of popular sovereignty, voters in Kansas would decide.

POPULAR SOVEREIGNTY

The problem was that there weren't many people in Kansas in 1854, so both parties (and their subsequent

Republican Party Explicitly antislavery party that emerged in the political turmoil of the 1850s; although not abolitionist, it favored "free-soil" movements to keep slavery out of the West

supporting groups) sent people to Kansas, just in time to vote in the election. Slaveholders in neighboring Missouri were fearful of having a free state just across their border. Being especially eager to see Kansas become a slave state, they encouraged slaveholding families to migrate immediately to Kansas. At the same time, abolitionists sent northern settlers to Kansas. One effort, led by New Englander Ely Thayer, sent nearly 1,250 settlers to Kansas, where they established Lawrence as a strong antislavery town. The tension between the two settling groups was palpable and violence flared up with increasing frequency, each side trying to frighten the other away.

THE STOLEN ELECTION

With both sides actively working to promote their own interests, Kansas became a bitterly divided territory. When the first territorial legislature was elected in 1855, throngs of men from Missouri, who came to be known as "border ruffians," crossed the border for the day and stuffed ballot boxes, electing a proslavery government. Only 2,900 registered voters lived in Kansas, but more than 6,000 ballots were cast. The advocates of slavery had stolen the election.

Kansas' new proslavery government immediately set out to crush its opposition and make Kansas a slave territory. It expelled antislavery representatives from the legislature and made it a crime to publicly advocate Free Soil principles or help fugitive slaves. Opponents appealed to the White House, but President Franklin Pierce supported southern interests. His opponents called him a "doughface," the derisive name for a northerner who openly supported the South. Forced to fend for themselves, antislavery Kansans formed a rival government in the city of Topeka. For a time, there were two functioning state governments in Kansas.

THE BLEEDING

Inevitably, this bitterly contested conflict erupted into violence. In 1856, a mob of proslavery men sacked the Free Soil town of Lawrence. The town was put to the torch, but no one was killed. This violence enraged John Brown, a zealous abolitionist who considered himself God's executioner of justice. To avenge the attack on Lawrence, Brown and his sons entered the town of Pottawatomie Creek, Kansas, rounded up five proslavery advocates, none of whom was a slaveholder, and butchered them. Brown's acts inspired more vigilantism, and

>> Throngs of men from Missouri (pictured here), who came to be known as "border ruffians," crossed the border into Kansas for the day and stuffed ballot boxes. Only 2,900 registered voters lived in Kansas, but more than 6,000 ballots were cast.

atrocities were met with counter-atrocities. As the newspapers reported, Kansas was bleeding.

KANSAS' CONSTITUTION

In June 1857, the people of Kansas elected another set of delegates to a convention in the town of Lecompton. The convention was charged with drawing up a state constitution. People opposed to slavery, however, boycotted the election on the grounds that the voting districts had been drawn so as to make it more difficult for them to elect antislavery representatives. Their boycott ensured that most of the men sent to the convention supported slavery, and predictably, they created a state constitution that made slavery legal in Kansas. Their constitution was called the **Lecompton Constitution**.

FREE SOILERS STRIKE BACK

In a provocative move, the convention refused to allow the citizens of Kansas a chance to challenge or reject the Lecompton Constitution. In the popular referendum that followed, Kansans were allowed to vote only on whether *more* slaves would be allowed into the territory, not on the legality of slavery itself. President James Buchanan, elected to succeed Pierce in 1856, was eager to satisfy the southern branch

Lecompton Constitution The 1857 state constitution that made slavery legal in Kansas; subsequently defeated in 1858

of the Democratic Party, so he backed the Lecompton Constitution despite what he knew about the antidemocratic convention that had created it. Senator Stephen Douglas, however, refused to support something so questionable, even though doing so angered the southern members of his party. President Buchanan pulled enough political strings to get the Senate to accept the constitution without Douglas's support, but he could not garner enough votes for it to pass in the House of Representatives. When no agreement could be reached on the issue, Congress sent the Lecompton Constitution back to Kansas for another vote by its people. This time, the Free Soilers participated in the vote and resoundingly rejected the pro-slavery constitution.

OUTCOMES

Although the Lecompton Constitution was ultimately defeated, the shenanigans surrounding its creation disgusted northerners, and the controversy convinced many northern Democrats to switch to the Republican Party. With each new political crisis, the sectional divide between northern Republicans and southern Democrats became more and more profound.

14-2d "Bleeding Sumner"

Events in the Senate only intensified the animosity. The reports from Kansas had caused emotions to run high among America's congressmen. No one was more vocal in his outrage than Charles Sumner, a Republican from Massachusetts who was perhaps the Senate's most outspoken opponent of slavery. Shortly before the burning of Lawrence (and John Brown's subsequent retaliation in Pottawatomie Creek), Sumner delivered a speech in Congress entitled **"The Crime Against Kansas,"** which blamed slavery for all the violence. In addition, Sumner made personally insulting remarks about Andrew P. Butler, a proslavery senator from South Carolina, leading many in attendance to believe that Sumner was deliberately provoking an attack.

THE CANING OF SUMNER

Butler was not at the capitol to defend himself, and he was too old and feeble to do so anyway. But his nephew Preston Brooks, a South Carolina representative in the House, stepped in on Butler's behalf. Brooks himself

SOUTHERN CHIVALRY — ARGUMENT versus CLUB'S.

>> The Caning of Sumner. With his first blow, Brooks opened a gash in Sumner's head and sent him careening to the floor. Brooks pounced on Sumner and continued to strike him in the head, even after his cane had shattered to pieces. To Northerners, his action came to symbolize Southern barbarity.

The New York Public Library/Art Resource, NY

had been a southern moderate before being galvanized by the events in Kansas. On May 22, 1856, just two days after Sumner delivered his vilifying speech, Brooks entered the Senate chamber and proceeded to beat Sumner senseless with his metal-topped cane. With his first blow, Brooks opened a gash in Sumner's head and sent him careening to the floor. Brooks then pounced on his victim and continued to strike him in the head, even after his cane had shattered to pieces. It took more than three years for Sumner to recover from his injuries.

In the opinion of many northerners, "Bleeding Sumner" came to match "Bleeding Kansas" as a symbol of southern barbarity. Certain southerners were proud of the caning, however, for its literal and symbolic value. Many of them mailed new canes to Brooks, with messages like "Hit Him Again." The episode captured in a moment the nation's breakdown of reason on the eve of civil war.

"The Crime Against Kansas" Speech delivered in Congress by Charles Sumner, Republican of Massachusetts, that blamed slavery for the violence between pro- and antislavery activists in Kansas

> "In the opinion of the court, the legislation and histories of the times, and the language used in the Declaration of Independence, show, that neither the class of persons who had been imported as slaves, nor their descendants, whether they had become free or not, were then acknowledged as a part of the people, nor intended to be included in the general words used in that memorable instrument . . . They had for more than a century before been regarded as beings of an inferior order, and altogether unfit to associate with the white race, either in social or political relations; and so far inferior, that they had no rights which the white man was bound to respect; and that the negro might justly and lawfully be reduced to slavery for his benefit."
>
> —CHIEF JUSTICE ROGER TANEY, IN THE DRED SCOTT DECISION, 1857

Slave Power Conspiracy Specter raised by antislavery Republicans who believed that, in order to preserve slavery, southern leaders would be willing to attack and silence anyone who advocated against slavery; allegedly the conspiracy intended to outlaw free speech and make all Americans accept proslavery principles

14-2e The Election of 1856

THE REPUBLICANS

Bleeding Kansas and the caning of Sumner were featured as central images in the 1856 Republican presidential campaign. The Republican candidate, John C. Frémont, founder of the free state of California, ran on a platform that denounced slavery as a "relic of barbarism." Frémont called for Kansas to be admitted to the Union as a free state, as the most recent vote there had suggested. There were several central themes in the Republican agenda, including expanding internal improvements and embracing the Market Revolution. But none were more important than the promotion of personal independence and free labor. Blocking the expansion of slavery in the territories, argued the Republicans, was essential to giving free white men the opportunity to establish homesteads for themselves in the West.

THE SLAVE POWER CONSPIRACY

The Republicans openly condemned the South's planter class. They argued that slaveholders were a minority group wielding a disproportionate amount of power. They believed that, in order to preserve slavery, southern leaders would be willing to attack and silence anyone who spoke out against slavery. According to Republican propaganda, the **Slave Power Conspiracy** intended to outlaw free speech and make all Americans accept proslavery principles.

THE ELECTION

Northerners comprised the majority of the American population, and Republicans believed it was time for the northern majority to control the national government. In 1856, Republican rhetoric proved powerful at the ballot box, but not quite powerful enough. Out of the sixteen free states, Frémont won eleven. Millard Fillmore, the American Party candidate, managed to take only Maryland, a slave state. Meanwhile, the Democratic candidate, James Buchanan of Pennsylvania, won thirteen of the fourteen slaveholding states, as well as the five free states that eluded Frémont. It was just enough for Buchanan to get into the White House.

RESULTS

The election made two things clear: (1) American voters were largely divided into sectional parties, and (2) despite Buchanan's victory, the Republicans were close to having enough support in the North to win a presidential election without winning a single southern state. The South was politically outnumbered and knew it.

14-3 THREE EVENTS THAT CATAPULTED THE NATION INTO WAR

In this heated atmosphere, three events pushed sentiments over the top: (1) the Dred Scott controversy, (2) John Brown's raid, and (3) the election of 1860. The events of the 1850s had pushed American politics to the brink of collapse. These three events would finish the job.

14-3a The Dred Scott Controversy

On March 4, 1857, Buchanan was inaugurated as president, and two days later, he confronted a controversial Supreme Court decision that threatened to intensify sectional tensions.

DRED SCOTT

A Missouri slave named Dred Scott had been taken by his owner to live for a few years in Illinois and the Wisconsin territory, where slavery was illegal. Eventually, however, Scott and his master returned to Missouri, where slavery was legal. With the help of antislavery advocates, Scott sued for his freedom on the grounds that his residence in a free state and a free territory had made him a free man.

The case went all the way to the U.S. Supreme Court and forced the court to rule on whether Scott's residence in Illinois and Wisconsin made him free. By a 7-to-2 decision, the Supreme Court ruled against Dred Scott. As Chief Justice Roger Taney explained, Scott had returned to Missouri before attempting to claim his freedom, and within Missouri he was a slave.

SLAVERY AS LAW OF THE LAND

But Chief Justice Taney, a Marylander who owned, but then freed, his own slaves, used the case to do much more than make a simple adjudication. Taney added remarks to his opinion that were intended to prevent black slaves from suing for their freedom ever again. In an incredibly bold statement, Taney asserted that the law Scott had cited— the Missouri Compromise— was unconstitutional because Congress had no right to prohibit slavery anywhere in the United States. A slaveholder could thus take his slaves anywhere he or she wanted within the Union, including free states, without losing title to them. By this logic, any attempt to restrict the westward march of slavery was prohibited by the land's highest court. This meant the Compromise of 1850, California's free-state status, and every state law prohibiting slavery ran afoul of the Constitution.

Republicans were outraged, interpreting the Dred Scott decision as proof that the Slave Power Conspiracy was as strong as ever. With the prohibition of slavery declared illegal by the Supreme Court, Republicans wondered if the South would attempt to renationalize slavery, as it had been before the Revolutionary War. Taney had, after all, declared that the federal government had no power to outlaw slavery.

Northerners could not accept this. Their fears made antislavery forces in the North all the more determined to reduce the South's political power in the country, deepening the sense of alienation and crisis between the two regions.

14-3b John Brown's Raid

Following the Dred Scott decision, John Brown, the radical abolitionist who had provoked some of the violence in "Bleeding Kansas," intensified the sectional crisis again. In October 1859, with eighteen of his followers, he raided the federal arsenal at Harper's Ferry in northwestern Virginia. Brown envisioned that, after seizing the armory, he would rally slaves in the surrounding area to join him in revolt against their oppressors.

To Brown's surprise, however, no slaves joined his side after he daringly seized control of the arsenal. Most were afraid Brown would be unsuccessful and did not want to risk their lives for the actions of a crazy man. Within three days, federal troops under the command of Colonel Robert E. Lee captured Brown and six of his cohorts. They were summarily tried for treason. Brown refused to give up the fight; throughout his trial, he spoke passionately against slavery and accepted his conviction and death sentence with the

>> John Brown.

>> The 1858 Lincoln-Douglas debates, depicted in this painting, where Douglas advocated "popular sovereignty."

calm resignation of a martyr. On December 2, 1859, the state of Virginia hanged him.

RESULTS

John Brown's raid was a dismal failure that horrified even some northerners. A few high-profile northerners praised Brown in no uncertain terms, though. Ralph Waldo Emerson, the prominent philosopher and abolitionist, publicly proclaimed Brown a "saint." Although views like Emerson's were probably in the minority, southerners fixated on such remarks as evidence that the North was out to destroy slavery and crush the "southern way of life." Brown failed to arouse the revolt he had planned, but he did succeed in inspiring a keen sense of fear and loathing among the southern public.

Lincoln-Douglas Debates Public debates on slavery between Stephen A. Douglas and Abraham Lincoln as they competed for the Illinois Senate seat in 1858

What the Dred Scott decision was to northerners, John Brown's raid was to southerners: an unfathomable, appalling episode that highlighted the gulf between the regions.

14-3c The Election of 1860

The implosion of national party politics and the sense of isolation felt in the North and the South came to a head in the election of 1860.

THE DEMOCRATS

In April of 1860, the Democratic Party held its convention in Charleston, South Carolina, and the sectional divide between northern and southern members generated palpable tension. Stephen A. Douglas was a clear favorite for the nomination, but southern Democrats had become disgusted with his leadership after he refused to endorse Kansas' proslavery constitution. Moreover, to nominate Douglas meant accepting the idea of popular sovereignty, which Douglas still supported and which contained within it the chance that antislavery forces would carry the day. Douglas had articulated his advocacy of popular sovereignty in the 1858 **Lincoln-Douglas Debates**, when Douglas and his opponent for the U.S. Senate seat in Illinois, Abraham Lincoln, publicly debated the issue of slavery. After the Dred Scott decision, southern Democrats wanted their party to agree with the Supreme Court that slavery could not be barred from any U.S. territory. Douglas would not accede to such a demand. Thus, the Democrats could not agree on a candidate who would satisfy the party's northern and southern members. They somewhat remarkably decided instead to adjourn the convention and reassemble in Baltimore in July.

The second Democratic convention nominated Douglas, but the southern delegates refused the nomination and walked out. That move confirmed the long-standing divide within the party, and the Democratic Party officially split into northern and southern wings. The northern branch stood behind Douglas, and southerners backed the current vice president, John C. Breckinridge of Kentucky, on a platform that called for the creation of a national slave code protecting slavery everywhere in the Union.

THE REPUBLICANS

The Republicans, meanwhile, nominated Abraham Lincoln, who was an attractive candidate for two reasons. First, Lincoln had become known after the Lincoln-Douglas Debates as a moderate on the slavery question. Although he believed that slavery was an evil institution, he did not aspire to end slavery in the southern states where it already existed. Republican leaders felt that this position would appeal to the general public of the North, which hoped to avoid greater conflict if possible. Second, Lincoln was from Illinois, a state the Republicans had failed to carry in 1856. If the Republicans were to win in 1860, they needed to win Illinois.

THE FINAL SECTIONAL DIVISION

In addition to Republicans (who had nominated Lincoln), northern Democrats (Douglas), and southern Democrats (Breckinridge), a fourth party entered the race with hopes that a showdown between North and South could be averted. The Constitutional Union Party nominated John Bell of Tennessee as their presidential candidate. Its simple platform was to avoid all discussion of slavery in an attempt to raise the Constitution and the Union above all schisms.

Despite the best intentions of the Constitutional Union Party, the election was not really a national contest. In the North, only Lincoln and Douglas held any popular appeal; in the South, the race was between Breckinridge and Bell. When all the votes were in, Lincoln emerged with the most votes, but not a majority of them. But because his base of support was in the populous states of the North, Lincoln won 180 votes in the Electoral College, just enough to secure victory.

RESULTS

Lincoln won the presidency as a sectional candidate. He did not win a single southern state (Map 14.2), and his

Counties Carried by Candidates in the 1860 Presidential Election

Candidate (Party)	Electoral Vote		Popular Vote	
Lincoln (Republican)	180	59.4%	1,865,593	39.8%
Douglas (Northern Democrat)	12	3.9%	1,382,713	29.5%
Breckinridge (Southern Democrat)	72	23.8%	848,356	18.1%
Bell (Constitutional Union)	39	12.9%	592,906	12.6%
Territories, no returns				

Map 14.2 The Election of 1860

>> A map of the election of 1860, showing how Lincoln won without winning a single county in the southern states.

The Reasons Why...

There were at least four major reasons why slavery plunged the nation into civil war in 1861:

Economics. The New England and Middle Colonies in the North had developed differently than the Chesapeake and Southern Colonies in the South, with those in the South more reliant on staple crops and, after the decline of indentured servitude in the 1680s, on slavery as well. These differences only accelerated during the Market Revolution. In the first half of the nineteenth century, states and territories in the North embraced internal improvements and the communication and transportation revolutions of the time, while wealthy landowners in the South were slow to embrace such changes, content that their plantations' reliance on rivers would be sufficient to enrich the region. With slave-grown cotton at a premium during the period, they were right. However, this gamble made them reliant on cotton, and on the slaves that cultivated it.

Westward expansion. After the Revolution, many northern states began the long process of ending slavery in the North. They recalled the arguments made against Britain about the importance of liberty, and they were not as economically dependent on a handful of slave-grown crops, as was the case in the South. In the South, however, the invention of the cotton gin in 1793 made cotton easier to cultivate, and a farmer who owned a little land and a few slaves could become wealthy. Thus, any talk of abolition in the South ceased, and these smaller farmers began pushing west, looking for land on which they could grow cotton and bring their slaves. For their part, most white northerners wanted to keep slavery out of the West, not because they hated the institution of slavery (though some did), but

principally because they did not want to compete against those with access to unfree labor.

Political breakdown. The westward expansion of slavery immediately created political problems. The House of Representatives and the Senate had agreed to develop a balance between slave states and free states, but with the proposed admission of new western states, the balance was threatened. A series of compromises in 1820, 1850, and 1854 allayed a few of the most problematic western additions, but the compromises took their toll on the various political parties, as many supporters would not abide by their party's compromises. By 1856, there were no longer any nationally unified parties, only sectional ones. After the newly formed Republican Party won the election of 1860 with support only from northern states, several states in the South seceded and attempted to drive American forces from the new Confederate States of America. Lincoln vowed to keep the nation together, and fought back.

An enraged populace. Not all northerners eagerly supported Lincoln, but many did. They did so because they viewed the South and slavery as barbarous and backward, and they were afraid that southerners wanted to renationalize slavery. If they were white, this "Slave Power Conspiracy" would limit their options as free white people, allowing slavery to sneak into areas in the West where they had the most to gain financially. They may not have been abolitionists, but they wanted to keep slavery from expanding. Many southerners, for their part, viewed the North as intent on ending slavery, and they were personally hurt by claims that they were backward and barbarous. These tensions led to violence in the West and even on the floor of the Senate. After the election of 1860, the enraged tempers meant that many people would be willing to fight for their side.

platform revealed his intention to halt the westward expansion of slavery. Although Democrats still controlled Congress, the North's ability to dictate the 1860 presidential election outcome confirmed the southern states' worst fear: they had lost control of national politics. The institution of slavery was in peril.

 14-4 SECESSION AND CIVIL WAR

In the eyes of many southerners, Lincoln's election spelled the end of the southern way of life as they knew it. Although Lincoln had actually affirmed the rights of

Map 14.3 Southern Secession

>> A map of the eastern United States showing the order in which the southern states left the United States in order to become a new nation, the Confederate States of America.

the states in his campaign speeches, the South saw his opposition to the spread of slavery in the West as a serious threat. If all the western territories became free states, southerners assumed Republicans would amend the Constitution and outlaw slavery everywhere. Many southerners believed it would be better to leave the Union before the horrors of abolition were inflicted upon them. (For more on slavery's role in the start of the Civil War, see "The Reasons Why . . .")

Americans had considered secession in the past. Ever since the founding of the nation, defenders of "states' rights" had argued that any state should be able to "nullify" laws passed by the federal government and even withdraw from the Union should it so desire. In 1798, Thomas Jefferson claimed the right of nullification in his Kentucky Resolution; disgruntled New England Federalists threatened to leave the Union during the War of 1812; and South Carolina's great statesman John C. Calhoun had in the 1830s defended the South's right to "disunion" in order to protect it from what he called "northern aggression." In these prior cases, however, only the most hotheaded ideologues urged secession. Until 1860, everyone had held back from dividing the country. That changed with Lincoln's election.

14-4a The Deep South Secedes

South Carolina took the lead. On December 20, 1860, a state convention repealed South Carolina's ratification of the U.S. Constitution and voted to withdraw from the Union. It did not want to be part of a nation in which it had no control. Over the next six weeks, severaother southern states—Mississippi, Florida, Alabama, Georgia, Louisiana, and Texas—followed suit (See Map 14.3). Together, on February 7, 1861, they established the Confederate States of America: an independent slave republic. The Confederate States of America elected Jefferson Davis of Mississippi as the new nation's first president.

LOWER SOUTH VERSUS UPPER SOUTH

Seceding was not a unanimous choice for these southern states. The planter class was the driving force behind the movement. Those counties that had a large number of slaveholding families tended to vote for secession in the secessionist conventions, while those areas with few slaves typically voted against it. Therefore, the initial wave of secession was confined to the Deep South (Louisiana, Mississippi, Alabama, Georgia,

>> The first flag of the Confederate States of America, called "the Stars and Bars," was flown from March 5, 1861, to May 26, 1863.

Table 14.1	Events Leading Up to the Civil War
1846	Wilmot Proviso
1850	Compromise of 1850
1852	*Uncle Tom's Cabin*
1854	Kansas-Nebraska Act
1856	"Bleeding Kansas," "Bleeding Sumner"
1857	Dred Scott decision
1859	John Brown's raid at Harper's Ferry, Virginia
1860	Abraham Lincoln elected president
1861	Southern states secede
April 12, 1861	Firing on Fort Sumter

South Carolina, Texas, and Florida), where slave-based agriculture was more fully established. The Upper South (Virginia, North Carolina, Arkansas, Kentucky, and Tennessee), by contrast, had a more diversified economy. Those states chose not to secede in the winter of 1860–1861. It would take actual battle to drive them to pick sides.

14-4b Conciliatory Efforts

A handful of attempts were made to prevent the situation from exploding into war, notably by John Crittenden and Abraham Lincoln.

CRITTENDEN COMPROMISE

The first last-ditch effort at reconciliation was spearheaded by John Crittenden of Kentucky. Crittenden proposed that the Missouri Compromise line of 1820 be resurrected and extended all the way to the Pacific, excluding California. All land north of the line would be free, all land south of it would be open to slavery. Moreover, he recommended that an "unamendable amendment" be made to the Constitution, guaranteeing the preservation of slavery in the southern states where it already existed.

Crittenden Compromise Reconciliation proposal advocating that the Missouri Compromise line of 1820 be extended all the way to the Pacific, excluding California, with all land north of the line free, all land south of it open to slavery; also included an "unamendable amendment" to the Constitution, guaranteeing the preservation of slavery in the southern states where it already existed

The **Crittenden Compromise** proved unworkable. Secessionists in the Deep South had no interest in returning to the Union. The Republicans, who had been elected to office on a platform that called for prohibiting the expansion of slavery, did not want to renege on their campaign promises. Thus, the Crittenden Compromise was a nonstarter, and the only question

>> Abraham Lincoln circa 1860.

>> Pictured here is the bombardment of Fort Sumter.

In early April 1861, President Lincoln organized a relief expedition to the fort. Hopeful that war could be avoided, Lincoln assured the governor of South Carolina that the ships sent to supply Fort Sumter would contain only food, not guns or ammunition. Jefferson Davis, however, declared that any attempt to send provisions to Fort Sumter would be considered an aggressive act against the Confederacy. As a preemptive move, Davis ordered General Pierre Beauregard, the Confederate Army commander in Charleston, to demand Fort Sumter's immediate surrender. If the garrison of eighty-five men refused to surrender, Davis ordered Beauregard to open fire. On April 12, 1861, when Beauregard's demands were rejected, Confederate batteries began shelling Fort Sumter. By the evening of April 13, the garrison capitulated.

remaining was whether the states of the Deep South would be permitted to withdraw from the Union.

LINCOLN'S MIDDLE COURSE

After his inauguration on March 4, 1861, Lincoln attempted to chart a middle course. He sought to reassure southerners that he would not interfere with slavery in the states where it already existed. Slave states that did not secede would be allowed to maintain slavery. At the same time, Lincoln, like Andrew Jackson before him, maintained that the Union was perpetual and that no state could withdraw from it. Furthermore, he insisted that federal property in the southern states (forts, arsenals, and customs houses) still belonged to the Union.

Lincoln put the ball in the Confederacy's court. It was up to the southern states to either return to the Union or face civil war. He had invited them back and granted them slavery where it already existed, maintaining the status quo. What would the Confederates do?

14-4c Fort Sumter

Army rations became the deciding factor. The deadlock was shaken when the federal garrison at Fort Sumter, South Carolina, located just off the coast of Charleston (now a city in the Confederate States of America), ran low on food. Provisions needed to be sent to the U.S. troops there, or they would have to surrender the fort to the Confederacy. By March 1861, only six weeks of supplies remained.

>LOOKING AHEAD···

In the wake of Fort Sumter's surrender, Abraham Lincoln called for 75,000 volunteers to put down the southern rebellion. Northerners eagerly rallied behind Lincoln and resolved to bring the secessionists to their knees. Lincoln had been savvy. By inviting the South to attack a U.S. fort, he had allowed a broad swath of northerners to support the suppression of the insurrection without forcing them to take a stand on slavery. The South was also coming together. In response to Lincoln's attempt to "coerce" the rebel states back into the Union, the Upper South states of Virginia, Tennessee, North Carolina, and Arkansas threw their lot in with the Confederacy; they too seceded from the Union.

Battle lines were now drawn. What was destined to become the bloodiest war in American history had begun. Later, in Abraham Lincoln's Second Inaugural Address, he said, "all knew" that slavery "was somehow the cause of the war." But it took time and a variety of factors before it became the driving force in the breakup of the Union. The political crisis of the 1850s, sparked by the question of whether slavery would be allowed in the West, finally erupted into civil war.

STUDY TOOLS 14

READY TO STUDY? IN THE BOOK, YOU CAN:

❏ Rip out the Chapter Review Card, which includes key terms and chapter summaries.

ONLINE AT WWW.CENGAGEBRAIN.COM, YOU CAN:

❏ Collect StudyBits while you read and study the chapter.

❏ Quiz yourself on key concepts.

❏ Find videos for further exploration.

❏ Prepare for tests with HIST5 Flash Cards as well as those you create.

❏ Read Calhoun's speech.

❏ Read the Kansas-Nebraska Act.

❏ Learn more about John Brown's raid.

❏ Read a contemporary account of the "sacking of Lawrence."

❏ Learn more about the history of Lecompton, Kansas.

❏ Read the first Lincoln-Douglas debate on the spread of slavery.

❏ Read Lincoln's powerful "House Divided" speech.

❏ Read South Carolina's declaration of the causes of secession.

❏ Read the Crittenden Compromise.

❏ Explore further information about Fort Sumter.

❏ Read Lincoln's Inaugural Address.

CH14 TIMELINE

		What Else Was Happening
		1842: Abraham Lincoln accepts a challenge to a duel from James Shields, the Democratic state auditor. (The duel never takes place.)
		1845: The rubber band is patented.
1846	Wilmot Proviso's ban on slavery from new territories alarms southerners. It never passes.	
1848	Whigs divide in presidential election; Free Soil Party emerges.	
1850	Compromise admits a free California, leaves slavery in territories to popular sovereignty, bans slave trade in D.C., expands Fugitive Slave Act.	Taiping Rebellion in China begins. This civil war, which lasts fourteen years, will see 20 million people die before the restoration of the Qing dynasty.
1853–1856	As Free Soilers and slaveholders race to settle Kansas, violence ensues.	Crimean War pits Russia against Britain, France, the Ottoman Empire, and the Kingdom of Sardinia. It is considered the first "modern" war because of the tactical use of railroads and the telegraph. It is also the war in which Florence Nightingale pioneers modern nursing.

1854 Kansas-Nebraska Act leaves slavery to popular sovereignty in territories.

1856 Republican Party draws Free Soilers, Whigs, Know-Nothings with antislavery stance.

Multiparty presidential election of James Buchanan highlights sectional rift.

1857 Supreme Court's Dred Scott decision prohibits Congress from restricting slavery.

Kansas' proslavery Lecompton Constitution splits Congress.

Indian Rebellion, protesting British colonial rule, lasts a year before the British finally suppress the rebellion.

1860 **November:** Republican Lincoln wins presidential election as sectional candidate.

December: South Carolina secedes in reaction to Lincoln's election; Deep South follows.

December: Crittenden Compromise fails.

1861 **April:** South Carolina attacks federal Fort Sumter near Charleston.

February 11: Both Abraham Lincoln and Jefferson Davis leave their homes to be inaugurated president.

15 | The Civil War

LEARNING OBJECTIVES

After reading this chapter, you should be able to do the following:

15-1 Describe the areas of strengths of each side at the beginning of the Civil War.

15-2 Explain why both sides believed the war would be brief, and describe the early conflicts that made that outcome unlikely.

15-3 Explain how preparing for and prosecuting the Civil War contributed to the transformation of the United States into a fully modern state.

15-4 Describe the actions of those who opposed the war in the North and the South.

15-5 Discuss the events of 1863 and 1864 that demonstrated Lincoln's eventual determination that the end of the war should bring a definite end to slavery.

15-6 Describe and discuss the events that finally led to the defeat of the South and the end of the war.

15-7 Assess the significance of the Civil War for the nation.

AFTER FINISHING
THIS CHAPTER
GO TO **PAGE 288**
FOR STUDY TOOLS

In hindsight, we know the Civil War was four years of prolonged and bloody battles. At the outbreak of fighting, however, neither northerners nor southerners took the prospect of fighting one another all that seriously. Both sides expected a short war with few casualties. Southerners believed that northerners were effete cowards lacking the mettle to endure a prolonged battle. They thought that once the northern armies caught a glimpse of the South's determination, northerners would drop their guns and let the South secede. Northerners, meanwhile, were certain that only southern slaveholders supported secession, and, because slaveholders were a tiny minority in the South, the lack of support would quickly become evident. Northerners also considered southerners ill prepared and ill equipped to take on the U.S. Army.

As a consequence, northerners and southerners predicted that the war would not change their societies very dramatically. Southerners presumed that their plantation-based, slaveholding civilization would continue to thrive as it had for decades. Northerners imagined that the southern states would realize their error and return to the Union to resume amicable relations. Southerners would keep their slaves, most northerners thought, but slavery would be prevented from spreading westward.

All these predictions proved inaccurate. The fighting between North and South quickly became fierce and vindictive, and casualties were high. In addition, when the North and South emerged from the war in 1865, both were transformed from what they had been in 1861. In short, the war ended slavery and accelerated America's modernization, shaping the nation we live in today.

> In terms of military-age white males, the Union outnumbered the Confederacy four to one.

15-1 EACH SIDE'S STRENGTHS

15-1a Northern Advantages

In some ways, northern expectations for a quick victory were reasonable, because the Union possessed overwhelming material advantages over the South. The North's primary advantages were (1) more people, (2) more materials, and (3) more industry.

POPULATION

In 1861, the total population of the Union was around 22 million, compared to 9 million in the Confederacy. This statistic becomes even more impressive when one considers that 3.5 million of the Confederacy's people were slaves, people clearly unwilling to fight on behalf of the perpetuation of slavery. In terms of military-aged white males, the Union outnumbered the Confederacy four to one.

MATERIALS AND INDUSTRY

The northern states had other advantages as well. The North had an existing navy and produced more firearms than the South. It also produced more of the essential provisions of war, including coal, textiles, corn, and wheat. By all estimates, the North was better able to outfit its men with weapons, clothing, shoes, and food. The North also had a more extensive network of railroad lines for transporting those supplies and a larger pool of money to finance its war effort. The Union possessed about $200 million in bank deposits, while the Confederacy had only $47 million.

15-1b Southern Advantages

The Confederacy did have certain strengths, however, including (1) the will to fight, (2) the fact that it is easier to fight a defensive battle, and (3) a large number of talented military leaders.

WILL TO FIGHT

First, northerners severely underestimated the southern will to fight. While only slaveholders had taken the lead in the secession movement, by April 1861, most southerners supported the bid for Confederate independence, and they were willing to fight for it.

◀◀◀ The Civil War turned out to be a long and bloody struggle that dramatically reshaped the nation. Soldiers often commented on how loud and violent the weapons of modern warfare truly were. This painting depicts the violence about to come when the two sides clashed.

A DEFENSIVE BATTLE

The Union also had to wage an offensive war to occupy the South in order to bring it back into the nation, while the Confederacy had the simpler task of fighting on the defensive. The Confederacy did not have to overwhelm or occupy the North; it merely had to frustrate northern efforts to conquer it.

MILITARY LEADERS AND MORALE

At the beginning of the war, the South also had more well-trained military leaders and a stronger tradition of military service. Many of the West Point-trained officers in the U.S. Army, including Jefferson Davis, Robert E. Lee, Albert Sydney Johnston, Thomas "Stonewall" Jackson, and James Longstreet, sided with the Confederacy. In addition, living in a rural environment, most men in the South were more comfortable with firearms than soldiers raised in the urban North. And, in terms of morale, the Confederacy had the advantage of fighting for its existence.

 ## 15-2 THE FALLACY OF AN "EASY WAR": 1861–1862

The fallacy of both sides expecting a brief war became apparent at the first major battle.

15-2a The Battle of Manassas (Bull Run)

On July 21, 1861, Union general Irvin McDowell moved 30,000 troops toward the Confederate soldiers clustered at Manassas Junction, just south of Washington, D.C. At the same time, civilians and congressmen from the capital packed picnic lunches and made the twenty-five-mile journey to witness the battle. After all, they anticipated fighting to be light and the battle to end shortly.

To the surprise of both sides, the Battle of Manassas, called the Battle of Bull Run by the Union (the North named battles after nearby creeks or rivers, the South after nearby towns), was hard-fought and bloody. Some 22,000 Confederate soldiers, led by General Pierre Beauregard, battled tenaciously against McDowell's men, and Confederate reinforcements under General Joseph E. Johnston, including the heroic Thomas "Stonewall" Jackson, turned the tide decisively in the South's favor. When McDowell ordered a retreat, his troops panicked and stampeded from the fray.

>> Filling cartridges at the U.S. Arsenal at Watertown, Mass., 1861, shows the conversion to the wartime economy.

A COSTLY CONFEDERATE VICTORY

Although the Confederates had won the field of battle, they were not prepared to pursue the fleeing federal troops. The victory had been too costly. Each side had suffered nearly 10 percent casualties, with the northern forces having had 2,896 killed, wounded, or missing and the southern forces suffering 1,982 similar casualties. In light of such carnage, northerners and southerners alike were stripped of their assumptions about an easy war. The change in tone was especially marked in the North. After the defeat at Manassas, fearing that victorious southern forces would head straight to Washington, D.C., Congress authorized, and received, the enlistment of 500,000 volunteers. They were now preparing for a major armed conflict, a bigger war than anyone had predicted.

>> At first, the armies of the Civil War were a ragtag bunch of soldiers, like those pictured here, eager to fight a quick battle. Note the collection of "uniforms" worn by these Confederate soldiers in 1861. Hopes for a quick war faded fast.

LIMITED WAR

Although northerners no longer believed that the war would be won quickly, they clung to the idea that most southerners still loved the Union but had been pressured into fighting by a small clique of powerful slaveholders. They viewed it as a rich man's war but a poor man's fight.

In keeping with this view, the Union Army in 1861 and 1862 fought a limited war, which meant that, in attacking the Confederacy, Union troops were careful not to assault southern civilians or damage their property. Their goal was to occupy southern territory and defeat the Confederate Army. They were not aiming to subjugate the southern people. They attempted this strategy of "limited war" in three theaters: (1) the water, (2) the West, and (3) the East (see Map 15.1).

15-2b The Water

The imposition of a naval blockade of Confederate ports was a key part of the Union strategy. Not only would it deprive the South of food, clothing, and other supplies coming from Europe, but it would also demonstrate to the world that the South was unable to defend itself, thus keeping Britain and France from recognizing, and perhaps allying with, the Confederacy. These nations did, after all, need the South's cotton. In April 1861, Lincoln formally declared a blockade of the southern coastline.

Cutting the Confederacy off from sea-borne commerce proved difficult at first because the U.S. Navy had only forty-two ships to patrol 3,550 miles of Confederate coastline. After the first year of the war, however, blockading the South became easier, as the Union took control of several southern coastal locations, including Roanoke Island in North Carolina, the sea islands of South Carolina, and New Orleans.

Taking New Orleans was a significant coup; it was the South's largest and richest city and its biggest port, and it opened the Mississippi River valley to invasion from the south. If the Union could not yet beat the Confederacy on the battlefield, it could prevent European goods from reaching it and eventually starve southerners into submission.

The blockade effort also stimulated the development of the ironclad battleship. Instead of wood, these ships used iron (later steel) siding and sat low in the water to ram targets more efficiently. One in particular, the USS *Monitor*, had

>> "You come to see the gladiator's show, But from a high place, as befits the wise: You will not see the long windrows of men Strewn like dead pears . . ."—From Stephen Vincent Benét, "The Congressmen Came Out to See Bull Run." In this latter-day photograph, Civil War re-enactors watch the Battle of Bull Run while picnicking in their bonnets.

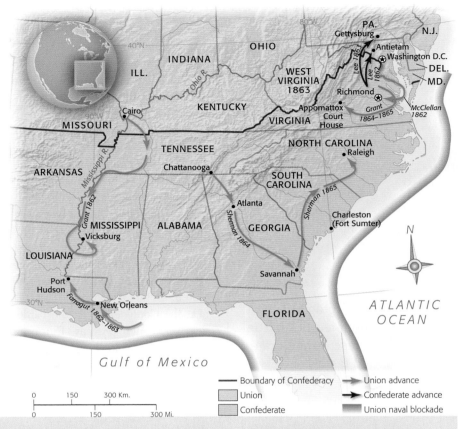

Map 15.1 Northern Strategy and Southern Resistance, 1861–1865

>> A map of the eastern United States showing the Union naval blockade and the major battles of the Civil War.

Confederacy won many of the battles waged in 1861 (including those at Wilson's Creek, Lexington, and Belmont), Union general Ulysses S. Grant earned the first decisive victories in the first half of 1862 in the western theater of the war. In February 1862, with the support of Union gunboats, Grant's forces captured Fort Henry on the Tennessee River and then Fort Donelson on the Cumberland River.

SHILOH

These losses forced Confederate troops to withdraw from Kentucky and Tennessee, states on the northwestern border of the Confederacy. A few months later, as Grant's army moved farther south, they encountered fierce resistance from Confederate troops under the command of General Albert Sidney Johnston. Johnston's army took Grant's men by surprise near the Tennessee-Mississippi border in April 1862. The ensuing **Battle of Shiloh** (or the Battle of Pittsburg Landing) was incredibly bloody, resulting in 23,000 combined north-

a two-gun rotating turret on top. The first battle between ironclads, a four-hour barrage in March 1862 between the USS *Monitor* and the CSS *Virginia*, ended inconclusively. But the news coverage it garnered signaled to the world a shift in military technology. Notably slow, however, the ironclads were only marginally successful in stopping Confederate blockade runners throughout the war.

15-2c The West

SOME UNION SUCCESSES

While the Union Navy was taking control of the southern coast, the Union Army achieved some success in the western theater of the war, located west of the Allegheny Mountains (see Map 15.2). Although the

Battle of Shiloh Bloody conflict near the Tennessee-Mississippi border in April 1862; also called the Battle of Pittsburg Landing; 23,000 casualties

ern and southern casualties. Grant took the victory on the second day, but at a heavy price. The casualties at Shiloh alone exceeded American losses in the Revolutionary War, the War of 1812, and the Mexican-American War put

>> Crew of the Union ironclad ship *The Monitor*, showing off the most modern of warships.

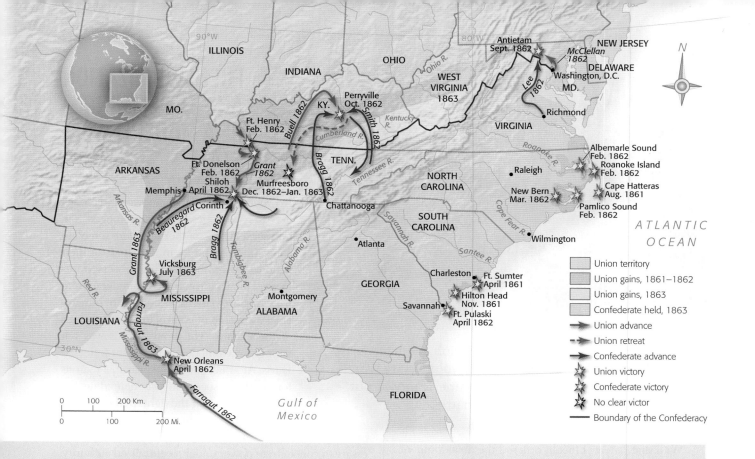

Map 15.2 The War in the West

>> A map of the eastern half of the United States, focusing on the large number of battles along the Mississippi River and throughout Tennessee and Kentucky.

together, and they were almost five times as great as the losses suffered at the Battle of Manassas. It would turn out to be only the ninth bloodiest battle of the Civil War, but the enormity of the fatalities was felt nationwide. The North was securing the western theater, but it was doing so at a tremendous cost. Not only would this be a massive war, it would be a tragic one as well. This was evident as early as 1862.

15-2d The East

The Union Army was less successful in the East, mainly because General McClellan was less decisive than Robert E. Lee, the respective generals over the Union and Confederate armies there.

McCLELLAN

In the East, General George B. McClellan headed the Union's Army of the Potomac. Despite his outward arrogance, McClellan was an insecure man and an excessively cautious commander. He thought the South should be coaxed back into the Union, not beaten back in. His troops appreciated his reluctance to expose them to bloody battles, but McClellan's self-defeating attitude hurt the Union cause.

Throughout most of 1861, McClellan resisted pressures to pursue the Confederate Army in Virginia, insisting that he needed time to discipline and drill his men. In spring 1862, McClellan finally decided to make a move on Richmond, the Confederate capital. After transporting his troops to the mouth of the James River, McClellan slowly made his way up the peninsula between the James and York Rivers. But his procrastination had given the Confederate Army a chance to organize and respond. On May 31, 1862, McClellan was within 5 miles of Richmond when General Joseph Johnston and the Confederacy's Army of Northern Virginia attacked his troops at Fair Oaks (or Seven Pines). Johnston was badly wounded in the battle, but he succeeded in halting McClellan's advance.

ROBERT E. LEE

Matters only worsened for McClellan after Robert E. Lee replaced Johnston as the head of the Army of Northern Virginia. Lee was as audacious as McClellan was cautious, and Lee repulsed the Army of the Potomac during the Seven Days' Battles, which raged from June 25 to July 1, 1862. The Army of the Potomac was pushed north, out of Virginia.

FULL MOBILIZATION AND THE MAKING OF A MODERN STATE

>> The casualties at the Battle of Shiloh, depicted here, exceeded American losses in the Revolutionary War, the War of 1812, and the Mexican-American War put together. It was a truly horrifying battle.

In order to amass the manpower and money necessary to wage a serious prolonged war, northerners and southerners were forced to concentrate authority in the hands of their national governments. This process transformed the Union and the Confederacy into truly modern nations with intricate bureaucracies capable of controlling the resources of their states. The irony of this was felt strongly by Confederate president Jefferson Davis. After all, one of the principal reasons for southern secession was defending the rights of states over the rights of the national government. Yet in order to secure the South's independence, Davis found it necessary to concentrate power under a centralized authority. Of course, in this the South wasn't alone. Northerners, too, felt the tightening grip of the federal government.

With that defeat, Lincoln ordered the abandonment of McClellan's peninsula campaign, removed McClellan from his post, and made General John Pope the Union's top eastern commander. Pope, though, was no more successful than McClellan had been. At the second Battle of Manassas, on August 29, 1862, Lee routed the Union troops and disgraced Pope. Lincoln had little choice but to reinstate McClellan as his top eastern commander. The Union armies were generally successful in the West and on the seas, but they were unable to beat their opponents where it mattered most—in Virginia, the heart of the Confederacy.

RESULTS

The initial battles in these three theaters were hard fought, suggesting that the war would last longer than anyone had expected. War would require each side to mobilize its resources and, in the end, establish what is thought of today as a modern nation-state.

>> "If General McClellan does not want to use the army, I would like to borrow it for a time."—attributed to Abraham Lincoln, 1862. McClellan is pictured here.

15-3a Raising Armies

Nowhere was this truer than when it came to raising armies.

THE CONFEDERACY

During the first year of the war, the Confederacy had only a small national army. Most soldiers volunteered for service through state militias controlled by state governors, not through the Confederacy. However, Jefferson Davis understood that engineering a strong war effort required greater coordination. So he convinced the Confederate Congress to implement a national draft in April 1862.

All men between eighteen and thirty-five became eligible for military service in the Confederate Army. Exemptions could be purchased, traded in return for supplying a substitute, or simply granted to wealthy landholders who owned twenty or more slaves. This "20 Negro Law" was designed to keep the planters producing their valuable cotton yield. The Confederate Conscription Act also contained occupational exemptions, whereby workers at gun and munitions factories would not be forced to leave jobs valuable to the war effort (the list of occupational exemptions immediately became political, such that, by the end of the war, the list of war-related jobs could not be contained on two finely printed pages). By 1863, the Confederate government, not the various state governments, had assumed control of the army.

THE UNION

The North implemented a national draft in 1863. Like the Confederacy, the Union had initially relied on state armies to enlist soldiers, but the high desertion and low enlistment rates of state officers forced the federal government to establish a national conscription law, making all able-bodied men ages twenty to forty-five eligible for the draft. To ease the burden of conscription, the Union also established volunteer quotas for each of its states. Only when a state failed to provide its allotted number of volunteer soldiers was the draft employed in that state.

Very few men were ever drafted; most volunteered. Others tried to fail medical exams in order to escape the war altogether. Similarly, under the conscription law, a person could be exempted until the next draft by paying a $300 **commutation fee**. The Union draft law, too, allowed men to be exempt from service by hiring a substitute to take their place. Some men, known as bounty jumpers, would receive a bounty to take another man's place in the army, then desert, only to do the trick again and again. Thus, in both the Union and the Confederacy, exemptions were made for rich men, who could afford to buy their way out of service, while ordinary workers and farmers could not. The accusation that this was a rich man's war but a poor man's fight applied to both sides of the conflict.

15-3b Suspension of Civil Liberties

The expansion of federal control also affected people's freedoms, and in the first year of the war, both Union and Confederate governments suspended civil liberties.

IN THE UNION

Abraham Lincoln took the lead. From the start of fighting in April 1861, some northerners opposed the war and worked to hamper the Union effort.

>> Recruiting soldiers was not always easy, and included short tours of duty and bounties. This recruitment poster shows the efforts made to sign up soldiers in New York.

For instance, on April 19, 1861, Confederate sympathizers in Baltimore (a large Union city) destroyed telegraph lines, sabotaged railroads, and attacked Union soldiers who were passing through on their way to Washington, which was threatened after the Battle of Manassas.

"20 Negro Law" Exemption from Confederate military service granted to wealthy landholders who owned twenty or more slaves; designed to keep the planters producing their valuable cotton yield

commutation fee Sum of money that guaranteed a draft-age man's exemption from enlisting in the Union Army until the next draft

To deal with the dissent, Lincoln used his authority as commander-in-chief to suspend the writ of habeas corpus in Maryland, which made it possible for Union soldiers to arrest any northern civilians suspected of disloyalty and imprison them without benefit of trial. Eventually, Lincoln suspended the writ in all other states, hoping to control disloyalty and dissent everywhere in the North. During the course of the conflict, roughly 14,000 people were arrested for undefined reasons.

IN THE CONFEDERACY

Jefferson Davis followed Lincoln's lead. As in the North, antiwar sentiment existed in the Confederacy from the outset, especially in poorer areas with few slaves. Several military losses in 1862 incited a level of dissent that provoked Davis to action. Unlike Lincoln, Davis himself did not suspend the writ of habeas corpus. Instead, he sought approval from the Confederate Congress, which granted the request and gave Davis the power to clamp down on citizens who opposed southern independence.

15-3c Taxation

Both sides also exercised new controls over their national economies. Before the war, the federal government had depended mostly on tariff revenues and land sales to finance its operations. In fact, aside from the tariffs, the federal government had levied no taxes on the American people since the War of 1812. That would have to change to pay for the war.

TARIFFS, TAXES, AND BONDS IN THE UNION

At the outbreak of hostilities in the Civil War, the U.S. Congress began raising tariff rates in order to pay for the war, and by 1865 the average tariff rate was an astronomical 47 percent. Despite these rates, tariffs failed to generate enough revenue to fully finance the military operation.

To compensate, Congress introduced direct taxation measures. During the first year of the war, it enacted a

3 percent income tax. Then, in 1862, Congress enacted a graduated tax schedule to bring in more revenue from wealthier citizens. It also passed a comprehensive tax bill that levied new occupational and licensing taxes, corporate taxes, stamp taxes, insurance company taxes, dividend taxes, sales taxes, food taxes, and so-called sin taxes on alcohol and tobacco. To streamline the collection of these new levies, Congress created the Internal Revenue Service in 1862.

The U.S. government also tried to raise money by selling war bonds, or bonds that a person or corporation could buy that would earn interest over a fixed period of time. Bondholders could then redeem the bonds within five to twenty years for their initial investment plus interest (they were called **five-twenties**). New York banker Jay Cooke took the reins on this project and rapidly sold more than $500 million worth of bonds, to both large corporations and individual buyers.

INFLATION AND IMPRESSMENT IN THE CONFEDERACY

At first, the Confederacy resisted creating a national system of taxation. It preferred instead to finance the war by simply printing more and more paper money—a plan

>> The Confederacy preferred to finance the war by simply printing more and more paper money of the kind pictured here—a plan that succeeded only in creating runaway inflation.

five-twenties War bonds, or bonds that would earn interest over a fixed period of time; the bondholder could redeem the bond in anywhere from five to twenty years for the initial investment plus interest

iStock.com/I.petter

that succeeded only in creating runaway inflation. The cost of living at the end of the war was an astounding ninety-two times what it had been before the war began. Only in 1863, once Confederate currency became nearly worthless, did the Confederate Congress institute a graduated income tax similar to the Union's. Nevertheless, while these types of taxes financed 21 percent of the Union's expenses, they furnished only 1 percent of the Confederacy's.

In addition, the Confederacy enacted a policy of impressment, authorizing armies to seize food, supplies, and even slaves for use in the war effort. Theoretically, citizens would be compensated, but many people complained that the government paid too little and that the payments were made in inflated and increasingly worthless Confederate dollars. The war was a financial disaster for the Confederacy, which never figured out the best method to pay for it.

15-3d A Changing Nation

Between the new system of conscription, suspension of the writ of habeas corpus, and taxes, the Union and the Confederacy became powerful nation-states with great control over the lives of their citizens. Before 1861, Americans had little contact with their federal government. Most Americans encountered the federal government only when the U.S. postal service delivered their mail. By 1865, however, northerners and southerners lived under large and powerful national governments. After the war, the writ of habeas corpus was restored, but other powers assumed by the federal government were not rolled back. The Civil War established innovative and permanent changes in the scope of government authority in the United States.

15-4 DISSENT

These changes stirred dissent, and governments in both the North and the South found themselves confronted by those who opposed the war.

15-4a Dissent in the North

The entire body of Lincoln's policies came to elicit a great deal of opposition on the northern home front.

PEACE DEMOCRATS

For example, a minority of Democrats refused to support the war. These Democrats came to be called

> "Although it filled the broad street from curbstone to curbstone, and was moving rapidly, it took between twenty and twenty-five minutes for it to pass a single point. A ragged, coatless, heterogeneously weaponed army, it heaved tumultuously along toward Third Avenue."
>
> —JOURNALIST JOEL TYLER HEADLEY, PEN AND PENCIL SKETCHES OF THE GREAT RIOTS [OF 1863], 1877

"Peace Democrats" or "Copperheads." They believed that secession was legal and that the Union had no right to force southern states to remain within it. Although their numbers were small in 1861, the Peace Democrats soon capitalized on popular dissatisfaction with Lincoln's leadership to become a formidable force in northern society.

LINCOLN THE TYRANT

The Peace Democrats jumped on Lincoln's suspension of the writ of habeas corpus as proof that the president was a tyrant undeserving of popular support. Although the Constitution did allow the government to suspend the writ in times of national crisis, it had always been assumed that the power rested with Congress. Lincoln, however, acted without prior consent from Congress. This gave rise to the notion that Lincoln, like Jackson before him, was a dangerous tyrant, ready to sacrifice liberties in order to exercise and expand his own power. The still-active partisan presses utilized this image widely throughout the war.

THE DRAFT

Even more than suspension of habeas corpus, the draft became an important symbol of Lincoln's supposedly dictatorial ways among Peace Democrats. Conscription seemed to contradict America's commitment to individual freedom. In addition, the 1863 draft law seemed

>> The 7th New York Regiment firing into a crowd of draft rioters who refused to go to war. It took four days to restore order, and more than one hundred people were killed. Not all Northerners, then, supported the war.

unfair to poor men, who, unlike the wealthy, could not afford to buy their way out of fighting.

THE NEW YORK DRAFT RIOT

This inequity generated violence as well as political opposition. In July 1863, when the first national draft was about to be held in New York City, Democratic working men, most of them Irish, rampaged through the streets and shut down the draft office. They attacked anyone who was rich or known as a pro-war Republican. The rioters also expressed hostility to the idea of fighting to free slaves, and in the 1863 riot they acted most violently toward black people, who had recently been used to replace Irish longshoremen during a labor strike. It took four days before order was finally restored, and by then, more than one hundred people had been killed. This was the largest loss of life caused by any civilian riot in American history up to that point.

15-4b Dissent in the South

The South faced its own problems on the home front.

ECONOMIC WOES

The prospect of a long war had put the Confederate economy in desperate straits by 1863. With the institution of slavery disintegrating (as explained in the following pages), the women and men who remained on the southern home front were unable to maintain sufficient production of corn, grain, and other foodstuffs. The shortages caused the price of food to skyrocket. Manufactured goods also became scarce as the Union blockade of the Confederacy cut off the region from European suppliers. Merchants made matters worse by hoarding goods, which also drove prices up.

RIOTS

In this economy, the average southerner could not afford basic necessities. High prices and food shortages provoked riots throughout the Confederacy in 1863. In April, in the Confederate capital of Richmond, three hundred women and children took to the streets armed with knives and pistols, broke into stores, and stole items they needed but could not afford.

In the face of months of scarcity and starvation, many women on the Confederate home front started to lose their will to sacrifice for independence. Jefferson Davis and the other leaders of the Confederate States of America were ineffective in sustaining popular morale. This was not due to their personal qualities, but principally because the South's poor transportation networks, never fully developed during the Market Revolution, hindered leaders from making rallying trips across the land. In addition to this inability to communicate with its citizens, the government did little to alleviate economic hardships. Focusing solely on the military problem of keeping the Union armies at bay, Davis made no attempt to provide his constituents with government assistance. Davis's wartime policies—cracking down on dissent, conscription, and impressments—only increased popular dissatisfaction. As in the North by 1863, there was a full-blown peace faction in the South working to undermine Davis's leadership.

By the midpoint of the war, both the Union and the Confederacy had become bitterly divided societies.

>> An engraving entitled "Sowing and Reaping" depicts southern women persuading their husbands to join in the rebellion (left) and the same women rioting for bread during the hard times of the war (right). As in the North, there was considerable dissent in the South as well.

15-5 THE TIDE OF BATTLE TURNS, 1863–1865

Wars continue despite dissent, of course. During the Civil War, men fought brutal battles, combining ancient methods of fighting (using sabers and knives) with modern warfare (using long-range rifles, cannons, and other instruments that could kill opponents without ever having to see them up close). The conflict deepened, and by 1863 the war had turned from a "limited war" focused on military struggles to an all-encompassing one that affected the entirety of both societies.

One key example of the broadening of the meaning of the war concerned slavery. As Lincoln struggled to keep up morale in the North, he by necessity performed a delicate political dance on the subject of slavery. But he knew that eliminating slavery would be a definitive move toward challenging the very existence of southern society.

15-5a Slavery and Emancipation

Lincoln had made no immediate move to end slavery; he understood that in 1861 most northerners did not support broad emancipation. Northern people generally agreed that slavery was an evil institution, but they also balked at the thought of creating a large, free black population in the United States.

Lincoln also feared that immediate emancipation would alienate the four border states that remained within the Union. Missouri, Kentucky, Maryland, and Delaware all retained slavery but still sought to preserve the Union. In order to defeat the Confederacy, Lincoln knew he needed to keep those states relatively happy, something emancipation would undoubtedly jeopardize. Therefore, as part of the Union's early "limited war" strategy, U.S. soldiers were initially instructed to leave southern slave property alone and return any escaped slaves who tried to hide behind Union lines.

OVERTURES TO EMANCIPATION

As the war dragged on, however, Union practice gradually deviated from this policy. The South depended on its slaves to provide food and manual labor for the war effort, so in May 1861, General Benjamin Butler of Massachusetts began the practice of treating runaway slaves as **contraband** (smuggled goods), refusing to return them to their owners. Then, in August 1861, Congress passed its first **Confiscation Act**, which officially declared that any slaves used for military purposes would be freed if they came into Union hands.

Congress also freed the 2,000 slaves living in the nation's capital, providing compensation to their owners. At the same time, it banned slavery from all U.S. territories, officially putting an end to the issue of the expansion of slavery that had aroused sectional tensions in the 1840s and 1850s. And in July 1862 Congress passed the Second

> **contraband** Smuggled goods; during the Civil War, it also referred to runaway slaves who had fled to the Union Army
>
> **Confiscation Act** Legislation that officially declared that any slaves used for military purposes would be freed if they came into Union hands

Confiscation Act, which stated that all slaves owned by rebel masters (not just those being used for military purposes) would be set free if they fell under Union control. With southerners absent from Congress, northern Republicans were making rapid strides toward eliminating slavery in the United States and southerners, now ostensibly in their own nation, could do nothing to stop it.

Although Lincoln signed the Second Confiscation Act, he generally ignored it. Lincoln wanted the slave states to choose emancipation, not to have it forced upon them. After the Second Confiscation Act became law, Lincoln summoned to the White House representatives from the border states of Missouri, Kentucky, Maryland, and Delaware and presented them with a plan to free their slaves. Unfortunately, the border states resisted any suggestion that they end the practice of slavery.

DECIDING ON EMANCIPATION

With few states eager to take the lead on the issue, Lincoln ultimately decided to initiate an emancipation policy himself, explicitly making slavery the central issue of the war. On July 22, 1862, Lincoln told his cabinet that he planned to issue a presidential proclamation freeing at least some of the slaves. Emancipation carried clear military benefits, he argued. For one thing, it would weaken the Confederacy by depriving southerners of slave labor. In addition, emancipation would earn moral support from the rest of the free world, making it difficult for nations such as Britain and France to ally with the Confederacy.

Taking the advice of his secretary of state, William H. Seward, Lincoln waited for a Union military victory before announcing his proclamation, in order to appear to speak from a position of strength, not desperation. Lincoln got his chance after the Battle of Antietam (Battle of Sharpsburg) on September 17, 1862, when the Union's Army of the Potomac forced Lee's Army of Northern Virginia to retreat from Union territory in Maryland back into the Confederacy. It was a major battle of the war, the single bloodiest day-battle in American history. The Union troops had done well at sea and in the West, but only after Antietam did they begin to get the upper hand in the vital lands of Virginia, Maryland, and Pennsylvania.

THE EMANCIPATION PROCLAMATION

Five days after the Battle of Antietam, on September 22, 1862, Lincoln made his preliminary Emancipation Proclamation, which declared that all slaves within rebel territory would be freed on January 1, 1863, unless the southern states returned to the Union. To make the proclamation more palatable to white northerners, Lincoln justified it by saying he had given the order out of military necessity. Emancipation would weaken the Confederacy, he argued, and as commander-in-chief, he was obliged to initiate and enforce such policies. In addition, it would not free a single slave in the slave states that were already part of the Union (thus keeping the Union's four slave states happy). When the southern states predictably failed to return to the Union as requested, Lincoln issued the formal Emancipation Proclamation on January 1, 1863. The North no longer fought for the reconstruction of the old Union. Instead it was seeking the creation of a new Union, one without slavery.

Although undeniably bold, the proclamation was far from a comprehensive plan for emancipation. Lincoln of course exempted Missouri, Kentucky, Maryland, and Delaware (the border states), as well as Tennessee and areas of Virginia and Louisiana that were already under Union occupation. Only areas actively engaged in rebellion were affected. Moreover, those places where the proclamation was intended to free slaves were precisely those places where the Union lacked the power to enforce its policies.

Library of Congress Prints and Photographs Division

>> Many African Americans were proud to fight for the Union cause—and for abolition. By the end of the war, more than 180,000 had, including this unidentified soldier with his wife and two daughters.

A FACTOR IN THE END OF SLAVERY, BUT NOT *THE* FACTOR

Even before Lincoln issued the Emancipation Proclamation, however, slavery was disintegrating, as the dislocations of war made it impossible for southerners to maintain control over their slaves. As more southern men left their farms to enter the army, slaves took more and more liberties and, in some cases, openly challenged white authority. They shirked work, and attempts to impose discipline only made them more defiant. When word spread that the Union Army was nearby, thousands of slaves would run away and attempt to take refuge behind Union lines.

Lincoln's proclamation thus did not end slavery; slaves themselves ended slavery—with the vital help of the Union Army. But the proclamation emboldened slaves to increase their resistance, and it offered hope that, if the Union won the war, slavery would be outlawed.

BLACK AMERICANS IN THE UNION MILITARY

The Emancipation Proclamation did something else as well. Black Americans had been trying to volunteer for service in the Union Army all along, but, afraid of the effect on white soldiers' morale, Lincoln rejected them. This changed with the Emancipation Proclamation, which included an announcement that black Americans would be accepted into the U.S. Army and Navy. During the next two years, 180,000 black men, up to 80 percent of them runaway slaves, joined the Union military. They faced difficult conditions, however, serving in segregated units headed by white officers and receiving only half the compensation paid to white soldiers. Despite the prejudicial treatment, the Union's black soldiers signed up readily, and, in June 1864, Lincoln persuaded Congress to grant them equal pay retroactively. By the end of the conflict, 37,000 black servicemen had lost their lives in the battle for the Union. Some historians contend that in the bitterly divided contest, African American soldiers were decisive in tilting the war in the Union's favor.

THE FORT PILLOW MASSACRE

Confederate soldiers resented the presence of African American troops in the U.S. Army. In one controversial incident, after a Confederate victory in the Battle of Fort Pillow, Tennessee, on April 12, 1864, Confederate soldiers, led by Major General Nathan Bedford Forrest (later the first leader of the Ku Klux Klan), massacred most of an African American regiment who may have been attempting to surrender. The interracial Union troops suffered defeat in the battle, and some witnesses said the Union troops were attempting to surrender when Confederate troops opened fire. Only about 20 percent of the black soldiers were taken as prisoners, while 60 percent of white soldiers were. The rest were casualties of war. The Fort Pillow Massacre became a rallying cry in the North at a pivotal time in the war.

CRITICISM OF LINCOLN'S PROCLAMATION

Although Lincoln's fellow Republicans generally supported the Emancipation Proclamation, many other northerners criticized it. Predictably, northern Democrats lambasted the proclamation as an act of tyranny. As they saw it, the government had no right to deprive anyone of his property. Moreover, the proclamation suggested that Republicans might actually allow black Americans to exist on a level of equality with white people in America. Given the depths of racism in the United States, the proclamation was hard for many northerners to accept, especially northern Democrats.

15-5b Union Military Triumphs

In 1863 and 1864, while both Union and Confederacy dealt with rising dissent and the expansion of their governments, the Union military won a number of important victories. Along with Antietam, the other key turning point was Gettysburg.

> "All that I had ever read in battle stories of the booming of heavy guns out-thundering the thunders of heaven and making the earth tremble, and almost stopping one's breath from the concussions of the air—was here made real, in terrific effect."
>
> —FROM "THE REMINISCENCES OF CARL SCHURZ," GENERAL AT GETTYSBURG

> "With malice toward none; with charity for all; with firmness in the right, as God gives us to see the right, let us strive on to finish the work we are in."
>
> —ABRAHAM LINCOLN,
> SECOND INAUGURAL ADDRESS

LEE'S HOPES

Before Gettysburg, Confederate forces under Robert E. Lee had won impressive victories at Fredericksburg, Virginia, in December 1862 and at nearby Chancellorsville in May 1863. With the momentum from these victories, Lee made a decisive gesture and invaded the North with 75,000 troops. By invading the North, Lee (1) sought to allow the southern soil time to recuperate from months of battle; (2) was hoping that, strategically, a major victory in the North would buttress the Union's peace movement and force Lincoln to accept Confederate terms for peace; and (3) thought a major victory in the North would also compel the British to reconsider recognition of the Confederacy, thus giving the Confederacy a valuable partner in the war.

GETTYSBURG

Despite Lee's intention of waging a northern battle in a major city, circumstances conspired to force a showdown at the small town of Gettysburg, Pennsylvania. Lee's Army of Northern Virginia had invaded Pennsylvania and had come close to taking Harrisburg, the state's capital. The Union's Army of the Potomac, however, now led by General George Gordon Meade, set off to chase Lee, ultimately confronting him in Gettysburg. The battle that ensued was one of the epic battles of the Civil War, and many historians consider it the turning point.

Engagement was vicious and bloody. After two days of trying unsuccessfully to break the Union line, Lee made an ill-fated move on July 3. In an attempt to split the Union forces, he sent about 12,500 men in a charge into the well-entrenched center of the Union line. This attack is known as Pickett's Charge because General George Pickett was one of the three division commanders leading it.

It was a disastrous move. Nearly two-thirds of the attacking Confederates were killed, wounded, or captured during the assault, and the Union took the victory. All told, Lee lost roughly 28,000 soldiers at Gettysburg (approximately one-third of his army) and never again had the manpower to go on the offensive. The federal losses numbered about 23,000, but the Union's great advantage in manpower made such losses tactically easier to overcome than for the South. Indeed, in his Gettysburg Address, Lincoln memorably used the battle to motivate his side to continue the struggle under the belief that what they were doing was right, destined to give the nation a "new birth of freedom."

VICTORIES IN THE WEST

Meanwhile, Union general Ulysses S. Grant continued to triumph in the West. On July 4, 1863, after a six-week siege, his troops forced the fortress town of Vicksburg, Mississippi, to surrender. Five days later, he captured Port Hudson in Louisiana. With those two victories, the Union controlled the entire Mississippi River, severing the Confederacy into eastern and western halves. The battle at Gettysburg received more public notice at the time, but Grant's victories on the Mississippi were perhaps more strategically important.

In light of Grant's success, Lincoln brought him east in March 1864 and made him commander of all the Union armies. From his new post, Grant prepared for an offensive against Lee in Virginia, while General William Tecumseh Sherman took over for Grant in the West.

NORTHERN MOMENTUM?

While northern momentum was strong, the Union again faced the strategic problem of having to completely subdue and conquer its enemy in order to win. In May and June 1864, Grant relentlessly pursued Lee's army in a bloody campaign from the Rappahannock River to the city of Petersburg, south of Richmond, Virginia. Outside Petersburg, the two armies settled into opposing trenches. The siege there lasted more than nine months. Between May and July 1864, Grant lost 60,000 men, and news of these heavy casualties demoralized the northern home front. Northerners began to fear that the Union armies could never fully defeat the Confederacy. Despite northern military momentum, was it possible to win a war when the opposition never had to attack?

15-5c The Election of 1864

In this atmosphere of uncertainty, the Union continued its pattern of predictable, regular elections as laid out in the Constitution and held a presidential contest. As the war stretched on, the impatience of the northern people during the summer of 1864 did not bode well for Lincoln. But, more than this, the election became a referendum on slavery and Lincoln's Emancipation Proclamation. Did they want four more years of Abraham Lincoln and, potentially, of civil war?

McCLELLAN

In 1864, Lincoln's Democratic opponent was none other than the overly cautious George B. McClellan, the former general of the Army of the Potomac. If elected, McClellan promised to restore slavery in the South and negotiate peace with the Confederacy (perhaps leading to the recognition of Confederate independence). His party's slogan was "The Union as it was, the Constitution as it is, and the Negroes where they are." After three years of war, northerners were despairing of the casualties and fearful of the outcome, and even Lincoln did not believe he would be voted into office for a second term. The struggle to bring the southern states back into the union while accepting the end of slavery seemed to require too much effort.

TIMELY MILITARY VICTORIES

The Union military, however, saved the day for Lincoln. On August 5, 1864, the Union captured Mobile Bay in Alabama, and less than one month later, Sherman took control of Atlanta. After months of stagnation, the momentum had swung fully to the Union. These victories heartened northern voters and gave them a renewed sense that the Confederacy could be beaten, and soon. On Election Day in November, Lincoln received 55 percent of the popular vote, giving him a landslide victory in the Electoral College.

15-6 THE DESTRUCTION OF THE SOUTH AND THE END OF THE WAR

With the tide of battle now fully turned and Lincoln reelected, the North sought to punish the South for what it had done to provoke this awful war.

The Art Archive at Art Resource, NY

>> Richmond in ruins, 1865. The Union had sought revenge for the awful war by destroying the southern infrastructure, as symbolized in this photograph of two war widows walking past the utterly destroyed ruins of Richmond, Virginia.

15-6a The Destruction of the South

General Sherman led the way. From November 15 to December 21, 1864, Sherman waged his famous **"March to the Sea,"** mowing a path of destruction 60 miles wide and several hundred miles long through Georgia. The March to the Sea stretched from Atlanta to the Atlantic. Sherman designed the move to encircle Lee's army, which was still in Virginia, and, more importantly, to prove to the southern people that the Confederate government lacked the ability to protect them. The soldiers burned fields, tore up vital infrastructure such as railroad ties, and killed and consumed all the livestock they encountered. By Christmas 1864, Sherman's soldiers had reached Savannah. As much as the Union soldiers relished this punishment of the rebels, they relished even more the prospect of moving north and destroying South Carolina, the birthplace of the Civil War. After hitting the coast, Sherman's troops continued their march through South and North

"March to the Sea" Path of destruction led by General William Tecumseh Sherman in late 1864; the March was 60 miles wide and several hundred miles long, from Atlanta to the Atlantic; Sherman's army pillaged all it encountered

Carolina, heading north to join forces with Grant in Virginia, an act that would encircle Lee's Army of Northern Virginia and end the war once and for all.

Sherman's March showed how much the war had changed since 1861. Having started with a strategy of limited war, intending to fight only against soldiers and leaving private property alone, by 1864 the Union was fighting a total war, one that affected all aspects of society, military and civilian, destroying railroads, bridges, cotton gins, and anything else that the rebels could plausibly use to support their war effort.

15-6b The Thirteenth Amendment Abolishes Slavery

Meanwhile, Lincoln sought to do politically what Sherman was doing militarily. In late 1864 and early 1865, Lincoln used all of the influence he had in Congress to ensure the passage of a constitutional amendment freeing all the slaves in the United States without compensating their owners. On January 31, 1865, Congress passed the Thirteenth Amendment, and by the end of the year, enough Union states had ratified the amendment to make it part of the Constitution, abolishing slavery from the United States forever.

THE SOUTH'S WILL TO FIGHT

The Confederacy's ravaged economy, the demoralization of its home front, and the dangers of the Union Army all combined to erode the southern people's will to fight. By the spring of 1865, more than half of Confederate soldiers had deserted. Meanwhile, Grant tenaciously attacked the Army of Northern Virginia, knowing that

when Lee surrendered, the South would be forced to give up entirely. Lee finally capitulated on April 9, 1865, at Appomattox Courthouse, Virginia. Although there was sporadic fighting in the West until the end of May, with Lee's surrender the war was effectively over. For the reasons why the North won the Civil War, see "The Reasons Why . . .".

 ## SIGNIFICANCE OF THE WAR

The four years of civil war were brutal for both the North and the South. One out of every twelve American men served in the war, and about 620,000 American men lost their lives, more Americans than were killed in World War I, World War II, the Vietnam War, and the Revolutionary War combined. For the Confederacy, of the roughly 1 million soldiers that fought, about 258,000 died from disease or battle. For the Union, its army of about 2,500,000 men lost around 360,000 men. In addition, for every 1,000 Union soldiers in battle, 112 were wounded. For every 1,000 Confederate soldiers, 150 suffered casualties. Of the 180,000 African American soldiers who fought, approximately one-third lost their lives. It was a brutal war indeed.

Beyond the grim number of dead, the American nation had turned into a battlefield. The various militaries had commandeered roads, pulled up enemy train tracks, destroyed factories, and killed livestock. The South bore the brunt of this destruction, but the entire nation felt the impact of the war. And there was more than just physical destruction. More than 4,000,000 men mobilized for war, meaning a major disruption of life back home. Labor relations had to be reworked and familial roles renegotiated. The large number of wartime dead also meant these transitions were often not temporary. With so many marriageable men deceased, for example, many young women had difficulty finding husbands. Some became teachers or went west or helped in the monumental effort to rebuild the nation after the war. And for the soldiers who did make it home, roughly 50,000 returned with one or more limbs amputated, physical reminders of the devastations of war.

Beyond this grim departure from daily life, the Civil War had at least six other long-lasting results.

15-7a The Impact on Federal Government

First, fighting its first modern war greatly increased the size and the power of the federal government. While this occurred in both the North and, ironically, the South, it was the North's expansion that set the course for the nation after the war.

To pay for the war, for instance, the federal government began, for the first time, to collect an income tax, targeting especially the wealthiest Americans (particularly those who earned more than $600). This brought the federal government into American lives in a whole new way. Rather than be charged a tax for goods purchased or imported, now some Americans had a tax placed on their annual income. Meanwhile, the federal government consolidated the nation's money supply, ending the era of wildcat banking begun by Andrew Jackson. During the Civil War, the federal government became the sole issuer of paper money, solidifying its importance in the financial future of the nation and extending its reach throughout the various regions. The federal government also expanded its budget twenty-fold between 1860 and 1865, with the 1865 national budget exceeding $1 billion for the first time in the nation's history. It took an army of clerks and tax collectors to manage this new endeavor, and by 1865 the federal government was the nation's largest employer. With the Civil War, the federal government possessed greater power than ever before and had a much larger bureaucracy to manage that newfound power.

In addition, with no southerners in the wartime Congress, Lincoln's Republicans passed a series of laws furthering the reach of the national government. For instance, to spur agricultural growth and to populate the West with free laborers, Congress in 1862 passed the Homestead Act, which offered 160 acres of free public land to any settler (including slaves) who had never taken up arms against the federal government and who lived on the land for five years. In 1862, Congress passed the Morrill Land Grant College Act, which gave states free federal land if they promised to develop colleges for the state's residents. The federal government also made huge land grants for internal improvements, including, most famously, giving 100 million acres to the Union Pacific and Central Pacific Railroads to build a railroad that stretched to the Pacific Ocean. (Each of these developments will be discussed more fully in Chapter 17.) The federal government thus increased its power during the Civil War, and it used this new power to shape the nation in a free-labor vision. The West would no longer be contested terrain. It would be filled with landowning farmers who could educate their children at local universities and take transcontinental railroads to get from one coast to another, all subsidized by the newly expanded federal government.

>> During the Civil War, women took on many new roles, including becoming professional nurses. Clara Barton was one of the most famous, going on to found the American Red Cross.

15-7b The Impact on Industry

But it was not entirely the free-labor vision that rose triumphant after the war. Rather, several leading manufacturers used the generosity of the federal government to create a vast industrial nation. Relying on profitable government contracts, several "captains of industry" consolidated their wealth during the Civil War, thus gaining a platform upon which they would plunge the nation into the Industrial Age of the late nineteenth century. Philip D. Armour, for instance, earned millions of dollars supplying meat to the Union Army during the war, using the exigencies of war to perfect the refrigerated railcar. He would become a major industrial magnate in the years after the war. Other industrial leaders, including steel baron Andrew Carnegie, oil magnate John D. Rockefeller, and financier J. P. Morgan, used the war to increase and consolidate their wealth, which allowed them to reshape the economy in the following decades. (These men too will be discussed more fully in Chapter 17.) The Civil War thus helped catapult the nation into the Industrial Age, allowing it to become one of the world's industrial powers.

15-7c The Impact on American Nationalism

Somewhat ironically, the war also unified the nation, pulling together the various states to form a more unified country. It is commonplace to say that before the war, the country was called the United *States* of America and after the war it was the *United* States of America. With a stronger federal government serving as a yoke to keep the nation together, the Civil War, like most wars, served as a centripetal force, shifting people's identities from one associated with a particular state to one associated more fully with the nation. The expansion of the federal government only secured a deeper movement toward national identity and American nationalism.

15-7d The Impact on Women

The Civil War also greatly impacted women, both in the work they did and in the way they were viewed within democratic society. Some four hundred women disguised themselves as men and fought during the Civil War. Many more worked with the various armies, serving as spies, cooks, and medical assistants. In addition to these battlefront contributions, the Civil War loosened up other opportunities for women. With millions of men off to fight, some never to return, women in both the North and the South took jobs that traditionally had been defined as male work. Women worked in munitions plants, as clerks in government offices, and as a sales force in retail businesses. While some of these gains were temporary (such as in munitions plants), others were not (such as in retail).

Women also revolutionized the nursing profession during the Civil War, a profession that had been dominated by men. In the North alone, more than 20,000 women served as nurses. Clara Barton was perhaps the most famous Civil War nurse, following troops into battle and working alongside doctors in makeshift battlefront hospitals. She once had a stray bullet go through her sleeve, killing the patient she was working on. After the war, Barton went on to found the American Red Cross.

Thousands of women in the North also served in the United States Sanitary Commission, the primary national relief organization, coordinating donations to the Union cause. While the national organization remained headed by men, women served as grassroots leaders, contributing directly to the ailing communities that were suffering from the departure of millions of working-age men, and emerging as community leaders.

Eon Images

>> During the Civil War, women not only moved into many new professions, but also served as spies, informers, and scouts. One Confederate spy, Antonia Ford, hid secrets in her hoop skirt after Union soldiers occupied her family's Virginia home. She was later imprisoned for espionage.

At a more political level, while the war temporarily stalled the nascent women's suffrage movement, women's increased role in public life, especially in the North, provoked many women to announce that they would fight for access to the ballot once the war stopped. Fulfilling their promise, several leaders of the late-nineteenth-century women's suffrage movement claimed to have been both inspired by their wartime efforts and frustrated by the traditional roles ascribed to them after the war.

15-7e The Impact on Religion

The war also changed the way people prayed, what denominations they belonged to, and how they viewed the Bible. Indeed, leading up to the Civil War, several large Protestant denominations split over the issue of slavery. Although the Bible clearly upholds the right to own slaves, several Protestant churches disagreed as to whether or not this was justifiable nearly 2,000 years after the life and death of Jesus. Even more problematic, they disagreed about whether or not religious denominations had any right to enter into political debates without debasing their faith. Divisions over these questions led Presbyterians, Methodists, and Baptists to split along northern and southern lines in 1837, 1844, and 1845, respectively. These divisions foreshadowed the larger political split that was to come with the Civil War. Indeed, because the words of ministers often served as moral guidance for the rest of society, by placing the question of slavery in biblical terms church leaders made the sectional split appear cosmic in nature, demanding decisive, even destructive action. While Lincoln continually took a humble approach toward faith and the question of which side, North or South, God was on, both sides often claimed to be fighting for the righteousness of the Lord. As one piece of evidence, the Civil War served to standardize the role and functions of military chaplains.

These divisions in turn foreshadowed a split that developed after the Civil War. Throughout the late nineteenth century, many northerners usually advanced a more liberal interpretation of the Bible, finding the institution of slavery to be vile and contrary to the spirit of the New Testament, thus placing great importance, they argued, on the spirit of the Bible rather than the literal words. Southerners, on the other hand, held onto a more literal interpretation of the Bible, which clearly accepted the practice of slavery. This split between liberal Protestants and their more conservative counterparts would only grow during the course of the nineteenth century, with one historian describing these years as the formative years of what has come to be called "the Bible Belt" in the South.

For African Americans, the war was also religiously transformative. Hundreds of new churches opened up throughout the South, often with the help of northern missionaries. Utilizing their new status as freed people, African Americans eagerly filled the pews.

For Jews, who numbered around 150,000 in the United States, the Civil War exposed a deep vein of anti-semitism in American life. Although about 10,000 Jews served in the war effort (on both sides) and many served in leadership roles (Judah P. Benjamin was secretary of state for the Confederacy), Jews were often used as scapegoats to explain the economic hard times many Americans experienced during the war. For instance, General Ulysses S. Grant expelled Jews from the areas of western Tennessee that were under his command. Although Lincoln quickly rescinded the order, Jews were nonetheless still expelled from several towns.

For Catholics, the vast majority of whom were recent Irish immigrants living in northern cities, the war provided an opportunity to assert themselves as Americans. Roughly 145,000 Irish Catholics served in the Union Army, and, while bishops preached a militant Catholicism that combated the varieties of nativism they had experienced since their arrival, in the battlefield Catholic leaders sought to ensure that Catholics fought bravely and acted responsibly. They often did. On the home front, though, many Catholics resisted the intrusions into their daily life by a federal government that had at times been overtly anti-Catholic. It was, for example, mostly Irish Catholics that formed the mobs of the 1863 New York City Draft Riots.

15-7f The Impact on Philosophy

While many northerners were accommodating themselves to a looser, nonliteral understanding of the Bible, still others grew disillusioned with any hard and fixed ideas. The passions invoked during the Civil War had led to violence, something democratic nations were not supposed to do. Thus the war discredited the beliefs and assumptions of the era that came before it, and there were very few guiding ideas to replace them. Oliver Wendell Holmes, Jr., and William James would use this disillusionment to fashion, after the war, a new philosophy called pragmatism. Pragmatism holds that ideas are not out in nature waiting to be discovered by smart people, but rather are tools, like shovels and hammers, to be used by people to cope with the world in which they live. This is not to say pragmatism allows someone to grasp on to any convenient truth available, but rather that humans should be open to new "truths" that might emerge, evaluating them in conjunction with their previously held beliefs. With this kind of flexibility, pragmatism's founders intended to create a worldview that made it harder for a nation to succumb to violence. Pragmatism, one of America's most important contributions to the world of philosophy, would be the predominant worldview in the United States until the middle of the twentieth century.

>LOOKING AHEAD...

Despite the reunification of the Union and the Confederacy after the war, exactly how northerners and southerners would come to live together again remained unclear. Reconstructing the nation would be a difficult process full of conflict and disappointment, and that story of frustration and success is the subject of the next chapter.

STUDY TOOLS 15

READY TO STUDY? IN THE BOOK, YOU CAN:

❏ Rip out the Chapter Review Card, which includes key terms and chapter summaries.

ONLINE AT WWW.CENGAGEBRAIN.COM, YOU CAN:

❏ Collect StudyBits while you read and study the chapter.

❏ Quiz yourself on key concepts.

❏ Find videos for further exploration.

❏ Prepare for tests with HIST5 Flash Cards as well as those you create.

❏ *Read a southern author's justification for southern independence, written in 1861.*

❏ *Learn more about the Battle of Manassas.*

❏ *Read about life in the armies of the Civil War.*

❏ *Read Lincoln's proclamation suspending habeas corpus.*

❏ *Read the Second Confiscation Act.*

❏ *Learn more about the Emancipation Proclamation.*

❏ *Read the Emancipation Proclamation.*

❏ *Take a virtual tour of the draft riots.*

❏ *Read Lincoln's Gettysburg Address.*

❏ *Read excerpts from Mary Boykin Chesnut's wartime diary from the South.*

❏ *Read the report from the congressional committee investigating Fort Pillow.*

❏ *Read Lincoln's remarkable Second Inaugural Address.*

CH15 TIMELINE

What Else Was Happening

▶ 1861

April: Lincoln orders blockade of southern coastline.

July 21: Battle of Bull Run (also known as the Battle of Manassas) in Virginia shatters hopes for an easy war.

August: First Confiscation Act frees captured slaves employed in military service.

1862

March: First battle of ironclads signals changes in military technology.

April: Union wins Battle of Shiloh, which exceeds all American casualties in history.

April: Confederate Congress implements draft.

June–July: Excessive caution at Richmond costs Army of the Potomac dearly.

July: Second Confiscation Act frees all slaves owned by rebel masters.

August 29: Lee defeats Union at Second Battle of Bull Run.

September 17: Union Army forces Confederacy back after Battle of Antietam.

September 22: Lincoln's Emancipation Proclamation declares freedom for rebels' slaves.

Serfdom is abolished in Russia.

Congress creates Internal Revenue Service.

The first black troops are used in battle, at Island Mount, Missouri.

The French go to war with Mexico after Mexican president Benito Juarez suspends interest payments to foreign countries. Mexican victory comes five years later, but the 1862 Battle of Puebla, an early Mexican victory, is now commemorated as Cinco de Mayo.

1863

July: Mostly Irish Democratic workingmen riot in New York over national draft.

July 3: Lee's army suffers devastating defeat at Gettysburg.

July 4: Union general Grant forces surrender of Vicksburg, Mississippi.

Former Union nurse Louisa May Alcott (author of *Little Women*) publishes a collection of wartime letters, "Hospital Sketches." During the Civil War women enter the male-dominated profession of nursing in huge numbers.

1864

April 12: Confederates kill surrendering black regiment in Fort Pillow Massacre.

June: Lincoln persuades Congress to grant black servicemen equal pay.

November 5: Military victories restore faith in Lincoln, who soundly defeats opponent for presidency.

The H. L. Hunley, a Confederate submarine, is the first sub to sink an enemy ship. It sinks the USS Housatonic on February 17, only to find itself sinking that same night.

Photograph of Lincoln is taken that appears on today's five-dollar bill.

1865

January 31: Congress passes Thirteenth Amendment abolishing slavery.

April 9: General Lee surrenders at Appomattox Courthouse.

16 | Reconstruction, 1865–1877

LEARNING OBJECTIVES

After reading this chapter, you should be able to do the following:

16-1 Describe the changed world of ex-slaves after the Civil War.

16-2 Outline the different phases of Reconstruction, beginning with Lincoln's plan and moving through presidential Reconstruction to Congressional Reconstruction.

16-3 Explain how Reconstruction evolved at the individual states' level.

16-4 Evaluate and understand the relative success and failures of Reconstruction.

AFTER FINISHING THIS CHAPTER GO TO **PAGE 306** **FOR STUDY TOOLS**

Confederate soldiers returned home to a devastated South in 1865. While northern trains and cities began to hum with activity, the South's farms and factories, its railroads and bridges—almost its entire infrastructure—had been destroyed by war. Nearly 23 percent of the South's fighting-age men had died in the war. Thousands more bore the physical scars of battle. The physical rebuilding of the region began quickly and progressed rapidly, but reconstructing southern society was a much more difficult process, especially considering (1) the political questions about how to integrate rebel states back into the nation and (2) the social questions about how to integrate 4 million newly freed slaves.

The North was also vastly changed, albeit in another way. Northern politicians seized the opportunity to pass many of the laws that southerners in Congress had long resisted. During and shortly after the war, Congress passed laws supporting internal improvements, outlawing slavery, and expanding the developments of the Market Revolution. Indeed, some historians argue that the Civil War was crucial in turning the Market Revolution of the 1830s, 1840s, and 1850s into the Industrial Revolution of the second half of the nineteenth century. Regardless of the term you use, the North after the Civil War was beginning to resemble what we think of today as a modern industrial society.

But, first, to the era of **Reconstruction**, defined as the country's various attempts to resolve the issues that remained after the Civil War, including: how free could former slaves be in the ex-Confederacy; how could the country re-incorporate the states that had voted to leave; and would the country undertake the dramatic transformations necessary to overturn two hundred years of slavery?

16-1 FREEDMEN, FREEDWOMEN

After the Civil War, black Americans encountered a new world of opportunities. After years of enslavement, or at least the perpetual threat of enslavement if they had been already freed, African Americans confronted a new question: what does it mean to be free? After the passage in 1865 of the Thirteenth Amendment outlawing slavery throughout the land forever, black Americans had to wonder: what does one do after the bonds of slavery have been broken?

The first thing many freed people did was move. They often left the plantations upon which they had labored as slaves, typically to put some distance between them and their former owners. They also moved in search of long-lost family members who had perhaps been sold to another owner during an era when the stability of slave families was always secondary to profits. The freedom of movement was the key.

This new mobility meant that black family life began to stabilize throughout the South. Men and women now had more control over their lives and their familial roles. Reflecting the priorities of nineteenth-century American society, ex-slaves often removed women from the fields so that they could occupy a "women's sphere of domesticity." Most black women still had to work for financial reasons, but they often began working as indoor domestics rather than field hands.

Meanwhile, freed families often desperately sought to purchase land in order to continue the planting life they knew best, sometimes by simply purchasing a piece of the land on which they had labored before the Civil War. In their new communities, African Americans also expressed their religious independence by expanding the independent network of black churches that had been established since the Revolution. During Reconstruction, the number of black churches grew exponentially.

The newly freed people also sought the education that had been denied them during slavery. Schools for African Americans opened all over the South, for parents and for children. Learning to read meant learning to understand contracts, engage in political battles, and monitor wages, new experiences for those who had only recently been deemed chattel.

Politically, African Americans sought to vote. They marched in demand of it. They paraded to advocate bills

Reconstruction The federal government's attempts to resolve the issues resulting from the end of the Civil War in order to reconstitute the nation

◄◄◄ **The process of reconstructing the nation after four years of civil war was long and exhausting, so long in fact that it may have even allowed the South to lose the war but win the peace. Here, new laws are explained at the office of the Freedman's Bureau in Memphis, Tennessee.**

endorsing it. They lionized black Revolutionary heroes in order to establish their credentials as vote-casting Americans. And they held mock elections to show their capacity and desire to participate in the American political process. Life for the newly freed was tumultuous but exciting, filled with possibilities.

16-1a The Freedmen's Bureau

While ex-slaves explored a life based on the free-labor vision, members of the defeated Confederacy sought to maintain as much of the old order as possible. To this end, they worked to prevent ex-slaves from acquiring economic autonomy or political rights. Although they had lost the war, ex-Confederates feared a complete turnover from the lives they had led before it. Indeed, one of the first organizations created after the war in the South was the **Ku Klux Klan**, founded in 1865 by six white Confederate soldiers concerned about the racial implications of black freedom. The Klan and

>> **What it means to be free** | After the Civil War, freedom was an expansive concept for African Americans in the South. They demonstrated this new freedom in numerous ways, large and small: many bought dogs and married, some purchased firearms, and several held mass meetings without white supervision. These were all actions often denied them under slavery. Pictured here is a group of "freedmen" in Richmond, Virginia circa 1865.

Library of Congress Prints and Photographs Division[LC-DIG-cwpb-00468]

other similar organizations, such as the Southern Cross and the Knights of White Camellia, served as quasi-military forces serving the interests of those who desired the restoration of white supremacy. Nathan Bedford Forrest, a Confederate general, was the Klan's first national leader.

To help mitigate this resistance, in 1865, Congress established the **Freedmen's Bureau**, a government agency designed to create a new social order by government mandate. Under the management of northerner O.O. Howard (after whom Howard University is named), Congress designed the Freedmen's Bureau to build and manage new schools, provide food and medical care to needy southern black and white people, and ensure equal access to the judicial system for southerners both black and white. It had some success with this Herculean task: the Freedmen's Bureau built 3,000 schools and expanded medical care throughout much of the South, paying particular attention to the freed slaves and the areas where they had settled.

Its task of redesigning economic relations would prove more challenging. Lincoln's Republicans in Congress succeeded in putting into the bureau's charter a provision that plantations be divided into 40-acre plots and sold to former slaves, thus the origin of the phrase "40-acres-and-a-mule" signifying promises (often broken) made to African Americans. However, that plan was upended by politicians intending to enforce their own plans for reconstructing the South. Because politics were vitally important in determining how Reconstruction would unfold—would wealthy southerners simply get their land back?—it is to politics we must turn.

Ku Klux Klan A quasi-military force formed immediately after the Civil War by former Confederate soldiers in order to resist racial integration and preserve white supremacy; after a temporary decline, the group reformed in 1915 and sporadically returned to prominence throughout the nineteenth and twentieth centuries

Freedmen's Bureau Government agency designed to create a new social order by government mandate; this bureau provided freedmen with education, food, medical care, and access to the justice system

>> "The Secretary of War may direct such issues of provisions, clothing, and fuel, as he may deem needful for the immediate and temporary shelter and supply of destitute and suffering refugees and freedmen and their wives and children, under such rules and regulations as he may direct."—Freedmen's Bureau Bill, 1865. The image shows the old and sick being issued rations at the Freedmen's Bureau.

16-2 POLITICAL PLANS FOR RECONSTRUCTION

Even before the war was over, President Lincoln had pondered what it would take to bring the South back into the nation. Unfortunately for him, many in Congress were more interested in punishment than in reconciliation.

16-2a Lincoln's Plan for Reconstruction and His Assassination

In 1863, while battle was still raging, Lincoln issued his **Ten-Percent Plan**, which offered amnesty to any southerner who proclaimed (1) loyalty to the Union and (2) support of the emancipation of slaves. When 10 percent of a state's voters in the election of 1860 had taken the oath to the United States, they could develop a new state government, which would be required to abolish slavery. Then that state could reenter the Union with full privileges, including the crucial apportionment to the House of Representatives and Senate. Although requiring just 10 percent of the population to declare loyalty to the Union, and sidestepping the issue of preserving rights for the millions of ex-slaves,

it is important to remember that the war was still being fought. Lincoln was simply attempting to drain support from the Confederacy and shorten the war by making appeasement look easy.

CONGRESS BRISTLES

Republicans in Congress, more interested in punishing the South than Lincoln was, bristled at Lincoln's leniency. In opposition to Lincoln's plan, they passed the **Wade-Davis Bill**, which would have allowed a southern state back into the Union only after 50 percent of the population had taken the loyalty oath. Furthermore, to earn the right to vote or to serve in a constitutional convention, southerners would have to take a second oath, called the **iron-clad oath**, that testified that they had never voluntarily aided or abetted the rebellion. The iron-clad oath was designed to ensure that only staunch Unionists in the South could hold political power. Lincoln vetoed the bill, thinking it too harsh, and the battle about Reconstruction continued.

LINCOLN'S ASSASSINATION

As the battle wore on between Congress and the president, the hostilities of the American Civil War finally ended. Although the South had lost the war, a few disgruntled southerners would attempt to get revenge. Three days after Appomattox, John Wilkes Booth, a local actor and Confederate sympathizer, shot and killed Lincoln during a play at Ford's Theater in Washington, D.C. Eleven days later, a Union soldier shot and killed Booth as he tried to escape from a burning barn. In the coming political showdown, Lincoln's deep empathy and political acumen would be missed, as the battle to reconstruct the nation now took place between defiant congressional Republicans and the insecure man who had stumbled into the presidency—Andrew Johnson.

Ten-Percent Plan Plan issued by Lincoln in 1863 that offered amnesty to any southerner who proclaimed loyalty to the Union and support of the emancipation of slaves; once 10 percent of a state's voters in the election of 1860 signed the oath, it could create a new state government and reenter the Union

Wade-Davis Bill Bill that would have allowed a southern state back into the Union only after 50 percent of the population had taken the loyalty oath

iron-clad oath Oath to be taken by southerners to testify that they had never voluntarily aided or abetted the rebellion

>> Shown here, in an act of retribution, actor John Wilkes Booth shoots Lincoln in the head just three days after the Civil War had ended.

16-2b Andrew Johnson and Presidential Reconstruction

Upon Lincoln's assassination, Andrew Johnson became president. Johnson was a native southerner, born poor to functionally illiterate parents in North Carolina, before the family moved to Tennessee. He didn't master reading and writing until he was in his twenties, and was trained to be a tailor. It was his wife who pushed him into politics and throughout the war Johnson proved a loyal Unionist. He served as Tennessee's military governor after the state was taken over by the Union Army. And, despite Johnson being a Democrat, in 1864 Lincoln selected Johnson as his running mate because Lincoln hoped to quiet dissent by running with a non-northerner and a non-Republican. While it may have helped him win the election, Lincoln's plan would ultimately backfire.

PRESIDENTIAL RECONSTRUCTION, 1865–1867

Johnson was a lonely man who had a tough time handling criticism. Since his youth, he had looked up to the South's planter aristocracy and constantly sought

> Even Robert E. Lee applied to be pardoned.

black codes Post–Civil War laws specifically written to govern the behavior of African Americans; modeled on the slave codes that existed before the Civil War

its approval. Reflecting these insecurities, within a month of assuming the presidency, Johnson unveiled his plan for Reconstruction: (1) scrapping the "40-acres-and-a-mule" plan suggested in the charter of the Freedmen's Bureau and (2) creating a tough loyalty oath that many southerners could take in order to receive a pardon for their participation in the rebellion. However, Johnson added a curious but vital caveat that Confederate leaders and wealthy planters—who were not allowed to take the standard oath—could appeal directly to Johnson for a pardon. Anyone who received amnesty through either of these measures regained his citizenship rights and retained all of his property, except for his slaves. Under Johnson's plan, a governor appointed by the president would then control each rebel state until the loyalty oath was administered to the citizens. At that point, southerners could create new state constitutions and elect their own governors, state legislatures, and federal representatives. Johnson's plan showed no concern for the future of black people in America.

Southern states made the most of the leeway Johnson afforded them. Even Robert E. Lee applied to be pardoned (although his pardon was never granted during his lifetime). A line of southern planters literally appeared at the White House to ask Johnson's personal forgiveness; doing so allowed the southern elite to return to its former privileged status. In the end, Johnson granted amnesty to more than 13,000 Confederates, many of whom had been combative leaders in the Confederacy. Once Johnson had granted these pardons, he ensured that there would be no social revolution in the South. With pardons in hand, wealthy southerners would not lose their land or their social control of the South.

BLACK CODES

Most of the new southern state governments returned Confederate leaders to political power. These leaders then created **black codes** modeled on the slave codes that existed before the Civil War. Although the codes legalized black marriages and allowed African Americans to hold and sell property, freed slaves were prohibited from serving on juries or testifying against white people in court. Intermarriage between black and white Americans was also strictly forbidden. Some states even had special rules that limited the economic freedoms of their black populations. Mississippi, for example, barred African Americans from purchasing or renting farmland. Most states created laws that allowed police officials to round up black vagrants and hire them out as laborers to white landowners.

In the end, these new laws hardened the separation of black Americans from white Americans, ending the intermingling and interaction that had been more common during slavery. With the rise of post-Civil War black codes, black and white southerners began a long process of physical separation that was not present before the war and that would last for at least a century. These black codes would also begin the process whereby black southerners after the Civil War were left with, in the words of one historian, nothing but freedom.

16-2c Congressional Reconstruction

Johnson did nothing to prevent the South from reimposing these conditions on the black population. In Johnson's eyes, reconstruction of the Union would be finished as soon as southern states returned to the Union without slavery. Conservative members of Congress agreed. However, a group that would come to be called the **Radical Republicans** heartily disagreed.

THE RADICAL REPUBLICANS

The Republican Party had never been squarely behind Lincoln's plan for Reconstruction, and in fact the Radical Republicans, defined as the wing of the party most hostile to slavery, had opposed Lincoln's plans fiercely. Radicals in Congress, including Thaddeus Stevens of Pennsylvania, Charles Sumner of Massachusetts (of "Bleeding Sumner" fame), and Benjamin Wade of Ohio, had pushed for emancipation long before Lincoln issued the Emancipation Proclamation, and they considered Lincoln's lenient Reconstruction program

outrageous. As they looked toward the end of the war, Radicals hoped to use the Confederacy's defeat as an opportunity to overhaul southern society. At the very least, they hoped to strip the southern planter class of its power and ensure that freed slaves would acquire basic rights.

THE RADICALS VERSUS JOHNSON

As we have seen, Johnson, considering himself somewhat of a moderate, took office intending to wrap up the process of Reconstruction quickly. Granting amnesty to former Confederate leaders and other wealthy southerners demonstrated as much. Radicals in Congress, however, continued to devise measures for protecting the interests of the newly freed black population. With no southerners yet in Congress, the Radical Republicans wielded considerable power.

Their first moves were (1) to expand the role of the Freedmen's Bureau, creating a stronger organization with greater enforcement powers and a bigger budget, and (2) to pass the important **Civil Rights Act**, which was designed to counteract the South's new black codes by allowing all citizens, black or white, the protection of the law, the right to enforce contracts, to sue and be sued, give evidence in court, and hold property. Johnson

Radical Republicans Wing of the Republican Party most hostile to slavery

Civil Rights Act Bill that granted all citizens mandatory rights, regardless of racial considerations; designed to counteract the South's new black codes

vetoed both bills, but Congress overrode the veto on the Civil Rights Act, making them the first laws ever passed over presidential veto. Their willingness to override a presidential veto suggests the importance that Radical Republicans placed on a meaningful reconstruction effort. It was the first of many vetoes the Radical Republicans would override.

THE FOURTEENTH AMENDMENT

Congress's success in circumventing Johnson's veto began a new phase of Reconstruction known as **Congressional Reconstruction** in which Congress wielded more power than the president. Congress introduced a constitutional amendment in 1866 that (1) barred Confederate leaders from ever holding public office in the United States, government (2) gave Congress the right to reduce the representation of any state that did not give black people the right to vote, and (3) declared that any person born or naturalized in the United States was, by that very act, an American citizen deserving of "equal protection of the law." This, in essence, granted full citizenship to all black people; by the power of the constitution, states were prohibited from restricting the rights and privileges of any citizen.

> There was nothing worse than being part of a nation and having no say in how that nation was governed.

To the frustration of Radicals like Thaddeus Stevens and Charles Sumner, the amendment, which became the **Fourteenth Amendment** to the U.S. Constitution, did not also protect the voting rights of African Americans. Nevertheless, Congress passed the amendment and it went to the states for ratification. Tennessee approved it and, in 1866, was invited by Congress to reenter the Union. Every other state of the former Confederacy rejected the amendment, suggesting that the Radicals' hopes for restructuring the South would not be realized easily.

CONGRESSIONAL RECONSTRUCTION, 1867–1877

Despite the strenuous labors of Andrew Johnson, the midterm elections of 1866 gave the Radical Republicans a two-thirds majority in both houses of Congress, and they began to push their program of Reconstruction more vigorously. The election was vicious, as Johnson and his supporters went around the country on what was called the "swing around the circle" to castigate and even threaten the execution of several Radical Republicans.

Despite Andrew Johnson's claim that Reconstruction was over, the Radical-led Congress easily passed (again over Johnson's veto) the **Military Reconstruction Act** in March 1867. This act divided the former rebel states, with the exception of Tennessee, into five military districts. In each district, a military commander took control of the state governments, and federal soldiers enforced the law and kept order (see Map 16.1).

Congress also made requirements for readmission to the Union more stringent. Each state was instructed to register voters and hold elections for a state constitutional convention. In enrolling voters, southern officials were required to include black people and exclude any white people who had held leadership positions in the Confederacy, although this provision proved easy to ignore. Once the conventions were organized, the delegates then needed to (1) create constitutions that protected black voting rights and (2) agree to ratify the Fourteenth Amendment. Only then would Congress ratify the new state constitutions and accept southern state representatives back into the national Congress. Holding a fair state election and agreeing to the Fourteenth Amendment became the litmus tests for reentry to the nation. Without doing so and thereby becoming full-fledged members of the Union again, the southern states would remain without congressional apportionment and under military control.

THE SECOND RECONSTRUCTION ACT

At first, these provisions proved to be both too harsh and too lenient. The Military Reconstruction Act so outraged southerners that they refused to enroll the voters needed

Congressional Reconstruction Phase of Reconstruction during which Radical Republicans wielded more power than the president, allowing for the passage of the Fourteenth and Fifteenth Amendments and the Military Reconstruction Act

Fourteenth Amendment Amendment to the U.S. Constitution passed in 1868 that extended the guarantees of the Constitution and Bill of Rights to all persons born in the United States, including African Americans and former slaves; it promised that all citizens would receive the "due process of law" before having any of their constitutional rights breached

Military Reconstruction Act Act that divided the former rebel states, with the exception of Tennessee, into five military districts; a military commander took control of the state governments and federal soldiers enforced the law and kept order

Map 16.1 Reconstruction in the South

>> Reconstruction in the South required continued military involvement, even after the end of formal hostilities. This map shows the five military districts created by the US government in order to keep the southern states in line with the demands of the United States.

to put Reconstruction into motion. But southerners also preferred military rule to civilian control by those hostile to the South. In response to these various objections (and to the South's subsequent foot-dragging), Congress passed the Second Reconstruction Act, authorizing the Union military commanders to register southern voters and assemble the constitutional conventions (since southerners were not eager to do this themselves). The southern states continued to stall, so, in the summer of 1867, Congress passed two more acts designed to force southerners to proceed with Reconstruction, including requiring universal manhood suffrage. President Johnson vetoed all these measures, but his vetoes were all overridden by Radical Republicans in Congress. He was helpless to stop Congress's actions.

Eventually, the southern states had no choice but to follow the Military Reconstruction Act's instructions. There was nothing worse than being part of a nation and having no say in how it was governed.

Southerners wanted congressional representation back, and, in order to get it, they had to acquiesce to Congress's demands. In June 1868, Congress readmitted representatives and senators from six states: North Carolina, South Carolina, Florida, Alabama, Arkansas, and Louisiana. By 1870, the remaining four southern states—Virginia, Mississippi, Georgia, and Texas—had also agreed to the required provisions and they too received permission to send congressmen to Washington. As more and more Confederate states came back into the Union, the Fourteenth Amendment became the law of the land in 1868.

FRUSTRATIONS

Although the Radical Republicans in Congress had considerable successes, in many important ways they did not produce the social revolution they had envisioned: (1) they did not redistribute land to freed slaves; (2) they did not provide black people with guaranteed access to education; (3) they did not forbid racial segregation; and (4) they did not call for absolute racial equality for black and white people. President Johnson's leniency at the outset of Reconstruction, allowing wealthy southerners to retain their land and possessions, had denied Republicans the ability to radically reform the social structure of the South.

16-2d Johnson's Impeachment

Still stung by Johnson's initial act of granting pardons to the southern aristocracy, Radicals were equally stymied by his constant string of vetoes. Frustrated by all this, Congress took steps to limit the president's authority.

THE TENURE OF OFFICE ACT

In 1867 Congress passed the Tenure of Office Act, which required the president to obtain the consent of the Senate before removing certain government officials from office. In essence, the law declared that Johnson could not fire anyone who had earned congressional approvals, especially Republicans who had been appointed by Lincoln. Johnson of course vetoed the act, but Congress once again overrode his veto.

THE IMPEACHMENT

A showdown over the new law occurred in August 1867, when Johnson wanted to remove from office Secretary of War Edwin M. Stanton. Stanton sympathized with the Radicals and had fallen out of favor with Johnson, so Johnson ordered his dismissal. The Senate, however, refused to authorize the firing. Undeterred, Johnson ordered Stanton to resign. When Republicans in the House of Representatives learned that Johnson had defied the Senate's Tenure of Office Act, they drafted a resolution to impeach Johnson. This could be the chance they had sought to eliminate a major obstacle to Congressional Reconstruction. The House made eleven charges against Johnson, stemming mostly from his refusal to heed the Tenure of Office Act, and a majority of the representatives voted in favor of putting him on trial. This made Andrew Johnson the first president in the nation's history to be impeached.

Radical Republicans in the House of Rep-resentatives (especially Thaddeus Stevens) powered the vote for impeachment, but the Constitution dictates that impeachment trials must take place in the Senate and must be judged by the chief justice of the U.S. Supreme Court. Moderate Republicans and Democrats in the Senate refused to join the House Radicals in condemning Johnson, and, by one vote, the Senate lacked the two-thirds majority needed to convict the president and remove him from office.

16-2e The Fifteenth Amendment

In 1868, there was no way the Republicans were going to allow Johnson to run for reelection. Instead, they nominated the war hero Ulysses S. Grant for president, hoping that Grant's tremendous popularity in the North would help them control the White House and propel their Reconstruction plans through the federal government. The Democrats nominated Horatio Seymour, the governor of New York. To the shock of the Republicans, the race between Grant and Seymour was relatively close. Although Grant obtained a majority in the Electoral College, he won the popular vote by only 300,000 ballots. Since an estimated 450,000 black people had voted for Grant, it was clear that a narrow majority of white Americans had cast their ballots for Seymour.

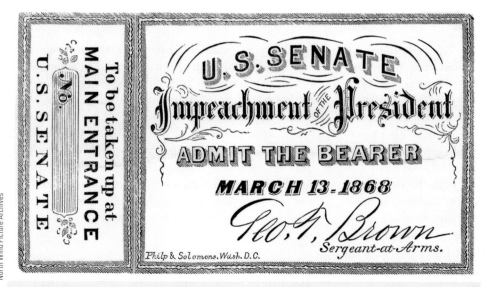

North Wind Picture Archives

>> Johnson was the first president ever to face an impeachment trial, and he held onto his job by only one vote in the Senate. Tickets, like the one pictured here, were sold at the trial.

Recognizing the importance of their newest support base—and aware that their time in power might be limited—Republicans in Congress moved quickly to create a constitutional amendment guaranteeing the suffrage rights of black males. It became the **Fifteenth Amendment**, which was ratified and adopted in 1870. The Fifteenth Amendment prohibited any state from denying citizens the right to vote on the grounds of race, color, or previous condition of servitude.

16-2f Women's Rights

The Fourteenth Amendment introduced the word *male* into the Constitution for the first time, and the Fifteenth Amendment ratified the notion that voting rights were solely intended for men. Many women, who had often supported the fight for black civil rights, fought back. Historically, advocates for the rights of women have often first fought for the rights of racial minorities, especially black people. This was the case in the 1830s and 1840s, and again in the 1860s and 1870s. Viewing the overhauling of the U.S. Constitution as a moment ripe for extending various freedoms to women, Elizabeth Cady Stanton, Susan B. Anthony, and Olympia Brown, veterans of the struggle to expand women's rights, pushed for a constitutional guarantee of women's suffrage. Using new journals such as *The Agitator* and *The Revolution*, women also pushed for a reform of marriage laws, changes in inheritance laws, and, as always, the vote.

But they were frustrated at almost every turn. Even Republicans declared that Reconstruction was designed solely for black men. Women were torn about whether or not to support the Reconstruction amendments, even if they excluded provisions for women's rights. These bitter differences led to divisions within the women's suffrage movement that would last until the 1890s.

16-3 GRASSROOTS RECONSTRUCTION

With all the political jockeying within the federal government, Reconstruction at the state level was even more rancorous. At the state level, freed slaves exercised more muscle, ensuring that Republicans

The Granger Collection, NYC

THE FIRST COLORED SENATOR AND REPRESENTATIVES.
In the 41st and 42nd Congress of the United States.

>> During Reconstruction, Hiram Revels of Mississippi (on the left in this image of seven African American congressmen) became the nation's first African American senator, while several other southern states voted African Americans to the House.

dominated all of the new state governments in the South. Newly freed slaves steadfastly cast their ballots for the party that had given them their freedom. To support this voter bloc, Republican politicians—from the North and the South—sought dramatic Reconstruction efforts. But at every turn they encountered strong opposition. Before long, it became evident that the process of reconstructing the South would be a process of two steps forward, one step back. And the most substantive change that could have happened—land and economic redistribution to the ex-slaves—remained perpetually frustrated.

16-3a Black Officeholders

Even with the admission of black voters, the proportion of government positions held by black Americans was still smaller than their proportion in the population. They were rarely elected to high positions, and until

Fifteenth Amendment Amendment that extended voting rights to all male citizens regardless of race, color, or previous condition of servitude

>> The Man with the (Carpet) Bags by Thomas Nast, 1872, Harper's Weekly. This political cartoon of Carl Schurz depicted as a carpetbagger, reflected Southern attitudes toward Northerners during Reconstruction. Many Southerners saw carpetbaggers as corrupt and lowly, although many came South with the intention of improving the life of America's black people.

1990 no black person was ever elected or nominated to serve as governor of a southern state. South Carolina was the only state where a black judge served in the state supreme court, and, because the state was 60 percent African American, only in South Carolina did African Americans form a plurality of the legislature. Nevertheless, more than 2,000 black citizens gained political office in the Reconstruction South. Some were policemen, some were sheriffs, some were tax assessors. Their roles were important because they ensured that fairness would be enforced and that the rule of law would be upheld.

16-3b Carpetbaggers and Scalawags

Yet white men held most of the offices in the new state governments, and many were Republicans supportive of

carpetbagger Northern-born white who moved south after the Confederacy's defeat

scalawag Southern-born white Republican; many had been nonslaveholding poor farmers

protecting black rights. Some of these new officials were northern-born white men who moved south after the Confederacy's defeat. Southerners called these men **carpetbaggers** because they supposedly journeyed to the South with nothing more than what they could carry in a ratty old carpetbag. The carpetbag was meant to symbolize corruption and lowliness, as supposedly poor and pretentious northerners headed south seeking to capitalize on the region's fall from grace. Not all the so-called carpetbaggers were corrupt, of course. Many of them came to the South with a desire to improve the lot of America's black people.

Southern-born, white Republicans were given the name **scalawag**, originally a term used by cattle drivers to describe livestock that was too filthy for consumption, even by dogs. Although southern Democrats insisted that only the "dirtiest" citizens became scalawags, in reality, many elite southerners joined the Republican Party, including Confederate generals Pierre Beauregard and James Longstreet. Most of the scalawags, however, had been nonslaveholding poor white farmers who worked and lived in the hill country. Many of these scalawags believed that participating in the Republicans' plan was the fastest way to return their region to peaceful and prosperous conditions.

SOUTHERN REPUBLICAN SUCCESSES

Although they faced considerable opposition from the old antebellum elite, southern Republicans managed to (1) construct the South's first public school system, (2) develop a system of antidiscrimination measures, (3) strengthen the rights and privileges of agricultural workers, and (4) begin efforts at internal improvements in the various states. Under the leadership of southern Republicans, for example, every state in the South financed a system of railroads and attempted to lure northern industries to the South. They met with mixed results, but they showed a newfound commitment to greater equality and to bringing the gains of the Market Revolution southward.

16-3c Sharecropping

Despite the new opportunities put forward by southern Republicans, freed slaves had to struggle hard to enjoy their new liberty. There was no serious land reform and the Market and Industrial Revolutions were slow to move southward, so most black southerners had no choice but to accept work as agricultural wage laborers for white landholders, many of whom had been slaveholders before the war.

THE BATTLE OF LABOR

Many of these landowners attempted to recreate as much of the slave system as they could, closely overseeing their workers, forcing them to work in gangs, and even trying to use the whip to maintain discipline. The freedmen, however, refused to be reduced to slavery again. They insisted on working shorter hours, and they often refused to work in gangs. To limit the amount of surveillance, freedmen often built their own log cabins far away from the houses of their employers. Unless they were willing to go beyond the rule of law, most landowners could do nothing to stop them.

THE SHARECROPPING SYSTEM

The power struggle between southern whites and the freedmen led former slaveholders to establish and develop the **sharecropping** system. As sharecroppers, families farmed a plot of land owned by someone else and shared the crop yield with the owner of the property. Typically, the farmer and the owner split the yield in half, but the owner often claimed an even larger share if he supplied the seeds or tools necessary for cultivating the crop or if he provided housing and food. Although black farmers had earned the right to work in a familial setting, as opposed to the gang labor system of the slave era, landowners had managed to curtail black freedom by preventing many of them from owning property.

Despite sharecropping's prominent place in southern black history, there were more white sharecroppers in the South than black. It was a sign of the South's poverty after the war. The sharecropping system offered little hope for economic or social advancement. Sharecroppers could rarely earn enough money to buy land, and they were constantly in debt to their landlords. The landlord was always paid first when crops were sold at market, so if crop prices were lower than expected, sharecroppers were left with little or no income. Although sharecropping was not slavery, it was still a harsh and limited form of economic existence that permeated the South after the Civil War. By 1900, 50 percent of southern whites and 75 percent of southern blacks lived in sharecropping families.

CONVICT LEASING

Southern landowners and politicians also began the practice of convict leasing during these years, whereby the state leased out prisoners to private companies or landowners looking for workers after the demise of slavery. Convicts usually were not paid for their labor and were often treated harshly. But the system was good for the state, which earned income from the practice, and the lessees, who exploited the labor of the prisoners. Convicts were used in railroad, mining, and logging operations, as well as on farms. And, although convicts of all colors were exploited by the system, African Americans were particularly targeted. During the three decades after the Civil War, the number of men in prison increased in nearly every state of the South, and the percentage of those prisoners who were black ballooned. Many were convicted on questionable charges, and more than one dirty judge was exposed for fraudulently convicting an innocent black man who would be destined to work as the leased property of the state. Some historians see convict leasing as just an extension of slavery, with only a different name.

 16-4 ## THE COLLAPSE OF RECONSTRUCTION

Despite the obvious setbacks, the reconstruction of the South did have some significant achievements, including two new constitutional amendments, the passage of the nation's first civil rights law, and the abolition of slavery. These positive achievements could have continued to accumulate, but they did not, for two reasons: (1) growing northern disinterest in the plight of America's southern black population and (2) increasingly violent resistance to Reconstruction from white southerners.

16-4a In the North

On the whole, the eight years of Grant's presidency (1869–1877) were not marked by great strides for African American civil rights. Instead, Grant's term became infamous for economic chicanery and corruption. The president's personal secretary was caught embezzling federal whiskey revenues in the so-called Whiskey Ring, while Grant's own family was implicated in a plot to corner the gold market. Charges of corruption even led to a split in the Republican Party, further draining support for Reconstruction efforts. As more upstanding

> **sharecropping** System in which a family farmed a plot of land owned by someone else and shared the crop yield with the owner

>> African American sharecroppers picking cotton during Reconstruction.

In addition to these flaws, the Civil Rights Act of 1875 proved ineffective anyway. The federal government did not enforce the law vigorously, so the southern states ignored it. And in 1883, in what would come to be called the **Civil Rights Cases**, the Supreme Court delivered a final blow to this last act of Reconstruction by declaring all of its provisions unconstitutional, except for the prohibition of discrimination on juries. In 1890, Henry Cabot Lodge, a Republican from Massachusetts, led the House of Representatives in passing a Federal Elections Bill that would have revived protection of voting rights for African Americans, but a Senate filibuster prevented the piece of legislation from becoming law. It would be nearly seven decades before another civil rights bill made its way through Congress.

political leaders became preoccupied with efforts to clean up the government and institute civil service reform, securing equal rights for black people in the South ceased to be the most pressing issue. Other things seemed to matter more. And, as Reconstruction moved into the background, northerners' racism—always just under the surface—became more visible.

Despite charges of corruption, Grant was reelected to the presidency in 1872, and during his second term, only one major piece of Reconstruction legislation was passed. Even that had key limitations. The **Civil Rights Act of 1875** forbade racial discrimination in all public facilities, transportation lines, places of amusement, and juries. Segregation in public schools, however, was not prohibited. Moreover, there was no effort whatsoever to legislate against racial discrimination by individuals or corporations, so discrimination in the workplace remained legal.

The failure of the Civil Rights Act of 1875 reflected a larger northern disinterest in Reconstruction. For many northerners, support for black rights had been an outgrowth of their animosity toward the South. In 1865, such feelings burned hotly, and northerners were willing to support federal efforts to guarantee the liberties of former slaves. As the bitterness of war faded, northerners were tired of the antagonism between North and South, so their interest in civil rights faded, too.

Instead, northerners became consumed with economic matters, especially after the United States entered a deep recession in 1873. The **Panic of 1873** erupted when overspeculation, high postwar inflation, and disruptions from Europe, emptied the financial reserves in America's banks. Rather than honor their loans, many banks simply closed their doors, which led to a panic on Wall Street. Although Grant acted quickly to end the immediate panic, many businesses were forced to shut down. The Panic lasted six years and left 3 million Americans unemployed. In the years after 1873, Americans became concerned more with jump-starting the economy than with forging new laws to protect the needs and interests of black citizens.

The Republicans, meanwhile, took the blame for the nation's economic troubles, so, in the congressional elections of 1874, they lost seventy-seven seats, thus losing control of the House. The party that had spearheaded civil rights legislation in America was no longer in a position to control federal policy. Instead, the Democrats were back.

Civil Rights Act of 1875 Act that forbade racial discrimination in all public facilities, transportation lines, places of amusement, and juries; it proved largely ineffective

Civil Rights Cases Cases in which, in 1883, the Supreme Court declared all of the provisions of the Civil Rights Act of 1875 unconstitutional, except for the prohibition of discrimination on juries

Panic of 1873 Financial crisis provoked when overspeculation, high postwar inflation, and disruptions from Europe emptied the financial reserves in America's banks; many banks simply closed their doors; this emergency focused northern attention on the economy rather than on civil rights

16-4b In the South

The decline of northern support for Reconstruction emboldened southern Democrats, who worked to reclaim political control of their region. In order to create white solidarity against Republican rule in the South, the Democrats shamelessly asserted white superiority.

Racism proved to be a powerful incentive for the Democratic Party, especially to attract poor southerners worried about their economic fortunes. Keeping black people as an underclass in southern society was important to poor white people's sense of self-worth (and economic well-being), and Democrats promised to protect the racial hierarchy as it had been before the Civil War. Democrats earned the backing of the vast majority of white southerners—mostly by championing continued white supremacy.

INTIMIDATION OF BLACK AND REPUBLICAN VOTERS

To control black votes, white Democrats often used economic intimidation. Throughout the nineteenth century, voting was not done by secret ballot, so it was easy to know how every individual cast his ballot. Democratic landowners fired tenant farmers who voted Republican and publicized their names in local newspapers to prevent other landowners from hiring them too. The threat of starvation and poverty thus kept many black citizens from voting for the Republican Party.

More than economic intimidation, however, southern Democrats used violence to control southern politics. A number of paramilitary groups, including the Ku Klux Klan, provided the ground troops. They harassed black and white Republicans, disrupted Republican Party meetings, and physically blocked black southerners from casting ballots in elections. They even assassinated Republican Party leaders and organizers. Their goal was to erode the base of Republican support in the South and to ensure election victories for the Democratic Party. For instance, prior to the presidential election of 1868, 2,000 people were killed or injured in Louisiana alone. In Texas, the federal military commander said murders were so common he could not keep track of them.

TERROR IN THE HEART OF FREEDOM

In addition to these more purely political forms of repression, southern white males also used rape and sexual violence against African American women as a form of political terror. Because black women now had the right to accuse white men of sexual crimes, historians have been able to determine that white men often staged elaborate attacks meant to reenact the antebellum racial hierarchy, when southern white men were firmly in control. African Americans of course fought back, but as Democrats grew increasingly powerful in the region, the claims made by southern black women often went unheard. Most damningly, these crimes indicated how limited black freedom had become in the decade after the Civil War. Not only were African Americans losing their political and social rights, they were also losing the right to basic safeties, the right to organize their life as they saw fit, and the right to live comfortably in a democratic nation.

GRANT'S RESPONSE

Although not known for its civil rights activism, the Grant administration did respond to the upsurge in southern violence by pushing two important measures through Congress: (1) the Force Act of 1870 and (2) the Ku Klux Klan Act of 1871. The new laws

"EVERY THING POINTS TO A DEMOCRATIC VICTORY THIS FALL."—Southern Papers.

The Granger Collection, NYC

>> The White League and other similar organizations were founded to use violence and intimidation to keep African American voters from the polls throughout the South. This cartoon from a Northern American newspaper of 1874 depicts the efforts of White League member in Louisiana attempting to intimidate and disenfranchise black voters.

declared that interfering with the right to vote was a felony; they also authorized the federal government to use the army and suspend the writ of habeas corpus in order to end Klan violence. Grant proceeded to suspend the writ in nine South Carolina counties and to arrest hundreds of suspected Klan members. These efforts crushed the Klan in 1871 (although it would resurge in the 1910s and 1920s).

THE MISSISSIPPI PLAN

Southern Democrats, however, did not relent. In 1875, Democrats in Mississippi initiated a policy called the **Mississippi Plan**, which called for using as much violence as necessary to put the state back under Democratic control. Democratic clubs began to function much as the Klan had, terrorizing Republican Party leaders and the black and white citizens who supported them. This time, the Grant administration refused to step in to stop the violence. Most northerners no longer seemed willing to support federal intervention into southern strife.

In 1876, the Mississippi Plan formally succeeded. By keeping tens of thousands of Republicans from casting ballots, the Democrats took charge of the state government. In the vocabulary of the time, Mississippi had been "redeemed" from Republican rule. In fact, it had been tortured into submission; official reports proclaiming as much were generally ignored.

"REDEEMERS" WIN THE PRESIDENTIAL ELECTION OF 1876

The presidential election of 1876 put the final nail in Reconstruction's coffin. Through violence and intimidation, the Democrats had already succeeded in winning control of all the southern states except Louisiana, Florida, and South Carolina. Now they intended to use the Mississippi Plan to "redeem" those three states and win the presidency as well. Perversely using the Christian language of redemption, the leaders of these efforts were widely called **Redeemers**.

The presidential campaign pitted Ohio Republican Rutherford B. Hayes against New York Democrat Samuel Tilden, who had a reputation as a reformer and a fighter against political corruption. The election was a mess. Violence prevented as many as 250,000 southerners from voting Republican, and, as southern Democrats had hoped, Democratic governors triumphed in Louisiana, Florida, and South Carolina. The Democrats in those states reported that the majority of voters favored Tilden for the presidency. Republicans were suspicious, however, and did a canvass of their own. They claimed that the Democrats had used violence to fix the results. Louisiana, Florida, and South Carolina, the Republicans argued, should have gone to Hayes. These disputed states carried enough Electoral College votes to swing the entire election one way or the other.

> Reconstruction was America's unfinished revolution, and a great chance to correct the colossal wrong that was slavery.

THE COMPROMISE OF 1877

After receiving two versions of the final tallies, Congress needed help deciding what to do. It created a 15-member electoral commission, with 5 members from the Senate, 5 from the House, and 5 from the Supreme Court. The commission was composed of 8 Republicans and 7 Democrats, and, by a purely partisan vote of 8 to 7, the commission gave the disputed states of Louisiana, Florida, and South Carolina to Hayes, the Republican. The Democratic Party leaders were furious, but, in order to prevent further violence, Republican leaders proposed a compromise that became known as the **Compromise of 1877** (see Map 16.2).

In the compromise, Republicans promised (1) not to dispute the Democratic gubernatorial victories in the South and (2) to withdraw federal troops from the region. The white redeemers would thus be in control throughout the entire South. In return, the Republicans asked the Democrats to (1) accept Hayes's presidential victory and (2) respect the rights of its black citizens. The Democrats accepted these terms, and, with that, Hayes withdrew the federal military from the South. Of course, without a federal military to protect black Americans, Reconstruction was over, and the South

Mississippi Plan 1875 Democratic plan that called for using as much violence as necessary to put Mississippi back under Democratic control

Redeemers A collection of southern Democrats and their supporters who used violence, intimidation, and the law to win political and social control away from those promoting greater racial equality in the region

Compromise of 1877 Compromise in which Republicans promised not to dispute the Democratic gubernatorial victories in the South and to withdraw federal troops from the region, if southern Democrats accepted Hayes's presidential victory and respected the rights of black citizens

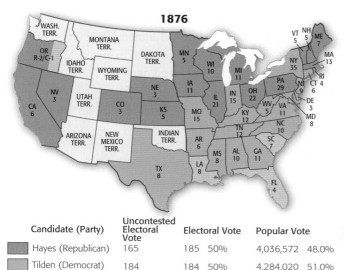

1876

Candidate (Party)	Uncontested Electoral Vote	Electoral Vote		Popular Vote	
Hayes (Republican)	165	185	50%	4,036,572	48.0%
Tilden (Democrat)	184	184	50%	4,284,020	51.0%
Contested					
Territories					

Map 16.2 The Disputed Election of 1876

>> An electoral map of the 1876 presidential election, showing the states that supported Hayes and Tilden, as well as the three contested states, where Democrats likely received more votes but only because of the violent suppression of Republican votes.

was left under the control of the Redeemers who used violence, intimidation, and the law to create the society they envisioned. Freed blacks progressively lost whatever political and social gains they had achieved during the previous twelve years. This failure ensured that racial oppression would continue. In the words of one historian, Reconstruction was America's unfinished revolution. A great chance to correct the colossal wrong that was slavery vanished. For more on why Reconstruction ended in 1877, see "The Reasons Why . . ." box.

>LOOKING AHEAD...

Why did Reconstruction fail? So boldly stated, the question is perhaps unfair. There were major accomplishments. Slavery was abolished. Federal laws were established that provided support for further political gains for America's black population. Following the 2016 elections, there have been only ten black senators ever elected to the U.S. Senate, but two of them were elected during Reconstruction (Hiram Rhodes Revels and Blanche K. Bruce, both from Mississippi). About 10% of the 139 black Americans ever to serve in the U.S. House of Representatives were elected during Reconstruction.

The Reasons Why...

There were three prominent reasons why Reconstruction ended in 1877, before equality could be ensured for southern African Americans.

Northern indifference. After the Panic of 1873, many northerners focused intently on economic matters. The passions inflamed by the Civil War had begun to fade by the early 1870s, and the economic turmoil provoked by the Panic led northerners to focus on their personal fortunes. Plus, with the Industrial Revolution ramping up in the North (see Chapter 17), northerners were even less likely to take big risks on behalf of black civil rights in the South.

Southern recalcitrance. With northern indifference becoming increasingly evident during the second

presidential term of Ulysses S. Grant, white southerners increased the level of violence—political, physical, and sexual—they used against African Americans and Republicans more generally. The Democratic Party in the South promised white superiority, and throughout the 1870s it was beginning to deliver.

National political ambivalence. By 1876, northern politicians had more at stake in reviving the sagging economy than in fighting for the rights of African American southerners. When it became clear that the results of the presidential election of 1876 were going to be disputed, northern Republicans willingly negotiated with southern Democrats, securing the Republicans the presidency at the cost of pulling federal troops out of the South. Without northern oversight, southern whites were free to reclaim their social and political power, and that is exactly what they did.

But there was a dramatic decline of black political participation in the South (where a large majority of black people lived) beginning in 1876 and lasting until after the Second World War. There was an even more dramatic increase in physical segregation between America's black and white populations during and after Reconstruction. The causes are many. President Johnson's unwillingness to participate in a wholesale social revolution meant that land would not be redistributed in the South, signifying that, for the most part, the wealthy would remain wealthy and the poor would remain poor. The development of sharecropping as an institution further paralyzed black advancements, especially after the emergence of black codes limited black Americans' abilities to protest economic injustices. Finally, the violence used by the southern Redeemers served as an emblem of the wrongs felt by white southerners, and, when northerners became more focused on the rollicking economy of the Industrial Revolution, there was no one left to monitor the henhouse. Plainly enough, most white southerners strongly opposed racial change, and after 1876, they were left in power to do as they wished.

As this happened, most Americans began to look away, focusing their attentions on another dramatic transformation in American life. It is to the development and ramifications of the great Industrial Revolution that we now must turn.

STUDY TOOLS 16

READY TO STUDY? IN THE BOOK, YOU CAN:

❑ Rip out the Chapter Review Card, which includes key terms and chapter summaries.

ONLINE AT WWW.CENGAGEBRAIN.COM, YOU CAN:

❑ Collect StudyBits while you read and study the chapter.

❑ Quiz yourself on key concepts.

❑ Find videos for further exploration.

❑ Prepare for tests with HIST5 Flash Cards as well as those you create.

❑ Read Lincoln's proclamation on vetoing the Wade-Davis Bill.

❑ View a Library of Congress picture gallery about Lincoln's assassination.

❑ View an oath of amnesty to the Union from Joseph Trimble.

❑ Read a *Harper's Weekly* editorial about the Civil Rights Bill.

❑ Read the Second Reconstruction Act.

❑ Find out more about the impeachment of Andrew Johnson.

❑ Analyze an image of the South Carolina legislature.

❑ Read the Fifteenth Amendment to the U.S. Constitution.

❑ Read the Mississippi legislature's black codes.

❑ Analyze a *Harper's Weekly* cartoon on the Panic of 1873.

❑ Analyze a *Harper's Weekly* cartoon on the Civil Rights Act of 1875.

CH16 TIMELINE

		What Else Was Happening
1863	Abraham Lincoln proposes the lenient Ten-Percent Plan.	
1864	Lincoln pocket-vetoes the stricter Wade-Davis Bill for Reconstruction.	**1865:** *John Wilkes Booth assassinates Abraham Lincoln.*

1865–1867 Johnson's presidential Reconstruction demands loyalty oath from Confederates. Congress establishes Freedmen's Bureau. Congress passes Civil Rights Bill.

1866 The Ku Klux Klan forms in Tennessee.

1867: *Congress enacts Military and Second Reconstruction Act.*

Benjamin Disraeli helps pass the 1867 Reform Bill in Britain, which extends the franchise to all male householders, including, for the first time, members of the working class.

1867–1877 During Congressional Reconstruction Congress enforces its rules for readmission.

1868 Fourteenth Amendment grants full citizenship to all persons born in United States.

North Carolina, South Carolina, Georgia, Florida, Alabama, Arkansas, Louisiana return to Union.

1869: *Opening of the Suez Canal in Egypt connecting the Mediterranean Sea and the Red Sea, allowing water travel between Asia and Europe without having to navigate around Africa.*

1873: *Marketing of Remington typewriter opens clerical positions for women.*

Financial panic causes severe recession and mass unemployment.

Mark Twain patents the scrapbook.

1870 Fifteenth Amendment bans state disfranchisement based on race but not gender.

Virginia, Mississippi, Texas return to Union.

First New York City subway line opens.

1871 Force Act of 1870 and Ku Klux Klan Act permit federal government to respond to Klan violence.

Euphemia Allen, age sixteen, composes simple piano tune "Chopsticks."

1875 Mississippi Plan calls for use of violence to restore Democratic control.

Civil Rights Act forbids racial discrimination in public places.

1877 To overcome election stalemate, Republicans grant Democrats home rule in return for presidency.

1883 In Civil Rights Cases, U.S. Supreme Court declares Civil Rights Act unconstitutional.

INDEX

In this index *i* indicates images, *m* indicates maps, and *t* indicates table. Defined terms are in **bold**.

A

abolition/abolitionists/abolitionism, 192, 220
  American Anti-Slavery Society, 221
  Beecher, Lyman and, 220
  Brown, John, 256, 259–260
  Chapman, Maria Weston and, 221
  Douglass, Frederick. *See* Douglass, Frederick
  Dred Scott controversy, 259
  free people of color and, 219–220
  gag rule and, 221
  Garrison, Lloyd and, 220–221
  in North, 221
  resistance to, 221
  Second Great Awakening and, 192
  The Liberator, 220–221
  Turner, Nat and, 224
  Weld, Theodore and, 220
Acadians, deportation of, 80*m*
Acuña, Rodolfo, 30
Adam-Onis Treaty, 177
Adams, Abigail, 90
Adams, John, 157
  Alien and Sedition Act and, 155–156
  Boston Massacre defense and, 94
  Declaration of Independence and, 108
  election of, 154–155, 157–158
  Federalists and, 153
  France and, 157
  Franco-American Alliance of 1778 and, 118
  image, 93*i*, 155*i*
  Instructions of the Town of Braintree to Their Representative, 91
  judicial appointments of, 163
  peace negotiations, 117
  Quasi-War and, 155
  separation of powers, 126
  tax protest and, 92*i*
  Treaty of Paris, 118
  vote to dissolve ties with Britain, 109
  XYZ Affair, 155
Adams, John Quincy, 198
  election of 1824 and, 198
  election of 1828 and, 199–200
  gag rule and, 221
Adams, Samuel
  as anti-federalist, 137
  boycott and, 94
  as patriot leader, 99, 100
Administration of Justice Act, 97
Africa, 12
  in 1500, 13*m*
  Catholic conversions in Kongo, 14
  early society in, 14
  on eve of contact, 15
  Ghana, 12
  Mali, 13–14
  North, Barbary Company and, 34
  politics in, 12–14
  pre-contact, 15
  religion and thought, early, 15
  repatriation of American slaves to, 192
  routes of exploration and, 25*m*
  slavery and, 14, 24, 76–77
  society, 14–15
  Songhay, Benin, Kongo, 14
  trade and, 15
African Americans, 287. *See also* civil rights; Colored Americans; race; racial discrimination; racism; segregation; slave society; slavery
  "40-acres-and-a-mule", 292, 294
  abolitionism and, 220
  black codes, 294–295
  black face, minstrel and, 219
  black officeholders, 299
  casualties, Civil War, 284
  Christianization of, 189
  citizenship, property restrictions and, 197
  distribution of in 1775, 119*m*
  election of 1868 and, 297
  Fifteenth Amendment and, 298–299
  as freedmen and freedwomen, 291–292
  free people of color in urban North, 219–220
  Liberia, abolition movement and, 192
  in Old West, 233
  population distribution, 1790, 119*m*
  racial discrimination and, 302
  racism in north, 201
  religion, war and, 287
  Seneca Falls Convention and, 192
  sexual crimes, post Civil War, 303
  sharecropping and, 300–301, 302*i*
  slavery, racism and, 79
  spirituals, music, 227
  temperance and, 220
  troops, 284
  as Union soldiers, 280*i*, 281
  violence against, 306. *See also* **Ku Klux Klan**
  voting restrictions on, 198, 303
  White League and, 303*i*
African Americans Masons, 120

African Methodist Episcopal Church (AME Church), 219, 220
Africans, 3
  of Lower Guinea, 14
  transition from servants to slaves, 57
African slavery, 75–79. *See also* slavery
  enslavement, 76–77
  labor demands of New World, 76*i*
  life under slavery, 78–79
  racism, 79
  slavery, 79
  spread of slavery, 77
Age of Discovery, 19
Age of Exploration, 26
Age of Jackson, 197
Agitator, The, suffrage journal, 299
Agrarian republic, 163
  land policies, 164
  Lewis and Clark, 163–164
  Louisiana purchase, 163
agriculture
  American Revolution and, 131
  Archaic era and, 5–6
  in Caribbean, 29
  in Carolina colony, 48
  in Chesapeake, 68–69
  chocolate, 30
  Columbian Exchange of, 29–30
  commercialized farming, 181–184. *See also* commercialized farming
  corn, 6, 31, 37
  cotton, 46, 181–182
  diversified farming, 63
  economy based in, pre-Columbian era, 6
  economy, of England, 33
  Erie Canal and, 180
  expanding territories and, Jefferson, 163
  feudalism and, 16
  indigo, 46
  localized commercial, 175
  in Lower Guinea, 14
  maize, 30–31
  matrilineal societies and, 8
  mechanization of, 184
  Mid-Atlantic tribes and, 9–10
  in Middle Colonies, 67–68
  in New England, 63
  Northeast, 8
  potatoes, 30
  Prairie India tribes and, 10–11
  in pre-Columbian era, 6
  Pueblo people and, 11
  rice, 78, 226
  sedentary, 6

  sharecropping and. *See* sharecropping
  slavery and. *See* slavery
  soil exhaustion, westward expansion and, 204–206
  Southeast tribes and, 10
  in Southern Colonies, 70
  southern economy and, 181
  sugar, 24, 29, 30, 31, 34, 35, 46, 47, 56, 78, 88, 206
  tariffs, nullification crisis and, 202
  tobacco. *See* tobacco
  tomatoes, 30
  Tribes of North America, 9*m*
  wheat, 67
Alabama
  Battle of Horseshoe Bend, 168
  Indian tribes of, 10
  Mobile Bay, capture of, 283
  Northern Strategy and Southern Resistance, 1861–1865, 272*m*
  Overland Trails, 237*m*
  Region and Race in Antebellum America 1830–1860, 214*m*
  Rivers, Roads, and Canals in 1825–1860, 179*m*
  secession of, 263
  statehood, 182
  Union, readmittance to, 297
  War in the West, 273*m*
  westward expansion and, 204
Alamo battle, Texas, 234
Alaska
  Beringia and, 3
  British Columbia and, 240, 241
  Oregon Boundary Dispute, 242*m*
Albany Congress, 81–83
Albany Plan, 81
alcohol, 219
  election of 1824 and, 199
  Know-Nothing Party and, 255
  temperance movement and, 191, 208, 216, 220
Alexander VI, (pope), 26
Algonquian communities, 54
Algonquian Indians, 9, 31
Alien and Sedition Acts, 155–156
Alien Friends Act, 155
Allegheny Mountains, 272
Allen, Ethan, 105
al Qaeda, 560, 561. *See also* terrorist/terrorism
American Anti-Slavery Society, 221
American Civil War, 293
American Colonization Society, 192, 220

Boston Harbor, 100
Boston, Massachusetts
    in 1775, 99*m*
    American resistance in, 89*m*
    anti-Catholicism and, 217
    battles of Lexington and
        Concord and, 99–100
    boycott in, 90
    British Settlement by 1760,
        65*m*
    committees of correspon-
        dence and, 95*m*
    European Settlements and
        Indian Nations in Eastern
        North America, 47*m*
    evacuation of, 108
    first newspaper, 74
    French and Indian War, 80*m*
    Hutchinson, Anne and, 40
    immigrants in, 216
    Irish in, 217
    New England During
        Metacom's War, 1675–
        1676, 54*m*
    patriot siege of, 105–106
    Population Density 1790–
        1820, 183*m*
    Powder Alarm, 99
    power loom in, 185
    Provincial Congress, 98
    Revolutionary War in the
        North, 112*m*
    Rivers, Roads, and Canals,
        1825–1860, 179*m*
    Seventeenth-Century New
        England, 40*m*
    Territories After Treaty of
        Paris, 1763, 82*m*
Boston massacre, 94
Boston News-Letter, 74
Boston Port Act, 97
Boston Tea Party, 96, 97*i*
Bowie, James, 234
boycotts, American resistance
    and, 90, 94
Braddock, Edward, 81
Bradford, Andrew, 73*i*, 74
Bradford, William, 73
Bradstreet, Anne, 73
Brazil, 31, 76
Breckinridge, John C., 260
Breed's Hill, 101
Bridger, Jim ("Old Gabe"), 233,
    234*i*
Britain. *See* England entries
British Army. *See* English Army,
    American Revolution and
British colonists, relations with
    Indians and, 52
British, foreign relations of
    Confederacy, 130
British Take over, 48–49
Brooks, Preston, 257
Brown, John, 259–260, 259*i*
Brown, Olympia, 299
Bruce, Blanche K., 305
Buchanan-Pakenham Treaty,
    242
Buchanan, James
    election of 1856 and, 258
    Kansas and, 256–257
buffalo. *See* bison
Bulfinch, Charles, 172
Bull Run, Battle of Manassas,
    Virginia, 270–271
bundling board, 67
Bunker Hill, American Revolu-
    tion and, 100–102

Burgoyne, John (general), 113
burned-over district, 189
Burr, Aaron, 164, 165
Butler, Andrew P., 257

C

cabinet
    of Lincoln, 280
    as part of executive branch,
        135
    of Washington, 144, 145
Cabot, John, 26
Cabral, Pedro, 27
Cahokia, 7
Calhoun, John C., 175, 176, 252*i*
    Compromise of 1850 and, 252
    Jackson and, 201
    nullification crisis, South
        Carolina and, 202–203
    right to disunion and, 263
    Texas and, 240
    Wilmot Proviso and, 250
California, 250
    "Bear Flag Revolt" in,
        244–245
    Compromise of 1850 and,
        251–252
    Crittenden Compromise and,
        264
    Frémont and, 258
    Louisiana Purchase and,
        162*m*
    Mexican-American War and,
        243–244
    as Mexican territory, 238
    Overland Trails, 237*m*
    paper money outlawed, 204
    ranchers & gold, 238–239
    Region and Race in Antebel-
        lum America 1830–1860,
        214*m*
    slavery and, 259
    statehood of, 251
    Treaty of Guadalupe Hidalgo
        and, 245
    tribal conflicts and, 238–239
California Republic, 244
California Trail, 237*m*
Calvert, George, 36
Calvin, John, 19
Cambridge, Massachusetts, 99
camels, 12
Canada
    French settlements in, 30
    Oregon border dispute and,
        241
    Treaty of Paris and, 81
canal era, transportation and,
    178
Canals, 179–180*m*
Caning of Sumner, 257, 257*i*
caning of Sumner, in Senate,
    257
Cape Horn, 31*i*
Cape of Good Hope, 24
capture, 76–77
carbon dating, 3
Caribbean, 29
    agriculture in, 29
    colonial holdings in, 45
    Columbian Exchange in, 30
    Dutch and, 31
    Haitian Revolution and,
        153–154
    King William's War/Queen
        Anne's War and, 59

pirates and, 131
proprietorship failure and, 47
slaves in, 29, 226
Spain and, 25*m*, 27
tobacco and, 35
Vespucci and, 26
Carnegie, Andrew, 286
Carolina colony, England and,
    46–48
    failure of proprietary owner-
        ship, 47
    life in, 48
    rice in, 47–48
Carpenter's Hall, Philadelphia,
    127*i*
carpetbaggers, 300, 300*i*
Carson, Christopher ("Kit"), 233
cash crops, 35
Cass, Lewis, 250
casualties, Civil War, 284–285
    Gettysburg & Petersburg, 282
    Manassas/Bull Run, 270–271
    Shiloh, 272–273
Catholic Church. *See also* anti-
    Catholicism; religion
    anti-Catholicism, 216
    Bible and, 19
    Church of England and, 32
    Civil War and, 287
    colonization and, 30–31
    crusades and, 17
    decline of in Europe, 18
    Elizabeth I and, 32
    in feudalism, 16
    feudalism and, 16
    Florida and, 29
    French colonies and, 31
    Irish, immigration and, 186,
        209, 216–217
    James II and, 79
    Know-Nothing Party and, 255
    Kongo people and, 14
    Ku Klux Klan, schools and,
        411
    in Maryland, 36–37
    in Middle Colonies, 68
    Native Americans and, 30–31
    parochial schools and, 217
    Portugal and, 26–27
    Protestant Reformation and,
        18–19
    Quebec act and, 98
    Second Great Awakening
        and, 188
    slaves, religious, beliefs and, 78
    Spain and, 51
    spread of, exploration and,
        23, 31
    Toleration Act of 1649, 37
    in Vietnam, 488
Catholic Europe, 18–19
    change, 18
    reformation, 18
Catholicism, 18, 186
Cato's Letters (Gordon &
    Trenchard), 107
cattle, 53, 300
centrism, 543, 555. *See also*
    Clinton, Bill
Chaco Canyon, 6
Chamberlain, Sam, 245*i*
Chancellorsville, Virginia, battle
    at, 282
Chapman, Maria, 192, 221
Charles I (King of England), 45
Charles II (King of England),
    46, 49, 50, 79
Charleston, South Carolina

boycott in, 90
Cornwallis in, 116*m*, 117
Democratic convention in,
    260
Fort Sumter and, 265
founding of, 47, 65*m*, 82*m*
Population Density 1790–
    1820, 182*m*
in Revolution, 116*m*
slave society in, 206
Chase, Samuel, 163
Cherokee Indians, 10
    slavery and, 205
Cherokee Nation v. *Georgia*,
    205–206
Chesapeake colonies, 68
    economy, 68–69
    governor's palace, 69*i*
    life on, 37, 37*i*, 69–70
    society, 69
Cheyenne Indians, 11
Chicago, Illinois, as westward
    hub, 204
Chickasaw Indians, 10
Child, Lydia Marie, 192
Chile, 6
Chinese immigrants, to
    California, 238
Chinook Indians, 11
chocolate, 30
Choctaw, 10
Christian humanism, 18
Christianity, spread of, 23
chronology. *See* timelines
Churchill, Winston, Church of
    England, 32, 37–38
Church of England, 38
Cincinnati, Ohio, as westward
    hub, 204
circular letter, 89
cities, growth of, 185
citizenship. *See also* Fifteenth
    Amendment
    property restrictions and, 197
    in U. S. Constitution, 143–144
city life, in North, 215–220
    abolitionism, 220
    class consciousness, 217
    congressional gag rule, 221
    "free labor", 221
    free people of color, 219–220
    Garrison and *The Liberator*,
        220
    immigrants, 216
    leisure time, 218–219
    racial and ethnic identities,
        216–217
    resistance to abolition, 221
    women and middle class,
        217–218
Civil liberties suspension,
    275–276
Civil Rights Act, 295, 296
Civil Rights Act of 1875, 302
Civil Rights Cases, 302
Civil War, 262, 269, 291, 303.
    See also North, in Civil
    War; *and entries for specific
    battles*; South, in Civil War
    American Nationalism im-
        pact, 286
    armies of, 271*i*
    battle of manassas, 270–271
    Battle of Shiloh, 272–273,
        274*i*
    changing nation, 277
    civil liberties suspension,
        275–276

motives for further expansion, 45
Quaker flight from, 49–50
Roanoke, 32–33
Sir Walter Raleigh, 32–33
Sir Walter Raleigh, Roanoke and, 32–34
textile industry in, 31–32
U. S. neutrality and, 165–166
War of 1812 and, 168–169
England, colonial control/expansion, 79
Albany Congress, 81–83
British soldiers, 88i
French and Indian War, 80–81
Georgia, 50–51
life on Chesapeake, 37, 37i
limiting settlement, 87–88
Maryland, 36–37
New Jersey, 50
New York, 48–49
Pan-Indianism, 83–84
paying off debts, 46
Pennsylvania, 49–50
raising revenue, 88–89
Salutary Neglect, 79–80
tightening control, 45–46, 87
Virginia, Jamestown, 34–36
England, colonies, 31–34, 45
Anglo-Dutch wars and, 49
expansion, Indian confrontation, 41
Jamestown, Virginia, 34–36
Lost Colony of Roanoke, 32–34
Maryland, 36–38
Massachusetts, 38–39
New England, 37–41
Rhode Island, 39–41
settlement by 1760, 65m
Treaty of Paris and, 81
West Indies, American ships banned from, 132
England entries, Britain, by 1700, 51
English Army, American Revolution and. See also American Revolution
Bunker Hill, 100–101
casualties, 118
Delaware crossing, 111, 113
Lexington and Concord, 99–100
Lord Cornwallis and, 116m, 117
to militias, 99
peace negotiations, 118
second phase 1776–1779, 111–115
in South, 115–117, 116m
strength of, 110–111
successes, 111
in the South, 115–117
third phase 1778–1781, 115–117
winter of 1777–1778, 114–115
Yorktown, 117
English Civil War, 45–46
English holdings in North America, 1660–1700, expansion of, 45
by 1700, 51
creation of colonies during and after restoration, 46–51
English motives for further expansion, 45–46
Spanish, 51

Enlightenment, 71–73. See also American Enlightenment
enraged populace, 262
enslavement, 8, 76
capture, 76–77
middle passage, 77
new life, 77
slave traders, 77i
enumerated articles, 46
environment, costs of market revolution, 185
Episcopal Church, 121
Era of Good Feelings, 170
Ericson, Leif, 26
Erie Canal, 178, 180i, 185
Erie Indians, 8
eternal taxes, 91
ethnic identities, 216–217
Euro-Indo relations, 52–56
Bacon's Laws, 55–56
Bacon's Rebellion, 54–56
Beaver Wars, 53
colonial land lust/democracy and, 53–56
King William/Queen Anne's Wars, 53
Metacom's War (King Philip's War), 53–54
Europe, 15. See also entries for individual countries
in 1492, 19
decline of Catholic Europe, 18–19
decline of feudalism, 16–18
exploration and discovery, 23–26
manors, 15, 16m
up to 1492, 15–16
European alignments, 52
European contact, Africa, 15
European Enlightenment, 71
Europeans, 3, 15
European Settlements and Indian nations in Eastern north America, 47m
Europe to 1492
decline of Catholicism, 18
manors, 15–16
Reformation, 18–19
Renaissance in, 16–17
society in, 16
trade, feudalism and, 17
eve of contact, Africa on, 15
ex-Confederates, 292
Executive branch
creation of, 144
how elected, 135
powers, 135
Executive Department, 144
exemptions from service, Civil War, 275
expansion
of franchise, 197–198
and Indian confrontation, 41
Massachusetts, 39
expansionist spirit rebounds, 239
manifest destiny, 242–243
Mexican–American war, 243–245
Oregon and American dominance in West, 241–242
Texas and rise of James K. Polk, 240–241
expansion of American slavery, 56

Africans' transition from servants to slaves, 57
slave codes, 57–58, 58i
transition from indentured servitude to slavery, 57
exploration and discovery, Europe
beginnings of European slavery, 24
eastern route, Portuguese, 23–24
fifteenth-century exploring ship, 24i, 27i
predecessors and followers, 26
routes of early exploration, 25m
western route, Spanish, 24–26
external duties, 93
external taxes, 91

F

factories, mechanization and, 184–185
failure of proprietorship, 46–47
family
in Chesapeake, 37
land, Massachusetts colony and, 39
lost, of slaves, 291
in Lower Ghana, 14, 15
Native American clan system, 8
in New England colonies, 66–67
plantations and, 33
sharecropping and, 301
slave culture and, 78, 226, 227
Federal Elections Bill, 302
federal government, 143
impact, 285
powers reserved for, 127
Federal Hall in New York city, 144i
federalism, 137
Federalist Party, 153
Federalists, 136i, 137, 146
Civil War and, 263
election of 1800, 157–158
election of 1828 and, 199
jailing of Democratic-Republican newspaper editors and, 156
Jeffersonian Democracy and, 161–166
Madison /War of 1812 and, 166–172
national bank and, 176
political cartoon, 136i
political divisions and, 146–152
ratification of Constitution and, 137–138
two-party politics and, 153–154
Washington and, 145
Federalists papers, 137
federal powers, 136
female reform societies, 191
Ferdinand (King of Spain), 24
Fern, Fanny, 219
feudal fiefdoms, 16
feudalism, 15, 16–18, 19
Black Death, 17, 17i
crusades, 17
expanding trade, 17
Hundred Years' War, 17

renaissance, 16–18
society, 16
fiber production, in American South, 181
Fifteenth Amendment, 298–299
"Fifty-four Forty or Fight!" border dispute, Canada, 241
filibusters, 252
Fillmore, Millard, Compromise of 1850 and, 252
financial impact, 30
financiers given preferential treatment, 147
Finney, Charles G., 188
First Amendment to U. S. Constitution, 138
First Bank of the United States, 147, 148
First Continental Congress, 98
First Great Awakening, 188
First National Bank, 176
Fitzhugh, George, 225
Five-twenties, 276
fleeing Britain, 49–50
Florida, 29, 51
Adam-Onis Treaty and, 177
explorers in, 29
secession of, 262–263
Seminole Revolt and, 206
Spain and, 29, 51
statehood, 182
Treaty of Paris and, 81–82
Union, readmittance to, 297
food riots, Civil War, 278
Force Act of 1870, 303–304
Force Bill, nullification crisis and, 202–203
Ford, Antonia, 286i
Ford's Theater, Washington, D. C., 293–294i
foreign policy. See also entries for specific treaties
Texas annexation and, 240
of Thomas Jefferson, 165–167
foreign relations, of Confederacy, 130–131
British, 130
Pirates, 131
Spanish, 130–131
Forrest, Nathan Bedford (General), 281
Forten, James, 220
Fort Laramie Treaty, 239
Fort Pillow Massacre, 281
Fort Sumter, 265, 265i
Fort Ticonderoga stamp, 106i
"40-acres-and-a-mule", 292, 294
48ers, the, 216
49th parallel, 249
"forty-niners," California gold rush and, 238
Fourteenth Amendment, 296, 296
Fourteenth Amendment, 299
France
in American Revolution, 113–114
colonization/settlements, 31
Florida and, 29
French and Indian War, 80–81
Haitian Revolution and, 153, 156i
Louisiana Purchase and, 162m, 163
Quasi-War and, 155
Treaty of Paris and, 81–82

Rhode Island, 40
    citizenship, property restric-
        tions, 198
    colony, 39–41
    First Continental Congress
        and, 98
    foreign trade and, 128
    Metacom's War in, 53
    new England in 1660s, 41
    Personal Liberty Laws and,
        252
    Puritans/Antinomianism in,
        40–41
    ratification of Constitution
        and, 138
rice, 47, 48i
    in Carolina colony, 47–48
    slavery and, 78, 226
Richmond in ruins (1865), 283i
Richmond, Virginia
    British Settlement by 1760,
        65m
    Confederate capital, 273
    food riots, 278
    Gabriel's Conspiracy and,
        153–154
    Northern Strategy and South-
        ern Resistance 1861–1865,
        272
    Revolutionary War in the
        South, 116m
    in ruins, 283i
    War in the West, 273m
right. See "New Right"
right of neutrality, 165–166
Rio Grande River, 243, 245
rioting, 90
riots
    American resistance and, 90
    draft, 278, 279i
    New York City Draft, 287
rise of slavery, 56
rivers, 178–179m. See also indi-
        vidual rivers
roads, 178, 179m
Roanoke, 12, 32–33, 33i, 34
Robinson, Harriet Hanson, 186i
Rockefeller, John D., 286
Rolfe, John, 35i
Roman Catholicism, 97
Rousseau, Jean-Jacques, 71
Rowlandson, Mary, 54
royal colony, 36
royal control, 36
rum, 67
runaway slaves, 228

S

Sacajawea, 164
Salem, Massachusetts, 40
Salem witch trials, 59i
Salt Lake City, Utah, 238
salutary neglect, 79–80, 87
Santa Domingo, Haiti, 153
Santa F, New Mexico, 29
Santa Maria, 24
São Tomé, Africa, 24
Savannah, Georgia, Cornwallis
        in, 116m, 117
scalawags, 300
school(s). See also education;
        universities
    Bible readings in, 192
    segregation, in public, 301
Schouten, Willem Cornelis,
        31, 31i

Scott, Dred, 259
Scott, Winfield, 205–206,
        244–245
seasoning, 36
secession, 262–265
Second Bank of the United
        States, 176, 204i
Second Confiscation Act, 280
Second Continental Congress,
        100
Second Great Awakening, 187,
        188–191
    abolition and, 220
    black church and, 219
    latter-day saints, 190–191
    in North, 215
    revival, 189
    slaves, Christianity and, 227
    spread of, 188–189
    theology of, 188
    Transcendentalists, 189–190
    Utopianism, 190
Second Reconstruction Act,
        296–297
second two-party system,
        199, 208
    constituencies, 209
    Election of 1840, 209i
    Jackson's democrats, 208
    political stability, 209
    Whigs, 208
secular press, American Enlight-
        enment and, 74
Sedentary existence, 5
Sedition Acts, 156, 156i
segregation
    in public schools, 301
    in representation, 305
self-rule, 37
selling of indulgences, 18
Seminole Revolt, 206
Senate
    apportionment and, 293
    black Americans serving in,
        305
    Bleeding Sumner and, 257
    Buchanan-Pakenham Treaty
        and, 242
    Buchanan and, 257
    caning of Sumner in, 257
    Chase, Samuel and, 163
    Compromise of 1877 and, 304
    Federal Elections Bill and,
        302
    Great Compromise and, 134
    Jackson, censure of, 204
    Lincoln-Douglass contest
        for, 260
    Mason gives Calhoun speech
        in, 252
    powers of, 135
    racial makeup, 305
    slaves parity in free/unfree
        states, 253, 262
    Tenure of Office Act and, 298
    Texas annexation and, 240
    Wilmot Proviso and, 250
Senate Tickets, 298i
Seneca Falls Convention, 192,
        193
separation of church and state,
        121
separation of powers, 126
Separatists, 38
Separatists, Mayflower Compact
        and, 38
serfs, 15
Serpent Mound in Ohio, 7i

settlement(s)
    of Chesapeake, 37m
    Dutch, 31, 31i
    English, 31–34
    European, Indian nations in
        Eastern North America,
        47m
    France, 31
    limiting, 87–88
    Lost Colony of Roanoke,
        33–34
    Massachusetts, 38–39
    Portuguese, 26–27
    Spanish, 27–31
Seven Days' Battles, 273–274
"Seventh of March" speech
        (Webster), 251
Seven Years' War, 81
Seward, William H., 280
sexual crimes, race and, 78, 303
Seymour, Horatio, 298
Shakers, religious movement,
        190
sharecropping system,
        300–301, 302i
    labor battle, 301
    sharecropping system, 301
    system of, 301
Shay, Daniel, 131–132
Shay's Rebellion, 131–132
shellfish, 9
Sherman, Roger, 108, 133–134
Sherman, William T., 283–284
ship building, in New England,
        64i
*Short Account of the Destruc-
        tion of the Indies, A* (de las
        Casas), 28
Shoshone Indian, Sacajawea,
        164
Shufelt, S., 241i
silver
    Aztecs and, 28
    as money, 203
    as Specie Circular, 206–207
    specie payments and, 131,
        203
Sioux Indians, 11
Sir Walter Raleigh, 32–33
Sixtus V, (pope), 32
Slater, Samuel, 185
slave auction, 58i, 78i
slave codes, 57–58, 58i
slave conspiracy, 252
slavedriver, 226
Slave Power Conspiracy, 258,
        261
slavery, 79
    20 Negro Law, 275
    "40-acres-and-a-mule", 292,
        294
    abolition of. See abolition/
        abolitionists in Africa, 14
    African. See African slavery
    African's transition to, 57
    American Revolution, impact
        of on, 119–120
    beginnings of, in Europe, 24
    Bible and, 287
    in Caribbean, 29
    in Carolina colony, 47
    Carolina colony and, 48
    in Chesapeake, 70
    Compromise of 1850 and,
        251–252
    congressional gag rule and,
        221
    Convention and, 134

defending, 223–224
    Democrats, the West and,
        249–250
    election of 1860 and, 260–261
    and emancipation, 279–281
    emancipation and, 278–281
    expansion of American, 56
    free states v. slave, Constitu-
        tional
    Fugitive Slave Law, 252
    Gabriel's Conspiracy, 153–154
    Haitian Revolution and, 153,
        156i
    idealized view of, 225
    ideology for, 224–225
    indentured servitude to, 57
    John Brown, Harper's Ferry
        raid and, 259–260
    Kansas-Nebraska Act and,
        253–254
    Kansas and, 256
    in Kansas and Nebraska, 252,
        254m
    as law of land, 259
    legal restrictions and, 224
    manumission of slaves and,
        119–120
    in Middle Colonies, 67–68
    misleading images of antebel-
        lum South and, 222
    Nat Turner, 223–224
    New York and, 49
    in Pennsylvania, 50
    Personal Liberty Laws and,
        252
    racism in north and, 201
    rape and, 78
    religious beliefs, Catholic
        Church and, 78
    in Revolutionary War, 106
    rise of, 56
    runaways, 228
    Seminole Revolt and, 206
    slave codes, 57–58
    in Southern colonies, 70
    in Texas, 234–235
    in the West, 183
    Thirteenth Amendment
        abolishes, 284
    trade and, 67
    treatment of, 206–207
    two-party politics and,
        153–154
    Underground Railroad and,
        228
    urban, 226
    Wilmot Proviso and, 250
slave society, 225
    community, 227–228
    culture and community,
        227–228
    family separations, 225
    living quarters, 227
    quarters, 227
    religion and, 227
    resistance and revolt, 227–228
    resistance and revolt, 228–229
    Underground Railroad, 228i
    work, 226–227
smallpox, 28, 29, 30
Smith, Adam, 17, 72
Smith, Hyrum, 237
Smith, John, 34
Smith, Joseph, 190, 236
social changes with market
        revolution, 185
    challenges to protestant con-
        sensus, 186

8000–13,000 B.C.E.
People of Paleo-Indian era develop different languages, economies, beliefs.

c. 7000 B.C.E. Kennewick man dies.

c. 500–8000 B.C.E.
Agriculture and sedentary existence become dominant in Archaic era.

500 B.C.E.–1492 C.E.
Pre-Columbian societies develop trade, cities, social hierarchies, science.

1 C.E. Rise of the Roman Empire, birth of Jesus Christ.

900–1150 Anasazi build multistory "apartment houses" in Chaco Canyon.

1000 Italian long-distance trade begins, empowering rich mercantilist city-states.

1096–1291 European crusaders try to capture Jerusalem; return with spices and luxury goods.

1100 Mississippian city of Cahokia has 20,000 inhabitants—the size of London.

1225–1274 Life of Thomas Aquinas marks the height of Catholic power in Europe.

1235 North African Muslims conquer trade and gold empire of Ghana.

1300s–1600s
Modern religion of Islam spreads rapidly through Africa, Middle East, Spain.

Urban wealth and expansion engender Renaissance of culture and humanism.

1337–1453 French and English Hundred Years' War prompts new trade routes, larger kingdoms.

1346 Bubonic plague kills one in three Europeans and weakens feudal order.

1440s Invention of printing press.

1500 Empires of Benin and Kongo rise with Mali's demise; first Catholic conversions.

1517–1648 Christian humanism and secular church practices trigger Protestant Reformation.

What Else Was Happening

c. 200,000 B.C.E.: *The earliest humans appear in Africa.*

16,000 B.C.E.: *The last Ice Age reaches its coldest point; people in Asia, across Beringia, live in huts made from woolly mammoth bones.*

2500 B.C.E.: *Age of the Egyptian pyramids.*

1023: *Paper money is printed in China.*

1300: *Timbuktu is Africa's cultural and artistic capital. Corsets for women are invented.*

1300s: *The Aztecs make "animal balloons" by creating inflated animals from the intestines of cats and present them to the gods as a sacrifice.*

1489: *The symbols + (addition) and − (subtraction) come into general use.*

1-1 **Explain current beliefs about how the first peoples settled North America, and discuss the ways in which they became differentiated from one another over time.** Scholars long held that ca. 10,000 b.c.e., humans first settled North America, following woolly mammoths from Asia across an Ice Age land bridge over the Bering Sea. Recent scholarship suggests humans may have come to America earlier, perhaps from both Europe and Asia. During the Archaic era, ca. 8,000–500 b.c.e., agriculture developed, offering a stable food supply and permitting permanent settlements. In the pre-Columbian era, ca. 500 b.c.e.–1500 c.e., societies became more complex and diverse, largely depending on what area a particular people settled. In what would become the northeastern U.S., Native Americans banded into loose confederations to defend against nearby enemies. Elsewhere Native Americans developed as their physical environment permitted: fishing in the Northwest, canyon "apartments" in the Southwest, buffalo hunting on the High Plains. Native peoples traded with each other across wide areas.

CHAPTER REVIEW | **CHAPTER 1 TIMELINE / KEY TERMS**

Paleo-Indians The first people to settle North America, roughly 10,000 to 15,000 years ago (p. 5)

Paleo-Indian era Era beginning about 15,000 years ago and ending about 10,000 years ago, characterized by initial North American settlement (p. 5)

Archaic era Era beginning about 10,000 years ago and lasting until about 2,500 years ago, characterized by increased agricultural development (p. 5)

sedentary existence Life in which settlers can remain in one place cultivating agriculture, instead of pursuing herd animals (p. 5)

pre-Columbian era North American era lasting from 500 B.C.E. to 1492 C.E., before Columbus landed (p. 6)

clan system Living arrangement in which a tribe was divided into a number of large family groups (p. 8)

matrilineal Family arrangement in which children typically follow the clan of their mother and married men move into the clan of their wives; most often seen in agricultural societies (p. 8)

polytheistic Belief system consisting of belief in many deities (p. 8)

animistic Belief system consisting of belief that supernatural beings, or souls, inhabit all objects and govern their actions (p. 8)

Iroquois Confederacy Group of northeastern tribes that joined to form a political and trading entity and later created an elaborate political system; also known as the Haudenosaunee Confederacy (p. 8)

Pueblo people Southwestern conglomeration of tribes including the Hopi, Taos, and Zuni, who lived in today's New Mexico and Arizona (p. 11)

wampum Beads made of polished shell, used as currency in trading for goods (p. 12)

roanoke Bracelet-like bands made of wampum (p. 12)

1-2 Describe the African societies that existed at the time the first Africans were brought to the New World as slaves. Most Africans brought to the New World were from West Africa, mainly Lower Guinea. West Africa had known sophisticated and powerful kingdoms, with wealth based on large gold resources and cities that were major trading centers. Political upheaval marked West African empires in the years just before European contact. West African societies relied on strong kinship networks, often matrilineal, and often polytheistic native religions rather than Islam or Christianity. Africans in Lower Guinea were mostly farmers, and many held slaves, often as a result of war. Slavery was not hereditary. On the eve of European contact, West Africans in general were members of sophisticated societies that had wealth and well-developed skills in the arts, politics, and learning.

Islam Modern religion that flourished throughout the world beginning in the fourteenth and fifteenth centuries; its adherents are called Muslims (p. 12)

Ghana West African kingdom that prospered from the eighth to the thirteenth centuries; famous for its gold deposits (p. 12)

Mali Flourishing Islamic kingdom; it enveloped the kingdom of Ghana by the thirteenth century (p. 14)

Timbuktu Principal city of the kingdom of Mali; cultural capital of Africa in the thirteenth century (p. 14)

Lower Guinea Southernmost part of Mali; home to the majority of the Africans who came to America (p. 14)

Songhay Empire Portion of Mali after that kingdom collapsed around 1500; this empire controlled Timbuktu (p. 14)

Benin African empire on the Malian coast (p. 14)

Kongo African empire on the Malian coast (p. 14)

1-3 Describe Europe's experiences during the last centuries before Columbus made his first voyage to the New World in 1492. Europe during the Middle Ages centered around large manorial holdings ruled by feudal lords; most of the people were tied to their lords' holdings as serfs with few freedoms. The Black Death in the mid-1300s and the Hundred Years' War both weakened feudal lords and strengthened kings and private citizens. The Crusades had also made a new class of people very wealthy and less accepting of feudalism's constraints. The decline of Roman Catholicism's dominance, invention of the printing press, and coming Protestant Reformation gave individuals more freedoms to think for themselves. The Renaissance led to a flowering of intellectual and artistic expression, making many people wealthier and more adventurous and curious about the world. New wealth and curiosity led to the "age of exploration".

manor Agricultural estate operated by a lord and worked by peasants in exchange for protection and sustenance (p. 15)

feudalism System of labor in which a lord granted control over a piece of land, and authority over all the land's inhabitants, to an upper-class ally, or vassal (p. 15)

serf Laborer in the feudal system; protected and controlled by the vassal of the estate (p. 15)

Renaissance Intellectual and artistic reconnection to the age of Greco-Roman antiquity, starting in the fourteenth century, that lionized the individual (p. 16)

mercantilism Theory that a nation or state's prosperity was determined by the total volume of its trade (p. 16)

Crusades Series of campaigns in which Europeans marched to the Middle East in an effort to seize the Holy Land of Jerusalem, which at the time was controlled by Muslims; battles lasted from 1096 to at least 1291 (p. 16)

Black Death Bubonic plague, which started to spread in 1346 and eventually killed one-third of all Europeans (p. 16)

Hundred Years' War War waged between France and England in the fourteenth century over who controlled the French throne (p. 16)

Catholicism Central religious force in western Europe; sole institution with moral authority and political power over all of medieval Europe (p. 18)

Christian humanism Belief in the importance of the singular individual, as opposed to

the institution of the Church; characterized by optimism, curiosity, and emphasis on naturalism (p. 18)

selling of indulgences Practice of popes using their authority to limit the time a person's soul spent in purgatory, in exchange for cash (p. 18)

Protestant Reformation Movement that challenged the Catholic Church to return to its unornamented origins; protesters criticized Church rituals, including the Mass, confession rites, and pilgrimages to holy sites (p. 19)

printing press Invention of the 1440s using metal letter faces to print words on paper, allowing for the quick, widespread dissemination of ideas, opinions, and scientific findings (p. 19)

What Else Was Happening

c. 1000 Scandinavian expeditions to North America.

1405–1433: *Chinese explorer Zheng He goes on seven expeditions to Arabia, East Africa, India, and Indonesia.*

1440s Portuguese begin trade with Africa.

1492: *First Spanish voyage of discovery: Christopher Columbus.*

1493 Pope Alexander VI draws Line of Demarcation.

1497 Englishman John Cabot lands in Canada.

1498: *Vasco da Gama reaches India via Cape of Good Hope:*

1512 First permanent Spanish settlements in New World.

1519–1522 Cortés conquers Mexico.
Magellan completes first circumnavigation of the world.

1532 Pizarro overthrows Incas in Peru.

1540: *The first horses arrive in North America, when Spanish explorer Francisco Vasquez de Coronado, traveling through Kansas, lets about 260 of them escape.*
1551: *What is now the National Autonomous University of Mexico is founded.*

1565 Spanish seize St. Augustine from French.

1585: *First Roanoke settlement.*
Sir John Harrington invents the first flushing toilet and puts one inside the palace of Queen Elizabeth, who deems it too loud.

1607 Jamestown founded by Virginia Company of London.

1608 Quebec founded as French trading post.

1620 Settlement of Plymouth.

1629 Massachusetts becomes a royal colony.

1630s Pequot War in New England.

1632 Founding of Maryland.

1644 Rhode Island receives preliminary charter as independent colony.

2-1 **Explain the reasons Europeans explored lands outside Europe, and trace the routes they followed.** Portuguese and other Europeans sought to explore new lands to alleviate a trade deficit (thus increasing wealth) and spread Christianity. This search drew Europeans to several locations around the globe, many of which quite accidentally. Portuguese sailors traveled down Africa's west coast seeking the passage to India and the Middle East. With Portugal's success, Spanish sailors began advocating a search for a western route to the Orient. Around the year 1000 C.E., Scandinavian explorers had already reached northeastern North America.

2-2 **Describe the founding of Europe's first colonies in the New World.** By the early 1500s, the Spanish had permanently settled Hispaniola, Cuba, Puerto Rico, Jamaica, and Panama. Also by this time, Spanish conquistadors led private armies to the New World—Hernán Cortés to Mexico, Francisco Pizarro to Peru, and others to Florida and the American Southwest. The French established several encampments in present-day Canada as French trading posts; the largest was Quebec. Sir Walter Raleigh founded the first English New World colony—Roanoke—in 1585.

Line of Demarcation Line drawn by Pope Alexander VI through a map of the Western Hemisphere; granted the eastern half to Portugal and the western half to Spain, in what could be considered the first act of modern European colonialism (p. 27)

conquistador One of the Spanish noblemen who sailed to the New World with small armies to vanquish kingdoms there (p. 28)

encomienda Tribute, usually payable in gold or slaves, that was demanded of conquered Indian villages by the conquistadors (p. 28)

viceroy Representative of the Spanish crown who governed conquered Indian villages (p. 28)

Columbian Exchange Biological crossover of agricultural products, domesticated animals, and microbial diseases from Europe to the New World and vice versa (p. 29)

price revolution Inflationary event, such as the huge influx of silver to Spain in the mid-1500s, that causes the price of goods to surpass the wages paid to laborers and landless agricultural workers (p. 30)

Atlantic World The complex interactions among the peoples and empires bordering the Atlantic Ocean from about 1450 to the 1800s (p. 31)

plantation Large farm staffed by an entire family in an agricultural economy (p. 33)

lost colony of Roanoke Second settlement by English colonists at Roanoke; deserted sometime before 1590 (p. 33)

joint stock company Company that sold stock to numerous investors in order to raise large sums of money (p. 34)

2-3 **Trace the expansion of England's holdings in the southern colonies.** Between 1600 and 1660, more than 150,000 English people left for the New World. Most went to the West Indies, but about a third settled eastern North America. Begun by the Virginia Company of London (a joint stock company), Jamestown was founded in 1607. In the early 1610s, English settlers there successfully cultivated tobacco. Following Virginia's success, in 1632 England's king granted present-day Maryland to George Calvert.

Jamestown English settlement of 1607 in present-day Virginia (p. 34)

starving time Winter of 1609–1610 in Jamestown, when food supplies were so scarce that at least one colonist resorted to cannibalism (p. 35)

Powhatan Confederacy Group of six Algonquian villages in present-day Virginia, named after its leader (p. 35)

cash crop Agricultural product grown primarily for sale. Examples include sugar and tobacco harvests (p. 35)

indentured servitude System of labor whereby farmers paid the Atlantic passage for English and Irish workers in exchange for four to seven years of their work on farms or plantations (p. 36)

head right A grant by the Virginia Company of 50 acres of land to any individual who paid his or her own passage across the Atlantic; put more property in private hands (p. 36)

"seasoning" Period of several years during which indentured servants were exposed to the New World's microbes; many did not survive (p. 36)

royal colony English settlement whose governor was chosen by the king (p. 36)

House of Burgesses Assembly of landholders chosen by other landholders, with which the royal governors were forced to work (p. 36)

proprietary colony Colony overseen by a proprietor who was allowed to control and distribute the land as he wished (p. 36)

Toleration Act of 1649 Act granting freedom of worship to anyone who accepted the divinity of Jesus Christ; meant that neither Catholics nor Protestants could be imprisoned for their faith (p. 37)

2-4 **Outline the reasons for and timing of England's founding of colonies in New England.** Despite harsh realities, the promise of wealth and religious freedom fueled English colonial desires. Separatists, receiving land from the Virginia Company, sailed on the Mayflower in 1620, destined for Virginia. Blown off course, they landed in present-day Massachusetts, where they founded Plymouth. In 1629, Massachusetts became a royal colony under the name of the Massachusetts Bay Company. Quickly, Massachusetts dissenters led by Roger Williams and Anne Hutchinson settled Rhode Island. Puritan dissenters continued to expand outward from Massachusetts throughout the 1630s, founding towns in what are now Connecticut, Maine, and New Hampshire. Rhode Island became an independent colony in 1644. Another charter in 1663 granted political and religious freedoms to the settlers.

Puritans Protestants who wished to reform or purify the Church of England by removing its hierarchy, its emphasis on work as payment to God, its allowance of prayers for communal salvation, and its promotion of missions (p. 37)

Separatists Group of believers who wished to separate completely from the Church of England because they believed it was irrevocably corrupted (p. 38)

Mayflower Ship containing Separatists who sailed from Holland and landed in Plymouth, in present-day Massachusetts, in 1620 (p. 38)

Mayflower Compact An agreement that bound each member of the Separatist group in Plymouth to obey majority rule and to promise to defend one another from potential eviction; set a precedent for democratic rule in Massachusetts (p. 38)

Antinomianism Theological philosophy stressing that only God, not ministers, determined who merited grace and that humankind's relationship with God was a continual process of divine revelation and not dependent on a single orthodox scripture; Anne Hutchinson led a group of Antinomian dissenters and was banished from Massachusetts for these beliefs (p. 40)

Pequot War Bloody battles of the 1630s between New England colonists and the Pequot tribe of Indians (p. 41)

1640–1680s	In Beaver Wars over French fur trade, Iroquois Confederacy defeats Huron.
1649	Oliver Cromwell's execution of King Charles I prompts English civil war.
1651	Parliament passes first of colonial trade regulations known as Navigation Acts.
1660–1685	Charles II's return to his father's throne signals a new era of royal Restoration.
1662–1690s	Colonial assemblies make slavery matrilineal, prohibit miscegenation, separate slaves from servants by race.
1664	Charles II invades Dutch colony New Amsterdam, grants it to brother, Duke of York.
1674	Penn and Quakers purchase West Jersey.
1675–1676	Wampanoags lead pan-Indian fight against Puritan encroachment in Metacom's War.
1676–1677	British freemen fight colonial nobility over Indian and land policies in Bacon's Rebellion.
1680	Pueblo Revolt expels and kills Spanish Catholic friars.
1681	William Penn exchanges father's royal debt claim for colony that offers religious freedom.
1689–1697	French–English rivalries reach colonies and Indian allies in King William's War.
1693	Rice cultivation expands rapidly in the Carolinas.
1698	Rapid growth of southern slave plantations prompts Carolina's split.
1701–1713	Europeans fight over French claim to Spanish succession, leaving English victorious in Queen Anne's War.
1705	Virginia slave code ties slavery to African origin.
1720	African slaves make up two-thirds of South Carolina's population.
1726	East and West Jersey unite as New Jersey.
1733	James Oglethorpe leads settlers to Georgia to create haven for "worthy poor."
1750	Non-native population in colonial America reaches 1 million.

What Else Was Happening

1655: The Dutch of New Amster-dam use lotteries to raise money for the poor.

1666: The Great Fire destroys three-fourths of London, killing only sixteen and helping halt the spread of the bubonic plague.
1670: Paris café starts serving ice cream.

1686: Christian Gabriel Fahren-heit invents the thermometer.
1688: The start of the Japanese Edo Renaissance, a cultural flow-ering that saw the development of Kabuki theater.

Expansion and Its Costs, 1660–1700

3-1 **Describe the development of the North American colonies from 1660–1700, and analyze the four distinct areas that began to emerge in British North America.** Civil war, the Restoration, and rising debt led the English to alter their treatment of the colonies as well as to develop several more. Carolina, New York, Pennsylvania, the Jerseys, and Georgia began as proprietary colonies. These colonies contained greater diversity than the ones first established, giving each a distinct character. The Spanish tried to preserve Southwest territories, despite two Native American uprisings. By 1700, the British appeared to have the upper hand over the Spanish in eastern North America.

commonwealth A kingless republican government (p. 45)

Restoration Period of English history when the Stuarts were restored to the throne (1660–1685) (p. 45)

Navigation Acts Regulations that dictated where colonial producers could ship their goods, stipulated that colonists must transport their goods in British ships, and listed a group of products that colonists were permitted to sell only to Britain (p. 45)

enumerated articles Goods (tobacco, sugar, cotton, indigo) listed in the Navigation Acts that colonists were permitted to sell only to Britain (p. 46)

proprietary colonies Colonies owned and ruled by an individual or a private corporation, rather than by the Crown (p. 46)

Quakers Protestants who believed that God's will was directly transmitted to people through "the inner light" of divine knowledge that a person possesses within his or her being; this belief was in direct opposition to the Bible-centered Protestant mainstream (p. 49)

Pueblo Revolt An uprising of several villages spanning several hundred miles across the New Mexican landscape in 1680, led by the shaman Popé (p. 51)

3-2 **Describe and analyze the English colonists' experiences up to 1700 with Native American peoples.** A "middle ground" of peaceful trade often existed between settlers and Native Americans. As the 17th century wore on, conflicts increased in frequency, intensity, and duration. With increasing settlement, native tribes were forced from traditional lands, spawning several wars (most notably Metacom's War and Bacon's Rebellion). The costly wars ended up splintering and greatly weakening Native tribes and confederations.

Beaver Wars Intertribal battles in the 1600s in which the Iroquois forced the Huron out of the Northeast (p. 53)

Metacom's War First large-scale conflict between colonists and Native Americans, waged in Plymouth, Massachusetts Bay, Rhode Island, and Connecticut (1675–1676) (p. 53)

King Philip's War British colonists' name for Metacom's War, because they referred to the Wampanoag leader Metacom as King Philip (p. 53)

Bacon's Rebellion Revolt among colonists, led by Nathaniel Bacon, that was triggered by Virginia governor Sir William Berkeley's unwillingness to listen to the demands of the laboring people who wanted to attack several nearby Indians (1676–1677) (p. 55)

Bacon's Laws Series of laws that democratized the politics of Virginia, granted the franchise to all freemen, inaugurated elections of the members of the legislature, and granted greater representation in taxation (p. 55)

3-3 **Understand the English colonists' experiences up to 1700 with African slaves.** Europeans' sugar cane plantations in the Caribbean and South America killed off much of the native populations, through hard work and disease, so Europeans then turned to Africa for slaves. English colonies at first relied on indentured servants; even some Africans were treated as such at first. Over time, Englishmen ceased indenturing themselves and more African slaves were needed for labor. Starting in 1662 colonists began to enact slave codes to ensure a labor supply. It was only then that laws began to forbid mixed marriages and to declare slavery hereditary.

slave codes Laws meant to govern the slave system of labor; these laws made it impossible for an African American to live as a free person (p. 57)

3-4 **Describe and analyze the European wars that had an impact on North America.** Both French and English had a strong North American presence (French fur traders, English settlers). Conflicts in Europe naturally bled over into America. In King William's War, New York's governor instigated warfare between native groups who supported the two nations. By war's end, the Iroquois were closer with the French, whom they had first attacked. English victory in Queen Anne's War brought a respite to the conflicts in Europe. English colonists seized the opportunity to move into the frontier areas and to take control of Hudson Bay. The tragic strangeness of the 1692 Salem witch trials reveals many of the anxieties of the era, including worries about warfare with Indians and gender and class uncertainties in a new land.

King William's War Battles between the Iroquois, French, and English colonists (1689–1697) (p. 59)

Queen Anne's War The New World name for the War of the Spanish Succession; twelve years of battle between the Spanish in Florida, the French in the North American interior, the English along the coast, and various Indian nations (1702–1713) (p. 59)

What Else Was Happening

1688 Protestants replace James II with William and Mary in Glorious Revolution.

1696 The Salem witchcraft trials signal demise of Puritans' religious utopia.

1709: *Bartolomeo Cristofori invents the piano.*

1712: *The last execution of an accused witch takes place in Britain.*

1720 Slaves make up 20 percent of Chesapeake population.

1734 New York Weekly Journal editor J. Peter Zenger is punished for government criticism.

1738–1745 In Great Awakening, itinerant preachers such as George Whitefield promote emotional Protestantism.

1739 South Carolina whites quell slaves' Stono Rebellion and in turn pass Negro Act.

1740 Fearful of slave insurrection, New York City convicts, burns, and hangs 35 suspects.

1744–1748 France and Britain continue imperial rivalries in King George's War.

1751: *Benjamin Franklin sends up a kite during a thunderstorm and discovers that lightning is a form of electricity.*

1752: *The first eraser is put on the end of a pencil.*

1754–1763 French and Indian war over trade in the North American interior escalates into a worldwide battle.

1754 At Albany Congress colonists for the first time discuss common concerns with war.

1760 Slaves make up 40 percent of Chesapeake population.

1773 Treaty of Paris evicts France from America, draws Proclamation Line, sets borders with Spanish Empire.

Brutal pan-Indian Pontiac Rebellion against growing British colonial empire fails.

4-1 **Describe the development of the English colonies during the 1700s, including a discussion of each of the four distinct groups of colonies: New England, the Middle Colonies, the Chesapeake, and the Southern Colonies.** By 1700, the English colonies had developed distinct differences and local governments of their own, and England found them more and more difficult to control. New England had long relied on farming, but now fishing and lumber led to trade with other countries. As population grew, a class system emerged and religion's importance began to recede. The Middle Colonies enjoyed a warmer environment, with individual, mostly self-sufficient farmsteads. The main industries developed around corn and wheat. With few cities, the Chesapeake revolved around self-sufficient tobacco farms. Aristocratic families controlled social, political, and religious institutions. Many poor whites eked out a living, and slaves comprised about 40 percent of the population. Southern colonies had little industry, with the main crops rice, indigo, and tobacco. The environment was poor, and colonists who chose to live there owned large plantations but lived in cities for comfort.

CHAPTER REVIEW / KEY TERMS

CHAPTER 4 LEARNING OUTCOMES

diversified farming System in which a single home could farm various crops to sustain the household throughout the year (p. 63)

Triangular Trade Pattern of trade in which fish, grains, spices, sugar, ships, slaves, and gold were traded between the New England colonies, England, southern Europe, the West Indies, and Africa (p. 63)

jeremiad A long speech or literary work emphasizing society's fall from purity and grace to its current, depraved state (p. 66)

4-2 **Discuss the impact of the Enlightenment and the Great Awakening on colonial America.** European Enlightenment thinkers spread the idea of "natural rights" that no government could deny. America's "Great Awakening" personalized and individualized religion for people who had once accepted the idea of deferring to church authorities without question.

Enlightenment A movement to prioritize the human capacity for reason as the highest form of human attainment (p. 71)

Great Awakening America's first large-scale religious revival, originated by preachers who stressed that all were equal in Christ (p. 75)

Old Lights Protestant leaders who condemned emotionalism and advocated a more rationalistic theology favored by elements of the Enlightenment (p. 75)

New Lights Protestant leaders who supported evangelism, the new methods of prayer, and equality before Christ (p. 75)

4-3 **Chronicle the development of slavery in the American colonies, and analyze the reasons for changes in attitudes and in the legal system that helped the distinctively American slave system flourish.** The Atlantic slave trade took Africans to many parts of the Americas, but in the American colonies, especially the South, slavery became deeply entrenched. The "middle passage" sea voyage took up to two months, during which many Africans died. Slaves might serve their masters in many ways, as domestic servants and field hands. Slave life on Chesapeake and Southern plantations made it possible for Africans to retain some aspects of their native culture, but white slave owners soon placed heavy restrictions on slaves.

Atlantic slave trade Huge system of trade and migration that brought millions of slaves to the New World and Europe in the 1600s and 1700s (p. 76)

middle passage The perilous journey across the Atlantic endured by captives from Africa (p. 77)

Stono Rebellion Slave rebellion in South Carolina in 1739, the largest slave uprising of the century (p. 78)

Negro Act South Carolina state law that consolidated all the separate slave codes into a single code that forbade slaves from growing their own food, assembling in groups, or learning to read (p. 79)

4-4 **By 1763, American colonists had become used to making their own decisions and taking care of their own needs. Describe the events in England that contributed to this situation, and explain their effects on the colonists.** The mid to late 1600s in England saw religious differences boil into political turmoil many times, culminating with the bloodless "Glorious Revolution" of 1688. The Glorious Revolution heralded a 75-year run of looser government and "salutary neglect." The French and Indian War of 1754–1763 for control of the Ohio Valley brought this neglect to an end. The war ended up involving several major countries in Europe and numerous Indian tribes in America. England won the war. But through it, the colonists began to develop unity among themselves that they no longer felt with the mother country.

salutary neglect Hands-off style of relations between the Crown and the colonies; a loose system of oversight whereby the Crown ignored governance of its colonies and enforcement of its trade laws so long as the colonies provided England with cash and crops (p. 79)

Glorious Revolution of 1688 Overthrow of King James II by Protestant factions; his exit left the crown to William and Mary (p. 79)

King George's War Continued New World battles between Britain and France (1744–1748) (p. 80)

Seven Years' War European label for the world war (1754–1763) between France, Britain, Austria, Russia, Prussia, Spain, and numerous Indian tribes (p. 81)

French and Indian War Colonial label for the Seven Years' War (p. 81)

Albany Congress Meeting of representatives from seven colonies in Albany, New York, in 1754, the first time the mainland British colonies met for a unified purpose (p. 81)

Albany Plan Concept for the first-ever colonial union, drafted by Benjamin Franklin (p. 81)

Treaty of Paris 1763 Agreement between Spain, Britain, and France that made the Mississippi River the boundary between Britain's holdings and Spain's, and evicted France from North America (p. 81)

pan-Indianism Movement in which many of the tribes of Native America shifted from favoring a tribal identity to assuming a racial one; a way in which the various Indian nations of North America came together to oppose the British (p. 83)

Neolin Prophet from the Delaware tribe who began preaching a return to old Indian ways (p. 83)

Pontiac's Rebellion Brutal battles between Ottawa Indians and British troops in 1763 (p. 84)

Chapter 5 Timeline

1751 Writs of Assistance allow British search and seizure in private homes.

1760 Privy Council issues "Orders of Council" to rein in smugglers and absentee officials.

1763 Proclamation Line tries to stop western land sales and settlement, makes Indians royal subjects.

1764 Sugar Act cuts taxes and increases enforcements.

1765 Quartering Act requires colonists to house and feed British troops. Stamp Act stirs powerful opposition against direct taxation of official paper.

1766 Declaratory Act asserts Parliament's right to legislate colonies. Restraining Act suspends New York Assembly for violating Quartering Act.

1767 New external duties in Townshend Act stir boycotts, revolutionary ideology.

1770 In Boston Massacre, British soldiers shoot into rowdy crowd, killing five.

1773 Tea Act cuts duties but establishes monopoly for East India Company. Colonists in Indian disguise board ship to destroy tea cargo in Boston Tea Party.

1775 In Concord and Lexington, Minutemen engage Redcoats in guerrilla tactics.
Second Continental Congress creates Continental Army under Washington.
Battle of Bunker Hill triggers colonists' solidarity and British resolve.

What Else Was Happening

1700s: *American innkeepers think nothing of requesting that a guest share his bed with a stranger when accommodations become scarce.*

1760s: *Because the British Macaroni Club's members are known for having affected manners and long, curled hair, "macaroni" becomes a slang term for "dandy." The song "Yankee Doodle" is invented by the British to insult American colonists. The section where Doodle puts a feather in his cap and calls it macaroni is a slap at the ragged bands of American troops.*

1769: *Shoelaces are invented in Britain.*

1772: *Joseph Priestley invents soda water.*

1774: *Coercive Acts close Boston harbor and Massachusetts government, tightening Quartering Acts to protect British officials from colonial courts. Parliament grants Quebec jurisdiction over land west of Proclamation Line. First Continental Congress signals colonial unified resistance, not submission. Empress Catherine II's Russian troops defeat Turkey, adding the Southern Ukraine, the Northern Caucasus, and Crimea to the Russian Empire.*

5-1 **Explain Britain's main reasons for attempting to overturn salutary neglect.** During and after the French and Indian War, Britain's Privy Council made decisions that angered many in the colonies. To re-exert its control, Britain cracked down on smuggling by colonists trying to avoid taxes. To protect British manufacturing, the Proclamation of 1763 banned settlement west of the Appalachian Mountains (keeping settlers closer to the coast and to British trading vessels). To pay for the war, Britain instituted the Sugar Act (1764), the Quartering Act of 1765, and the Stamp Act (1765).

Privy Council A group of close advisors to the Crown that offered suggestions on how the Crown should best exercise its executive authority (p. 87)

Sugar Act of 1764 Act that reduced taxes on molasses and sugar, laid taxes on indigo, pimento (allspice), some wines, and coffee, and increased enforcement of tax collection; signaled the end of the era of salutary neglect (p. 88)

Quartering Act of 1765 This act required the colonies to feed and house British troops stationed in their territory (p. 88)

Stamp Act of 1765 This act mandated the use of stamped (embedded) paper for all official papers, including diplomas, marriage licenses, wills, newspapers, and playing cards (p. 88)

5-2 **Explain how the colonists responded to the new acts, and trace the evolutionary process that brought the colonies closer to rebellion.** The Stamp Act affected virtually everyone, not just rum traders as the Sugar Act did. Colonists appealed to Parliament and boycotted British goods (shutting down the port of New York). The Sons of Liberty coordinated riots, and newspapers proclaimed "no taxation without representation." Without support from the king, Parliament repealed the Stamp Act, and the protesters claimed victory. Parliament's Declaratory Act reasserted its right to legislate for the colonies "in all cases whatsoever."

circular letter Communication among a number of interested parties that was sent from colony to colony to keep the disparate colonies together, or united; a primary form of communication for the colonies during the revolutionary period (p. 89)

Stamp Act Congress Gathering of colonial leaders from nine states in New York City in October 1765 to discuss resistance to the Stamp Act; one of the early instances of collaboration between colonies and of identifying Parliament as the opposition rather than the king (p. 89)

Daughters of Liberty Group of colonial American women who organized boycotts of tea and other imported British goods and who produced homespun clothes as a protest of British imported clothing (p. 90)

Sons of Liberty Groups of colonial leaders who organized protests and intimidated stamp officials; their actions caused the resignation of all known stamp officials (p. 90)

Radical Whigs Political activists and pamphleteers who vigorously defended the rights and liberties of Englishmen and who coined the phrase "no taxation without representation" (p. 90)

external taxes Duties designed to protect the British Empire; part of Parliament's right to regulate trade, as argued by Benjamin Franklin and Daniel Dulany (p. 91)

internal taxes Duties that directly affected the internal affairs of the colonies; according to Benjamin Franklin and Daniel Dulany, this internal legislation threatened private property (p. 91)

virtual representation Theory endorsed by Parliament that said the House of Commons represented the interests of all the king's subjects, wherever they might reside; this was the pretext for rejecting the colonists' demand for actual representation (p. 92)

deputy representation The practice of the people's interests being advocated by a deputy; also known as actual representation (p. 92)

Declaratory Act Passed by Parliament in 1766, this act affirmed its authority to legislate for the colonies "in all cases whatsoever"; largely symbolic, it became one of the nonnegotiable claims that Parliament was unwilling to relinquish throughout the struggle (p. 93)

5-3 Trace the path to revolution from the Townshend Acts of 1767 to the meeting of the First Continental Congress. In 1767 Charles Townshend, new Chancellor of the Exchequer, declared broad-based Townshend Acts. Colonists resisted and violence ensued. The "Boston Massacre" resulted in 5 deaths among the rioters. Tensions escalated, and committees of correspondence came together to disseminate current news. Colonists began to choose sides; those loyal to the Crown were most often wealthy urban residents and those with the most to lose in the Southern Colonies and the Chesapeake. The Tea Act of 1773 lowered the tax on tea so as to give the East India Company a monopoly, resulting in the Boston Tea Party. That in turn led to the Coercive Acts in 1774. Parliament closed the port of Boston, ordered colonists to house and feed British troops, and removed most of Massachusetts's rights to self-government. Representatives of twelve colonies met in Philadelphia as the First Continental Congress.

Restraining Act In this act, Chancellor of the Exchequer Charles Townshend suspended the New York Assembly for failing to comply with the Quartering Act (p. 93)

Townshend Acts These acts of 1767 instituted duties on glass, lead for paint, tea, paper, and a handful of other items (p. 93)

Boston Massacre Incendiary riot on March 5, 1770, when British soldiers fired into a crowd and killed five people (p. 94)

***Gaspée* incident** Conflict that occurred when colonists from Providence boarded and burned the British naval vessel *Gaspée* (p. 95)

committees of correspondence Organized groups of letter writers who would provide quick and reliable information throughout the colonies (p. 95)

Tea Act Passed in 1773, this act was designed to give the East India Company a monopoly on the sale of tea to North America (p. 95)

Boston Tea Party Protest staged December 16, 1773, when an organized squad of roughly sixty colonists dressed as Mohawk Indians boarded Hutchinson's ship and dumped 342 chests of tea into Boston Harbor (p. 96)

Coercive Acts Four separate acts, passed in 1774, that were meant to punish Massachusetts for the Tea Party: the Boston Port Act, the Massachusetts Government Act, the Administration of Justice Act, and the Quartering Act (p. 97)

Intolerable Acts Colonists' collective label for the Quebec Act and the Coercive Acts (p. 98)

First Continental Congress Meeting of twelve colonies at Philadelphia in May 1774 to consider the American response to the Coercive Acts (p. 98)

Continental Association Group that supervised a boycott of British trade; the association was prefaced with a "Declaration of Rights" that affirmed the natural rights of "life, liberty, and property" (p. 98)

5-4 Explain how the American Revolution began, and describe the first battles of the conflict. Colonists began to make military preparations. Britain responded by requesting 20,000 new troops. In April 1775, General Gage sent troops to Concord to capture weapons held there by the colonists. Colonial "Minutemen" responded and drove the Redcoats back to Boston. Colonists convened the Second Continental Congress, creating an army headed by George Washington. The Congress stopped short of declaring war, but the king declared them in rebellion. The first major conflict took place at Boston's Bunker Hill (actually Breed's Hill). Though forced from their hilltop position, the colonists inflicted heavy casualties and claimed victory. Parliament declared a state of open rebellion and began a blockade of American ports.

Minutemen Nickname for American militia soldiers because of their reputation for being ready on a minute's notice (p. 100)

Second Continental Congress Gathering of colonial leaders in May 1775 to determine the colonies' response to the battles of Lexington and Concord; they passed resolutions supporting war that included a sharp rejection of all authority under the king in America (p. 100)

Olive Branch Petition A 1775 declaration to King George III that the colonists were still loyal to him and imploring the king to seek a peaceful resolution to the conflict (p. 100)

Battle of Bunker Hill Outbreak of fighting on June 17, 1775, near Boston Harbor; the first all-out battle of the Revolutionary War (p. 101)

American Prohibitory Act This act declared the colonies to be "in open rebellion," forbade commerce with the colonies by blockading their ports, and made colonial ships and their cargo subject to seizure as if they were the property "of open enemies" (p. 102)

What Else Was Happening

1775

August: King George III denounces colonists as rebels.

November: Dunmore promises slaves freedom for fighting alongside British.

1776

January: Thomas Paine's pamphlet Common Sense calls for independence.

March: Continental Army forces British to evacuate Boston, ending eleven-month siege.

June 7: Committee for Declaration of Independence forms, with Jefferson as draftsman.

June 28: Continental Congress debates and edits Declaration of Independence.

1776

July 2: Continental Congress unanimously approves Declaration of Independence.

August–December: Continental Army escapes British in New York.

December 26: General Washington defeats British with surprise move in Trenton, New Jersey.

1779

Under Cornwallis, British land in South Carolina and advance quickly.

1780

To weaken British, patriots draw fighting deeper into South Carolina.

1781

Cornwallis gives up South Carolina and awaits reinforcements in Virginia.

October 19: American and French forces trap Cornwallis army on Yorktown peninsula.

1782

John Jay, Benjamin Franklin, John Adams travel to Paris for peace talks.

1783

September: Treaty of Paris grants American independence and rights to the West.

1785

Revolution inspires formation of freedom churches such as the Unitarians.

What Else Was Happening column:

1777 September 19: *Patriot victory at Battle of Saratoga leads to Franco-American Alliance.*

September 26: *Under General Howe, British take the new capital of Philadelphia.*

July 4: *The United States celebrates its first birthday. Ships lined up on the Delaware River discharge thirteen cannon shots in honor of the thirteen states.*

Franco-American Alliance against British expands the war to the Atlantic.

New Orleans businessman Oliver Pollock creates the $ symbol.

1784: *A new trade route opens for Americans when the Empress of China sails from New Jersey around Cape Horn in South America to China.*

1787: *The first U.S. penny, designed by Benjamin Franklin, is minted.*

1789: *The French Revolution begins, initiating a long battle in France over "liberty, equality, and fraternity."*

1790: *All states but South Carolina and Georgia outlaw slave import from abroad.*

The cornerstone of the mansion known as the White House is laid.

6-1 Describe the long-term causes and more immediate events that led the colonists into a true revolution against Britain. British colonists in America had forged a society very different from the one in Britain. Class differences were less important in the colonies, and there was a greater sense of community. When Britain passed its acts in the 1760s–70s free men and women from all classes drew together. As each colony had its own government, colonists knew they were capable of governing themselves. As the disagreements with Britain escalated, more colonists began to talk of complete separation, while Parliament and King George became more determined to clamp down on the rebellion. It became clear that the split between the two had become too wide to repair.

Hessians German soldiers hired by Britain to fight against the rebelling American colonies (p. 106)

republicanism The theory that government should be based on the consent of the governed and that the governed had a duty to ensure that their government did not infringe on individual rights (p. 107)

Cato's Letters Book that spread republican ideas throughout the colonies; written by British authors John Trenchard and Thomas Gordon (p. 107)

Common Sense Influential political pamphlet written by Thomas Paine, published in January 1776, containing a simple wording of republican ideals (p. 107)

Declaration of Independence Statement adopted by the Second Continental Congress declaring that the thirteen American colonies, then at battle with Britain, constituted a free and independent state; drafted primarily by Thomas Jefferson and adopted in 1776 (p. 108)

6-2 Enumerate the various phases of the American Revolution, and analyze the circumstances that eventually helped the colonists win a conflict that Britain, by rights, should never have lost. At the outset of hostilities, most analyses would have predicted that Britain would prevail. Washington's troops were ill equipped, while the British troops were well equipped, clothed, and fed. The British understood the first phase of the war from 1774 to 1777 as a police action. Once the suppression of the uprising had failed, the second phase brought a number of successes to the British, who hoped to deflect the colonial forces in the north without having to broaden the conflict further. After initial British advances, Washington won a victory at Trenton, New Jersey, at the end of 1776. The next year, the Continental Army's victory at Saratoga brought the French in on the American side. Hoping to enlist Loyalists, as well as hold on to the South, the British moved the war southward in the third phase of the war, and most remaining fighting took place there. However, many Loyalists joined America's cause. And guerrilla tactics began to take a toll on the British. At home the British people grew restless over taxes to pay for a distant war far too few felt strongly about.

bills of credit Currency printed by the Continental Congress during the Revolutionary War; printing these bills in huge numbers and without any backing led to high inflation (p. 110)

Battle of Saratoga Battle in New York State in 1777 between the Continental Army and General Burgoyne's British Army troops; Burgoyne surrendered, giving hope to the revolutionary effort (p. 113)

6-3 Assess the significance of the American Revolution to the following groups: colonists, slaves, Native Americans, and women. Joining together in the cause of liberty contributed greatly to the new sense of American nationalism. The war brought polarization between North and South over the slavery issue. Some northern states outlawed slavery immediately; by 1840 only 1,000 Africans in the North remained slaves. Southerners clung to their right to own slaves, even after the fight for their own independence. Native American tribes fared badly. Americans exacted revenge on several that had sided with Britain. Americans now began venturing west, which would bring many new conflicts with Indian nations as time went on. During the Revolution women upheld boycotts, raised war funds, and did everything in their power to help. A few states "rewarded" them with suffrage, but mostly women returned to traditional roles.

manumit To willingly free one's slaves (p. 119)

Virginia Statute on Religious Freedom Bill passed in 1786 that was originally drafted by Thomas Jefferson, articulating distrust of an established state church and the value of religious liberty (p. 121)

What Else Was Happening

1777–1781	States ratify Articles of Confederation.
1783	Continental Congress demobilizes Continental Army.
1784	Virginia cedes western land claims to federal government.
1786	In vain, Massachusetts farmers petition for debt relief.
1790	**May:** Rhode Island is last state to ratify Constitution.
1791	**December:** Bill of Rights goes into effect.

1785: *Frenchman J. P. Blanchard is said to be the first to actually use a parachute by dropping a dog in a basket, to which the parachute was attached, from a hot-air balloon. The dog survived, but fourteen years later, Blanchard suffered a heart attack, fell from one of his own balloons, and died of his injuries.*

1787: *Northwest Ordinance creates territorial governments, orders western development.*
January 26: *In Shays' Rebellion, Massachusetts farmers try to seize federal armory.*
May: *State delegate meeting in Philadelphia turns into Constitutional Convention.*
September: *Delegates present new Constitution to states for ratification.*
December: *Delaware, Pennsylvania, New Jersey ratify Constitution. Mozart composes his opera* Don Giovanni.
1788 June: *New Hampshire becomes ninth state to ratify Constitution. Australia is first settled by Europeans as a penal colony.*
1789 September: *Congress sends Bill of Rights to states for ratification. Mutiny takes place on H.M.S. Bounty.*

1793: *Reign of Terror begins in France, as rival revolutionary factions battle over the proper ways in which "liberty, equality, and fraternity" can be implemented in a modern nation-state. Between 15,000 and 40,000 French lose their lives during the fourteen-month Terror, many by the blade of the guillotine, which earns the nickname "National Razor."*

7-1 **Describe the first state constitutions written and adopted after the United States declared its independence.** Though differing in details, state constitutions provided models for the Articles of Confederation. Each included a bill of rights. Some allowed only Christians to participate politically; others retained property-owning qualifications. Women were usually excluded from voting, except notably in New Jersey. All envisioned a separation of powers, per Enlightenment thinkers, but only within individual states.

bill of rights In the American context, a list of "natural rights" that many Americans felt were threatened by Britain's prerevolutionary laws; most of the bills of rights included in early state constitutions guaranteed the freedom of the press, the right of popular consent before being taxed, and protections against general search warrants (p. 125)

separation of powers The concept of creating several different branches of government and giving each of them different responsibilities so as to prevent any one body from exerting an excess of authority (p. 126)

7-2 **Analyze the federal government as it existed under the Articles of Confederation.** The Articles laid out the operation of the federal government, and addressed states' rights and responsibilities. Drafted in 1777, the Articles did not take effect until 1781, because all states had to ratify it. A major weakness was that every proposed alteration required unanimous consent by all states. There was no provision for raising funds or overseeing internal trade, nor was the federal government authorized to settle newly arising issues between the U.S. and other sovereign nations.

Articles of Confederation Document that defined the colonies' collective sovereignty; drafted by the Continental Congress between 1776 and 1777, then ratified by the thirteen states by 1781 (p. 127)

7-3 **Enumerate the most significant issues that the United States had to deal with under the Articles of Confederation, and explain how the Articles failed to live up to the needs of the new country.** One of the first issues was how the country's new lands should be settled. With independence, America nearly doubled in size, extending from the Atlantic Coast to the Mississippi River. Some states claimed all of their settled lands north to south, plus all lands westward to the Mississippi. In 1784, Virginia ceded its western lands to the U.S. government; the other states then did as well. Congress had to develop plans for creating territories and then making them eligible for statehood. Britain was supposed to vacate U.S. lands, but without a military the U.S. couldn't have forced the issue. The U.S. was deeply in debt, unable to pay financiers, or provide backpay for the army. Shays' Rebellion clearly demonstrated the weakness of the Articles of Confederation.

Northwest Ordinance of 1787 Legislation that established territorial governments in the Great Lakes region and set a pattern for future western development (p. 129)

specie Gold or silver, which has intrinsic value, used as payment instead of paper money, which has extrinsic value (p. 131)

Shays' Rebellion Potential coup of January 26, 1787, when Daniel Shays led 1,200 men to seize control of the federal arsenal in Springfield, Massachusetts, to protest the state legislature's inability to address the debt problems of small farmers (p. 132)

7-4 **Explain the need for the Constitutional Convention that met in Philadelphia in 1787, and describe the process of writing the Constitution.** The meeting was officially to amend the Articles, but in reality to create a new plan of government. The two main plans presented highlighted the problems of trying to unite diverse states. The body was composed of the wealthy and educated, believers in strong government, who feared too much democracy. The Virginia Plan represented large states, the New Jersey plan small states; both sought a two-house legislature. Most matters required compromise, such as how to count population for representation in the House. The awkward "three-fifths clause" accepted slavery but counted slaves as less than whole people. Another compromise permitted the slave trade to continue for another 20 years so the U.S. economy could get established. The new plan gave the federal government the power to regulate the admission of new states.

Virginia Plan This proposal, known as the large states plan because it favored those states, sought to scrap the Articles of Confederation and create a Congress with two houses, with representation in Congress being determined by population (p. 133)

New Jersey Plan This proposal suggested revising the Articles of Confederation rather than replacing them altogether (p. 133)

Great Compromise Plan to grant each state equal representation in the upper house (to be called the Senate) and representation that was proportional to population (1 representative for every 30,000 people) in the lower house (the House of Representatives) (p. 134)

three-fifths clause Section of the Constitution that allowed southerners to include three-fifths of their slave population for both representation and the apportionment of federal taxes (p. 134)

7-5 **Describe and explain the major provisions of the Constitution created by the Philadelphia convention, especially concerning the separation of powers and the rights given to individual states.** The new Constitution let Congress collect taxes, regulate commerce, maintain an army, declare war, and make modifications to the Constitution itself. Each state retained a great deal of power over its own internal affairs. Powers were separated through the division of duties into three branches of government. Congress was designed to be the most powerful branch, with the ability to make new laws. The executive branch consisted of an elected president and a cabinet of advisors that he appointed. Presidential powers included making treaties, overseeing the military, and vetoing acts of Congress. The election process was removed from direct voter control, since the framers feared too much democracy. Instead, an Electoral College would meet after a general election to override any "bad" decision made by the citizenry. The judicial branch included the Supreme Court (the ultimate interpreter of the Constitution) and regional courts.

Electoral College Group composed of delegates from each state equal in number to its total apportionment in Congress (number of senators plus number of representatives); these delegates cast votes for president (p. 135)

7-6 **Explain the procedure established for ratification of the Constitution, describe the actions of its supporters and its opponents, and explain how and when ratification was eventually achieved.** The framers agreed that it would become the law of the land when nine states had ratified it. Some states ratified it immediately. Most larger states held off, wanting to ensure states' rights. The Constitution's supporters, known as Federalists, campaigned with a series of newspaper articles known as the Federalist Papers. Much Anti-Federalist opposition evaporated after the Federalists pledged to add a Bill of Rights. New Hampshire's ratification in June 1788 gave the Constitution legal status. Rhode Island eventually made acceptance of the Constitution unanimous.

Federalists Framers of the Constitution who emphasized that the new government would not end state autonomy; they also contemplated a Bill of Rights that would prevent the new centralized government from infringing on what were thought of as natural rights (p. 137)

Federalist Papers Essays written by John Jay, Alexander Hamilton, and James Madison in 1787, meant to influence the Constitution ratification debate in New York State; the essays defended the Constitution article by article and addressed many of the complaints of opponents, such as the concerns about the size of the new nation (p. 137)

federalism Philosophy of government in which states and the nation share the responsibility of government, with no one group or agency possessing sufficient power to dominate the other (p. 137)

Anti-Federalists A group of American patriots who preferred a weaker confederation of states and a more direct democracy; they objected to the concentration of power in a centralized government regardless of how it divided power (p. 137)

1788 First federal election.
Judiciary Act creates three circuit and thirteen district courts.

1790 Naturalization Act limits citizenship for immigrants to free white persons.
Indian coalition attacks American settlers north of Ohio River.
Indian Trade and Intercourse Act puts trade with natives under federal control.

1792 Jefferson becomes leader of Democratic-Republican Party.

1793 Genêt affair further splits Democrat-Republicans and Federalists.

1794 Western settlers resist federal authority in the Whiskey Rebellion.

1796 Pinckney Treaty with Spain opens Mississippi River to American trade.
Federalist John Adams becomes second president of the United States.

1797 XYZ Affair prompts quasi-war with revolutionary France.

What Else Was Happening

1791: Congress charters First Bank of the United States.
Haitian Revolution becomes only successful slave rebellion in hemisphere.
Early bicycles are made in Scotland.
France begins using the metric system.

1795: Conciliatory Jay Treaty with Britain angers Democratic-Republicans.
Treaty of Greenville forces Indians west out of Ohio Valley.
Tula Slave Rebellion in the Dutch Caribbean colony of Curacao lasts a month before finally being suppressed. August 17 is still celebrated in Curacao as a day of freedom.

1798: Adams tries to control political conflict with Alien and Sedition Acts. In response, Virginia and Kentucky formulate doctrine of nullification.
The first soft drink is invented.
1800: Virginians crush Gabriel's slave conspiracy and tighten slave laws.
Jefferson's election demonstrates peaceful political change in the republic.

8-1 **Describe the creation of the federal government under the new Constitution.** The new Constitution was unclear about how the three-branch government should function. Elections for the first Congress were held in 1788; members met in New York City to begin crafting a federal system. The Judiciary Act of 1789 established the federal court system. Congress adopted the Bill of Rights, handled matters of finance, citizenship, and the cabinet, and agreed on the title "president." George Washington was unanimously selected first president. He negotiated treaties, then obtained Senate consent. He also supported delivering a state of the nation speech to Congress once a year. Washington filled his cabinet with men of opposing political views, hoping they'd work together for the country's good.

Naturalization Act of 1790 Legislation which declared that, among immigrants to the United States, only "free white persons" could become citizens (p. 143)

patronage System of granting rewards for assisting with political victories (p. 144)

Hamilton Tariff of 1789 Act that imposed a 5 to 10 percent tariff on certain imports to fund the new government (p. 144)

cabinet Group of the heads of departments within the executive branch; one of George Washington's innovations as president (p. 145)

8-2 **Show how disagreements over how the United States should be governed led to political divisions, and discuss some of the individuals who took strong stands on each side.** The new government faced issues of how to finance its work and how to deal with foreign policy. Federalists (supporting strong federal government) included Washington and Hamilton. The group that became the Democratic-Republicans (with Jefferson and Madison) wanted weaker federal, and stronger states', rights. Treasury secretary Hamilton laid out a plan to pay wartime loans, establish a national bank, and raise revenue for government operation. Opponents resisted nationalization of state debts; many felt a national bank benefited only the wealthy. In an unlikely compromise, those opposed to the bank allowed Hamilton's plan to pass in Congress, and the nation's capital was established along the Potomac River, in the new city of Washington, D.C. Washington quelled the tax-fueled Whiskey Rebellion, establishing supremacy of the federal government. The Pinckney Treaty was a foreign policy success, allowing the U.S. to use the mouth of the Mississippi River; Jay's Treaty with Britain revealed great and deep partisan divisions between Federalists and anti-Federalists. Continuing conflict with Native Americans pushed Native tribes ever westward, and spawned restrictive Indian Trade and Intercourse Acts.

implied powers Congress's power to do anything "necessary and proper" to carry out its delegated powers, even if those actions are not explicitly named in the Constitution (p. 147)

loose constructionism Interpretation of the Constitution suggesting that the Constitution should be flexible to accommodate new demands (p. 147)

Democratic-Republicans Faction that coalesced in opposition to Alexander Hamilton's economic policies and Jay's Treaty; led by Virginians like Thomas Jefferson and James Madison; also known as the Jeffersonians (p. 147)

strict constructionism Literal interpretation of the Constitution, arguing that the original meaning of those at the Constitutional Convention should not be adapted to fit more recent times (p. 147)

Whiskey Rebellion Conflict in which Pennsylvania farmers fought a tax on whiskey, eventually rioting and overrunning the city of Pittsburgh in 1794, where they were to be tried for tax evasion (p. 149)

impressment Practice of capturing and forcing sailors from other nations into naval service (p. 150)

Jay's Treaty Treaty in which the British agreed to evacuate military posts along the frontier in the Northwest Territory and make reparations for the cargo seized in 1793 and 1794 while the United States lifted duties on British imports for ten years (p. 151)

Pinckney Treaty of 1796 Agreement with Spain that opened the Mississippi River to American shipping and allowed Americans the "right of deposit" at New Orleans, which meant that American merchants could warehouse goods in the city (p. 151)

Treaty of Greenville Agreement that forced the Indians of the Old Northwest westward across the Mississippi River in 1795 (p. 151)

Indian Trade and Intercourse Acts Laws that made it illegal for Americans to trade with Native Americans without formal consent from the federal government and also made it illegal to sell land to or buy land from Native Americans without similar federal consent (p. 152)

8-3 **Outline the country's development of a two-party political system.** By 1792, opposing groups had coalesced into formal Federalist and Democratic-Republican parties. Federalists tended to be wealthy property owners and conservative farmers with strength in New England and the Mid-Atlantic. Democratic-Republicans sought limited government, supported slavery, and were strongest in the South and along the frontier. Federalists supported the 1791 Haiti slave revolt, while Democratic-Republicans backed the French attempt to quell it. Gabriel's Conspiracy, along with a second failed slave rebellion, led to the passage of harsh slave laws.

Federalist Party Faction of American leaders that endorsed Hamilton's economic policies and Jay's Treaty (p. 153)

Gabriel's Conspiracy Slave rebellion in 1800 in Richmond, Virginia; twenty-six rebels were hanged (p. 154)

8-4 **Discuss the issues of John Adams's presidency, and explain how he and the country dealt with them.** After two terms, Washington retired, warning against "entangling alliances" with foreign governments and urging Americans to abandon the two-party system before it became too entrenched. The two presidential candidates were Federalist Adams and Democratic-Republican Jefferson. Because of an electoral glitch, Adams became president and Jefferson vice president. Foreign policy dominated the new presidency, as French-British trade wars embroiled the U.S. As diplomacy broke down, French and Americans raided each others' ships, and war seemed imminent. Fearing partisan battles in the U.S. during a potential war, Adams promoted the Alien and Sedition Acts. The acts backfired; Virginia and Kentucky passed resolutions claiming the right of states to ignore federal law. Such states' rights resolutions anticipated the doctrine of nullification that would lead later to Civil War.

XYZ Affair Foreign policy crisis with France over the trade wars; three agents designated X, Y, and Z attempted to extort money from American envoys as a prerequisite for negotiations (p. 155)

Alien and Sedition Acts Legislation signed by President John Adams; included the Alien Enemies Act, the Alien Friends Act, and the Sedition Act; opponents called them a violation of the First Amendment's guarantees (p. 155)

Virginia and Kentucky Resolutions Declarations written by Thomas Jefferson and James Madison and adopted by the legislatures of Virginia and Kentucky, proclaiming that the Sedition Act was an infringement on rights protected by their state constitutions and that states had the right to nullify federal laws within their borders (p. 156)

doctrine of nullification The theory that each state had the right to nullify federal laws within its borders (p. 156)

8-5 **Explain the convoluted political process that made Thomas Jefferson president in 1800, including the constitutional change designed to mend the problem.** The election of 1800 proved that the U.S. could hold together even when a different political party took over. Adams's party divided on the French peace treaty. Jeffersonian unity led to a Democratic-Republican win. The outcome was decided in the House of Representatives between Jefferson and his vice presidential candidate. The Twelfth Amendment sprang from this, stating that electors would elect a president and then a vice president.

lame-duck Politician who is not returning to office and is serving out the rest of his or her term with little influence; a soon-to-be-out-of-office politician or Congress (p. 158)

	What Else Was Happening

1800 — Land Act creates federal offices for sale of western land to settlers.

1801–1835 — Chief Justice John Marshall builds Supreme Court's constitutional authority.

1803 — John Marshall introduces judicial review in *Marbury* v. *Madison;* Napoleon Bonaparte sells Louisiana territory.

1804 — Aaron Burr kills Alexander Hamilton; his supposedly secessionist plans lead to trial for treason.

1804–1806 — Lewis and Clark expedition sparks Americans' fascination with the West.

1807 — Embargo Act stops American exports and foreign trade, and imperils economy.

1808: *End of legal slave importation in the United States.*

1810: *Peter Durand invents the tin can.*

Father Miguel Hidalgo begins the movement for Mexican independence.

1811: *William H. Harrison attacks Tecumseh's tribal alliance at Tippecanoe.*

Steamboat service begins on the Mississippi River.

1812 — War with Britain over American neutrality, alleged collusion with Indians. Invasion of British Canada a fiasco.

1813 — Andrew Jackson defeats Creek Indians in battle over land in Georgia.

1814 — Treaty of Ghent ends hostilities without resolving causes of war.

March: Creeks lose their land to United States after Battle of Horseshoe Bend.

August: British burn White House in assault on Washington, D.C.

October: Defense of New Orleans against British forces makes Jackson national hero.

December: New England Federalists invoke states' rights at Hartford Convention.

1815: *Battle of Waterloo ends the Napoleonic Wars and the reign of Napoleon.*

1815–1824 — Decline of Federalist Party ushers in nonpartisan "Era of Good Feelings."

9-1 **Define Jeffersonian Democracy, and explain how Jefferson's presidency both defined and contradicted that political philosophy.** "Jeffersonian Democracy" describes the political style and belief system of Democratic-Republicans. Early on, it sought to involve "the people" in elections; its appeal helped elect Jefferson in 1800. The term broadened into a philosophy of less federal control, more control to states and "the people." Jefferson, a strict interpretationalist, felt it wrong for any branch of government to go beyond what was explicitly included in the Constitution and its amendments. Democratic-Republicans demonstrated Jeffersonian Democracy during the 1800 election: through partisan newspapers, personal appeals for votes, and concern for needs and hopes of common people. Jefferson's ideal republic, after all, was a nation of industrious and successful yeoman farmers. Jefferson's realism was evident in his desire to open the frontier and purchase New Orleans. Napoleon Bonaparte's France needed money, and offered to sell the Louisiana Territory to the U.S. The Constitution did not explicitly allow a president to acquire territory, but Jefferson's decision to complete the Louisiana Purchase almost doubled the size of the country.

Jeffersonian Democracy Innovation introduced by Jefferson's Democratic-Republicans when they cultivated popular opinion through newspaper editorialists who put yeoman farmers at the center of their political ideology (p. 161)

yeoman A person who cultivates a small farm, thus situating themselves below the gentry class but above common laborers (p. 161)

***Marbury* v. *Madison* (1803)** Court decision declaring that William Marbury deserved his appointment but that the Court could not force the president to grant it because a federal law was unconstitutional; first U.S. Supreme Court decision to declare a law unconstitutional (p. 162)

doctrine of judicial review Right of the courts to judge the constitutionality of federal laws; established the Supreme Court as the ultimate interpreter of constitutional questions (p. 163)

Louisiana Purchase Tract of 828,000 square miles that stretched from the Mississippi River to the Rocky Mountains; Jefferson bought the rights to it from Napoleon for $15 million in 1803 (p. 163)

revitalization movement Revival of old ways of tribal life and pan-Indianism preached by Tecumseh and the Prophet (p. 164)

Embargo Act of 1807 Legislation that stopped American exports from going to Europe and prohibited American ships from trading in foreign ports (p. 165)

9-2 **Discuss the reasons for and results of the War of 1812.** James Madison, firm Democratic-Republican, was elected in 1808, but the Federalists showed strength. Fearing Federalist popularity, Congress repealed the Embargo Act even before Madison took office. The new Non-Intercourse Act stated that the U.S. would trade with all European nations except Britain and France. Napoleon agreed first, leading the president to reestablish trade with France and reassert the British embargo. Congressional "war hawks" pushed for war against Britain. Democratic-Republicans believed the U.S. must fight again with Britain before it would truly recognize the sovereignty of the United States. President Madison asked for a declaration of war against Britain. While Congress debated, Britain recognized U.S. neutrality; still, Congress voted to declare war. Madison won reelection in 1812, supported by western states and war hawks. A series of U.S. victories in 1813 were followed by major British advances in 1814. The war formally ended in 1814, but the Battle of New Orleans in January 1815 made General Andrew Jackson a hero. Federalist opposition to the war, and their Hartford Convention in 1814, destroyed their support. The war left Democratic-Republicans as the only viable national party, in an "Era of Good Feelings." It also proved that the U.S. did need a stronger central government and military, a national bank, and better infrastructure. It also fanned nationalism and a true, distinctly non-British, American culture.

Non-Intercourse Act Legislation passed in 1809 that allowed American ships to trade with all nations except Britain and France and authorized the president to resume trade with those countries once they began respecting America's neutral trading rights (p. 166)

Hartford Convention Meeting of New England Federalists in 1814 in which they proposed constitutional amendments limiting the government's ability to restrict American commerce and repealing the three-fifths clause to limit the power of the South in Congress (p. 170)

"Era of Good Feelings" Period of non-partisan politics following the implosion of the Federalist Party, roughly 1815–1824 (p. 170)

CHAPTER 10 TIMELINE

Year	Event	What Else Was Happening
1789	Samuel Slater builds first American spinning factory.	
1793	Cotton gin makes fiber a profitable cash crop and revives plantation slavery.	
1800	Land Act creates federal offices for sale of western land to settlers.	
1807	First steamboats introduced to American rivers.	
1811	Congress fails to recharter First Bank of the United States.	
1813	Lowell system combines all processes in textile production in one factory.	**1815:** John Roulstone writes the first three verses of "Mary Had a Little Lamb" after his classmate Mary Sawyer comes to school followed by her pet lamb.
1816	Democratic-Republicans push for Second Bank of the United States. Congress discourages foreign imports with high tariff.	
1817	State of New York begins construction of canal from Albany to Buffalo.	
1819	Supreme Court protects contract clause in *Dartmouth College* v. *Woodward*. Spain yields Florida and claims to Pacific Northwest in Adams-Onís Treaty.	
1820	Federal Land Act promotes western migration and farm settlements. Compromise admits Missouri as slave, Maine as free, states; sets slavery's northern boundary at 36° 30'.	
1820s–1840s	Second Great Awakening promises salvation through good works.	**1823:** Monroe Doctrine claims Western Hemisphere as American domain. The game of rugby is invented.
1825	364-mile-long Erie Canal connects eastern seaboard with Great Lakes.	
1826	American Temperance Society becomes century's largest reform movement.	
1828	Workingmen's Party formed; eventually spreads to fifteen states.	
1831	Cyrus McCormick's mechanical reaper transforms commercial agriculture.	**1833:** Britain outlaws slavery in response to the continued efforts of evangelical Christians and the politician William Wilberforce.
1834	National Trades' Union formed.	
1837	Horace Mann becomes secretary of the Massachusetts Board of Eduation, eventually developing the foundations for American public schools.	**1838:** Grimké sisters publish landmark tract in struggle for women's equality. Massachusetts prohibits the sale of liquor. One man gets around the law by painting stripes on a pig and advertising that, for 6 cents, a person could see the pig and get a free glass of whiskey.
1844	Samuel P. Morse "wires" first message "What Hath God Wrought?"	
1845	Irish potato famine further pushes European immigration to United States.	
1846	Mormons migrate west to escape persecution.	**1847:** Hanson Gregory, a New England mariner, invents the donut.
1848	Women's Rights Convention at Seneca Falls adopts Declaration of Sentiments.	
1854	Thoreau's *Walden* typifies Transcendentalist response to Market Revolution.	

10-1 **Describe the economic system known as the American System.** As younger men entered Congress, fears of a more powerful central government eased. Younger members embraced a program of internal improvements to promote economic growth. The American System focused on infrastructure, banks, and protectionist tariffs. The Second Bank of the United States was chartered in 1816. A 25% tariff was placed on all imported goods, so domestic goods would find a strong domestic market. Court cases also promoted business growth on a national level, often giving states little consideration. America was moving toward more federal control and less independence at the state level. Cotton planters in the South protested that laws helped only those in the North and the West.

Market Revolution A series of innovations that led to the creation of an integrated national marketplace; it included the long-distance coordination of the production, distribution, and consumption of goods (p. 175)

American System Economic plan based on the idea that the federal

government should encourage economic enterprise (p. 175)

internal improvements Building of roads and canals by the federal and state governments (p. 175)

Second Bank of the United States National bank established in 1816 to curb rampant currency speculation (p. 176)

Monroe Doctrine Declaration of 1823 proclaiming that any European nation attempting to colonize Latin America would be treated as a party hostile to the United States; President James Monroe announced that the Western Hemisphere was the domain of the United States and was to remain separate from the affairs of Europe (p. 177)

10-2 **List the three specific parts of the Market Revolution in early-nineteenth-century America, and evaluate how the United States developed during this era.** There were three concurrent "revolutions": transportation/communications; commercialized farming; and industrialization. Transportation included roads paid by taxes; new canals in the East; steamboats in the South; and a nationwide railroad network. Better transportation and invention of the telegraph revolutionized how businesses could operate. Better equipment allowed farmers to specialize in certain crops, selling surplus and buying goods. The cotton gin reshaped plantations in the lower South, and steamboats could ship cotton worldwide. With its huge possible profits, southern cotton contributed to a growing dependence on slave labor. Factories consolidated workforces and began to employ entire families, and cities continued to grow. Immigration provided needed workers, as did rural emigrants. An urban working class emerged.

Erie Canal Artificial river connecting the New York State cities of Buffalo and Albany; provided a continuous water route from the shores of the Atlantic to the Great Lakes; measured 364 miles long and 40 feet wide (p. 178)

Land Act of 1820 Legislation that promoted settlement west of the Appalachians by setting affordable prices for manageable plots of land (p. 182)

Tallmadge Amendment Proposal that would have enforced gradual emancipation in Missouri (p. 183)

Missouri Compromise Arrangement brokered by Henry Clay that set 36°30' as

the divider between free and slave territories and that allowed Missouri to enter the nation as a slave state if Maine were allowed to enter as free (p. 183)

"putting out" system Division of labor in which large manufacturers would pay one family to perform one task, then pass the item on to the next family or artisan to perform the next task (p. 184)

Lowell System A labor and production model for manufacturing textiles that, for the first time, brought all stages of textile production under one roof, with employees living near the factory in employee housing, away from their families; featured

mostly female employees, young women seeking to earn wages before getting married (p. 186)

Great Irish Famine Years of miserable poverty and hunger in Ireland that peaked during 1845–1851 and led millions of Irish to the United States (p. 186)

Workingmen's Party Union of laborers, made up from citywide assemblies, that formed in 1828; eventually spread through fifteen states (p. 187)

National Trades' Union First large-scale labor union in the United States; formed in 1834 (p. 187)

10-3 **Describe the growth of America's middle class during the first half of the 1800s, and discuss some of the stronger movements toward reform during the era.** Factory work required unskilled labor, but also record-keeping, bookkeeping, and planning. These jobs needed better education and commanded greater pay for their specific skills. "Management" became separate from "labor," even though all employees worked for the same company. Higher wages for a larger group of people led to a tremendous increase in the "middle class." Middle-class men now provided for their family without wife or children working outside the home. The Second Great Awakening led many middle-class individuals to look to help those less fortunate. Transcendentalists believed that mankind could create a perfect society; many tried but failed. Reform movements included temperance, public education, colleges, prison reform, and abolition. As women became deeply involved in various reform efforts, they began to perceive themselves as being left out of a major part of American life: politics.

burned-over district Area in upstate New York that had many converts who had been inspired by the fiery orators speaking the Word of God during the Second Great Awakening (p. 189)

Transcendentalists Group of thinkers and writers in the Northeast who believed that ultimate truths were beyond human grasp (p. 189)

lyceum circuit Schedule of lectures in which clergymen, reformers, Transcendentalists, socialists, feminists,

and other speakers would speak to large crowds in small towns (p. 190)

American Female Moral Reform Society Women's activist group that had more than five hundred local chapters throughout the country by 1840 and had successfully lobbied for legislation governing prostitution (p. 191)

American Temperance Society Group founded by temperance workers in 1826; they promoted laws prohibiting the sale of alcohol (p. 191)

American Colonization Society Organization founded in 1816 to advocate removing America's black population and repatriating them to Africa; the Society established the colony of Liberia on the West African coast for this purpose in the 1820s (p. 192)

Seneca Falls Convention Gathering of women activists in Seneca Falls, New York, in 1848; their goal was securing the vote for women (p. 192)

▶ **1819** Europe's postwar recovery hits U.S. agriculture, leading to financial panic.

1821: *Mexicans finally win an eleven-year war for their independence from Spain.*

1822–1834: *British mathematician Charles Babbage proposes constructing machines to perform mathematical calculations: the Difference and Analytical Engines, forerunners of the modern computer. He runs out of money before completing either.*

▶ **1824** Most states have expanded franchise to all free white men.

Jackson's complaint of Adams's "corrupt bargain" starts second party system.

Michael Faraday invents the first toy balloon.

1826 July 4: *Both John Adams and Thomas Jefferson—longtime friends, rivals, and, in the end, correspondents—die, on the fiftieth anniversary of the Declaration of Independence.*

▶ **1828** Jacksonian Democrats win presidency with mass appeal.

▶ **1830** Jackson's Indian Removal Act forces Indians to move west of Mississippi.

Simón Bolívar dies of tuberculosis in Colombia, after contributing to the independence of much of Latin America, including Venezuela, Colombia, Ecuador, Peru, and Bolivia.

▶ **1832** Supreme Court confirms Cherokee sovereignty in *Worcester* v. *Georgia*.
Tariffs cause nullification crisis between South Carolina and Washington.

▶ **1836** Jackson refuses to renew charter of Second National Bank.
Jackson's Specie Circular forbids government from accepting paper currency.

▶ **1838** 4,000 Cherokees die on the Trail of Tears from Georgia to Oklahoma.

1837 *Severe bank panic spreads from New York across the country.*

The first kindergarten, called "small child occupation institute," opens in Germany.

▶ **1842** Seminole Indians rebel against sugar planters in Florida.

Table 11.1 The Differences Between Jacksonians and Whigs

	Jacksonians	Whigs
Strength in government	Presidency	Legislature
Economics	Local growth	Nationalists
National Bank	Against	For
Internal improvements	Against	For
Constituents	Southerners, westerners, and the working class	Social conservatives, native born

11-1 **Describe the changes that took place in American politics during the first decades of the 1800s, and explain the reasons for these changes.** Boom and bust cycles, more men gaining the right to vote, elections that reeked of corruption—all of these led to greater participation in American politics by the time of the 1828 election. The Panic of 1819 affected the whole nation, as the U.S. realized that global markets affected domestic economy. Land prices fell, banks failed, bankruptcies escalated, and the U.S. experienced its first depression. Ordinary people demanded more government intervention during such economic crises. Removal of property restrictions extended the right to vote to all white males. Democratization of politics fed new factionalism that would create the second two-party system. The 1824 election caused many to view the current system as too corrupt to continue unopposed. All five presidential candidates were Democratic-Republicans, and no one received a majority of the votes. The House of Representatives decided the outcome, with Henry Clay throwing his support to John Quincy Adams. Andrew Jackson, who had won the most popular votes and the most electoral votes, was furious. Adams named Clay secretary of state; Jackson's supporters protested the "corrupt bargain."

"corrupt bargain" Alleged deal between John Quincy Adams and Henry Clay to manipulate the voting in the House of Representatives to install Adams as president and Clay as his secretary of state in 1824 (p. 198)

second two-party system Evolution of political organizations in 1824 into the Jacksonians and the Whigs (p. 199)

11-2 **Explain how Jackson's approach to the "spoils system," the nullification crisis, the National Bank, Indian removal, and the Panic of 1837 reflected his vision of federal power.** Jackson ran as a new Democrat in 1828 and handily defeated Adams, primarily in the South and West. During this era of the "common man," he rewarded supporters with jobs, in the "spoils system." Jackson's most serious problem was the issue of protective tariffs. Southerners objected to high tariffs and asserted a state's right to nullify federal law within its borders. South Carolina threatened to secede; Jackson obtained from Congress the power to send forces if it tried. Both sides compromised on the tariff and ended the crisis—temporarily. Jackson distrusted the Second Bank, and when Congress renewed the Bank's charter four years early, just before the 1832 election, Jackson vetoed, arguing the Bank was unconstitutional. After a landslide reelection, he ordered U.S. funds transferred from the National Bank to state banks. In 1836, Jackson ordered all payments to the U.S. government be made in gold and silver, or specie. This order, the "Specie Circular," contributed to the Panic of 1837 and a major depression. Westward expansion brought whites and Indians into greater conflict, and the position of the federal government came to be that the Indians should be "removed" from any contact with white Americans. The 1830 Indian Removal Act gave government the right to move Indians from east of the Mississippi to the west. Jackson seemed to believe he did the Indians a favor; in truth he did expansionists a favor.

patronage Exchange of a government job in return for political campaign work (p. 201)

nullification Assertion that the United States was made up of independent and sovereign states; states did not agree to give up their autonomy; and every state reserved the right to reject any federal law it deemed unconstitutional (p. 202)

Indian Removal Act of 1830 Legislation that allowed the federal government to trade land west of the Mississippi River for land east of the river, allowing the federal government to move Indians further west (p. 205)

Trail of Tears Forced removal of the Cherokee nation from Georgia to Oklahoma in 1838; the Cherokee were forced to travel more than a thousand miles (p. 206)

Specie Circular Executive order of 1836 requiring that the government cease accepting paper money as credible currency, accepting only gold or silver (specie) for all items, including public land (p. 206)

11-3 **Explain the development of America's second two-party political system between the Democrats and the Whigs.** Andrew Jackson and his supporters felt marginalized by the Democratic-Republican "old guard." The self-titled new Democrats were highly nationalistic and yet supported a smaller government. Those who continued to push for federal assistance for financial improvements, and who opposed Jackson's acting "like a king" in their eyes, took the historical name Whigs. Two strong parties again took center stage. The main difference was, Whigs simply detested Jackson. Whigs pushed for strong government support of the economy via internal improvements and banks. Democrats appealed to small farmers, disaffected workers, small businessmen, and anti-elitist Irish.

1816 African Methodist Episcopal Church becomes national organization.

1821 American Colonization Society promotes slaves' return to Africa and founds Liberia.

1831 Nat Turner's deadly revolt breeds repression and new defense of slavery. Lloyd Garrison becomes leading voice of abolitionists.

1838 Frederick Douglass escapes slavery with help of the Underground Railroad.

1840s–1850s A peak period of immigration to America, with nearly 1 million Irish escaping the potato famine.

Catholic parochial schools are established, with public schools becoming more visibly influenced by Protestantism.

1852 Harriet Beecher Stowe's *Uncle Tom's Cabin* popularizes abolitionism.

What Else Was Happening

1848 *Revolutions occur throughout Europe protesting industrial disorder and aristocratic rule. Most fail. Karl Marx and Friedrich Engels publish The* Communist *Manifesto.*
1849 *The first safety pin is patented.*
1850 *Beer is first sold in glass bottles. Before that, patrons had their beer poured into a bucket or cup that they brought with them.*

1857 *Elisha Graves Otis demonstrates his passenger safety elevator at the Crystal Palace Exposition in New York by cutting the elevator's cables as it ascends a 300-foot tower. The words and music to "Jingle Bells" are registered, under the title "One Horse Open Sleigh"—which didn't stick.*

Percentages of black people in the total population are shown for each state/territory.

States with less than 1% of black people are shown as <1%.

Free state by admission to Union
Free state by gradual abolition
Free territory by Act of Congress
Slave state by admission to Union
Territory open to slavery by Act of Congress
(1803) Date of abolition by State Constitution

12-1 **Describe social life in the commercial North as it developed between 1830 and 1860.** Despite rapid industrialization, many still lived in rural areas, maintaining close family and communal ties. Most embraced some consumerism. Improvements in transportation and communication ended their isolation, traveling lecturers brought new ideas, and newspapers provided both local and national news. Cities grew tremendously, from immigration and internal shifts. Urban immigrant communities arose. Irish Catholics became prime targets of discrimination because they arrived ready to work for whatever wages they could get, and workers already here feared for their jobs. Some immigrants moved westward and found greater acceptance on the frontier. City growth deepened class rifts; the new rich left downtown, the working-class lived in squalor. Some middle-class women managed to enter the work force, at least until they married. Boxing, horse racing, theaters, and a unique new literary movement engaged those with leisure time. Ethnic diversity included free blacks, who formed churches and advocated causes such as abolition. Lloyd Garrison's *The Liberator* went beyond the idea of returning blacks to Africa, instead seeking full emancipation. Southerners, as well as northern merchants and white laborers, often opposed abolition violently. Defying abolitionists, Congress in 1836 agreed to bar any discussion of abolition indefinitely.

the 48ers Germans who came to the United States in 1848, after a failed revolution in Germany forced many political dissidents to flee (p. 216)

nativism Political identity that defined an American as someone with a British background who was born in the United States; supporters formulated a racial and ethnic identity that proclaimed the superiority of their group, usually labeled "native Americans" (p. 216)

Uncle Tom's Cabin Antislavery novel published by Harriet Beecher Stowe in 1852; best-selling book of that period (p. 219)

African Methodist Episcopal (AME) Church National African American Methodist religious denomination founded by Richard Allen and Absalom Jones in the 1790s; doctrinally Methodist, it was the first major religious denomination in the Western world to originate for sociological, not theological, reasons (p. 219)

American Anti-Slavery Society Organization founded by journalist William Lloyd Garrison in 1833 that served as a point of contact for escaped slaves like Frederick Douglass and Harriet Tubman (p. 221)

gag rule Legal provision of 1836 that automatically tabled any discussion of abolition in Congress; under this law, slavery was not open for discussion (p. 221)

free labor The concept that most unified the diverse collection of people in the northern states, centered on a society filled with those who worked without a master and possessed the freedom to leave a job if and when they wished (p. 221)

12-2 **Describe social life as it developed in the South between 1830 and 1860 as a result of dependence on cotton.** The South contained (1) wealthy planters, businessmen, and politicians; (2) yeoman farmers who hoped to become wealthy at raising cotton, but who almost never did; and (3) a large slave population. Planters, self-proclaimed aristocrats, vacationed and schooled their children abroad, and entered politics because they felt it their duty to see that their society continued to run smoothly. Vast plantations were located on waterways so they could ship cotton to the North and Europe easily. Plantations provided virtually everything they needed. Thus, towns and cities were few in the South. Yeoman farmers sometimes managed to acquire small plots of land—usually not the best. They often hoped to gain enough wealth to move into the social world of the planters, but this seldom happened. Most blacks were slaves, with a large majority living and working on large plantations. Many whites owned no slaves, and many owned only a few. Almost all, however, supported slavery. Planters saw slave labor as the only possible way for them to make a decent profit on their cotton. Some purchased slaves to hire out as blacksmiths, carpenters, longshoremen, and such. Most blacks, however, had no special skills to speak of and thus were relegated to the plantation. African American slaves sought to hold on to their culture. Religion provided one bond, and after the Second Great Awakening, most accepted Christianity, though with overtones of African beliefs. Rebellions seldom occurred because legal restrictions let whites basically treat slaves as property. Uprisings were quickly put down, and those involved were usually executed in vicious ways. Some southerners espoused abolition, but their numbers remained so small as to be insignificant.

gang system Work arrangement under which slaves were organized into groups of twenty to twenty-five workers, supervised by an overseer (p. 226)

slavedriver Supervisor or overseer of slave labor, usually employed on a cotton plantation (p. 226)

task system Work arrangement under which slaves were assigned a specific set of tasks to accomplish each day; often employed on rice plantations and in domestic service situations (p. 226)

Underground Railroad Network of men and women, both white and black, who were opposed to slavery, sheltered runaway slaves, and expedited their journey to freedom (p. 229)

1822: *A yellow fever epidemic leaves New York City with 16,000 corpses and no readily available space to bury them.*

1829: *Mexico abolishes slavery.*

1821 Mexico's independence draws American settlers to northern province of Texas.

1830 Joseph Smith forms Church of Jesus Christ of Latter-Day Saints.

1834 Texas settlers rebel against Mexican ruler Santa Anna.

1835: *The Liberty Bell becomes cracked.*

1836 187 Texan rebels perish in Alamo after killing over 1,200 Mexican troops.

1840: *The saxophone is invented.*

1842: *The Treaty of Nanjing ends the First Opium War between Great Britain and China, which began when China protested the importation of opium by British merchants. The treaty mandates that China open trade relations with Great Britain, including the continued trafficking of opium, and it makes Hong Kong a British colony, which it remains until 1997.*

1844 James K. Polk wins presidency with promise of annexing Oregon and Texas.

1845 Admission of Texas sets stage for war with Mexico.

July: *John O'Sullivan coins term* manifest destiny.

"Mormon Wars" follow 1844 murder of Joseph Smith in Nauvoo, Illinois.

The New York Baseball Club plays the Knickerbockers in the first recorded baseball game, at Elysian Fields in Hoboken, New Jersey.

1846 **April:** Polk provokes war with Mexico and seizes northern provinces.
June: Rebels under John C. Frémont declare California independent republic.
June: Buchanan-Pakenham Treaty establishes Canadian–U.S. border in Northwest.

1847 Clashes between Oregonians and Indians show need for territorial government.
September: U.S. forces march into Mexico City; Santa Anna surrenders.

1848 **January:** Gold discovery in California triggers global gold rush.
January: Gold discovery in California triggers global gold rush.
America gains control of the Utah Territory one year after Mormons settle there.

1851 Fort Laramie Treaty with Plains Indians secures settler migration westward.

13-1

Describe the conquest and development of the West between 1820 and 1850 by white Americans. Settling the West, the area from Texas to California, presented many challenges and demonstrated Americans' true frontier spirit. Americans who moved to Mexico-controlled Texas settled eastern areas, where rainfall was plentiful. Santa Anna tried to stop the influx of immigrants, fearing they would attempt to separate from Mexico. That did happen in 1836, with a series of battles from the Alamo to San Jacinto. Texas gained independence, and would remain a republic until it gained U.S. statehood in 1845. A large migration to Oregon and nearby areas spread the fame of the route dubbed the Oregon Trail. Local Indians tried to fight off the intruders but were defeated.

Mormons, unloved by their neighbors for practicing polygamy and staying aloof from their local communities, first settled Illinois, then Utah. America gained control of the Utah Territory at the end of the war with Mexico in 1848. The Mormons there, under Brigham Young, had hoped their move to Utah would put them beyond government control, but chose to remain. In California, migrants were converging even before the discovery of gold in early 1848. The "gold rush" brought many. Most stayed on, concentrating not in old mining camps but new cities. The government resettled Native Americans on a few reservations scattered through the Southwest. Trappers roamed the Rocky Mountains, charting the lands for the rest of America.

manifest destiny Likely coined by journalist John L. Sullivan in 1845, refers to the idea that the United States was destined by God to expand from the Atlantic Ocean to the Pacific (p. 233)

polygamy The practice of having more than one spouse (p. 236)

Fort Laramie Treaty Agreement of 1851 between Plains Indian nations and the U.S. government; the government

agreed to make cash restitution for disruptions to the buffalo grounds, while tribal leaders agreed not to attack the large number of settlers moving through the area (p. 239)

13-2

Explain how the expansionist spirit in the West led to political conflict at home as well as conflict with Mexico, even as it gave the United States its modern boundaries. John O'Sullivan coined the term "manifest destiny" in 1845. The process, then underway, was soon complete. Ending years of argument within the U.S. government, Texas became part of the U.S. in March 1845. Hotly debated was whether to expand slavery; Texas' constitution guaranteed slavery would continue.

The debate affected the terms of three presidents; James Polk assumed office just after Texas joined. Polk set out to goad Mexico into war to win more Mexican territory, and succeeded in May 1846. The 1848 Treaty of Guadalupe Hidalgo ended the Mexican–American war and gave the Southwest to the U.S. for $15 million. Polk also negotiated British Canada's border, gaining all of the Oregon Territory up to the 49th parallel.

Liberty Party Political party created by northern antislavery activists who left the Whig Party because they were outraged at Henry Clay's reversing his position against annexation of Texas; their departure revealed cracks in the second two-party system (p. 240)

"Fifty-four Forty or Fight!" Rallying cry referring to the Americans' intended

latitude for the contested border between the United States and Canada; Britain was willing to settle for the 49th parallel (p. 241)

Buchanan-Pakenham Treaty Agreement of 1846 between the United States and Britain, agreeing on the 49th parallel as the border between the United States and Canada; the treaty gave the

United States uncontested access to the Pacific (p. 242)

Treaty of Guadalupe Hidalgo Agreement ending the Mexican War in 1848, which gave the United States control of Utah, Nevada, California, western Colorado, and parts of Arizona and New Mexico and established the Rio Grande as the border, in exchange for $15 million (p. 245)

What Else Was Happening

1842: *Abraham Lincoln accepts a challenge to a duel from James Shields, the Democratic state auditor. (The duel never takes place.)*
1845: *The rubber band is patented.*

1846 Wilmot Proviso's ban on slavery from new territories alarms southerners. It never passes.

1848 Whigs divide in presidential election; Free Soil Party emerges.

1850 Compromise admits a free California, leaves slavery in territories to popular sovereignty, bans slave trade in D.C., expands Fugitive Slave Act.

Taiping Rebellion in China begins. This civil war, which lasts fourteen years, will see 20 million people die before the restoration of the Qing dynasty.

1853–1856 As Free Soilers and slaveholders race to settle Kansas, violence ensues.

Crimean War pits Russia against Britain, France, the Ottoman Empire, and the Kingdom of Sardinia. It is considered the first "modern" war because of the tactical use of railroads and the telegraph. It is also the war in which Florence Nightingale pioneers modern nursing.

1854 Kansas-Nebraska Act leaves slavery to popular sovereignty in territories.

1856 Republican Party draws Free Soilers, Whigs, Know-Nothings with antislavery stance. Multiparty presidential election of James Buchanan highlights sectional rift.

1857 Supreme Court's Dred Scott decision prohibits Congress from restricting slavery. Kansas' proslavery Lecompton Constitution splits Congress.

Indian Rebellion, protesting British colonial rule, lasts a year before the British finally suppress the rebellion.

1860 **November:** Republican Lincoln wins presidential election as sectional candidate.
December: South Carolina secedes in reaction to Lincoln's election; Deep South follows.
December: Crittenden Compromise fails.

1861 **April:** South Carolina attacks federal Fort Sumter near Charleston.
February 11: Both Abraham Lincoln and Jefferson Davis leave their homes to be inaugurated president.

14-1 Describe the arguments that took place over whether slavery should be allowed to expand into the new territories, and explain how the Compromise of 1850 was supposed to settle the issue. Disagreements over slavery's expansion led to a realignment of parties after the U.S. defeat of Mexico. Southern Democrats wanted slavery allowed in new territories, to protect the southern economy. Northern Democrats opposed new slave territories because white people did not want to compete with black people for jobs. In the 1848 presidential election, Democrats proposed "popular sovereignty," allowing a territory's voters to decide about slavery. The Whigs, and Zachary Taylor, did not discuss the issue. Unhappy Democrats formed the Free Soil Party, proposing existing slavery remain but go no farther. The Free Soil Party made a good showing in the election, but Whig Zachary Taylor won. Because of the gold rush, California was ready to petition for statehood by the time Taylor took office. Southern Democrats feared California might enter the Union as a free state, tipping Congress's scales. In 1849, with Congress deadlocked, Henry Clay proposed a compromise: California would be free; other lands won from Mexico would decide themselves; slave auctions would end in Washington, DC; Texas would stop interfering with New Mexico; and Congress would enact a tougher Fugitive Slave Law. Taylor's successor, Millard Fillmore, allowed Congress to decide. The move toward allowing people to decide themselves worried northern abolitionists, who talked of a "slave conspiracy" in the South.

Wilmot Proviso Legislation proposed in 1846 to prohibit slavery from any new territories that the United States might acquire from Mexico (p. 250)

doughface Derisive name for a northerner who openly supported the South (p. 250)

popular sovereignty Proposal for letting the settlers in the territories decide whether or not they wanted slavery (p. 250)

Free Soil Party Political movement started by disaffected anti-South Democrats and headed by former Democratic president Martin Van Buren; they wanted new lands to be made available to small, ambitious white farmers (p. 250)

Compromise of 1850 Five-part bill proposed by Henry Clay, which outlined specific arrangements that accommodated both antislavery northerners and slave-owning southerners (p. 251)

Fugitive Slave Law Law passed as part of the Compromise of 1850 requiring that all runaway slaves be returned to their masters; those who willfully ignored the law were to be punished (p. 251)

Personal Liberty Laws A variety of laws designed to protect escaped slaves, such as by prohibiting the use of a state's jail for runaway slaves; these laws passed in many northern states in the 1850s (p. 252)

filibusters Adventurers who attempted to invade the island of Cuba to bring it into the Union as a slave state (p. 252)

14-2 **Explain how the Kansas-Nebraska Act affected the territories of Kansas and Nebraska, and describe the events that made "Bleeding Kansas" an accurate description for the region.** To finish a transcontinental railroad, the rest of the Louisiana Purchase needed to be settled. The Missouri Compromise had prohibited slavery in the northern part of the Louisiana Territory. Southerners, fearing several new slave-free states in those lands, opposed the railroad plan. Illinois Senator Stephen Douglas offered a compromise: two territories, Kansas and Nebraska, with their new populations to decide for themselves whether to allow slavery. The Kansas-Nebraska Act passed in 1854. People raced to populate Kansas for the vote on slavery. Slavery supporters crossed from Missouri in large numbers, as did abolitionists from New England. Kansas was divided, and violence became the norm. Abolitionist John Brown set out to avenge the sack of Lawrence; he and his sons killed five proslavery men in "Bleeding Kansas."

Kansas-Nebraska Act The 1854 act that created two territories, Kansas and Nebraska, and left the status of slavery in each territory open, to be decided by the popular sovereignty of those who settled there (p. 253)

Know-Nothing Party The American Party, a new political party of the 1850s that built its base of support on anti-immigrant and anti-Catholic sentiment (p. 254)

Republican Party Explicitly antislavery party that emerged in the political turmoil of the 1850s; although not abolitionist, it favored "free-soil" movements to keep slavery out of the West (p. 255)

Lecompton Constitution The 1857 state constitution that made slavery legal in Kansas; subsequently defeated in 1858 (p. 256)

"The Crime Against Kansas" Speech delivered in Congress by Charles Sumner, Republican of Massachusetts, that blamed slavery for the violence between pro- and antislavery activists in Kansas (p. 257)

Slave Power Conspiracy Specter raised by antislavery Republicans who believed that, in order to preserve slavery, southern leaders would be willing to attack and silence anyone who advocated against slavery; allegedly the conspiracy intended to outlaw free speech and make all Americans accept proslavery principles (p. 258)

14-3 **Discuss the events that propelled the United States into a civil war in 1861.** In the Supreme Court's Dred Scott decision, Chief Justice Taney declared that slaves were not citizens and could not sue in court. Further, slaves were property and could be taken anywhere by their masters without gaining freedom. Taney also declared the Missouri Compromise unconstitutional. Republicans were shocked that the high court validated slavery in any and all territories and states. John Brown raided Harper's Ferry, Virginia, to collect weapons and hopefully start a slave uprising. The uprising failed, and Brown was tried for treason, convicted, and hanged within a matter of weeks. By the presidential election in 1860, southern states were discussing secession if a Republican won. Between Republican Abraham Lincoln's victory and inauguration, seven southern states left the Union.

Lincoln-Douglas Debates Public debates on slavery between Stephen A. Douglas and Abraham Lincoln as they competed for the Illinois Senate seat in 1858 (p. 260)

14-4 **Explain why and how the southern states seceded from the Union, discuss President Lincoln's reaction, and describe the earliest physical conflict between the two sides.** Though seven southern states quickly came together in the Confederacy, the Upper South held off. Shortly after inauguration, Lincoln tried to resupply Fort Sumter, off Charleston, South Carolina. Confederate forces opened fire on the federal supply convoy and demanded that the fort surrender. With shots fired, the South was in full rebellion, and Lincoln would have no choice but to go to war.

Crittenden Compromise Reconciliation proposal advocating that the Missouri Compromise line of 1820 be extended all the way to the Pacific, excluding California, with all land north of the line free, all land south of it open to slavery; also included an "unamendable amendment" to the Constitution, guaranteeing the preservation of slavery in the southern states where it already existed (p. 264)

1861

April: Lincoln orders blockade of southern coastline.

July 21: Battle of Bull Run (also known as the Battle of Manassas) in Virginia shatters hopes for an easy war.

August: First Confiscation Act frees captured slaves employed in military service.

1862

March: First battle of ironclads signals changes in military technology.

April: Union wins Battle of Shiloh, which exceeds all American casualties in history.

April: Confederate Congress implements draft.

June–July: Excessive caution at Richmond costs Army of the Potomac dearly.

July: Second Confiscation Act frees all slaves owned by rebel masters.

August 29: Lee defeats Union at Second Battle of Bull Run.

September 17: Union Army forces Confederacy back after Battle of Antietam.

September 22: Lincoln's Emancipation Proclamation declares freedom for rebels' slaves.

1863

July: Mostly Irish Democratic workingmen riot in New York over national draft.

July 3: Lee's army suffers devastating defeat at Gettysburg.

July 4: Union general Grant forces surrender of Vicksburg, Mississippi.

Former Union nurse Louisa May Alcott (author of *Little Women*) publishes a collection of wartime letters, "Hospital Sketches." During the Civil War women enter the male-dominated profession of nursing in huge numbers.

1864

April 12: Confederates kill surrendering black regiment in Fort Pillow Massacre.

June: Lincoln persuades Congress to grant black servicemen equal pay.

November 5: Military victories restore faith in Lincoln, who soundly defeats opponent for presidency.

1865

January 31: Congress passes Thirteenth Amendment abolishing slavery.

April 9: General Lee surrenders at Appomattox Courthouse.

What Else Was Happening

Serfdom is abolished in Russia.

Congress creates Internal Revenue Service.

The first black troops are used in battle, at Island Mount, Missouri.

The French go to war with Mexico after Mexican president Benito Juarez suspends interest payments to foreign countries. Mexican victory comes five years later, but the 1862 Battle of Puebla, an early Mexican victory, is now commemorated as Cinco de Mayo.

The H. L. Hunley, a Confederate submarine, is the first sub to sink an enemy ship. It sinks the USS Housatonic on February 17, only to find itself sinking that same night.

Photograph of Lincoln is taken that appears on today's five-dollar bill.

15-1 **Describe the areas of strengths of each side at the beginning of the Civil War.** The North held a clear advantage over the South in population, with more than twice as many people. The North had four times as many fighting-age men as the South, and had a functioning navy. Industrialization allowed the North to produce its own firearms and material to outfit an army.

The North also had a better rail network and larger bankroll—and an established, stable currency. The South had strong morale, and many officers who had trained, and even taught, at West Point. Thanks to culture, most southern boys also rode, hunted, and could provide their own food.

15-2 **Explain why both sides believed the war would be brief, and describe the early conflicts that made that outcome unlikely.** The North knew its advantages and did not see how the South could withstand its forces for long. The South knew that it just had to maintain a good defense and fight off northern aggression. Neither side was prepared for actual warfare, or for the toll in casualties. The North began a naval blockade to

starve the South, and General Grant's troops seized key forts. The shocking Battle of Shiloh saw 23,000 combined casualties but didn't change the situation much. Union general McClellan trained his troops well but found it difficult to commit them to a major battle. Robert E. Lee's well-commanded Army of Northern Virginia meant few Northern successes in the East.

Battle of Shiloh Bloody conflict near the Tennessee-Mississippi border in April 1862; also called the Battle of Pittsburg Landing; 23,000 casualties (p. 272)

15-3 **Explain how preparing for and prosecuting the Civil War contributed to the transformation of the United States into a fully modern state.** Both sides had to give more power to central government, even the "states' rights" Confederacy.

As volunteers began deserting the long war, the Union, then the Confederacy, both instituted a draft. Both sides had to raise taxes to help finance the war. President Lincoln suspended some civil liberties to cut down on Northern disloyalty.

"20 Negro Law" Exemption from Confederate military service granted to wealthy landholders who owned twenty or more slaves; designed to keep the planters producing their valuable cotton yield (p. 275)

commutation fee Sum of money that guaranteed a draft-age man's exemption from enlisting in the Union Army until the next draft (p. 275)

five-twenties War bonds, or bonds that would earn interest over a fixed period of time; the bondholder could redeem the bond in anywhere from five to twenty years for the initial investment plus interest (p. 276)

15-4 **Describe the actions of those who opposed the war in the North and the South.** Northern Peace Democrats ("Copperheads") approved secession, strengthening as the war dragged on. The suspension of the writ of habeas corpus, then the institution of the draft, resulted in the New York draft riot in July 1863. Peace Democrats didn't want to fight for the rich, or to free

slaves since free blacks competed for jobs. In the South, women and even children rioted, looting stores, furious at shortages of basic goods. The Confederate government focused its support toward the military over those on the home front. By mid-1863, morale and support for the war were down considerably in both North and South.

15-5 **Discuss the events of 1863 and 1864 that demonstrated Lincoln's eventual determination that the end of the war should bring a definite end to slavery.** During the war's first year, Northern troops handled runaway slaves by declaring them "contraband." Shortly after Northern victory at the Battle of Antietam, Lincoln issued the Emancipation Proclamation. This document freed only slaves in the southern

states rebelling against the U.S. government. In July 1863, Lee was defeated at Gettysburg. Grant gained Vicksburg and the Mississippi River. 1864 brought new bloodshed and southern victories. Lincoln's reelection looked slim by that summer. McClellan ran against Lincoln, supporting slavery. But Lincoln held firm that slavery must end. General Sherman's march through the South raised Lincoln's numbers, and he handily won reelection.

contraband Smuggled goods; during the Civil War, it also referred to runaway slaves who had fled to the Union Army (p. 279)

Confiscation Act Legislation that officially declared that any slaves used for military purposes would be freed if they came into Union hands (p. 279)

15-6 **Describe and discuss the events that finally led to the defeat of the South and the end of the war.** General Sherman carried out a "scorched earth" policy in his "March to the

Sea." The war had become a war of attrition. By spring 1865, only half of the troops remained at their posts. Lee handed over his sword to Grant at Appomattox Courthouse on April 9, 1865.

"March to the Sea" Path of destruction led by General William Tecumseh Sherman in late 1864; the March was 60 miles wide and several hundred miles long, from Atlanta to the Atlantic; Sherman's army pillaged all it encountered (p. 283)

15-7 **Assess the significance of the Civil War for the nation.** The war wrought destruction, strengthened the federal government, and created an industrial nation. Civil war also unified the country, as the disparate states became truly one United States of America. Opportunities loosened for women, who resumed

the push for the vote. The war changed how people prayed, their denominations, and how they viewed the Bible. It led to the philosophy of "pragmatism," which would dominate the U.S. worldview until the 1950s.

	What Else Was Happening

1863 Abraham Lincoln proposes the lenient Ten-Percent Plan.

1864 Lincoln pocket-vetoes the stricter Wade-Davis Bill for Reconstruction.
1865: *John Wilkes Booth assassinates Abraham Lincoln.*

1865–1867 Johnson's presidential Reconstruction demands loyalty oath from Confederates.
Congress establishes Freedmen's Bureau.
Congress passes Civil Rights Bill.

1866 The Ku Klux Klan forms in Tennessee.
1867: *Congress enacts Military and Second Reconstruction Act. Benjamin Disraeli helps pass the 1867 Reform Bill in Britain, which extends the franchise to all male householders, including, for the first time, members of the working class.*

1867–1877 During Congressional Reconstruction Congress enforces its rules for readmission.

1868 Fourteenth Amendment grants full citizenship to all persons born in United States.
North Carolina, South Carolina, Georgia, Florida, Alabama, Arkansas, Louisiana return to Union.
1869: *Opening of the Suez Canal in Egypt connecting the Mediterranean Sea and the Red Sea, allowing water travel between Asia and Europe without having to navigate around Africa.*
1873: *Marketing of Remington typewriter opens clerical positions for women. Financial panic causes severe recession and mass unemployment. Mark Twain patents the scrapbook.*

1870 Fifteenth Amendment bans state disfranchisement based on race but not gender.
Virginia, Mississippi, Texas return to Union.
First New York City subway line opens.

1871 Force Act of 1870 and Ku Klux Klan Act permit federal government to respond to Klan violence.
Euphemia Allen, age sixteen, composes simple piano tune "Chopsticks."

1875 Mississippi Plan calls for use of violence to restore Democratic control.
Civil Rights Act forbids racial discrimination in public places.

1877 To overcome election stalemate, Republicans grant Democrats home rule in return for presidency.

1883 In Civil Rights Cases, U.S. Supreme Court declares Civil Rights Act unconstitutional.

16-1 Describe the changed world of ex-slaves after the Civil War. In Reconstruction South, African American were legally no longer any one else's property, but black codes and "Jim Crow" laws held freed slaves still in a state of servitude. Ex-slaves could move, buy dogs, learn to read, attend schools, and more, and the Freedmen's Bureau provided assistance to black people, and also poor white people, in the South. The Bureau opened thousands of schools and improved medical care across the South. But it would confront challenges everywhere, as many white southerners sought to return the South to its antebellum days.

Reconstruction The federal government's attempts to resolve the issues resulting from the end of the Civil War in order to reconstitute the nation (p. 291)

Ku Klux Klan A quasi-military force formed immediately after the Civil War by former Confederate soldiers in order to resist racial integration and preserve white supremacy; after a temporary decline, the group reformed in 1915 and sporadically returned to prominence throughout the nineteenth and twentieth centuries (p. 292)

Freedmen's Bureau Government agency designed to create a new social order by government mandate; this bureau provided freedmen with education, food, medical care, and access to the justice system (p. 292)

16-2

Outline the different phases of Reconstruction, beginning with Lincoln's plan and moving through presidential Reconstruction to Congressional Reconstruction. During the war, Lincoln wanted to allow southern states to return to the Union if 10 percent of voters signed a loyalty oath. The Wade-Davis bill wanted 50 percent to take the oath. Lincoln's assassination meant that neither became law. President Johnson pardoned most who took the oath—even military leaders and the wealthy, thus ending any hope for a property realignment after the war. Southern states, uncowed, returned the same people to office and enacted restrictive black codes. To counter this, Radical Republicans expanded the Freedmen's Bureau and passed a Civil Rights Bill. Their Military Reconstruction Act laid out strict guidelines for southern states: organizing state conventions, writing new constitutions, protecting black voting rights, and passing the 14th Amendment. After only 12 years, the North abandoned Reconstruction. There was to be no land redistribution, education guarantee for freedmen, or racial equality. Southern whites were freed to push segregation.

Ten-Percent Plan Plan issued by Lincoln in 1863 that offered amnesty to any southerner who proclaimed loyalty to the Union and support of the emancipation of slaves; once 10 percent of a state's voters in the election of 1860 signed the oath, it could create a new state government and reenter the Union (p. 293)

Wade-Davis Bill Bill that would have allowed a southern state back into the Union only after 50 percent of the population had taken the loyalty oath (p. 293)

iron-clad oath Oath to be taken by southerners to testify that they had never voluntarily aided or abetted the rebellion (p. 293)

black codes Post–Civil War laws specifically written to govern the behavior of African Americans; modeled on the slave codes that existed before the Civil War (p. 294)

Radical Republicans Wing of the Republican Party most hostile to slavery (p. 295)

Civil Rights Act Bill that granted all citizens mandatory rights, regardless of racial considerations; designed to counteract the South's new black codes (p. 295)

Congressional Reconstruction Phase of Reconstruction during which Radical Republicans wielded more power than the president, allowing for the passage of the Fourteenth and Fifteenth Amendments and the Military Reconstruction Act (p. 296)

Fourteenth Amendment Amendment to the U.S. Constitution passed in 1868 that extended the guarantees of the Constitution and Bill of Rights to all persons born in the United States, including African Americans and former slaves; it promised that all citizens would receive the "due process of law" before having any of their constitutional rights breached (p. 296)

Military Reconstruction Act Act that divided the former rebel states, with the exception of Tennessee, into five military districts; a military commander took control of the state governments and federal soldiers enforced the law and kept order (p. 296)

Fifteenth Amendment Amendment that extended voting rights to all male citizens regardless of race, color, or previous condition of servitude (p. 299)

16-3

Explain how Reconstruction evolved at the individual states' level. During Reconstruction, about 2,000 southern African Americans gained state and local political office. Some Northerners traveled to help; some Southerners became Republican to aid Southern recovery. Gains were short-lived in the turbulent political climate, which was still ruled by wealthy whites. White landowners devised a new "sharecropping" agricultural system to ensure sufficient field hands. Sharecropping oppressed black & poor white southerners (most of the population) until World War II.

carpetbagger Northern-born white who moved south after the Confederacy's defeat (p. 300)

scalawag Southern-born white Republican; many had been nonslaveholding poor farmers (p. 300)

sharecropping System in which a family farmed a plot of land owned by someone else and shared the crop yield with the owner (p. 301)

16-4

Evaluate and understand the relative success and failures of Reconstruction. During Reconstruction, protections were added to the Constitution, but most existed on paper only. Clinging to the Democratic Party, white voters reasserted control of elections. Society became controlled via harassment, intimidation, and murder, helped by the new Ku Klux Klan. Industrialized Northerners tired of trying to change Southerners, especially after the Panic of 1873. Many also feared an exodus of ex-slaves into the North, and long-held racist tendencies emerged. After the Compromise of 1877, federal troops left the South, leaving Reconstruction mostly a failure. In the "solid South," for decades African Americans existed as neither slave nor free. Only after WWII, and the modern civil rights movement, would Reconstruction-era laws be enforced.

Civil Rights Act of 1875 Act that forbade racial discrimination in all public facilities, transportation lines, places of amusement, and juries; it proved largely ineffective (p. 302)

Civil Rights Cases Cases in which, in 1883, the Supreme Court declared all of the provisions of the Civil Rights Act of 1875 unconstitutional, except for the prohibition of discrimination on juries (p. 302)

Panic of 1873 Financial crisis provoked when overspeculation, high postwar inflation, and disruptions from Europe emptied the financial reserves in America's banks; many banks simply closed their doors; this emergency focused northern attention on the economy rather than on civil rights (p. 302)

Mississippi Plan 1875 Democratic plan that called for using as much violence as necessary to put Mississippi back under Democratic control (p. 304)

Redeemers A collection of southern Democrats and their supporters who used violence, intimidation, and the law to win political and social control away from those promoting greater racial equality in the region (p. 304)

Compromise of 1877 Compromise in which Republicans promised not to dispute the Democratic gubernatorial victories in the South and to withdraw federal troops from the region, if southern Democrats accepted Hayes's presidential victory and respected the rights of black citizens (p. 304)

What Else Was Happening

Year	Event	What Else Was Happening
1860–1890	U.S. Patent Office issues 144,000 licenses, four times more than in 1790.	
1866–1868	In Erie Railroad War, Cornelius Vanderbilt and competitors exemplify new ruthless business practices.	
1867–1872	Crédit Mobilier railroad financing scandal tarnishes Grant administration.	
1868	Congress introduces eight-hour day in federal work projects.	
1869	Completion of transcontinental railroad.	
1872	Montgomery Ward launches mail order business.	
1873	Drastic wage cuts in Panic of 1873 anger and mobilize workers.	
1876	Alexander Graham Bell's telephone speeds up long-distance communication.	**1876–1882:** *The right arm and torch of the Statue of Liberty cross the Atlantic three times.*
1877	National railroad strike kills over 100, brings labor tensions to forefront.	
1878	Refrigerated rail cars permit long-distance transportation of perishable goods.	
1879	John D. Rockefeller's Standard Oil Company controls 90 percent of petroleum market.	*Thomas Edison completes experimentation on the incandescent light bulb.* *Knights of Labor emerge as nation's largest union.*
1883	Congress passes civil service reform with Pendleton Act.	**1884:** *N. Thompson, founder of Coney Island Luna Park, introduces the roller coaster, calling it Switchback.* **1886:** *Explosion at Chicago Haymarket protest kills seven, puts Knights of Labor in disrepute. Statue of Liberty is dedicated. The statue, a gift from France intended to commemorate the two nations' founding ideal of liberty, will come to symbolize American freedom to millions of immigrants.*
1892	Carnegie steel plant strike in Homestead pits workers against Pinkertons and militia.	
1893	Severe economic recession drives further labor organization.	
1894	Government intervenes on side of industrialists in Pullman strike.	**1895:** *Independent Labour Party founded in Britain.* **1896:** *The first comic strip character—the "Yellow Kid"—appears in the* New York Journal. **1899:** *Felix Hoffmann patents aspirin.*
1902	Theodore Roosevelt mediates miners' strike in favor of workers.	
1905	Colorado miners form anarcho-syndicalist International Workers of the World.	
1911	Triangle Shirtwaist Company fire.	

17-1 **Describe and discuss the development of the Industrial Revolution in America after the Civil War, concentrating on the major industries and their leaders.** Post-Civil War industrialization accelerated thanks to federal support and technological breakthroughs. In 1869 the new transcontinental railroad fed this growth, connecting cities and growing companies. Andrew Carnegie's steel industry included new business practices such as "vertical integration"—the ability to control all aspects of the industry, from the extraction of iron to shipping it to customers. The growth of petroleum promoted development of other, sometimes harmful, business practices. John D. Rockefeller perfected "horizontal integration," monopolizing the oil industry to control prices. Innovators and risk takers introduced the light bulb, telephone, steel skyscrapers, elevators. New business practices brought more wealth and product diversity. Entrepreneurs streamlined operations, improved bookkeeping, merged and grew their companies, and made use of corporations to gain more investors and decrease the likelihood of losing entire fortunes. Greater wealth flowed to many members of management, helping grow a much larger middle class. Stock manipulation, higher prices, and environmental damage were byproducts of this rapid growth.

Industrial Revolution Transformation in the way goods were made and sold, as American businessmen between 1865 and 1915 used continuing technological breakthroughs and creative financing to bring greater efficiency to their businesses, dramatically increasing the nation's industrial output (p. 310)

vertical integration The system by which a business controls all aspects of its industry, from raw materials to finished product, and is able to avoid working or sharing profits with any other companies (p. 312)

horizontal integration The system by which a business takes over its competitors in order to limit competition, lower costs, and maximize profits (p. 313)

17-2 Describe how the United States' regional and local markets merged into one national market and how this influenced consumer demand for products and services, as well as some of the costs associated with the transition.
Railroads could bring goods to customers, but businessmen now needed to advertise their availability. They created roadway billboards, placards on city streets, large newspaper ads, and ad agencies. By improving packaging, companies could ship farther, and brand-names became known nationwide. Celebrities wore specific brands, causing the general public to want the same thing. Chain stores grew national markets, as did mail order catalogues (such as Montgomery Ward, Sears, and Roebuck). The ability to order anything through the mail tied rural families into the country as nothing had before. To cut costs, workers were exploited by jobs that were grueling, monotonous, and dangerous. It took years for protective laws to be passed and even longer for employers to obey them.

Triangle Shirtwaist Company New York City garment factory; scene of a horrific fire in 1911 (p. 317)

sweatshop Crowded factory in an urban setting, often one where workers are exploited (p. 317)

17-3 Discuss the functioning of national, state, and local politics during the late 1800s.
"Corruption" is the best descriptor of American politics during the late 1800s. Urban growth and overpopulation overpowered local governments, which sought political "machines" with "bosses" to manage neighborhoods in return for government contracts and a sense of power. Reform was slow, thanks to Social Darwinism's "survival of the fittest" outlook. The successful often embraced novelist Horatio Alger's belief that if a man were willing to work, he would succeed. The working poor, who knew better, had no one to turn to when in need except the political bosses. The Crédit Mobilier scandal, involving railroad executives and even the vice president, spurred reform. New York's "Boss" Tweed had a hand in virtually every aspect of building the city's infrastructure. Political machines could have done good, but without checks, power bred corruption.

Social Darwinism The theory that "survival of the fittest" extended to the business realm; tycoons believed they were justified in their overbearing behavior because they had shown themselves to be the most successful competitors in an open market (p. 319)

Crédit Mobilier Company A construction company set up by the directors of the Union Pacific in 1867 in order to build part of their transcontinental railroad—in essence, they were their own subcontractors and awarded themselves generous contracts (p. 320)

Tweed Ring Friends and cronies of New York's corrupt "Boss" William M. Tweed (p. 320)

Tammany Hall A political organization known as a "machine," whose members regarded politics as an opportunity to get rich while providing favors to the urban underclass (p. 320)

mugwumps The machine's mischievous nickname for Republicans who supported Democrat Grover Cleveland in the 1884 election only because Republican candidate James Blaine was considered a product of machine politics (p. 322)

17-4 Describe the formation of the early labor unions in the United States, including their goals, activities, and confrontations at the end of the nineteenth century.
While entrepreneurs and owners got rich, the working poor lived and worked in pitiful, unsafe places. Assembly lines took their toll, with tens of thousands of workers (kids and adults) killed each year. Employers disliked unions because of "strength in numbers"; they wanted employees under control. Over time, several unions gathered strength, including the International Ladies' Garment Workers' Union, the Knights of Labor, the American Railway Union, and the American Federation of Labor. All pushed for better, safer working conditions, decent wages, and a shorter workweek. Early successes gave way to frustration and failure during the economic depression of 1893. Strikes at Carnegie's Homestead Steel and McCormick Harvester Company led to violence, as did the nationwide Pullman Strike. The violence frightened people, and union numbers plunged. Union organizers began working with rather than against the political system, which proved helpful.

yellow dog contract Contract stipulating that an employee would not join a union (p. 323)

blacklist A compilation of known union activists in a particular area; employers refused to hire anyone whose name appeared on one (p. 323)

strikebreakers Workers who agreed to work while union workers were on strike (p. 323)

International Ladies' Garment Workers' Union (ILGWU) Major New York City union that often conducted its union meetings in five different languages simultaneously (p. 324)

Contract Labor Law Passed in 1885, this prohibited employers from forcing immigrants to work to pay off the costs of their passage to America (p. 324)

American Federation of Labor (AFL) The leading labor organization in America, founded in 1881 by Samuel Gompers and composed of craft unions rather than a single national union (p. 326)

craft union Union of skilled laborers, the type of union assembled under the American Federation of Labor (p. 326)

American Socialist Party Political party formed in 1901 and led by Eugene V. Debs that advocated replacing the nation's capitalist system (p. 326)

International Workers of the World (IWW) A collection of militant mining unions founded in 1905 in Colorado and Idaho; sought to use labor activism to overthrow the capitalist system (p. 326)

anarcho-syndicalism A radical form of political protest that advocates the use of labor activism to overthrow the capitalist system (p. 326)

What Else Was Happening

1862	Republican Homestead Act grants 160 acres of western lands to farming settlers.
1864	In Sand Creek Massacre, Colorado militia kills over 200 Cheyenne following land disputes with white gold seekers.
1866	Edward Pollard's *The Lost Cause* turns Civil War into Old South mythology.
1869	Completion of transcontinental railroad.
1873–1875	Federal government forces economy back on gold standard at farmers' expense.
1874	Barbed wire closes open range, signaling the decline of cattle drives.
1877	In *Munn* v. *Illinois*, Supreme Court finds that states can regulate businesses within their borders that operate in the public interest.
1879	John D. Rockefeller's Standard Oil Company controls 90 percent of petroleum market. Thomas Edison completes experimentation on the incandescent light bulb.
1882	Exclusion Act bans most Chinese immigration and citizenship.
1887	With single plots of land, Dawes Act tries to turn Plains Indians into family farmers.
1890	Second Mississippi Plan models legal black voter disfranchisement for New South. 39 soldiers and 146 Indians die in Wounded Knee Massacre after ritual Ghost Dance.
1892	Carnegie steel plant strike in Homestead pits workers against Pinkertons and militia. Southern and western farmers form backbone of new People's Party (Populists).
1894	Populist Jacob Coxey leads unemployed in march on Washington demanding jobs.
1895	New York's Coney Island amusement park opens.
1896	In *Plessy* v. *Ferguson*, Supreme Court declares racial segregation constitutional. Democrat-Populist presidential candidate William Jennings Bryan loses to William McKinley.
1899	Economist Thorstein Veblen describes "conspicuous consumption" of the rich.
1903	American and National League teams play first World Series.
1909	Niagara Movement establishes NAACP.

1876: *Sioux and Cheyenne warriors wipe out General Custer's division at Little Big horn.*

Alexander Graham Bell's telephone speeds up long-distance communication.

1885: *The first modern hamburger is made in Seymour, Wisconsin.*

Pharmacist Caleb Bradham produces "Brad's Drink" as a digestive aid and energy booster; in 1898 it would be renamed Pepsi-Cola.

1893: *The melody for "Happy Birthday to You" is copyrighted.*

18-1 **Describe the urbanization and immigration in the North during the second half of the nineteenth century, and how those two factors shaped the region's social relations, including its disparities of wealth.** Urban population grew 500 percent, and 25 million immigrants arrived, most settling in Eastern cities. Cheap housing for workers resulted in densely populated, disease-ridden, polluted living conditions. Those who could flee slums did so, and the wealthy lived in ostentatious mansions meant to impress. The excesses of the rich led Mark Twain to coin the term "The Gilded Age." Earlier immigrants to America came from western and northern Europe. As economic conditions there improved, they were replaced with Europe's poor, often uneducated and discriminated against at home. New immigrants sought people like themselves to find jobs, learn English, and "become American." Jobs were usually low-paying, and management often exploited their ignorance of American ways. Urban entertainment was diverse, with large amusement parks geared toward families, the widely popular sport of professional baseball, and the more salubrious dance halls and saloons.

tenements Crowded slum houses in urban areas, which housed mostly immigrants (p. 332)

Coney Island Public amusement park opened in New York in 1895; it featured roller coasters, water slides, and fun houses (p. 333)

National League The first professional baseball league, begun in 1876 with eight teams (p. 334)

American League The second professional baseball league, begun in 1901 (p. 334)

World Series Baseball competition between the National League and the American League, played for the first time in 1903 (p. 334)

greenhorns European newcomers to America (p. 335)

Ellis Island Immigrant gateway to New York City from 1892 to 1954 (p. 335)

18-2 **Evaluate the accuracy of the term *New South* in describing the post-Civil War South, and discuss ways in which the term was and was not appropriate.** After the Civil War, cotton remained "king," but some industrialization spread into parts of the South. Textile mills developed, selling much more expensive finished products, rather than just raw cotton. Urbanization was slow, with Birmingham, Alabama, the standout. Slavery was replaced with a mix of laws and codes that held blacks to barely second-class citizenship. After Reconstruction, black people were systematically disfranchised, often illegally, sometimes by law. When a case did reach the Supreme Court (*Plessy* v. *Ferguson*), the court upheld segregation. Booker T. Washington and W. E. B. Du Bois brought hope, but also demonstrated the lack of consensus from the African American community.

"Second Mississippi Plan" Plan that established legal barriers (the poll tax, literacy tests, and property qualifications) to prevent African Americans from voting in Mississippi; served as a legislative model for other states (p. 338)

Jim Crow laws State and local laws, usually passed in southern states, that mandated racial segregation in public facilities, including schools, restaurants, and rail cars (p. 338)

Louisiana Separate Car Act 1890 law mandating that black people and white people ride in separate train cars; challenged by Homer Plessy (p. 338)

hierarchy of races A theory based on the idea that some racial groups are superior to others; in the nineteenth and twentieth centuries, many Americans used purported scientific evidence and social science data to argue that white people from British descent sat atop the hierarchy, while racial minorities and new immigrants were less sophisticated and less capable of self-rule (p. 339)

Plessy v. Ferguson 1896 Supreme Court case that declared that segregation laws were constitutional, claiming that, as long as the accommodations were "separate but equal," it was legal to have separate facilities for black and white Americans (p. 339)

Atlanta Compromise Speech delivered by Booker T. Washington in 1895 encouraging black economic development and assuaging white fears of racial intermingling; black and white people, he said, should remain as separate as the fingers on a hand, but they should work together to reach common economic ground (p. 340)

Niagara Movement An attempt at political organization among black activists in the early 1900s; W. E. B. Du Bois drafted a "Statement of Principles," which declared that African Americans should fight for their rights rather than accept abuse and separation (p. 340)

Juneteenth A celebration marking the date that slaves were formally freed in Texas: June 19, 1865 (p. 342)

Tuskegee Institute College established for African Americans in Tuskegee, Alabama, by Booker T. Washington in 1881 (p. 342)

18-3 **Describe the development of the American West that took place during the second half of the nineteenth century, addressing both industrialization and the general defeat of Native American nations on the plains.** With the population growing rapidly, Americans began to flood westward toward the receding frontier. The 1862 Homestead Act lured families to the Plains, but acreage limitations hampered its success. When small plots consolidated and grew, Plains farmers began to provide the food needed by cities. Mechanization provided by new industry made it possible to move these crops in sufficient quantities. Railroads contributed to a short-lived cattle industry (killed by the 1874's invention of barbed wire, which carved up the formerly open plains). Westward growth meant uprooting the Plains Indians, who were herded onto numerous reservations.

Homestead Act Federal act, passed in 1862, that awarded 160 acres to settlers who occupied the land for five years (p. 343)

sodbusters American pioneers who settled the northern Great Plains (p. 343)

bonanza farms Giant farms on the Great Plains, covering thousands of acres and employing hundreds of workers (p. 343)

Dawes General Allotment Act Federal law, passed in 1887, declaring that lands held by Indian nations were to be divided among families, and the Indians were not allowed to sell their lands because the government held these lands in trust for twenty-five years, after which individual Indians were to receive title to the land and become U.S. citizens (p. 347)

"Ghost Dance" The central ritual for the Plains Indians, this was a dance lasting five days that would supposedly raise the Indians above the ground while the land below them was replaced with new land, effectively sandwiching the white men between the two layers of sod, removing them forever (p. 348)

Wounded Knee Massacre 1890 conflict in which the U.S. Army fired on the Sioux, triggering a battle that left 39 U.S. soldiers and 146 Sioux dead (p. 348)

Chinese Exclusion Act of 1882 Act that banned the immigration of Chinese laborers for ten years and prohibited the Chinese who were already in the United States from becoming citizens (p. 349)

18-4 **Discuss the problems that confronted America's farmers in the North, South, and West during the late 1800s, and describe how their attempts to solve those problems led to the formation of a new political party.** Purchases of machinery led to debt; distances led to isolation and higher shipping costs for products. Railroads favored large farmers; sharecropping took its toll; and lack of specie made repayment hard. As the price of purchased goods rose, the price of sold goods dropped. Farmers began to unify, from the Grange to the national Farmers' Alliance and the People's Party. These "Populists" developed a platform based on reforms, which were then taken up by major parties.

Populist Party A political party of the 1890s that championed the "farm" cause of land and crops over the powers of banking and credit (p. 350)

gold standard An economic plan using gold as the primary form of currency while taking paper money and silver coins out of circulation (p. 350)

***Munn v. Illinois* (1877)** A Supreme Court case that declared states could regulate businesses within their borders if those businesses operated in the public interest (p. 350)

Subtreasury Plan An economic plan advocated by the Farmers' Alliance, in which crops would be stored in government-owned warehouses and used as collateral for low-cost government loans to struggling farmers (p. 351)

remonetize To turn a certain commodity (for instance, silver) back into an acceptable currency (p. 351)

Year	Event

What Else Was Happening

1882 Electric lights are first used on a Christmas tree.

1883: *Germany institutes the world's first universal health care system.*

1889 Jane Addams founds Hull House in Chicago, the nation's second but most renowned settlement house.

1890 Sherman Antitrust Act is federal government's first effort to curb monopolies.
Founding of National American Woman Suffrage Association (NAWSA).

1893 Temperance activists form Anti-Saloon League to pass laws on state and local level.

1900 National Civic Federation tries to build partnership between workers and owners.
Hurricane kills more than 8,000 in poorly prepared Galveston, Texas, prompting city reform.

1902: *The teddy bear ("Teddy's bear") is created by a Brooklyn shop owner after he sees a newspaper cartoon depicting hunter Theodore Roosevelt with a bear cub.*
1903: *President T. Roosevelt forms Bureau of Corporations to investigate monopolies. Crayola crayons go on sale.*

1906 Hepburn Act caps railroad prices and introduces federal oversight.
Upton Sinclair publishes novel *The Jungle* about life in Chicago meatpacking plant.
Congress passes Pure Food and Drug Act and Meat Inspection Act to protect consumers.

1908 Supreme Court upholds maximum-hours law for women in *Muller* v. *Oregon*.

1911–1914 Women gain suffrage in California, Oregon, Kansas, Arizona, Montana, Nevada.

1911: *Great Britain passes the National Insurance Act, creating a system of social welfare to protect workers against illness and unemployment, as well as providing retirement pensions.*

1912 Disappointed with successor Howard Taft, T. Roosevelt forms Progressive Party.

1913 Seventeenth Amendment replaces senators' election by state legislatures with popular vote.
Founding of National Women's Party led by Alice Paul.
Alice Paul leads march of 5,000 women to White House, demanding suffrage.
Woodrow Wilson signs Federal Reserve Act establishing new banking system.
Wilson signs Underwood Tariff to expose monopolies to competition.

1914 Clayton Antitrust Act defines and outlaws unfair business practices.
Federal Trade Commission investigates and rules on legality of business practices.

1916 Keating-Owen Child Labor Act prohibits employment of children under sixteen.

1920 Nineteenth Amendment grants women the right to vote.

19-1 Discuss the reform efforts of the Progressive era and the groups involved in those efforts. Political and social causes occupied the reformers of the Progressive era. Middle-class women spearheaded the Women's Christian Temperance Union. Settlement houses did a great deal to help individuals and families mired in poverty.

Social Gospel An early-twentieth-century Protestant-inspired movement advocating widespread reforms to curb the worst abuses of the Industrial Revolution; its leaders included Washington Gladden and Walter Rauschenbusch (p. 358)

settlement houses Safe residences in poor neighborhoods where reformers could study local conditions and where residents could hold meetings and receive free health care (p. 358)

Hull House The second but most renowned settlement house in the United States, founded in Chicago in 1889 by Jane Addams; its residents lobbied the government to pass better construction and safety laws to improve conditions in the surrounding tenement houses (p. 359)

19-2 Describe the methods used by the various states to bring about reforms in state governments during the Progressive era. Progressives sought to bring openness and democracy to politics, most successfully at the state level. Reformers pushed for and won a constitutional amendment in 1913 for direct election of senators. Implementation empowered citizens to petition their state governments to place specific issues on the general ballot, whether state legislatures supported the issue or not. Primaries and recalls gave citizens a greater voice in candidate selection and oversight of officials. States adopted rules for hiring government workers, including civil service exams to replace cronyism.

Galveston hurricane Devastating hurricane that killed more than 8,000 people in Galveston, Texas, in 1900; helped spur demands that local and state governments be more responsive to people's needs (p. 361)

initiative A legislative device designed to allow citizens more control over state law; they could advocate a specific idea and introduce it on the ballot (p. 362)

referendum A legislative device designed to allow citizens more control over state law; citizens could collect a few thousand signatures on a petition in order to advance a specific idea and introduce it on the ballot (p. 362)

primary A preliminary election designed to let voters choose which political candidates will run for public office (p. 362)

recall A device by which petitioning citizens can, with a vote, dismiss state officers, governors, and judges who are deemed to have violated the popular interest (p. 362)

19-3 Compare and contrast the progressivism of Theodore Roosevelt and Woodrow Wilson. As "activists," both believed in encouraging Congress to enact laws to improve the lives of citizens. Roosevelt involved himself with environmental causes, including creating the National Forest Service. He also disliked trusts, and the "trustbuster" set out to break ones he considered the worst. Wilson supported legislation designed to make the entire society work more effectively and equitably. His efforts helped create the Federal Reserve, Clayton Antitrust Act, and Federal Trade Commission. Roosevelt is known as quite Progressive; Wilson's Progressivism was overshadowed by World War I.

Sherman Antitrust Act Passed in 1890, the federal government's first attempt to break up monopolies (p. 363)

trustbuster A nickname for those in government advocating antitrust laws (p. 363)

National Forest Service Government agency created by Theodore Roosevelt to preserve land and protect local animal species (p. 363)

Progressive Party Political party created by Theodore Roosevelt in 1912 to win back the presidency from Taft (p. 364)

"The New Freedom" Woodrow Wilson's platform message pledging to use government power to destroy big businesses and give smaller ones greater ability to compete (p. 364)

Federal Trade Commission A government agency charged with investigating unfair business practices (p. 364)

19-4 Discuss the involvement of women's groups in Progressive-era reform movements. Women were at the core of most reform movements. Many pushed for suffrage for all women, helping usher in the Nineteenth Amendment in 1920. National suffrage culminated decades of perseverance by women for a right long denied them. Women supported each other in social work, and their organizations evolved into groups dedicated to improving life in specific communities as well as across the country.

19-5 Describe ways in which American culture was influenced by the Progressive movement. Reform-minded people found creative ways to raise awareness of important problems. Literature was one way; Upton Sinclair and Jacob Riis shined light on the state of the working poor. Partly because of their works, the Pure Food and Drug Act and Meat Inspection Act passed in 1906. Ida Tarbell and Lincoln Steffens contributed; Tarbell targeted Standard Oil for ill treatment of workers. Frederick W. Taylor developed the business practice of "scientific management." It increased production efficiency and gave Americans better and cheaper consumer goods, improving many lives. In general, reformers sought practical and needed reforms in almost all areas of American life.

muckrakers Investigative writers who exposed bad conditions in American factories, political corruption in city machines, and the financial deceit of corporations (p. 366)

Pure Food and Drug Act Passed in 1906, this act, along with the Meat Inspection Act, gave the federal government responsibility for ensuring that meat would reach its customers fresh and disease-free (p. 367)

scientific management Pioneered by Frederick W. Taylor, the detailed study of the best ways to schedule, organize, and standardize work tasks (p. 368)

Progressive Education Association Formed in 1919, this national association supported and advocated for education reforms that taught children to make good moral and political choices (p. 368)

eugenics An early-twentieth-century movement centered on the belief that it was possible to improve the human species by discouraging or outlawing reproduction by various people thought to have undesirable traits (p. 368)

What Else Was Happening

Year	Event	What Else Was Happening
1844	Treaty of Wanghia opens Chinese ports to U.S. trade.	
1853	U.S. Navy in Tokyo Bay pressures Japan to open to West.	
1867	United States purchases Alaska from Russia.	
1895	Cleveland administration invokes Monroe Doctrine in Venezuela Crisis with Britain.	*Cubans rebel against heavy-handed Spanish rule.*
1898	Spanish-American War transforms United States into major overseas power. **June:** Filipino leader Emilio Aguinaldo declares Philippines' independence from Spain. **July:** Rough Riders' capture of Santiago, Cuba, forces Spain's surrender.	
1899–1902	Americans fight vicious anti-insurgency war against Filipino nationalists.	*Anti-Imperialist League forms in opposition to annexation of Philippines. The Second Boer War in southern Africa between Great Britain and a handful of small African nations leads to the conversion of several small African republics into parts of the British Empire.*
1899	United States turns former naval base on Samoa into protectorate of American Samoa. U.S. Secretary of State John Hay demands Open Door policy from China.	
1900	After thirteen years as an American-led republic, Hawai'i becomes part of United States. Republican expansionist McKinley defeats Democrat Bryan in presidential election.	*United States joins multinational military expedition to suppress Boxer Rebellion in China.*
1901	Platt Amendment to Cuban constitution grants U.S. right to military intervention. Roosevelt encourages Panamanian independence after negotiations with Colombia fail.	
1903	U.S. support for Panama's rebellion leads to U.S. rights to 10-mile-wide Canal Zone.	**1904:** *Russo-Japanese War breaks out because of each nation's imperial ambitions over Manchuria and Korea.*
1905	President Roosevelt negotiates end to Russo-Japanese War, wins Nobel Peace Prize.	
1909	Taft administration supports coup in Nicaragua in the interests of U.S. mining company.	**1912: April 15:** *The Titanic sinks. First passenger meal is served on an airplane in flight.*
1914–1916	**June 28:** Assassination of Archduke Franz Ferdinand throws Europe into World War I. **August:** Germany invades France. Wilson administration sends troops into Mexican civil war to restore order. Wilson administration sends more troops into Mexican civil war to restore order.	**1915: May 7:** *German U-boat sinks British Lusitania; 128 U.S. civilians die; protests follow.*
1917	**January:** Zimmerman Note from Berlin to Mexico suggests alliance against United States. **February:** Bolshevik Revolution in Russia prompts talks over separate peace with Germany. **April 2:** Woodrow Wilson asks Congress for declaration of war against Germany. Espionage Acts punish protests and criticisms of draft.	
1918	**January 8:** Wilson proposes conciliatory postwar peace settlement in Fourteen Points. **February:** Both sides sign armistice; World War I ends.	
1919	**June 28:** Treaty of Versailles demands German reparations, adopts few of Wilson's ideas.	
1920	League of Nations meets for first time without U.S. participation.	

20-1 Explain the major reasons for the growing call in the late 1800s for the United States to develop an empire. "Manifest destiny" and an expanding frontier gave generations a chance to improve their lives. Historian Frederick Jackson Turner claimed the frontier made Americans what they were. As more lands became settled, many talked of a need for a "new" frontier; business leaders sought new colonial materials and markets; religious leaders wanted to take Christianity around the world. The race for colonies by European countries brought them great rewards Americans wanted.

Turner Thesis Argument put forward by historian Frederick Jackson Turner that the presence of the western frontier had shaped the American character and allowed the development of democracy and capitalism, necessitating in the wake of its 1893 disappearance "a wider field for its exercise"; was used to buttress attempts to propel American interests abroad (p. 373)

dollar diplomacy The use of a country's financial power to extend its diplomatic interests, including but not limited to using private capital from the U.S. to further American interests overseas (p. 374)

20-2 Describe the first moves the U.S. made toward empire. After the Civil War, the U.S. determined to show other countries that it deserved respect. Alfred Thayer Mahan advocated warships, merchant ships, and colonies for supplies: imperialism. America purchased Alaska in 1867; next, Samoa and Hawaii came under American influence. The U.S. then became involved with Mexico and Venezuela because of natural resources.

Treaty of Wanghia Agreement between China and the United States signed in 1844, opening several Chinese ports to American trade (p. 374)

20-3 Explain the major reasons for the Spanish-American War of 1898, and discuss the controversy over imperialism that developed after the war. With U.S. business interests menaced by Spanish expansion, the U.S. fought Spain in 1898 over Cuba. The sinking of an American warship in Havana Harbor and an intercepted telegram led to the war. Though refusing to take over Cuba, victory did give the U.S. Guam, Puerto Rico, and the Philippines. The Filipinos warred with the U.S. for four years. Dealings with Cuba also remained strained.

yellow journalism Journalism that shows little dependence on fact or research and instead uses sensationalized headlines and storylines in order to sell more newspapers or magazines; pioneered by Joseph Pulitzer and William Randolph Hearst during the buildup to the Spanish-American War (p. 377)

Teller Amendment Legislation that barred the United States from annexing Cuba, forcing it to leave Cuba independent once the Spanish-American War was over (p. 377)

Rough Riders The most colorful contingent of the American forces in the Spanish-American War, led by Theodore Roosevelt (p. 378)

Platt Amendment Legislation intended to overrule the Teller Amendment and then added to the Cuban constitution, allowing the United States to militarily intervene on the island whenever revolution threatened (p. 380)

20-4 Describe the growth of American imperialism during the Progressive era. Under Roosevelt and Wilson, America became involved in China (with the "Open Door" policy), Central America (with the Panama Canal), and many Western Hemisphere areas under the Roosevelt Corollary. Americans remained divided over imperialism, but it was clearer the U.S. would play a vital role in world affairs. Isolationists wanted no part of such a role.

Boxer Rebellion Conflict that erupted in China in 1900; Chinese nationalists attacked embassies in Beijing in an attempt to oust foreigners (p. 381)

20-5 Discuss World War I, including reasons for the war, American experiences during the war, and effects of the treaty ending the war. World War I's prelude involved alliances, distrust among European states, and economic competition. The assassination of Austria-Hungary's archduke by a Serbian nationalist set the war in motion. At first neutral, Americans leaned toward Britain and France, as German subs sank U.S. merchant ships. Germany's declaration of unrestricted submarine warfare, following the Zimmermann Note, in which Germany attempted to goad Mexico into war against the U.S., brought America into the war in 1917. The significance of American participation is disputed, but U.S. troops clearly impacted later battles. The war ended in November 1918, with Germany suing for peace under Wilson's Fourteen Points plan. The Versailles Treaty punished Germany. The Allies pushed aside Wilson's ideas on self-determination. Germany had to pay reparations with money it lacked. Its bitterness would lead to the rise of Hitler.

U-boat Primitive but effective submarine invented by the Germans and used extensively in the First World War (p. 386)

war bonds Securities bought by ordinary people to fund and support the war effort (p. 388)

Espionage Act Legislation that meted out large fines and twenty-year jail terms to anyone who protested the draft or said anything that might impede the war effort (p. 388)

Fourteen Points Declaration by President Wilson that outlined the principles he believed should shape the postwar peace settlement; a blueprint for what he called "a world made fit and safe to live in" (p. 389)